Here's what America's to newspapers and readers are saying about Skiing America — They love it.

"Ski vacationers will want to look at Skiing America and Ski Europe."
—*Consumer Reports*
Travel Letter

"When Leocha talks about something he finds lacking, there is no sugar coating . . . when he writes about something he likes, you know you're getting the truth."
—*Wood River Journal*
Sun Valley/Ketchum

"It provides independent evaluation of the ski terrain and offers more extensive information than found in other guides."
—*Skier News*

"If you're planning a ski vacation . . . this guide should serve you well."
—*Ski Magazine*

"Up-to-the-minute info, so accurate that even ski resort personnel peruse these pages . . . The only guidebook you'll ever need. The latest edition is packed chockablock with detailed information about the ski experience at every major resort in the United States and Canada."
—*Robb Report*

"Charlie Leocha is first a skier, then a writer. He shuns the party line of the big ski corporations, preferring instead to talk to locals. *Skiing America*'s perspective is direct, credible, and no-holds-barred."
—*Daily Record*, NJ

"Detailed information on lift ticket prices, cross-country facilities, nightlife and more."
—*Powder Magazine*

"The flavor, feel and personality of each resort."
—*Boston Globe*

"Includes everything needed to make an educated decision about which slopes to hit."

—*PhysiciansFinancial News*

"Let's you know where the action is . . . on and off the slopes."
—KFYI, Phoenix AZ

"I finished reading your book and wanted to tell you how useful and informative I found it to be. In particular, it appears (with great relief) that the information is totally reliable. For those ski resorts of which I have personal knowledge, I found your comments and observations to be *totally* in accord with my own feelings."

—JLC, Toronto, Canada

"Your book made the planning of the trip a breeze and my husband was thrilled with the skiing."   —JSH, Dallas TX

"Your book is, in our experience, unique and we will certainly rely upon it when we next plan a vacation."   —MIG, Burlington VT

"We are enthusiastically looking forward to our trip—mostly because of your book; the gracious responses to the phone calls we made, the wonderful down-to-earth descriptions you gave us of what we should expect and the clear concise information. (The book is going with us to Colorado.)"   —JR, Media PA

"Thanks for a great vacation. I used your book to great advantage with planning a two-week trip . . . keep up the good work."
—KSH, Philadelphia PA

"I hope my comments help one-100th of what yours have helped me. Thanks for the book, It's a wealth of information."

—TR, Sherman Oaks CA

"Packed with information for ski resorts across America."
—Good Morning Houston

"Simply the best ski guide you can buy."
—The Sports Final

Skiing America '96

by Charles A. Leocha

Diane Slezak Scholfield, executive editor

with
Steve Giordano
Katy Keck
James Kitfield

WORLD LEISURE CORPORATION
Hampstead, NH   Boston, MA

Help us do a better job

Research for this book is an ongoing process—we have been at it for more than a decade. Each year we revisit many of these resorts, and every winter we speak with locals from all of them.

If you find a new restaurant, hotel, bar or disco that you feel we should include, please let us know. If you find anything in these pages that is misleading or has changed, we would like to hear that too. If we use your suggestion we will send you a copy of next year's edition.

Send your suggestions and comments to:
Charlie Leocha, *Skiing America*, World Leisure Corp.
Box 160, Hampstead NH 03841, USA

Distributed to the trade in USA by
Login Publishers Consortium, 1436 West Randolph Street, Chicago, IL 60607; tel. (312) 733-8228, (800) 626-4330.

Distributed to the trade in Canada by
E.A. Milley Enterprises, Inc., Locust Hill,
Ontario L0H 1J0, Canada; tel. (800) 399-6858.

Distributed to the trade in U.K. by Roger Lascelles,
47 York Road, Brentford, Middlesex TW8 0QP; tel. 081-847 0935.

Mail Order, Catalog and Special Sales by
World Leisure Corporation, 177 Paris Street, Boston, MA 02128;
tel. (617) 569-1966, fax (617) 561-7654.

ISBN: 0-915009-40-4   ISSN: 1072-8988   LCCN: 93-643936

Contributors to *Skiing America '96*

Charlie Leocha has skied virtually every major international resort. He is also author of *Ski Europe*, a guidebook to the Alps' top ski resorts, and writes about travel and skiing for scores of magazines and newspapers. His most recent books are *Travel Rights*, a pocket guide to your rights while traveling, *Getting To Know You* and *Getting to Know Kids in Your Life* both about activities and ways to get to know other people better.

Steve Giordano is a Pacific Northwest travel and recreation writer and photographer who contributes to the *Bellingham Herald*, *Adventure Northwest* and *Northwest Skier* magazines. He is president of the Pacific Northwest chapter of the North American Ski Journalists Association (NASJA).

Katy Keck worked in France under chefs at Michelin-star restaurants. She owns and runs Savoir Faire Foods, a consulting company in New York specializing in food styling, recipe development and catering. She is co-owner of a New York City restaurant, New World Grill at 329 W. 49th Street.

James Kitfield was awarded the Gerald R. Ford prize for distinguished reporting, and the Jesse H. Neal award for excellence in reporting. His first book, *Prodigal Soldiers*, was recently published by Simon & Schuster.

Diane Slezak Scholfield writes a weekly ski column for *The San Diego Union-Tribune*. She has written for *Ski*, *Skiing*, *Snow Country*, *Ski Impact*, *Adventure West*, *The Miami Herald*, *The Washington Post* and many other publications. She has been named Ski Writer of the Year three times by NASJA.

Other contributors: **Karen Cummings**, various Colorado and New Mexico resorts; **Colleen Maloney**, Big Sky; **Christopher Elliott**, various nightlife updates; **Mary Jo Tarallo**, mid-Atlantic; **Tom Carter**, Santa Fe and mid-Atlantic; **E d Blumstein**, Poconos; **Mike Terrell**, Midwest; **Dave Barrell**, Jay Peak, Smugglers' Notch and Okemo.

Contents

How to get the most out of Skiing America

How many times have you looked in a guidebook and said, "Thanks for the facts, guys, but what's this place *really* like?"

Well, we're going to tell you. This is a straightforward, honest, opinionated guide to North America's top resorts. We know that a ski vacation is made up of much more than the number of chair lifts or ski trails. We describe the personality of each resort, where we found the best skiing, where we liked to eat and where we enjoyed the liveliest off-slope fun. And we give you all the facts you'll need—hotel and restaurant descriptions, lift ticket and lesson prices, day-care programs, nightlife activities, and where to call or write for more information. All skiers and snowboarders have various likes and dislikes, and ski resorts have different personalities. Our goal is to match you with the right vacation spot.

Most of the ski areas we describe are destination resorts—ones that can support five to seven days of ski and non-ski activity without becoming repetitious. Smaller areas near major cities are included for skiers who want to take day trips.

What's new in this edition

We added new chapters on Silver Mountain and Schweitzer, two up-and-coming resorts in Idaho. We greatly expanded the Big Sky chapter: that Montana resort added an aerial tram to its summit, and now claims the longest vertical drop in the nation, 4,180 feet (41 feet higher than Jackson Hole, which held that honor for many years).

And as always, each chapter is full of new resort information and price changes for everything from lift tickets to day care and ski school.

A note about prices

We make every attempt to include prices for the current 1995/96 ski season. Unfortunately, as of late July many resorts had not announced their new prices. Where we have been unable to obtain current prices we have noted the 94/95 prices in the text. Where there is no notation, assume the prices are from last season (94/95).

The prices provided in this guidebook are in no way official and are subject to change at any time; ski resorts sometimes announce one price in July and change it by November. Some resorts even change announced prices during the season. Our intention is to provide you the best possible information for planning and comparison.

Chapter organization

Each resort chapter has several sections. We begin by sketching the personality of the place—is it old and quaint, or modern and high-rise? Clustered at the base of the slopes, or a few miles down the road? Remote and isolated, or freeway-close? Family-oriented or catering to singles? Filled with friendly faces or an aloof herd of "beautiful" skiers?

The **Mountain Facts** box outlines the basic statistics of each resort. We note the **base and summit altitudes,** an important consideration for those with altitude-related medical difficulties or sea-level dwellers who are planning a rigorous week on the slopes. The **vertical drop** provides one indicator of the amount of skiing, top to bottom. This, combined with the total **skiable acreage** and **number and types of lifts,** will give you a good idea of how much skiing is available. **Uphill lift capacity** is the number of skiers the lift system can carry up the mountain each hour—a larger uphill lift capacity normally means shorter lift lines. **Bed base** is the approximate number of people who can be accommodated overnight near the resort. Most destination resorts try to keep uphill capacity much bigger than bed base to ensure short lift lines. (Resorts with great uphill capacity/bed base ratios may still have long weekend lines if they are near major cities—we try to identify these.)

An important note about our stats: They reflect *lift-served* terrain. Examples: Breckenridge, Colorado, lists its vertical as 3,398 feet; we list it at 2,546. If you want that maximum vertical, you must hike the extra 852 feet to the in-bounds summit. Grand Targhee has two mountains totalling 3,000 acres of skiing, but half of that acreage is on a mountain reserved for snowcat skiing. Exceptions such as these are explained where they occur.

A detailed description of **Where to ski** is next, followed by a **Mountain rating.** The first describes various sections of the mountain and how to find your way around. The second will tell you what the resort has for beginner, intermediate or expert skiers. Also, we suggest which resorts may be too tough for the beginner or too mild for the expert. (Where trail maps are included, they are only for reference when planning your trip. Use the official maps provided by the resorts when you ski.)

Cross-country information will tell you which resorts have Nordic trails, as well as significant cross-country and backcountry skiing opportunities near the resort.

Snowboarding outlines special snowboard facilities such as halfpipes and parks.

The **Lessons** section details instructional programs for adults and children, including any special workshops.

Child care facilities cover nursery and day care programs, either at the resort or nearby.

Lift ticket prices are listed for adults, children and seniors. We've organized them in a chart that has one-day, three-day and five-day prices, with any additional information listed in paragraph form following the chart. Where possible we list the 95/96 prices, but when prices are from last season, assume an increase of a couple of dollars.

Under **Accommodations** we list both the most luxurious places and many of the budget lodges, including amenities such as slopeside location, pools and spas, health clubs and intra-resort transportation. We also suggest lodging that is particularly suited to families.

The **Dining** recommendations always include the best gourmet restaurants in town, but we don't leave out affordable places where a hungry family or a skier on a budget can chow down and relax. We have compiled these suggestions from dozens of interviews with locals and tourists, then combined them with our own dining experiences. For a few resorts—the Aspen area, Crested Butte and Steamboat—Katy Keck visited the top restaurants and wrote a Savoir Faire chapter.

Après-ski/nightlife describes places to go when the lifts close, and where to find entertainment later in the evening. We tell you which bars are loud, which are quiet, which have live music and what kind. Non-skiing activities and facilities—such as shopping, tennis, fitness clubs, sleigh rides, dog sledding and snowmobiling—are included under **Other activities**.

Finally, we give detailed **Getting there and getting around** instructions and finish with key phone numbers and addresses for **Information/reservations**. An important note: Every chapter ends with the local area code. We don't list the local area code for every number because you probably will use local numbers most often while you're at the resort (in the case of restaurants, for instance). But if you need it while you're at home, that's where you'll find it.

Types of accommodations

A **hotel** is relatively large, with 25 rooms or more, and comes without meals. If hotel rates include any meals, that is noted.

An **inn** usually has fewer rooms than a hotel. Many have packages that include breakfast and dinner.

A **bed-and-breakfast (B&B)** tends to be even smaller, with just a few rooms. More B&Bs have private baths now, so if guests must share a bath, it is noted. Breakfast is included and some B&Bs also offer dinner.

Motels don't have the amenities of a hotel or the ambiance of a B&B, and often are further from the slopes. Motels are good for families and budget-minded skiers.

Condominiums have become the most affordable group lodging at American ski resorts because of their separate bedrooms and kitchen facilities. Many are ski-in, ski-out, or within easy walking distance of the lifts. They usually have a central check-in facility. Most condominiums have daily maid service for everything but the kitchen.

When you call the resort central reservations number, ask for suggestions. Most of the staff have been on lodging tours and can make honest recommendations based on your needs.

High and low season

Ski resorts have several pricing seasons. The highest prices are during the Christmas-New Year holidays. The Regular Season usually runs all of February and March, but at some resorts, March may be considered high season. Value Season is in January after New Year at some resorts. Low Season usually is the first weeks of December, and April until closing. These vary from resort to resort, so ask for more information when you call. The most noticeable change is in the cost of accommodations, but some resorts also lower the prices of lift tickets, especially in the pre-season and in spring.

Skier ability levels

These are the terms we use in the "Where to ski" sections:

Never-evers are just what the name implies. We apply the term to the novice for the first couple of days on skis.

Beginners can turn and stop (more or less) when they choose, but still rely on snowplow turns.

Lower intermediates can link snowplow turns and are beginning to make parallel turns.

Intermediates can negotiate any blue trail and can parallel ski (more or less) on the smooth stuff. They go back to survival rules on expert trails, and struggle in heavy powder and crud.

Advanced skiers can ski virtually any trail with carved turns, but are still intimidated by deep powder, crud and super steeps.

Experts can always ski anything, anytime, anywhere. They are few and far between.

A warning about **ski-area trail ratings:** In North American ski areas, green circles designate the easiest runs, blue squares show the more difficult ones and black diamonds designate the toughest. However, the system only shows the relative difficulty of the runs at that particular ski area, not as they compare to other resorts.

Ratings are largely determined by steepness, but are also influenced by other factors, such as the trails's width and frequency of grooming. When you ski at a new area, *always* warm up on a run rated one color below what you usually ski—that way you'll avoid nasty surprises.

Skiing for everyone

Skiers and snowboarders come in all abilities, genders, interests and ages. Better equipment and slope grooming techniques mean that skiing is easier to learn and you never have to give it up as you age. As more people are attracted to the sport, resorts are putting more emphasis on teaching how much fun you can have with downhill, cross-country or snowboarding. These are sports that combine the best of Mother Nature with the best of friendly people out to enjoy themselves.

The first step is learning We touch on the basics of lessons, equipment and clothing, then explore special programs for older skiers, disabled skiers, women and advanced levels.

Throughout this book, we use the word "ski" in a general sense, meaning skiing or snowboarding. Our staff includes boarders who like to ride some days and ski on other days. So, boarders, please don't take offense. We're trying to think of one neutral word that takes in both sports—so far, no luck.

The experience of beginning to ski

When you ski or snowboard, you escape from your everyday routine. No matter your level of expertise, you find challenge, beauty and a balance with nature. This is a sport where beginners to experts can have fun amid clean air and stunning scenery. It's also a sport where you'll easily meet other people.

Learning is not difficult if you don't try to teach yourself. We firmly believe that lessons are the only way to go for never-evers, whatever their athletic ability. Natural athletes may quickly develop balance, but they'll also develop bad habits that will hinder later progress. Toddlers can start as young as two (though three or four is usually better) and you're never too old to learn—really. And learning will not break the bank: many resorts offer heavily discounted lessons for beginners.

After only four or five downhill lessons, most beginners have improved enough to negotiate their way down more than half the marked ski trails in North America. For cross-country you need only a couple of lessons to begin gliding through the forests and across rolling meadows.

How do you get started? Call any of the resorts listed in this book and ask about learn-to-ski packages. Most include lift tickets, rental equipment and lessons. Or visit your local ski shop for information.

While learning to ski, rent your equipment. Renting is much less expensive than buying at this point, because as you get better you'll need more advanced gear. Ski shop pros will help you with the correct ski length and type, bindings and adjustments. As you improve, they can suggest how to upgrade. The two principal places to rent are ski shops near home or at the resort; the choice will probably be based on the way you get to the resort—flying or driving—and how much time you'll spend there. If possible, rent near home or at the resort the night before you start skiing. You'll get better attention if you're not part of the masses the morning of your first lesson.

Proper clothing also is important. You don't need the latest, most colorful ski fashions—what you can find in your closet should do just fine, provided you can find such basics as a pair of long johns, a sweater, a waterproof or water-resistant jacket, wool or acrylic socks and a pair of wool trousers or nylon wind pants. One warning: because your backside will be spending time in contact with the snow at first, don't wear jeans or other cotton pants. In fact, don't wear anything made of cotton next to your skin, such as cotton socks or a T-shirt. Cotton soaks up and holds moisture—either sweat or snow—and you will soon be cold. If you are missing any of the basics, borrow from a friend. The secret to staying just warm enough is layering. A few lightweight garments are better than one heavy one, since layers trap the air. Remove or add layers as temperatures change.

Wear a hat—50 percent of your body heat can escape through your head! Wear gloves—they will keep your hands warm and protected. Ski gloves are padded and reinforced in ways different from any other gloves you're likely to have on hand, so these may have to be a specific purchase if you can't borrow them. Though you can get by with sunglasses on your first few days (do wear some: high-altitude sun is very nasty to unprotected eyes), amber goggles are *vital* for seeing trail contours on overcast days. Use sunscreen—at high altitudes the sun's rays are stronger and the reflection of rays off the snow increases your total dose.

Your first lessons will teach you how to walk, slide and—very important—stop. Then the lessons focus on how to get up after falling (you may have already practiced that lesson on your own). You will learn the basic wedge turn, also called a snowplow turn. With this turn you will be able to negotiate almost any groomed slope. Your instructor will show you how to use the lifts, and you'll be on your way. You'll be surprised how much you're enjoying it from the start, and how fast you improve.

You don't have to start with downhill skiing. Many skiers go right to cross-country or to snowboarding. Just pick the sport that suits you best. Enjoy!

Getting in shape

How important is it to be in shape for skiing? Well, we aren't going to lie to you—the more fit you are, the more fun you'll have and the better you'll ski.

But this doesn't mean you have to devote half your life to jogging and hamstring stretches. We won't lie to you about this, either—most of the contributors to this book would never be mis-taken for Jane Fonda or Arnold Schwarzenegger, writing being the sedentary profession it is. But we all have learned—some-times the hard way—that if we get lax about exercise at home, we pay for it when we're doing our on-slope research.

A moderate exercise program—about an hour three to four times a week—is all it takes. Here are key things to include:

•**Aerobics**. Get that heart pumping so your whole body will process oxygen more efficiently. A good portion of America's skiers—especially those who buy guidebooks—live at or near sea level. Most of the Rocky Mountain ski areas are at 8,000- to 11,000-foot elevations where the air is thin. Those who lead unathletic lives where the oxygen is plentiful will be exhausted after a short time where there's less of it. You've spent big money for your ski trip—why waste a minute?

• **Flexibility**. Stre-e-e-tch those muscles, particularly the ones down the backs of your legs. Sometimes your skis decide to head in different directions, and your feet may stay attached. If your hamstrings or inner-thigh muscles are tight, a fall like that could put you out of commission for the rest of your vacation.

• **Strength**. Most skiers, even new ones, know that strong leg muscles make skiing a lot easier. Muscles just as important, but ignored by many skiers, are the ones in your upper body. Have you ever had to push yourself across a long flat section of the mountain? Have you ever carried 15 pounds of ski equipment from your car or lodge to the chair lift? Have you ever pushed yourself up off the snow after a fall? Sure you have, and you do all those things with your arms and shoulders.

Of course, it's important to consult your doctor before going from a chair-bound lifestyle to a regular exercise program. And it's best to get some professional help regarding the best program for you. Fitness centers—especially in cities that have a lot of skiers—often have ski-conditioning classes during the fall months focusing on exercises that mimic skiing movements. Such a class can give you a real head start on the season.

If you can't find a ski-conditioning class in your area, you can take one with your VCR. Several ski-conditioning videos are on the market now, such as Patty Wade's "In Shape To Ski." Wade, a fitness instructor in Aspen, teaches a ski-conditioning class each autumn that many of the locals swear by. Her 60-minute video workout offers a thorough and tough workout (even Patty breathes hard during the workout). You can adjust the pace to your level by not doing the exercises as long as she does. Call (800) 925-9754 for ordering information if you can't find it at a local video outlet.

Mountain maladies

Even those skiers in the best of shape can find themselves spending their vacation in the condo if they aren't careful. These four skier maladies are easily avoidable. Here's how to keep from being a victim.

•**Altitude sickness.** Caused by a too-fast gain in elevation, the symptoms are a bit like the flu—nausea, headaches, insomnia. The best way to avoid it is to go easy the first day or so—ski slow and easy, eat light and drink lots of water but little alcohol. If this is a persistent problem for you, go to ski areas where the base elevation is below 8,000 feet.

•**Snow blindness.** Always wear sunglasses or goggles when you ski, and be sure they protect your eyes from damaging rays. Sun reflecting off bright snow can easily "sunburn" your retinas. Your eyes will feel as if someone has dumped a load of sand in them, and the only cure is resting in a darkened room for a day or two—no reading, no TV and definitely no skiing.

•**Hypothermia.** It's 10 degrees outside, the wind is howling and you don't want to wear a hat because it will flatten your hair? Your vanity could make you sick. When you lose body heat faster than you can replace it, you're risking hypothermia. Wear enough clothes so you're warm, but not so many that you're soaked through with sweat. (Cold weather and wet clothing act as a hypothermia magnet.) If you start to shiver, get inside. Add a layer of clothes. If you still are shivering, quit for the day. Better to lose a few hours than several days.

•**Frostbite.** This happens to fingers, toes, cheeks, noses and ears when body tissue starts to freeze. If any of these start to feel cold, check to see if your skin is turning white. If it is, get inside, drink something warm and non-alcoholic, and cover the affected part with extra clothing or warm it with body heat. Don't rub it or hold it near a fireplace, this could do further damage.

Programs for older skiers

Skiing isn't just for youngsters anymore. One of the fastest growing age groups in skiing is 55 and older. By the year 2010, 37 percent of all skiers are expected to be in that age group.

Some of those skiers learned when they were young and never stopped skiing, but others started late in life. Many resorts have started programs that cater to the upper age group. Nearly every ski area in North America offers free or heavily discounted lift tickets to skiers when they reach 60, 65 or 70.

And thanks to clubs such as the Over the Hill Gang and the 70+ Club, older skiers always have companionship. The 70+ Club started in 1977 with 34 members; now it has more than 10,000—all 70 or older—in several countries.

Here is a partial list of clubs and programs for older skiers. New programs are starting every season, so give the ski school at your area a call.

Clubs: Members of the **70+ Ski Club** wear distinctive red-and-white patches that identify them as part of this elite group. A $5 lifetime membership fee, plus a copy of a legal document that clearly shows date of birth (such as a passport or driver's license), is all it takes to join. Founder Lloyd Lambert was a pioneer in getting discounts for older skiers. About 19 members are still skiing in their 90s. For membership information, write to Lambert at 104 East Side Drive, Ballston, Lake NY 12019.

The Over The Hill Gang is for skiers 50 and older. This nationwide group has local chapters all over the country whose members not only ski, but also play volleyball and tennis, go hiking and sailing and enjoy the outdoor life. Contact the Over The Hill Gang at 3310 Cedar Heights Dr., Colorado Springs, CO 80904; (719) 685-4656.

Members of the **Over Eighty Ski Club** get their names inscribed on a Scroll of Distinction at the U.S. Ski Hall of Fame. The club began in 1985, and the list has included kings (the late Olav V of Norway was a member) and commoners. To become a member of this special group, send a minimum donation of $25 to the U.S. Ski Hall of Fame, (Attn: Ray Leverton), Box 191, Ishpeming MI 49849-0191.

Elderhostel offers learn-to-ski programs several times a year at Sunday River Ski Resort in Maine. The skiing is combined with other academic courses. This is the first Elderhostel campus to offer skiing. For information, call Elderhostel in Boston at (617) 426-8056.

Ski area programs: Special instruction or social programs for seniors are offered at Purgatory, Colorado; Park City, Utah; Badger Pass, California; Northstar-at-Tahoe, California; Waterville Valley, New Hampshire; Aspen, Colorado; Stratton, Vermont and Sun Valley, Idaho, among other resorts. Some are day programs; others are week-long vacations with big-band dances and wine-and-cheese parties. Resorts keep adding programs every year in order to attract this important age group.

Women's ski instruction

Nearly every major ski resort, and many of the smaller ones, has some sort of program just for women.

Why segregate? Annie Vareille-Savath, Telluride's Ski School Director, observes, "The skill level of women often drops when a man enters their ski class. Even strong, successful women, assertive in their own fields, sometimes feel intimidated and humiliated when they are in a mixed skiing atmosphere. They crumple into self-conscious inability or regress to silliness, stiffness or fear."

The goal of such seminars is not to segregate women from their male friends on the slopes permanently, but to provide a temporary environment geared to eliminating learning barriers so that "women only" instruction ultimately becomes unnecessary.

Because lessons usually are with the same instructor each day, improvement is both dramatic and clearly recognizable.

Discussions address issues particular to women skiers, such as fear of speed and equipment selection to compensate for a woman's body build. Most programs incorporate video sessions. Some seminars are as heavy on social fun as improving skills; others are directed toward higher-ability skiers who want to learn to race, ski moguls or ski powder.

There are women's programs that have received very high reviews at Squaw Valley, where instructor Elissa Slanger originated this type of program two decades ago; Telluride, where Vareille-Savath's influence as ski-school director shows through, and Crested Butte, where Kim Reichhelm, a former amateur and professional ski racer who also has been the Women's World Extreme Skiing Champion (for successfully skiing ultra-steep slopes), will operate her Women's Ski Adventures program. Information about the Telluride and Squaw Valley programs are available from those ski areas; for Reichhelm's program at Crested Butte, call (800) 992-7700.

Three of the contributors to *Skiing America* have participated in a women's seminar within the past five years and all three reported vast improvement in their skiing ability. We can recommend these programs wholeheartedly.

Research on helping women ski better is ongoing and extensive. Some of the latest discoveries are included in *WomenSki*, a book by award-winning Colorado ski journalist Claudia Carbone and published by World Leisure Corporation.

Skiing for the physically challenged

At more and more areas, you're likely to see a few empty wheelchairs next to the ski racks in the base area. Skiing is a great sport for physically challenged people, because gravity plays such a major role. Specially designed equipment is available for just about any type of disability. At most resorts that cater to this group of skiers, if they don't have the right equipment, they'll invent it. There is no reason why an otherwise disabled skier can't ski as fast as an able-bodied one; in fact, sometimes they're faster—a real ego boost for those who must proceed a little slower than most on dry land.

Winter Park, Colorado has been the pioneer in this area, and it still has one of the best programs. Hal O'Leary, founder and director of the **National Sports Center for the Disabled**, began with a few sets of borrowed skis and a broom-closet office. Now with a full-time staff of 13 and a volunteer organization of 850, Winter Park handles 2,500 participants with 45 types of disabilities, and gives 14,500 lessons yearly.

Among those who can ski are amputees, wheelchair users, the blind and those with cerebral palsy and multiple sclerosis. Write to Hal O'Leary, Director, **National Sports Center for the Disabled**, Box 36, Winter Park, CO 80482; tel. (970) 726-5514.

Disabled Sports USA (formerly National Handicapped Sports), has chapters and programs in more than 60 cities and resorts, and reports that more than 12,000 individuals are in learning programs each year. Write to 451 Hungerford Dr., Suite 100, Rockville, MD 20850; tel. (301) 217-0960.

Among the other ski schools for the disabled:

Tahoe Handicapped Ski School at Alpine Meadows; offices at 5926 Illinois Avenue, Orangevale CA 95662; (916) 989-0402. Onsite phone number: tel. (916) 581-4161.

Bear Mountain (two and a half hours east of Los Angeles) Box 6812, Big Bear Lake, CA 92315; tel. (909) 585-2519.

Breckenridge Outdoor Education Center, Box 697, Breckenridge, CO 80424; tel. (970) 453-6422.

New England Handicapped Sportsmen's Association. The program is at Mt. Snow/Haystack in Vermont; offices are at 26 McFarlin Rd., Chelmsford, MA 01824; tel. (508) 256-3240.

Ski Windham; offices at 1A Lincoln Ave., Albany, NY 12205; tel. (518) 452-6095.

Park City Handicapped Sports Association, Box 680286, Park City, UT 84068; tel. (801) 649-3991.

Clinics for advanced skiers

Advanced skiers hardly ever take lessons, and it's no wonder. Until recently, advanced skiers were taught just like beginners: groups of four to six make a few turns, then listen to the instructor give generalized tips on improvement. That format works well for lower-level skiers, all of whom need to learn the same skills. But while most skiers develop bad habits as they progress, not all develop the same ones. One skier may need to work on pole plants; another may need to keep his shoulders square to the hill and a third may be sitting too far back on her skis. Just like World Cup racers, these skiers need fine-tuning. They need a coach, not an instructor: someone who will observe the way they ski and then give very specific tips on breaking the habits that keep skiers from progressing to the next level.

Resorts are responding to advanced skiers' needs with lessons that are vastly different from the ones offered to lower-level skiers. First of all, they aren't called lessons—they are "workshops" or "clinics." Instead of the standard ski-stop-listen format, most of these clinics are heavy on ski, ski, ski and listening to the instructor as you go or while on the lift. Quite a few work on the "condition du jour"—powder, moguls, crud, etc. Many have video feedback.

If you're an intermediate or advanced skier, look into these programs. But when you're at the ski school office, here are a few tips to be sure to get what you want:

• Don't use the word "lesson." Ask what type of clinics or workshops are offered for upper-level skiers.

• Be specific when asking about the format. How much time is spent skiing? What skills will we work on?

• Insist that the instructor address each students' needs. Some instructors won't target individuals for fear of offending them. That's fine for beginners, but not for better skiers who need specific advice.

• If after the clinic you don't feel you got your money's worth, go to the ski school office and politely tell them why. ("I expected to actually ski moguls during the mogul clinic, not practice short turns on groomed slopes.") If the ski school is smart, they'll get you in the right workshop.

One instructional method we can recommend heartily is **Perfect Turn®**, which began at Sunday River, Maine, and has spread to Mt. Bachelor, Oregon; Sugarbush, Vermont; Attitash/Bear Peak, New Hampshire; Jiminy Peak, Massachusetts; and Blue Mountain, Ontario. Perfect Turn operates on total positive reinforcement. The ski pros (they aren't called instructors) never tell you what you're doing wrong; only what you're doing right.

Example: a non-Perfect Turn ski instructor would first tell a student, "You're sitting back too far on your skis," then illustrate how to correct that—perhaps by telling the student to push her shin against the tongue of her boot just enough to keep a hundred-dollar bill from flying away. The Perfect Turn ski pro skips the critical comment and goes right to the correctional tip. Additionally, the pro identifies what the skier does very well and compliments those skills lavishly.

Because he makes you feel confident about your current skills, you believe that you can take on a bigger challenge and do that well, too. Jump off that cornice into those igloo-sized moguls? Sure, coach, if you say I can do it, I can.

It may sound hokey but it works. One of our contributors, halfway between intermediate and advanced, took one Perfect Turn lesson early last season, then merrily led two *Skiing America* staffers—both advanced skiers—down a slope of cut-up powder. Throughout the season she skied black diamonds with more confidence than ever before. If you learn faster when you get positive strokes, take a trip to a ski area that offers this program.

Lake Tahoe Area

Alpine Meadows
Squaw Valley USA
Northstar-at-Tahoe, Sierra-at-Tahoe
Kirkwood, Heavenly
Diamond Peak, Sugar Bowl
with Reno, Nevada

Few regions on the North American continent have the ski-resort diversity of the Lake Tahoe region. When you consider the elements of a perfect ski vacation—variety of terrain, good snow, comfortable lodging, beautiful scenery, a wide choice of restaurants and nightlife, a myriad of other activities, accessibility—Lake Tahoe would rank near the top in all but a couple of categories (and it would be above the median in those).

Lake Tahoe, one of the largest and most stunning mountain lakes in the world, straddles the border of California and Nevada about 200 miles east of San Francisco. The lake is surrounded by five world-class ski areas, plus several smaller resorts (some of which have more than 1,000 skiable acres).

Tahoe is best divided into three regions for vacation purposes. Though you can run yourself ragged by trying to ski at every major area in a week, it's better to concentrate on the North Shore, South Shore or northeast Nevada corner. The South Shore is highly developed, lined by high-rise casino-hotels hugging the California-Nevada state line. The Nevada Northeast Shore is quiet but upscale, with fewer and smaller casinos. The California North Shore has mom-and-pop cabins, some stylish B&Bs and upscale lakefront condos.

Tahoe's ski nightlife is unique. No other ski area has 24-hour casinos and big-name entertainment on a regular basis. Whatever skiing, lodging or nightlife you like, you'll probably find it somewhere around the 72-mile perimeter of Lake Tahoe.

Because this region is so huge, we need two chapters to describe it all. This one will detail everything but the skiing. You'll find descriptions of the eight largest resorts in the next chapter.

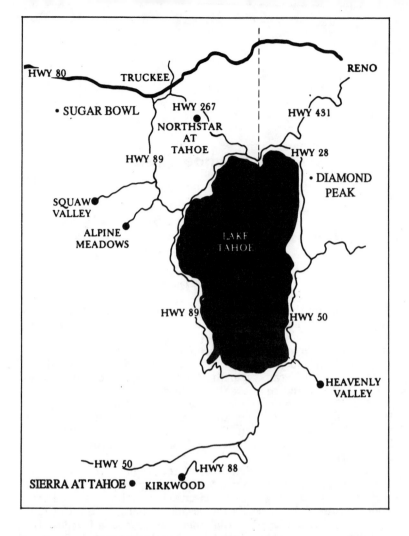

Cross-country (94/95 prices)

The Lake Tahoe region may have the greatest concentration of large cross-country ski areas in the U.S., with more than 800 km. of groomed trails. We have listed the bigger operations; local tourist offices can direct you to smaller and less expensive centers. Many of the ones we list here also have full-moon tours and snowshoe rentals and tours; call for information.

Seven of these Nordic centers offer a Lucky Seven interchangeable trail pass. They are Royal Gorge, Diamond Peak, Northstar, Spooner Lake, Squaw Creek, Tahoe Donner and Lakeview. The pass is $40 for 4 days, $48 for five and $54 for six. If you use the pass at Royal Gorge, there is a $4 surcharge.

Cross-country—North shore

The largest single area, without question, is in California at **Royal Gorge** (916-426-3871) just off I-80, west of Donner Summit at the Soda Springs exit. Royal Gorge has nearly 9,000 acres of terrain, and more than 300 km. of trail with a skating lane inside the tracks. They also make snow and use modern snowcats. Adult trail fees are $19.50, for children 7–14 $8.50; there are discounts for midweek, multiday tickets and skiers 65 and older.

Northstar-at-Tahoe (916-562-1010) has 65 km. of groomed and marked trails. Trail fees, adults $15, children 5–12 $8; lessons (one-and-a-half hour) with equipment, $20.

The Tahoe Donner Cross-Country Area (916-587-9484) is also off I-80 at Donner State Park exit. This area has 70 km. of trails, all double-tracked with wide skating lanes, and a day lodge with cafe. Tahoe Donner has California's only lighted night cross-country skiing. Day trail fees are $15 for adults, $13 for teens 13–17 and seniors 60–69, and $9 for kids 6–12. Those younger than 6 and older than 69 ski free.

Squaw Creek Cross-Country Ski Center (916-583-6300) is at the Resort at Squaw Creek, which has rentals and lessons. Trails cover 18 km. and range from beginner to expert. Trail fees are $12 for adults, $10 for children. Child care is available for ages 3-13.

Lakeview Cross-Country Ski Area (916- 583-9353) is two miles east of Tahoe City. It has 65 km. of groomed skating lanes and tracks, a lodge, cafe, lessons and rentals. Trail fees are $14 for adults, $11 for teens 13–17 and seniors 60–69, and $5 for children 7–12. Those older than 69 and younger than 7 ski free.

Cross-country—Nevada

Diamond Peak Cross-Country Area has more than 35 km. of groomed tracks and skating lanes for all levels. Trail fees are $13 for adults. Children 6-12 and seniors 60–69 pay $8. Those older than 69 and younger than 6 ski free. Rentals and lessons are available, as is a warming hut with food and beverage.

Spooner Lake Cross-Country (702-887-8844) on Highway 28 about a half-mile north of the junction with Highway 50, has more than 100 km. of trails, nearly all of which are machine groomed with one 19-km. backcountry trail. Adult trail fees are $10, children $3. Rentals and lessons are available.

Cross-country—South Shore

Kirkwood Cross-Country (209-258-7248) has 80 km. of machine-groomed tracks, skating lanes and three interconnected trail systems with three warming huts, including the 1864 Kirkwood Inn, a trappers' log cabin full of nostalgia. The White Pine trail has an environmental theme: signs along the trail discuss the flora and wildlife. Trail fees, $14 adult, $5 children, $10 seniors.

Hope Valley Cross-Country Ski Center (916-694-2203) is near the junction of Highways 89 and 88. It has about 100 km. of marked trails, a quarter of which are groomed, plus lessons and rentals. Trail fees are by donation.

Accommodations

The Tahoe basin has hundreds of options. Here, we divide them into these categories: 1) at the resorts (listed in the next chapter), 2) North Shore, 3) South Shore, 4) Reno. Skiers concentrating on Squaw, Alpine, Northstar, Diamond Peak and Sugar Bowl will find the North Shore handiest, with Reno close behind (and less expensive). Those skiing Heavenly, Sierra-at-Tahoe or Kirkwood should head to South Lake Tahoe.

Accommodations—North Shore

The North Shore of Tahoe is relatively quiet. It has bed-and-breakfast inns, cabins on the lake, plush or spartan condominiums, and medium-sized casino hotels—a place for everyone. Ours is a very small list of properties that we've toured, stayed in or had recommended by readers or trusted locals. **Tahoe North Lodging Information & Reservations** is at (800) 824-6348 (TAHOE-4-U). That agency also can also suggest private homes and condos.

The most upscale bed-and-breakfast is the **Rockwood Lodge** (916-525-5273), originally built in the mid-1930s. There are four rooms, two with private bath. It has antique furnishings, plush carpet, brass-and-porcelain bath fixtures, and down comforters on the beds. The lodge is next to the Homewood Ski Area, on the west shore of Tahoe about seven miles south of Tahoe City. Rates: About $100-$150 per night. NOTE: this is a No-Smoking inn and does not accept children.

The **Mayfield House** (916-583-1001), another B&B, was once a private residence in Tahoe City. The atmosphere is elegant and romantic. Full breakfasts come with the rate, which is $85 to $135. None of the six rooms has a private bath, but the owners hoped to add them for this ski season.

Just south of Tahoe City is the **Sunnyside Lodge** (916-583-7200, or in California only, 800-822-2754), located directly on the lake. There are 23 rooms, all with a lake view and a few rooms have fireplaces. No. 39 makes a great honeymoon suite, but reserve early because there is a four- to six-week waiting list. This is an excellent property with a lively bar après-ski and a good restaurant, the Chris Craft. Rates are $95 a night for standard rooms and up to $175 for lakefront suites.

Perhaps the most luxury for the money on the North Shore is the **Tahoe Vista Inn & Marina** (916-546-4819) in Tahoe Vista. The six units here are spectacular and sited directly on the lake.

The Jacuzzi tubs are big and the picture windows looking onto the lake are massive. Rates range from $160 a night for the smallest unit to $240 for a one-bedroom suite with a panoramic lake view.

Among the casinos just over the border, the top property is the **Cal-Neva Lodge Hotel Spa Casino** (800-225-6382 or 800-CAL-NEVA) of Frank Sinatra and Marilyn Monroe fame. Every room has a lake view, the best from the deluxe suites on the top three floors. There are also honeymoon bungalows with heart-shaped tubs, round beds and mirrored ceilings. Rates midweek are below $100, and on weekends below $125.

For families or anyone looking for a great deal, **North Lake Lodge** (916-546-2731) in Kings Beach only a few feet from the shore, is one of the oldest hotels but still in great shape. Continental breakfast is included and the shuttlebuses stop just across the street. Rates start under $100.

River Ranch (916-583-4264) on Highway 89 near Alpine Meadows, is another moderately priced lodge, with rooms in the $59 to $125 range. .

The least expensive lodging we could find is **Hostel at Squaw Valley** (916-581-3246) with dorm beds for about $25.

Away from the lake in Truckee, but convenient to Northstar and Sugar Bowl, is the **Truckee Hotel** (916-587-4444), which has been welcoming guests since 1873. Mostly it housed timber and railroad workers, but one of the residents was a madam who reportedly ran a little business on the side. It has been renovated, but you'll still feel like you're sleeping in the Old West. Some rooms have baths—the old-fashioned claw-footed kind. Those rooms cost $90–$115. Shared-bath rooms are $70–$105. Some rooms are large enough to sleep six, and there is a restaurant, The Passage, that serves lunch and dinner.

Another recommended lodge is the **Best Western Truckee-Tahoe Inn** (916-587-4525) with 100 rooms, with complimentary breakfast.

Accommodations—South Lake Tahoe

These divide into three categories: the casinos hugging the Nevada border for great views and nonstop nightlife; the top of Kingsbury Grade, near the base of Heavenly's Nevada side, for upscale condominiums and top-quality hotels; and along the California lake shore for moderately priced motels. **Central Reservations for South Lake Tahoe** is at (800) 288-2463 (AT-TAHOE). Again, we list just a tiny slice of what's available.

For casinos, try **Harvey's** (800-648-3361 from outside Nevada or 702-588-2411 from Nevada) and **Harrah's** (800-648-3353 or 702-588-3515), which has everyone's highest ratings, from AAA to Mobil. Other casino-hotels within walking distance of the state line are **Caesars Tahoe** (800-648-3353) and the **Lake Tahoe Horizon Casino Resort** (800-648-3322). For the Nevada side of Heavenly accommodations, there are scores of condos at Stagecoach Base and Boulder Base areas. At the base of Kingsbury Grade on Highway 50 you'll find the **Lakeside Inn & Casino** (800-624-7980), which offers some of the best deals. The rooms are simple and motelish but access to the mountain is excellent. Rates are $70–$100 a night. The California side of South Lake Tahoe has many small motels lining Lake Tahoe Boulevard for miles. The most luxurious hotel is the **Embassy Suites Resort** (800-362-2779 or 916-544-5400), which appears to be one of the casino-hotels, but is actually on the California side (so, no casino). Rates range $130–$220.

Among the best of the motel bunch are two Best Western properties—**The Timber Cove Lodge** (800-528-1234 or 916-541-6722), located on the beach; and **Station House Inn** (800-822-5922 or 916-542-1101), within walking distance of the casino area, on the California side of the border. Both have rooms from $88–$100.

Inn By The Lake (916-542-0330) is less than 100 feet from the lake and two miles from the casinos. It has 100 guest rooms (including nine suites with kitchens), free continental breakfast, heated pool, bi-level spa, sauna and free shuttles to the slopes. Rates start at $84 for smaller rooms to $370 for multi-bedroom suites. Midweek and AAA rates available.

Lakeland Village (800-822-5969) has a hotel and collection of condominiums right on the lake with convenient shuttlebus service to the bases of Heavenly and Kirkwood. Expect to pay $85 for a studio or $130 for a suite with loft in the Lodge. Townhouses cost from $165, for a one-bedroom unit not on the lake, to $395 for a four-bedroom, three-bath unit on the lake front. For those who want a room just across from Heavenly's lifts on the California side, the **Tahoe Seasons Resort** has received good reviews from everyone locally (916-541-6700).

One more, for couples only: The **Fantasy Inn** (800-367-7736, 916-541-6666) has about 60 rooms designed for romance. Tahoe had another Fantasy Inn a while back that was quite tacky, but this one is very tastefully done. Each room has one bed in a choice of several shapes (round, heart-shaped, water or regular mattress, king-size), a private spa for two, an in-room music system with 30 channels, adjustable peach-colored lighting and showers with double shower heads. Sixteen of the rooms are theme or theme deluxe suites, such as Rain Forest (plants and rattan decor), Caesar's Indulgence (a sexy black decor), and Romeo and Juliet (the honeymoon suite that we didn't see because it was continually booked during our visit). A wedding chapel is on the premises. Per-night rates are $110

Sunday-Thursday and $150 Friday and Saturday for the Princess room, $130/$170 for the Royal room (it's a little bigger), $170/$210 for the theme rooms and $190/$230 for theme deluxe (these have sunken tile Jacuzzis). Ask about special ski and/or wedding package rates. If you can swing it financially, rent a theme room—you won't forget it.

Accommodations—Nevada Northeast

Reno offers big-time casino atmosphere closer to the North Shore and at lower prices than you'll find at the South Shore. Reno also has a planetarium and two major museums, and is 30-45 minutes by car from the North Shore resorts. Some hotels have ski shuttles, but most visitors here probably will want a car. **Central Reservations** is at (800) 367-7366 (FOR-RENO).

Incline Village is a quiet upscale community that is home to Diamond Peak ski area. It has several very fine hotels and condo units, some of which we list in the Diamond Peak section. Call (800) 468-2463 (GO-TAHOE) for information.

Dining

North Shore (all 916 area code unless noted)

For those not concerned with price:

Glissandi at the Resort at Squaw Creek (583-6300) brings New York and San Francisco style and service, all overlooking Squaw Valley. Reservations suggested.

Captain Jon's (546-4819) in Tahoe Vista serves excellent seafood and French country specialties. Closed Mondays.

Le Petit Pier (546-4464) in Tahoe Vista presents upscale French cuisine. Reservations needed. Open daily.

Swiss Lakewood Restaurant (525-5211), in Homewood, is Lake Tahoe's oldest and one of its finest dining experiences. Cuisine is French-Swiss and classic continental, service impeccable. Closed Mondays, except holidays.

Wolfdales (583-5700) in downtown Tahoe City has superb dining. Reservations are suggested. Closed Tuesdays.

Graham's is a new restaurant that locals recommend, located in Squaw Valley at the Christy Inn (581-0454).

Katy Keck's recommendation: **Christy Hill** in Tahoe City (115 Grove Street, reservations recommended, 583-8551) is a real find. Just on the edge of the Lake Tahoe North Shore, Christy Hill offers superb lake views in an intimate, casually elegant atmosphere. Chef-owner Matt Adams and his wife Debbie are charming hosts, which makes every visit a delight.

The menu, which changes several times each week, is loaded with the freshest fish and specialty produce. Matt's fascination with eastern flavors is evident, but his style is pure California. The restaurant is open for dinner only from Tuesday through

Sunday from 5:30 p.m. Appetizers are $8-$10 and entrées range from $18 to $24.

On the other side of the lake, in Incline Village, head for **The Lone Eagle Grill** at the Hyatt Regency (702-832-1234) for some of the best food that the Nevada lakeshore offers in one Tahoe's most spectacular architectural and natural settings. The soaring stone and timber, with a massive fireplace blend with magnificent views across the lake at sunset, and the cuisine and extensive wine list provide accomplished accompaniment.

For more moderate fare try:

Ristorante D'Aosta in Olympic House at Squaw Valley USA (583-2614) provides an elegantly casual setting, or ride the cable car to the top of Squaw Valley USA and dine at the **Alexander's** (583-2555) overlooking Granite Chief and Emigrant Peaks.

The Basque Club Restaurant (562-2460) in the Northstar-at-Tahoe Golf Clubhouse serves a family-style five-course meal of traditional Basque cuisine—be sure you're hungry. There are always two entrées, plus many side dishes you think are entrées before the real thing is served. Sleigh rides depart hourly from the clubhouse.

Black Bear Tavern (583-8626) is in a historic log building just south of Tahoe City on Highway 89, with gourmet dinners at moderate prices. **A.J.'s Ristorante** (546-3640) in Tahoe Vista is new, featuring Northern Italian cuisine and beautiful lake views.

In Truckee: **The Passage** in the Truckee Hotel has good soups and interesting salads; the bar is cozy but the dining-room is uninviting and small. **OB's** has a pleasantly cluttered decor with old farm antiques and very creative tastes (example: potato-asparagus soup with nutmeg) at cheap prices.

Others to try closer to the lake: **River Ranch** at the access road to Alpine Meadows; **Jake's on the Lake** (583-0188) in Tahoe City; **La Playa** (546-5903) in Tahoe Vista; **Gar Woods** (546-3366) in Carnelian Bay; **Za's** (583-1812) in Tahoe City for moderately priced Italian; **Grazie!** (583-0233) in the Roundhouse Mall for "nouveau" Italian food and great lake views. **The Soule Domain** (546-7529) in Crystal Bay received consistent raves from people at both ends of the lake. For Mexican with a big dose of margaritas and a shoulder-to-shoulder crowd on weekends, a good choice is the **Hacienda del Lago** (583-0358) in Tahoe City in the Boatworks Mall.

For lots of good food at very reasonable prices:

Bacchi's (583-3324) just outside Tahoe City or **Lanza's** (546-2434) in Kings Beach, both serving good Italian fare. **The Family Tree** in Tahoe City has perhaps the best all-round family food. **Bobby's Cafe** (546-2329) serves great ribs, **Willii B's** (583-0346) is known for great Cajun, and **Bridgetender** (583-3342) for burgers and an extensive beer selection.

The casinos on the Nevada border all serve inexpensive breakfast, lunch and dinner specials.

For the best pizza, try **Pizza Junction** (587-7411) outside of Truckee, where they make their own Truckee River Beer, or **Lake House Pizza** (583-2222) where you can enjoy a great view of Lake Tahoe, as well as **C.B's Pizza** (546-4758) in Kings Beach.

Azzara's (702-831-0346) in Incline Village serves good reasonable Italian food.

The best breakfasts are at the **Squeeze In** (587-9814) in Truckee where the list of omelets requires a speed-reading course. The Squeeze In has all the atmosphere you could want in a breakfast joint, built in a former alley and only 10 feet wide. On weekends expect to wait a while—this place is popular. Down the street is the **Coffee And**, which also serves up a good basic breakfast. Also try **The Fire Sign** about two miles south of Tahoe City, and for those further to the north, try the **Old Post Office** in Carnelian Bay or the **Log Cabin** in Kings Beach. Near Alpine Meadows, try **The Alpine Riverside Cafe** for breakfast and lunch.

South Lake Tahoe

For the best restaurants in the higher priced category:

Evan's American Gourmet Café on State Route 89 has become one of the best-liked restaurants on the south shore. The chef prepares California Cuisine with an unusual flair. Expect to pay for his efforts, but they are reported to be well worth it. **Primavera Restaurant** in Caesar's Hotel & Casino serves Italian poolside in an atmosphere reminiscent of quaint European cafes with excellent service, quality and wine list.

For good reasonable restaurants, try:

Fresh Ketch for fish, **Cantina Los Tres Hombres** or **Bueno Rico's** for Mexican, or head to one of the casinos' great buffets or fixed-price dinners. **Harvey's** has a reasonably priced seafood buffet with large portions. **Zackary's Restaurant** in Embassy Suites has the best blackened salmon. **Bennigan's** is in Bill's Tahoe Casino across from the High Sierra. Others to try are **Beacon**, on the lake with blackened prime rib a speciality; and **Nephies**, which serves California cuisine in a cozy setting and has private hot-tub rentals.

For great breakfasts head to **The Red Hut**, where you can pack into a small room and listen to the talk of the town. A new branch opened on Kingsbury Grade handy for skiers heading to the Nevada side of Heavenly. At **Heidi's**, you can get anything from dozens of Belgian waffles to chocolate pancakes. The other two locals' spots for morning gossip and breakfast, **Frank's** and **Ernie's**, just about face each other on Route 50 south.

At Heavenly, table linen lunch service is offered at **Top of the Tram** Restaurant. Heavenly also has a new gourmet picnic service, **Heavenly Mountain Caterers** (916-542-5153). Place your reservation by 10 a.m. and enjoy a steak or chicken lunch, either at one of the lodges or in a secluded outdoor location with great views. It's $25 per person (plus tip and tax), two people minimum.

And just in case you crave a malt "so thick it holds the straw up," head to the **Zephyr Cove Resort**. Try the banana-chocolate shake.

Après-ski/nightlife

South Shore: Head to **Carlos Murphy's** immediately after skiing or stop in the **California Bar** at Heavenly's Base Lodge, with its famous California brown bear. If you want quieter après-ski with a flickering fireplace, stop in at **Christiana Inn** across from the Heavenly ski area.

Later in the evening, **Turtle's**, a Tahoe institution which relocated to the Embassy Suites, has good dancing. **Wild West**, in the Round Hill Mall, plays a mixture of C&W, R&B and Top 40.

And of course, the casinos have musical reviews that are extravaganzas of sight and sound with top-name performers.

North Shore: At Squaw, local hangouts include **Slopes** at the Squaw Valley Inn and **Bullwackers** at the Resort at Squaw Creek. Also try **River Ranch** on the Alpine Meadows access road, which was voted top après-ski in North Lake Tahoe.

In Tahoe City, places to head include **Pete 'n' Peter's**, **Rosie's Café**, **Pierce Street Annex** behind Safeway near the Boatworks Mall or **Sunnyside**, just a couple of miles south of Tahoe City on the lake. **Hacienda del Lago** in the Boatworks has nachos till 6 p.m. or try **Humpty's** across from Safeway.

In Truckee there is occasional music at **The Passage** in the Truckee Hotel and at the **Bar of America** and the **Pastime Club**, both at Commercial Row. The **Cottonwood Restaurant** overlooking Truckee on Highway 267 has jazz. The casinos on North Lake Tahoe have entertainment every night. Sure bets are the **Cal-Neva Lodge**, **The Crystal Bay Club**, **Hyatt Lake Tahoe** and the **Tahoe Biltmore**.

A hot, relatively new après-ski spot is **Naughty Dawg** on the main road in Tahoe City, where you can get munchies and speciality drinks served in dog dishes and "shotskis," a ritual of drinks served in an unusual way.

Getting there and getting around

By air: Reno-Tahoe International Airport has more than 90 nonstop flights a day from various parts of the country. The airport is 45 miles from Squaw Valley USA, 50 miles from Alpine Meadows, 35 miles from Diamond Peak, 38 miles from Northstar-at-Tahoe, 55 miles from Heavenly and 70 miles from Kirkwood.

The Lake Tahoe Airport, near South Lake Tahoe and 10 minutes from Heavenly, has service from California including two daily nonstops from Los Angeles on Reno Air jets. Buses and hotel shuttles take skiers to the resorts from both airports.

By train: Amtrak serves Truckee and Reno on the California Zephyr line, running Oakland to Chicago. Call (800) 872-7245.

By boat: The Tahoe Queen Ski Shuttle, an authentic Mississippi sternwheeler, double-decked and heated, takes South Shore skiers for $18 across Lake Tahoe to and from the big North Shore resorts. (Buses take skiers from the dock to the ski areas.) A breakfast buffet and dinner are served; price extra. The return trip includes dancing and cocktails. Call (916) 541-3364 for reservations, and confirm a day before, because departures depend on ice conditions on the lake.

By bus: Shuttles run from almost every major hotel to each principal ski resort. Check for schedules when you arrive. Most of the shuttles that cruise around the North or South Shores are free, but when you need to go from one end of the lake to the other, expect to pay about $4 round-trip. Call the ski areas or hotels for more information.

Sierra Nevada Gray Lines (800-822-6009 or 702-329-1147) operates a daily ski shuttle between downtown Reno and Alpine Meadows, Northstar-at-Tahoe (except Saturdays) and Squaw Valley USA from mid-December through the end of March. **Tahoe Casino Express** runs 14 times daily between Reno airport and South Shore for about $15 each way.

By car: Driving time from Reno is about an hour to any major resort except Kirkwood, which is approximately 90 minutes. San Francisco is about four hours away, by I-80 to the North Shore and Highway 50 to South Lake Tahoe. During storms, the police don't let anyone up the mountains without chains or a 4-wheel-drive vehicle, so come prepared.

Sugar Bowl is off I-80 just west of Donner Lake. Alpine Meadows and Squaw Valley are on Highway 89 and Northstar-at-Tahoe is on Highway 267 (both highways run between I-80 and Highway 28, which hugs the North Shore). Diamond Peak is on Highway 28 in Nevada on the lake's east side, Heavenly is right off Highway 50 in South Lake Tahoe and Kirkwood is on Highway 88 (follow signs from South Lake Tahoe).

Though we hate to make this recommendation, (because it adds to the congestion and pollution around this beautiful lake), bring a car if you intend to move frequently from north to south, or if you are staying in North Lake Tahoe. You can get along fine without a car if you station yourself in South Lake Tahoe and use public transportation. Based on personal experience, we also recommend that you concentrate on either the North Shore or South Shore during a trip to avoid running yourself ragged.

The Tahoe Area Ski Resorts

Squaw Valley USA

> ### Squaw Valley USA Facts
> **Base elevation:** 6,200'; **Summit elevation:** 9,050'; **Vertical drop:** 2,850 feet
> **Number of lifts:** 33—1 cable car, 1 six-passenger gondola, 4 quad superchairs,
> 8 triple chairs, 15 double chairs, 4 surface lifts
> **Percent snowmaking:** 10 percent; **Total acreage:** 4,000 lift-served acres
> **Uphill capacity:** 49,100 per hour; **Bed Base:** 1,600 within 3 miles

Squaw Valley USA is perhaps the best-known ski resort in the region, having hosted the 1960 Winter Olympics. It offers some of the finest skiing in the United States. Opening the trail map of Squaw, you'll notice that there aren't any trail-cut runs, just wide-open snow fields—4,000 acres of them. Anything within the boundaries can be skied by anyone daring enough to challenge the mountain. Super skiers test themselves here.

Access starts at the base with a six-person gondola or the 150-skier cable car. Or start with the Squaw One superchair and then connect to others. Six separate peaks, each with every conceivable exposure, overlook Lake Tahoe.

Extreme skiers will be in heaven at Squaw. Two popular spots are the Palisades above Siberia Bowl and Eagle's Nest at the top of KT22. Locals will take you to where you can ski terrain that resembles an elevator shaft.

Experts who like to keep their skis on the snow will find plenty of challenging terrain. The entire KT22 side of Squaw Valley is expert. Try Chute 75, the Alternates, and the Dead Tree Chute, or the National Chute off the Palisades. At Elevation 8200, on the upper mountain, try the Funnel or the Elevator Shaft, or hike to the top of Granite Chief. These are very black diamonds.

The intermediate terrain also has challenge and variety. By taking the Headwall Lift, skiers can opt for Chicken Bowl or drop over the back of the ridge to Sun Bowl. Up Siberia Express, experts turn to the left getting off the lift, intermediates traverse to the right. There Newport, Mainline, Gold Coast and Emigrant serve wide-open intermediate slopes. Intermediates will like the Shirley Lake area served by a detachable quad and a triple chair. The Mountain Run is a great end-of-the-day cruise: top to bottom, it's a hefty 3.5-mile run. Another great heading-home cruise is Home Run. Or give the new intermediate Olympic High ski run a try. It follows the route of the original 1960 Olympic men's downhill, won by France's Jean Vuarnet of current sunglasses fame. It begins above the bottom shack of Headwall and heads to the base, bypassing the Mountain Run entirely.

Though Squaw Valley's well publicized black-diamond terrain has given it a menacing reputation, it has a little-known surprise: this is a great spot for never-evers to learn. Squaw has a gentle bowl at the top of the cable car known as Bailey's Beach, served by two slow-moving lifts. Though Bailey's Beach is not physically separated from the other terrain, better skiers rarely use it. Beginners usually long to head toward any summit just like the big boys and girls, and here they can. They just ride the cable car up to High Camp (where they'll also find restaurants, shelter and an outdoor ice rink), and at the end of the day, ride the cable car back down.

Snowboarding

Snowboarding is permitted on all sections of Squaw Valley USA. Squaw has a halfpipe, lessons, special clinics, rentals and a terrain park adjacent to the Riviera Lift.

Lessons (95/96 prices)

Never-evers get a **First-Timer Package** for either skiing or snowboarding that includes a beginner lift ticket, equipment rental and a two-hour lesson—skiing costs $54 and Snowboarding is $59. Call the ski school at (916) 581-7263.

Lower intermediate to intermediate skier levels get instruction through a **Ski Your Pro** format where instructors are assigned to training areas on the mountain, and skiers can join in on the half hour for as long as they want for $29. Higher-level skiers get two-hour **workshops** that center on a specific skill, such as moguls, powder or gate training, also for $29.

Private lessons cost $60 an hour and $20 for each additional person. All-day private lessons run $300.

Children aged 4–12 can take an all-day lesson, including lunch, lift ticket, activities and ski instruction for $60. The half-day price is $40 and includes a snack instead of lunch.

Child care (95/96 prices)

Squaw Valley USA's Children's World has licensed care for toddlers, ages 2–3. All-day care is $60 with lunch, activities and supervision, while half-day care is $40 (no lunch). Parents must provide current immunization records. A one-and-a-half-hour ski option is available for 3-year-olds for an extra $7. Reservations are required; call (916) 583-5585.

Lift tickets (95/96 prices)

	Adult	Child (Up to 12) Senior (65+)
One day	$45	$5
Three days	$120 ($40/day)	$15 ($5/day)
Five days	$120 ($38/day)	$25 ($5/day)

No, that's not a misprint. Children and seniors ski for $5 here, less than the cost of a single cable car or gondola ride, which is $13 for adults, $5 for children.

Squaw has an unusual "No-waiting-in-line-or-your-money-back" program. For $1, skiers register as beginner, intermediate or expert; if the average wait in the registered category is more than 10 minutes, the skier receives a full refund and skis the rest of the day free.

Accommodations

Squaw Valley has several lodging choices. All lodges give easy access to the slopes, but evening activities are limited. Even if you are staying at Squaw, it is best to rent a car if you'd like to explore dining and nightlife in Truckee and Tahoe City.

Resort at Squaw Creek (800-327-3353) is a luxurious hotel that, despite being several stories tall, blends well with the valley. This hotel connects with the ski area by its own lift, and is virtually a self-contained resort. No restaurant problem here: there are five. Squaw Creek also has three pools (one of which is open in winter), several hot tubs, a complete fitness center, cross-country skiing and an ice-skating rink. Rates start at $198 per night midweek, $270 weekends in high season.

Squaw Valley Lodge (800-992-9920; in California, 800-922-9970) is only a few yards' walk from the lifts. The lodge boasts a fully equipped health club, free covered parking and kitchenettes in the units. Cost: $160 a night and up for a studio midweek in high season.

The Olympic Village Inn, (800) 845-5243 (800-VILLAGE) or (916) 583-1501, has five hot tubs, and all units have kitchens. Rates: $195 a night on weekends, $165 Sunday-Thursday.

The **Squaw Valley Inn,** (800) 323-7666 or 916-583-5176 is more like a basic hotel, across from the gondola and cable car. Rates start at $145 midweek, $185 on weekends.

Squaw Valley USA also has **central reservations:** (800) 545-4350 or (916) 583-5585.

Alpine Meadows

Alpine Meadows Facts
Base elevation: 6,835'; **Summit elevation:** 8,637'; **Vertical drop:** 1,802 feet
Number of lifts: 12–2 quad superchairs, 2 triple chairs, 7 double chairs, 1 surface lift
Percent snowmaking: 12 percent, runs from 10 lifts
Total acreage: 2,000 skiable acres
Uphill capacity: 16,000 per hour; **Bed base:** 10,000 (N. Lake Tahoe Area)

For every level of skier, particularly intermediate and advanced, Alpine Meadows has something to offer. It has expert terrain, overwhelming intermediate bowls and trails, and an excellent beginner area. Alpine may seem like a relatively small area until you take the Summit Chair and see it unfold beneath you.

As you ride up the lift, to the right are the expert Wolverine Bowl, Beaver Bowl and Estelle Bowl; to the left spreads the seemingly endless Alpine Bowl, graded as intermediate.

Experts approaching Alpine Meadows have plenty of great bowl skiing and enough steeps to keep their hearts in their throats. Here's a route suggestion: take the expert bowls, to the right ascending the Summit Chair, then take the Summit Chair again and cruise down into the blue territory of Alpine Bowl. Finally, take the Alpine Bowl Chair and traverse to the Sherwood Bowls on the backside of the area or take the High Yellow Traverse to the Saddle Bowl. When you come up the Sherwood Chair, drop down Our Father—and you can say a few enroute—then head to Scott Chair and try out Scott Chute for a direct plunge, or take it easy on tree-lined roundabouts. By then your knees will have earned a cruise. Nearby, the Promised Land has great tree skiing for top skiers.

Intermediates, especially those who are better than average, will find this ski area perfect. Stay here all day using the Alpine Bowl Chair, or make endless runs off the Roundhouse, Lakeview and Kangaroo Chairs. Beginners will find themselves limited to a small but sheltered area close to the base lodge.

In the Lake Tahoe area, Alpine Meadows has traditionally been the ski area with the earliest and longest season (it stayed open until July 4, 1995 with top to bottom skiing).

Snowboarding
Not allowed.

Lessons (95/96 prices)
Alpine Meadows divides its lessons into ones for beginners, and those for everyone else. A two-day **adult learn-to-ski** program includes beginner lifts, equipment and four hours of instruction for $82. Skiers can take two morning sessions, or morning and afternoon. Additional two-hour sessions are $10 and you can take as many as you need. Other **group lessons** are $32 for two hours, $25 for each additional two-hour session. Alpine also offers a coupon book of five two-hour lessons for $140 ($28 each). Anyone may use the coupons, so this is a good deal for families where everyone wants to take a refresher.

Private lessons are for 1-2 people with rates that vary depending on time. From 9–10 a.m. or 9–11 a.m., the cost is $50 per hour. During prime time, 10 a.m.–noon, the cost is $70 per hour; from noon–4 p.m. $60 per hour. For three or more people, add $20 a person.

Telemark lessons and rentals are offered for the same prices as downhill.

Children's lessons: The youngest age accepted by the Alpine Meadows Snow School is 4 years. Snow school for children 4–6 costs $62 a full day and $57 for an additional child from the same family; $42 a half day and $39 per additional child. Reservations are recommended but not required.

Kids Ski Camp is for children 6–12, and it sounds like so much fun we want to enroll too. Kids get lessons, of course, but they also visit and learn about snow grooming, avalanche dog rescuers, ski patrol and other mountain services. For never-evers, a two-hour program with lessons, rentals and lift ticket is $45, plus $10 for additional sessions. For children who already ski, the cost is $32 per two hours, which includes a lift ticket. A supervised lunch option includes an hour lunch and an hour more of lessons for $25 between noon and 2 p.m.

Child care
Alpine Meadows has no child care.

Lift tickets (95/96 prices)

	Adult	Child (7–12)
One day	$45	$18
Three days	$123 ($41/day)	$48 ($16/day)
Five days	$198 ($39.60/day)	$75 ($15/day)

Seniors 65-69 ski for $30, children 6 and younger ski for $6, 70+ ski free.

Accommodations
Alpine Meadows doesn't have lodging at the base, but has lodging-lift packages. Call Alpine Meadows at (800) 441-4423.

Northstar-at-Tahoe

Northstar-at-Tahoe Facts
Base elevation: 6,330; **Summit elevation:** 8,610; **Vertical drop:** 2,280 feet
Number of lifts: 12–1 gondola, 4 quad superchairs, 2 triple chairs, 2 double chairs, 3 surface lifts
Percent snowmaking: 50 percent of developed acres
Total acreage: 2,000 total acres, 500 developed acres
Uphill capacity: 19,400 per hour; **Bed Base:** 3,500 at resort

---

Unlike Squaw and Alpine, Northstar is a planned resort area, designed to make skiing easy. Condos line the lower slopes, and the runs are laid out for family skiing. Here an intermediate can feel like a World Cup racer. The grooming is impeccable—you'll have to look hard for bumps—and the entire area management and operations are squeaky clean.

Although Northstar's Mount Pluto is an extinct volcano, you won't find bowls and cornices as at Squaw or that other massive Western volcano, Mammoth. The skiing is all trail-cut.

Advanced skiers or those aspiring to the upper levels of intermediate will find some challenge in the drops off the East Ridge (labeled as black diamonds, but the mapmaker was being generous). Normally at least two of the runs are groomed and the others have moderate bumps. Tonini's is the longest, but The Plunge is the steepest. The only bad part is that it's over too soon. Chute, Crosscut and Powderbowl are also fun—short but sweet. If you're an air skier, you'll be disappointed; these blacks would be blues at Squaw.

Instead of getting your exhilaration by plummeting down some shaft, enjoy the longer rides with moderately steep and sustained pitch off the backside via Lookout Chair and the long traverse called Back Door. This run makes you feel as though you're in another mountain range, far away from any crowds; eight stretched-out swaths provide some of the longest continuous pitches in the West, all served by the Backside Express quad lift. Though they're all labeled as advanced runs, an intermediate will have no difficulty in good conditions.

The gem of Northstar lies between these runs, through the trees. Start down Rail Splitter, then take off into the woods to the right or left. After a storm, Northstar is one of the prime areas where locals can enjoy powder through the trees long after Squaw's powder has been skied off.

Intermediates will enjoy the smooth blues that descend from the two ridges into Main Street, the intermediate run that nearly every other run on the mountain feeds into. Avoid Main Street except when you need to get to a lift.

Northstar is a good never-ever and beginner resort because its gentlest terrain is below the gondola, while all the other runs are above it. Better skiers leave this terrain to the learners except at day's end, when some of them use it to practice tucks. Luckily for everyone, this is fairly flat terrain, so no one can keep up excessive speed.

Snowboarding

Boarding is allowed on all areas of the mountain. Snowboard lessons are available and boards may be rented at the Village Ski Rental Shop. A free one-hour clinic is offered Monday mornings at 9 a.m. except on holidays.

Lessons (95/96 prices)

Beginner group lessons: Intro to Skiing I is a 1 3/4-hour lesson with beginner lift access and equipment for $43; Intro to Skiing II is the same program but with expanded lifts for $63. Three-day programs for skiing, boarding, women, men and seniors, with lessons and lifts, are $225 (Seniors 60–69 pay $153, those 70 and over pay $103).

Skill improvement clinics for higher level skiers are $25 for a 1.75-hour lesson. Specialty three-day clinics for women, seniors and snowboarders are offered a few times per year. There is a free one-hour seniors' (age 60+) clinic is every Wednesday at 9 a.m. Free one-hour women's or men's clinics are Tuesdays at 9 a.m.

Northstar has a Ski With The Legends clinic program for advanced skiers, taught by well known former U.S. Team skiers and freestyle champs. Clinics are twice daily and cost $25; call for instructor schedule. On Thursdays there is a free one-hour clinic with the legends.

Private lessons run $60 per hour with each additional person $20. Take your private lesson at 9 a.m. and you'll save $10.

The **Starkids** all-day program for children 5 to 12 is $60 a day with lifts, lessons and lunch (add $11 for ski gear; $21 for snowboard equipment). An introduction to skiing program costs $35 for the first level and $45 for the next higher level.

Child care (95/96 prices)

Minors' Camp licensed day care accepts toilet-trained children 2-6 years old. The program combines skiing with other activities, including art, snow play, science, drama and language development. Reservations are suggested; call (916) 562-2278. Costs: all day, $45; slightly more for ski instruction. Hours: 8 a.m. to 4:30 p.m.

Lift tickets (95/96 prices)

	Adult	Child (5–12)
One day	$43	$19
Three days	$116 ($38.66/day)	$51 ($17/day)
Five days	$190 ($38/day)	$78 ($15.60/day)

Senior rate is $22 a day for skiers 60 to 69, and $5 for those over 70. A gondola ride costs $5/$3. Children under five with a parent ski free.

NOTE: Northstar's parking lot sometimes fills on busy days, and skiers are turned away at the entrance. If you can figure out a way to get to the window, though, you can still ski.

Northstar also has an electronic frequent-skier program called Club Vertical that offers discounted lift tickets, prizes for achieving certain vertical-feet totals, and a separate chair lift entrance to help you speed through lift lines.

Accommodations (95/96 prices)

This area was created for condo living. The village has a convenient lodge, with rooms from $149 a night, two-night minimum. The condo rates range from $139 a night for a studio to $280 for a two-bedroom, two-bath unit. Northstar also has full-sized homes for rent, accommodating five to eight people for $356 to $585 a night. Special packages include lifts, rentals and lessons. Reservations: (800) 466-6784.

Sierra-at-Tahoe

Northstar has a sister resort, Sierra-at-Tahoe, at the south end of Lake Tahoe. It also is a family-oriented area, but leans more toward a day crowd than a resort atmosphere. With 10 lifts,

2,000 acres and a 2,212-foot vertical, it definitely is worth a trip for those staying at the southern end of the lake. Lift tickets are less than $40 for adults, with discounts for teens, children and seniors.

Among its best features are a snowboard park with halfpipe, a summit sundeck with lake views, and a children's day care and ski center with care for ages 2–5 and lessons for ages 4-12, including a Magic Carpet lift (best described as a slow moving conveyor belt) exclusively for kids' classes. Sierra-at-Tahoe also operates the Club Vertical program, so club members can build reward points at either spot. Sierra-at-Tahoe has no on-site accommodations, but free shuttles run from lodging at South Lake Tahoe, 12 miles west on Highway 50.

For more information, call (916) 659-7453.

Heavenly Ski Resort

Heavenly Ski Resort Facts

California Side–Base: 6,540'; **Summit:** 10,040'; **Vertical drop:** 3,500 feet
Nevada Side–Base: 7,200'; **Summit:** 10,040'; **Vertical drop:** 2,840 feet
Number of lifts: 24–Aerial tram, 3 quad superchairs, 8 triple chairs, 7 double chairs, 5 surface lifts; **Percent snowmaking:** 66 percent (240 acres)
Total acreage: 4,800 patrolled acres (1,084 skiable trail acres)
Uphill capacity: 29,000 per hour; **Bed Base:** 22,000 in S. Lake Tahoe

---

Heavenly is big. It ranks Number One at Lake Tahoe for highest elevation (10,040 feet), greatest vertical rise (3,500 feet) and longest run (5.5 miles). Except for its famous face run—Gunbarrel—and Mott Canyon, the resort is most appropriate for the giant intermediates and advanced skiers category: 90 percent of America's skiers.

Heavenly is also the only two-state ski resort—you can start out from either California or Nevada.

The California base, on Ski Run Boulevard from Highway 50, strikes awe in all but the best skiers because the world seems to drop straight down into Lake Tahoe. Gunbarrel and East Bowl are straight ladders of bumps 1,700 feet high, often with dangerous-looking rocky protrusions in early winter or late spring. Leap over that by taking either the Gunbarrel Chair or the aerial tram. Then head down Patsy's (a horrible bottleneck on weekends, unfortunately) to the Waterfall Chair, which gives access to superb intermediate and advanced runs off Ridge, Canyon and Sky Express Chairs.

From the top of the Sky Express, the best of the California side opens up. After you have admired the inspiring view of Lake Tahoe, drop down Ellie's if you are looking for bumps—or if you want long smooth cruising, head to the right when you get off the chair and steam down Liz's, Canyon, Betty's or Ridge Run. Sometimes you can catch Ellie's when it's groomed.

When you have had enough of California, strike out for Nevada, where 50 percent of the terrain is located. (The connecting trail now has snowmaking coverage.) You get to the Nevada side from the top of Sky Express; go left along the Skyline Trail, which requires a bit of pushing. Now here's the trick for advanced intermediates who want the best of the Milky Way Bowl: the Skyline Trail will dip a bit after you get off the Sky Express Chair. You then have to make a small climb and the trail starts down again. Just as you begin dropping, look to your right for tracks leading into the trees and follow them. After a short traverse you will end up at the top of the Milky Way Bowl with about twice the vertical you would have found had you stayed on the trail. The same traverse applies to skiers riding on the Dipper, which is the summit chair on the Nevada side. If you ski from the top of Milky Way to the bottom of Mott Canyon in one long run you will drop over 2,000 vertical feet through black and blacker terrain.

The Nevada side has even better cruises. From the top of the Dipper are the Big Dipper and Orion. Advanced intermediates with moguls on their minds can bump down Big Dipper Bowl or traverse a bit further and try the Little Dipper. Another good advanced run is through the ponderosa pines on either side of Little Dipper. The Galaxy Chair is a good spot for low intermediates to gain confidence. For a cruise that seems to take forever, take Olympic Downhill to Stagecoach Base.

Skiers can also start from the Nevada side by driving on the Kingsbury Grade to either the Stagecoach or Boulder bases. Most skiers start from California, so doing this is often a good way to avoid the crowds.

Super-experts who used to scorn Heavenly now have their own playground, Mott Canyon. This north-facing wall is peppered with pines and has half-a-dozen advanced expert chutes. This lift-served area can only be entered through designated gates.

Home to California means taking the Dipper Express to the top and traversing right to the California Trail. Or take Comet and then cruise the 49er run. The runs meander into a small depression where the three-mile winding Roundabout trail down the face gets most of the intermediate traffic at the end of the day (beginners may want to ride the tram back down). Or with a short lift up, mogul maniacs can get to the top of Gunbarrel and East Bowl.

Though Heavenly is exactly that for intermediates and up, never-evers should pick another resort for their skiing baptism. Except for a tiny learning section at the California base, Heavenly's green terrain is smack in the middle of a place where four lifts have their boarding areas. Skiers dart in every direction, making a most intimidating scene.

Snowboarding

Snowboarding is allowed on both sides of the mountain. When there's enough snow, Heavenly constructs a halfpipe, and The Airport is a snowboard park under Olympic Chair in Nevada. Lessons and rentals are available on the Nevada and California sides. A never-ever snowboard lesson is three hours long and includes a limited-access lift ticket for $35, while an intermediate or advanced Mountain Adventure lesson is $28. This lesson has a You Be The Judge guarantee—if you didn't learn anything new, you can repeat the lesson.

Lessons (95/96 prices)

Group lessons include a never-ever special for $45 that includes a three-hour lesson, rentals and access to the beginner lifts.

Group lessons for other levels are in the form of **special workshops.** The Adult Mountain Adventure is $29 for two hours, $78 for three lessons and $125 for five. These do not have to be used consecutively, and all have the You Be The Judge guarantee, where you can repeat the class if you didn't learn anything new. Daily Specials show how to master the conditions of the day— powder, crud, moguls. Twenty-minute Quick Tip clinics cost $10.

Heavenly has special three-day **clinics** for for women, Seasoned Skiers (50+) and "Be Strong To Ski Strong," which includes instruction for muscle-strengthening and reflex-sharpening to help improve on-hill performance. Each clinic is offered once a month January through March (the women's also runs in December), usually midweek. Call for specific schedules.

Private lessons are $55 an hour per person between 9 and 10 a.m., and $65 per hour at 10 a.m. or after, which the resort suggests for beginners only. Each additional person is $30. Two-hour private lessons cost $100 for one person, three hours cost $160, and all-day private lessons are $350 for one to five people. Reservations suggested. Call (702) 586-7000, ext. 6244.

Ski Explorers is a **children's program** for ages 4-12. Full day ($60) includes instruction, lunch, snacks and lift access. Half day ($40) is from 10 a.m. to noon, without lunch. On heavy snow days or for children who can't ski a whole day, Ski Explorers also includes some behind-the-scenes field trips to see a grooming snowcat, how the ski patrol works, or avalanche dog demonstrations.

Child care

Heavenly has no child care program.

Lift tickets (95/96 prices)

	Adult	Child (6–12) Senior (65+)
One day	$44	$19
Three days	$129 ($43/day)	$54 ($18/day)
Five days	$205 ($41/day)	$90 ($18/day)

Youth (ages 13–15) ski for $31 a day, $90 for three days, $120 for five days. Children 5 and younger ski free with a paying adult.

Accommodations

Heavenly's base area is in South Lake Tahoe, which means plenty of lodging (see the South Lake Tahoe Accommodations section). **Heavenly Central Reservations** can arrange an entire ski vacation including airfare, transfers, lessons, rentals, non-ski activities, skiing and lodging. Midweek packages are a particularly good deal. (800) 243-2836 (2-HEAVEN) or (702) 588-4584.

Kirkwood

> ## Kirkwood Facts
> **Base elevation:** 7,800'; **Summit elevation:** 9,800'; **Vertical drop:** 2,000 feet
> **Number of lifts:** 11–6 triple chairs, 4 double chairs, 1 surface lift
> **Snowmaking:** none **Total acreage:** 2,300 patrolled acres; 1,500 skiable trail acres
> **Uphill capacity:** 15,000 per hour; **Bed Base:** 10,500 in S. Lake Tahoe

After the bustle of Heavenly and its casino-laced hometown, Kirkwood is like taking a trip back into the wilderness. The lovely drive through Hope Valley to Kirkwood from South Lake Tahoe takes only about 45 minutes, but it is light-years away in altitude and ambiance. There are no bright lights, no ringing jackpots, no wide blue lake, no high-rise buildings and no urban noise. Instead, you have the feeling that you are entering a special secret place, known to a select few.

Kirkwood is a great area for skiers who have mastered the stem christie and who are just into paralleling, and it will thrill any expert, even super-expert, with its steeps and dozens of chutes. Kirkwood's northeast exposure in a snow pocket gives light, dry conditions and produces storms that linger and dump more. Last season, Kirkwood stayed open until May 29, with good late-season conditions.

Right now, Kirkwood has no snowmaking—the only major California ski area that has none. By the time you read this, however, Kirkwood may be covering some of its popular runs with machine-made snow, including one top-to-bottom run.

Beginners will find a great learning area served by Snowkirk Chair to the east, and the beginner area reached by Bunny Chair at the far west. Intermediates choose to ski either on the lower sections of the face, using the Hole 'n' Wall and Solitude Chairs, or work their way over Caples Crest (Chair Two), then stay high on the trail (far right) and traverse to the Sunrise section. Here is plenty of groomed intermediate terrain to the east of Chair Four (Sunrise). This area is called The Wave because it gets a cornice that looks like a giant rounder. On the right, or west, side of the chair the half dozen runs of Thunder Saddle keep powder for three days after a snowfall because it takes two chairs to get skiers there. Watch your step along the ridge. When you get toward the bottom of the steeps, after dropping down One Man Chute, Bogie's Slide or Corner Chute, tuck and keep your speed up for the flat run back to the Wagonwheel or Cornice chairs.

Chair Ten (Wagonwheel) had a new entry cut to eliminate the leap formerly required to get into the black runs below the Sisters. Some of the best skiing is further west, below False Peak through chutes and trees that an aggressive intermediate can negotiate with care. But intermediates should first try the Cornice (Chair Six), which is almst a true advanced run. By working the mountain from east to west, as described here, you can keep finding powder as well as new challenges.

The Sentinel Bowl gets groomed every three days or so and is beautiful for anyone looking for super-smooth steeps. If you want bumps, try Olympic, Look-Out Janek, Zack's or Monte Wolfe, which drop to either side of the Cornice Chair.

Snowboarding

Boarding is permitted on all areas of the mountain. The area has numerous naturally occurring halfpipes and quarterpipes. Boards may be rented at the Mountain Outfitter ski shop at the base, and the ski school has lessons.

Lessons (95/96 prices)

Kirkwood's Ski School offers **Pro Turn Ski Clinics** for all levels except beginners. These are 90 minutes long and cost $12, and are designed to smooth out rough edges, rather than teach the basics from scratch. **Private lessons** cost $55 for an hour, $20 each additional person.

A **Learn To Ski package** including a lesson, beginner lift ticket and rental equipment costs $30. The ski school guarantees that a never-ever will be able to ski the beginner area by the end of the day, or return for a free lesson. Days 2 and 3 for beginners also cost $30.

Kirkwood runs **special clinics** for women, and skiers aged 40 and older, each day Friday through Monday. These 90-minute programs cost $12. More intense three-day clinics run several times a season; call for details.

Children's lessons are for ages 4–12 and called Mighty Mountain. This includes equipment, lessons and lifts and costs $55 for a full day with lunch, $45 for a half day.

Child care

Kirkwood Day Care accepts toilet-trained children 3–8 years. All day costs $35 including lunch, half day is $25. Hourly charges are $5.

Lift tickets (94/95 prices)

	Adult	Child (Up to 12)
One day	$40	$5
Three days	$114 ($38/day)	$15 ($5/day)
Five days	$185 ($37/day)	$25 ($5/day)

Ages 60 and older ski for $20; students ages 13–24 ski for $30, but older students will need to present a photo ID to verify age.

Accommodations

Many skiers would rather stay here than put up with the nearly one-hour commute from South Lake Tahoe. Of the condo complexes the top choice is Sun Meadows, which is across from the Solitude and Cornice chairs and about as centrally located as you can get in Kirkwood. The second choice is The Meadows, between Timber Creek and the Cornice Chair. The Whiskey Run condos are a favorite with families because the Mighty Mountain children's ski school is on the ground floor. Rates for all condos are the same. In regular season a studio costs $110 on weekends and $75 midweek. A one-bedroom unit, which sleeps up to four, runs $155 on weekends, $120 midweek. A two-bedroom premium unit will cost $220 on weekends and $160 during the week. Reservations: (209) 258-7000.

Tahoe Interchangeable tickets (95/96 prices)

The Ski Lake Tahoe interchangeable lift pass is good at Kirkwood, Heavenly, Sierra-at-Tahoe, Northstar, Alpine Meadows and Squaw Valley USA. Five of six consecutive days costs $215, and six of seven, $258 (both $43 per day).

Diamond Peak

> ### Diamond Peak Facts
> **Base elevation:** 6,700'; **Summit elevation:** 8,540'; **Vertical drop:** 1,840 feet
> **Number of lifts:** 7–1 quad superchair, 6 double chairs
> **Percent snowmaking:** 80 percent **Total acreage:** 675 acres
> **Uphill capacity:** 7,500 per hour **Bed Base:** 6,000

Big is not always better, nor desirable. For skiers who don't want the expansive terrain of most Lake Tahoe resorts, let us recommend Diamond Peak, a medium-sized but exquisite jewel that skiers too often overlook. If we were to rate Tahoe's best family resorts—meaning superb non-extreme skiing and excellent accommodations—we'd rank Northstar first, followed by Diamond Peak. Northstar gets the edge only because it has slopeside lodging. And in rating best lake views, Diamond Peak, Heavenly and Homewood (a day area on the west shore that we don't cover here) are tops.

Diamond Peak is primarily an intermediate mountain, though its Solitude Canyon area has the greatest concentration of advanced terrain. The rest of the skiing falls from a single ridge that starts at the summit and ends at the octagonal Snowflake Lodge overlooking Lake Tahoe. These runs are gentle blacks and blues, relatively short toward the bottom and longer near the summit. Crystal Ridge off Diamond Peak is a long blue (with a stunning view of the lake), while the canyons and gullies off it are labeled advanced. Most of the expert terrain here would be labeled intermediate at Squaw.

This is a great learner's mountain because of its friendly atmosphere and manageable size. (Unfortunately, the amount of beginner terrain is a bit limited.) Diamond Peak employs about 100 instructors—equal to much larger areas—another indication that it's a good place to learn to ski, service clearly is a high priority. A strong point is that even the highest chair, Diamond Peak, is sheltered so that it can run when heavy winds shut down unprotected chairs at other resorts.

This is a very friendly area, relatively uncrowded and peaceful. Take a camera—the view is absolutely awesome.

This season Diamond Peak will become the first U.S. ski resort to install a "launch pad" loading system, a conveyor belt that is covered with a skiable felt surface. Similar to the moving walkways at airports, the system will allow Diamond Peak to run its two fixed-grip quad chair lifts at maximum speed and simulate a detachable quad chair experience, but without the million-dollar cost.

Snowboarding

Snowboarding is allowed on all parts of the mountain except on three runs served by the Red Fox lift (marked with pink shading on the trail map). Boarders have a mountaintop park that is off-limits to skiers. Rentals and lessons are available.

Lessons (95/96 prices)

All-day **group lessons** are $36; half day is $23 (ski or snowboard). **Private lessons** are $50 an hour, with discounts for additional hours or early-bird lessons. A **Learn-to-Ski Special** including beginner lifts, rentals and two-hour lesson is $32. Learn-to-Snowboard is $45. **Children's** programs are for ages 4–6 (all day with lunch is $57) and for ages 7–12 (all day including lunch is $55). For children 7–12, Sierra Scouts mixes ski instruction with the natural history of the Lake Tahoe region.

Child care (94/95 prices)

Diamond Peak has the Bee Ferrato Child Ski Center, named for its director, an energetic and kind New Zealand native whom every kid will want to adopt as a grandmother. Diamond Peak will expand the center as part of its 95/96 improvements. Child care is available for ages 3-6, but reservations are a must. Call (702) 832-1130; prices are $20 for a two-hour session; $35 for four hours. Supervised lunch is an extra $10.

Lift tickets (95/96 prices)

	Adult	Child (6–12) Senior (60–69)
One day	$35	$14
Three days	$99 ($33/day)	$36 ($12/day)
Five days	$165 ($33/day)	$60 ($12/day)

Younger than 6 and older than 69 ski for free. Diamond Peak has a super Family Package, good any day of the season. It starts with a lift ticket good for one adult and one child for $42. Four additional family members may be added at these prices: adult, $30; child or senior, $5; teen (13–17), $25. (Only one adult can be added.)

Accommodations

Incline Village has several hotels and condo complexes. Two worthy of mention are **Hyatt Regency Lake Tahoe Resort and Casino** and **Inn at Incline Motor Lodge and Condominiums.** The Hyatt is a four-star luxury hotel with rates from $75 to $230 a night, while the Inn at Incline has more modest facilities and rates (starting around $60 a night.) The town of Incline Village, with the highest per-capita income of any Nevada city, has several excellent restaurants.

For off-slope fun, check out the **Incline Village Recreation Center**, which has aerobics, basketball court, weight room and an indoor pool, among its amenities. Visitors can use the facilities for $10 per day or $25 per week. Discounts are available for children, teens, seniors and families. Another good spot for family fun is **Bowl Incline** with far more than bowling. There are pool tables, other pinball gizmos and video poker built into the bar. You'll also find a golf simulator where you can play seven world-class courses, such as Pinehurst, Banff Springs and Mauna Kea. Greens fees are $24 per hour and it takes about a hour to play 18 holes.

Sugar Bowl

Sugar Bowl is one of the oldest resorts at Lake Tahoe and the oldest chair lift-served resort in California. From the moment you step out of your car and board the Magic Carpet gondola to ride *down* across a pristine valley to the lifts, you feel you're stepping back in time.

Sugar Bowl is another of Tahoe's overlooked ski areas, at least by destination skiers. That's a shame, because it has great variety. Beginners have beautiful long runs off the Christmas Tree and Jerome Express chairs and a decent learning area at the base. Lower intermediates will find the best runs off the Christmas Tree chair. Intermediates should progress to the Jerome Hill Express quad on 8,238-foot Mt. Judahand the Silver Belt lift to the top of 8,383-foot Mt. Lincoln takes you to intermediate and expert trails.

The third mountain, 7,953-foot Mt. Disney, has some advanced runs off either drainage of a ridge, with wide intermediate terrain to the far right for cruising.

Sugar Bowl is recommended for a day's change of pace from the larger Tahoe resorts. However, remember that it's one of the first ski areas on the drive from the San Francisco, Oakland and Sacramento and gets its biggest crowds on weekends.

Sugar Bowl Facts
Base elevation: 6,883'; Summit elevation: 8,383'; Vertical drop: 1,500 feet
Number of lifts: 9—1 gondola, 1 quad superchair, 2 quads, 5 double chairs
Percent snowmaking: 8 percent Total acreage: 1,110 acres
Uphill capacity: 8,500 per hour; Bed Base: 460

Snowboarding
The entire mountain is open to snowboarders and all ski school programs offered to skiers also are available to boarders.

Lessons (94/95 prices)
A two-hour group session is $25. Private lessons are $45 an hour, with each additional person $20. The ABC package of lift, lesson and rental for never-evers through intermediates is $45 for adults ($40 without rentals), $35 for children. PowderKids all-day program for ages 6–12 is $52, which includes lifts, equipment, two lessons and lunch.

Child care
Sugar Bears Child Care is a licensed center for ages 3–6 with educational and recreational activities as well as skiing and quiet time. The program includes snacks, lunch and ski equipment. All day is $48, and half day (without lunch) is $35.

Lift tickets (94/95 prices)

	Adult	Child (5–12)
One day	$37	$10
Two days	$65 ($30/day)	$20 ($10/day)

Other than the two-day ticket, which must be on consecutive days, Sugar Bowl does not have multiday discounts. (Most skiers are here for one or two days at a time.) Seniors 60 and older pay $17 on non-holiday weekdays, full price on weekends. Adults who turn in their all-day lift ticket by 12:30 p.m. receive a credit coupon for $13 off another day's ticket.

Accommodations

Sugar Bowl has a lodge that is certainly unusual, and possibly unique at American ski resorts: a base lodge that also is a hotel. It is reached by the same four-passanger that brings skiers to this part of the mountain. In addition to the usual services on the ground floor, Sugar Bowl's base lodge also has 28 rooms on the upper two levels. Though it was built in 1939, the rooms have been remodeled for a combination of historic charm and modern convenience. The dining room preserves the grace of a former era with its decor and jacket-required dress code. Room rates, based on double occupancy, start at $110 per night. Bed-breakfast-lift packages, available Sunday through Thursday, non-holiday, are $136 single occupancy, $170 double, $215 triple and $255 quad. Five-day ski weeks with two meals a day also are available; call for prices.

The lodge rooms are very popular (we were unable to tour them, because all were booked.) Call (916) 426-3651 for reservations, well in advance.

Information/reservations

Lodging: South Lake Tahoe: (800) 288-2463 (AT-TAHOE); **North Lake Tahoe:** (800) 824-6348 (TAHOE-4U); **Reno:** (800) 367-7366 (FOR-RENO).

Squaw Valley USA, Box 2007, Olympic Valley CA 96146; information (916) 583-6985; snow phone (916) 583-6955; reservations (800) 545-4350.

Alpine Meadows, Box 5279, Tahoe City CA 95730; information (800) 441-4423 or (916) 583-4232; snow phone (916) 581-8374.

Northstar-at-Tahoe, Box 129, Truckee CA 95734; information and reservations: (916) 587-0200 or (800) 533-6787.

Sierra-at-Tahoe, 1111 Sierra-at-Tahoe Road, Twin Bridges, CA 95735; (916) 659-7453; 24-hr snow phone (916) 659-7475. South Lake Tahoe bus route information: (916) 541-7548.

Heavenly, Box 2180, Stateline NV 89449; information (702) 586-7000; reservations (800) 243-2836 (2-HEAVEN).

Kirkwood, Box 1, Kirkwood CA 95646; information (209) 258-6000; snow phone (209) 258-3000; reservations (209) 258-7247 or (800) 967-7500.

Diamond Peak, 1210 Ski Way, Incline Village NV 89451; 24-hour information (702) 831-3249; snow phone: (702) 831-3211; lodging reservations (800) 468-2463 (GO-TAHOE).

Sugar Bowl, Box 5, Norden CA 95724; information and reservations (916) 426-3651; ski conditions (916) 426-3847.

Mammoth Mountain
June Mountain
California

When you stand at the base lodge and scan the mountain you can't even see a quarter of the ski terrain. The encircling ridge, all above treeline, promises dramatic skiing, but what you don't see can be even better. This is what remains of a massive prehistoric volcano. Even now with most of the cone missing, it gives access to half a dozen wide bowls with the largest, once the interior of the cone, a whopping 13,000 feet across. In addition lower peaks like Lincoln Mountain, Gold Hill and Hemlock Ridge, all with groomed swaths and moguled canyons, stretch six and a half miles in width. Mammoth is one of the nation's largest ski areas in size, and is at times the nation's busiest, with more than 14,000 skiers swooping over its slopes on an average weekend. And yet, outside of California, it is not well known.

When you come to Mammoth Mountain, you come to ski—at the top of the mountain road there's not much to distract you. There is a labyrinthine base lodge with ski school, lift ticket windows, rental shops and hundreds of season lockers for locals and coin lockers for visitors. Across the parking lot is the Yodler chalet, brought piece by piece from the Alps and rebuilt to house a restaurant and bar. Nearby is the Mammoth Mountain Inn.

At the bottom of the mountain road lies the small but spread-out town of Mammoth Lakes. Here is just about all you need for a ski vacation short of luxury hotels. Don't expect a cozy picturesque small-town atmosphere, though. As the town grew to support the ski area's success, newcomers haphazardly transplanted Southern California sprawl and mini-malls to themountains. Most visitors drive from Southern California, but the few who don't may feel the need for wheels—not much is within easy walking distance. However, there is a free town bus that runs day and night.

Mammoth Mountain Facts
Base elevation: 7,953'; Summit elevation: 11,053'; Vertical drop: 3,100 feet
Number and types of lifts: 31–2 quad superchairs, 4 quads, 7 triple chairs, 14 double chairs, 2 gondolas, 2 surface lifts Acreage: More than 3,500 skiable acres
Percent of snowmaking: 6 percent (200 acres)
Uphill capacity: 53,000 skiers per hour Bed base: 30,000

If size intimidates you, Mammoth's little sister June Mountain, a half-hour drive from Mammoth Lakes, will appeal. Its Old-World village atmosphere in a sheltered canyon is on a more human scale. That is not to say it's a puny resort: seven chair lifts and an aerial tram scale a 2,590-foot vertical rise (as opposed to 3,100 feet at Mammoth).

June Mountain Facts
Base elevation: *7,545';* **Summit elevation:** *10,135';* **Vertical drop:** *2,590 feet*
Number and types of lifts: *8–2 quad chairs, 5 double chairs, 1 "QMC" tram*
Acreage: *500+ skiable acres*
Uphill capacity: *12,000 skiers per hour* **Bed base:** *30,000 region, 2,000 local*

Where to ski

First-time visitors cannot help but smile at the size of the mountain. Forget knowing the names of peaks at this resort—everything goes by number. The mountain is crisscrossed with a network of chair lifts numbered in the order they were built. Chair 22, for example, is not anywhere near Chair 23. It makes perfect sense to skiers who grew up with the mountain, but it's confusing to the first-timer who hears regulars planning their day football-quarterback style, "Take one to three, then backside to 23, down the ridge to 14, then to 13 and lateral to 19."

With massive weekend crowds the lines at the base lifts can be long, but since the area is so expansive you can easily avoid the them if you avoid the main base area. From left to right on the trail map, try Chairs 9, 18, 25, 22, 21, 10, 5, 12, 13 and 14.

Expert yaa-hoo skiers will strike out for the ridge, reachable by the gondola or a series of chairs. There any chute or path will open into a wide bowl. Mammoth's signature run, a snarling lip of snow called The Cornice, looms large in every expert's memory bank. Other runs dropping from the ridge are considered steeper and more treacherous. Reached from the gondola, Hangman's—Mammoth's toughest—is an hour-glass-shaped chute hanging from the summit and bordered by wicked rocks; at its narrow part there's space for only one turn—a perfect one. Other expert shots can be found off Chair 22, and on powder days you often can find untracked or less-tracked snow on the far east Dragon's Back off Chair 9, or the far west Hemlock Ridge above Chair 14.

One of the most popular advanced areas is the group of bowls available from Chair 3. They're great warm-up runs for experts, but plan to get here early. By 9:30 or 10 a.m. on weekends, the line is outrageous, although it diminishes at lunch time. At busy times knowing skiers head for Chair 19, which offers half a dozen runs hidden in a glen; these resist crowds and keep their grooming late into the day. Also, Chairs 22 and 25, which provide access to Lincoln Mountain and its intermediate runs and advanced chutes, rarely have lines.

Chair 1, a high-speed detachable quad, takes off from the Main Lodge. It is especially popular because experts can either plunge down Gravy Chute or weave through The Wall, a panel of bubbly moguls, while their intermediate friends can coast down wide, smooth Broadway and meet them at the bottom.

The mid-to-lower mountain lets the intermediate traverse vast expanses and crisscross runs. Hidden canyons like Lower Dry Creek are full of swoops and surprises, and require tighter turns. For long cruising, head to the eastern edge of the ski area and Chairs 15 and 24. Other intermediate playgrounds are served by the tree-lined runs dropping from Chairs 8, 4, 16, 20, 21, and 10 between Hut 2 and the Chair 2 Outpost. At the other extreme of the area, a local secret when lines are long, is Chair 12 and the drop over to Chairs 13 and 14.

Beginner trails like Hansel and Gretel weave gently through evergreens, and there are sheltered slopes for learning, tucked away from the paths of speed demons shooting down from the top. (Look out for this breed on Stump Alley, a crowded all-out raceway down to Chair 2.) Hidden gullies give variety even to the beginner; the never-ever slopes (off Chairs 11 and 11B at the Main Lodge and Chair 7 from Hut 2) have terrain as interesting as the more difficult ones.

June Mountain: Beginners and intermediates will find June Mountain challenging, though it has none of the high broad bowls that make Mammoth Mountain famous. The steepest terrain at June, The Face, is as steep as anything at Mammoth. Because it is on the lower mountain, it unfortunately doesn't keep the snow as long as the upper runs—intermediate cruisers and expert chutes like Dave's Drop and Pro Bowl. Since June is more sheltered than Mammoth and none of its slopes is above the tree line, June tends to hold powder longer than Mammoth's more exposed bowls and the snow doesn't crust up so quickly.

Mountain rating

Mammoth Mountain has terrain for all levels of skiers—and no matter what yours is you won't be shortchanged. If you are visiting for the first time, take a trail map and if you're with a group, decide where to meet if you get separated (we usually pick a centrally located short chair, such as Chair 20, rather than Mid-Chalet or the base lodge, which are usually loaded with bodies looking for other bodies—we just keep skiing that chair and watching from the lift until we all hook up). This is a huge mountain, and because of the crazy lift numbering system, it's hard to figure out how to get back to your starting point without the map.

June doesn't have quite Mammoth's range of terrain, but most skiers will enjoy it. The pace at June is slower, the crowds considerably fewer and sometimes nonexistent (locals come here on weekends and holidays), and the atmosphere friendly.

Cross-country

Twenty to 25 miles of groomed trails, actually summer roads, wind around four of the dozen or more high Alpine lakes, for which the town of Mammoth Lakes is named. **Tamarack Lodge** (934-2442) a 50-year-old summer hunting and fishing lodge, maintains these trails and charges $15 for access ($10 for those 11-17, free younger than that). The Lakes Basin includes many trail heads into the backcountry, where no fee is charged. Rentals and lessons are available. On weekends it's advisable to reserve.

Just out of town at the 8,000-foot level is **Sierra Meadows Ranch Ski Touring Center** (934-6161). A 25-km. network of mainly flat, machine groomed trails gives a magnificent view of Sherwin Bowl (now planned as another downhill area). Trail access is $10 for adults, $5 for children. Rentals and lessons available. Make reservations for advanced, telemark and children's lessons. A moonlight dinner tour is $40.

Snowboarding

Both Mammoth and June offer snowboarding on all runs. June Mountain is the snowboard center with national competitions, a halfpipe and a snowboard park featuring steep jumps, a quarter pipe, table jumps, and other treats. Snowboarding lessons and rentals are available at both areas.

Lessons (95/96 prices)

At peak season, Mammoth's ski school has 400 instructors. At either Mammoth or June, an all-day **group lesson** for six to eight, is $41; half day is $30. A book of five all-day group lessons is $190.

Children's group lessons for ages 4—12 called Mammoth Explorers begin at 10 a.m. and include a supervised lunch, as well as four hours of lessons. The cost is $65 per child. Half-day sessions are $30; full day without lunch is $41.

Teens 13—17 have specially developed clinics starting at 10 a.m. Cost is $38 for a full day and $25 for either the morning or afternoon.

Private lessons for adults or children cost $60 for one hour, $10 for each additional person. A five-day **Advanced Skiing Clinic,** conducted from 9 a.m. to 4 p.m. at Mammoth Mountain only, is $475. This clinic is offered just once a month, on the first Monday and is restricted to seven participants; reservations required.

All lessons are available at both the Main Lodge and Hut II. Reservations are not necessary, but questions can be answered at 934-0685 for Main Lodge, 934-0787 for Hut II. June Mountain Ski School number is 648-7733.

Child care (95/96 prices)

The **Small World Day Care Center** at Mammoth Mountain Inn, just across the street from the Main Lodge and at June Mountain offers these services:

Child care for newborn to two-year-old children is $54 per day, $39 for a half-day. Care for kids 2–12 years is $44 for a full day and $33 for a half-day. Additional children in a family get a $5 reduction. Fees include snacks and lunch, except for infants.

The combined day care and ski school rates at Mammoth Main Lodge for ages 4–12 include supervised activity from 8 a.m.– 5 p.m. and a ski lesson from 10 a.m. until noon. Rate is $70, including lunch. Call 934-0646.

Lift tickets (95/96 prices)

	Adult	Child (6–12) Senior (65+)
One day	$43	$22
Three days	$112	$56
Five days	$187	$94

Lift tickets are interchangeable for Mammoth and June Mountains; however, if you just ski June it's $35 for adults, $18 for kids. Mammoth introduced a teen price for ages 13–18, which is $33 at Mammoth and $25 at June. Children 5 and younger ski free, as do never-evers taking a ski school lesson. The multiday rates listed here are non-holiday. During holidays, regular per-day rates apply, though you still can buy a multiday ticket.

Anyone who skis Mammoth more than six days in a season should buy a Mammoth Club Card. It costs $60, but allows you to buy lift tickets for $33.

Ticket offices are at the Main Lodge, Warming Hut II and Chair 15 areas, as well as June Mountain. Additional satellite offices at Chairs 4, 10 and 2 are open weekends and holidays.

Accommodations (94/95 prices)

One of the nicest places to stay, **Mammoth Mountain Inn**, is also closest to the slopes—just across the parking lot. Lodging is deluxe to moderate, including hotel units with room service, motel and condominium units. Weekend rates (midweek is cheaper) are $99 for rooms to $400 for a condo that sleeps eleven; (800) 228-4947.

Mammoth Lakes has been called Condo City of the Sierras. Just beyond town, **Snowcreek** (934-3333; 800-544-6007) is huge and wooded with athletic club including racquetball and basketball. It's actually a neighborhood. Units are spacious one-, two- and three-bedroom loft style, $105-$350.

Closer to the slopes, in fact next to Hut II, two other large condominium complexes have a range of units. **Sierra Megeve** (934-3723; 800-227-7669), **Mountainback** (934-4549; 800-468-6225) **1849 Condominiums** (934-7525) and **Aspen Creek** (934-3933; 800-227-7669) cost $155–$495 depending on size and amenities.

In the middle of town, only a walk to restaurants and a shuttle to the lifts, you'll find **Sierra Nevada Inn** (800-824-5132; 934-2515) has hotel rooms starting at $65 and chalet units up to $280. **The Snowgoose Inn** (800-874-7368, California only; 934-2660) is one of three bed-and-breakfast inns in town. Decorated with antiques, breakfast served communally in a friendly atmosphere, approximate rates are $78–$168.

The least expensive private rooms ($40-$58) are at **Motel 6** (934-6660) but it takes no reservations. Three places offer dorm rooms: **Kitzbuhel Lodge** (934-2352) is good for groups and young people, with a huge dining room and group kitchen. Three to 14 beds are in each room. Cost is $20 a night for men and women. Besides motel rooms and large suites, **Alpenhof Lodge** (934-6330) has dorm rooms for $64 for men only, with three beds to a room and the bath at the end of the hall. **Ullr Lodge** (934-2454) is a European-style dorm for men only, mainly share-a-bath rooms, for about $20 a night. They will rent to women if four take one room. The last two are on the shuttle line right in town.

These are just a few of the places to stay. For more ideas, call **Mammoth Lakes Visitors Bureau** (800-367-6572), or for condos, call **Mammoth Reservation Bureau** (800-527-6273; 800-462-5571 from Southern California).

June Mountain: June has two large condominium complexes. **Interlaken** charges from $85 for studios midweek to $185 for three-bedroom units. Weekend prices are $120–$240. **Edgewater** has only one size unit, suitable for six to nine people, for $105 midweek to $165 on weekends. All other lodgings at June are small and quaint, even funky. **The Haven** has studios for $65. Call June Lake Properties Reservation at (800) 648-5863 (648-JUNE) or Century 21 Rainbow Ridge at (800) 462-5589 for condominium reservations.

Also try **Fern Creek Lodge** (800-621-9146), **Whispering Pines** (800-648-7762), or **Boulder Lodge** (648-7533), all of which have rooms and cabins in the $50 to $100 range.

Dining

Mammoth Lakes has nearly 60 dining options, from gourmet French cuisine to delicatessen sandwiches and quick take-out. The top-of-the-line menu is found at **Anything Goes** (934-2424), served daily in a cozy dining room. The choices change each week. Here the focus is on great presentation combined with healthy, generous portions. A bit pricier and a bit more elegant is

Natalie's (934-3902) where the atmosphere is romantic with lace curtains and a coordinated decor. **O'Kelly and Dunns Restaurant** (934-9316) leans toward American country with dried flowers, grasses and quilts gracing the walls.

For the most romantic (and expensive) dining head out to **Lakefront Restaurant at Tamarack Lodge** (934-3534) where the menu is basic but excellently prepared. The atmosphere is Old World in a small dining room decorated with photos of movie stars who used to hang out here. After dinner wander into the lodge and have after-dinner drinks in front of the fireplace. On a night with a full moon, make plans to head out to **Convict Lake Restaurant** (934-3803) south of Mammoth Lakes on Route 395. On nights when the moon reflects on the lake, there is no prettier setting for dining in front of a flickering fire.

Nevados (934-4466) receives good recommendations, but expect to pay handsomely for continental cuisine with unusual dishes. Mammoth Mountain Inn's **Mountainside Grill** (934-0601) is worth the trip up the mountain from town.

For the best steaks and prime rib head to **Whiskey Creek** (934-2555), or try **The Mogul Restaurant** (934-3039) and the **Chart House** (934-4526) which also serves fish dinners.

Families (or anyone with limited funds) will want to stop in at **Berger's** (934-6622) for big, big portions. The tuna salad is massive and you can have not only burgers but also chicken, salad or Canadian stew. Another family spot is **Angel's** (934-7427) with great ribs, beans and barbecue.

The **Old Mammoth Pasta House** (934-8088) dishes out huge plates of fresh pasta and friendly service. Locals consider **Nik-N-Willie's Pizza** (934-2012) the best in town. Pizza also appear at **Giovanni's** (934-7563) or **Perry's Italian Cafe** (934-6521). The best Mexican food is at **Roberto's** (934-3667) with homemade tortillas and authentic big servings, but no margaritas. If you can't live without a margarita, head to **La Sierra's** (934-8083), **Gringo's** (934-8595), known for its "almost world famous Rotisserie Chicken," or **Gomez's** (924-2693).

Grumpy's (934-8587) holds the distinction of the town's best greasy chicken and big steaks, also the best cole slaw, all presented in a big-screen TV, sports bar atmosphere. (Warning: Grumpy's can get very smoke-filled on busy weekends.)

Shogun (934-3970) has Japanese cuisine and a sushi bar. Try **Matsu** (934-8277) for inexpensive Chinese-American.

Ocean Harvest (934-8539) is the prime seafood restaurant, offering fresh fish caught from the owner's boat.

The best breakfast in town is served at **The Stove** (934-2821) with biscuits 3 or 4 inches high, though it could be challenged by **Breakfast Club** (934-6944) at the intersection of Old Mammoth Road and Highway 203. We tried to eat there, but couldn't get a parking space—two *midweek* days in a row. Or head to the **Swiss Cafe** (934-6196) for excellent croissants. Coffee lovers, your choices are **Looney Bean** (934-1345) on Main Street next to the Chevron station or **World Cup Coffee** (924-3629) on Old Mammoth Road across from the movie theater. Both have in-house bakers for rolls and muffins. For very good baked goodies and good but non-gourmet coffee, try **Paul Schat's Bakery and Cafe** (934-6055) on Main Street, which serves breakfast on weekends, fresh-baked goodies every day.

For dining on the mountain for lunch or dinner the best bet by far is at the **Mountainside Grill** (934-0601) in the Mammoth Mountain Inn. Surprisingly, the prices are not much more than the cafeteria. Or head over to the more crowded **Yodler** (934-0636). If you are in town for a quick lunch check out the **Gourmet Grocer** (934-2997).

Après-ski/nightlife

Lively après-ski gets underway across the parking lot from the Main Lodge at the **Yodler** or in the **Thunder Mountain Bar** in the Main Lodge, decorated with photos of early Mammoth days. **Josh Slocum's** in town is the après-ski hangout for ski patrol and instructors. At **Austria Hof**, singer and guitarist Gayle Louise entertains after skiing. Entertainment also is at the **Ocean Club** and at Mammoth Mountain Inn's **Dry Creek Bar**.

Dancing and general meet markets are at **Whiskey Creek** and **The Rafters**. For a great night out where you are sure to meet someone, try Country & Western dancing on Thursday and Saturday nights at **Annie Rose's**.

There's plenty of nighttime hoopla at **Grumpy's**. Featured are five giant-screen TVs, pool, foosball, inexpensive chili and burgers. If you want to shoot pool, head to **Kegs & Cues**.

Shogun has karaoke singalong on Tuesday and Saturday nights with a sushi bar, tempura, sukiyaki and teriyaki, which you can wash down with sake and imported beer.

Other activities

Shopping: Mammoth's shopping is oriented as much for the local population as for tourists. You won't find many trendy boutiques here, though there is a small factory outlet center on Main Street . A favorite store with an eclectic inventory of jewelry, soothing CDs, nature books and mountain survival supplies is The Great Outdoors on Old Mammoth Road.

Snowmobiles can be rented from DJs Snowmobile Rentals, 935-4880; Center Street Rentals, 934-4020; or Mammoth Snowmobile Rental, 934-9645. Bobsledding down a designated track is available through Sledz, 934-7533. Sleds are available at Kittredge Sports, 934-7566. Dogsled rides are offered by Dog Sled Adventures, 934-6270.

Sleigh rides with (or without) a cozy ranch-house dinner are offered at Sierra Meadows Ranch, 934-6161. Hot-air balloon trips with High Sierra Ballooning Company (934-7188) take off from Mammoth Meadow. Snowcreek Athletic Club (934-8511) has a variety of indoor and outdoor facilities.

Mammoth Lakes also has two movie theaters (one with two screens), Minaret Cinemas and Plaza Theater (both at 934-3131). The Mammoth Times, a free weekly newspaper, is a good source for special events listings.

Getting there and getting around

Getting there: Mammoth is 300 miles north of Los Angeles on Highway 395 and 170 miles south of Reno on the same road. June Mountain is also off 395, 20 miles north of Mammoth Lakes. It is difficult to reach Mammoth in winter from the San Francisco Bay area, because the shortest route, Highway 120 through Yosemite, is closed in winter. Northern Californians can use either I-80 or Highway 50 to reach Highway 395, but those roads pass by Lake Tahoe and its multitude of ski areas, so not many Bay Area skiers make it here.

TW Express (800-421-9353) has daily service to the Mammoth Lakes airport from Burbank, Los Angeles, Orange County and San Francisco. **United Express** has daily flights from Los Angeles, Sacramento, Ontario and San Diego. **Eastern Sierra Auto Rentals** (935-4471) is available at the airport, or you can catch a bus into town.

Getting around: The resort operates a free shuttle that runs throughout the town and to Mammoth's Main Lodge (four miles out) and to Warming Hut II and Chair 15. A nightly shuttle makes half-hourly loops around town until midnight during the week, 1 a.m. on Friday and Saturday nights. Most visitors have a car.

Information/reservations

Mammoth Lakes Visitors Bureau, 934-8006 or (800) 367-6572, handles accommodations, car and ski rentals, airline and lift tickets, ski school, child care and even restaurant reservations. **June Mountain** has three booking agencies: 648-5863 (648-JUNE), (800) 648-6835, and (800) 462-5589. The last two numbers are within California only.

Twenty-four-hour **snow report** for Los Angeles is (213) 935-8866; Orange County, (714) 955-0692; San Diego, 231-7785. Road information is 873-6366.

Mammoth Mountain Ski Resort business office is 934-2571. **June Mountain Ski Resort** office is 648-7733.

Unless otherwise noted, all area codes are 619.

Southern California Areas

Bear Mountain, Snow Summit
Snow Valley

Quick: which of the following is *not* found in Southern California: Sun. Palm trees. Golf. Smog. Surfboards. Skiing. Movie stars.

Okay, it's a trick question. You can find *all* of the above in Southern California. When winter rain falls on Southern California's palm trees, snow falls on the mountains that ring the Los Angeles basin.

These mountains are home to nine ski and/or snowboard areas, most of which lie between 6,500 and 8,800 feet. Three of them—Bear Mountain, Snow Summit and Snow Valley, all in the San Bernardino mountain range—attract the majority of the skiers, and are the only ones that aren't strictly day areas.

Ask just about any Southern California skier what he or she thinks of the local ski areas, and they'll probably tell you they never ski here—they only ski Utah, Colorado or Mammoth. Well, *someone* is skiing here: combined, these nine areas record nearly a million and a half skier visits a year.

Southern Californians just don't know how good they have it. On many a sunny winter day, it is entirely possible to spend the

Bear Mountain Facts
Base elevation: 7,140'; Summit elevation: 8,805'; Vertical drop: 1,665 feet. Number and types of lifts: 11–1 quad superchair, 1 quad, 3 triples, 4 doubles, 2 surface lifts. Acreage: 175 skiable acres Percent of snowmaking: 100 percent Uphill capacity: 15,000 skiers per hour Bed Base: 2,500 within 5 miles

Snow Summit Facts
Base elevation: 7,000'; Summit elevation: 8,200'; Vertical drop: 1,200 feet. Number and types of lifts: 12–2 quad superchairs, 2 quad chairs, 2 triple chairs, 5 double chairs, 1 surface lift Acreage: 230 skiable acres Percent of snowmaking: 100 percent Uphill capacity: 17,850 skiers per hour Bed Base: 2,500 within 5 miles

Snow Valley Facts
Base elevation: 6,700'; Summit elevation: 7,898'; Vertical drop: 1,198 feet. Number and types of lifts: 13–5 triple chairs, 8 double chairs Acreage: 230 skiable acres Percent of snowmaking: 74 percent Uphill capacity: 18,550 skiers per hour Bed Base: 1,700 within 15 miles

morning skiing in the San Bernardino mountains and the afternoon playing a round of golf in Palm Springs. The few out-of-staters that venture to Big Bear Lake, site of the two leading ski areas, are usually astonished at the skiing that's available.

That's not to imply that skiing here is on a par with skiing in Utah, Colorado or Mammoth. The Southern California areas have much less terrain and often rely on snowmaking to cover the runs. All three have extensive snowmaking; however, Bear Mountain and Snow Summit have a more reliable water supply. Even if the season has been dry, you'll find surprisingly good snow on the runs. And if the winter has been a wet one, the conditions can be quite good.

The Big Three are very similar in that all have 175-250 skiable acres on largely intermediate terrain. The differences are in accessibility and visitor amenities. Snow Valley is a little easier to reach, but its lodges and restaurants are fewer in number and farther from the slopes. Bear Mountain and Snow Summit are a longer trip, but are in the resort town of Big Bear Lake, where lodging and restaurants are pleasant and plentiful.

Where to ski

Beginners, intermediates and snowboarders will have the most fun at these areas. All have limited amounts of advanced terrain and all embrace snowboarding.

At **Bear Mountain**, beginners have their own area under the Inspiration triple chair, with wonderfully expansive, nearly flat terrain. Lower intermediates will be happiest with runs off the Goldmine or Showdown mountains, while upper intermediates will like Silver Mountain. Advanced skiers should head for the top of Bear Peak, which has the area's only real hair-raising run, Geronimo. When natural snow conditions permit, advanced skiers may go off-trail within the ski area boundaries for some of the best tree and glade skiing you'll find in Southern California.

Beginners at **Snow Summit** also have a private, gentle slope, served by Chairs 4 and 8. Those with at least a few trails under their skis can head for the green runs under Chair 9, which is a Family Ski Park, meaning no snowboarders allowed on busier days. Intermediates will love Miracle Mile, a long cruiser that descends from the summit (8,200 feet) to the base (7,000 feet), and the trails served by Chairs 1, 2, 3, 5, 7 and 10, the latter of which will be converted to a high-speed quad this season. Upper intermediates will enjoy the runs under Chair 11, a surprisingly underskied section of the mountain.

Advanced skiers have the steep (but short) pitch of The Bowl runs served by Chair 6. The Bowl is almost always skiable, thanks to snowmaking, but also attracts a lot of hotshots who think they ski better than they can. Snowboarders have a 3,600-foot freestyle park on the Westridge run with bumps, jumps and obstacles. The park is open to skiers, but mostly used by boarders.

Snow Valley has the gentlest overall terrain of the three. Never-evers have several acres of flat runs at the base, strong beginners can handle the blue runs, and strong intermediates can handle most black-diamond trails. Solid intermediates especially should head for Chairs 4, 8 and 9, rated black on the trail map, but often deserted. A nice touch here: the base of each chair has a large vertical sign on it, clearly stating the number of the chair and the symbols for the difficulty of terrain it serves.

Snow Valley's toughest area, Slide Peak, is not visible from the parking lot. It is a wide face with a respectable pitch. Half the face is groomed, while the other half is left alone to build moguls. Last season Snow Valley added snowmaking to this slope.

• • •

If you have the choice, don't ski on Saturdays or holidays! The parade of cars crawling up the roads combined with the parade of skiers careening down the slopes is not conducive to a relaxing day. Sunday is the much better choice, if weekends are your only option.

During dry winter seasons, chances are that these areas will be operating: all have very good snowmaking systems covering much of their terrain. In winters with a lot of natural snow, consider these smaller areas that have limited or no snowmaking—all are less crowded than the Big Three and all have lower prices: **Mt. Baldy,** north of Upland; **Ski Sunrise,** next to Mountain High in Wrightwood; **Big Air Green Valley,** near Running Springs (for snowboarders only) and **Kratka Ridge** and **Mt. Waterman,** both on the Angeles Crest Highway north of La Cañada-Flintridge.

Mountain High, via Highways 138 and 2 from I-15, is one of the largest Southern California ski areas, with 205 acres, snowmaking, night skiing and 11 chairs, but it is strictly a non-resort experience. We have not yet discovered any lodging suitable for a weekend getaway; what we've found is rustic, in the worst sense of the word.

Mountain ratings

These areas are most suitable for intermediate skiers, although beginners will find them comfortable, unintimidating places to learn on uncrowded days. Advanced skiers can be entertained if snow conditions cooperate, but experts will be bored after a couple of runs. Those who dislike sharing the slopes with snowboarders may not like these areas—Southern California is a hotbed of snowboard activity.

A tip for upper-level skiers: After a snowfall, head for **Mt. Baldy,** off I-10 north of Upland. This lesser-known area has the steepest slopes and the largest vertical drop (2,100 feet) in

Southern California. Its biggest problems are very little snowmaking and one double chair lift from the parking lot to the upper mountain, where much of the skiing is. On super powder days, the line waiting to board that chair is agonizingly slow.

Cross-country

Although drought sometimes makes it tough for Southern California Nordic centers to operate, they do exist. The **Palm Springs Nordic Center,** which is at 8,500 feet on 10,800-foot Mt. San Jacinto, is accessible only by the Palm Springs Aerial Tramway. Skiers may use the ungroomed trails for free (the tram ticket is $15.95). Ski and snowshoe rental equipment is available. Lessons are given on weekends. Call (619) 327-6002 for the Nordic Center and (619) 325-1391 for tramway information. Note: This is not near any of the downhill ski areas, but it overlooks those great Palm Springs golf courses.

Nearer to downhill skiing is the **Green Valley Lake Cross-Country Center,** just beyond Running Springs in the town of Green Valley Lake. It has about five miles of set tracks, and many more miles of ungroomed trails in the San Bernardino National Forest. The longest trail is 13 miles from Green Valley Lake to Fawnskin. The trail fee is $5. Group lessons and rentals are available. The phone number is (909) 867-7754, but it's seasonal. If you get a recording that says the number is not in service, wait for snow and call again.

The **Rim Nordic Ski Area Inc.** is five miles east of Running Springs across from the Snow Valley ski area. It has 14 km. of groomed and tracked trails, lessons and rentals. There is also a snowshoe trail with rentals available. Trail fees are $6 for adults, free for children 10 and younger, $3 for ages 60 and older. Call (909) 867-2600.

Snowboarding

It's not too surprising that the ski areas in the surf and skateboard capital of the U.S. celebrate snowboarding. All three major ski areas not only allow boarders, but they also have excellent snowboard parks, halfpipes, rentals, lessons and many contests and competitions. Most ski and sporting goods shops near the areas also rent snowboards. One of the smaller areas, **Big Air Green Valley** (909-867-2338), is one of just a few areas in the entire nation devoted entirely to snowboarders.

Lessons (94/95 prices)

Bear Mountain has an especially good new skier and snowboarder program. It starts with an orientation video, then progresses to a very flat and isolated slope where never-evers go through a series of skill development stations at their own pace. The beginners package for skiers or snowboarders (rentals, lifts and lessons) is $39, which includes a discount card for future lessons, plus the promise of a free lift ticket after they complete the third day of lessons.

Group lessons are $22; a lesson and lift package is $59; add ski rental to that package and it's $73, and add snowboard rental and it's $84. Private lessons are $50 an hour, $35 for each additional person, with multi-hour discounts available. Bear Mountain also has the only disabled-skier school in Southern California. Children's lessons (ages 4-12) are $50 for a full day with lunch, and $35 for a half day. Equipment rental is $10 extra.

Snow Summit offers a beginner package for $40 midweek ($45 weekends). Its two-hour group lessons are $20; private lessons are $60 per hour. Snow Summit last season offered free video analysis on its Log Chute run, with a ski instructor who offered a couple of free tips.

Children 8-12 can get all-day instruction (four hours) for $35, or a half day (two hours) for $20. Children 4-9 have several options, including day care and ski lessons, ranging from $20 for a two-hour lesson to $50 for two two-hour lessons, day care for the remainder of the day, lunch and snacks. Children's prices include lift access during the lesson. Snow Summit also has a Family Private Lesson that groups parents and up to two children for $100 (parents, who must be of at least intermediate ability, learn how to teach their children).

Snow Valley's beginner package (lesson, lifts and rentals) costs $35 for ages 6 and older. Ninety-minute adult or child group ski lessons are $18; a snowboarding lesson is $22. Private lessons are $50 per hour. SKIwee for children is $55 per day with lunch and rentals included. Snow Valley has a fun terrain garden set up for children called AdventureSki™.

Child care

The only area that has had child care is **Snow Summit,** which has its Little Bear Care Center for ages 2-9 (must be toilet-trained). Activities include crafts, games, videos for all ages and ski lessons for 4-year-olds (ages 5–7 can enroll in regular children's ski school). A telephone hotline at the tops of Chairs 2 and 10 gives parents access to the care center. The cost (94/95 prices) is $40 for all day (nine hours with lunch), $25 for four hours. Reserve by calling (909) 866-5766, ext. 354.

Snow Valley has plans to offer child care for ages 2 and older (toilet-trained) for 95/96. Call the ski area at (909) 867-2751 for prices and information. Snow Valley's AdventureSki™ program includes a heated play tent, but parents must supervise.

Lift tickets (94/95 prices)

	Adult	Child (6–12)
Bear Mountain	$38	$21
Snow Summit	$41	$21
Snow Valley	$39	$22

These are one-day weekend prices. Specific ticket information for each area follows:

Bear Mountain: Buy a ticket for two or three consecutive days and the price drops $5 per day for adults and $4 for children. Midweek specials: Seniors 65 and over ski for $21, one adult and one child ski together for $48 ($10 for each additional child), and ages 13–23 with valid picture ID ski for $28.

With Bear Mountain's Permanent Ticket you can charge your lift ticket through Ticketmaster any time up to the night before you ski, then bypass the ticket window line and head straight for the lifts. Better yet, you save a dollar off the ticket-window price. Call the ski area for full details on how this works and how you can get your free Permanent Ticket, (909) 585-2519, ext. 235.

Snow Summit: Seniors (60 and older) and ages 13-22 can ski midweek for $32. Night skiing is $24 for adults, $13 for kids, 3–9:30 p.m. You can ski free on your birthday by showing ID at the ticket window. Children 7–16 pay $15 for an all-lifts ticket when skiing with a parent, but reservations are required.

Snow Summit sets limits on ticket sales; to reserve in advance with a credit card, call (909) 866-5841, or you can buy Snow Summit lift tickets at RealTime kiosks located at many Southern California ski shops and sporting goods stores, including Chick's and Sport Chalet branches.

Snow Valley: Tickets bought through Ticketmaster are $29 (plus service charge), good any day. The day lift ticket is good the same night as well; night skiing alone costs $24. Ages 65-69 ski for children's prices; older than 69 or younger than 6 ski free.

Snow Valley also has an Option Pass, a point-ticket system that allows skiers to pay only for what they ski and save the unused points for use on a return visit. This is a great alternative for those who don't ski a full day.

Accommodations

Southern California skiing is overwhelmingly day skiing. Nearly everyone drives up from the urban valleys, skis, and drives home. However, the town of Big Bear Lake, home of Bear Mountain and Snow Summit, is trying to change this. Downtown Big Bear Lake (called "The Village") now looks and feels like a cozy mountain resort. Old-style streetlights and planter boxes create a setting that is very inviting for an evening stroll. The only thing left for the chamber of commerce to do is to convince more of the downtown stores to stay open past 6 p.m.

A new hotel, **Northwoods Resort Hotel,** opened in spring, 1995, with 153 rooms, lodgepole-style decor, a restaurant, ski shop, pool, hot tub, exercise room, sauna and free shuttles to the ski areas. Room rates are $99-$129 weekends, with lower rates midweek; and ski packages starting at $59 per person, double occupancy. The hotel is in Big Bear Village, a mile or so from the ski areas. Call (800) 866-3121 for reservations.

Mountain Vista Resort (909-585-7855), has lodging within walking distance of Bear Mountain. **Snow Summit Townhouses** (800-445-2223) and **All Seasons Condominums** (800-722-4366) are next to the Snow Summit base area.

The **Big Bear Inn** is very unusual, a conglomeration of marble floors and walls, ornate statuary, oversize Oriental antiquities, Baroque chandeliers and a lobby ceiling with a painting of a cloud. Rates for its 80 rooms run from about $90 to $200, depending on room size and time of year. Reservations: (800) 232-7466 (BEAR-INN).

For a lake view, try **Marina Riviera** (909-866-7545), with a pool, spa and Jacuzzi tubs; or **Forest Shores Inn,** with studios and one, two, and three bedrooms (909-866-6551).

The town has a lot of mom-and-pop motels, small lodges and cottages, some on the lake, others in nicely wooded areas, still others on the single main boulevard. Two groups of cabins that are particularly quaint are **Oak Knoll Lodge** (909-866-2773) and **Cozy Hollow Lodge** (800-822-4480).

For B&Bs, try these: **Gold Mountain Manor** has a triple diamond rating from AAA and is furnished in antiques and Western artifacts. (909-585-6997). **Eagle's Nest B&B** is moderately priced and offers free shuttle service to ski areas (909-866-6465). **Janet Kay's B&B** is beautifully funished, with rooms that have fireplaces or canopied beds (800-243-7031).

Ski packages are available. The best place to start for general lodging information is the **Big Bear Lake Resort Association**, (909) 866-7000. It represents more than 1,200 lodging units—cabins, motels, hotels, B&Bs, home rentals, etc.

Lake Arrowhead is a small resort town about 30 miles west of Big Bear Lake and about 10 miles from the nearest skiing at Snow Valley. The largest hotel is the **Lake Arrowhead Resort**, with 261 rooms ranging from $99 to $199. This is a full resort hotel, featuring lakeview rooms, a health club and spa, and meeting and banquet facilities. Reservations: 336-1511 or (800) 800-6792. The next largest lodge is **The Saddleback Inn**, with 34 rooms in a central building and outlying cabins. Other properties include B&Bs, cabins and condos.

Call the **Lake Arrowhead Accommodations and Lodging Information** at (800) 545-5784 for more information.

Dining

In **Big Bear Lake** (all area codes 909): Dining prices are either moderate ($12-$22 for entrees) or budget. **The Iron Squirrel** (866-9121) is not only considered the finest dining by locals, it is an entirely No-Smoking restaurant. Two others in this category, both relatively new, are **Ché Faccia** (878-3222), which serves fine Italian meals in a casual atmosphere, and **Madlon's** (585-3762), which has great breakfasts, unusual specials and romantic evenings in a gingerbread-house setting.

More moderate, **The Blue Ox** (585-7886) serves hearty meals. **The Old Country Inn** (866-5600) specializes in better-than-average German, Italian and American food at moderate prices. **Mandarin Garden** (585-1818) serves a fine shrimp curry and good Szechwan dishes. **Captain's Anchorage** has steak and seafood (866-3997), and **The Blue Whale** is good for prime rib and seafood (866-5771). The **Log Cabin** (866-3667) has great specials for German and American food, a bakery and a bar with a large assortment of imported beers.

Many places are inexpensive. For Mexican food, try **La Montana** (866-2606) or **Nacho's** (866-6309). **Maggio's Pizza** (866-8815) has full dinners, as well as Italian subs and calzones. **Pong's Place** serves oriental specialties (866-8688). Check out **Paoli's** for Italian food (866-2020). **Boo Bear's Den** (866-2932) has the widest variety—from burgers to Australian lobster. The **Cowboy Steak House** serves up big portions of barbecue and home style food (866-1486).

In or near Lake Arrowhead or Snow Valley:

Snow Valley has been improving its restaurant services and has a sit-down restaurant, **WR's Eatery**, that serves dishes such as parchment-wrapped tarragon shark and New York steak with peppercorn sauce. Call 867-4160 or 867-2751.

The **Cliffhanger Restaurant** on Highway 18 leading to Lake Arrowhead has Greek and Italian specialties in the $13-$30 range. Lunch runs $7–$15. Great views of the San Gabriel Valley (if the smog isn't too thick.)

Lake Arrowhead Village has about 20 restaurants ranging in atmosphere and price from **McDonald's** to the lakeside **Candlewood Restaurant**.

Après-ski/nightlife

Because these areas attract many more day skiers than overnighters, après-ski is more plentiful than night life. Each ski area has a bar at the foot of the slopes where skiers relax before heading down the mountain; live music is standard on weekends, recorded music during the week.

Big Bear Lake has most of the night life that exists. One hot spot is **Slicks Mountain Sports Pub** on Big Bear Boulevard. It has karaoke, video trivia contests, a big-screen TV, a varied beer selection and nightly appetizers. Other places to try: **Prospector's, The Moonridge Club** at the Big Bear Inn, the **Pine Cone, Chad's,** and **the Sugarloafer**.

Other activities

Shopping in Big Bear Lake is a pleasant diversion, but not the reason to come here. Some fun shops in Big Bear Lake include **Adora Bella** and **Room to Room** for some unusual home and kitchen accessories, and nearly everyone's favorite for funky selection and decor, **Bear Mountain Trading Company**, on the road up to Bear Mountain ski area. As noted, many of the stores are open only during the day.

Lake Arrowhead's village has many fine shops in a layout very conducive to strolling and window-shopping.

Getting there and getting around

Getting there: For overnight visits, the only option is to drive. Carry chains: the California Highway Patrol will not let unchained vehicles past its checkpoints during and sometimes even a couple of days after storms.

From Los Angeles:

Bear Mountain and Snow Summit: The least crowded route is to take I-10 east to the Orange Avenue exit. Follow the signs to Highway 38, which leads to Big Bear Lake. The shorter but most crowded route is I-10 east to the Mountain Resorts exit and follow Highways 30, 330 and 18 through Running Springs to Big Bear Lake. Tip: To avoid bumper-to-bumper traffic in the city of Big Bear Lake, take Highway 38 around the north side of the lake through Fawnskin, and turn right on the Stanfield Cutoff on the east end of the lake.

Snow Valley: Take I-10 east, then take the Mountain Resorts exit and follow Highways 30, 330 and 18 east, just past the town of Running Springs. To reach Lake Arrowhead, take Highway 18 west from Running Springs.

Getting around: Southern Californians are surgically attached to their cars. Traffic and parking at the two areas is okay midweek, but awful on weekends. The town has a trolley system that costs $1 for adults, 75 cents for students and 50 cents for ages 60 and older and disabled persons. It requires exact fare, and it services both ski areas in town; however, the trolley comes around only about once per hour and makes a lot of stops. If you're staying in Lake Arrowhead, you will need a car.

Information/reservations

Bear Mountain: Box 6812, Big Bear Lake, CA 92315, (909) 585-2519. Snow report: (213) 683-8100 (LA number), (619) 238-5555 (San Diego number).

Snow Summit: Box 77, Big Bear Lake, CA 92315, (909) 866-5766. Snow report: (310) 390-1498 (LA number), (619) 294-8786 (San Diego number.)

Snow Valley: Box 2337, Running Springs, CA 92382, (909) 867-2751. Snow report: (800) 680-7669 (680-SNOW).

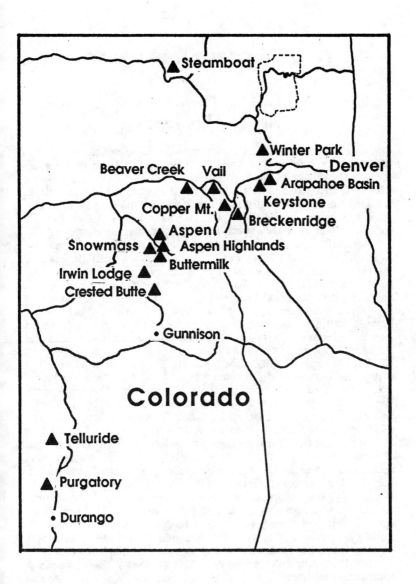

Aspen Area, Colorado

Aspen Mountain, Buttermilk Mountain Aspen Highlands

Ask a crowd of non-skiing Americans to name a ski resort, and you can bet a bundle that Aspen will be one of those they name, though they'll probably know more about the rich and famous who frequent the resort than about its equally notable skiing. With four mountains within a 12-mile radius, offering 40 lifts, 270 trails and more than 4,000 skiable acres, a trip to Aspen just for the skiing would be well worth it. But Aspen has much more.

Aspen fits a niche unique among North American ski resorts. Sure, other resorts attract wealth, but Aspen's wealth glitters and sparkles with a "look-this-way" flamboyance. Sophisticated New York and Hollywood fashions shimmer against turn-of-the-century brick façades. Learjet pilots wait patiently for parking spaces on the airport tarmac. The newest Bogner ski outfits are beyond being *de rigueur;* they're commonplace. And paparazzi aim their lenses at every celebrity in town so that supermarket tabloids can keep their pages filled.

But the great fun about Aspen is that if you aren't a multimillionaire and you aren't part of the "in" crowd of celebrities and their friends, it's just as much fun to observe them. Ski bunny-ism is taken to new heights by perfectly groomed "skiers" who ride up the Silver Queen Gondola to the top of Aspen Mountain, lounge in their skin-tight outfits on The Sundeck, and then ride the gondola back down. But you also can observe serious celebrity skiers, such as Martina Navratilova, attempting to meet the challenge of double black diamonds off Loge Peak at Aspen Highlands.

If all your information about Aspen comes from *People* magazine, you probably think you can't afford to ski there. True, the lift ticket is one of the pricier in America, but it's a little-known fact that lodging and restaurants have a huge price range, starting out quite inexpensive and topping out at stratospheric.

Another fact that often gets lost is that Aspen is also a Victorian mountain town, albeit a large one. Not every Aspen resident aspires to come up with the most original license plate or throw the most spectacular party. There's also a side to Aspen where perfectly painted lips, careful coiffure and cosmopolitan style are not the rule. Aspen has women and men who exude a natural freshness, whose smiles are spontaneous rather than reserved for photo sessions. Aspen has restaurants where one can eat without taking out a loan and bars that have never seen a fur coat. Children play tag, mothers attend PTA meetings and men go out for a beer after work.

Aspen also draws skiers who couldn't care less about the off-mountain scene. They come for the skiing, which has received rave reviews for decades. The region has four separate ski areas, all owned by the Aspen Skiing Company. Aspen Mountain, or Ajax as it's often called, challenges intermediate and advanced skiers. Buttermilk is a nub by contrast, but serves as the perfect beginner and cruising mountain. (This mountain was first called Buttermilk, then Tiehack, and now it's back to Buttermilk.) Aspen Highlands is the most varied, with skiing for experts and beginners, cruisers and bumpers. Snowmass, larger than the other three combined, is several miles farther down the road. Though it is one of the four Aspen Skiing Company areas and included in that lift ticket, it also has its own accommodations, restaurants and shops, and is covered in the next chapter.

Aspen in fact has more happening in winter than just about anyplace else. Make no mistake—money is the fuel that runs this action machine, but Aspen also has places to stay and eat that are no more expensive than any other ski area. So take your choice: If you want glamour and you don't mind paying for it, you can find it here. If you don't, there are ways to avoid it.

Where to ski

Aspen's four mountains are close to each other, but not interconnected. This chapter covers Aspen Mountain, Aspen Highlands and Buttermilk. Snowmass has its own chapter.

Free mountain tours orient skiers. Tours last 90 minutes, outline the history and nature of the area, and point out different runs. Buttermilk and Snowmass tours meet Sundays at 9 a.m. at the ski school rendezvous. Aspen Mountain tours are Monday at 9:30 a.m. at the base of the gondola.

Aspen Mountain is one of skidom's best intermediate and expert playgrounds; indeed, it may be the only ski mountain in America that has no designated green-circle runs. Beginners shouldn't even think about tackling this terrain, and with Buttermilk so close they don't need to. The Silver Queen Gondola

---

Aspen Mountain Facts
Base elevation: 7,945'; **Summit elevation:** 11,212'; **Vertical drop:** 3,267 feet
Number of lifts: 8–1 gondola, 1 quad superchair, 2 quad chairs, 4 double chairs
Snowmaking: 33 percent **Total acreage:** 631 skiable acres
Uphill capacity: 10,775 per hour **Bed Base:** 15,000

whisks skiers to the summit of Ajax. From here 3,267 feet of uninterrupted vertical drops to the gondola base.

The basic guideline for Aspen Mountain is that intermediate terrain is on the top knob around the summit and in the gullies between the ridges. The expert stuff drops from the ridges into the gullies. The gentlest terrain—Dipsy Doodle, Pussyfoot and Silver Bell—funnels into Spar Gulch. Ruthie's Road along the ski area boundary connects with Ruthie's Run, and Copper Bowl is a long intermediate run, serving a dozen expert trails from the Bell Mountain Ridge and Gentleman's Ridge.

Buttermilk Mountain Facts
Base elevation: 7,870'; **Summit elevation:** 9,900'; **Vertical drop:** 2,030 feet
Number of lifts: 7–1 high-speed quad, 5 double chairs, 1 surface lift
Snowmaking: 27 percent **Total acreage:** 410 acres
Uphill capacity: 6,600 per hour **Bed Base:** 15,000

Buttermilk Mountain is all that Aspen Mountain isn't. Beginners can experience top-to-bottom runs as soon as they master snowplows or halting stem christies. Intermediates will enjoy an ego boost, and wise experts will let their skis go and enjoy no-stress, no-crowd cruising.

The beginner terrain concentrates under the Buttermilk West chair. Tom's Thumb, Red's Rover, Larkspur, Westward Ho and Blue Grouse will keep beginners improving. The Homestead Road turns back to the Savio chair and lazily winds its way to the Main Buttermilk area.

Intermediates with confident turns will have fun on Jacob's Ladder and Bear, which drop from the Cliff House to the main area, but the real playground is Tiehack. This area is colored black on the trail map, but don't get too excited—it's only black on the map. You'll discover good solid intermediate trails that make inspiring cruisers. In one day you can ride the Upper Tiehack chair a dozen times, taking a different cruise on each run. Buckskin, Ptarmigan, Sterner, the Glades, Tiehack Parkway and Racer's Edge (where the Mahre brothers trained) all offer 1,500 feet of dipping and sweeping curves. Smile in the evening when you overhear others scoffing about what a waste Buttermilk is for real skiers, and savor memories of 15,000 feet of vertical in just one afternoon.

Aspen Highlands, between Aspen Mountain and Buttermilk, used to be independent but for the past two seasons has been part of the Aspen Skiing Company family. Aspen Highlands is the best-balanced mountain of the three with slopes for every level of skier, and it's the locals' favorite. No need for fur-trimmed Bogner outfits here; you can be comfortable if you appear for lunch at mid-mountain in jeans and gaiters. The vertical rise is one of the highest in Colorado (Steamboat goes a few feet higher). The Aspen Skiing Company has constructed two high-speed quads this season that dramatically cut the time needed to reach the summit.

From the top of Loge Peak, the run back to the base is an uneven series of steeps, catwalks and gentle runouts. This mountain has some fantastic long cruises. The ridge, knifing directly to the summit, has thrilling pitches down both sides.

Beginners are best served by the trails from the Exhibition II chair and the Grand Prix Poma—Prospector, Norway, Nugget, Exhibition and Apple Strudel. Intermediates will want to take the next series of lifts: Cloud 9, Olympic and Loge Peak. (The easiest of the intermediates are off Cloud 9.) Experts should head for the steeps at the top of Loge Peak with Kessler's Bowl, Snyder's Ridge, Sodd Buster, Garmisch and St. Moritz. Dropping from Cloud 9 are The Wall and Le Chamonix, which will test any skier. The Olympic Bowl area has mostly expert terrain. After short steep drops you traverse back to Robinson's Run.

Also check out the lower mountain. The Nugget Chair will take you to the top of Bob's Glades or Upper Stein, or you can drop into Thunderbowl and ski virtually anywhere you want. The Thunderbowl area is served by a chair from the base and a Poma for its upper reaches.

The Merry-Go-Round restaurant at the top of the Exhibition II lift is one of the better cafeterias you'll find on a mountain. The apple strudel here is the real thing and an Aspen tradition, made with Gretl Uhl's original recipe. Freestyle competitions are held Fridays at noon on Scarlett's Run facing the Merry-Go-Round.

Aspen Highlands Facts
Base elevation: 8,040'; **Summit elevation:** 11,675'; **Vertical drop:** 3,635 feet
Number of lifts: 9–2 quad superchairs, 5 double chairs, 2 surface lifts
Snowmaking: 20 percent **Total acreage by trails:** 619 skiable acres
Uphill capacity: 9,145 per hour **Bed Base:** 15,000

Mountain rating

Everyone gets something at Aspen. Beginners will have the most fun at Buttermilk. Intermediates probably will have a more varied day at Aspen Highlands than on Aspen Mountain, but the longest runs sweep down Ajax, and it's hard to beat the exhilarating cruising on Buttermilk. Experts have a tossup between Aspen Highlands and Aspen Mountain.

Snowboarding (95/96 prices)

Unlimited snowboarding is permitted at Aspen Highlands and on Buttermilk Mountain. Boarding is not allowed on Aspen Mountain, and is controlled on certain parts of Snowmass.

Snowmass and Buttermilk have halfpipes and terrain parks. All areas offer special snowboard lessons following a format similar to their ski lessons. At Snowmass, a one-day lesson is $50; three days cost $135 (lessons only). Buttermilk has a three-day learning program for $129 including rentals, lessons and lifts.

Champion professional snowboarder Kevin Delaney runs a learn-to-snowboard two-day camp for adults at Buttermilk that is designed to "provide adults with a smooth and safe entry into the sport of snowboarding" with "fewer falls and more fun." Delaney speaks a language that 30-plus adults readily understand, ideal for anyone who thinks snowboarding looks like a lot of fun, but can't relate to the snowboard culture.

Aspen Highlands offers 2.5-hour beginner lessons twice a day for $45 per session which includes lesson and board rental (you can rent boots, but the number is limited.)

Rentals are available throughout the Aspen area.

Cross-country

Craig Ward organized the most extensive free Nordic trail system in America, 80 km. of groomed trails called "Aspen's fifth mountain." The **Aspen Nordic Council's** free system is accessible from Aspen or Snowmass and includes easy golf-course skiing as well as more difficult trails rising up to Snowmass.

In addition to the free trails provided by Aspen's Nordic Council, **Ashcroft Touring Unlimited** has 30 km. of groomed and set trails, and backcountry skiers can use summer hiking trails. Hut systems connect Aspen with Vail on the Tenth Mountain Trail and with Crested Butte over the Pearl Pass.

Cross-country contacts and centers (R=rentals, L=lessons, G=guides, F=food, T=trail fee, TL=telemark lessons): **Ashcroft Ski Touring** (R,L,T,F) 925-1971; **Aspen Touring Center** (R,L,TL,G) 925-7625; **Snowmass Touring Center** (R,L,F) 923-3148; **Ute Nordic Center** (R,L,F) 925-2849; **Fred Braun Hut** (information on trails to Crested Butte) 925-6618; **Tenth Mt. Trail Association** (Aspen to Vail hut system) 925-5775.

Lessons (95/96 prices)

The **Aspen Skiing Company ski school** offers an extensive traditional lesson program. For reservations and information, call 925-1220 or (800) 525-6200.

Group lessons for all levels are taught at Aspen Highlands, Buttermilk and Snowmass. (Intermediate and advanced specialty clinics are taught at Aspen Mountain.) Adult group lessons cost $52 a day. Classes meet daily at 10:30 a.m.

Private lessons start at $115 for 90 minutes for one student, $135 for two to five people. Two hours of lessons cost $165 for one to five people. Full-day lessons run $350 for one to five people. A book of coupons for five full-day lessons costs $1,775 for up to five students.

Specialty clinics: Three-hour racing clinics cost $45 a day or $129 for three days. Bump, powder and video clinics all cost $35 for each two-hour session. The Mountain Masters program for intermediate and advanced skiers provides a guide who will run you for four days, until your legs feel weak, for $295. A special women's seminar costs $295 for four days.

The Magic of Skiing is a one-week program administered separately from the ASC ski school, but using ASC instructors. "Magic" approaches skiing from a mind-body perspective. Theoretically this approach to skiing should permeate your entire lifestyle. The cost varies from $1,695 to $2,855, which includes lift tickets, lodging, breakfast, instruction, videotaping and training in relaxation, relationships, fitness and health, and mind-body coordination. For reservations and information, call 925-7099 in Aspen or (716) 924-7302 in New York.

Teen and children's programs are held at Buttermilk, Aspen Highlands or Snowmass. For children first grade through 19 years the fee is $60 a day (four hours). Special kids' and teens' five-day programs include lessons, fun races, a picnic and video at a cost of $275.

All children 3 to 6 are enrolled in either Powder Pandas at Buttermilk, Snowpuppies at Aspen Highlands or Big Burn Bears at Snowmass. Children from 18 months to 4 years are enrolled in Snowcubs at Snowmass. The programs cost $68 a day including lunch and lifts, $340 for five days.

Child care

Aspen Skiing Company does not have a day-care center. Children aged 18 months to 4 years can enroll in Snowcubs at Snowmass, which has snowplay activities and very basic ski instruction.

A local preschool, the **Aspen Sprouts** (920-1055), accepts children 2 to 5 years and concentrates on typical preschool activities. Call for reservations.

Other private day-care and babysitting services are available in both Aspen and Snowmass through the Aspen or Snowmass reservations offices, **Supersitters** (923-6080) or **Night Hawks** (923-0571).

Children from fifth through 12th grade can mingle with local kids at the **Aspen Youth Center** in downtown Aspen. The center has games, ping-pong, pool tables, movies and a dance room. The center does special programs depending on the season. Admission is free and a hotline gives weekly activities information, 925-2139.

The four Aspen-area mountains are far from any other ski resorts and far from metropolitan areas. Consequently, just about all the visitors ski for more than one day. (There is a one-day ticket, but the price was not available at press time). Tickets are valid at all four mountains.

Lift tickets (95/96 prices)

	Adult	Child (7–12)
Three days	$147 ($49/day)	$81 ($27/day)
Five days	$225 ($45/day)	$135 ($27/day)
Six days	$254 ($42.33/day)	$156 ($27/day)

Ages 65 to 69 can buy these tickets for $99 for three days, $160 for five and $186 for six. Ages 6 and younger and 70 and older ski free. One little-known way for beginner and low-intermediate skiers to save on Aspen's ticket prices is to buy a one-day lower-lift ticket at Snowmass or Buttermilk for $12.

If you ski before mid-December, or in April, you'll pay less— $111 for a three-day pass, $185 for five days and $222 for six. Call (800) 525-6200 to order lift tickets.

Accommodations

Accommodations in Aspen range from luxurious to inexpensive. Reservations for virtually all properties are available through **Aspen Central Reservations**, (800) 262-7736 or (970) 925-9000.

Hotel Jerome 330 East Main Street, (800-331-7213 or 920-1000) is a historic hotel that has been restored to more elegance than the silver barons ever knew. The lounges are furnished with overstuffed chairs and framed in etched glass. Rooms are filled with antiques, and each has a brass or carved wooden bed. Baths feature Jacuzzis, marble counters and telephones. Rates in regular season are $225–$1,650.

For those searching out a smaller, more intimate hotel, the **Sardy House** (920-2525 or 800-321-3457) on East Main Street is a restored Victorian mansion. A more modern addition has been tacked onto the rear, but we suggest you try to get one of the original rooms in the main house. Rooms in regular season are $299–$359 and relatively small suites range from $399 to $599.

The Little Nell Hotel (800-525-6200) has 92 rooms and suites, only steps from the Silver Queen Gondola at the base of Aspen Mountain. All rooms have fireplaces, sofas, oversized beds with comforters, and marble bathrooms. There is a spa and heated outdoor pool. Rates are $400–$440 a night. Weekend stays require a four-night minimum.

Other top-rated luxury hotels are the **Aspen Club Lodge** (800-882-2582), the small **Hotel Lenado** (800-321-3457), the **Gant** (800-345-1471), **Hotel Aspen** on Main Street (800-527-7369), **Molly Gibson Lodge** (800-356-6559) and the **The Ritz Carlton Aspen** (800-241-3333).

Other Aspen room rates drop from this stratospheric level to $85–$130 a night for a double.

Our favorite place in Aspen, a lodge of a kind that's disappearing all too fast, is **The Mountain Chalet** (925-7797). This place is just plain friendly to everyone, including families. If you can't stand a 3-year-old crawling over a lounge chair in the lobby or families howling over a game of Monopoly, then don't stay here. Rates are reasonable and include a hearty breakfast served family-style. Call early for rooms, because folks reserve space here well in advance.

Other places that treat guests very well are the **Alpine Lodge** (925-7351), **Mountain House** (920-2550), and **Crestahaus Lodge** (925-7081).

Also try **Skier's Chalet** (920-2037) across from Lift 1-A with a heated outdoor pool, the **Christiana** (925-3014) at 501 West Main Street and the **St. Moritz Lodge** (925-3220), only five blocks from the center of town.

Good rooms are also available for under $100 each night at the **Little Red Ski Haus** (925-3333), the **Christmas Inn** (925-3822), **Innsbruck Inn** (925-2980), **Ullr Lodge** (925-7696) and budget champion **Tyrolean Lodge** (925-4595).

Both the **Maroon Creek Lodge** (800-356-8811, ext. 223) and the **Heatherbed Lodge** (925-7077), opposite Aspen Highlands, are great places to stay out of Aspen's bustle. Rates are about $100 per night, depending on season.

Several management companies rent condominiums. For luxury condos right on the slopes, try **Mountain Queen Condominiums** (925-6366); all are three-bedroom units. The **Aspen Club Management** (800-443-2582 in Colorado, 800-882-2582 nationwide) controls two luxurious condominiums, the Aspen Club and the Clarendon. Expect a unit with two bedrooms and two baths to run $500 and up in the regular season.

Coates, Reid and Waldron, 720 East Hyman Ave. (925-1400 or 800-222-7736), is the largest management company in the area. Chateau Eau Claire and Chateau Roaring Fork are two of their most popular units. Two-bedroom, two-bath units run $330 a night in regular season. Shadow Mountain is not so luxurious, but has a ski-in/ski-out location. Its two-bedroom, two-bath unit is $300 in regular season. Pomegranate, near the base of Buttermilk, is perfect for cross-country skiers who will pay $290 a night during regular season for a two-bedroom, two-bath unit. There are units in every corner of town, but none would be rated luxurious. They also handle home rentals.

Condominiums directly on the slopes with similar prices are the **Fasching Haus** (925-5900), **Fifth Avenue** (925-7397) and **Durant** condominiums (925-7910). They are available through the Aspen Central Reservations.

Just outside town, the **T-Lazy-7** (925-7254) offers apartments. You'll pay $60 for a double bed in a small studio and $300 for five bedrooms and living area that easily sleeps 10. If you can

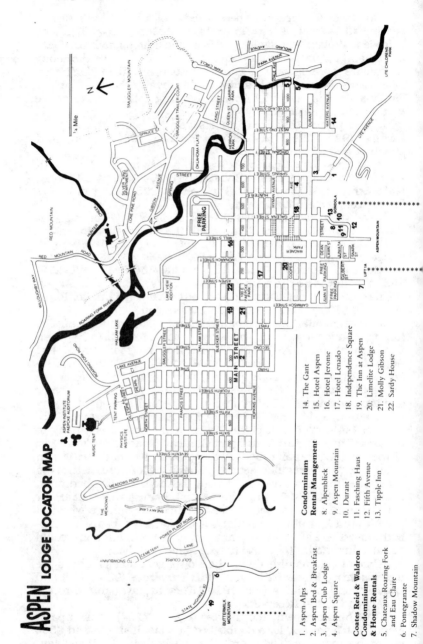

ASPEN LODGE LOCATOR MAP

1. Aspen Alps
2. Aspen Bed & Breakfast
3. Aspen Club Lodge
4. Aspen Square

Coates Reid & Waldron Condominium & Home Rentals

5. Chateaux Roaring Fork and Eau Claire
6. Pomegranate
7. Shadow Mountain

Condominium Rental Management

8. Alpenblick
9. Aspen Mountain
10. Durant
11. Fasching Haus
12. Fifth Avenue
13. Tipple Inn

14. The Gant
15. Hotel Aspen
16. Hotel Jerome
17. Hotel Lenado
18. Independence Square
19. The Inn at Aspen
20. Limelite Lodge
21. Molly Gibson
22. Sardy House

fill these apartments, they are a deal that's hard to beat, and they're on a real working ranch where kids have no end of exploration. However, you will need a car.

Dining

Let's start with *the* place to eat breakfast, **The Wienerstube** at 633 E. Hyman and Spring. Come here for Eggs Benedict, Austrian sausages and homemade Viennese pastries. **Pour la France!** at 413 E. Main is good for croissants and pastries, quiches and waffles, with superb coffee in a high-tech coffee-shop atmosphere. **Main Street Bakery** (925-6446) has home-made baked goods, granola, fruit, eggs and great coffee for reasonable prices.

Our expert on top-level gourmet dining, Katy Keck, covers **The Little Nell, Sage, Syzygy, Piñons, Crystal Palace, Renaissance, The Golden Horn, Cowboys, Ashcroft Pinecreek Cookhouse, Ajax Tavern** (where Shlomo's used to be), **Krabloonik** and several on-mountain dining choices in the following Aspen Savoir Faire chapter.

Other recommendations: **Fireside Tavern** (925-8845) at the corner of First and Cooper is an elegant little place with many European and American dishes. **Smuggler Land Office** (925-8624) at 415 E. Hopkins in the historic Brand Building has tasty Cajun and Creole food, including Cajun popcorn with a spicy ré-moulade. **Cache Cache** (925-3835) on the lower level of the Mill Street Plaza is highly recommended by locals for Mediterranean cuisine. The polenta niçoise, wild mushroom cannelloni and per-fectly grilled yellowtail were favorites. **Mezzaluna** at 600 E. Cooper (925-5882) serves highly rated Italian cuisine. **La Cocina** (925-9714), 308 E. Hopkins, is a very popular Mexican place with locals, but **The Cantina** (925-3663) at the corner of Mill and Main is a trendier alternative. **Boogie's Diner** at 534 E. Cooper (925-6610) is a real '50s diner with oldies like Elvis' "Hound Dog," blue plate specials and meatloaf. The **Flying Dog Brew Pub** (925-7464), which gets its name from a Sherpa guide's misinterpretation of the term "bird dog," has home-brewed beers and affordable menu selections. It's downstairs at 424 E. Cooper. **Little Annie's Eating House** (925-1098) at 517 E. Hyman is still the ribs, chicken, hamburger and potato pancake champ. **The Skier's Chalet Steak House** (925-3381) at 710 S. Aspen has been around since 1951 and is a great food institution, and very inexpensive. **The Steak Pit** (925-3459), at the corner of Hopkins and Monarch, also has some of the best steaks in Aspen. **Asia**, 132 W. Main Street, was recommended for the best Chinese (Szechwan, Mandarin and Hunan) food. It is in an opulent Victorian setting, but has free delivery if you prefer (925-5433).

The T-Lazy-7 Ranch (925-7254) organizes a Western night every Wednesday and Thursday. It includes sleigh rides, cooking your own steak and chicken on an open grill and a Country & Western band cookin' up some footstompin' music.

Reader recommendation: Andrew S. Zieve of Milwaukee enjoyed the fine Italian cuisine at **Carnevale Ristorante** (920-4885) located at 430 E. Hyman.

Après-ski/nightlife

Ajax Tavern, in the Little Nell Hotel, draws a big crowd as the lifts start to close. If you don't find what you want there, the crowd spreads out to **Little Annie's, Cooper Street Pier,** the **Red Onion** and **O'Leary's. Legends of Aspen,** a sports bar; **The Cantina,** with its very happy hour (have a margarita in the compadre size) and the **Hotel Jerome Bar** are all great après-ski meeting places—Legends filled with locals, the Cantina loud, the Jerome quiet.

At night, the music and dance beat begins to take over. Our Aspen Savoir Faire chapter has details on the **Crystal Palace Theater Restaurant.** Earlier in the evening, the high-energy place to find out who's in town is **Mezzaluna,** with its brassy horseshoe-shaped bar. You have to be a member of the **Caribou Club,** which often is packed with celebrities. On the Mall, head to **Silver Nugget Saloon. Planet Hollywood** and the **Hard Rock Cafe** attract a lot of tourists looking for celebrities, but few celebs. A slightly lower-keyed dancing place is the **Tippler. The Ritz Carlton** has live music in the lounge, and **The Little Nell** bar has jazz.

For a good singles bar, head to **Mezzaluna** for the best in upscale people-watching. A relatively mixed crowd with normal pedestrian tastes congregate in the **Red Onion, Little Annie's** and **O'Leary's.** The **Cooper Street Pier** is very much a local and college student hangout. **Shooter's,** on Hyman Avenue, is a very dark and smoky Country & Western bar with great deals on shooters and beer and great dancing. **The Silver Nugget Saloon** also is C&W, while **Flying Dog Brew Pub** has live bluegrass. For the best "last call," try **Mother Lode.**

Other activities

Shopping: This town is a shopper's heaven. Two of our favorites are **Gracy's,** a secondhand clothing store that stocks some drop-dead-gorgeous designer outfits for a fraction of what their original owners paid for them; and **Boogie's,** which has many unique clothing and accessories items in a 1950s setting. Part of the decor is a 1955 red Corvette that Elvis Presley bought for $3,500 (you can easily blow that much in this entertaining store).

Arts lovers will enjoy Aspen's 30 galleries, its three resident theater groups, three movie houses (including art films) and its winter classical concert series. The Aspen Chamber Resort Association has more information, 925-1940.

Several companies have winter **fly-fishing** trips—the waters in the Aspen/Snowmass area are rated "gold medal." Outfitters to call include **Oxbow Outfitting Co.** (925-1505), **Taylor Creek Angling Services** (920-1128) and the **Snowmass Falls Outfitters Ltd.** (923-6343).

The **Aspen Center for Environmental Studies** (925-5756) has daily self-guided Hallam Lake snowshoe touring, and daily two-hour naturalist-guided snowshoe walks atop Aspen Mountain twice a day for $35. Free guided environmental interpretive ski tours are offered on one or more of the Aspen Skiing Company's four mountains each day. For the schedule, call 925-5756.

Go for a hot-air balloon ride with **Unicorn Balloon Company** (925-5752). Daily departures, weather permitting, leave from Aspen and Snowmass. Another balloon company is **Adventures Aloft II** (925-9497).

Sleigh rides, part of the Western party night noted in the dining section, take place at the **T-Lazy-7 Ranch**. The ranch also hosts private sleigh rides for $10 a person, with a five-person minimum. Call 925-7040. **The Aspen Carriage Company** (925-4289) offers one-hour carriage rides.

The **Aspen Athletic Club** (925-2531) is open to the public from 7 a.m. to 10 p.m. on weekdays and 8 a.m. to 8 p.m. on weekends for a $15 daily fee.

Getting there and getting around

Getting there: United Express offers connections from Denver into **Aspen Airport**. Delta, United, Northwest and American fly into the **Eagle County airport** near Vail, roughly one hour's drive from Aspen. Ground transportation companies, such as **High Mountain Taxi** (925-8294 or 800-528-8294) take skiers from Eagle to Aspen.

Amtrak has daily service to Glenwood Springs, where skiers can get ground transportation the rest of the way. **Greyhound** offers daily bus service between Glenwood Springs and Denver International Airport.

Getting around: Aspen has a free shuttle, the RFTA, with several routes in town and to the various ski mountains. Not only is a car unnecessary, parking is a pain.

Information/reservations

For Aspen area information or transfers, hotel rooms and lift ticket bookings, call **Aspen Central Reservations** at (800) 262-7736.

Aspen Skiing Company: (800) 525-6200.

Unless otherwise noted, all area codes are 970.

Aspen Savoir Faire

This mountain town with Victorian roots has enjoyed an un-paralleled culinary revolution that has bypassed sole meunière for a more exotic "beach party" shellfish. There are black trumpets and white truffles, edible nasturtiums, a veal dish called "@*#?&!," and just everybody is into lemon grass. Aspen is a place where you can enjoy the fine restaurants thoroughly, knowing that the next day you'll ski off those calories.

One of Aspen's long-time favorites had a culinary rebirth a few years back. The **Little Nell** at 675 E. Durant (920-4600) specializes in contemporary American cuisine. When Chef George Mahaffey arrived from Los Angeles' Bel Air, he imple-mented a light, updated menu at the Little Nell. The menu is a delight: pan-seared shrimp, scallop and lobster potstickers with sambal potatoes; leeks and herbs; and homemade basil gnocchi with Santa Barbara prawns, truffles and asparagus.

Mahaffey's creativity in choosing Alpine ingredients, carries throughout the menu. The restaurant serves three meals daily. Dinner starters range from $6 to $12.50, and entrées from $22 to $32. For fine dining, it's one of the best values in town.

Like the Little Nell, the Snowmass Lodge & Club is owned and operated by Aspen Skiing Company. Its new bistro, **Sage,** offers food as distinctive and flavorful as Mahaffey's, with a casual unpretentious atmosphere and at more moderate prices. Executive Chef Ford Fry's style is best described as American, but often incorporates global influences. Start with the warm romano-crab spread with crusty bread or split a southwest pizza with jack cheese and cilantro. Entrées includes a roast of the day, complete with Yorkshire pudding and a hefty 16-ounce grilled cowboy steak with spiced white beans and crispy onions. Starters are reasonably priced between $3.50 and $8.50, while entrées range from $12 to $20. Call 923-5600 for reservations.

Syzygy is a favorite among locals. Chef Charles Vresilovic combines French, southwestern, Oriental and Italian cuisines. Don't be put off by the hard-to-pronounce name (Siz i je) or the obscure explanation of its meaning on the menu (the con-junction or opposition of three or more heavenly bodies—for us earthlings, that's fine food, good service, and elegant atmo-sphere.) At 520 E. Hyman Avenue (925-3700, reservations required); the atmosphere is intimate yet casual. The menu changes frequently, but a few menu staples continue to sell out. Get there early for the Syzygy roll—a roasted lamb loin wrapped in soft rice paper with glass noodles, carrot and mint pesto—it's rarely there by the last seating.

Start with the seared ahi with Korean spinach, baby lettuces and mango-chili oil. Try the slash-and-burn snapper—fresh red snapper filet marinated in coconut milk, then slathered in achiote barbecue sauce and grilled. Sample the mixed grill: tenderloin of buffalo with chipotle ketchup; wild boar ham with black currant glace; and veal sweetbreads with sweet mustard sauce. Plan on spending a stiff but worthwhile $12 to $14 for appetizers and $22 to $34 for entrées; it's a meal well worth remembering. Open daily 6 to 10 p.m.

Piñons (second floor at 105 S. Mill; 920-2021), decorated in a cozy western ranch style, with aged stucco walls, a big leather bar and huge brass bowls filled with corn tortillas, specializes in Colorado Cuisine. The wild pheasant quesadillas with sour cream, salsa and guacamole were rivaled only by the lobster strudel, a flaky combination of phyllo dough, morels and chanterelles. While other appetizers are not nearly so inspired in design, they are all perfectly executed. Try the salmon spring roll with daikon and cucumber salad.

Entrées range from a simple grilled chicken with roasted portobello mushrooms to pan-seared local pheasant breast with foie gras and truffles. The ahi is sautéed with a macadamia nut crust and lime butter, and the elk tournedos, served with ginger and pink peppercorn sauce, is perfectly grilled. All meats and fish are grilled over mesquite and cherry wood. Desserts vary daily, but will usually include the white chocolate macadamia nut tart. You may need a chainsaw to get through it, but it's worth every effort for its nutty caramel taste. Prices are steep ($23 to $33 for entrées), but you didn't come to Aspen to save money. Open daily 6 to 10 p.m.; reservations recommended.

If you think that at these prices they should entertain you and clean your apartment for a year, one man will at least do the former. Mead Metcalf has been playing to **The Crystal Palace** sellout crowds each evening (6 and, on some nights, a second seating at 9:15 p.m.) for the last 36 years. At 300 East Hyman Avenue (925-1455; reservations may be necessary several weeks in advance), the Crystal Palace adds wit and satire to the old notion of barbershop quartets. Amid stained glass and crystal chandeliers, the talented staff not only cranks out a full dinner and bar service, but then belts out a cabaret revue spoofing the media's latest victims. You'll hear skits on O.J., Madonna, Dr. Jack Kevorkian, Bill and Hillary, and Fergy and Di. For about $50 per person, you can choose from perfectly pink beef tenderloin with Madeira sauce, roast duckling with sauce bigarade (a piquant sauce flavored with Cointreau and brandy), rack of lamb or prime rib. The food doesn't have to be good, but it is.

On the outside chance there's still a platinum card burning a hole in your parka, try Aspen's latest in exquisite dining: **Renaissance,** 304 East Hopkins (925-2402). Chef/owner

Charles Dale (who grew up in the palace in Monaco with Caroline and Albert) claims his is one of three restaurants in the world to have a daily changing degustation or tasting menu (five courses), as well as offering course-by-course, by-the-glass wine pairings. The menu itself is $65, or with wine, $95. Dale offers modern French cuisine, with a touch of Colorado. A leader in ecological awareness in Aspen, Dale's menu reflects his concerns: all fish are line-caught or farm-raised. Start with a warm tumbleweed scallop salad with lemon tarragon dressing, then proceed to perfectly cooked-under-a-brick chicken with potato gnocchi. Wine gets special attention at Renaissance, with an impressive selection by the glass. The list has won the Wine Spectator Award of Excellence. And don't miss the grand dessert with more chocolate than Switzerland! A la carte entrées cost $24 to $32. Open daily, 6 to 10:30 p.m. Reservations recommended.

The Golden Horn Restaurant, at the corner of Mill and Cooper (925-3373), dates back to a 1949 nightclub. Klaus Christ, chef-owner since 1972, has always offered savory Swiss specialties with a wine list cited by The Wine Spectator for nine consecutive years as one of America's top 100. But in a departure from many other menus in town, recently Christ introduced a new lighter menu, in addition to the traditional Swiss fare, which includes fondue, stroganoff (albeit salmon), and wienerschnitzel. Called Cuisine Minceur, from a style developed in southern France, it offers three full-flavored courses for less than 450 calories. The menu changes daily, but generally begins with a soup, such as fresh tomato basil, followed by an entrée such as grilled veal chop or swordfish, and completed with fresh berries. Open daily; reservations are advised.

The hottest place in Snowmass is Cowboys (923-5249) in the Silvertree Complex. Open for lunch and après-ski appetizers, Cowboys also serves dinner daily from 5:30 to 10 p.m. Chef Mark Bolton has fired up a menu sure to thrill even the boldest cowboy. The Colorado loin of lamb is stuffed with achiote and roast garlic pesto and served with a rosemary tomato cream. The mesquite-grilled T-bone is served cowboy-style, branded with a sweet and mild barbecue sauce. Shrub-dusted tournedos is saddled on a cornbread crouton and served with campfire tomatoes. They claim on the menu to be able to meet special dessert needs, but no one could tell me if they serve S'mores. Come for the food and stay for the live music nightly.

For a real adventure, head out to the Ashcroft Pinecreek Cookhouse (925-1044) for a casual evening and solid fare. At an elevation of 9,725 feet, this rustic log cabin in the midst of towering pines beneath Elk Mountain peaks some 12 miles from Aspen. The Cookhouse is accessible by a one-and-a-half mile cross-country trek, or by a sleigh drawn by a team of Percherons. Reservations are essential (two to four weeks in advance), as the logistics of running a kitchen not reached by road in winter is no small matter. The Cookhouse feeds several hundred people each day, and all that food comes in by snowmobile. Meals are prepared right in front of you in the open kitchen and will be served by one of your cross-country guides. Dinner is a prix fixe for $55 plus tax and tip ($15 extra if you are one of the 29 who choose to take the sleigh). The menu changes daily, but includes choices of venison, lamb, fresh trout, or a pasta, such as fettucine with sun-dried tomatoes and shrimp. After the 40-minute trek or the nippy sleigh ride, the cozy cabin with tables adorned with deerhorn and candle centerpieces seems perfect. After the meal and a bit of wine, the trip back to the Touring Center doesn't seem nearly so long or cold.

Dining on the mountain

Unlike the majority of U.S. resorts, the Aspen Skiing Company puts restaurant contracts up for public bidding, so real restaurateurs end up with them, and the food is a far cry from the usual cafeteria and steam-table fare.

The latest example of this phenomenon is the arrival of Real Restaurants, the famed restaurant group from San Francisco whose crown jewels include Fog City Diner, Mustards, Gordon's and Tra Vigne. They've formed a new start-up called Colorado Culinary Capers and have opened **Bumps** at the Buttermilk base area. The menu features foods from a wood-fired rotisserie, brick ovens and a pit smoker. While turning out rustic foccacia pizzas, the owners have not forgotten the 10 children among them. A "no green stuff" pizza is offered, as well as a hip macaroni-and-cheese with applewood smoked bacon and cheddar. Stop in for a bowl of buffalo chili with black beans and cilantro gremolata.

This group also has taken over **Shlomo's** at the base of Aspen Mountain and opened the **Ajax Tavern** last season. Ajax Tavern's broad-based menu boasts Mediterranean influences in a handsome clubby room. Grilled and cedar-planked loin of tuna, herb salad and sweet potato chips in a roasted pepper vinaigrette, garlic shrimp cassoulet baked with fennel sausage, and rocky range chicken breast slow roasted on wild mushrooms highlight the dinner menu. Lunch offers skiers a hearty selection of pastas, salads, and sandwiches with outdoor seating.

While not a sit-down restaurant, **Bonnie's**, just above Lift 3 on Aspen Mountain, feeds some 1,500 hungry skiers per day between 9:30 a.m. and 2:30 p.m. Go before noon or after 2 p.m., unless you love lines. (If you do find yourself there at peak hours, there's an outdoor fajita express line for $3.85 that will get you on your way in a hurry.) At $3.25 per slice, owner Bonnie Rayburn's gourmet pizza on freshly made crust is a huge crowd pleaser. Choose from smoked chicken with pesto, spinach with goat cheese, or spicy mushroom and eggplant. Homemade soups, such as the Colorado white-bean chili, are served with large crusty pieces of fresh French bread. The apple strudel, with homemade pastry and local apples, is famous.

A relative newcomer at the top of Lift 1A on Aspen Mountain is **La Baita** (literally, "mountain eatery"), run by Farfalla, one of Aspen's hottest restaurants. The innovative Italian buffet cafeteria features traditional Italian fare with gourmet pizzas, panini and a variety of lasagnas. The sit-down restaurant (920-0728), with the best views of town, offers relaxed dining over such dishes as white polenta with wild mushrooms, grilled pheasant, creative pastas, and Aspen's best tiramisu.

Café Suzanne is at the bottom of Elk Camp Lift 10 at Snowmass and specializes in French Country Cuisine. Although it's a cafeteria, the food is a pleasant surprise, with a daily assortment of entrée crêpes, such as buckwheat crêpes with spinach, mushroom or chicken, and dessert crêpes. Suzanne McPherson has taken her classical French training and customized it to the fast-food needs of the mountain. There is a daily hot entrée special, generally a Provençal or Norman dish, and a special soup with a homemade sourdough boule. You won't find a Parisian hot dog with gruyère and Dijon in any other mountain restaurant around here. Also, some menu items, such as chicken breast marinated in herbes de Provence, are flagged with a heart logo, indicating American Heart Association heart-healthy selections. Open daily 9 a.m. to 3:30 p.m.

Also at Snowmass, try **Gwyn's High Alpine Restaurant**, at the top of Alpine Springs (Lift 8), for fine dining. Gwyn offers a sit-down breakfast daily from 9:30 to 10:30 a.m. Lunch is served from 11:30 a.m. to 2:30 p.m. Reservations are essential (923-5188). If you take the first chair up, but aren't quite ready to brave the cold, you can relax with an orange blossom and enjoy a zucchini frittata, fresh-fruit pancakes, or Alpine potatoes while sipping a cup of Kona coffee. At noon, you can warm up with the special appetizer—Prince Island mussels steamed and served with a roasted red pepper sauce, a fresh garden vegetable fondue, a pasta special, the catch of the day—perhaps Rocky Mountain ruby red trout served with a cranberry-orange butter, a variety of buffalo burgers or the warm vegetable strudel (such as zucchini, mushroom, tomato, or smoked cheddar).

Krabloonik (923-3953) is located at the base of Campground off the Dawdler Catwalk, and serves both lunch and dinner. Famous for its 300 Alaskan sled dogs, Krabloonik also serves legendary cuisine. While the restaurant is accessible by skis at lunch, a dogsled ride is the kickoff to a four-course feast at dinner. The house specialty is wild game, including boar, caribou, elk, moose and pheasant. Krabloonik smokes these ingredients in true Alpine fashion.

by Katy Keck

Aspen Area, Colorado
Snowmass

Though it is lumped into the Aspen experience by geography, Snowmass can stand on its own as a ski destination. Measuring by skiable acreage, Snowmass is one of the top ten resorts in America in size, and it's the second-largest in Colorado (after Vail). It covers more than 2,600 acres—more than Aspen Mountain, Buttermilk and Aspen Highlands combined. It has four mountain peaks and a vertical of more than 3,600 feet. The lift system, which includes five high-speed quads, can move more than 23,000 skiers an hour.

Snowmass will get even bigger for 95/96. A new base area, called Two Creeks, will have a new high-speed lift, a day lodge, parking for 200 cars, a mass transit terminal and 125 acres of new intermediate ski trails. The new Two Creeks quad superchair will connect with an upgraded Elk Creek lift (it used to be a double), getting you to the top of Elk Camp in under 20 minutes. This new base area will become the most convenient entrance to this vast playground if you're staying in Aspen.

Snowmass is a wonderful intermediate and advanced area. The Big Burn allows you to activate your autopilot, and the run from the top of Elk Camp to Fanny Hill is a four-mile-plus cruise. But Snowmass has steeps such as Hanging Valley Glades and Hanging Valley Wall that pucker up intermediates and delight advanced skiers.

Snowmass village seems to stretch forever. Like Keystone, Copper Mountain and Steamboat, this is a purpose-built ski resort. A village mall has a cluster of shops, restaurants, bars and ski administration facilities. Hundreds of condos are spread out around the lower part of the ski area, and about 90 percent of the lodging is ski-in/ski-out. It doesn't get much more convenient than Snowmass.

Snowmass Facts
Base elevation: 8,223'; **Summit elevation:** 11,835'; **Vertical drop:** 3,612 feet
Number of lifts: 17–7 quad superchairs, 2 triple chairs, 6 double chairs, 2 surface lifts
Snowmaking: 3 percent **Skiable acreage:** 2,625 acres
Uphill capacity: 23,979 per hour **Bed Base:** 6,000 in resort

Where to ski

Beginners have a wide gentle area parallel to the village. Fanny Hill eases down by the mall, Wood Run lift opens another easy glide around the Wood Road side of the village, and further to the left a long straightaway, Funnel, will give beginners the feeling they're really covering terrain. Beginners who want to see more of the mountain can head up to Sam's Knob, eat lunch, enjoy the view and head down a meandering trail bearing the names Max Park, Lunchline and Dawdler, which turns back to Fanny Hill. (Avoid the blue runs on the face of Sam's Knob because they are not for beginners.) The next step up would be Elk Camp, labeled blue but very gentle.

Intermediates will be in their element. The Big Burn is legendary cruiser fun. It's an entire side of a mountain that was reportedly set aflame by Ute Indians in the 1880s as a warning to advancing white settlers. The pioneers settled anyway, but the trees never grew back thickly, so the run, dotted by a few spruces, is a mile wide and a mile and a half long.

If the pitch there is not quite to your liking, head over to High Alpine, which is perhaps five degrees steeper. (Once you're on the mountain, the lift system will keep you at the higher altitudes until you decide to come down.)

Advanced skiers and experts ready to burn up steep-pitched cruising will think they've found nirvana when they make the first descent into the Campground area. Here is a wonderful long run for solid intermediates or advanced skiers: to come off the top of Big Burn on Sneaky's, schuss to avoid the uphill stretch at Sam's Knob, cut south around the Knob and head into the blacks of Bear Claw, Slot, Wildcat or Zugspitze to the base of the Campground lift. All offer great cruises and patches of moguls normally of the mellow sand-dune variety.

Advanced skiers will get an adrenalin rush by dropping through the trees in the Hanging Valley Glades or into steep open-bowl skiing on the Hanging Valley Wall. Both are labeled double black diamonds. To get there quickly on powder mornings, take Wood Run, Alpine Springs and High Alpine Chairs. The ski school offers guided tours back here. Check at their desk at High Alpine.

Another extreme playground is the Cirque, a scooped-out place between Sheer Bliss and High Alpine lifts. Don't try this unless you're comfortable on Hanging Valley Wall: you'll have to be deft of foot on Rock Island and KT Gully. Even more challenging is AMF at the top. It's not on a trail map, but a local says it's awesome and stands for "Adios, My Friend."

Mountain rating

This is an intermediate mountain even though it has pockets of advanced terrain and beginner smoothies. Skiers who love cruising will think they have arrived in heaven. Few competent skiers who have returned from Snowmass have been heard complaining. That's the best recommendation of all.

Snowboarding

Snowboarding is allowed on the mountain. However, three chutes are controlled based on snow conditions. Just below the Naked Lady chair on the Funnel trail is a 500-foot long, 50-foot wide halfpipe with eight-foot sides. The resort also has a snowboard park. Private and group lessons are available, and D&E Snowboards in the village has rentals.

Cross-country

See the Aspen chapter.

Lessons

See the Aspen chapter.

Child care

Children's ski programs are detailed in the Aspen chapter, but if you have very young children, we recommend Snowmass rather than Aspen—the condos are more convenient and of the four areas, Snowmass has the only programs for children younger than 3. A snowplay program for children 18 months to 4 years is called **Snowcubs.** Reservations are suggested; call 925-1220 or (800) 525-6200.

Little Red School House (923-3756) offers licensed day care for children 2 1/2–5 years; the **Little Red School Toddler Center** (923-5020) has day care for kids 12 months to 3 years. **Kelly's Kids** (923-2809) provides sitters.

Lift tickets

See the Aspen chapter.

Accommodations

As noted there are few hotels but thousands of modern luxurious condominiums. You can't beat their slopeside positioning or soaring cathedral ceilings and wide-open, glassed-in living rooms. All rates below are for the regular season with double occupancy. We have not listed all of the condos; for other recommendations, and reservations, call **Snowmass Accommodations** (800-598-2004).

A range of prices are listed here. The low price is for value season, normally before Christmas, in January and in early April. The high price is the holiday rate, usually valid during the two-week Christmas holiday and Presidents' Weekend in February. Regular-season rates will be somewhere in the middle.

Hotel accommodations are relatively limited:

The Snowmass Lodge and Club is below and outside the village, but upscale. It serves as the Nordic center and has a deluxe athletic club. There are regular shuttles to the slopes. Rates, including lift tickets: $225-$430 a night.

These two are the class acts in Snowmass Village. The contemporary **Silvertree** ($140-$375), which has been open since the ski area began in 1967 and is the largest property in the area, has redone 80 of its guest rooms to make them warmer and brighter. Across the street is the more rustic **Wildwood Lodge**, with rates a little less at $66-$295. Both are comfortable with beautiful rooms, and close to everything in Snowmass.

Mountain Chalet costs $179-$205 during regular season with rooms as inexpensive as $105 during low season. The **Pokolodi** normal season rates are $130-$140 with low season costs as low as $65.

Condo rates given here are per-night, for two-bedroom units designed to sleep four. Smaller and larger units are available.

The **Woodrun V** units are the most luxurious and roomiest, with multilevel design, private hot tubs and elegant furnishings. Rate: $317-$677. **Shadowbrook** is probably the best in the village area, with rates running $300-$525.

The **Top of the Village** two-bedroom units run $200-$455. The **Timberline** condos cost $240-$473 in regular season. Both are a good 5- to 10-minute climb above the village mall.

The **Stonebridge** in the center of the village has two-bedroom units for $225-$450. The **Terracehouse, Willows** and **Lichenhearth** are clustered together two levels below Village Mall; two-bedroom units range from $200 to $330. The Willows are unusual because they are separate buildings, either cozy studios with kitchenettes ($119-$180 for two) or two bedrooms for $238-$330. Above the village is the **Sonnenblick**, which has only large units, three to five bedrooms ranging from $430-$1,200.

Dining

Snowmass claims two of the best restaurants in the area. **Krabloonik** (923-3953) has become an institution, even when measured against the more trendy competition in Aspen. It's a formal dining experience featuring wild game and seafood amid spectacular views and the howling of sled dogs in the kennels outside. With a bit of imagination you can imagine yourself in Doctor Zhivago country. The chef at **La Boheme** (923-6804), Maurice Couturier, was once the chef for the King of Jordan but now offers up some specialties such as lamb, pheasant, deer and caribou. He also oversees the cooking at the less expensive **La Brasserie** (923-6803), which specializes in pasta and fish dishes and has live jazz performances. Other top quality spots are **Cowboys** on the Village Mall with gourmet Colorado cuisine (see the Aspen Savoir Faire chapter), **Il Poggio** (923-4292) and **The Conservatory**.

Midrange dining can be found at **The Tower, Cottonwoods** (with live jazz on weekends), **Pippins Steak and Lobster, Butch's Lobster Bar** (formerly Moguls), **Brothers' Grille** (which reportedly has the best hamburgers in the valley) and **Mountain Dragon,** (for Chinese).

Every restaurant in Snowmass has children's menus, but for affordable and hearty meals for the family, **The Stewpot** features soups, tasty and unusual stews and sandwiches. Also for soups and sandwiches, try **Paradise Bakery** in Silvertree Plaza. Or go to **S'noBeach Café** (featuring "eggs S'noBeach" for breakfast). A popular hangout is **La Piñata** for fair Mexican food at fair prices, where sombreros and wild art line the walls and locals play darts and table shuffleboard.

Snowmass excels with mountaintop cookery (see Aspen Savoir Faire).

Après-ski/nightlife

The **Timbermill** and the **Brothers' Grille** are the hubs of après-ski with live music. The Timbermill tends to be more crowded and rowdier. Brothers' has five different draft beers and almost a dozen hot drinks for quick warmups. **Cottonwoods** and **La Brasserie** have live jazz on weekends.

At night Snowmass is quiet. The hottest action in town is in the **Tower,** where Doc Eason performs magic throughout the night. For those with dancin' boots, head to **Cowboys** where they strike up C&W.

Other activities

The **Anderson Ranch Arts Center** (923-3181) in Snowmass Village exhibits work by visiting and resident artists throughout the winter. The center also offers a series of workshops in ceramics, woodworking and photography from January through April. Call for current events.

Krabloonik Kennels in Snowmass (923-3953) has dogsled rides. Two-hour rides cost $185 and include lunch.

Also see the Aspen chapter.

Getting there and getting around

See the Aspen section.

Information/reservations

Snowmass runs one of the best reservation systems in the country. Staff members will take care of your entire ski vacation from air transportation and transfer to lodging and lift tickets, lessons and child care. Call (800) 598-2004, or 923-2010.

Unless otherwise noted, all area codes are 970.

Summit County, Colorado

Some winter vacationers aren't satisfied with skiing at just one place. When they return to the office, they want to drop ski resorts names and compare the black-diamond plunges. For these skiers, we suggest Summit County.

Summit County, about a 90-minute drive from downtown Denver, has four well-known ski areas—Breckenridge, Copper Mountain, Keystone and Arapahoe Basin. Each resort has its own village with lodging, shopping and restaurants. (Okay, A-Basin's lodging is a few miles down the road at Keystone.)

If you plan to do most of your skiing at just one area, stay at that resort, but if you want to experience them all and save some money—then set up your base camp in Dillon, Frisco or Silverthorne, three small towns that around Dillon Reservoir off I-70.

This tri-town area is smack in the center of the ski action. Breckenridge is about nine miles in one direction, Copper Mountain five miles in another, and Keystone and A-Basin seven miles away in a third. Having a car is nice, but not really necessary. The reliable Summit Stage, the free bus system subsidized by sales tax revenue, runs between the towns and the ski areas all day.

Summit County deserves its lofty name. Each of the ski areas, and each of the three mountain towns, has a base elevation above 9,000 feet. (If you have problems with high altitudes, take note. If you like spring skiing, also take note. High elevations usually mean a longer ski season. Each of these areas stays open at least until late April in normal snow years, and Arapahoe Basin—the base lodge of which is above 10,000 feet—runs lifts well into June.)

Keystone, Arapahoe Basin and Breckenridge are owned by the same company and offer an interchangeable lift ticket. You'll have to buy a separate ticket to ski at Copper Mountain, but the skiing there is worth the trip to the ticket window.

This chapter lists accommodations, dining, nightlife and non-ski activities in the tri-town area of Frisco, Dillon and Silverthorne.

Separate chapters detail the skiing, lodging, dining and nightlife at Breckenridge, Copper Mountain and Keystone/Arapahoe Basin.

Accommodations

Frisco: This is our first choice for a home base, for several reasons. One, it is the closest town to Breckenridge and Copper Mountain, and Keystone isn't far away. Two, its downtown area along Main Street has lots of funky shops and restaurants, perfect for a late afternoon or evening stroll. And three, we like friendly mountain inns, and found a couple of good ones.

Twilight Inn is tucked behind a bookstore at 308 Main Street, (800) 262-1002 or (970) 668-5009. Though not as fancy as the Galena Street Mountain Inn, this B&B is down-home friendly, the kind of place where you'll probably get to know all the inhabitants in record time. Its 12 rooms have a variety of bed arrangements ranging in cost from $90-$128. Examples: A first-floor room with one queen bed and private bath costs $108. A third-floor, shared-bath room with a double-sized bunk bed, a regular-sized bunk bed and a sofa sleeper costs $90 for the first two bodies and $15 for each additional. Rooms on the first and second floors have private baths; the four third-floor rooms share two large bathrooms, one for men and one for women. Guests may use the kitchen, hot tub, steam room, laundry room and two common rooms filled with books, games and magazines (plus a TV in one of the rooms).

The **Galena Street Inn**, First Avenue and Galena Street (one block off Main Street), (800) 248-9138 or (970) 668-3224, was built three years ago. Its 15 rooms have private baths, televisions and phones, and all are nicely furnished. Two large common rooms, a locked ski storage area, a hot tub and sauna are among the amenities. A full breakfast with hot entrée is included, as are après-ski refreshments. No Smoking, no pets. Nightly room rates, based on double occupancy, are about $120 during February and March; about $95 in January (it depends on the specific room). Extra people in a room cost $15 each.

Dillon/Silverthorne: The **Best Western Ptarmigan Lodge** in the Dillon town center is one of the best bargains. Rooms are about $100 per night, sometimes a little lower during the shoulder seasons and in January. (800) 842-5939 or (970) 468-2341.

Off the interstate in Silverthorne are side-by-side chain hotels—**Hampton Inn** (800-321-3509 or 970-468-6200) and **Days Inn** (800-329-7466 or 970-468-8661). The Summit Stage stops at their doors, and they are convenient to the Factory Stores (see Other Activities). Rates are about $135 in high season for the Hampton Inn and $120 at Days Inn.

Budget travelers should stay at the **Super 8** motel in Dillon, across from the City Market shopping center. Most of the best cheap restaurants are in this center, and rooms are less than $100.

The towns have many more B&Bs, chain hotels, private homes and condos. **Summit County Central Reservations** (800-365-6365) can help you find them and can book lodging at the three ski resorts.

Dining

Frisco: The fanciest restaurant in town is the **Blue Spruce Inn** (668-5900) in a historic log cabin at the corner of Madison and Main. Entrées include such dishes as filet béarnaise, vegetables en croûte, grilled venison and scallops dijonaise. Prices are in the $15–$28 range. The food is good, though a little sauce-heavy, and the atmosphere and service are excellent. Reservations recommended.

More moderate fare is found at **Charity's** (668-3644) 307 Main Street, which features Mexican and Southwestern dishes with pasta, chicken and seafood for variety. Another Southwestern-styled restaurant is **Golden Annie's** (668-0345) corner of 6th and Main. Prices are $8–$15 at both; the difference is atmosphere. Charity's is historic saloon, while Golden Annie's is yuppie faux-adobe.

Budget eats: The smells coming from **Smithwick's Bar-B-Q Smokehouse Restaurant** (668-3729) at 400 Main St. are divine. The Smithwicks barbecue a splendid variety of meat: beef, pork, turkey, buffalo and venison. The atmosphere is very casual, with vinyl chairs and linoleum floors.

Locals recommended **Ge-Jo's**, upstairs at 409 Main St. (668-3308), for inexpensive Italian fare, **Whiskey Creek**, near Wal-Mart at 908 N. Summit Blvd. (668-5595), for Mexican dishes, **Szechuan Taste** at 310 Main St. (668-5685) for Chinese food and **Barkley's**, downstairs at 620 Main St. (668-3694) for prime rib and Mexican food. Frisco also has many chain fast-food restaurants, most along Summit Boulevard.

Halfway between Frisco and Breckenridge, in an area called Farmer's Korner, are neighboring restaurants that are quite different. **The Blue River Saloon** (453-4068) is a no-frills local hangout with great burgers, $2 draft beers and a 10-ounce sirloin for $7.95. **The Swan Mountain Inn** (453-7903) offers a nightly four-course meal (about $25) in a seven-table dining room with a fireplace. The inn also has a weekend brunch.

Dillon & Silverthorne: Locals and visitors alike rave about **Silverheels Southwest Grill** (468-2926) 81 Buffalo Drive in Silverthorne. Fine Southwestern fare and a Spanish tapas bar are the specialties here. The restaurant, located in a hacienda-style building in the Wildernest area, is a bit off the main drag but worth the search. When you call for reservations ask for directions.

Another choice for finer dining is **Ristorante Al Lago** in the Dillon town center (468-6111), which serves Northern Italian meals in the $13 to $19 range.

For slightly more casual dining in Dillon, try **Antonia's** (468-5055) in the same building as Christy's Sports on Highway 6, **Pug Ryan's**, (468-2145) in the Dillon town center, or **Wild Bill's Stone Oven Pizza**, (468-2006) also in the Dillon town center. In Silverthorne, you can cook your own meat over an open grill at **The Historic Mint** (468-5247) or enjoy inexpensive Tex-Mex food at **Old Dillon Inn** (468-2791).

Budget diners: the City Market center on Highway 6 on the Dillon-Silverthorne border has several highly recommended restaurants, including **Sunshine Cafe** (468-6663), jammed with locals; **Roberto's** (468-5878) for the least expensive Mexican food this side of Taco Bell; and **Nick-N-Willys** (262-1111) for very good take-out pizza.

Breakfast: The best breakfast in the tri-town area is **Claimjumper**, on Summit Boulevard in Frisco across the street from Wal-Mart (668-3617). Not only does it have an extensive omelet-and-pancake menu, it has $1.99 breakfast specials that taste great and fill both the plate and stomach.

A close second is the **Arapahoe Cafe** on Lake Dillon Drive in the Dillon town center (468-0873), a huge favorite with locals. The cafe building used to stand in the old town of Dillon, but was moved in the 1960s when the new reservoir flooded the area. The service is great, the menu names are creative (Arapahuevos Rancheros, Hans and Franz Power Breakfast, etc.) and eavesdropping on the neighboring table will educate you about the local politics. Both restaurants also have inexpensive lunch and dinner menus.

Definitely in the running for the Best Breakfast title is **Sunshine Cafe** in the City Market center.

For those who prefer a lighter breakfast, head for the **Butterhorn Bakery**, 408 W. Main Street in Frisco (668-3997). Muffins, pastries, bagels and gourmet coffee are the highlights here. Or, try **Java Mountain Summit** (668-1400), another gourmet coffee establishment next to Safeway on Summit Boulevard in Frisco.

Après-ski/nightlife

Frisco: Most locals head to **Barkley's Margaritagrille** on Main Street or **Whiskey Creek** on Summit Boulevard for happy hour. Several of the Main Street restaurants listed in the Dining section also have happy hours.

Dillon/Silverthorne: This seems to be the choice for late-night fun. **Tommy C's**, which is behind Antonia's restaurant and Christy Sports in Dillon, is the leading sports bar with large-screen TVs, darts, pool tables and foosball. The menu is Chicago sandwiches and pizza.

Old Dillon Inn has live Country & Western music on weekends, and the best margaritas in town. Its 120-year-old bar definitely has authentic Old West atmosphere. The building was pieced together from bits of defunct establishments, and the whole thing was moved in 1961 when the old town of Dillon disappeared under the aforementioned lake.

Other popular choices are the **Pub Down Under**, underneath the Arapahoe Cafe in Dillon, or the **Corona St. Grill** or **Pug Ryan's**, both in the Dillon Town Center. For a smoky, low-key locals' hangout with pool and darts, try the **Virgin Islands Lounge** in the City Market Plaza on the Dillon-Silverthorne border.

Child care

Services of the Summit, Inc. (668-0255) in Frisco has professional babysitters aged 18-65 who are insured, bonded and child-care trained. They will come to your hotel or condo anywhere in the county.

Other activities

Shopping and services: Pack an extra suitcase. Better yet, buy a bag at one of the four luggage stores in the **Silverthorne Factory Stores.** Then starting filling it with bargains at nearly 70 brand-name stores. This is probably the largest factory outlet center in Western ski country. Among the stores are Carole Little, Anne Klein, Liz Claiborne, Guess?, Nike, Great Outdoor Clothing Co., Pfaltzgraff, Dansk, Corning/Revere, Bass Shoes, Capezio Shoes, American Tourister and Samsonite.

Collectibles and antiques lovers will go nuts at **Junk-Tique**, 313 Main St. in Frisco. It has an excellent inventory of collectible housewares, clothing and furniture at very attractive prices. The store also stocks some new jewelry and knickknacks items. Kids will love the huge black locomotive that is the centerpiece of the store.

For those items you forgot and don't want to pay resort prices for, try **Wal-Mart** on Summit Boulevard in Frisco. Near-normal grocery prices are at the **City Market** in Silverthorne or **Safeway** in Frisco. Note: only 3.2 beer is sold in Colorado grocery stores. If you want the stronger stuff, or wine or hard liquors, go to a liquor store (conveniently, right next to each of the markets). **Cozy Cleaners**, a 24-hour laundromat, is at 109 Dillon Mall in Dillon.

Snowmobiling, sleigh rides, dogsled rides: The **Summit Adventure Park**, (453-0353) on Highway 9 between Frisco and Breckenridge, has many family-oriented activities. They offer day and dinner snowmobile trips, day and dinner horse-drawn sleigh rides, a snoscoot track, (snoscoots are kid-sized motorized snow scooters), a tubing hill and an Old West variety dinner show featuring "gamblers, gunslingers and dancehall gals." Reservations are advised for the latter event.

Other companies in the area that offer snowmobiling and/or sleigh and dogsled rides are **Tiger Run Tours**, 453-2231; **Swan River Adventure Center**, 453-7604 or 668-0930; and **Two Below Zero Dinner Sleigh Rides**, 453-1520.   In the Dillon/Silverthorne area, call **Eagles Nest Equestrian Center**, 468-0677.

Cross-country skiing is available at the **Frisco Nordic Center** on Highway 9 about one mile out of town toward Breckenridge. Trail passes are $8 for adults and $6 for those 55 and older or 12 and younger. Rentals and instruction are available. Call 668-0866.

Getting there and getting around

Getting there: Frisco, Dillon and Silverthorne are just off I-70, about 75 miles west of downtown Denver. **Resort Express** has regular vans connecting the resort with Denver International Airport. (800) 334-7433 or 468-7600. Another option is **Vans to Breckenridge**, (800) 222-2112 or 668-5466.

Getting around: Frisco is laid out nicely for walking along Main Street. Otherwise, take the Summit Stage, the free bus system that links the towns with each other and the ski areas. A car is an option here; most distances are too far for walking, but the Summit Stage is reliable. Call 453-1241 for route info, or pick up a route map and schedule from the chamber of commerce or the stores that carry them. If you really enjoy nightlife and want to do extensive exploration of the restaurants and bars, we recommend a car.

Information/reservations

Summit County Central Reservations, (800) 365-6365 or (970) 468-6222, can help with lodging reservations and general information.

Summit County Chamber also has information and many helpful brochures and booklets, (970) 668-0376.

The local area code is 970.

Breckenridge, Colorado

Breckenridge has become one of the ski industry's giants, attracting more than a million visits each season. A good number are what is called Front Range skiers, who live in Denver and its suburbs. Another large portion are destination skiers. And a third fast-growing group are skiers from Great Britain, Mexico and other countries.

Undoubtedly many are attracted by Breckenridge's vast ski mountain: the numerous white ribbons that descend from its four peaks are readily visible from town (as well as from the slopes of its sister resort, Keystone). Skiers also like the restored Victorian downtown and its close proximity to Denver, about a 90-minute drive.

Breckenridge has a split personality, but it's been that way from conception. It was named for a man who became a Confederate brigadier general, but its streets are named for Union heroes—Lincoln, Grant and Sherman. When a former slave, Barney Lancelot Ford, opened one of the most successful saloons between St. Louis and San Francisco (it's still in business), townspeople initially welcomed him, but later unceremoniously ran him out of town. The Victorian buildings lining the streets witnessed wild revelry during gold and silver booms and the discovery of Colorado's largest gold nugget, but they also stood silent over windswept, vacant streets when Breckenridge joined the list of Colorado ghost towns.

Though the closest Breckenridge comes to being a ghost town these days is during the mud season in May, it still displays its inherited division. Modern architecture around the base area is a contrast to the restored Victorian downtown. The ski industry brought economic life back to Breckenridge, and the local residents have preserved the town's Victorian ginger-bread soul. Thus, visitors may submerge themselves in glass-fronted condos, pulsating spas, modern fitness facilities and nightclubs.

Breckenridge Facts

Base elevation: 9,600'; *Summit elevation:* (lift-served) 12,146';
Vertical drop: 2,546 feet.
Number and types of lifts: 17—4 quad superchairs, 1 triple chair, 8 double chairs and 4 surface lifts *Skiable acreage:* More than 2,000 *Snowmaking:* 43 percent
Uphill capacity: 24,430 skiers per hour *Bed base:* 23,000

They also have in Victorian Breckenridge hundreds of boutiques, scores of pubs and dozens of restaurants packed into brightly colored restored buildings.

Because Breckenridge is so close to Denver, weekend skiers stream into the town. But with superchairs on Peaks 8, 9 and 10 normally there's a wait of less than 10 minutes, and with the skiing now spread over four mountains, there is plenty of room for skiers even on peak days.

You'll find your fellow skiers a mixed bag. Though the general atmosphere still is more down-to-earth than at some other Colorado resorts, Breckenridge is starting to attract more of society's upper crust. Many shops now carry more upscale goods, and some of the sales personnel have adopted snooty attitudes to match. Restaurant and ski-area workers remain as friendly as ever though, and long-time Breckenridge locals still retain much of the devil-may-care attitude of their 19th-century predecessors, which helps balance the others out. For now, the Breckenridge crowd is not as free-spending as that of Aspen or Vail, nor as laid back as Crested Butte. It's a middle-of-the-road, comfortable atmosphere with plenty of great skiing.

Where to ski

Breckenridge, on four peaks covering nearly 2,000 acres, is the largest of the Summit County ski areas. At the main base facility, at the bottom of Peak 9, the Quicksilver high-speed quad chair powers skiers from the village to Peak 9's higher lifts, which will connect with Peak 10's blue and black trails. The Beaver Run superchair takes skiers to the heights of Peak 9 or a Peak 8 connection.

Years ago Breckenridge was known as an excellent beginner and intermediate resort, but the opening of the back bowls off Peak 8, the North Face of Peak 9, and Peaks 7 and 10 added hundreds of acres of expert terrain. Today, Breckenridge boasts a very high percentage of black-diamond terrain (55 percent overall) and some of the highest in-bounds skiing in North America, but still maintains its wide-open well-groomed runs for beginners and intermediates.

Imperial Bowl, crowning Peak 8, tops out at nearly 13,000 feet, creating a total vertical that's only two feet shy of 3,400. If you noticed that our statistic box shows a much smaller vertical, it's because we list the highest *lift-served* terrain. Imperial Bowl is in bounds but not lift-served. If you want to ski it, you must hike first. Likewise Peak 7, you can ski from the 12,677-foot summit, but only if you hoof it to the top. Locals love it; visitors from sea level often pass up the opportunity.

Beginners probably will stick to the front side of Peak 9 area unless they are enrolled in the Peak 8 ski school, which has the best never-ever terrain. Peak 9's terrain is a good intermediate and beginner mix. The easiest are Silverthorne, Eldorado and Red Rover, all skiable from the top of the Quicksilver lift. For more challenge, intermediates should take Lift B to the summit and ski down Cashier, Bonanza and Upper Columbia. More advanced intermediates enjoy American, Gold King and Peerless, which might be rated black at a smaller resort.

For the best cruising, head to Peak 10 and alternate between Centennial and Crystal. These runs are slightly easier than the ones on Peak 9, but the combination of a high-speed lift and mostly expert-marked terrain keeps the crowds lighter. Everything else on Peak 10 is in the black-diamond category, with Mustang, Dark Rider and Blackhawk boasting monstrous bumps. Cimarron, marked black on the map, often is groomed. The Burn, dropping to the left of the high-speed lift, offers limited short-but-sweet tree skiing.

The North Face on the back of Peak 9 is expert territory. Plenty of good skiers have begged for a rest after playing with Tom's Baby, and even prayers won't help lower intermediates who accidentally find themselves in Hades, Devil's Crotch or Inferno—once you drop down the face from Chair E, there is no escape or easy traverse.

Peak 8, where skiing at Breckenridge began, is the most varied of the mountains. Beginners practice wedge turns near the base facility; intermediates can ski alongside the high-speed Colorado lift down Springmeier, Crescendo and Swinger; experts and advanced skiers can play in Imperial Bowl or drop down a half dozen runs, such as Spruce and Rounders, to the right of the Colorado lift on the trail map. Experts can take the T-bar up to wide-open Horseshoe Bowl and the smaller, steeper Contest Bowl. (These bowls are wide—solid intermediates can ski them.)

Mountain rating

Breckenridge has many ingredients for the perfect ski vacation: lots of good terrain for all levels, plenty of slopeside lodging and a charming town. It's urban enough to have a good variety of restaurants and shops, yet not so urban that you'll feel as if you never left home. And if you don't find enough here to keep you busy, Copper Mountain and Keystone are nearby.

Cross-country

The **Breckenridge Nordic Ski Center,** near Peak 8 base on Ski Hill Road, has 28 km. of groomed, double-set trails for all skiing abilities. Trail passes are $10 for adults, $6 for 55 and older and 12 and younger. Equipment rentals, lessons, and guided backcountry tours are available. You can also rent snowshoes. Call 453-6855.

Lessons (94/95 prices)

Group lessons cost $44 for a full day; $84 for two days of lessons. **Private lessons** are $70 for one hour, $190 for three hours ($165 in the afternoon); add $25 for extra students.

Special workshops and clinics include three- or four-day women's seminars, early-season ski and racing clinics, telemark lessons, lessons for disabled skiers and several clinics for advanced skiers, such as bumps, racing and powder.

The **children's ski school** operates from its two children's centers at the bases of Peak 8 and Peak 9. Ski instruction starts at age 3 with a special ski-school morning program. Child care is available beyond ski-school hours at an additional charge.

Junior Ski School is for 4 and 5 year olds, and again, the program is a combination of ski lessons and day care. Half day (no rentals) is $50; all day is $60.

Older children 6–12 have their own classes at the same pricing as adult instruction. Ticket prices are the same as those for the adult program.

NASTAR races are held daily, 10 a.m.–3 p.m., on Country Boy on Peak 9 and on Freeway on Peak 8. Register at the top of the course. Fees are $6 for two runs and $1 for additional runs. A self-timed course is open on Peak 8 at Freeway (10 a.m.–3 p.m.) and on Country Boy on Peak 9 (10 a.m.–3:30 p.m.) for $1 a run.

Child care

The Peak 8 Children's Center accepts children from 2 months to 5 years. Infant care for children up to 2 years is $55 a day, $45 a half day. Parents must provide diapers, formula, food, change of clothes, etc.

Child care for 3 to 5 year olds is $55 a day and $45 for half days. Children this age can go to either the Peak 8 or Peak 9 children's centers. A Snow Play program allows preschoolers to build snowmen, go sledding and do other outdoor activities.

Reservations are required; call 453-3258 for Peak 8 Children's Center, 453-3259 for Peak 9 Children's Center.

Another possibility for child care and instruction is **Kinderhut** (800-541-8779 or 453-0379) a privately owned children's ski school and licensed day-care center. It accepts children aged 6 weeks to 8 years.

Lift tickets (94/95 prices)

	Adult	Child (6–12)
One day	$42	$19
Three days	$111 ($37/day)	$45 ($15/day)
Five of six days	$175 ($35/day)	$75 ($15/day)

The asterisked prices are from last season. Multiday tickets for 2-6 days are available. Ages 60-69 can buy a daily lift ticket for $19; 70 and older and children 5 and younger ski free. All lift tickets are good at Breckenridge, Keystone and Arapahoe Basin.

Accommodations

Breckenridge boasts extensive ski-in/ski-out lodging. Early December and all of January are the most affordable times, as is April. Breckenridge's lifts can keep running into May some years, but one caveat: many of the town's shops and restaurants start closing down at the end of April. Double rooms in all of these accommodations will range from $130-$225 depending on the time of the season and the particular lodge you select.

The Village at Breckenridge (reservations and information: 800-800-7829; local: 453-2000) surrounds the Peak 9 base area. Try to get into Plaza 1, 2 or 3, which are the most spacious units. The three-bedroom units here are giant. Many amenities are available: on-site health club facilities, indoor/outdoor pools, hot tubs, racquetball, steam, sauna and exercise room.

Beaver Run (reservations and information: 800-525-2253; local: 453-6000). This complex is slopeside on Peak 9. It has restaurants, outdoor hot tubs, indoor/outdoor swimming pools, a giant indoor miniature golf course and a great game room for kids. The Kinderhut child-care center, located in the hotel, will take children from the ages of 1 to 3; kids 3 to 6 can take ski lessons.

The Breckenridge Hilton (reservations and information: 800-321-8444; Denver: 825-3800; local: 453-4500) This hotel is almost but not quite ski-in/ski-out; it's only 50 yards from the slopes. The rooms here are massive, about 40 by 12 feet. There is an indoor swimming pool, whirlpool spas and a fitness and exercise room.

The River Mountain Lodge (800-325-2342; 0800-897-497 United Kingdom direct; local 453-4711) This collection of studio to four-bedroom suites is in the heart of Breckenridge, only steps away from Main Street. The ski bus stops across the street. This is one of the most reasonable accommodations in Breckenridge.

In town, try **The Wellington Inn** at 200 N. Main St., (800-655-7557 or 453-9464). This four-room B&B inn opened a couple of years ago in one of Breckenridge's Victorian houses. The rooms are fairly spacious and beautifully decorated. All have outside decks and excellent private bathrooms with spa-jet tubs. No Smoking and no pets.

Another attractive mountain inn is the **Allaire Timbers Inn** at 9511 Hwy. 9/South Main St., (800-624-4904 outside Colorado; locally 453-7530). Each of the 10 rooms has a private bathroom (most with the standard tub and shower) and private deck. No Smoking, no pets and no children younger than 12. Prime season rates (mid-February through March) are $130-$190 with breakfast. Christmas holiday rates are $15-$30 higher; regular-season rates are about $15-$30 lower.

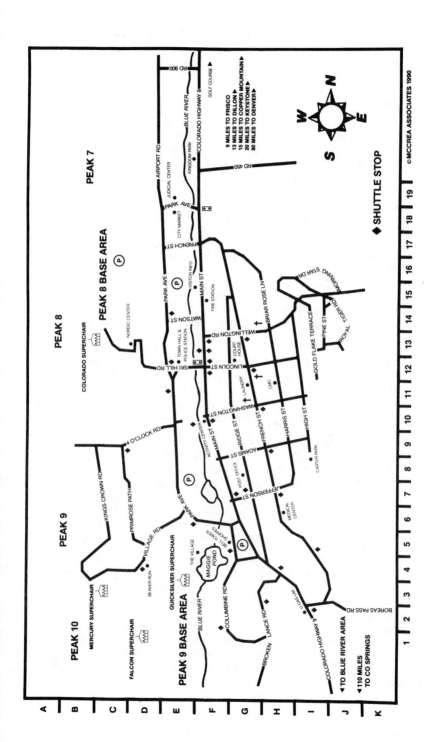

©MCCREA ASSOCIATES 1990

9 MILES TO FRISCO
13 MILES TO DILLON ▶
15 MILES TO COPPER MOUNTAIN ▶
20 MILES TO KEYSTONE ▶
80 MILES TO DENVER ▶

◆ SHUTTLE STOP

For most other lodging, call **Breckenridge Resort Chamber**, (800-221-1091, 800-800-BREC or 453-2918). In the United Kingdom, call toll-free 0800-89-7491.

Dining

Breckenridge has not gained a reputation for gourmet dining, and it probably won't in the near future. It's not bad by a long shot, but even the best restaurants in town won't set a Michelin taster's tongue to quivering. Our general comment on the top-of-the-line restaurants: heavy sauces and overpriced wine.

Our top choices in the expensive category (entrées in the $15-$25 range) are:

The Wellington Inn, 200 N. Main Street, 453-9464, with the best Victorian ambiance in town and some of the best food. Cuisine is German, featuring sauerbraten and schnitzels, or lobster, pasta primavera, steaks and honey dijon chicken. Reservations suggested.

St. Bernard Inn, 103 S. Main Street, 453-2572, has what most consider the best northern Italian food in town. Reservations suggested.

Cafe Alpine, 103 E. Adams St., 453-8218, has an interesting mix of cultural entrées, such as Greek spanekopeta, Thai curried pork, Italian tortelloni, American trout and a Spanish tapas bar. The restored Victorian atmosphere is quiet and intimate.

Other recommendations for finer dining: **Pierre's** (French), 453-0989; **Poirrier's Cajun Café**, 453-1877 and **Adams Street Grill** (Southwestern), 453-4700. All are on Main Street. **The Gold Dredge**, on a converted dredge boat sitting in the Blue River behind Le Bon Fondue, has pastas, prime rib, etc.

Best of the moderate ($10-$15) restaurants:

Tillie's, 213 S. Ridge Street, 453-0669, has good basic food. The menu is limited but so are the prices. The hand-carved bar, tin ceiling and stained glass provide a good period effect. The Tillie's crowd could often form a quorum for a town meeting.

The Hearthstone, 130 S. Ridge Street, 453-6921, is in a great Victorian house that served as a bordello in the old mining days. Prices are reasonable, food acceptable and ambiance hard to beat.

Other moderate recommendations: **Main St. Bistro**, 453-0514, for mix-and-match pastas and sauces; **Blue River Bistro**, 453-6974, winner of the Annual Taste of Breckenridge contest; **Pasta Jay's**, 326 S. Main St., 453-5800, has pasta with plenty of garlic; and **Le Bon Fondue**, 453-6969, serves crêpes and four kinds of fondue.

Some suggestions for good cheap eats (less than $10):

Beer lovers should try the **Breckenridge Brewery & Pub**, 600 S. Main St., 453-1550. The menu has good variety, and the micro-brewed beer is excellent.

Mi Casa, 600 Park Ave, 453-2071, across from the base of Peak 9, has Tex-Mex food. **Colt's Down Under**, 401 S. Main, 453-6060, has satellite TV for the big sports events and good inexpensive food until late. **The New York Delicatessen**, 110 S. Ridge St., 453-0413, has an extensive Big Apple menu of Coney Island hot dogs, bagels, potato knishes, brisket and more.

Breakfast: For one of the best breakfasts at any ski resort, the hands-down winner is **The Prospector** at 130 S. Main Street (453-6858). The Huevos Ranchero will test your facial sweat glands. Another favorite with the eggs-and-pancake crowd is **The Blue Moose**, 540 S. Main St. (453-4859). For muffins, pastry and gourmet coffee, try **Mountain Java** upstairs at 118 Ridge St. (453-1874) or **Clint's**, 131 S. Main St. (453-1736). The best bargain breakfast is at the **Copper Top** in Beaver Run.

Après-ski/nightlife

Breckenridge's liveliest après-ski bars are **Tiffany's** and **Copper Top** in Beaver Run, the **Village Pub** in the Bell Tower Mall, and **Mi Casa**, with great margaritas by the liter.

Tiffany's at Beaver Run rocks until the wee hours, but after dinner most of the action moves into town. **Downstairs at Eric's**, downstairs at 109 Main Street, has a raucous younger crowd with loud live music and long lines on weekends. A slightly older group with plenty of locals gathers at **Shamus O'Toole's**, 115 S. Ridge Street, a wide-open roadhouse with live music on most evenings and an eclectic crowd, ranging from absolute blue-collar to those yuppied-up for the evening. Some nights the mix is intoxicating, and on others merely intoxicated, which often sets off fireworks. **Horseshoe II** on Main Street gets packed and there is dancing at **Johsha's** on Park Avenue across from the Village at Breckenridge. For a non-dancing, quieter time, try the **St. Bernard** on Main Street; a cozy bar in the back is often packed with business-class locals. **The Breckenridge Brewery & Pub** has live music and beer specials, and **The Alligator Lounge** on Main Street has touring blues-and-jazz acts, plus local musicians' nights in an unfinished-sheet-rock atmosphere.

The old **Gold Pan**, 103 N. Main Street, is the legacy of Barney Lancelot Ford. It is the oldest continuously operating bar west of the Mississippi. This was once one of the wildest places in the Wild West, with a miner or two known to be thrown through the saloon doors. A long century-old mahogany bar presides over a now worn, dimly lit room with a pinball machine tucked into the back corner and a couple of well-utilized pool tables. The crowd had shifted toward preppie pool players a few years ago, but a local tells us that it recently shifted back to the more usual crowd of truckers, pool sharks sporting earrings, and the temporarily unemployed.

Other activities

Exploring the old town of Breckenridge is great fun, either with a formal **historical tour** or on your own armed with a free guidesheet.

Shopping: Downtown has scores of boutiques, most of which seem to be T-shirt shops. Some of our non-T-shirt favorites: **Skilled Hands Gallery**, 110 S. Main St., with paintings, jewelry, ceramics and other beautiful items hand-crafted by Colorado artisans; **The Twisted Pine**, two locations on Main Street, for elegant leathers and furs; **Lift Off Sportswear**, 111 S. Main St., for unusual women's clothes with a Southwestern flair; **Mountain Kids**, in Towne Square on Main Street, for children's ski clothing; and **Goods**, near the intersection of Main Street and Lincoln Street, for classic mountain clothing for men and women and funky accessories.

For active types of non-ski activities, see the Summit County chapter.

Getting there and getting around

Getting there: Breckenridge is 98 miles west of Denver International Airport by I-70 to Exit 203, then south on Highway 9. It is a 110-minute drive. **Resort Express** has regular vans connecting the resort with the airport. Telephone: 468-7600 or (800) 334-7433. Another option is **Vans to Breckenridge**, 668-5466 or (800) 222-2112.

Getting around: Nearly everything is within walking distance. The town trolley and buses cruise the streets regularly and the Summit Stage links Breckenridge with neighboring Ski the Summit resorts Keystone, Arapahoe Basin and Copper Mountain, as well as the towns of Dillon, Silverthorne and Frisco. Both the town transportation and the Summit Stage are free.

Information/reservations

The **Breckenridge Resort Chamber central reservation office** handles transfers, lodging and lift tickets. Call (800) 221-1091 or 453-2918.

Breckenridge Ski Corporation: 453-5000 or (800) 789-7669. Snow report: 453-6118. In the United Kingdom, call 0800-89-7491.

The local area code is 970.

Copper Mountain, Colorado

If ski resorts were people, Copper Mountain Resort would be the ultra-organized type—the kind of guy whose sock drawer has navy dress socks neatly folded on the left side, black dress socks stacked on the right, and white athletic socks nesting in the middle. Copper's trail system and base village are similarly arranged in a logical, easy-to-find manner.

As you face the mountain, the beginner slopes are to the right, the intermediate trails are in the middle and the most difficult runs are on the left. The base village, built from the ground up a couple of decades ago, has clusters of restaurants and shops surrounded by multi-story condo buildings, with an efficient free shuttle system connecting the whole thing. Even getting there is a well-organized snap. Drive about an hour and a half west of Denver on I-70, and the resort and its base village appear on the left side of the freeway.

This is not to imply that Copper Mountain is a dull place for a ski vacation. The bowls at the top of Copper and Union peaks have plenty of chutes, cornices and powder stashes. Copper's layout makes for a convenient vacation. Just as Mr. Neat doesn't waste time finding a matching pair of socks, you won't waste it consulting the trail map or riding endless lifts to find your type of terrain.

Don't expect to find any old copper mines or even a miner's turn-of-the-century saloon—Copper is strictly a creature of modern-day master plan. Its condominium villages are divided into three sections. The heartbeat of the resort thumps from the Village Center, where you'll find the high-speed American Eagle and American Flyer quads, as well as most of Copper's dining and nightlife. The condos in this section tend to be more upscale. The East Village, centered at the base of the B lift, offers less expensive accommodations, plus a few bars and restaurants.

Copper Mountain Facts

Base elevation: 9,712'; **Summit elevation:** 12,313'; **Vertical drop:** 2,601 feet.
Number and types of lifts: 20–3 quad superchairs, 6 triple chairs, 7 double chairs, and 4 surface lifts
Acreage: 2,790 skiable acres **Snowmaking:** 20 percent
Uphill capacity: 29,450 skiers per hour **Bed base:** 2,800

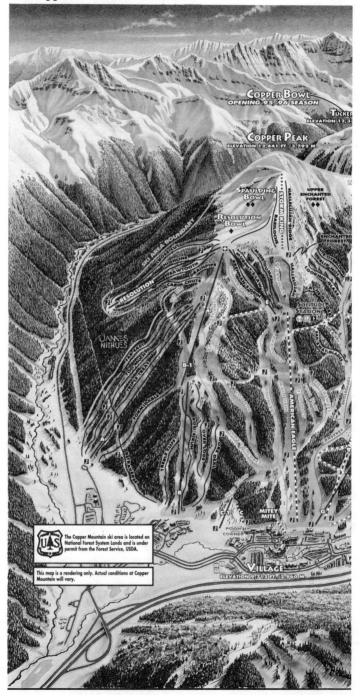

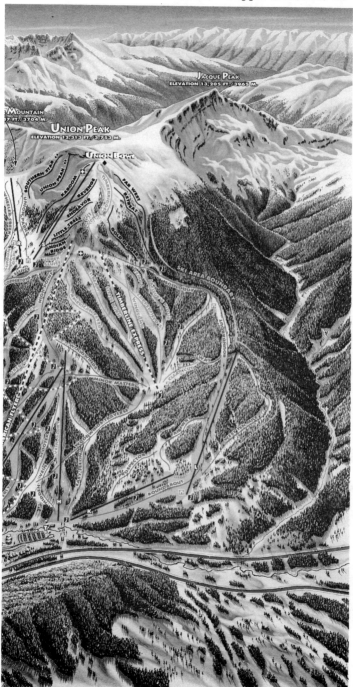

The West Village, close to the Union Creek area, is home to Club Med, some upscale properties and the cross-country center.

Copper mountain plans to install a double chair by January 1996 to bring skiers into the 700-acre Copper Bowl. the terrain, on the back side of Union Peak will provide advanced above treeline skiing as well as excellent glades. The snowcat tours of this area will end.

Where to ski

Beginners and intermediates should first hop on the high-speed American Flyer lift, or the H lift in the Union Creek area. Nearly the whole side of the mountain under Union Peak consists of sweeping runs lined by trees, perfect for the advanced beginner and lower intermediate.

For a long run to the bottom, beginners should bear left when getting off the high-speed quad and take Coppertone for an easy cruise. Beginners who take the H lift can head right, down Woodwinds to the Timberline Express quad chair, ride to the top and ski the equally sweeping Soliloquy to Roundabout connection to the bottom. The K and L lifts, which constitute the far right border of the resort, also are custom-made for the beginner. In fact, this is one of the most extensive networks for the beginner that we've seen.

Intermediates should exit to the right of the American Flyer quad and try the American Flyer, I-Beam and Windsong runs under the Timberline Express lift. Better yet, take the American Eagle quad chair from Village Center and dart down any of the runs under this lift. If you're patient enough to continue up the mountain on the E lift, you'll have the best intermediate runs of the resort at your feet. Both Collage and Andy's Encore are worthy challenges for the intermediate, offering good grade without the heavy moguls or tight funnels that can turn a blue run black (and an unwary intermediate black and blue).

Experts need not despair. Powder monkeys can find a virgin slate—and the best views—at the top of Union Peak. It doesn't come without a price, however: take the S chair after exiting the high-speed American Flyer, then hike 100 yards up the ridge to whatever spot above Union Bowl strikes your fancy. (This hike also takes you into Copper Bowl that will have new lifts installed). All three runs that parallel the E lift are short and steep, and Brennan's Grin in particular will bring a smile to a serious bump skier's face. Bear far right off the E lift and you can find serious tree skiing on Enchanted Forest (even more serious tree skiing, albeit unmarked, is available if you bear left about halfway off the Çollage run). If you take the Storm King surface lift instead of heading down Enchanted Forest, you'll come to the side of Copper reserved strictly for experts. After you drop into steep Spaulding Bowl (lose a ski here and you'd better hope to have an uphill friend), you can choose from several very worthy expert runs to the bottom of the Resolution lift. Because this lift serves only expert runs, there's rarely a wait.

Mountain rating

This is one of the best ski trail layouts in America. Various skill levels are kept separated so that no one needs to feel intimidated or slowed down by fellow skiers. The beginner area is wonderful and there's plenty of intermediate and expert terrain— 51 percent of the mountain is rated advanced.

In the midst of all this order, however, is a confusing lift-naming system. Six of the 19 lifts have names; the others are lettered. But instead of a logical progression through the first 13 alphabet letters, the order goes like this: A, B, B1, C, C1, E, G, and so on, skipping letters at random until finally ending with T, a tiny lift at the Union Creek base area. This may be old hat to locals, but it's baffling for first-time visitors, especially if they use the lifts as meeting places. Adding to the confusion are the American *Eagle* and American *Flyer* chairs. If you're meeting someone at the top of one of those chairs, be very specific: they start in the same general area but unload on different peaks.

Snowboarding

Boarding is permitted on all sections of the mountain. Copper Mountain has an annual snowboard race series. Lessons and rentals are available.

Cross-country (95/96 prices)

Copper Mountain has created an excellent and varied cross-country trail system. Some 25 km. of set tracks and skating lanes fan out from the Union Creek cross-country center. The center offers rentals, lessons and clinics.

Track fees for adults are $10; children 5 and under and those 70 and older ski free. A package for cross-country first-timers, including half-day lesson, track pass and equipment rental is $34. The never-ever telemark package includes a half-day lesson, equipment rental and beginner lift ticket for $55.

Group lessons are $28 for a half day. The telemark program costs $50 and includes all lifts. Private lessons are $40 an hour per person; $17 per hour for each person additional.

Skiers with multiday lift tickets may trade a day of downhill skiing for the Newcomer Track Package. Overnight hut tours, a gentle ski tour with a four-course progressive meal and various telemark camps are among the special Nordic programs.

The **Copper Mountain Cross-Country Center** phone is 968-2318, ext. 6342.

Lessons (95/96 prices)

Group classes for those 13 and older are from 9:30 a.m. to noon and 12:45 to 3:15 p.m. Never-evers through near-intermediates meet at the Union Creek area; upper ability levels meet in front of the Center Building. Costs are $39 a day if you have a lift ticket or $65 including lifts. An introductory package, including lesson, beginner lift and rentals, is $55.

An excellent package program includes lessons, lifts and rentals for the seasoned skier for $69.

Private lessons lasting 90 minutes cost $80 for one or $90 for two to four skiers. Half-day private lessons run $150 for one, and all-day lessons for one are $240; up to four skiers are $350.

Specialized programs include Women's Skiing Seminars, two- and three-day seminars offered several times a season; snowboard camps for adults or children; an Advanced Skiing Seminar and the Copper Mountain Adaptive Ski Program.

Children's classes are for ages 4–12 for Alpine skiing and 8–12 for snowboarding. All-day programs include lunch and a lift ticket for $60. Two days are $110 and three days are $160. A half-day lesson for never-ever skiers, including a half-day lift ticket, is $34. The Kids Value Package (all-day lesson, rental, lift and lunch) is $65, with additional days $55.

Child care (95/96 prices)

The **Belly Button Bakery** and **Belly Button Babies** (968-2318, ext. 6345; or (800) 458-8386) are two of the most innovative child care programs in Colorado. In-room babysitting services require 24-hour advance reservations or cancellations, and cost $7 per hour, plus $1 for each additional child.

Belly Button Babies accepts children 2 months to 2 years. Full day costs $42 and includes lunch. Parents should provide diapers, extra change of clothing, a blanket and a favorite toy.

The Belly Button Bakery, for kids over 2, has "soft" ski play programs and indoor activities. One day with lunch is $47.

Reservations are required.

Lift tickets (95/96 prices)

	Adult		Child (6–14)
One day	$42	$18	
Three days	$108 ($36/day)		$30 ($10/day)
Five days	$180 ($36/day)		$50 ($10/day)

Multiday tickets are available for 3–6 days, and are valid over a 14-day period (children's multiday tickets are valid the whole season). Skiers aged 60–69 pay $27 per day, those 70 and older and 5 and younger ski free. A ticket for beginner lifts only is $17.

Copper Mountain has Kids Ski Free/Stay Free packages during December, January and April that allow children 14 years and under to ski and stay free when accompanied by parents. There is a Seniors Ski Free program for those 60 and older when they stay at Copper Mountain at certain times.

Accommodations

Copper Mountain Lodging Services has one-stop shopping for accommodations. Call (800) 458-8386. The **Copper Mountain Resort Chamber** provides information for the Copper Mountain area at (800) 525-3891, or 968-6477 in Colorado. All Copper Mountain Lodging Services properties include membership in the Athletic Club (see Other Activities).

Lodging is designated according to the village—Village Center, East Village and West Village. All condos are in the same general price range; those managed by Copper Mountain Lodging Services are newer, concentrated in the Village Center and West Village area. Top condo choice is the **Spruce Lodge** because it's so close to the lifts. The **Telemark Lodge** in West Village has a small bar and crackling fireplace, and sits equidistant from the downhill lifts and the cross-country area. Next door are the **Beeler Place Townhomes** with glass-enclosed patios (and creaky floors; if you're a light sleeper, pick the bedroom on the top floor). The **Mountain Plaza** has some hotel rooms.

Westlake Lodge and **Bridge End**, both costing the same as Spruce Lodge, are significantly farther from the lifts. The Lodging Services properties are $120-$190 a night for a hotel room, $130-$245 for a one-bedroom condo, $219-$415 for a two-bedroom unit, and $279-$480 for three-bedroom units. These prices are higher at Christmas.

The East Village condominiums are a bit older, slightly less expensive and convenient to the intermediate and expert lifts. However, they will be quite out of the way if your group includes beginners. Of these properties, the **Peregine** is perhaps the most luxurious and **Anaconda** follows. These Carbonate Property Management units start at $99 for a hotel room, $139-$170 for one-bedroom units, $169-$239 for two-bedroom condos, and $230-$300 for three-bedroom units. The **Best Western Foxpine Inn** is the distant poor cousin of Copper Mountain properties.

Excellent packages combine lodging and lifts. From early January through mid-February, packages start around $107 per day per person, double occupancy. In early or late season, packages start at $59 per person, a virtually unbeatable deal. Copper Mountain also has one of the few single-occupancy packages, which start at $98 in early December and mid-April to closing, rising to $195 in February and March. Call (800) 458-8386 or 968-2882.

Club Mediterranée is the first Club Med built in North America and still its only U.S. winter club. Rooms are small. Programs and activities are nonstop, and everything is included in the price except drinks. There are ski lessons, dancing, and sumptuous spreads for breakfast, lunch and dinner. In fact, Club Med guests rarely venture outside the Club Med world except to ski—and even then they are still lesson-wrapped in the Club Med cocoon. For reservations, call (800) 258-2633 (CLUB MED).

Dining

Copper Mountain's range of restaurants is fair for a resort of compact size. **Pesce Fresco** (968-2318, ext. 6505) in Mountain Plaza is the most upscale restaurant. Reservations are suggested. **O'Shea's** in the Copper Junction building has great bargains, and the best breakfast buffet for miles.

Rackets Restaurant (968-2318, ext. 6386) located in the Racquet and Athletic Club has a southwestern menu and a great salad bar.

The East Village has the best restaurants. Virtually everyone's favorite was **Farley's** (968-2577) in the Snowflake building, which serves up heaping portions of prime rib, steaks and fish. Reservations are a good idea—don't hesitate to ask for the table next to the fireplace.

Another favorite for light fare and great burgers is the **B-Lift Pub**, which has a lunch and dinner menu and is by far the best bar in town.

The **Village Square** shopping area has some specialty choices: **Imperial Palace** for Chinese food and **That Soup Place** for a fair eggs-and-pancake type breakfast and excellent soup-in-a-bread-bowl lunches. **Lizzie's Bagelry**, in the same building but facing toward West Village, has bagels, muffins and other items for a light breakfast. The **Corner Grocery** is in Village Square, for those who prefer to dine in their condos. Prices are typical resort; those with rental cars may wish to stop along I-70 to stock up.

Copper Mountain also offers a **Progressive Dinner** on Wednesdays that tours five resort restaurants via horse-drawn wagon. Another unusual program offered several nights a week is **Dining In the Woods**, a four-course barbecue dinner served in a miner's tent with wood-burning stove and reached by horse-drawn sleigh. Either dinner experience costs $39.95. Call 968-2318, ext. 6320 for more information or reservations.

Après-ski/nightlife

This is one of Colorado's better immediate après-ski resorts. The **B-Lift Pub** rocks from 3 p.m. to 5 p.m. It's a great spot to meet avid skiers, because the bar anchors the mountain's expert and intermediate sections. **Kokomo's Bar** in the Copper Commons gets overflow après-ski, and **O'Shea's** hums as well.

Later in the evening, **O'Shea's, Farley's** and the **B-Lift Pub** are always a good time. If you like to dance, though, you'll have to head for other parts of Summit County or perhaps to Vail.

Other activities

Shopping: Copper Mountain's shopping opportunities are limited to a few souvenir and clothing shops. **The Copper Collection,** in the Village Square center, has some nice upper-end sweatshirts and T-shirts, plus elegant knickknacks, some handcrafted by Colorado artisans. **Turning Point Sports,** a few doors down, also has some nice gift items among its main inventory, which is skiwear.

The **Copper Mountain Racquet and Athletic Club** is the primary nonskiing activity. Membership is included when you stay in Copper Mountain Lodging Services properties. Amenities include a lap pool, sauna, steamroom, exercise classes and two indoor tennis courts (the latter for an extra fee). Call 968-2318, ext. 6380 for information.

For other activities see the Summit County chapter.

Getting there and getting around

Getting there: Copper Mountain is about 90 miles west of Denver International Airport on I-70. **Resort Express** runs vans between the airport and your lodge, with many daily departures. You can make arrangements when you reserve lodging, or call Resort Express at 468-7600 or (800) 334-7433.

Getting around: A free shuttle runs within the Copper Mountain village, but you can easily walk between the outlying condos and the village center. The free Summit Stage buses can take you to three nearby ski areas—Breckenridge, Keystone and Arapahoe Basin—as well as the towns of Dillon, Silverthorne and Frisco. If you plan to head over to Vail or to the other Summit County areas frequently, you'll probably want a car, otherwise you don't need one. If you are not staying at Copper, one warning about parking: Two lots nearest the center lifts cost money ($9 per day last season). There are several free lots; try the B Lift lot for upper-level skiers, or the Union Creek lot for lower-level.

Information/reservations

Call **Copper Mountain Lodging Services** at (800) 458-8386. **Copper Mountain Resort Chamber** provides information only at (800) 525-3891, or 968-6477 in Colorado. All local area codes are 970.

In the United Kingdom, call 0800-89-4964; in Australia, call 0014-800-127348; in New Zealand, call 0800-44-0755; in Germany call 0130-81-9770; and in Mexico call 195-800-826-7773.

Keystone/Arapahoe Basin Colorado

Keystone has no 19th-century Victorian charm. Most of its restaurants and lodging are too far apart for a comfortable walk. Yet it is one of those resorts where everything works.

Keystone is one of the best intermediate playgrounds in Colorado. It also has one of the nation's best summit-to-base beginner runs (Schoolmarm), and advanced skiing on North Peak and The Outback. Add in the Alps-like terrain of nearby Arapahoe Basin, and it meets the needs of every ability level.

Its management has created a smoothly humming community with buses shuttling to every corner, foot-of-the-mountain child care, the Rockies' largest snowmaking system and one-number central reservations. Keystone's employees also deliver Service—with a capital S and a smile. Even late in the season, when personnel at many resorts get snappy from too many long days, Keystone workers are happy and helpful, including ski-shop technicians, lift attendants, cafeteria workers, hotel staff and instructors.

Right now, Keystone has no real center, even though it has a collection of shops, restaurants and condos called Keystone Village. But the village has no pulse—it is too far from the base area to be a center for après-ski activity and too isolated to be much more than a promenade for guests at the Keystone Lodge and the closest condominiums.

Keystone/North Peak/Outback Facts
Base: 9,300'; Summit elevation (lift-served): 11,980'; Vertical drop: 2,680 feet
Number and types of lifts: 19—2 gondolas, 3 quad superchairs, 1 quad chair, 3 triple chairs, 6 double chairs, 4 surface lifts.
Acreage: 1,737 skiable acres Snowmaking: 49 percent
Uphill capacity: 26,582 skiers per hour Bed base: 5,000

Arapahoe Basin Facts
Base elevation: 10,780'; Summit elevation: 13,050'; Vertical drop: 2,270 feet
Number and types of lifts: 5—1 triple chair, 4 double chairs
Acreage: 490 skiable acres Snowmaking: none
Uphill capacity: 6,066 skiers per hour Bed base: 5,000

Even so, guests don't seem to mind. The resort is perfect for families, couples or small groups of friends who want to spend time with each other.

Where to ski

Unlike other areas that have separate peaks side by side, Keystone has three peaks that stack up one behind another. In front is Keystone Mountain, with beginner and intermediate terrain. In back of that is North Peak, and finally, the Outback. Other than one snaking green-circle trail, these latter peaks have just blue and black terrain.

This unusual arrangement lends an exploratory quality to a ski day. As you get farther from the base area, the skiing feels a little wilder, a little more off-piste.

Keystone Mountain is one of the better intermediate mountains in Colorado, maybe in America. Snowmaking covers 100 percent of the mountain, and the slope grooming may be surpassed only by Utah's elite Deer Valley. The Mountain House base area has three chair lifts taking skiers up the mountain, and the other base area, River Run, is the lower station of the Skyway Gondola.

The gondola serves the night-skiing area until 9 p.m. This is the largest single-mountain night ski operation in the United States and covers 13 runs.

If you see a trail going up and down the mountain, you can be assured that it is intermediate. These are great cruises with enough twists, turns and dips to entertain the most jaded skier. Paymaster, the Wild Irishman, Frenchman and Flying Dutchman are runs that play with the mountain's terrain. The twists and natural steps on these cruisers represent nature at its best, and they obviously did not have the character bulldozed out of them.

Trails cutting across the mountain are principally for beginners. You can take most of them traversing from the top of the Peru Chair, or take Schoolmarm along the ridge and drop down Silver Spoon or Last Chance.

Advanced intermediates and experts have really only one trail on Keystone Mountain that develops pitch—Go Devil, dropping down the far right edge of the area. Skiers at this level should head for Keystone Mountain's summit, then drop down the super-long groomed Mozart to the base of **North Peak**. The descent to the North Peak base can also be negotiated down Diamond Back, which maintains a steeper pitch and is infrequently groomed. (Skiers also can ride the Outpost Gondola to the beautiful restaurant at the top of North Peak.) These North Peak runs are almost all advanced or expert and are a great spot for working on technique and steeps. Starfire is a superb steep, groomed run, and a good warmup for this area. Black diamonds that plunge off this run are Ambush, Powder Cap or Bullet. On the other side of the lift, Cat Dancer and Geronimo offer a challenge, and experts can break their own tracks through the trees directly beneath the lift. Two groomed intermediate runs, Anticipation and Spillway, lead to **The Outback.**

The 889-acre Outback is a mix of open-bowl skiing, natural chutes and tree-lined glades. The quartet of Timberwolf, Bushwacker, Badger and The Grizz are visible from North Peak and allow tree-skiing fans to pick how tight they want their trees. Two black-diamond bowls are accessible by a short uphill hike from the top of the Outback Express high-speed quad. (This inbounds skiing tops out at 12,200 feet, giving Keystone a 2,900-foot vertical descent, slightly more than is listed in the stat box.) Solid intermediates also can enjoy this peak, with four groomed runs under the high-speed quad. Two other trails, Wildfire and Wolverine, are a bridge between blue and black.

Arapahoe Basin, long a legend with die-hard skiers, was folded into the Keystone package about 10 years ago. Though it is not connected physically to Keystone, you'll sometimes see references to Keystone/Arapahoe Basin, as if it were one area. This stark ski area is only a short five-mile shuttlebus ride from Keystone, but it's another world when it comes to skiing. Arapahoe is the highest lift-served skiing in North America, with a high point of 13,050 feet. Arapahoe Basin's above-timberline terrain is subjected to howling winds, plummeting temperatures, and white-out conditions. This is the closest thing Colorado has to skiing the high Alps.

For all its gnarly reputation, Arapahoe has excellent beginner terrain. Never-evers start on their own lift, called Molly Hogan, and the flat, nearly separate terrain beneath it. Wrangler is a very wide and flat trail on the far left side of the map. Chisolm and Sundance are the next steps up the ability ladder. All three wind down from the top of the Exhibition chair lift. Intermediates can test themselves from the top of either the Lenawee or Norway chairs and enjoy this above-timberline bowl skiing.

The "Pali" side of Arapahoe was created for the strong, hardy skier who braves bumps, weather, wind and super-steep terrain to push his or her envelope of experience. The entire east wall has chutes, gullies and steeps regularly searched out by experts, and dozens of expert runs drop from the top of the Palivacinni Lift. When all is said and done the heart of Arapahoe for experts is the "Pali," a legendary avalanche chute, a steep stamped in nature.

Thanks to its elevation, Arapahoe doesn't hit stride until late January when the gullies fill in and the rocks have sufficient cover. It's skiable until June, and sometimes into early July.

Mountain rating

These mountains break easily into categories, with some exceptions as noted above. Keystone weighs in as great beginner and cruising terrain. North Peak is for advanced skiers with expert tendencies. The new Outback is for upper intermediates and experts. Arapahoe Basin is for strong intermediates, advanced and very expert experts, but beginners won't be left in the base lodge. The night skiing is for everyone.

Snowboarding

Keystone is not open to snowboarders. Boarding is permitted at Arapahoe Basin without limits. Lessons and rentals are available there.

Cross-country

Keystone has also developed one of the most extensive cross-country touring areas in Colorado. The touring center (468-4275) at the Ski Tip Lodge services 24 km. of groomed trails around the resort and is open from 8 a.m. to 5 p.m. There are an additional 57 km. of extensive backcountry skiing trails to ghost mining towns in the Montezuma area.

Trail fees are $7.50 a day or $5 for a half day. Lesson packages range from $29 to $45. There are special children's classes for $24. Rentals are available from the touring center. Cross-country activities include moonlight tours for $30 and mountain tours. A women's cross-country seminar is held every spring, focusing on total development for the cross-country experience.

Lessons (94/95 prices)

Keystone's ski school is as smooth-running as its shuttle system, and the mountain is perfect for lessons of every type.

Group lessons meet daily at 10:25 a.m. and 1:30 p.m. for a two-and-a-half-hour session at all three locations (base of Keystone, River Run Plaza and Arapahoe Basin). These sessions cost $32 each. Beginners have a lesson that includes lift tickets for $40, or $54 with rentals included. The Advanced Skier Workshop with three days of instruction is $290.

Private lessons are $70 for one hour and $90 for 90 minutes. A private half-day lesson (three hours) for one to three people is $200. Full-day lessons (six hours) are $300.

The Mahre Training Centers are held here exclusively. These are five- and three-day sessions conducted in part by either Phil or Steve Mahre, Olympic medal winners. The skiing, for all levels, teaches fundamentals. In the evening there is a classroom session where on-slope activities and techniques are reviewed, and one of the Mahre brothers is available to answer questions. The three-day program costs $390 and the five-day program costs $650. Both include lifts, six hours of instruction daily, video, races and time for fun. Lodging is not included. The Mahre programs run through mid-January.

For **children** there is a Minor's Camp Program for ages 5 to 12 with all-day supervision. The daily rate of $62 includes rental equipment, lift ticket, lesson and lunch. The Mini-Minors is a program for kids 3 or 4 years old. Full day with lunch is $62, half day with lunch, $52. Keystone puts a big emphasis on families and children's lessons. It has parts of the mountain that are designated Children Only, and they try to keep classes small, usually no more than five students.

For ski school, call (800) 255-3715; in Colorado, 468-4170.

Child care (94/95 prices)

The **Children's Center at Keystone Mountain** base accepts infants as young as 2 months, and the nursery at Arapahoe takes children from 18 months. Reservations are required; call 468-4182 or (800) 255-3715.

Child care for children 2 months and older is $46 for a full day and $38 for a half day, either morning or afternoon. Both include lunch. The Snowplay Program, designed for children 3 and older, costs $46 for a full day of activities and lunch, and $38 for a half day of fun.

Lift Tickets (94/95 prices)

	Adult	Child (6–12)
One day	$42	$19
Three days	$111 ($37/day)	$51 ($17/day)
Five of six days	$170 ($34/day)	$85 ($17/day)

Keystone, Arapahoe and nearby Breckenridge are owned by the same company, so the tickets are interchangeable. Keystone has an additional pricing twist because of its night skiing. Day lift tickets are valid until 9 p.m. Children and young seniors get discounted full-day and multiday lift tickets, but no discounts for afternoon, twilight or night tickets. Ages 65–69 pay $25 per day; 70 and older ski free. Note: lift tickets limited to Arapahoe Basin are $35 a day.

Twilight tickets (2–9 p.m.) are $31, night (4–9 p.m.) $25, and late night (7–9 p.m.) $17.

Accommodations

Keystone, a condominium community, has three hotels. One is the modern **Keystone Lodge**, which also houses the main restaurants and dozens of conference rooms for business meetings. Another is **The Inn**, a 103-room hotel within walking distance of Keystone Mountain.

The other embodies the only "past" that Keystone exhibits, and is a personal favorite of several *Skiing America* staffers. The quaint **Ski Tip Lodge**, which was a stagecoach stop in the late 1800s, is a near-perfect ski lodge. Rooms are rustic (in the best sense of the word) with true ski history, the dining room elegant and the sitting room warm and inviting.

The Ski Tip Lodge only rents rooms with breakfast and dinner included. Private rooms have baths, and the dorm rooms share one. The rooms are not huge but are comfortable and the food usually is very good. Private rooms in regular season based on double occupancy are $110 per person a night; dorm rooms cost $84 per person a night. Call (800) 222-0188.

Condo accommodations are broken into ratings of Bronze, Silver, Gold and Slopeside. Each group has a central swimming pool and, except for the slopeside units, all have about equal access to the lifts, thanks to the excellent shuttle system.

Slopeside condominiums are virtually ski-in/ski-out—they are right across the street from the Keystone Mountain Base Area. The **Chateaux d'Mont** condos are spectacular, by far the most luxurious and worth every penny. We strongly recommend trying to get one of these units. Those renting at the **Keystone Mountain Inn** are paying mainly for location rather than amenities.

Gold condominiums seem to be priced in a higher category because of more lavish decoration and because they are closer to the Keystone Village and Keystone Lodge. This is logical because they would be the best locations for any company planning a meeting at Keystone. However, they are not worth a premium to skiers or their families.

The Silver condominium grouping offers the best value for money and are considered more "homelike." **The St. John** units have spectacular views and were built with just about every amenity. In the Silver category these units are clearly the leader. In the deluxe group we also highly recommend the **Pines** condominiums. Bronze condos are a little older and less expensive.

Kids 12 and under stay free in the same lodge room or condo with their parents, provided minimum occupancy is met and maximum occupancy not exceeded.

Dining

There are three dining experiences visitors to Keystone should try to have—**The Keystone Ranch**, the **Ski Tip Lodge** and the **Alpenglow Stube**, perched at 11,444 feet at the top of North Peak.

All are sophisticated gourmet restaurants, perfect for romantic dinners or groups of adults (and not at all suitable for young children). All require reservations, which you can make before leaving home by calling (800) 222-0188 (outside Colorado). If you're staying at a resort property, dial extension 4130. If you're staying elsewhere in Summit County, call 468-4130. Use these numbers for all the restaurants we list here.

The Keystone Ranch is a restored log ranch house of the 1930s. Reportedly, the only completely original part of the house standing is the fireplace. The Ski Tip Lodge exudes a homey, rustic flavor.

The Alpenglow Stube is located in The Outpost, which features rough-hewn timbers, massive fireplaces, vaulted ceilings and expansive windows. It is reached by a ride on the Skyway and Outpost gondolas. The restaurant, seemingly inspired by Heidi and decorated by a Victorian Martha Stewart, features a six-course menu (for a fixed price of $68 per person) of such non-traditional skiing fare as wood-grilled salmon, grilled venison chops and roasted boar tenderloin. Ask to sit at the chef's counter; only eight people get to do it each sitting. You'll see the chefs preparing the meal on open grills, get to taste dishes they're working on for future menus, and receive a little more attention than the other diners.

You say your kids want to ride the gondola, too? Take the family to **Der Fondue Chessel,** also at The Outpost. Ride the gondola to the top of North Peak and then enjoy fondue, raclette and wine by candlelight with music by a Bavarian band.

In the Keystone Lodge, **the Garden Room Steakhouse** offers fanciful gourmet fare and buffalo or beef steaks at hefty prices ($18-$25 for entrées, with side dishes another $4 or so).

For more casual dining, try **Nonnino's Italian Restaurant**, in Keystone Village, where you choose a pasta and a sauce that is then served family-style, or **RazzBerrys,** in the Keystone Inn, serving grilled items and pastas. For truly casual dining, we got a tasty individual-sized pizza and a draft beer sitting at the bar in the **Snake River Saloon.**

Après-ski/nightlife

Keystone's nightlife is limited, at least in the categories of leaning on a bar, knocking back a few brews and dancing.

The best bet for a good night out dancing and meeting the other nightlife denizens is at **Bandito's.** Across the highway you will find the **Snake River Saloon,** which has good action with a slightly older crowd. **MonteZuma's** in the Village has a huge dance floor with live bands or DJ music, pool and foosball tables and a basketball toss game. **Keysters** in River Run Plaza offers karaoke.

For immediate après-ski activity, try the **Last Lift Bar** in the Mountain House at Keystone Mountain base or the **Snake River Saloon. Tenderfoot Lounge,** in Keystone Lodge, has piano entertainment and a 15-foot fireplace. Locals give high marks to après-ski at **China Café.**

Other activities

Shopping: You'll find a few of the standard souvenir and T-shirt shops in the Village, but nothing memorable. Head for

Breckenridge or the Silverthorne Factory Stores (see the Breckenridge and Summit County chapters).

Keystone has a good **athletic club** with two indoor tennis courts. Tennis lessons are available for $45 an hour.

Sleigh rides to the Soda Creek Homestead, including a dinner with all the fixins, will cost adults $49.50; children under 12, $30. The sleigh ride without dinner is $11 a person. Call (800) 354-4386 or 468-4130.

Ice skating in the middle of Keystone Village is open each day and night. The rink, which is smoothed twice a day, has a fee of $7; ice skates can be rented for $6.

Getting there and getting around

Getting there: Keystone is 90 miles from Denver International Airport via I-70. Transportation between the airport and the resort can be booked with the central reservations number, (800) 222-0188.

Resort Express has several daily round trips. Call (800) 334-7433 or check in at the counter when arriving in Denver.

Getting around: The **Summit Stage** provides free transportation between Dillon, Silverthorne, Frisco, Breckenridge and Copper Mountain. Call 453-1241 for information. Keystone and Breckenridge also operate a free shuttle, the Ski KAB Express, between those two resorts from 8 a.m. to 11 p.m.

Within Keystone a free shuttle system runs continuously from 7:30 a.m., passing every 15 minutes. In the evenings the shuttles run every 20 minutes until midnight on weeknights, until 2 a.m. on Fridays and Saturdays. Bartenders and hotel doormen will call the shuttle to ensure pickup in the evenings and late at night, 468-4200. If you are staying and skiing mostly at Keystone, you won't need a car.

Information/reservations

For all reservations except air, call **Keystone Condominium Reservations** at (800) 222-0188 or 534-7712 (toll free from Denver), or the **Keystone Lodge** at (800) 541-0346.

General information: 468-2316 or (800) 222-0188. **Ski report:** 468-4111. **Denver-direct ski report:** 733-0191.

Activities/dining information and reservations (800) 354-4386 (354-4FUN).

In Great Britain, call 0800-89-8727; in Mexico, call 195-800-222-0188.

Unless otherwise noted, all area codes are 970.

Crested Butte
Colorado

Great skiing—especially for advanced and expert skiers—and down-home western friendliness make Crested Butte one of our favorite resorts.

Many Colorado resorts cater to the well-to-do celebrity or CEO skier, and that's fine. But this is one place you can come if you want to avoid that scene. You won't find flashy ski outfits, you won't hear talk of yesterday's movement in 30-year bonds, you won't be caught in the middle of a disagreement between a movie star and his agent, and you won't hear much griping about slow lifts or cruddy snow. Crested Butte has a laid-back attitude and the locals have a way of looking at the better side of life. After a few days here, it's contagious.

Entering the town, which has been designated a National Historic District, is like stepping back to the turn of the century. A walk down Elk Avenue, the main street, takes you past the old post office, built in 1900; the hardware store, where old cronies still reminisce around a pot-bellied stove; and The Forest Queen, reputed to have once been a brothel. More than 40 historic structures are tucked in and around the town.

In contrast, the ski area, about three miles away, is surrounded by modern condominiums and a couple of hotels, with more in the planning stages. With the shuttlebus system you won't need a car after you arrive.

Crested Butte has also made a major commitment to snowmaking, which has ensured excellent coverage for early-season skiing. The snowfall statistics speak for themselves. Crested Butte has one of the highest average snowfalls of any ski town in Colorado.

Crested Butte Facts
Base elevation: 9,100'; **Summit elevation:** 11,875; **Vertical drop:** 3,062 feet
Number of lifts: 13–2 quad superchairs, 3 triple chairs, 4 double chairs, 4 surface lifts
Snowmaking: 35 percent **Acreage:** 1,162 acres
Uphill capacity: 15,960 per hour **Bed Base:** 5,750

Where to ski

The Crested Butte skier seems to like the terrain just as nature left it. There are plenty of groomed trails for intermediates and beginners, but you'll notice that named trails only cover about half the terrain. Looking at a trail map, on the left is a huge area called the North Face with a series of double diamonds punctuating the mountainside; and on the far right is another grouping of double diamonds hard against the area boundary.

Let's make sense of it all. Beginners have extensive terrain, served by the Keystone lift. However, this is not stuff you want to attempt with the skiing ability you learned from a book on the plane. Never-evers should head to the Peachtree lift, take a couple of lessons and practice for a day or two before attempting the Keystone lift. When you're ready for Keystone, get off at the second stop and try Houston and Painter Boy.

Intermediates in search of long cruising runs should go up Keystone or Silver Queen, and head down Treasury, Ruby Chief, Forest Queen, Bushwacker, Gallowich and variations of the same. The Paradise Bowl at the top of the Paradise lift gives intermediates a taste of powder on good days. Advanced intermediates can manage most of the runs down from the Silver Queen superchair. The short and steep Twister and Crystal both have good bail-out routes about halfway down. Tree skiing off the Teocalli and the high-speed quad lifts let skiers test themselves on natural slalom courses.

This area of Upper Forest, Hot Rocks and Forest (all part of the North Face) and the Phoenix Bowl offers what experts claim is the best extreme skiing in Colorado, comparable to Utah steeps. The resort has free tours of the mountain for all levels, including the extensive expert terrain. Call 349-2251 for information on the tours. The North Face normally opens in mid-January.

Mountain rating

Crested Butte has terrain for every level of skier. It needs it, because there are no alternatives in the near vicinity, with the notable exception of 2,000 acres of snowcat powder skiing at nearby Irwin Lodge, the largest such operation in North America.

Cross-country

Crested Butte is linked with one of the most extensive cross-country networks in Colorado. For those on skinny skis, the adventures are virtually limitless. Crested Butte was the pioneering resort in the rediscovery and popularization of telemarking; it has more of these skiers per capita than any other big-time ski resort.

In April hundreds of free-heel skiers scramble up the North Face and drop 1,200 vertical feet through deep snow competing in the Al Johnson Memorial Uphill/Downhill Race. Johnson used to deliver mail on Nordic skis to 1880s mining camps. Every month the Crested Butte Nordic Center sponsors a different race event, ranging from citizens' races to team relays and the Alley Loop race.

The **Crested Butte Nordic Center** is located at the edge of town, on 2nd Street between Sopris and Whiterock Streets. The town maintains about 20 km. of Nordic tracks, which begin a few yards from the Nordic Center. Trail fees are $6 for adults and $3 for children and seniors. The center also has hot tubs and racquetball courts for après-Nordic activity. There are more than 100 miles of backcountry trails. Call 349-1707 for pricing on lessons and rentals. Group lessons, half-day and all-day tours are scheduled several times each week, but private lessons and special tours must be requested two days in advance.

Snowboarding

Snowboarding is allowed on the entire mountain including the double-diamond Extreme Limits. Crested Butte has a snowboard park with slides, quarter pipes and other features, accessed by the Keystone Lift. Snowboard lessons are $30 per two-hour session. A first-timer's package that includes a four-hour lesson, lift ticket and all-day rental equipment is $55.

Lessons (95/96 prices)

Group lessons: Adult group lessons are $30 for a half-day (two-hour) lesson, skiing, telemarking or snowboarding. A three-day introduction to skiing package costs $146, and includes an all-day lesson, two two-hour lessons and a three-day lift ticket.

Private lessons: One and a half hours are $76 for one person, two hours cost $98, three hours are $140, and six hours cost $285. Additional persons may be added for $35.

Special workshops for seniors, bumps, powder, Ski the Extreme, and turning fundamentals cost $45 for two hours. A workshop that shows how to ski on the new parabolic, or hourglass skis, also is $45 and includes free equipment rental. A North Face workshop is $60.

NASTAR races cost $5 for two runs and $1 for each additional run. Race clinics include coaching and a race for $45 for adults; $35 for kids. A two-hour private racing clinic can be arranged for $98, children or adults; additional persons cost $35.

Children aged 8–12 enroll in Buttebusters. Half-day lessons are $45; full-day, lunch included, is $55. Miners is the program for children aged 4–7. Half-day lessons are $49; full-day with lunch, $59. Mites is for toilet-trained 2 and 3 year olds with shorter ski lessons and day care for $47 half day, $57 full day.

All programs include lessons and lift tickets (except Mites, but most kids that young will ski free under lodging promotion plans, or they pay their age), and the Mites and Miners programs include ski rental and supervised daycare after the lesson. More experienced child skiers have classes separate from beginners.

Registration and reservations for all programs are at the ski school desk in the Gothic Center, 349-2251.

Child care

The **Children's Ski Center** cares for kids from infants to age 7. Registration and information are in the Whetstone Building at the base of the Silver Queen Lift; 349-2259. Hours: 8:30 a.m. to 4:30 p.m.

Care for infants up to six months is $8 per hour, two babies per staffer. Day care for toddlers through age 7 costs $48 per full day and $38 per half day. All day-care programs include crafts, games, snow play and other activities, but no ski lessons, and toddlers have separate programs from the older children.

Lift tickets (94/95 prices)

	Adult	Child (0–12)
One day	$42	$**
Three days (consecutive)	$126 ($42/day)	$**
Five days (of 6)	$185 ($38/day)	$**

Crested Butte doesn't charge for lift tickets in its low season. That's right: FREE SKIING November 17 through December 16 this year, and free never-ever lessons for people 7 and older. As a bonus, Crested Butte also will have free skiing April 8–21, 1996. A limited number of tickets will be available on Nov. 24 and 25, Thanksgiving weekend. Call (800) 754-3733 for more information (800-SKI-FREE).

During regular season, other multiday tickets also are available. Skiers 70 and older ski free; 65-69 ski for half price.

**When children 12 and younger are skiing with one full-paying adult, they pay their age per day. This program has no blackout periods, nor any limits to the number of children, but proof of age may be required.

Accommodations

Most of the accommodations are clustered around the ski area in Mount Crested Butte. The historic town has a handful of lodges, but they are not as modern nor as convenient to the slopes. They are less expensive and closer to the nightlife however and offer a taste of more rustic Western atmosphere. A free bus service takes skiers right to the slopes, so the primary inconvenience of in-town lodging is the short bus ride.

Crested Butte Vacations can take care of everything from your plane tickets to hotel room, lift tickets and lessons with one phone call. It also offers some of the best packages available. Before you make any arrangements, call (800) 544-8448 and ask for the best possible deal.

Mountainlair Hotel was brand-new last season and is 200 yards from the Silver Queen superchair. It has 126 large rooms with two king-sized beds in each, two outdoor hot tubs and a coin-operated laundry. Rates are $70–$175 per night.

Grande Butte Hotel (800-341-5437 or 349-7561), has ski-in/ski-out lodging with a tasteful decor and nice-sized rooms. Mountain hotels don't get much better than this, at least in this price range. Room rates are $99–$600 per night, depending on room size and season.

Crested Mountain Village is perhaps the top luxury group of properties at the mountain. It has a series of spectacular penthouse suites that open onto the slopes.

The Buttes are well-appointed condos 35 yards from the lifts. Rooms range in size from studios to three bedrooms; prices are $84–$506 per night.

The Gateway, across from the Peachtree lift and about a two-minute stroll from the Silver Queen, is perhaps the best value of any condo on the mountain when you trade price for space and amenities. One-, two- and three-bedroom units range $185–$475 per night. Gateway units are managed by several competing agencies. It is best to book through Crested Butte Vacations, (800) 544-8448.

The Plaza, about 80 yards from the Silver Queen superchair, is one of the most popular condo projects on the mountain. It gives excellent value and is especially popular with groups because special functions can be easily arranged. Two- and three-bedroom units cost $131–$579 per night.

Wood Creek and **Mountain Edge** are convenient to the lifts, but not particularly well appointed. The **Columbine** is an excellent ski-in/ski-out property. These three, together with nine others within shuttlebus distance of the lifts, are managed by Crested Butte Accommodations at (800) 821-3718 or 349-2448. Rates are $110–$475 per night.

The Crested Butte Club (349-6655) on Second Street in town, is the upscale old-world elegance champion of the area. Though the lifts are a bit far, this place is worth the inconvenience. Seven suites have been individually furnished with Victorian furnishings including double sinks and a copper-and-brass tub, as well as beautiful four-poster or canopied beds and a fireplace. The amenities include the fitness club, with heated swimming pool, two steam baths, three hot tubs, weight room, and massage and weight trainer. This is a No-Smoking property. Room rate is $75–$225.

The Claim Jumper, 704 Whiterock Street; 349-6471, a historic log-home bed-and-breakfast, is the class act in town. Jerry and Robbie Bigelow run it and have filled it with a collection of memorable antiques. Bedrooms have themes and are furnished with brass or old iron beds. There are only five rooms, four with private bath. Room rates are $59-$170 per night including a full breakfast. Children are not encouraged; No-Smoking. The Claim Jumper can arrange catered special-occasion wedding receptions.

The Cristiana Guesthaus, 621 Maroon Ave.; (800) 824-7899, 349-5326, is only a block from the ski shuttle and a five-minute walk from downtown. This has a mountain inn atmosphere and most of the guests manage to get to know one another. The rooms are small, but most guests spend their time in the hotel's living rooms so this doesn't really matter. Let the owners know if you need quiet, because some rooms get quite a bit of traffic from the owner's family and folk using the washers and dryers. Rates are $65-$87.

The Forest Queen, corner of Elk and 2nd, 349-5336, is inexpensive, with a double with bath for $40-$70.

The Elk Mountain Lodge around the corner from the Forest Queen on 2nd Street has simple but comfortable rooms, all with private bath, for $79 to $108 per room per night. Call 349-7533. Ask for Room 20 on the third floor with lots of space, a balcony and a great view.

Other B&Bs in town worth a look are **Alpine Lace,** 726 Maroon, 349-9857; and **Whiterock Lodge,** 505 Whiterock Ave. and Route 135, (800) 783-7052 or 349-6669.

Rocky Mountain Rentals at 214 6th Street, 349-5354, offers rentals in private homes in the area as well as in many special condominiums. If you are looking for something out of the ordinary, check with them for help. Another possibility is **Crested Butte Properties,** 349-5780.

Dining

Crested Butte is blessed with more excellent, affordable restaurants than any other resort in the West. You can dine on gourmet French cuisine or chow down on platters of family-style fried chicken and steaks.

For information on the top of the line restaurants, **Le Bosquet, Timberline, Soupçon, Penelope's, Giovanni's Grande Cafe, Idle Spur** and the **Powerhouse Bar Y Grill,** see the following Crested Butte Savoir Faire chapter.

For hard-to-beat group and family dining, head to **The Slogar** (349-5765). It used to be the first bar the miners hit when returning from the mines and is decorated in old bordello decor. Slogar's offers a skillet-fried chicken dinner with mashed potatoes, biscuits, creamed corn, ice cream and even some other extras for a flat price of $11.50 each ($5.95 for children 2-12; kids younger than 2, no charge). It also offers a family-style steak dinner. Reservations recommended.

For other substantial meals, head down Elk Avenue to **Donita's Cantina** (349-6674), where the margaritas are giant and strong and Mexican food comes in heaping portions. Be early or be ready to wait. No reservations. For a quick meal, try **Angelo's** (349-5351) for pizza and Italian food. **The Gourmet Noodle** (349-7401) has many pasta dishes prepared fresh daily, espresso and cappuccino and tempting desserts, such as peanut butter pie and chocolate mousse.

The best breakfast by far is served in the **Forest Queen**. The atmosphere is Old West and turn of the century. Ask for the "baggins." You won't find it on the menu—it has developed as a specialty for most of the locals. The Forest Queen also serves lunch and dinner. For the gourmet coffee and pastry crowd, **Crested Butte Coffee Roasting & Breakfast House** has granola, waffles, muffins, croissants and all the Seattle-style coffee drinks.

For breakfast on the mountain head to **The Tin Cup** or **The Avalanche**. For a good lunch try **Rafters,** the **Smiley's Deli** in the Treasury Center, or for a more elegant setting try **The Artichoke** and start off with artichoke soup. The **Swiss Chalet** serves Alpine fare, such as fondues and raclette, plus a good selection of European beer.

Crested Butte has several outdoor dining experiences, such as the **Twister Fondue Party**, every Sunday, Wednesday and Friday when at 4:30 p.m., diners board the Keystone Lift for a three-course on-mountain fondue dinner, followed by a gentle ski to the base by torchlight. The cost is $35 for adults, $25 for children. **Paradise Sleigh Ride Dinners** are every Tuesday, Thursday and Saturday via snowcat-drawn sleigh. Call 349-2211 or 349-2213 for either of those. Another company offering dinner sleigh rides is **Just Horsin' Around** (349-9822). You also can ride a snowmobile to dinner at **Irwin Lodge**; see that chapter for more information.

Après-ski/nightlife

Here nightlife means wandering from bar to bar. The immediate après-ski action is centered in **Rafters** at the base of the lifts. Then it begins to move downtown to the **Wooden Nickel**, with some wild drinks, and **The Bistro**, which has a very happy hour from 10 p.m. to 11:30 p.m. and karaoke. **Talk of the Town** is a smoky locals' place with video games, shuffleboard and pool tables. **Kochevar's** is another local favorite. **The Idle Spur** has its own micro brewery and live music on weekends. Cover charges are $3 to $8, depending on the talent, and it has dancing, sometimes even a polka or two.

Rafters has dancing and good singles action most nights in Mount Crested Butte, plus it's within stumbling distance of most of the lodging. Those staying in town can take an inexpensive town taxi service if they miss the last bus of the night.

For a combination dinner and show, try the **I-Bar Ranch** Western barbecue and show, advertised as family-style fun with dancing. Call 641-4100.

Other activities

Shopping: Lots of great shops at the resort and in town. Among them: **Diamond Tanita Art Gallery**, for jewelry, glass, ceramics, paper, forged iron and other functional art pieces; **Cookworks, Inc.**, a gourmet kitchen shop; **Book Cellar**, with local maps, Western art and collectibles; and **Minor's Closet**, out-of-the-ordinary children's gifts.

Crested Butte has several more active things to do. These include snowmobiling, snowmobile dinner tours to Irwin Lodge, snowcat dinner tours to Paradise Warming House on Crested Butte Mountain, winter horseback riding, sleigh rides with and without dinners, and ballooning—weather permitting. Call Mt. Crested Butte or **Crested Butte Chamber of Commerce** at 349-6438 for brochures and information. For resort activities, call 349-2211.

Getting there and getting around

Getting there: Despite its seemingly isolated location, Crested Butte is quite convenient to reach. United Express and Continental Express offer several flights daily from Denver, plus nonstop jet service from Atlanta, Dallas and Houston into Gunnison, a halfhour from the resort.

Alpine Express (800-544-8448) meets every arriving flight and takes you direct to your hotel or condo for $34 round-trip ($22 for children; one-way fares available). For reservations, call Crested Butte Vacations. .

Getting around: No need for a car. Crested Butte's free town-resort shuttle is reliable and fun to ride, thanks to some free-spirited and friendly drivers.

Information/reservations

Crested Butte Mountain Resort, Box A, 12 Snowmass Road, Mount Crested Butte CO 81225; 349-2333; **Crested Butte Vacations:** (800) 544-8448 or 349-2222. **Snow reports:** 349-2323.

All local area codes are 970.

Crested Butte Savoir Faire

For a town of its size, Crested Butte has an impressive number of fine dining choices, most within steps of one another. At the far end of Elk Avenue is **The Timberline Restaurant.** Chef Tim Egelhoff spent five years as sous-chef at Creme Carmel in Carmel, California before opening Timberline a few years ago. He combines seasonal products to create a Café French Cuisine, whose roots are classic French, with a pinch of California and a dash of the Rockies. Served in a quaint old private home, the menu changes often. Start with the goat cheese and vegetable terrine splashed with balsamic vinaigrette. Or try the sesame ahi tuna, rolled in sesame seeds, seared rare, and sliced and served with soy and wasabi. I fell in love with the Alaskan caribou, roasted medium rare and finished with a port and blackberry reduction. Timberline also offers a selection of reasonably priced boutique wines. Open nightly from 6 p.m. For reservations call 349-9831.

Soupçon Restaurant is hidden in the alley behind Kochevar's Bar. This log cabin started at half its current size in 1916 as a private residence to the Kochevars. While there have been several restaurants over the past 30 years, Soupçon itself dates back almost 20 years. Current owners Maura and Mac Bailey have created an innovative French cuisine, with menu items posted daily on a chalkboard. Reserve two to three days ahead for one of two seatings, 6 and 8:15 p.m. (349-5448.)

A special appetizer often on the menu is oysters aioli, poached in a spicy broth and served with a garlicky aioli on the side. Catalan onion almond soup finished with a hint of orange zest is another frequent offering. Entrées range from $17.75 for roast duckling glazed with soy and honey and served with plum wine and hoisin to $24 for Australian rack of lamb with a honey lavender sauce.

The Baileys' other establishment across Elk Avenue, is **Penelope's,** a restaurant in a greenhouse. Featuring exceptional American cuisine, Penelope's offers a terrific fresh rainbow trout, sautéed and covered with roasted hazelnuts, then laced with an orange honey beurre blanc. Start with the Kendallbrook smoked salmon, served with diced egg, red onion, and capers. Starters range from $3.50 for the Mediterranean white bean soup to $8.50 for the brie en croûte. Entrées are priced from $12.50 for a vegetarian four-cheese lasagna to $25.95 for rack of lamb dijonaise. Call 349-5178; open daily 5:30 to 10 p.m.

Those up for serious suds should head to the **Idle Spur Steakhouse and Microbrewery**. Always crowded, always noisy, it offers the finest hand-cut steaks in town. Other choices are burgers (including vegetable and elk—sounds better than it is), Mexican entrées and a selection of fresh fish, all reasonably priced. Six beers are brewed in-house from the White Buffalo

Peace Ale to the full-bodied Rodeo Stout. For $3.50, you can sample four 4-ounce tastes of the home brew. For reservations, call 349-5026. Brewery tours 2 to 5 p.m. daily during happy hour.

Next to the Old Town Hall bus stop (130 Elk Avenue) is the **Powerhouse Bar Y Grill.** Known for its Mexican specialties, like cabrito, fajitas, tamales, and tacos, the Powerhouse also offers some surprises. Try the pork tenderloin Guadalajara—medallions of tangy marinated pork tenderloin with fried banana, pineapple, jicama, and yams, served with black beans and rice; or the chicken borracho—mesquite-grilled breast of chicken with orange chipotle sauce on "drunken" vegetables. Prices are quite reasonable and portions are huge. Be prepared for a wait though—this popular restaurant doesn't take reservations, and the line for tables can be more than an hour.

The best Italian restaurant in town is actually in Mt. Crested Butte. **Giovanni's Grande Cafe** is located on the plaza level of the Grand Butte Hotel. Open daily from 5:30 to 10 p.m. (349-4999), Giovanni's offers great service and a Wine Spectator award-winning wine list.

Entrées are preceded with an antipasti plate and a head of roasted garlic served with fresh warm bread. Try the risotto with wild mushrooms and truffle oil, or the lasagna with grilled eggplant, squash, spinach, peppers and goat cheese. Game lovers will love the boar scaloppini with caramelized pearl onions. Most starters are $7, with entrées ranging from $14 for the farfalla with garlic and vegetables to $25 for rack of lamb with fresh rosemary and walnuts.

For gourmets with a sense of adventure, join a snowmobile tour to the **Irwin Lodge.** The Irwin Lodge is an immense cedar structure maintained in an 1890s tradition. Start with the toasted ravioli, a.k.a. the Jamaican postage stamp, stuffed with a conch ricotta filling and served with an orange beurre blanc. Entrées range from elk Wellington stuffed with chanterelles and chilis to ahi, cooked black and blue, and served with rice noodles with ginger and wasabi. Four new selections each day of the week come from an eclectic 28-item rotating menu. After one visit, you'll realize that a week's stay is needed to sample all the chef's greats. Entrées are priced from $17 to $26.

Snowmobile tours and the dinner are priced separately, so call (970) 349-2441 to inquire about prices and make arrangements to join a tour. Plan at least one week in advance.

The **Princess Wine Bar** at 218 Elk Avenue is the place to finish your night on the town. Serving a limited menu of mostly soups and salads, there are a few tempting desserts to enjoy with cappuccino or a fine dessert wine. With no doubt the best selection of quality wines by the glass, Princess also carries a full list of cognacs, ports, and single malts. Come relax by the fire. Open daily from 10 a.m. to "whenever."

Irwin Lodge, Colorado

Irwin Lodge at Lake Irwin, 12 miles west of Crested Butte, is Colorado's most exclusive and remote ski area. Virtually unlimited skiing stretches over 2,200 acres with an overall 2,100-foot vertical drop, but you won't find a chair lift or a snowmaking gun anywhere, and only 50 or so skiers can use the area at a time. Irwin Lodge specializes in snowcat skiing.

The lodge was built by an eccentric millionaire with a vision of the perfect ski lodge. The only way in is by snowmobile, snowcat or cross-country skis. There are no phones (the only contact with the outside world is two-way radio), no network television, and one lodge, perched on a ridge, that sleeps about 50.

As you approach the massive wooden building you see the imposing edifice presiding over the frozen lake and an army of rugged pines and spindly aspens. Inside, the lodge is even more impressive. The 120-foot-long living area stretches almost the length of the building and soars two stories to the ceiling. The living area is the most important room; it takes up 60 percent of the structure, with the rest dedicated to the guest rooms.

Mornings begin with breakfast from 8 to 9:30 a.m. Snowcats make their first climb to the ridge at 9:30 a.m. loaded with skiers, and cross-country skiers take off on organized tours a bit later.

Where to ski

Here's a nice surprise: skiing is available for every level of ability. We don't recommend this for a first-time ski experience, but we do recommend it for a first time in powder. Two groomed slopes serve the needs of intermediates and beginners, one slope for each. The top of Dan's Delight leads to the advanced areas as well as the groomed slopes. The 70 MPH Basin dropoff opens more difficult terrain.

One run to the left off Dan's Delight starts in a relatively tame bowl. You can continue down through the gladed Central Park area or turn to the left and drop down an expert chute into the wide-open Banzai Bowl. Twenty-five or thirty turns later you enter the trees to begin running nature's slalom gates through the Lumber Yard, where some of the Ponderosa pines are only three to five feet apart. The 70 MPH Basin offers truly advanced terrain which bottoms out at the West Wall, where skiers have a choice of almost a dozen chutes running down the face, starting with open glades and ending through tightening trees.

Normally skiing starts at 9:30 a.m. and continues until 4:30 p.m. From 12:30 to 1:30 p.m. everything stops for the lunch buffet while the snowcats are serviced and the skiers fuel up for the afternoon.

Irwin also offers snowmobiling and guided cross-country skiing as well as ice fishing and snowshoeing.

Snowboarding

Boarding is permitted but it is difficult if you need to traverse in deep powder: a problem known as postholing occurs when the free leg sinks into the snow. Board rentals are available in Crested Butte.

Prices (95/96 rates)

The way to do Irwin is to purchase a package that combines lodging, meals, activities and round-trip transportation from Crested Butte. To the nearest dollar, these are the starting per-person prices for various inclusive packages: three-day/three-night: $957; four-day/three-night, $1,079; five days/four night, $1,450 and seven days/six night, $2,052. These packages include snowcat skiing, snowmobiling and/or cross-country skiing.

Folks coming up to ski from Crested Butte pay $195 a day for snowcat skiing, including transportation from Crested Butte and lunch.

Irwin Lodge rents fat skis designed for easier powder skiing to overnight guests only for $25 per day. Day skiers who want fat skis must rent them in town before they come.

Getting there

Round-trip transportation from Crested Butte is included in all packages; see Crested Butte chapter for other transportation information.

Information/reservations

Contact Irwin Lodge, PO Box 457, Crested Butte, CO 81224, (303) 349-5308, or (800) 247-9462 (800-2-IRWIN-2).

Purgatory, Colorado

If you are ever banished to Purgatory, consider yourself lucky—that is, if your exile is to this resort in southwestern Colorado, 25 miles north of Durango.

Purgatory is a ski area that feels comfortable right from the start. It draws heavily from Arizona, New Mexico, Texas and to a growing extent Southern California and the Southeast. Its clientele includes skiers who take one trip a year, or even one every other year. What draws them are low prices (winter is off-season in Durango), great weather and a welcoming attitude.

Purgatory attracts families, college students and people turned off by ostentatious displays. Flaunting one's wealth in Durango is not looked upon with favor. And though Purgatory has challenging terrain that attracts many talented skiers, there are quite a few folks doing the flying snowplow—skis in pizza position, arms akimbo, big smiles on their faces, barreling downhill while flirting with control. No one makes fun of them or makes them feel unwelcome, not even the other visitors.

The skiing is fun, thanks largely to the area's undulating terrain. Millions of years ago glaciers scraped this valley, leaving narrow natural terraces on the mountainside. Purgatory's runs plunge downward for a bit, then level off, then plunge, then level off—all the way to the bottom. The effect is rather like a roller coaster ride. It's super for skiers who love to get air. Those who don't can use the flat spots to rest before the next dropoff.

The ski area is 25 miles from town. For years skiers stayed in Durango and drove the 50-mile round trip, but with the growth of Purgatory Village at the base area you now have a choice. There's little going on nightlife-wise in the village, but it has the big advantage of being slopeside. Durango has lots to do and a very charming setting, but it's far from the slopes.

Purgatory owes its name, indirectly, to a 16th-century Spanish explorer who drowned in the river that flows through Durango. His companions christened the river "Rio de las

Purgatory Resort Facts
Base elevation: 8,793'; **Summit elevation:** 10,822'; **Vertical drop:** 2,029 feet
Number of lifts: 9—1 quad superchair, 4 triple chairs, 4 double chairs
Snowmaking : 29 percent **Skiable acreage:** 745 acres
Uphill capacity: 13,600 per hour **Bed base:** 3,120 near resort, 7,000 in Durango

Animas Perdidas," River of Lost Souls. A witty 19th-century mapmaker named a brook that flows into the river Purgatory Creek. The ski area was built along the creek and adopted its name. The trail names were inspired by the Divine Comedy, Dante Alighieri's 14th-century epic poem that described a journey through Hell, Purgatory and Paradise (they must have paid attention in school).

Where to ski

This season Purgatory installed its first quad superchair, and at the same time gave all the lifts names. The lifts formerly had numbers from 1 to 9, based on the order of installation. We'll give you the new name, with the old number in parentheses.

At Purgatory, skiers enjoy a nice progression from beginner to expert terrain. Never-evers have their own learning area, Columbine Station. An intra-area shuttlebus takes beginners here after they have bought their rentals and lift tickets. After a couple of lessons on the terrain under the Columbine Lift (Lift 9), they are ready to board Graduate Lift (Lift 7), which takes them back to the base area. Purgatory offers *free* beginner lessons to adults, and more than 11,000 skiers take advantage each season.

Beginners will like the runs under the Twilight Lift (Lift 4). The easiest of these is Pinkerton Toll Road, a gently winding catwalk trail. Divinity and Angel's Tread are wide gentle runs, and Columbine winds through stands of trees, giving beginners the feeling of being deep in the woods. As they progress, they may want to head down Salvation toward the Hermosa Park Express (Lift 3), a new high-speed quad that goes straight to the summit. From there they can descend The Bank or Silvertip to West Fork, where they have many choices for getting back down.

The next step is the intermediate runs off the Engineer Lift (Lift 2). Snowmaking on these runs ensures a good surface. After skiers feel comfortable on What, Limbo, and West Fork, they should head for Peace and Boogie, two wide intermediate runs off the Hermosa Park Express. Still not enough of a challenge? Head down blue-square The Legends toward Dead Spike, the widest of Purgatory's runs, or continue on The Legends to the mid-loading station on the Legends Lift (Lift 8). From the top of this lift, Sally's Run is not as steep as Chet's, but both are challenging blues.

Still not enough to make your heart leap into your throat? Go for Wapiti, a black run under the Grizzly Peak Lift (Lift 5) where the moguls grow to small igloo size. Or try Catharsis or No Mercy, two short black runs under Spud Lift (Lift 1) and Needles Lift (Lift 6). Or try Pandemonium, a long black diamond under the Spud Lift that gets steeper and bumpier the farther down you go (Pandemonium is often groomed and then it's really a blast).

If you have this wired, then you're ready for Bull Run, a double-black trail that starts just below Dante's Restaurant off the Grizzly Peak Chair (Lift 5). It has a tough pitch as well as funnels and moguls (and once you're on it, you're stuck). Other advanced areas include the short steep runs at the bottom of the Legends Chair (Lift 8), which sometimes are winch-cat groomed, and Styx and Hades off the Spud and Needles lifts.

Purgatory's trails are quite long. Most stretch from summit to base, and have lots of dips, twists and turns to keep them interesting. The gentler runs wind around stands of pine, passing islands of aspens and picnic tables. The more difficult runs make a beeline for the bottom, straight, true and fast.

A tip for powder hounds and other natural-terrain fans: the vast majority of Purgatory's skiers like groomed terrain, so after a storm the powder between the timber is often still fresh long into the afternoon. Tree hounds might like the aspens between Pandemonium and Lower Hades. Beginning adventure skiers can try the easier powder stashes between Peace and Boogie or Snag for a bit steeper terrain. Paul's Park, below the Legends Lift, has chutes for gladed skiing. The trees here were thinned last season, but they are still a challenge.

Mountain rating

Purgatory may be a place where souls suffer before being allowed into Paradise, but that's in Dante's poem. Intermediates get to bypass the limbo stage and head straight for the blessed abodes, such are the variety and plenitude of trails for this level.

This resort also is an excellent place to learn, because of a completely separate learning area and a generous free-lesson offer for first-time skiers and snowboarders. Advanced skiers will have a great time, too. Only super-experts looking for extremes may feel that they are somewhat in Purgatory.

Cross-country

The **Purgatory Nordic Center** is just north of the Alpine ski area across Highway 550 and is maintainted by the Durango Nordic Ski Club. It has 16 km. of trails groomed for skating and diagonal skiing. Nordic skiers will find the same undulating terrain as the ski area, with appropriate terrain for various ability levels.

Rentals are available and trail fees are $8 for adults and $4 for seniors older than 65 and children 12 and younger. A lesson, rental and trail fee package is $30. As part of Purgatory's Total Ticket program, one Alpine ski day can be exchanged for the Nordic package.

Snowboarding

Purgatory has welcomed snowboarders since 1985. It has a snowboard park and boarding is permitted on all runs (except one skis-only run that is intended to offset the snowboard-only park.) However, you won't find many snowboarders in the

Legends area, because the only way to return to the base is BD&M Expressway, a very long, very flat run (locals say the initials stand for Boring, Dull, and Monotonous; actually, the run is named for three of Purgatory's pioneers).

The Purgatory Village Center houses the **Inferno Snowboard Company**, which sells equipment and clothing, rents equipment, does tuning and repairs, and arranges backcountry tours led by experienced snowboard guides.

Lessons (95/96 prices)

Purgatory has a very generous offer for never-ever skiers and snowboarders—free lessons. The **Start 'Em Off Right** program offers half-day adult (13 and older) beginner lessons FREE with the purchase of a lift ticket. That means a saving of $30.

Group lessons cost $30 for a half day and $45 for a full day. **Private lessons** are $110 for two hours, with one-hour lessons available very early or very late. Additional skiers are $20 apiece.

Purgatory also has **special workshops** for telemark skiers, conditions of the day, racers, older skiers, women, men and snowboarders. Some are daily, some are weekly and some are for designated weeks or weekends, so call the resort for details. The school also runs a Mountain Guide service for three to six skiers of similar abilities who want to find the local secrets. New this season will be an Introduction to Parallel Skiing workshop using Elan SCX "hourglass" skis, designed specifically to make carving a parallel turn effortless.

Children's lessons are for ages 3–12. Purgatory participates in the SKIwee program. The full-day program is $52, which includes lunch and morning and afternoon sessions. The half-day program ($43) includes either a morning or afternoon session with no lunch. All kids 12 and younger get free lift tickets.

For information on any of the ski school programs, call 247-9000 or (800) 525-0892.

One of the country's outstanding instruction programs for **disabled skiers** is here. For information, call 259-0374.

Child care (95/96 prices)

Children aged two months to 3 years old can be enrolled in day care for $45 for a full day with lunch and $35 for half day. Toddlers (2-3) get outdoor snowplay, arts and crafts, games, movies and storytime.

If you're not sure whether to put your child in day care or lessons, Purgatory's **Kids Central service,** located on the second floor of the Village Center, will help. The staff will assess your child's abilities and interests, then escort him or her to the appropriate spot.

Make reservations, especially on weekends and holidays. The day care staff also can recommend a babysitter who can watch your kids while you enjoy a night out. Call 247-9000.

Lift tickets (95/96 prices)

	Adult	Child (Up to 12)
One day	$39	Free
Three days	$114 ($38/day)	
Five days	$160 ($32/day)	

Children ski free here. Parents do not have to buy a ticket, and there is no limit to the number of free child tickets per family. Block-out dates are Christmas (Dec. 23, 1995–January 5, 1996) and spring break (March 11–22, 1996). During those times, children ski for $20, but those in ski school still ski free.

Ages 70 and older ski free; seniors 62–69 ski at a discount, about half the adult price.

Purgatory started an unusual program last season called **Total Ticket**. Skiers with four-day or longer multiday tickets may exchange a day of downhill skiing for cross-country skiing or one of several major vacation activities in southwest Colorado, examples of which are the Durango & Silverton Narrow Gauge Railroad train (which runs year-round), a soak and massage at Trimble Hot Springs, a dinner sleigh ride, or a tour of Mesa Verde National Park, a collection of ancient cliff dwellings that have been named a World Heritage site. Call for complete details on this program.

Accommodations

Purgatory has three lodging areas. The condos at the base are the most expensive; hotels and condos within 10 miles of the ski area are a little less so, and lodging in Durango is dirt cheap, but 25 miles away.

Base-area lodging is at the **Purgatory Village Hotel**, **Best Western Lodge at Purgatory** and the following condo complexes: **Angelhaus, Brimstone, East Rim, Edelweiss, Graysill, Sitzmark** and **Twilight View**. Condos have full-service units (kitchens, fireplaces, common-area hot tubs and laundry facilities) from $75 for a studio to $420 for some three-bedroom suites. Prices vary slightly for similar-size units in the various complexes. Hotel costs are $85-$250.

Several other complexes are one to ten miles from the ski area. The prices at **Cascade Village, Needles, Silver Pick** and **Tamarron** range from $85 to $395. Most of the outlying condo complexes have free shuttles to and from the ski area. (Even if you brought your own car, leave it behind and take the shuttle: it will get you closer.) And many of them, such as Tamarron, have their own restaurants and sundries shops, so you can get just about anything you need.

Durango, like Banff, Jackson, and Lake Tahoe, considers winter low season with prices below the summer rates. Winter rates are as low as $25 a night for a one-bed unit in a clean but frills-free motel, and several motels have this low-end price.

Prices go as high as $165 per night, but the average is about $50-$60.

Much of the lodging in Durango is unadorned motels and chain hotels, but four historic lodging properties are worth mentioning. **The Strater Hotel** (800-247-4431) and the **General Palmer Hotel** (800-523-3358) are multi-story, brick hotels that date back about 100 years. Both are in the heart of the walkable downtown. **Leland House Bed & Breakfast** and **T h e Rochester Hotel**, (800-664-1920 for both) across the street from each other on East Second Avenue, were bought by the same family and completed renovated. The Leland House has a Durango history theme, with the rooms named after local historic figures. The Rochester Hotel has a Hollywood theme, with each room named for a film shot at least in part in Durango. "Butch Cassidy and the Sundance Kid," "Around The World in 80 Days" and "City Slickers" were all filmed in or around the town, and you can read about how they were made in framed narratives researched and written by one of the owners, Frederic Wildfang. Rates at these four historic properties range from $62 to $165.

All Durango and Purgatory lodging can be booked through **Durango Central Reservations,** (800) 525-0892.

Dining

Purgatory base area offers **Purgatory Creek** (nice food and atmosphere), **Sterling's** (upgraded cafeteria food and atmosphere) and **Farquahrt's** (bar food and atmosphere) for local eateries. For some of the best fish in Colorado, flown in daily, and for local game, try the **Cafe Cascade**, two miles north of Purgatory (259-3500), elegant dining in a rustic setting with entrées $16-$22; everyone who has eaten here raves about it. **Sow's Ear** (247-3527), just north of the Purgatory entrance, is famed for its large hand-cut steaks.

Café de los Piños, at the midway loading station of the Grizzly Peak Chair (Lift 5), offers sit-down gourmet dining at lunch, accessible only by skis or snowboards. **Dante's**, in the same building, offers a quick bite to eat as does **The Powderhouse** near the Engineer Lift (Lift 2).

Durango is where you'll find most of the restaurants. Two things to know when trying to find a Durango street address: One, nearly all of Durango's streets have numbered names. The streets *parallel* to Main Avenue are called "avenues" and the numbers often are spelled out (Second Avenue, for example). The streets that *intersect* Main all are "streets" and the number is seldom spelled out. Most tourists hang out between 5th Street and 11th Street, and occasionally venture onto Second or Third Avenue, but if you get directions such as "at the corner of Second and 8th," you'll know it isn't a mistake. Second thing to know: 6th Street was re-named College Drive last year.

The Palace Grill, 1 Depot Place (247-2018), has continental cuisine such as honey-glazed duck, with most entrées $14 to $20; it's been one of Durango's top restaurants for years. A new entry in the fine dining arena is **Lola's Place** (385-1920) next to the Leland House Bed & Breakfast at 721 E. Second Avenue. It has a colorful and casual decor, and excellent food. **Ariano's**, 150 East College Dr. (247-8146), serves north Italian cuisine for $9 to $20.

The Ore House, 147 College Dr. (247-5707) is an Old West steak house, rustic and casual with entrées in the $10-$20 range; **The Red Snapper**, 144 East 9th St. (259-3417) also has fresh seafood and saltwater-aquarium decor. Entrées are about $11-$16 and wonderful vegetables and salads.

Pronto Pizza and Pasta, 160 E. College Dr. (247-1510) is for families and those looking for a bargain, and features thin-crust pizza and fresh pasta. They feature an all-you-can-eat pasta buffet every weekend and offer deliveries in Durango. **Gazpacho**, 431 E. Second Ave., (259-9494), has northern New Mexican cuisine that can get very spicy.

Olde Tymer's Cafe, 1000 Main Ave. (259-2990), is one of our top choices, with the best hamburgers in town and huge margaritas. Daily specials include $2.95 burgers Monday nights, $1.25 taco night on Friday—locals jam the place on these evenings. Mexican food on weekends. **The Golden Dragon**, 992 Main Ave. (259-0956) serves Chinese food in huge portions.

Carver's Bakery and Brew Pub, 1022 Main Ave. (259-2545) is the best place in Durango for breakfast; muffins and bagels are fresh daily. It's a hangout for locals. If you prefer the eggs-and-bacon-type breakfast, head for the **Durango Diner**, 957 Main Ave. (247-9889). Sunday brunch at the **Red Lion Inn** is outstanding and a good choice for skiers departing on Sunday, since the inn is between the ski area and the airport.

Après-ski/nightlife

Skiers congregate in three places after the lifts close: **Farquahrt's**, where the music is the liveliest; **Purgatory Creek**, slightly more sedate; or **Sterling's**, which is the quietest. Nightlife at the ski area is limited to Farquahrt's, which has live bands Thursday through Sunday.

A popular après-ski spot is the **Trimble Hot Springs**, about 20 miles from the ski area toward Durango. Natural mineral springs bubble into two outdoor therapy pools, one heated to 90 degrees and the other to 105. Private tub rentals and massages are available.

If you really want to tango, go to Durango. Catch the Durango Lift from the base area, $7 round trip; everything in town is in walking distance. Depending on the time of year, Durango is either jumping or mildly hopping. Spring Break, which goes on for several weeks in March, brings thousands of college students and the bars schedule lots of entertainment.

Durango has quite a variety of musical entertainment. Try **Farquahrt's** downtown for dancing, or the **Sundance Saloon**. Farquahrt's has an eclectic clientele—hippies, neo-hippies and clean-cut college students. The music ranges from reggae to blues, rock 'n' roll, and oldies. The Sundance Saloon is a cowboy bar with Country & Western music and dancing.

Just-opened **Lady Falconburgh's Barley Exchange** (382-9664) has live jazz and a selection of microbrews on tap. It serves dinner as well and has become an instant local hangout.

Carver's Bakery and Brew Pub has strong and tasty locally brewed beers accompanied by fresh rolls from the bakery. To tourists who ask why a bakery is also a brewery, locals quote the sage who said, "Beer is just a modified form of bread."

The bar on the second floor of **The Pelican's Nest** restaurant (658 Main Ave., 247-4431) has live jazz on the weekends and a jam session on Thursdays—bring your own instrument and join local amateur jazz musicians. Other nights, talented entertainer Ron Urban sings a variety of music. On football Sundays, the best big screen in town is **A.J.'s Grill & Sports Bar** (128 E. College Dr.; formerly 6th St.; 247-5085), with pool tables, pinball and other games. Live bands and comedians play here occasionally.

The other popular hangouts are the **Old Muldoon**, furnished in a dark Victorian style, and the **Solid Muldoon**, which is worth a visit just for the decor. Everything imaginable—typewriter, kayak, bubble gum machine (with gumballs), and the kitchen sink—hangs from the ceiling. They spin a wheel of fortune every so often, setting the price of drinks for the next few minutes. Over at the **Diamond Belle Saloon** in the Strater Hotel, where the genuine cowboys hang out, a player piano plunks out hit tunes from the Gay 90s—1890s, that is.

Other activities

Shopping: Downtown Durango has tons of great stores. Among our favorites: the **Bula Factory Outlet** on College Drive for fantastic savings on ski hats and headbands (Bula is headquartered here); **New West Galleries** between 7th and 8th, worth a visit to view the colorful and whimsical Markus Pierson sculptures; **Toh-Atin's Art On Main**, 865 Main Ave. and **Toh-Atin Gallery** on 9th Street for Western, Southwestern and Native American clothing and art; **The Bookcase**, 601 E. Second Ave., with a fine inventory of used and collector books; and **O'Farrell Hat Company**, on Main near the General Palmer Hotel, where you can buy a cowboy hat custom-made to fit "all the bumps and shallows of your head." Durango also has 20 **factory outlet stores**, some in a little mall on 13th Street and others scattered throughout downtown.

Durango has a couple of off-slope activities unique in the ski industry. One of America's finest national parks is then nearby **Mesa Verde**. Anasazi Indian cliff dwellings dating back more than 800 years have been preserved here. Another unique activity is the **Durango & Silverton Narrow Gauge Railroad**. Until a couple of years ago, this historic train ran only in the summer. During the winter, it goes halfway to Silverton, then returns to Durango. The fare is $36.15 for adults, $18.05 for 12 and younger. The train leaves at 10 a.m. and returns at 3 p.m. Though the cars are enclosed, warm clothing is recommended.

Sleigh rides, snowmobiling and other traditional winter activities can be booked through the Purgatory Ski Concierge, on the second floor of the Village Center.

Getting there and getting around

Getting there: The Durango-La Plata County Airport, 44 miles south of Purgatory and about 20 miles from Durango, is served by America West Express, Continental Connection and United Express (Mesa Airlines). American Airlines has daily flights from Dallas from December 15 and March 30. From the airport, **Durango Transportation** (259-4818) charges about $13 one-way to Durango and $20 to Purgatory.

By car, the resort is 25 miles north of Durango, 350 miles southwest of Denver, 232 miles northwest of Albuquerque and 470 miles northeast of Phoenix. There are no major mountain passes from the south or west. Nevertheless, if you don't have four-wheel drive, carry chains.

Getting around: The Durango Lift shuttle service runs four to five times a day between town and resort for $7 round trip. If you stay in Durango and use the shuttle just to get to and from skiing, you can get along without a car. Same thing if you stay at Purgatory and use the shuttle for an evening excursion to Durango.

If you're planning to stay anywhere beyond a couple of blocks of Durango's main street, you'll want to rent a car.

Information/reservations

With one call you can arrange lodging, transportation, lifts, transfers, ski rentals, and lessons. Call **Durango Central Reservations** at (800) 525-0892. Ski area information is 247-9000.

Local area code is 970.

Steamboat, Colorado

Its ad campaign would have you believe that horses outnumber the cars in the ski area parking lot, that cowboy hats and sheepskin jackets are the preferred ski wear and that you should watch out for tobacco plugs on the dance floors. In reality, this is a big, sleek, modern ski area with few spittoons in sight.

Steamboat Village, the cluster of condos, shops and restaurants next to the ski mountain, is unpretentiously upscale. Boutiques offering elegant high-priced goods are intermixed with T-shirt shops; gourmet restaurants are within steps of ribs-and-hamburger eateries. You will see an occasional socialite swathed in fur, but right behind her will be someone wearing a 15-year-old ski parka. Everyone looks right at home.

In Steamboat Village, the only cowboy hats you're likely to see grace the heads of Steamboat's resident celebrity, Billy Kidd, and the ticket punchers in the gondola building. Venture into downtown Steamboat Springs, though, and you may see cowboys sauntering down Lincoln Avenue. Northwest Colorado still has many cattle ranches, so they'll probably be the real thing.

The downtown area—about 10 minutes by car and about a half hour by shuttlebus—squeezes into its dozen blocks a hodge-podge of old Victorian buildings, 1950s storefronts and a gas station or hardware store here and there. Good restaurants and nightlife havens are at the village, downtown, and on the highway linking the two. A shuttlebus runs between slopes and town every 10 minutes during the day (every 20 minutes at night) making it easy to enjoy the village, town and everything in between.

Steamboat is also a great place for non-skiers. In addition to great shopping, Steamboat has activities that go beyond the usual sleigh rides and snowmobile tours. See Other Activities.

Steamboat Facts

Base elevation: 6,900'; **Summit elevation:** 10,568'; **Vertical drop:** 3,668 feet.
Number and types of lifts: 20–1 gondola, 2 quad superchairs, 1 quad chair, 6 triple chairs, 7 double chairs, 3 surface lifts
Acreage: 2,500 skiable acres **Snowmaking:** 13 percent of groomed trails.
Uphill capacity: 29,941 skiers per hour **Bed base:** 15,500

INSET: BURGESS CREEK AREA
as seen from the base of Burgess Creek Lift, looking toward Thunderhead

◆◆ CHUTE TWO
◆◆ CHUTE THREE
◆◆ CHRISTMAS TREE BOWL
◆◆ EAST FACE
(◆◆ HIKE TO ... EXPERTS ONLY)

MT. WERNER

Steamboat.

Recreation on this public land is provided by a unique partnership between the Steamboat Ski & Resort Corporation and the Routt National Forest.

The Steamboat Ski & Resort Corporation is committed to the wise use of our natural resources, as well as the preservation and enhancement of the Routt National Forest. We hope you will join us in our commitment to preserve our environment by helping to keep your National Forest lands beautiful.

Steamboat Recycles: Please use recycling containers.

STEAMBOAT TOURING CENTER

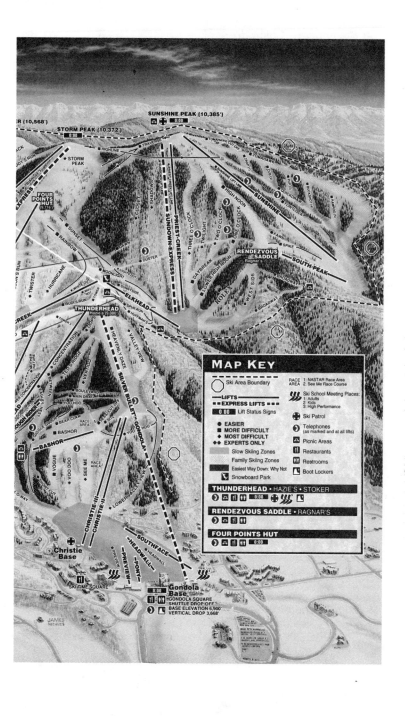

Where to ski

Expert skiing here means trees and lots of them. Steamboat has only a few extreme steeps, but the runs from the Priest Creek and Sundown chairs are tree skiing developed to an art. These trails have been expertly thinned, trees about 50 feet apart along the center and as close as 10 feet at the edges. That may sound like a lot in the safety of your living room, but when you're gathering speed with not much room to bail out, those trees will seem inches apart.

Such trails, natural slalom course where the poles ain't spring-loaded, produce gallons of adrenaline, even for the best skiers. To avoid a trip down in a ski patrol sled, you must substitute control and technique for simple daring: few skiers choose to repeat an intimate encounter with a silver aspen or lodgepole pine.

Other good areas for advanced and expert skiers are The Meadows area off to the north of Storm Peak. There, Chutes 1, 2 and 3, the Christmas Tree Bowl, the Ridge and Crowtrack provide great challenges. A favorite locals' area known as the Toutes was incorporated into the ski area recently. This is extreme powder skiing at its best, and the short hike needed to reach it keeps all but the truly dedicated away.

Many of the black-diamond runs aren't as intimidating as you might think. Though the terrain gets steep in spots and the moguls pretty high, the trails are generally wide, allowing ample room for mistakes and recoveries. Westside, a black trail off Rendezvous Saddle, is steep but usually groomed. It's a good starting point for intermediates wondering if they can handle the other black runs.

Among the great cruisers are all the blue trails from the Sunshine Chair (locals scornfully call this area "Wally World"), Sunset and Rainbow off the Four Points lift and Vagabond and Heavenly Daze off Thunderhead Peak. The Sunshine Chair blues also have spots where beginning tree skiers can get some practice. If the crowds build in any of those areas, head for the short intermediate runs reached by the Bashor chair, which often is deserted.

Although Steamboat has plenty of terrain marked with green circles, it is not the best place for never-evers to learn. Novices start on gently sloping terrain at the bottom of the mountain, but there are two problems: the natural fall line is different than the direction of the trail returning to the lifts, and this area crowded with skiers heading back home at the end of the day. With more than a million skiers a year, that's a lot of people whizzing by the slow-going snowplowers.

With the exception of some gentle terrain served by the Bashor and the two Christie chairs, most of the green trails higher on the mountain are cat trails. Although they have a gentle grade, they also have very narrow spots, they intersect advanced runs (where bombers are likely to use the intersection as a launching pad for the next black section), and they have some very intimidating dropoffs on the downhill side. If beginners are part of your group, *insist* that they enroll in ski school so that they will have a pleasant experience.

Mountain rating

Excellent tree skiing for experts, nice mogul runs for advanced intermediates, great cruisers for intermediates. Passable for beginners; not so great for never-evers.

Cross-country

The **Steamboat Ski Touring Center** at 2000 Golf Course Rd. (879-8180) has about 30 km. of groomed, set tracks winding along Fish Creek and the surrounding countryside. The touring center has group and private instruction for all ability levels, rentals at $10 a full day or $8 a half day, a restaurant, and backcountry guided tours. Trail fees are $9 a full day, $7 a half day after 1 p.m.

Track skiing also is available at **Howelsen Hill** in downtown Steamboat (879-2043) and at **Vista Verde** and **Home Ranch**, both guest ranches in the town of Clark, about 25 miles from Steamboat.

For a real thrill, take a tour to **Rabbit Ears Pass** (guided tours available through Steamboat Touring Center and Ski Haus, 879-0385); you'll be skiing on the Continental Divide. The marked backcountry ski trails range from 1.7 to 7 miles, from relatively gentle slopes to steep and gnarly, but on a clear day you can see forever. On a day after a little snowfall, the new powder feels like heaven. Call or visit the U.S. Forest Service Ranger Station (57 10th Street in downtown Steamboat, 879-1870) to get current ski conditions and safety tips. Other popular backcountry areas are **Buffalo Pass, Pearl Lake State Park, Stagecoach State Recreation Area** and **Steamboat Lake State Park.**

Snowboarding

Snowboarding is allowed on all lifts and trails. Lessons are offered daily and cost $55 for all day, including lunch but no lift ticket. Private lessons also available. Children must be at least eight years old for snowboard lessons. Steamboat has a snowboard park, Dude Ranch, with various jumps, slides and obstacles.

Lessons (95/96 prices)

Adult **group lessons** are $34 for two hours; $50 for all day, with multi-day discounts available. Lift/lesson packages start at $233 for three two-hour lessons and four days of lifts. **Private lessons** are $75 for one hour, $140 for two and $190 for three.

Steamboat has **special clinics** for telemark skiing, snowboarding, bumps, powder, skiers 45 and older, women, disabled skiers—even a style clinic to teach those who can parallel how to look more graceful. Group clinics last three hours and cost $50 to $55.

Steamboat also has the **Billy Kidd Center for Performance Skiing** for intermediate and higher-level skiers. The clinics, which are offered only on specific dates throughout the season, refine the skier's technique in the bumps, through race gates and on tough terrain. The cost is $155 per day for adults; $140 for ages 13-17; $125 for kids.

Children have the **Rough Rider** program (ages first grade-15), **Sundance Kids** (ages 4-kindergarten) and **Mavericks** (ages 3 1/2-4). The Rough Rider lessons are $34 for two hours and $55 for all day (with lunch). Sundance Kids and Mavericks cost $40 for half day; $55 for full day and lunch. Ages 2-kindergarten also can opt for **Buckaroos**, a one-hour private lesson and all-day child care for $110, including lunch.

Steamboat Teens is for intermediate and advanced skiers aged 13-17. An all-day lesson is $55 including lunch. This program is offered Monday through Friday and during some holiday periods.

A special Ski Week package for adults is offered Monday through Friday and costs $143 for five two-hour lessons, an on-mountain barbecue, video analysis, NASTAR racing and a Ski Week pin. A similar children's program is $225, but the lessons are all day and all lunches are included (and the kids get a T-shirt!). Lift tickets are extra.

Child care

Steamboat has a well-deserved reputation for building a family-friendly ski resort with excellent day care.

The **Kiddie Corral** takes children from 6 months to first grade. They get games, puppet shows, movies, crafts, rest time and stories for $55 all day (lunch included) or $40 for half day. Three or more days costs $50 per day, lunch included. Parents must provide a lunch for children under 2.

Kids Adventure Club at Night is an evening care program for children 2 1/2 to 12 years every Tuesday through Saturday from 6 to 10:30 p.m. Snacks, games, video and rest time are included for $8 per hour. A second child is an additional $2 per hour, and three or more children are $12 per hour for the group.

Reservations are required for all care programs, and must be prepaid. Cancellations must be 24 hours or more in advance to avoid being charged. Call the **Kids Vacation Center**, 879-6111, ext. 469 or make reservations through Steamboat Central Reservations, (800) 922-2722.

Lift tickets (95/96 prices)

	Adult	Child (Up to 12) Senior (65-69)
One day	$44	$25
Three days	$132 ($44/day)	$75 ($25/day)
Five days	$215 ($43/day)	$125 ($25/day)

Children don't get multi-day discounts, but can qualify for the Kids Ski Free program, which works like this: one child skis free for each parent who buys a lift ticket valid for at least five days and stays in a participating Steamboat property. If the parent rents skis, the child gets free rentals. The program is not available during the Christmas vacation period, and only two children per family may ski free, and then only if both parents are skiing. Kids approaching the cut-off age should bring proof of age. Seniors 70 and older ski free.

Prices are lower during the value season, from the ski area's opening through mid-December, and again the first two weeks of April.

Accommodations

In general, lodging in Steamboat Village is more expensive than in town. Condos outnumber hotel and motel rooms. Many properties have rates that vary throughout the season. Before mid-December and after March 31 are the cheapest; January comes next, and Christmas and Presidents' Weekend are most expensive.

The **Sheraton Steamboat Resort**, (800-848-8878; 800-848-8877 in Colorado; 879-2220 locally) the only luxury full-service hotel, sits at the center of Steamboat Village 60 feet from the Silver Bullet Gondola. Nightly rates are about $160 to $229.

Nearly all the other lodging at the ski area is in condominiums—hundreds of them surrounding the base area.

Torian Plum (879-8811 or 800-228-2458) is one of the best, with spotless rooms and facilities, an extremely helpful staff, and the ski area out one door and the top bars and restaurants out the other. Prices start at about $150 a night for the smallest units and top out close to $700 for the largest ones during prime times.

Torian Plum's sister properties, **Bronze Tree** and **Trappeur's Crossing**, have similar prices. Bronze Tree has no one-bedroom units; its smallest units are two bedrooms. Trappeur's Crossing is about two blocks from the lifts.

Generally, prices are based on how close the property is to the lifts. Among those in the expensive category ($160 per night and up for hotel rooms and small condo units) are the **Best Western Ptarmigan Inn** (800-538-7519 or 879-1730; close to lifts, but farther from shopping and night life), **Storm Meadows Resort** (800-525-2622 or 879-5555) and **Thunderhead Lodge and Condominiums** (800-525-5502 or 879-9000).

More moderate facilities ($110-$159 for hotels and $136-150 for smallest condos) include **Norwegian Log Condominiums** (800-525-2622 or 879-0720) **Timber Run Condominiums** (800-525-5502 or 879-7000; three outdoor hot tubs of varying sizes), **the Harbor Hotel** in downtown Steamboat (800-543-8888; 800-334-1012 in Colorado; 879-1522 locally; free bus pass is included with your stay), **The Lodge at Steamboat** (800-525-5502 or 879-6000) and **The Ranch at Steamboat** (800-525-2002 or 879-3000; great views of the ski hill and the broad Yampa Valley).

Economy lodging ($109 and lower for hotels/motels and $95-$135 for condos) includes **Alpiner Lodge** (800-538-7519 or 879-1430; downtown), **Shadow Run Condominiums** (800-525-2622 or 879-3700; 500 yards from lifts), **Alpine Meadows Townhomes** (800-525-2622 or 879-3700; 800 yards away) and **The Rockies** (800-525-7654 or 879-7654; one mile away).

The Steamboat Bed and Breakfast, (879-5724) just a few years old, is located at 442 Pine Street. The B&B has rooms filled with antiques. Winter rates are about $75-$110 per double room with breakfast. No children, no pets.

Travelers who enjoy elegance will want to know that in the nearby town of Clark is one of only a handful of U.S. Relais et Chateaux properties, **The Home Ranch**. Cabins are nestled in the aspens of the Elk River Valley. A stay here includes three gourmet meals per day in the main house and a shuttle to the ski area. Call 879-1700.

Steamboat Central Reservations will make suggestions to match your needs and desires. Let the reservationist know the price range, location and room requirements (quiet location, good for families, laundry or other special amenities). The number is (800) 922-2722.

Dining

Steamboat has a great variety of restaurants—varied menus, varied atmosphere and varied prices. The area has more than 50 restaurants, including one or more Cajun, Chinese, French, Italian, and Scandinavian. Look for the Steamboat Dining Guide in your hotel or condo—it has menus and prices.

Katy Keck covers some of Steamboat's finest dining in detail in her Steamboat Savoir Faire chapter. Here are some that have moderate prices ($15-$20 per meal, including drinks) and a casual atmosphere:

At the ski area or close by:

Dos Amigos (879-4270) serves large portions of Tex-Mex food and sandwiches and is part of the infamous "Steamboat Triangle" après-ski circuit along with **Tugboat** and **Mattie Silks'** bar, and **The Cathouse Cafe.**

Grubstake (879-4448) serves hamburgers, steak sandwiches and the like.

Downtown:

Old West Steakhouse (879-1441) is somewhat expensive, but packs in the crowds for steaks and seafood.

Giovanni's (879-4141) has not only Brooklyn-style Italian fare, but also what may be the largest collection of Brooklyn memorabilia this side of the borough. For more moderate Italian, head to the relocated **Riggio's** (879-9010) on Lincoln. Seafood and veal are especially good, and be sure to leave room for their homemade desserts.

BW-3 (879-2431) has several flavors of beef and buffalo burgers, and **The Cantina** (879-0826) is downtown's equivalent of Dos Amigos in food and bar. **Mazzola's** (879-2405), between downtown and the ski area, has the best pizza in the region.

You never need to leave the mountain for lunch. **Hazie's** and **Ragnar's**, both on the mountain, are wonderful for lunch as well as dinner. **The Grubstake** and **Tugboat** are both good base-area spots to grab lunch, or try **Buddy's Run.**

If you're in town for breakfast or lunch, try the **In-Season Bakery and Deli** (879-1840), which serves homemade soup, sandwiches and salads. Soothing classical music is played, and the pastries are excellent. For some quiet time and a light lunch (sandwiches, homemade pasta salads and soups) head to the **Off The Beaten Path** bookstore and coffeehouse (879-6830) across from the Harbor Hotel. We like the bookstore (we're authors, and besides, it stocks *Skiing America*), the great gourmet coffees and the linger-as-long-as-you-want attitude.

Good breakfast spots are **Winona's** or **The Shack Cafe** downtown, or **The Tugboat** at the base area. Avid skiers can board the gondola at 8 a.m. and have breakfast at **The Early Bird Breakfast Buffet** at the top of the gondola until the slopes open. Biscuits and gravy are a specialty, with other high-fuel fare also served, cafeteria-style.

Après-ski/nightlife

For immediate, relatively rowdy après-ski, the place to go is the **Inferno**, just behind the base of the Silver Bullet gondola. Skiers pack into the bar where each hour the bartender spins the shot wheel, setting prices anywhere from 35 to 95 cents. When 35 cents comes up, revelers buy shots by the tray.

Dos Amigos, as noted, is one leg of the "Steamboat Triangle." You have margaritas here, then head for the **Cathouse Cafe** and **Tugboat** for beer or mixed drinks. Friday is Zoo Night at the Cathouse, where any beer that has an animal on the label or in the name is $2.

Downtown, the **Old Town Pub** and **The Steamboat Yacht Club** are popular après-ski locations.

Quieter après-ski locations on the mountain include **HB's** in the Sheraton or **Time Out**, which had a guitar player singing folk/pop/country tunes the week we were there. Steamboat also has two brew pubs, **Heavenly Daze**, in Ski Time Square at the ski area, and **Steamboat Brewery & Tavern** downtown.

Late-night places include **Inferno, Dos Amigos, Heavenly Daze** and **Tugboat**, all with live music and lots of people.

Downtown, the lively spots include **BW-3, The Steamboat Saloon** (where you'll find many cowboys who drink long-necked beers and dance the two-step) and **The Old Town Pub**. On Wednesdays, head for **the Steamboat Yacht Club** to watch the ski jumping on Howelsen Hill.

Steamboat has two movie theaters downtown and one at the mountain, if that's your idea of nightlife. A night trip to Strawberry Park Hot Springs is great fun (see Other Activities). **Buddy's Run** usually has comedy Tuesday through Friday night, and occasionally a big-name artist such as Lyle Lovett will perform at the **Sheraton**.

Other activities

Steamboat has so much to do *off* the mountain, it's tempting to skip the skiing. Here is a mere sampling:

• Soak in the natural thermal waters at **Strawberry Park Hot Springs**, about 10 miles north of the ski area. Admission to the hot springs is $7; a tour (transportation and admission) is $18. Unless you have four-wheel drive, spend the extra for the tour—the road to the springs is narrow, slick and winding. Strawberry Park is open from 10 a.m. to 10 p.m. during the week and stays open a couple of hours later on weekends (879-0342). Helpful info: after dark, many bathers go without suits (unless it's a clear, moonlit night, you won't see much). The only place to change is an unheated teepee, so wear your swimsuit under your clothes, but take dry clothes. You will need a large trash bag to store your clothes; otherwise steam from the pools and the cold air will freeze them. (The tour company will provide you with one.)

Families might prefer the Steamboat Health and Recreation Center, which has hot springs pools and a water slide that kids enjoy. Call 879-1828.

• Ride in a hot-air balloon. Three balloon companies offer rides. **Balloons Over Steamboat** (879-3298) is the oldest company in town; others are **Pegasus Balloon Tours** (879-9191), and **Aerosports, Ltd.** (879-7433). A half-hour balloon ride runs about $80—sounds steep, but the view and experience are spectacular.

• Learn to drive on ice. Now in its 12th season, the **Bridgestone Winter Driving School** (879-6104) teaches how to drive skillfully and confidently on ice and snow. Half-day, full-day and multi-day lessons on a specially constructed course are a unique experience.

• **Shopping** opportunities are many and varied, both in the village and downtown.

• Two companies that can suggest and make reservations for activities are **Windwalker Premier Tours** (879-8065; 800-748-1642) or **Steamboat Fun Brokers** (879-9116 ; 800-257-6985).

Getting there and getting around

Getting there: Yampa Valley Airport at Hayden, about 20 minutes away, handles jets—American, Continental, United, United Express and Northwest have direct flights from more than 100 North American cities. Several ground transportation companies provide service from the airport; Avis, Budget and Hertz have rental cars available.

Panoramic Coaches' Steamboat Express is available daily from Denver's Airport. For schedule and information, call (800) 825-8383, or ask Steamboat Central Reservations about it.

Steamboat is 157 miles northwest of Denver via I-70 through the Eisenhower Tunnel, north on Highway 9 to Kremmling, then west on U.S. 40 to Steamboat Springs.

Getting around: A car is optional. Steamboat has an excellent bus system between town and ski area running every 20 minutes. The fare is 50 cents each way. Exact change is necessary, but a buck will pay for two people. If you are going to commute between town and ski area a lot, rent a car; otherwise, take the bus.

Information/reservations

Steamboat Central Reservations is a one-call service that can book airlines, lodging, lifts, transfers and many activities. The number is (800) 922-2722. Telephone area codes are 970 unless otherwise noted.

Steamboat Savoir Faire

Without a doubt, the most impressive evening in Steamboat starts at Gondola Square at the Silver Bullet terminal. Here, you set off on the complimentary journey into the stars on the Silver Bullet. This roomy gondola (in New York, we would call it an apartment with a view) is complete with blankets for the crisp ride to the top of Thunderhead. The view is breathtaking.

Once on top, **Hazie's** (879-6111) offers exquisite nouvelle continental cuisine, with unbeatable views. The Steamboat Mountain executive chef, Danish-born Morten Hoj, has created a menu that will intrigue any palate. Choose from one of five delicious appetizers. The second course features soup du jour or clam chowder, or the Hazie's salad with mixed greens, grapefruit, roasted hazelnuts, peppers and mushrooms.

Try the very popular Châteaubriand Béarnaise or rack of lamb roasted with garlic. Seafood might include charbroiled salmon with pear salsa. Several daily specials, might include grilled swordfish and veal prime ribs, both cooked to perfection. Dessert offerings vary, but are sure to include the ethereal white chocolate mousse. Let the sommelier help you choose from Hazie's list of over 90 wines. Open from Tuesday to Saturday, Hazie's offers this prix-fixe four-course dinner, including the gondola ride and an after-dinner drink, for $45 (discounts for children aged 6 to 12, those 5 and younger eat free).

Hazie's also serves lunch (reservations recommended) from 11:30 a.m. to 2:30 p.m., featuring an assortment of soups and salads, and entrées like Maryland crab cakes, lemon pepper chicken breast, or the popular Hazie's burger.

If you find your skiing keeps you over in the Sunshine Peak area, however, try **Ragnar's** at Rendezvous Saddle featuring Scandinavian and continental cuisine in a more rustic atmosphere. Reservations for lunch are suggested—879-6111. Start with a smorgasbord platter, an assortment of Scandinavian herring, salami, ham, Danish paté and Nordic cheeses. Entrées range from daily specials such as mesquite-grilled chicken Florentine to wienerschnitzel and chicken breast Lillehammer. Prices range from $8.25 for a mesquite-grilled hamburger to $12.95 for Norwegian salmon.

At night, five times a week (Tuesday through Saturday), Ragnar's offers a prix-fixe Scandinavian menu at $59 for adults. This evening also starts at Gondola Square, but once off the Silver Bullet at the top of Thunderhead, you climb into a sleigh to continue your journey to Rendezvous Saddle. You'll want at least one mug of hot spiced glögg before relaxing to music and enjoying the meal. For reservations call 879-6111, Ext. 320.

For Steamboat's pinnacle of French dining, try **L'Apogee** (911 Lincoln Avenue, 879-1919). Chef-owner Jamie Jenny has created a casually elegant ambiance where he serves some of the area's finest French food. Several specials, often wild game, are offered each day. Menu staples include the center-cut filet of beef, seared with Szechuan peppercorns and sizzled tableside with a soy-bacon vinaigrette. Appetizers start at $7 and entrées range from $18 for half a duckling glazed with a green apple curry to $26 for twin medallions of south Texas Nilgai antelope.

While the food cannot be too highly praised, it is the wine list that is truly impressive. There are more than 500 wines, ranging from $12 to $1,000 a bottle, all maintained in three temperature-controlled cellars. L'Apogee also features Steamboat's only cruvinet system, serving over 30 wines and ports by the glass.

This talented crew also services the more casual **Harwig's Grill** (same address, no reservations). Here, the menu reflects a passion for Southeast Asian flavors. Start with Shu Mei dim sum, chestnut and pork-filled wontons with a fiery soy dipping sauce; raclette fondue; or flaky filo triangles filled with garlic-herb cheese or spinach, ricotta and mushrooms. Offerings range from Black Forest Hunter's stew to Down Under lamb burgers, but the chalkboard tells the real story of the day. Fish can be ordered sautéed, poached or grilled. First-time clients are often surprised when they see jackalope on the board, but will take Jenny's humor more seriously after trying the delicious mignonette of rabbit tenderloin and émincée of elk, with a chasseur sauce. Prices range from $3.95 for appetizers to $7-$11 for entrées. The list of 60 wines here is less than $21 per bottle. Daily from 5 p.m.

As if Jenny et al. weren't busy enough with L'Apogee and Harwig's, they also are in the kitchens at **Cipriani's** and **Roccioso's** in the Thunderhead Lodge. These restaurants are open daily, serving fine cuisine in the evenings only, 5:30 to 10:30 p.m. Call 879-8824 for reservations.

Cipriani's offers traditional northern Italian fare, with Jenny's special flair: tender dry-aged Colorado filet is stuffed with gorgonzola and wrapped with pancetta, then char-grilled to perfection and finished with a light Balsamic shallot sauce; Muscovy duck breast is marinated in Montepulciano wine, garlic, shallots, juniper and cracked black pepper, then finished with sun-dried tomatoes, artichokes and a red wine juniper duck sauce. Entrée prices range from $15.25 for cannelloni with peppers and squash in a fresh spinach pasta to $24.50 for center-cut Colorado lamb chops with a hearty cacciatore sauce.

Roccioso's maintains this Italian flair, but at more moderate prices. Starters include polenta grilled with fresh herbs and mozzarella with a fresh basil vinaigrette. Entrées are mostly less than $11. Try the el diablo con limone—bay shrimp or chicken sautéed with broccoli, garlic, mushrooms and red chilis,.

The newest addition in fine dining is **Antares**. Not coincidentally, all the principals are alums from the L'Apogee campus. Serving new American cuisine, this star from the

Scorpio constellation is housed in the historic Rehder building, built in the early 1900s, at the site of the old Gorky Park restaurant, (57 1/2 Eighth St., 879-9939). "Starters and Lite Fare" range from $4 to $11, and include Thai chili prawns and lemon fire shrimp with penne. Many dishes on the menu are flagged with a "V," indicating vegetarian cuisine, and all are light, and exotic interpretations of Mediterranean and Pacific Rim classics. Try the jalapeño cheese cutlets with pineapple-ginger glaze or the roasted root vegetables with carrot-tomato sauce over pasta. Open daily 5:30 to 10:30 p.m.

For more than Mex, don't miss **La Montaña,** (879-5800) located at 2500 Village Drive. Chef Michael Fragola has created an inventive menu that goes way beyond tacos and fajitas. Start with the grilled braided sausage, a trio of elk, lamb and chorizo sausages, braided together and mesquite-grilled. The chef's keen understanding of southwestern ingredients is reflected well in an ever-changing list of specials. Try mesquite grilled sea scallops on smoked corn salsa with a guajillo prickly pear sauce or the yellowfin tuna steak seared with a pepita crust. The filet medallions, pan-seared with garlic and cumin and served with goat cheese mashed potatoes and a red chili demi glace, is an updated southwestern twist on meat and potatoes. The fajitas are cooked to sizzling perfection—and not just chicken and beef. They also are available in pork, shrimp and elk.

Chef Fragola has a light cuisine menu as well, with such greats as sweet pepper relleño, stuffed with corn, chilis, mushrooms and low-fat mozzarella. Appetizer prices are about $7 and entrées about $10 for Tex-Mex taco dinners and $16 to $22 for the southwestern specials. Save room for the fried ice cream with three sauces—caramel, chocolate and raspberry.

Now in its fifth season is the **Steamboat Smokehouse** at 912 Lincoln Ave. Here, in a no-credit card, no-reservations, no-nonsense atmosphere, are some of Colorado's best Texas-style hickory smoked barbecued anything—you name it—brisket, sausage, turkey, chicken, ham and even a daily road kill special.

A popular seafood restaurant is the **Steamboat Yacht Club,** at 811 Yampa Avenue (879-4774). The dining room overlooking the river is perfect for watching night skiing or Wednesday night ski jumping on Howelson Hill. Offering both lunch (11:30 a.m. to 2:30 p.m.) and dinner (5:30 to 10 p.m.) daily, it has a menu designed to mix and match fish, cooking techniques and sauces to suit your tastes. Try the yellowfin or mahi mahi, grilled or blackened, then choose from a citrus mango butter, a Szechwan style or Santa Fe style sauce. Prices are a reasonable $15.50. The Yacht Club also has a selection of meat and poultry.

If you are unable to choose between these excellent dining spots, plan a trip back for the Annual Sizzlin' Chefs Classic, a grilling contest sponsored by the local culinary association.

Telluride, Colorado

You wouldn't imagine anyone sticking a ski resort way out here, starting from scratch—that would be crazy. No, Telluride is the creation of the era of gold and silver mining. The energies poured into digging out precious metals also created the world's first practical alternating-current electrical system for mine equipment, and one of the best town water supplies. But gold meant money, money meant banks, and banks attracted robbers: here Robert Leroy Parker, a.k.a. Butch Cassidy, robbed his first bank. He reportedly practiced his getaway over and over before the robbery, timing his escape down the main street.

Jack Dempsey worked here as a bouncer and dishwasher before becoming famous. Telluride was even witness to politics (of a relatively harmless variety): in 1903 William Jennings Bryan delivered one of his renowned renditions of the "Cross of Gold" speech from the front of the New Sheridan Hotel.

In 1964, Telluride was declared a national historic landmark *in toto*. The main street still appears much as it did when Butch Cassidy began his career, and the original houses around the town have remained unspoiled as residents work to restore the old Victorian finishes. And the mountains surrounding the town remain as imposing, beautiful and majestic as ever.

What has changed is the skiing. Telluride will celebrate its 23rd year as a ski resort, changing from a place dedicated to the extremely steep to an all-around area with some of the best beginner terrain in Colorado.

In addition to its historic town, Telluride also has a different face, built on the opposite side of the ski mountain, and called Mountain Village. This development offers excellent access to the mountain, but is quite different in look and feel. Mountain Village is a master-planned community anchored by what is considered the most luxurious hotel in the area. The resort has big plans to complete a long-delayed gondola that would link town with the Mountain Village. If the 2.5-mile gondola can be

---

Telluride Facts

Base elevation: 8,725'; **Summit elevation (lift-served):** 11,890'; **Vertical drop:** 3,165'
Number and types of lifts: 10—2 quad superchairs, 2 triple chairs, 5 double chairs, and 1 surface lift. **Acreage:** 1,050 skiable acres **Percent of snowmaking:** 15 percent.
Uphill capacity: 10,000 skiers per hour **Bed base:** 4,000

completed by December 1995, it will replace an eight-mile drive by car or bus, and indeed it is intended more as public transportation than as a ski lift, which is why we don't list it in our stat box. The gondola will operate roughly 16 hours per day to transport guests between the two areas, both of which have restaurants and hotels. The gondola ride also is free, but just a common-sense warning: don't board at 8:30 a.m. toting skis and expect to get off at the top without a lift ticket.

Where to ski

Start with what put Telluride on the skiers' map—The Plunge and Spiral Stairs. This duo, where left ungroomed, is as challenging a combination of steep bumps as you can find anywhere. If you manage to get down without too many bruises or sore spots, you can savor a sense of accomplishment. Mammoth is an alternate trail but not any easier. Formerly untamed Bushwacker is just as steep, but these days its massive bumps have succumbed to winch-cat grooming.

Even skiers dropping down below the base of Chair 9 will find a very narrow trail, about two or three moguls wide, which requires better than intermediate skills to negotiate well. For the intermediate who glides off at the top of Chair 9, the alternatives are to follow See Forever around to Lookout, to the blue runs under Chairs 3 and 4, or down the Face. The Plunge is now half blue, half black because it is groomed regularly, but only on one side. Telluride does this with several of its tough runs. Groomed, this run is a thrill, allowing experts to play on a steep cruise not found on many other mountains in North America, and letting advanced intermediates ski gingerly down.

Perhaps the drive to label The Plunge and its sister super-steep trails as intermediate has been spearheaded by what many perceive as Telluride's limited intermediate terrain. The only true intermediate terrain is under Chairs 3, 4 and 5, but the Telluride Face with its half-and-half grooming is now acceptable for advanced intermediates. In fact, even without adding terrain, increased grooming is making more runs acceptable for intermediates each year.

The most fun for an intermediate would be repeated trips up Chair 4, and down Peek a Boo, Humboldt Draw, Pick and Gad and Tomboy. The runs off Chair 6 are also short and manageable.

Another good area for experts is the 400 acres of glade and above-timberline skiing in the Gold Hill area. These double-diamond runs require a hike to the 12,247-foot mark (if you want to go to the top of in-bounds skiing), which makes Telluride's legal vertical drop 3,522 feet.

Beginners will find this one of the best places in the world to learn to ski. The Meadows has for years been considered a perfect beginner area. Sunshine Peak, which for several years had carried blue colors on the trail map, has now been mostly reclassified green, as it should be. Telluride divides its runs into six categories instead of three or four. One green circle is easiest, then double greens, then single blues, then double blues, single black and double black. This allows an easier progression for those who still are developing their skills.

Mountain rating

Telluride is a rite of passage for experts. It's a chance to test oneself against consistent steeps and monstrous bumps. For intermediates, Telluride is making a serious effort to groom more formerly expert slopes, and plenty of challenges exist for anyone trying to graduate to the expert level. If you are an intermediate whose trademark trails are long, mellow cruising terrain, head elsewhere. For beginners, there are few better places to be introduced to skiing.

Snowboarding

Snowboarding is allowed on the entire mountain. Beginner lessons cost $75, including lift and rentals.

Cross-country

Here again the spectacular scenery makes cross-country a joy to experience. For high-mesa cross-country skiing this area is difficult to beat. The **Telluride Nordic Center** offers a 30-km. network of groomed trails around town and the ski area.

Lessons are also available. Track fees are free or $12, depending on which you use. Adult and children's group lessons are priced at $35. Full day backcountry tours cost $60. Equipment rentals—skis, boots and poles—for a full day are $12 for adults or children.

Guided tours wind through the San Juan Mountains and a five-hut, 45-mile network. Huts are approximately six miles apart and each is equipped with padded bunks, propane cooking appliances and a big potbelly stove. The same rates apply to all programs: about $19 per person cabin fee and $25 a day for provisions, which covers breakfast, lunch and dinner. The $100-a-day guide fee is split between the members of the group. Groups are held to a maximum of eight skiers.

Lessons (95/96 prices)

Telluride's 150-instructor ski school, run by Annie Vareille-Savath for the past 16 years, has a good reputation. A successful learning experience usually requires two main ingredients: good instruction and appropriate terrain. Telluride has both.

Group lessons cost $35 for a half day (two and a half hours). If you start in the morning, you can add on the afternoon for $20, or the next day for $30. A full-day clinic is $50. A never-ever package for Alpine skiers, telemarkers, Nordic skiers or snowboarders is $70 for skiers and $75 for snowboarders and includes lessons, lifts and rentals.

Private lessons are $70 an hour, with each additional skier paying $20. A full day is $380, $60 for each additional skier.

Special workshops include a highly acclaimed Women's Week program that includes lifts, races, video analysis, seminars, and wine and cheese parties. Perhaps because Telluride's ski school is run by a woman, this program is one of the best and longest-running of this type. Two of our contributors have participated, and both made big strides in skiing ability. A five-day session is $400, while a three-day session is $330.

Ski school also offers racing clinics. NASTAR two-hour courses cost $35, or practice on your own for $5 (two runs) and $1 for each additional run.

The **Children's Ski Center** (728-7545), takes ages 3 to 12. Lessons and lunch cost $45 per half-day; $62 full-day; $156, three days; $260, five days.

Lift ticket rates for children in Children's Ski School are $12 a day for those from 7 to 12 years and free for those 6 and younger. Rental equipment per day costs $12.

Child care (95/96 prices)
Children's ski and day-care programs are in the Village Nursery and Children's Center near the Mountain Village Base Facility.

The **Village Nursery** takes children 2 months to 3 years. Cost is $49 for a full day; $39 for a half day. For reservations and information, call 728-6727 or (800) 544-0507.

Lift tickets (95/96 prices)

	Adult	Child (6–12) Senior (65–69)
One day	$45	$25
Three days	$129 ($43/day)	$50 ($25/day)
Five days	$200 ($40/day)	$125 ($25/day)

Telluride's shoulder-season discounted rates, good November 22–December 15 and March 30–April 14, are $30 per day for adults, and $15 for children 6–12, and $22 for seniors 65–69. Other multiday discounts are available. Skiers aged 70 and older and children 5 and younger ski free.

Accommodations
In Telluride you can stay down in the old town or in the Mountain Village. We start with some of our favorite spots in town; lodging in the mountain village is listed at the end of this section. Some lodging prices include lift tickets.

The San Sofia Bed & Breakfast (800-537-4781) the upscale property in town, is near the Oak Street lift. Rates are

$130–$195. This cozy B&B is considered one of Telluride's best, with exceptional service.

The historic **New Sheridan Hotel** (728-4351) is a step back in time. It's on Colorado Avenue close to everything, with a skiers' shuttle stop outside the front door. Rates: $100–$145.

The Johnstone Inn (728-3316 or 800-752-1901) is a B&B with eight small quaint rooms with private bath and a full breakfast every morning for $125–$145 per night, and **Bear Creek Bed & Breakfast** (728-6681 or 800-338-7064) has ten rooms with private bath and TV, roof deck and sauna and steam room for $60–$155 per night.

The Ice House Lodge, a block from the Oak Street lift, has been turned into a luxury hotel. You'll get 6-foot tubs, comforters, balconies, and custom furniture. Rates are $120–$385 a night.

The **Manitou Bed & Breakfast** (800-237-0753 or 800-233-9292 in Colorado) is decorated with country fabrics and antiques. It is near the Oak Street lift and is a two-minute walk from the center of the town. Each room has a double bed, and the price includes continental breakfast, rates are $145–$197. **The Riverside Condos** are perhaps the nicest in town and located near the base of the Oak Street lift. **The Manitou Riverhouse** is just as close to the lifts but be ready for lots of stairs if you rent here. Around the Coonskin Base check into **Viking Lodge, Etta Place** and **Cimarron Lodge,** where you can almost literally fall out of bed and onto the lifts, and the **Tower House** about two blocks from the lifts. More moderately priced units are **West Willow** and **Coronet Creek.** All the properties in this paragraph (and others not listed) are managed by **Telluride Resort Accommodations,** (800) 538-7754 (LETS-SKI).

In the Mountain Village

The most luxurious property is the **The Peaks at Telluride.** The massive 181-room ski-in/ski-out resort hotel boasts one of the largest full-service spas in the country. Rates for deluxe accommodations with daily spa access range $220–$800 per night. The "Ski, Spa Free" package, based on double occupancy, in early December and April is $99 per night and includes one lift ticket per day (three nights minimum); from January 2–13 the same package is $130 per night. Call 728-6800 or (800) 789-2220 for information.

Pennington's (800-543-1437) is the B&B of choice for the utmost in elegance. The rooms are giant and the views magnificent. The only problem is that you are not really in Telluride. Prices are $150–$260 per room with breakfast.

For deluxe accommodations on the mountain, try the **Telemark Condominiums** for $535–$775 for a group of eight to ten people, **Columbia Place,** $180–$300 for four persons, or **Kayenta Legend House,** $380–$525 for six people. All are either ski-in/ski-out or close to the lifts and cost $180–$700 .

These and several other properties are managed by **Telluride Mountain Village Accommodations**, (800) 544-0507.

Telluride has also organized a **Regional Half-Price Program** with several neighboring towns. If you stay in one of these spots, you can get half-price lift tickets in the early season—lodging and lifts starting at $42. For more information on this program, call (800) 228-1876 for Ouray; (800) 253-1616 for Cortez, Dolores and Rico; (800) 754-3103 for Ridgway and (970) 249-3495 for Montrose.

For lodging and information, call **Telluride Central Reservations**, (800) 525-3455.

Dining

Telluride has about 30 restaurants in town and the Mountain Village. Upscale dining is found in three downtown restaurants—all with entrées in the $15-$28 range. **La Marmotte** near the Ice House Lodge serves French cuisine; 728-6232. **McCrady's** is a new Southern-cookery restaurant highly recommended by locals and visitors (728-4943, 115 W. Colorado) in Silverglade's old location. **221 S. Oak** (it's both the name and address; 728-9507) is in a Victorian house with regional American specialties that vary daily in response to the freshest products available.

One of our readers recommended **Campagna**, which serves Italian specialties.

For more casual and moderate dining: **Leimgruber's** serves German cooking and beer imported from Munich with Gemütlichkeit: 728-4663. **Eddie's** serves up great pizzas. **The Floradora** claims the best burgers in town. **Excelsior Cafe** is known for mid-priced good-value North Italian cuisine.

Coffee houses have hit Telluride, and skiers have four from which to choose: **The Steaming Bean, Maggie's, The Creamery** and **Between the Covers.**

The T-ride Restaurant and Sports Bar offers cook-your-own steaks and seafood. **Sofio's** serves good Mexican cuisine but be prepared for a long wait. It's worth it—have a margarita. The **Powderhouse** serves local specialties as well as their secret Powderhouse Cocktail. **The San Juan Brewing Company** (known locally as the Depot) provides good basic chicken, fish and beef with local brew.

In the mountain village, try **Legend's at the Peaks** (728-6800) with Southwestern cuisine. **Evangeline's** (728-9717) has good Cajun Creole cooking.

If you are staying in a condo you can call for deliveries. Eddie's delivers pizza—728-5335. **Telluride Room Service** (728-4343) delivers gourmet meals from the town's restaurants.

Après ski/nightlife

For immediate après-ski, stop at **Leimgruber's Bierstube** near the Coonskin Lift (Lift 7) for a selection of great beer and a sure shot at meeting folks. For live music the place to be is the **Fly Me to the Moon Saloon** with live entertainment Thursday through Saturday. **The Last Dollar Saloon** has the best selection of imported beer in Telluride, plus pool tables and dart boards. The old Victorian **New Sheridan Bar** is one of the "must sees" in Telluride to experience the essence of the Old West.

Other activities

Shopping: Telluride's main street seems to be populated by T-shirt shops, but you can find some gems, such as **The Bounty Hunter**, 226 W. Colorado, with authentic leather Western wear and handmade cowboy hats; **Mendota**, 129 W. Colorado, with Native American jewelry and artifacts; and **At Home in Telluride**, 137 E. Colorado, a quaint shop with distinctive housewares. They'll ship your purchases home.

Helicopter skiing is run by Helitrax for downhill and cross-country enthusiasts. Box 1560, Telluride CO 81435; 728-4904.

Telluride also has **sleigh rides** from Deep Creek Sleigh Rides, 728-3565; **hot-air ballooning** from San Juan Balloon Adventures, 626-5495; **snowmobile tours** from Telluride Outside, 728-3895 and a town **ice-skating rink**.

Getting there and getting around

Getting there: Telluride has a small weather-plagued airport five miles from town. United Express and Continental Connection have daily flights from Denver; and America West Express has daily flights from Phoenix. Montrose, 65 miles from Telluride, is where most skiers arrive, either by plan or by a diversion from Telluride because of weather. It is served by United Express and Continental Connection from Denver, United from Chicago and Los Angeles, Continental from Houston and America West Express from Phoenix.

Ground transport is provided by **Telluride Transit** (728-6000); **Skip's Taxi** (728-6667); and **Western Express** (249-8880). Call 24-hours in advance for Montrose airport pickups.

Getting around: A car is unnecessary. The town is just eight blocks long,—you can walk anywhere. A free bus service runs in town and to the Mountain Village, and if the gondola is up and running this season, it will decrease the need for a car even more.

Information/reservations

Telluride Central Reservations (800) 525-3455 (nationwide) or 728-4431. One call handles everything.

For **Telluride Mountain Village Accommodations** call (800) 544-0507 or 728-6727.

Telluride Resort Accommodations also can help with lifts and lodging: (800) 538-7754 (LETS-SKI) or 728-6621. In Great Britian ring 0800-894957, in Mexico call 95-800-8357669.

The local area code is 970.

Vail
Beaver Creek Resort
Colorado

In skier survey after skier survey, Vail usually is found near the top—never, it seems, lower than two or three. It is a *complete* area, lacking none of the essential ingredients that form the magical stew of a world-class ski resort for the masses. Vail has an ersatz Old World village atmosphere and condominum convenience, raucous nightlife and quiet lounges, fine dining and pizzeria snacking. Its off-slope activities are unsurpassed—shopping, skating, movies, museums, sleigh riding and so much more—everything lots of money can buy. Bring lots of money. But village and expenses aside, there is above all The Mountain.

Vail Mountain is a single stoop-shouldered behemoth so massive that every crease and wrinkle in its cape becomes another entire section to ski or bowl to explore. Though it does not have the ultra-steeps or deeps of some of its Rocky Mountain cousins, what it has is a huge front face of long and very smooth cruisers, and an enormous back-bowl experience of wide-open adventure unlike anything this side of the Atlantic.

Vail Facts
Base elevation: 8,120'; Summit elevation: 11,450'; Vertical drop: 3,330 feet.
Number and types of lifts: 25—9 quad superchairs, 1 gondola, 1 quad chair,
3 triple chairs, 6 double chairs, 5 surface lifts
Acreage: 4,014 skiable acres Snowmaking: 9.75 percent
Uphill capacity: 42,570 skiers per hour Bed base: 41,305 within 10 miles

Beaver Creek Resort Facts
Base elevation: 8,100'; Summit elevation: 11,440'; Vertical drop: 3,340 feet
Number and types of lifts: 10—3 quad superchairs, 3 triple chairs, 4 doubles
Acreage: 1,125 skiable acres Snowmaking: 33 percent.
Uphill capacity: 17,540 skiers per hour Bed base: 4,700 at resort, 4,000 in Avon

Arrowhead-at-Vail Facts
Base elevation: 7,400'; Summit elevation: 9,100'; Vertical drop: 1,700 feet
Number and types of lifts: 2—1 quad superchair, 1 surface lift
Acreage: 180 skiable acres Snowmaking: 40 percent Uphill capacity: 1,707 skiers/hour
Bed base: About 80 at the base; much more nearby

Vail's network of nine quad superchairs is also the largest in the country. Combined, the mountain and its lift system let you do more skiing and less back-tracking than almost any other resort you can name.

As important as it is, skiing only constitutes part of the total ski vacation experience. A true world-class resort has to have amenities and atmosphere, and Vail is one of a kind in both areas. You'll find city conveniences such as 24-hour pharmacies (which you don't appreciate until you need medication in a more rural ski resort), but you won't find the typical Colorado mining-town atmosphere: Vail never was a mining town. About 35 years ago, it was a sheep pasture; developers who saw the potential of the mountain built a village styled after an Austrian ski town. Vail gets a lot of ribbing about its Europe-in-the-USA look, but lots of people apparently like it—Vail consistently gets about 1.5 million skier visits each year, more than just about any other ski area in the United States.

Because of its immense size, Vail is ultimately urban skiing. This city-town just doesn't feel rural. It bustles with traffic and people jams in peak periods. You won't see too many stars at night—too many streetlights. And far too many shop personnel are standoffish at their best and downright rude at worst—vacationing New Yorkers feel a certain déjà vu.

But for many of Vail's urban-dweller guests, Vail is just rural enough to make them feel they are getting away from it all. They find the well-lit streets comforting. They don't want to engage in small talk with every shopkeeper in town and they are used to high prices. Vail's bargains are few and extremely far between—even the parking (in a multistory garage) costs $8 a day.

Beaver Creek Resort

Don't visit Vail without spending a day at Beaver Creek Resort, Vail's sister area 10 miles west on I-70. Beaver Creek Resort is a master-planned complex of condominiums, hotels, a small shopping mall and excellent base facilities. Its purpose, quite simply, is to plop those with a taste for being pampered squarely in the lap of luxury.

Beaver Creek is a monument to the excesses and comfortable decay of the '80s. The initial marketing concept came across as something like, "If you aren't worth a million dollars, don't even bother coming here." That pretentiousness has been toned down quite a bit, but remnants still linger. It doesn't happen as often as it used to, but Beaver Creek sometimes projects an air of country-club-style exclusivity—if you aren't a member, you really ought to ski elsewhere.

Though one can still search out a few party types listening to live après-ski music in the main lodge, most Beaver Creek skiers disappear into expensive condos or multimillion-dollar homes that dot the golf course on the way up to the resort.

Vail Associates recently purchased a small ski resort, Arrowhead, which has an upscale golf resort at its base. They eventually plan to connect Arrowhead to Beaver Creek, with another Disneyesque Alpine village built in between them.

To get a fix on Beaver Creek Resort, drive up the mountain and pay to park in the underground parking (shuttlebuses to Vail also depart on the half hour for a cost of $2, or you can park free at the Beaver Creek base and take a free shuttle up). As you go from the parking garage directly into the main base-lodge area, stop at the roaring fire pit outside the Hyatt Regency. Order a hot toddy from the waiter and wave to the guests in the outdoor heated pool or bubbling and steaming Jacuzzis. Wonder what the poor slobs back at the office are doing. Now you're in a Beaver Creek state of mind.

Where to ski

Vail Mountain is one of the biggest single ski mountains in North America. But it is segmented: you can concentrate on separate bowls and faces for a morning or afternoon, always having the choice of a new path down the mountain. And none of these runs seems intimidating, although there is plenty of challenge for every level of skier.

One suggestion: if you're skiing with a group, arrange a meeting place in case you get separated. This is a big mountain.

Beginners have areas at Golden Peak and Lionshead. A series of crisscrossing catwalks named Cub's Way, Gitalong and so on allow beginners to work their way down the mountain, shifting from trail to trail.

Intermediates will probably run out of vacation time before they run out of trails to ski. Few other mountains offer an intermediate the same expansive terrain and seemingly countless trails. Especially worthy cruising areas include the long ride down the mountain under and to the right of the Lionshead gondola, almost any of the runs bordering the Avanti express chair, the Northwoods run, and the relatively short but sweet trio down to Game Creek Bowl—The Woods, Baccarat and Dealer's Choice. Our vote for best run on the mountain, and one available to advanced intermediates (though parts are rated black), is the top-to-bottom swath named Riva Ridge.

Much of the intermediate skiing on Vail Mountain is good enough that experts won't notice they're not being stretched to their limits. Those who want more challenge, however, should head to the far left of the mountain face to a trio of double black diamonds named Blue Ox, Highline and Rogers Run. The straight-down-the-lift, waist-high, mogul-masher Highline is the stiffest test of the three. Nearby Prima is almost as tough, and the short drop of Pronto down to the Northwoods chair lets you strut your mogul-mauling stuff in front of the lift lines. The only authentic gut-suckers on the front face are the tops of South and North Rim off the Northwoods lift, leading to a tight but nice Gandy Dancer.

Experts can drop down the Northeast Bowl or come off Prima Ridge through tight trees on Gandy Dancer, Prima Cornice or Pronto to the Northwoods area.

Solid skiers, of course, will also want to explore Vail's famous Back Bowls. Stretching seven miles across, they provide more than 2,600 acres of choose-your-own-path skiing. On a sunny day, these bowls are about as good as skiing gets. Confident intermediates also can enjoy the bowls, but should stick close to China Bowl and Tea Cup Bowl trails that the grooming machines make each night. That way, if you get tired or frustrated with the natural conditions, you can bail out easily. Skiers who have skied Vail for years say they now ski the front side only when they come down at the end of the day. The bowls also are an excellent way to escape crowds that may have built up on the front side of the mountain.

Beaver Creek Resort

Somehow in its enthusiasm to sell itself as a resort to pamper the well-off, Beaver Creek Resort acquired a reputation as strictly a beginner and intermediate cruiser mountain. Not so. Advanced skiers and experts should spend at least a day here and maybe more. Our advice is to choose a Saturday or Sunday, when the lines at Vail can climb over the 15-20 minute barrier, yet be nonexistent at Beaver Creek Resort.

The mountain is laid out upside down, with the easiest skiing at the top, down the Stump Park lift. Intermediates and advanced skiers should turn their skis loose down one of America's best unheralded cruisers, which dips and turns under the Centennial Express lift down the lower half of the mountain.

What's most surprising about Beaver Creek Resort is the amount of truly tough stuff. The Birds of Prey runs rival anything Vail offers—all long, steep and mogul-studded. While somewhat shorter, Ripsaw and Cataract in Rose Bowl, and Loco in Larkspur Bowl, are equally challenging. Grouse Mountain provides even more great expert terrain and is being outfitted with snowmaking. The skiing at Grouse Mountain is the steepest you will find. It is for advanced intermediates and above, but adequate width allows uncertain intermediates to traverse their way down.

Arrowhead-at-Vail

This area has just two lifts—one surface tow for beginner lessons, and one high-speed quad that shoots to the top. It also has plenty of wide-open cruising trails, with a winding beginner run (Piece O' Cake) to the left of the trail map, and a couple of isolated advanced plunges (Lone Pine Canyon) to the right. It's a great spot for any group that wants to stick together without having to be within sight of each other at every moment. Lose sight of your friends or family at Vail, and you may not find them again until the end of the day.

Mountain rating

Vail is one of the best ski mountains in the world for all but the extreme fringes of the skier ability chart. Super experts will miss the extreme skiing of a Snowbird, Jackson or Squaw Valley, and frankly, Vail is a little overwhelming for a first-timer's adventure on skis. But for skier ability levels 2-9 (on a scale of 10), Vail offers much. Experts have the Back Bowls, with acres of powder skiing. Advanced and intermediate skiers have long cruisers, and beginners have many runs to choose from.

Beaver Creek is the spot for aggressive, bump-hungry experts with the Birds of Prey and Grouse Mountain runs. Lower intermediates will also be happy at Beaver Creek Resort with its long runs and virtually no lift lines. In fact, anyone who does not want to see anything resembling a line should take a trip to Beaver Creek Resort.

Arrowhead is best for families with young children, or any group that wants to stick together. It also is quite good for those who like moderately pitched, groomed trails.

Cross-country

For a truly different Nordic experience at an Alpine ski area, head to the McCoy Park cross-country center at the top of the Strawberry Park Lift at Beaver Creek. Instead of skiing on the flats (usually a golf course) at the base of a ski area, you'll be on a 32-km. system at the summit, with spectacular views in every direction. Groomed and tracked for both skating and diagonal skiing, the trail system has one advanced (and exciting) loop, the Wild Side trail, but basically beginner and intermediate. Skiers can either download on Chair 12 or take the very gradual Home Comfort trail (6 km.) all the way down. It's great fun if there's some new snow to slow you down but a little too speedy if there isn't.

Adult fees are $15 for an all-day pass, $12 for a half day beginning at noon; $7 and $5 for children. If you bought the resort's new Mountain Plus Ticket™, you can exchange one day for a cross-country pass and rental equipment or a half-day Nordic lesson with equipment.

For more experienced Nordic skiers, there are several one-day or multiday backcountry tours available from Vail's Golden Peak Nordic Center at the base of Lift 6. All-day tours cost $53; afternoon tours are $37; Gourmet Tours, with lunch, cost $67.

For more information on Nordic skiing, call the Beaver Creek Cross-Country Center at 476-3239; or Paragon Guides (926-5299).

Snowboarding (94/95 prices)

Boarders are welcome at all three ski areas. At Vail, snowboarders will want to head for the halfpipe on Golden Peak. Beaver Creek has a snowboard park called Stickline, located off the Centennial Express chair.

At Vail and Beaver Creek a full-day Discover Boarding lesson is $75 plus $25 for a lift ticket. Lessons for levels 2–9 are $100 for the lesson and lift. Half-day lift-and-lesson prices are $60. Brian Delaney, a national snowboarding champion, teaches two-day learning camps at Beaver Creek.

Lessons (94/95 prices)

In Vail, the ski school has offices and meeting places at Vail Village near the base of the Vista Bahn Express, at Lionshead next to the gondola, at Golden Peak next to Chairs 6 and 12, at Mid-Vail next to Chairs 3 and 4, at the Eagle's Nest at the top of the gondola; at Cascade Village near the Westin, and at the Two Elk Restaurant near China Bowl. Private lessons meet at Vail Village. Call the Vail Ski School at 476-3239.

In Beaver Creek Resort, the school locations are in Village Hall next to Chair 1 and at Spruce Saddle atop the Centennial Express lift. Call the Beaver Creek Ski School at 845-5300.

Skiers watch a video that demonstrates the nine levels of skiing skills the school uses to form classes, then place themselves in classes ranging from never-evers to advanced.

A free Ski Tips program meets at 11 a.m. daily at Mid-Vail, Eagles Nest or Spruce Saddle. The session gives you a chance to ski down a gentle slope alongside an instructor who will provide a critique and suggestions on which ski-school program will offer the best benefits.

Private lessons (for one to five people) cost $90 for an hour, two hours cost $180; half day (three and a half hours) costs $255, and full day (8:30 a.m.–3:30 p.m.) costs $370.

Group lessons are $55 for a full day (10 a.m. to 3:30 p.m.) for any level skier. Packaged full-day lessons that include a lift ticket are $75 for never-evers through level 2, $100 for levels 3–9. Three-day packages with rentals cost $210 for levels 1–2, and $285 for levels 3–9.

Special workshops concentrate on specific skills or snow conditions, such as skiing parallel or handling bumps. Most are morning or afternoon three-hour workshops.

Pepi's Wedel Weeks were created in the European tradition, which allows skiers to start off the ski season with an inexpensive lesson package. These are held for three weeks only, in November and early December. It's a seven-day program with breakfast, lessons every morning and afternoon, races, a welcome reception, an evening party, a fashion show and a farewell dinner. Call (800) 445-8245 or (800) 433-8735 in Colorado.

The Children's Ski School is quite good. Vail has built a real adventure for kids, starting outside the high walls of Fort Whippersnapper atop the Golden Peak lift. Here children enter a magical land and follow in the tracks of the little Indians Gitche and Gumee, as they accompany Jackrabbit Joe and Sourdough Pete on a quest to find the treasure of the Lost Silver Mine. This adventure is just part of the program offered by the Golden Peak Children's Ski Center, which has the most extensive facilities at Vail for children of all ages. There are also special Kids Nights Out featuring dinner, theater and special games.

Vail has two children's centers: Golden Peak (479-2040) and Lionshead (479-2042), and Beaver Creek has one (845-5464). Registration is from 8–9:15 a.m., or pre register the day before.

Children 3 1/2–6 years have a supervised playroom and programs when not skiing, and the prices include lunch and snacks. Special children's rental shops are available in the Golden Peak and Beaver Creek Resort centers. Beginner equipment for 3 to 6 year olds is available at Lionshead.

Children 6–12 can spend their day on the mountain, be entertained with videos and have supervised meeting rooms. Lunch is also supervised but not included in the price ($7 is suggested as adequate lunch money). Group lessons are $64 a day for lessons and lifts. Information on Kids' Night Out and Family Night Out dinner theater programs is available by calling the Family Adventure line, 479-2048.

Teens aged 13–18 have daily all-day classes with members of their age group. Prices are the same as adult lessons.

Child care

The child care facility is run by the ski school. Reservations are advised, especially during the holidays. A nursery facility, **Small World Play School,** is in Beaver Creek Resort (845-5325), with another in the Golden Peak base area (479-5044) at Vail. Children aged 2 months to 6 years may be enrolled in the program. Costs are $55 a day. Half-day programs are available on a space-available basis for $30, either morning or afternoon. For babysitters call 479-2292 or 476-7400.

Lift tickets (94/95 prices)

	Adult	Child (Up to 12)
One day	$48	$33
Four days	$172 ($43/day)	$124 ($31/day)
Seven days	$252 ($36/day)	$189 ($27/day)

We list four- and seven-day prices in this chapter rather than three- and five-day prices for two good reasons: because most Vail skiers are there for a few days to a week, and because

Vail has a ticket program called Mountains Plus Ticket™. Any skier who buys a lift ticket for four or more days may exchange a day for credit toward other Vail Valley activities, such as snowmobile tours or cross-country rentals and trail fees.

Senior citizens 65–69 years usually get a discount equal to the lowest multiday day rate, and those 70 and older ski free.

We always warn you that prices are subject to change, but we want to emphasize it here. Corporate greed at Vail has few bounds. Last season, Vail did something no other ski resort has done in our collective ski journalists' memories: it raised the one-day ticket price from $46 to $48 midway through the season. Most resorts stick with their prices once they've been announced.

Arrowhead-at-Vail offers a bargain alternative in this region. Until it is connected with Beaver Creek, which could happen by next season, it will have separate pricing. Adults ski for $30, children 16 and younger ski for $20. An adult three-day pass is $85, while a Family Pass (two adults and up to three children 16 and younger) is a very attractive $90. Ages 65–69 pay $25, and older than that ski free. A ticket for the surface lift alone is $10.

Accommodations
Vail Village and Lionshead

Vail's premier properties are clustered in Vail Village at the base of the Vista Bahn Express. Selecting the best place in town is a virtual tossup between four hotels.

The Lodge at Vail (476-5011 or 800-237-1236) is the original, around which the rest of the resort was built. It is only steps away from the lifts, ski school and main street action. **Gasthof Gramshammer** (476-5626) is located at the crossroads of Vail Village. Our favorite and the most economical within this group of hotels is the **Christiania** (476-5641). **The Sonnenalp Hotel** (476-5656 or 800-654-8312) is a group of buildings that exude Alpine warmth and charm. All are expensive. Regular season seven-night/six-day ground packages cost around $1,700.

At the Lionshead end of town the **Marriott at Vail** (476-4444) is the top of the line and has an excellent location only three minutes' walk from the gondola. The seven-night/six-day package will cost about $1,300.

The Westin Hotel (476-7111) in Cascade Village is also luxurious. The Cascade Athletic Club is across the parking lot from the hotel and is available without extra charge to Westin guests. The hotel has a dedicated ski lift, which makes getting to the slopes a pleasure. The seven-night/six-day package costs $1,500–$1,800.

Condominiums are plentiful in the Vail region and the prices are sky-high. The most reasonable for those who want to be on the shuttlebus route are found in Lionshead, clustered around the gondola. Village studio units go for about $200 a night; two-bedroom units for about $500; three-bedroom units for about $700 a night with lifts.

The **Vailglo Lodge** (476-5506) is a 34-room hotel that operates like an elegant B&B. In Lionshead, it has easy access to the slopes and town. Room rates are $108 in low season to a high of $224 at Christmas. For other relatively more affordable lodging, try **West Vail Lodge** (476-3890) in West Vail; **Antlers** (476-2471) in Lionshead; **Manor Vail** (476-5651) in Gold Peak; the **Holiday Inn at Vail** (476-5631) and **Vail Village Inn** (476-5622).

Beaver Creek Resort

In Beaver Creek Resort most properties are clustered around the base area and the Beaver Creek Resort village.

Hyatt Regency Beaver Creek has rates ranging from as low as $215 for a standard room to $285-$480 for a mountain view room. The hotel also features an unusual program which matches up singles who want to take advantage of the double occupancy rates. Call (800) 233-1234 for information about Single Share or reservations. The Hyatt also has organized a fun story-telling program which started out for kids but has gained widespread interest.

The **Centennial Lodge** (800-845-7060) and **Creekside Lodge** (949-7071) are just about 300 yards from the base of the Centennial Lift. The seven-night/six-day hotel/lifts package will cost about $1,500 based on double occupancy.

The **Charter Lodge** (949-6660) is a bit more expensive and exclusive. **The Poste Montane** (845-7500) is located directly in Beaver Creek Resort Village as are **The Inn at Beaver Creek**, **Pines Hotel**, **B.C. Lodge** and **St. James Place**.

The absolute bargain condominiums are in Avon at the beginning of the Beaver Creek Resort access road, about a 20-minute drive from Vail's slopes. The Avon condominiums are served by a shuttlebus system. Prices in Avon are $170–$220 for a one-bedroom unit.

Comfort Inn (949-5511) has five-night packages with four days of lifts for about $460 per person in value season and seven-night packages with six days of lifts for about $760 per person, double occupancy, regular season. Or try the **Christie Lodge** (949-7700).

Dining

Vail Village and Lionshead

Vail has a collection of acceptable restaurants, but has not developed the gourmet reputation of Aspen, Deer Valley or even Steamboat. After speaking with scores of locals and tourists, we have these recommendations:

If you have deep pockets, this first group of restaurants is worth testing. **The Tyrolean Inn** (476-2204) has fine game and is a favorite among visiting Europeans. **Ambrosia's** (476-1964) and **La Tour** (476-4403) also receive consistent and excellent ratings. **Sweet Basil** (476-0125) was recommended by both upscale and blue-collar folk as a great place for lunch and dinner. **Lancelot** (476-5828) has the best prime rib in town, with prices from expensive to moderate. **Alfredo's** (476-7111) in the Westin has perhaps the best Northern Italian fare. **Windows Restaurant** (476-4444) in the Radisson has great dining and a great view.

For more moderate prices, stop at the **Ore House** (476-5100) in the village and the **Chart House** (476-1525) in Lionshead for steaks. **Blu's** (476-3113) can be moderate if you choose carefully, and **Bully Pub** (476-5656) in the Sonnenalp's **Bavaria Haus** keeps prices traditionally low. **Garton's Saloon** in the Crossroads Shopping Center has a Mexican menu.

Those on a budget should try **Pazzo's** (476-9026) across from Crossroads, which offers spaghetti or soup and pizza for less than $6. **Bart and Yetti's** (476-2754) in Lionshead is a good place to head for lunch or light dinner.

The Jackalope (476-4314) in West Vail is a great spot for inexpensive basic good eats and a local atmosphere.

In Beaver Creek Resort, try the **Golden Eagle Inn** on the mall, a restaurant run by Pepi Langegger of the Tyrolean Inn. **Legends** (949-5540) in the Poste Montane has the best fish in the area. **Mirabelle** (949-7728) at the bottom of the Beaver Creek Resort access road serves well-prepared nouvelle cuisine. **Covered Bridge Cafe** in the Park Plaza is the most moderately priced of the resort area restaurants. In Avon try the **The Brass Parrot** and **Cassidy's**.

Visitors who are looking for something special, and have a car or are willing to take a taxi, head to nearby Minturn. Here, you'll find the **Minturn Country Club** where you choose your own T-bone, filet or swordfish steak, and then cook it yourself over open grills. Just across the street, the area's best Mexican food is dished out at the **Saloon** or **Chili Willy's**. Casual to the nth degree, they offer pitchers of margaritas and Mexican food so authentic that both will bring tears to your eyes.

Up on the mountain make it a point to have lunch at the beautiful **Two Elk Restaurant**. This is what every on-mountain cafeteria dining experience should be.

A memorable Vail dining experience is a night at **Beano's Cabin** at Beaver Creek Resort. Groups meet at the base of the mountain and are served hot chocolate or coffee. They are bundled onto a 40-person sleigh and pulled up the mountain under the stars by a snowcat. Unfortunately the ride up isn't the romantic experience it might be: the sled is steel, decorated with plastic evergreens; you'll be forced to listen to loud and bad singing and stories of marauding black bears, and depending on the wind you may suffer diesel exhaust fumes. All in all, the ride is more appropriate for spring break than romance. Once you get there, though, Beano's Cabin is beautiful, modern and rustic, completed by a roaring stone-hearth fire, log beams, an 11-point buck head, and exciting, well-prepared cuisine. The cost is $69 per person. Reservations, 949-5750.

Another experience of this type, but on a much smaller scale, is an evening at Arrowhead's **Anderson Cabin**. Originally built by John Anderson, one of the bachelors that homesteaded in the Bachelor Gulch area, the cabin was restored in 1985. It has no electricity, so up to 20 can dine by lanternlight and watch the chef cook a five-course gourmet meal on a wood stove. Lunch is $60, including a lift ticket at Arrowhead (diners ski in and out); dinner is $80, including a snowcat ride in and the meal, but without alcohol, taxes and tip. Call 926-3029 or (800) 332-3029 for more details.

Après-ski/nightlife

Après-ski in Vail is centered in the Village or in Lionshead. In the Village, try **Sarah's** in the Christiania for squeezebox music with Helmut Fricker on Tuesdays, Wednesdays and Fridays; and **Vendetta's**, which normally has live music. **Mickey's** at the Lodge at Vail is the top piano bar après-ski spot. Several restaurants have house entertainers who are long-time career musicians; we liked Mike Moloney's personable mix of ballads and country-rock at **Pepi's.**

In Lionshead, **Sundance Saloon** fills up with locals and probably has the best drink prices in town, especially at happy hour in the late afternoon. There are pool tables, a locals' keg party on Thursdays and live music on the weekends. **The Hong Kong Café** is also a hot locals' bar.

For later nightlife with live music, dancing and such, try **Nick's**, which has rock 'n' roll with a disc jockey. **The Club** normally offers acoustic guitar music. **Garton's Saloon** has live alternative music. On weekends the **Sundance Saloon** in Lionshead and the **Jackalope** in the West Vail shopping center have live music.

Other activities

Shopping: Plenty of boutiques and shops, many of the pricey variety. The better stores are concentrated in Vail Village.

Vail has a number of athletic clubs. **The Cascade Club** across from the Westin has indoor tennis courts, squash courts, racquetball courts, Nautilus and free weights, indoor track, outdoor heated pool and thermal spa. The **Vail Athletic Club** (476-0700) also has fitness facilities in Vail Village. The **Vail Racquet**

Club (476-3267) in East Vail has indoor tennis, squash and racquetball courts, swimming pool, Nautilus and weight room.

Steve Jones Sleigh Rides on the Vail Golf Course can be booked by calling 476-8057.

Vail also has a ski museum worth looking at, a movie theater, an ice skating rink and many other things to do.

Getting there and getting around

Getting there: These resorts are right on I-70, 100 miles west of Denver and 140 miles east of Grand Junction.

Flights land at the **Vail/Eagle County airport**, about 35 miles west of Vail, and the Denver International Airport 110 miles east. Eagle County airport is served by American, America West, Delta, United and Taesa Airlines.

Ground transportation between Denver and Vail is frequent and convenient. The trip to Vail takes about two and a half hours. Contact **Colorado Mountain Express** at (800) 424-6363; or **Vans to Vail** at (800) 222-2112.

Getting around: If you are staying in Vail Village or Lionshead, a car is a big pain. Vail has a reliable free shuttle, and the town is designed for strolling. Parking is a head-ache, and costly, too. The Vail/Beaver Creek shuttlebus is $2. If you plan to commute frequently between Vail and Beaver Creek, you may want to rent a car. If you are planning a late- or early-season trip ask about the resort transit systems—schedules are often curtailed.

Information/reservations

Vail/Beaver Creek Reservations at (800) 525-2257 (Vail) or (800) 622-3131 (Beaver Creek) handles air tickets, transfers and lodging.

In the Great Britain, ring 0800-891-673; in New Zealand, dial 0800-44-0827; in Australia, call 0014-800-128088; and in Mexico, call 95800-010-1028.

All area codes are 970 unless otherwise noted.

Town Map
Winter Park

Kings Crossing

40

Sitzmark Lodge

Hi Country Haus

Idlewild Lodge

Braidwood

Olympia

Alpenglo

Alpine Vista

Forest Trail

Tall Pines

Silverado I

Silverado II

Timber Ridge

Lions Gate

High Season

Sundance West

Timber Run

Mountain View

Sundowner Motel

Winter Park

Viking Lodge

Woodspur Lodge

Hideaway Road

Arapahoe Road

Creekside

Millers Inn

Vasquez Road

Cooper Creek Way

Crestview

Snowblaze Athletic Club

Valley Hi Motel

Hideaway Village

Vasquez Run

Rio Grande Railroad

2 Miles

Beaver Village

Key

ⓐ Mary Jane Ski Area
ⓑ Winter Park Ski Area
ⓒ Crestview
ⓓ Cooper Creek Square
★ Winter Park Resort Chamber

ⓔ Winter Park Center
ⓕ Park Plaza Shopping Center
ⓖ Idlewild Lodge
ⓗ Park Place Center
ⓘ Kings Crossing

Old Town Winter Park

Timber House

Brenger's Ski Chalet

Winter Park Place

Corona (Rollins) Pass

40

High Country Inn

Trail Road

Iron Horse Resort

Vintage

Moffat Tunne

← Denver 70 miles

N

Winter Park
Colorado

Winter Park doesn't have the glamour of Aspen or Vail, nor the quaint Victorian charm of Telluride, Breckenridge or Crested Butte. What Winter Park has is a great mountain with a phenomenal variety of terrain and some of the most affordable big-mountain skiing in the United States.

Early this century, when the Moffat Tunnel through the Rockies was completed, Denverites began to ride the train to the area. The shacks first built for the tunnel construction crews made perfect warming huts for hardy skiers who climbed the mountains and schussed down on seven-foot boards. Eventually the ski area became part of the Denver public parks system, which explains its name. Today Winter Park ranks as one of the largest ski areas in Colorado.

Winter Park has no massive condo complexes lining the roads, and no built-up center of town. Both the ski area and most of the lodgings are tucked into the woods off the main highway. A traveler might well ride through Winter Park and never realize that the town can sleep over 13,200 in some 100 properties.

Lodging is designed with families in mind, the ski school is one of Colorado's most respected and the children's center is one of the biggest and most advanced of any ski resort.

Although Winter Park has maintained a great family reputation, it is surprisingly a good destination for singles. The Mary Jane section of the resort has tough skiing, as difficult as any in Colorado; the town benefits from having only a few, but good, nightlife centers, meaning that you get to meet most of the other skiers in town if that's what you desire; and the mountain inn lodging gives singles a great opportunity to meet other vacationers over dinner and drinks, or while enjoying the hot tubs. If you are looking for a solid good time without the fanfare, Winter Park presents you with one of the best.

Winter Park Facts
Base elevation: 9,000'; **Summit elevation:** 12,060' **Vertical drop:** 3,060 feet
Number of lifts: 20–6 quad superchairs; 5 triple chairs, 9 double chairs
Snowmaking: 20 percent **Skiable acreage:** 1,358
Uphill capacity: 33,700 per hour **Bed Base:** 13,200 in Fraser Valley

Where to ski

Visitors who have read most reports about Winter Park arrive expecting a good intermediate resort with plenty of lower-intermediate and beginner trails. Yes, that's all here—what is surprising is the amount of expert terrain.

Though the mountain is completely interconnected by its lifts, it has separate base areas: Mary Jane and Winter Park. The Winter Park base area serves most of the beginner and intermediate trails, with a handful of advanced trails dropping down the left side as you look up. Beginners can ride to the top of the mountain to Sunspot and then ski down Allan Phipps, March Hare and Mad Tea Party, or they can ski all the way back to the base using the Cranmer Cutoff to Parkway. Intermediates starting from the same mountaintop can play down Jabberwocky, White Rabbit and Cheshire Cat.

The Vasquez Ridge area also has an excellent collection of intermediate cruising runs and is served by a quad superchair. (The only drawback to the Vasquez Ridge area is a long runout down the Big Valley trail; the Buckaroo trail lets you avoid the runout.) If you find yourself on the other side of the ridge, keep up your speed and tuck for the run back to the Pioneer Express lift. Gambler and Aces and Eights are two short steep mogul runs that take you to the Olympia Lift. To change mountains, green-circle Gunbarrel takes skiers to the High Lonesome Express superchair for a drop into the Mary Jane area.

For advanced skiers, the most popular lift on the Winter Park side probably will be the Zephyr Express Superchair. It skirts the far left boundary of the area and allows drops down Bradley's Bash, Balch, Mulligan's Mile and Hughes—all good advanced terrain. From the top of Zephyr, bump fanatics can dance down Outhouse and end up at the base area of Mary Jane.

Now on to the Mary Jane side of the resort: a blast for any solid intermediate or advanced skier, with some chutes that will make the hair stand up on the expert's neck. The Sunnyside lift has excellent runs for intermediates. If you can handle these with no trouble, try Sleeper, one of Winter Park's "blue-black" designated runs that help intermediates advance to blacks. If that doesn't shake you, head for the black runs off the Iron Horse chair, and if you're still standing, then you're ready for the runs off the Challenger chair—all black-diamond, all ungroomed, and all tough as a bag of nails.

For experts who believe in super-steeps, try the chutes accessible only through controlled gates: Hole in the Wall, Awe Chute, Baldy's Chute, Jeff's Chute and Runaway, all reached by the Challenger lift.

The only bowl skiing is in Parsenn Bowl, 200 acres of open space that opened in 1992. Though rated blue on the trail map, it can be a good workout. Winds often close the Timberline lift, which provides the only access. Even if the lift is open, the cold wind can harden a thin surface layer into breakable crust, which makes turning a bit of a chore. If you can hit Parsenn on a good day though, you're in for a treat. The naked upper part is wide open and of medium steepness, while the gladed bottom part is an absolute delight, especially for those just learning to ski between trees.

Winter Park is one of the best ski areas in the nation for never-evers. Its $2-million Discovery Park, which won an award from *Snow Country* magazine in 1995 for best special project, is 20 acres of excellent gentle, isolated learning terrain for adult beginners, children and disabled learners, served by a high-speed detachable chair lift that slows down for loading and unloading. Winter Park also has a wonderful device for first-time skiers—a "Magic Carpet" conveyor belt that transports adult and child beginners up the learning slope, eliminating the need for side-stepping. It is very heartening to see a major ski area invest money and planning in the very things that make learning easier for beginners of all ages.

Mountain rating

Winter Park is one of the few ski areas on the continent that can truly serve the needs of all skier ability and interest levels. Very few mountains have both the nearly flat, isolated terrain that never-evers need, and the precipitous plunges that experts adore. Winter Park is lucky enough to have both, plus plenty at every stage in between.

Snowboarding

Snowboarding is allowed on the entire mountain. Many of the rental shops in the area have boards for hire. Lessons include a 4 1/2 hour first-time lesson for $20 with the purchase of a full-day, all-lifts ticket. There is a series of three-hour workshops for $55. Private lessons are $90 for an hour and a half.

Cross-country

Devil's Thumb Cross-Country Center (726-8231) offers great views of the mountains and 105 km. of trails groomed for both skating and classical. National-level competitors race and train here. The center is located near Tabernash on County Road 83. Trail fees are $9 a day for adults and $6 for children and seniors; half days cost $6 adult and $4 for children; children 6 and under ski free. Private lessons are $30 an hour. A learn-to-ski package costs $25 for lessons, rental and trail fee. Children and seniors: $20.

Snow Mountain Ranch (726-4628), eight miles west of Winter Park on Highway 40, offers 100 km. of groomed trails through a variety of terrain—open, wooded, hilly and flat. The system includes a lighted 2.2 km. loop for night skiing. The instruction staff includes national-level coaches and racers. Ski lessons, rentals, lodging, dining and child care are available. The trail fee is $8 a day, and children younger than 12 pay $4. Group lessons are available for $12 and private lessons are $20 an hour. Snow Mountain Ranch also is a YMCA with inexpensive dorm lodging.

Lessons (94/95 prices)

Recently rated by the *Rocky Mountain News* as one of the most innovative in Colorado, Winter Park ski school has something for everyone from never-evers to hot skiers and snowboarders.

An example: In the three-hour **Performance Lab**, instructors will analyze your skiing and your ski equipment, then combine equipment adjustments with private lessons to enable most skiers to advance beyond their previous level. The cost is $210, not much more than the three-hour private lesson alone. The relationship between proper equipment alignment and ability improvement is only beginning to be addressed, particularly with women, so Winter Park is quite cutting-edge with this workshop.

The Winter Park side is the focus of most **group lessons**. Beginners can get a $20 four-and-a-half-hour lesson with the purchase of their first lift ticket. Lessons for two days on skis cost $45, and for three days the price will be $75.

Intermediate and advanced skiers can choose from several **workshops**, including Parallel Breakthrough for $45, and Bump Workshop or Style and Technique for $50.

Private lessons are $90 for 90 minutes for 1-4 persons. Six hours of private lessons cost $320; three hours, $160.

Children's programs operate out of the children's center. Ute is for 3-4 year olds; $55 gives all-day lessons with rentals. Cheyenne is for kindergarteners, Navajo is for first through third graders, and Arapaho is for fourth grade through 12 years old. All three programs, including lifts and lunch, cost $60 without rentals; $70 with.

Winter Park operates the leading **disabled skiing instruction** program in the world. It also has a full-time race training program for disabled skiers. The programs help physically-challenged skiers reach their potential for full mountain enjoyment. Instruction is available for all levels, and the race program is open to advanced intermediate level or above.

Child care

Here, Winter Park clearly stands far above much of the winter resort world. Winter Park has always been a leader in creative children's ski programs and its commitment is evident in the multistory center built for the purpose. On some days the program handles more than 600 children—anyone who has organized anything for a group that size (of whatever age) knows what an undertaking this is. The center is open from 8 a.m. to 4 p.m.

Child care for ages 2 months to 5 years, including lunch, costs $45 a day; $30 half day. Instructional programs for older children are detailed in the Lessons section.

Reservations are required for all child care. Reservation forms may be obtained from Winter Park Central Reservations, or write to: Children's Center, Winter Park Resort, Box 36, Winter Park, CO 80482.

Lift tickets (94/95 prices)

	Adult	Child (6-13) Senior (62-69)
One day	$40	$18
Three days	$102 ($34/day)	$54 ($18/day)
Five days	$165 ($33/day)	$90 ($18/day)

Children younger than 6 and seniors 70 and older ski free. The resort also has a limited-lift ticket program called Preference Pricing, a great idea that more ski areas would do well to adopt. The beginner-only lift at Mary Jane costs $5 a day. For $19 a day ($12 for kids), skiers have access to six lifts (Galloping Goose and Pony Express at Mary Jane, and Arrow, Gemini, Endeavor and Discovery at Winter Park) servicing 200 acres of terrain on both sides of the resort with up to 1,000 feet of vertical. These lift tickets should be perfect for parents skiing with children and lower-level skiers who don't need access to all the terrain.

Accommodations

Winter Park has a group of mountain inns unique in Colorado: they are like small bed-and-breakfasts but with dinner thrown in as well. They all serve meals family style so that guests get a chance to meet one another easily. Most inns have transportation to and from the slopes, making a car unnecessary. The food is usually fantastic and plentiful, and the inn owners go out of their way to please their guests.

There are eight mountain inns in Winter Park. Perhaps the most upscale is the **Gasthaus Eichler** (726-5133). This inn is very European and the rooms are well decorated with down comforters on the beds. Each bathroom is equipped with a Jacuzzi tub. It's perfect for those wanting quiet elegant lodging in the center of town within walking distance of restaurants and nightlife. Rates based on double occupancy are approximately $70 per person in regular season for bed, breakfast and a massive dinner. This is a quality bargain that is hard to beat.

Arapahoe Ski Lodge (726-8222 or 800-338-2698) also located downtown, is a pleasant, friendly No-Smoking mountain inn that feels like home. The rooms have private baths. It features a large spa and indoor swimming pool. Prices based on double occupancy are $74 per person per night with dinner, breakfast and transport to the slopes. Single skiers pay $98.

The Woodspur Lodge (726-8417 or 800-626-6562) The lodge living room is massive with a fireplace, soaring roof and plenty of space. This central area makes a perfect meeting place for the guests. The rooms here are of two types—newly restored and old style. Ask for one of the updated rooms if you are staying as a couple and one of the older rooms for larger groups. The lodge is served by local buses as well as lodge vans that shuttle skiers to the area and the town. Rates based on double occupancy are $70 per person including breakfast and dinner.

The Timber House Ski Lodge (726-5477 or 800-843-3502) is tucked into the woods at the edge of the ski area. A private trail lets you ski directly back to the lodge. You can meet other guests in the giant living room with its stone fireplace, sitting at long tables with food served family style, or soaking in the outdoor hot tub. Rates based on double occupancy are $57–$88 per person with breakfast and dinner.

The remaining mountain inns are outside of town toward Tabernash. **The Outpost Inn** (726-5346) is the most comfortable and homey. Here Jerry and Susie Frye serve homecooked meals and nonstop hospitality. Vans shuttle skiers to and from the ski area. A spa attached to the building becomes a social center in the evenings. A maximum of 20 guests at a time stay at the inn. Rates are $68 per person double occupancy.

High Mountain Lodge at Tally Ho Ranch (726-5958) is a rambling lodge more akin to a motel in its room arrangements, but with a cozy group living room and dining area. It has a swimming pool. The inn overlooks a frozen lake and gives splendid isolation. Transportation to the ski area is provided. Rates are about $68 per day with breakfast and dinner.

The next lodges are not part of the Mountain Inn Association, but offer similar accommodations.

The Pines Inn (726-5416), is a B&B just around the corner from the Timber House with a personality of its own. It is accessible from the ski area by the Billy Woods Trail, which also ends at the Timber House. Rates based on double occupancy are $67 per night including breakfast.

Beau West B&B (726-5145 or 800-473-5145) is only 500 yards from Winter Park base and features gourmet breakfasts. It has a hot tub and great views. Rates are $60-$75 per person based on double occupancy.

The **Engelmann Pines Bed & Breakfast** (726-4632), in the nearby town of Fraser in a mountain-style home, has some rooms with fireplaces and Jacuzzi tubs for less than $100.

The next two inns are located at cross-country areas in Fraser. **Morningstar Ranch** and the **Devil's Thumb Ranch**.

Both charge about $55 per person for two sharing a room, including breakfast.

The condos of Winter Park are the mainstay accommodations for most skiers. The most luxurious is the **Iron Horse Resort** (726-8851), the closest that Winter Park has to true ski-in/ski-out, though that stretches the definition a bit. There is a swimming pool and a fitness center. The condos range from studios to two-bedroom suites. One-bedroom units cost $125-$320 a night, and two bedrooms $185-$395. Iron Horse is a bit outside of the town center, but has excellent shuttle service for those who want to strike out for nightlife.

The Vintage (726-8801) is also slightly out of the center of town but right next to the ski areas. It features a restaurant, fitness room, swimming pool and good shuttle service into the town. One of the finest properties in Winter Park, the Vintage has studios from $195, two-room suites for $225-$400, and three-room suites for $250-$500.

For some of the best condominiums in the center of town, try either the **Snowblaze** or **Crestview Place**. Both are virtually across the street from Cooper Creek Square. Snowblaze (726-5701) also features a full athletic club with racquetball court, swimming pool and fitness center, which are included in the price of the condo. The units are all equipped with color TVs. Studio units normally come with a Murphy bed, and two- and three-bedroom units have baths for each bedroom, private saunas and fireplaces. Approximate costs: two-bedroom units cost $130-$237; and three-bedroom units, which sleep up to eight, $187-$316.

Crestview Place (726-9421), just remodeled, does not have an athletic club or private saunas, but has fireplaces and full kitchens. Costs: two-bedroom units, $204-$264 a night; three-bedroom units, $272-$352.

One of the most popularly priced condominiums is the **Hi Country Haus** (726-9421). These condos are spread out in a dozen buildings and share a recreation center with four hot tubs, sauna and heated swimming pool. They are within walking distance of town and are on the shuttlebus routes. Costs: two-bedroom units, $180-$222; three-bedroom units, $240-$296.

For the least expensive lodging we could find, try **The Bunk House** (726-4657) at $15 per night for a dorm room.

Dining

Winter Park isn't packed with high-priced restaurants; instead, the emphasis is on good, solid cooking.

The **Gasthaus Eichler** (726-5133) in the center of Winter Park has an Austrian/German-influenced menu. Locals all raved about **The Last Waltz** (726-4877), which is in the King's Crossing Shopping Center on Highway 40. One resident claims the Last Waltz has the best breakfast in town and the others give unanimous thumbs up to the American and Mexican menu, which features homemade dishes with very fresh ingredients. Save room for dessert.

For venison and fondue, head to the **Chalet Lucerne** (726-5402). **The Divide Grill** (726-4900) in the Cooper Creek Square serves up Northern Italian dishes and has a good salad bar. **Deno's** (726-5332) also has excellent pasta dishes as well as chicken, steak and shrimp selections. And surprisingly, **The Slope** (726-5727), also known as one of the town's top nightlife spots, gets excellent marks for its table.

For family fare try the **Crooked Creek Saloon** in Fraser for basic steaks and down-home cooking. **Lani's Place** is the spot for Mexican food at great prices.

Hernando's Pizza & Pasta Pub with its fireside lounge is highly recommended by locals, but is often crowded. You can opt for free delivery, though. A new place to try is the **Winter Park Brewing Co.**, called The Pub and located downtown, which offers traditional pub fare and has 15 beers on tap, including microbrew specials.

For the best breakfast in town head straight to **The Kitchen** and ask Rosie to rustle up some eggs. You probably won't find Rosie doing much cooking but if she's around she'll liven up the crowd. **Carver's Bakery & Café** behind Cooper Creek Square serves hearty breakfasts and healthy lunches and dinners.

On the slopes, the best lunch is found in the **Club Car** restaurant at the Mary Jane base area. The new **Lodge at Sunspot** atop the mountain is a spectacular setting for a gourmet lunch. Winter Park has long had a fun way to order a pizza for lunch. Head for the telephone at the top of the Winter Park section of the mountain, call **Mama Mia's Pizzeria** in Snoasis and your pizza will be waiting when you arrive.

For something different, ride one of the new gondola cars for dinner at the **Lodge at Sunspot**, the spectacular summit mountain restaurant. A six-course menu is $49 inclusive, except for alcohol and gratuity. Winter Park's Zephyr Express lift has 20 gondola cabins that are used to transport dinner guests to the Lodge at Sunspot. During the day, it's a high-speed quad. Call 726-5514 for information and reservations.

Après-ski/nightlife

For après-ski, the **Derailer Bar** in the West Portal of the Winter Park Base area is the place to be. **The Slope**, close to the base area on the road leading out to Highway 40, also gets a good crowd at happy hour, 4-6 p.m. If there are any sports events on tap, the place to go is **Deno's Mountain Bistro**, which has a half-dozen TV sets, plus more than a hundred types of beer and

200 wines. **Lani's Place** in Cooper Creek Square serves up excellent happy-hour $1.50 margaritas and tacos.

The dancing nightlife centers in two spots: **The Slope**, which has live music most nights, and **The Foxxes** in the Cooper Creek Square, which has disc jockeys and infrequent live bands. For a quiet drink without the loud music head down to **Hideaway Bistro & Pub**. It has a fondue evening every Wednesday with live music from 7 to 10. The **Iron Horse** often has a guitar player in the bar, and a Comedy Club every other Wednesday in ski season.

The **Crooked Creek Saloon** in downtown Fraser also has food and music. Diehards using public transportation, take note: After midnight, you're on your own (get a taxi, or hope you made a friend in the bar).

Other activities

Shopping: There are a few shops here and there, especially for sports equipment and clothing, but this is not Winter Park's forte.

Winter Park's extensive mountain biking trails are used in winter for **snowshoeing**, one of the fastest growing winter sports. The trails are easy to follow and often packed down by snowmobile riders. The Winter Park/Fraser Chamber of Commerce has maps and more information.

Jim's Sleigh Rides in Fraser (726-5527) and **Dashing Through the Snow** (726-5376) have old-fashioned sleigh rides with a stop for refreshments around a roaring campfire. **Dinner at the Barn Sleigh Rides** (726-4293) offers a ride to a 90-year-old ranch, gourmet dinner and period entertainment.

Dog Sled Rides of Winter Park (726-8326) takes tours through miles of spectacular backcountry.

Snowmobile tours are available with **Trailblazer** (726-8452) or **Sporting Country Guide Services** (726-9247). Snowmobile tours run $35 for one hour, $55 for two hours and $100 for four hours. For dogsled rides call 726-8301.

Snoscoots are scaled-down snowmobiles that drivers aged 8 and older can operate around a marked, flat track. **Snoscoots** (the business) is on the highway between Winter Park and Fraser.

One rare but eminently enjoyable activity at ski resorts is tubing—sliding down a hill upon an inflated inner tube. The **Fraser Valley Tubing Hill** (726-5954) has what you'll need for a night of tubing—a hill, rental tubes and two rope tows to pull you back to the top. It's a blast.

Getting there and around

Getting there: Winter Park is 67 miles northwest of Denver on U.S. Highway 40. Take I-70 West to Exit 232, then head toward Granby on Highway 40. **Home James** vans take skiers from the

Denver International Airport to Winter Park. The one-way fare is $33 from the airport to Winter Park; $64 round trip. Reserve through central reservations, or contact the van lines directly. Home James: 726-5060 in Colorado; or (800) 525-3304.

Amtrak's California Zephyr, which runs between Chicago and San Francisco, makes a daily stop in Fraser, only a few miles from the ski area. However, certain parts of Amtrak routes have been cut to two or three times per week, so check with Amtrak on current schedules. Skiers from Chicago can board the train in the afternoon and arrive in Winter Park the next morning. West Coast skiers board in the morning and arrive by the next afternoon (Los Angeles passengers ride the Desert Wind train and change to the Zephyr in Salt Lake City.)

Sleeper cars are available, but sleeping in the coaches is not as bad as you might think. There's lots of leg room, and the seats recline nearly all the way. Special packages make the trains very affordable. Call Winter Park Central Reservations for details.

Call Amtrak for information and train-only reservations: (800) 872-7245 (USA-RAIL).

The **Rio Grande Ski Train** is an unusual treat. This special train leaves Denver on weekends mid-December to April.

Operating for more than 50 years, it brings 800 passengers from Denver directly to the Winter Park base area, chugging along 56 miles and climbing 4,000 feet. The train snakes through the Rocky Mountains, through 28 tunnels and across canyons, ravines, and ice-crusted rivers. The scenery is as gripping as any we have seen in the Swiss and Austrian Alps. The train leaves Denver at 7:15 a.m. and departs Winter Park at 4:15 p.m. Parking is available at Denver's Union Station for $3 all day.

Two classes of service—club and coach—are available; club car includes a continental buffet. Rates are $45 club and $30 coach (94/95 rates). For information and reservations, call (303) 296-4754.

Getting around: Destination skiers are advised to rent a car for any extensive restaurant and bar-hopping. If you plan to stick close to your lodging at night and your lodge has transportation to the slopes you won't need a car. In fact, a car is a pain at the ski area—though both base areas have parking, it fills up fast, especially on weekends, with heavy traffic from Denver.

Information/reservations

Winter Park Central Reservations, Box 36, Winter Park CO 80482; (800) 453-2525 (nationwide); or 726-5587. Winter Park is in the part of Colorado that changed its area code in April, 1995. All area codes are now 970 unless otherwise noted.

Utah skiing
and staying in Salt Lake City

Name a big city with a small-town friendly feel, which is also a major airline hub and an hour's drive from seven major ski areas. If you said Salt Lake City without hesitation, you must be a skier.

Utah has the most convenient major skiing in the country. It is blessed with incredible snow—light, fluffy and abundant. But that's not all. It is also blessed with resorts that don't feel the need to be carbon copies of their neighbors. Each of the seven nearby ski areas has a distinct mood. If you think variety is the spice of life, get ready for a well-seasoned feast.

An hour by car from Salt Lake City, you can find one ski resort that pampers guests like few others do (Deer Valley), one with a rugged feel (Alta), one with a youthful feel (Wolf Mountain), another with a bustling urban atmosphere (Park City), one with a cosmopolitan ambiance (Snowbird), and a couple that are particularly affordable and family-friendly (Brighton and Solitude). Some of Utah's ski towns resound with the deep bass

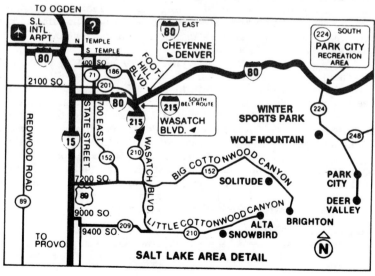

of live rock bands; in others, the loudest night noises are the snores of exhausted weekend athletes. Utah has ski areas with frightening precipices and with gently undulating meadows.

Utah's biggest blessing is its accessibility. No other region has so many major ski areas so close to a major airport (Lake Tahoe comes close, but Reno doesn't have anything like Salt Lake City's 300-plus arrivals per day). Transportation is well-organized and efficient, so you don't even need a car.

Many skiers still believe that finding a palm tree in Maine is easier than buying a drink in Utah, but liquor laws have changed radically in the last decade. In most places, you won't notice a difference between buying a beer here and at home. In fact, Salt Lake Cith claims more micro breweries per capita than any other western metropolitan city. And as far as entertainment goes, Salt Lake City is unsurpassed in variety. You can watch a pro basketball game, see a ballet, symphony or theater performance, laugh at a comedy club, and rock the night away in a rowdy night spot, the dance floor packed.

You're going to hear a lot about Salt Lake City in the next several years. It has been chosen to host the 2002 Winter Olympics, and will be the third U.S. site to have that honor (Lake Placid in 1932 and 1980; Squaw Valley in 1960.) Alpine ski events will be at Park City Ski Area, Deer Valley and Snowbasin.

Salt Lake City

Salt Lake City is a great spot to stay, for several reasons. One, you're centrally located to sample all the major ski areas. Two, hotels are very inexpensive, perhaps a result of having more than 10,000 rooms available for nightly use. Three, Salt Lake City has a ton of fun stuff to do at night.

The **Utah Transit Authority** (287-4636) has a very efficient ski bus system serving Brighton and Solitude in Big Cottonwood Canyon and Snowbird and Alta in Little Cottonwood Canyon. The buses are clean, pleasant and inexpensive, and go directly from downtown to the ski areas. UTA has a free fare zone downtown, convenient for sightseeing and evening activities. Unlike many other urban areas, downtown Salt Lake City is safe for groups to walk at night. **Lewis Brothers Stages** (800-826-5844 or 359-8677) has a SkiExpress service that picks up skiers from downtown hotels and takes them to one of seven ski areas. Many of the hotels include the service in their rates.

Unless otherwise noted, all area codes are 801.

Accommodations

Although rates are a little higher downtown than in outlying parts of the city, it is worth the extra few bucks to be close to Salt

Lake City's major attractions. Here are some recommendations (all rates are per night, double occupancy):

Salt Lake Marriott (531-0800 or 800-345-4754) is across from the Salt Palace Convention Center and is connected to the Crossroads Plaza shopping mall. Rates are $69–$159. **Howard Johnson Hotel** (521-0130 or 800-366-3684) is across the street from Temple Square. Rates are $51–$165.

Red Lion Hotel (328-2000) is a few blocks farther south on West Temple, but it's within stumbling distance of the Zephyr nightclub (see Après-ski/nightlife). Rates are $79–$115. Another choice in this area is the **Peery Hotel** (521-4300; $59–$109), historic, nicely elegant, but subject to street noise.

In the vicinity of West Temple and 500 South are several good hotels. **Little America Hotel and Towers** (363-6781) has some of the largest rooms we've ever seen in a hotel—great for spreading out all the junk that skiers bring. Rates are $63–$114. Also recommended are **Embassy Suites Hotel** (359-7800; $70–$129) and the **Salt Lake Hilton** (532-3344; $95–$140).

The **University Park Hotel** (581-1000; $94–$104) is near the University of Utah, a little farther from downtown but closer to the resorts.

Those looking for the coziness of an inn can try **The Brigham Street Inn** (364-4461), on East South Temple near the university. Three B&Bs in historic buildings are clustered about seven blocks from Temple Square: **The Anniversary Inn at Kahn Mansion** (13 "theme" rooms; 363-4900), **Anton Boxrud Bed & Breakfast** (six rooms; 800-524-5511) and **The Armstrong Mansion B&B** (14 rooms; 800-708-1333).

For budget lodging, try the **Salt Lake City Center Travelodge** (531-7100), **Travelodge Temple Square** (533-8200), **Deseret Inn** (532-2900), **Emerald Inn** (533-9300) or **Best Western Olympus Motel** (521-7373). All are $35–$80.

For more lodging, contact the **Salt Lake Convention and Visitors Bureau**, (800) 541-4955 or (801) 521-2822.

Dining

Downtown Salt Lake City has more than 60 restaurants. While you will feel comfortable in most of them with casual wear, you may want to dress up a bit for the finer establishments.

For a commanding night view of the state capitol and downtown, try **Nino's** (136 E. South Temple, 359-0506) at the top of the University Club Building for elegant Italian dining. More casual Italian dining can be found at **Baci'Trattoria** (134 W. Pierpont Ave., 328-1500), **Ferrantelli Ristorante Italiano** (300 Trolley Square, 531-8228) with its New York atmosphere, **Firenze Market** (358 S. West Temple; 532-1055) and **Della Fontana** (336 S. 400 East, 328-4243), which is in a converted church with stained-glass windows and a waterfall cascading from the ceiling.

For Asian dining, **Charlie Chow** (277 Trolley Square, 575-6700) has the most interesting atmosphere, but **Pagoda** (26 E St., 355-8155) has been around the longest, since 1946. **Mikado** (67 W. 100 South, 328-0929) has private Japanese zashiki rooms.

Cafe Pierpont (122 W. Pierpont Ave., 364-1222) and **Rio Grande Cafe** (270 S. Rio Grande, at the Amtrak Station, 364-3302) are downtown's best bets for Mexican food.

American and steak and seafood restaurants abound. **New Yorker** (60 Post Office Place, 363-0166) has an elegant atmosphere in the dining room. Its more casual neighbors, **Market Street Grill** (322-4668) and **Oyster Bar** (531-6044) emphasize seafood, but also serve steaks and chicken. **Lamb's** (169 S. Main, 364-7166) is Utah's oldest restaurant, dating back to 1919 and still packed today. **The Green Parrot** (155 W. 200 South, 363-3201) plays rock-jazz-blues while serving the renowned cuisine of Chef Glen Austin. Another spectacular night view awaits diners at **Room at the Top** (150 W. 500 South, 532-3344), the Salt Lake Hilton's fine restaurant. **Shenanigan's** (274 S. West Temple, 364-3663) has a fun atmosphere.

At the base of Little Cottonwood Canyon is **La Caille at Quail Run** (942-1751) which gets rave reviews not only for its French cuisine, but also for its setting, built to look like a French chateau and surrounded by gardens filled with swans, peacocks, rabbits and other animals.

Après-ski/nightlife/other activities

Utah's liquor laws: A few years ago, getting a glass of wine here was a major effort, requiring a trip to the state liquor store before going to a restaurant, then paying a set-up fee before you could consume your own brown-bagged bottle. Now, it's much easier. Drinking establishments fall under three categories:

Restaurants can serve alcohol from noon to midnight "to customers intending to dine." If you order wine or a cocktail with dinner, for example, you won't notice any difference.

"Bars" don't exist in Utah, at least, not by that name. If you are planning just to drink, not eat, you'll do so at a **private club**. Utah residents buy an annual membership costing $25–$35 for each club. Visitors pay $5 for a two-week membership, valid for the visitor and five guests. Because the annual memberships also allow for five guests, some visitors just approach a local outside the club and ask if they can be a guest. Once inside, they thank their "sponsor" and split for separate tables. If you lack such audacity, just think of the membership as a cover charge.

Taverns are open to the public and may or may not serve food, depending on the establishment. The only alcohol served at taverns is beer.

For an unusual happy hour, stop by the **Cotton Bottom Inn** (273-9830) at the base of Big and Little Cottonwood Canyons. This is a raucous, sawdust-on-the-floor tavern with great garlicburgers and an earthy crowd. The address is 2820 E. 6200 South, but it's a little hard to find. Ask a local to direct you.

For lively après-ski downtown, try the **Dead Goat Saloon** (Arrow Press Square, 165 S. West Temple). A quieter, pleasant location is **D.B. Cooper's** (19 E. 200 South), which Salt Lake City's career crowd seems to favor.

Salt Lake City has three brew pubs, **Squatter's Pub** (147 W. Broadway, 363-2739) **Fuggles** (367 West 200 South, 363-7000) and **Red Rock Brewing Co.** (254 South 200 West, 521-7446). All brew their own beer on the premises (Fuggles does free tours on Saturdays) and serve excellent pub fare.

This isn't the typical ski-town nightlife activity, but classical music lovers shouldn't miss the free 8 p.m. Thursday night **rehearsals of the Mormon Tabernacle Choir**. You can drop in and leave as you wish.

Bella Vista, the private club next to Nino's Restaurant, has a great view of the state capitol building and downtown lights. And for high-energy dancing, it's **Zephyr** (301 S. West Temple), which lives up to its billing as "Salt Lake City's premier showcase for local and national entertainment." Other rowdy night spots include **Club Max** at the Red Lion Hotel, **Power Plant** on South Highland Drive and **Nickelodeon Club**, at the University Park Hotel for dancing to DJ music.

You can go shopping at **Trolley Square,** shops and boutiques in a restored trolley barn; attend a **Utah Jazz** basketball game, or attend theater, symphony, dance or opera performances. Now what other ski town can offer all that?

The Interconnect Adventure Tour

Experienced skiers can ski to as many as five different resorts in a single day via backcountry routes on this all-day tour. Six to 14 skiers are led by mountain guides. Some traversing and walking is necessary, so you need to be a confident skier and in condition. The four-area tour (Solitude, Brighton, Alta and Snowbird) is offered three days a week, while the five-area tour (those four and Park City) goes the other four days. Each tour costs $95, including return transportation and lunch. Reservations are required. Call (801) 534-1907 and have a credit card.

Park City Area

Park City, Deer Valley, Wolf Mountain

Walk outside the Alamo Saloon on a wintry dusk, just as the lights of Main Street begin to twinkle seductively and the sidewalks fill with après-ski traffic, and you can almost imagine the tinkling sound of spurs. Squint your eyes slightly and the strolling figures become the miners and cowboys who roamed this same street a hundred years ago, swaggering between more than 30 saloons in what was one of the largest silver mining towns in the country. Just as suddenly, the vision is gone, and the strolling figures are once again well-heeled skiers and funseekers. Yet the flamboyant atmosphere of a gold-rush town remains. Park City is one western ski resort whose authenticity runs as deep as the local silver mines.

That unstrained air of originality is evident in the century-old buildings on Main Street, many of which are included in the National Register of Historic Places. It is there in the clapboard houses, which seem to tilt precariously on the mountainsides, and in the old weathered mine buildings, which share the mountains above town with adjacent ski runs. It's there in the very un-Utah-like funkiness and live-and-let-live attitude of the Park City locals.

That attitude of quirky independence is perhaps not surprising in this town in the Wasatch Mountains, which was originally founded by soldiers who had been sent west to discourage Brigham Young from seceding from the Union. After surviving a period between 1930 and 1950 when it was all but a ghost town, Park City now can rest its hat on the stand reserved for world-class ski resorts.

In one category, Park City stands above all competition. This is the most accessible destination resort of its caliber in the country. Lying just 30 miles outside of Salt Lake City by six-lane Interstate 80 and Utah 224, it is a 45-minute drive from the airport, door to door. Skiers from either coast who carefully chart days of actual skiing per vacation time taken can get one and a half extra days on boards per trip because they don't have to devote an entire day to getting here and back. Accessibility was one of the key factors that helped Salt Lake City get the 2002

Winter Olympics. Park City, which is headquarters for the U.S. Ski Team, will host a number of the Olympic events. Park City Ski Area and Deer Valley will host the slalom, giant slalom and freestyle, while bobsled, luge and ski jumping will be at the Winter Sports Park.

Park City is home to three ski areas that appeal to quite different crowds, which makes it a versatile ski destination. Park City Ski Area itself is a massive, round-shouldered mountain that will appeal to the skier who demands expanse and skiing diversity. Nearby Deer Valley has built a reputation for pampering at a price, but its slopes include tougher trails than it gets credit for. Wolf Mountain is unpretentious and inexpensive, and extends the only welcome mat in the area to snowboarders. With the Main Street of Park City as the spiritual epicenter, this trio combines to form one truly world-class ski destination.

Park City Ski Area—Where to ski

At the base area, the Three Kings and First Time lifts service excellent learning terrain. Beginners, even those just getting into their snowplow turns, can take the gondola to the Summit House and ski a very long run back. This trail starts with Claimjumper, shifts to Bonanza, then finishes at the base area on Sidewinder. And for an adventure and a chance to see a different part of the mountain, take the Webster Run down to the Pioneer Lift, where you can have lunch at the Mid-Mountain Restaurant and watch experts bouncing down the steep face of Blueslip Bowl.

Intermediates have mind-boggling choices. If you want to start with a worthy cruiser, take PayDay from the top of the lift by the same name. The views are spectacular on this run, and at night it becomes one of the longest lighted runs in the Rockies.

Probably the most popular runs for intermediates are the 11 trails served by the King Consolidated quad superchair (called "King Con" by just about everyone). These runs have a steep, wide and smooth pitch.

Both intermediates and advanced skiers will enjoy the runs under the Prospector quad chair.

Experts looking for a solid challenge will find Park City most accommodating. Start off with a trip to the top of Blueslip Bowl. Reportedly, when this was the boundary of the ski area, resort workers regularly slipped under the ropes, made tracks down the

---

Park City Ski Area Facts
Base elevation: 6,900'; Summit elevation: 10,000'; Vertical drop: 3,100 feet
Number of lifts: 14—1 gondola, 2 quad superchairs, 1 quad, 6 triple chairs,
4 double chairs Snowmaking: 40 percent Total acreage: 2,200
Uphill capacity: 23,000 per hour Bed base: 12,000

bowl and then skied back into the resort. The management regularly passed out blue (you're fired) slips to anyone caught floating through this powder bowl. If you can ski Blueslip with confidence, then try Jupiter Bowl and its neighbors—McConkey's, Puma and Scotts Bowls.

Jupiter Bowl has every type of steep expert terrain. To reach the Jupiter lift, take the Jupiter access road from the top of the Pioneer or Thaynes lifts. To the left as you get off the Jupiter lift are wide-open faces, especially on the West Face, which is the easiest way down (a relative term). Narrow gullies and chutes, such as Silver Cliff, 6 Bells and Indicator, drop vertically between tightly packed evergreens. Or head to the right as you get off the chair and try Portuguese Gap, a run more akin to having the floor open below you, or traverse to Scotts Bowl, which is just as steep as Portuguese Gap. The adventurous (and those with parachutes) will find definite thrills in the McConkey's Bowl and Puma Bowl areas. When open, these are reached by a long traverse across the West Face ridge and some climbing and hiking over the Pioneer Ridge. We asked Park City officials why they don't put a lift in to access these bowls, but they prefer to keep them a wild and untamed reward for those willing to make the hike. We're of two minds on that philosophy, but it certainly makes sense for skiers who want to make virgin tracks in a powder bowl. The cornice at the top of both bowls deposits skiers into steep faces and chutes, which empty out into the Pioneer lift area.

A tip to avoid lift lines: the Town triple chair lift takes skiers from the lower part of Main Street to the mid-station of the gondola. Even on holidays or peak periods, the Town lift is usually empty, so those faced with a long line at the bottom of the mountain may want to take the free shuttle here and avoid the crowds. If the gondola has a line—not unusual in peak season—try the PayDay and Ski Team chairs. From PayDay, you can ski to the Crescent Chair and then to Pioneer. From Ski Team, ski down Claimjumper or King Con to the Prospector Chair.

Mountain rating

Most reviews of Park City characterize this area as a cruising paradise for intermediates, which is true enough. While it may not have as much steep and "gulp!" as Snowbird or Alta, its bowl skiing and chutes are serious—even on the expert scale.

On the other end, Park City has plenty of open and gentle terrain for beginners and lower intermediates. Though the green-circle trails up on the mountain are wide and gentle, they wind in and around tougher stuff. If you're just starting out and concerned about getting in above your head, carry a trail map and pay attention to the signage.

Snowboarding

Snowboarding is not allowed at Park City, but boarders are welcomed at nearby Wolf Mountain (formerly ParkWest).

Park City—Lessons (95/96 prices)

Group lessons cost $45 for a full day (four hours) and $37 for a half-day program. Three consecutive days cost $125 and five consecutive days are $197.

Private lessons cost $78 per hour up to $370 for a day (six hours). An early-bird private lesson, 8:45 to 9:45 a.m. is $48. Additional persons can be added for $15.

Park City Mountain Experience classes are for high intermediates and advanced skiers. The classes explore Jupiter Bowl, off-trail skiing and deep powder. These are four-hour classes with an instructor/guide. Classes, 10 a.m. to 2 p.m.: $45. Park City also offers a **Women's Ski Challenge**, three-day camps hosted by U.S. Ski Team member Kristi Terzian.

Kinderschule ski lessons, for children 3 to 6 years, can be combined with a day-care option. The combined day care and ski lessons are $50 for a half day, either morning or afternoon, including a snack. A full day, including lunch and lessons morning and afternoon, costs $68; and a three-day course is $178. For lessons only (90 minutes), the cost is $37 for a half day and $42 for a full day. Private lessons are also available for $59 an hour, $64 with two children; $69 for three.

Children aged 7 to 13 can take a two-hour group lesson for the same cost as adults. An all-day lesson that includes a supervised lunch is $70. Three days is $200; five days is $322. Multi-half-day discounts also are available.

Call for details on any of the ski school programs, (800) 227-2754. Park City Ski Area does not have child care for children younger than 3.

Park City—Lift tickets (95/96 prices)

	Adult	Child (Up to 12)
One day	$45	$20
Three days	$135 ($45/day)	$63 ($21/day)
Five days	$210 ($42/day)	$95 ($19/day)

One-day rates are from 94/95; expect them to rise a dollar or two. Multi-day passes also are valid for night skiing.

Utah multi-area books (coupons good for a day of skiing at Park City, Wolf Mountain, Deer Valley, Alta, Snowbird, Brighton, Solitude or Sundance): five of six days, $230 for adults, $95 for children; six of seven days $276 and $114. At resorts with low lift ticket prices, these coupons and combined with credits for ski school, restaurants, and gift shops.

Deer Valley—Where to ski

Deer Valley is renowned for pampering its guests with top-flight gourmet meals, palatial accommodations, attentive service and impeccable slopes. Some of the many amenities include guest service attendants who help get skis off car racks as you pull up to unload, tissues at every lift, restaurants to make a gourmet salivate, a free ski corral service where you can safely leave the best equipment, and grooming crews that comb the snow so pool-table smooth it will make any beginner into an instant intermediate. Experts who sneer at the daily slope manicure can go somewhere else. Deer Valley fills a marvelous niche in the ski world, satisfying those who want to be pampered and are willing to pay a little more for the privilege.

This season Deer Valley will enlarge its base facility, the Snow Park Lodge, by an additional 33,000 square feet. It also will offer snowcat skiing tours of a 640-acre area called Empire Canyon that will become lift-served in 1996-97. This new area is northwest of Flagstaff Mountain, and it borders McConkey's Bowl at the Park City Ski Area.

If you want to be seen, and have plenty of company and beautiful scenery, the best runs are Sunset, Birdseye and Success. But if you head for Mayflower Bowl or Perseverance Bowl you'll have these steeper trails virtually to yourself. Run after run down Legal Tender, Wizard, Keno and Nabob are a blast. The Mayflower and Perseverance expert sections are not all groomed, but with so little traffic the bumps never grow monstrous. Orient Express and Stein's Way are perfect cruisers with good advanced pitch, and Perseverance, coupled with the initial steeper sections of Thunderer, Blue Ledge and Grizzly, are just right for advanced intermediates.

Flagstaff Mountain has both moguls and cruising runs; it's easy to see from the lift which is which. For experts, a short traverse to the left off the top of this lift will open up an entire mountain face of wide-open Ontario Bowl, and challenging tree skiing. Don't miss this experience.

Experts also can find some fun terrain in Mayflower Bowl, to the far left of the trail map. Here you can find moguls on Morning Star, Fortune Teller, Paradise and Narrow Gauge. These are long trails bordered by glades you can dart in and out of. You also can request an "experts only" trail map (it has a white cover), which points out advanced runs and several gladed and chute areas.

Deer Valley Facts

Base elevation: 7,200'; **Summit elevation:** 9,400'; **Vertical drop:** 2,200 feet
Number of lifts: 13—2 quad superchairs, 9 triple chairs, 2 double chairs
Snowmaking: 20 percent **Total acreage:** 1,100 acres
Uphill capacity: 22,800 per hour **Bed base:** 12,000

Though Deer Valley has two short lifts for never-evers, we recommend other resorts for a first ski experience. The novice area is gentle enough, but it's a big step to the next level. Deer Valley's green runs (most on Bald Eagle Mountain) are also access runs that better skiers use to reach the base area. A beginner will feel as though he or she is riding a scooter on a freeway. One beginner run we recommend is Sunset, a gentle scenic route that descends from the top of Bald Mountain—but head back to the base before day's end or you'll find yourself acting as a human slalom pole.

Daily complimentary tours of the mountain leave from the base of the Carpenter Express lift, Snow Park Lodge, at 9:30 a.m. for advanced skiers and 10 a.m. for intermediates.

Mountain rating

On a scale of one to ten, one being a never-ever and ten being a top-flight expert, we'd say that Deer Valley is best for levels three through eight. And that's no slam: the vast majority of skiers fit that profile.

Snowboarding

Not allowed. Boarders should head for Wolf Mountain.

Deer Valley—Lessons (95/96 prices)

Group all-day lessons (11 a.m. to 4 p.m.) for ages 13 and older cost $57.

Private lessons for one or two cost $80 for one hour, $143 for two hours, $222 for a full morning or afternoon and $406 for a full day of instruction.

Children's (6 to 12 years) group lessons are $62 for the full day, including lunch. The Reindeer Club program is for ages 4 1/2 through kindergarten for $67 with lunch.

Special clinics include a black diamond workshop for advanced skiers, a style clinic, a women-only clinic and a mountain extreme class for skiers 18 and older. The Black Diamond workshop runs from 11 a.m. to 4 p.m. and costs $57; the others are 1–4 p.m. and cost $60.

Deer Valley—Child care (95/96 prices)

Deer Valley has a state-licensed facility that handles children 2 months to 12 years. Full-day child care, including lunch, costs $48. Half-day programs, morning or afternoon, cost $37 without lunch. Full-day infant care, including lunch, is $65, and half-day without lunch, either morning or afternoon, is $45.

Designed for 3- to 5-year-old beginners, the Bambi Special program runs from 9 a.m. to 4 p.m. Cost is $84 including lift tickets, a private lesson, lunch and children's activities. Child care phone number is 645-6612; call for reservations.

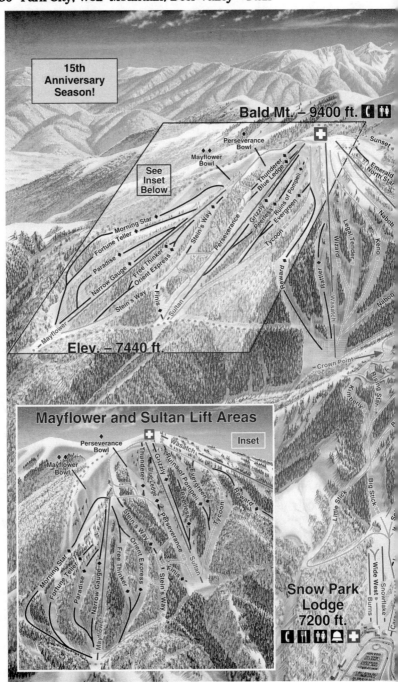

15th
Anniversary
Season!

Bald Mt. – 9400 ft.

Sunset

Emerald
North Star

Perseverance
Bowl

Mayflower
Bowl

See
Inset
Below

Thunderer
Blue Ledge

Nabob
Way

Grizzly
Peerless
Ruins of Pompeii
Evergreen

Legal Tender

Keno

Morning Star
Fortune Teller

Stein's Way

Perseverance

Tycoon

Wizard

Nabob

Paradise

Free Thinker
Orient Express

Reward

Rattler

Wasatch

Narrow Gauge

Stein's Way

Finis

Mayflower

Sultan

Elev. – 7440 ft.

Crown Point

Rising Star

Kimberly

Mayflower and Sultan Lift Areas

Inset

Perseverance
Bowl

Mayflower
Bowl

Thunderer
Blue Ledge

Wasatch
Ruins of Pompeii
Grizzly

Sunset
Evergreen

Morning Star
Fortune Teller

Stein's Way

Perseverance
Peerless

Reward

Tycoon

Big Stick

Paradise

Free Thinker
Orient Express

Narrow Gauge

Stein's Way

Finis

Sultan

Little Stick

Mayflower

Snow Park
Lodge
7200 ft.

Snowflake
Wide West
Burns

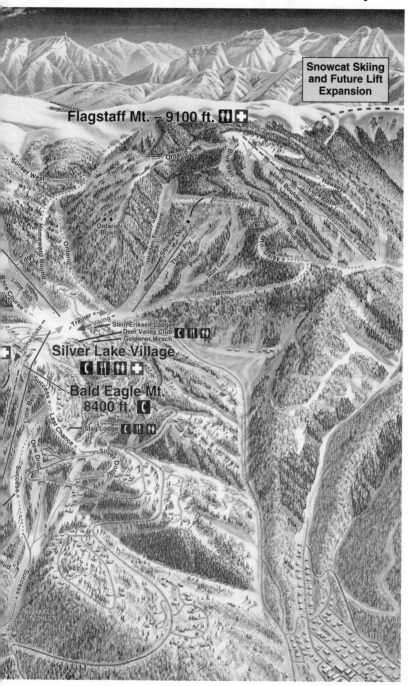

Deer Valley—Lift tickets (95/96 prices)

	Adult	Child (Up to 12)
One day	$49	$27
Three days	$141 ($47/day)	$75 ($25/day)
Five days	$230 ($46/day)	$120 ($24/day)

Skiers 65 and older ski for $34 for a single day, $96 for three days and $155 for five days.

For seven days between Christmas and New Year's, Deer Valley sells a pass for $364 ($52 per day) for adults, $210 ($30/day) for children and $259 ($37/day) for seniors. The single-day rate during that period will be $52/$30/$37.

Ticket sales are limited to 4,500 skiers, so on holidays the extra few bucks to ski Deer Valley are worth it.

Multi-area books (coupons good for a day of skiing at Park City, Wolf Mountain, Deer Valley, Alta, Snowbird, Brighton, Solitude or Sundance): five of six days, $230 for adults, $95 for children; six of seven days, $276 and $114.

Wolf Mountain—Where to ski

Wolf Mountain (formerly ParkWest) is a family-oriented, bargain-priced ski area that came under new ownership a couple of seasons ago. Though big changes are planned for the future to upgrade this 25-year-old ski area, including high-speed lifts and terrain expansion, right now it resembles a day area more than it does a resort.

Wolf Mountain is the only Park City ski area that allows snowboarding. It's also a few miles away from the historic town, though it is serviced by the free city bus service. Its atmosphere is non-glitz and unhurried and its lift ticket prices—$25 for adults and $15 for children in 94/95—are far less expensive than those of its neighbors.

Most of Wolf Mountain's terrain is not visible from the base area. What you can't see are some chutes and gullies as extreme (in fact, impossible to ski without deep powder) as any in Utah. There also is bowl skiing and a spread of black and blue runs. Wolf Mountain has some good terrain for beginners, visible from the base area. Lessons, rentals and child care are available.

On top of being the only choice in town for snowboarders, Wolf Mountain is smart for rugged advanced and expert skiers, for price-conscious intermediates and families and for lower-level skiers who don't want to pay top dollar for terrain they aren't using.

Wolf Mountain Facts
Base elevation: 6,800'; **Summit elevation:** 9,000'; **Vertical drop:** 2,200 feet
Number of lifts: 7 double chairs **Snowmaking:** 7 percent
Acreage: 850 skiable acres **Uphill capacity:** 6,700 per hour **Bed base:** 12,000

Cross-country

White Pine Touring (649-8701 or 649-8710) offers track skiing, lessons and tours at the Park City golf course. Rates are $8 daily ($4 after 3 p.m.), and those 12 and younger and 70+ ski free. A ten-punch pass costs $60 and is completely transferable, so that a family with three teens or a group of friends can use it and save a few dollars. There are 18 km. of set tracks, plus mountain tours.

The **Norwegian School of Nature Life** (649-5322) offers cross-country lessons and guided backcountry tours.

Accommodations

In and around the Park City Area are bed-and-breakfasts, country inns, hotels and condominiums. At Deer Valley the lodging has a decidedly upscale flavor and tariffs to match.

Park City's accommodations are roughly grouped either in the old town surrounding the Resort Center Complex or in the Prospector Square area. All are served by the free shuttlebus system. In general, low rates reflect early and late season prices in the smallest room or unit; high rates are the holiday rates for the largest unit.

In old Park City the best is the **Washington School Inn**, (800) 824-1672 or 649-3800. This is a very elegant country inn built in a former schoolhouse. Each room's name honors a former Park City teacher and everything is definitely first class. It has a hot tub and steambath, and is steps away from the center of the old town. If you are on your honeymoon, ask for the Miss Urie Room. Room rates range from $75 to $300 and include breakfast and afternoon tea. No children under 12 or pets.

The **Blue Church Lodge & Townhouses,** 649-8009 or (800) 626-5467, is a unique property, constructed around an old church. It is a block from Main Street and is a grouping of seven condominiums ranging from one to four bedrooms in the church, with four additional townhouses across the street. Again, this is rated as a B&B because breakfast is provided in a common area each morning, though it doesn't fit the category of B&B in the classic sense. It has indoor and outdoor spas and laundry facilities. Rates are $90 to $475.

If the three keys to lodging, as in real estate, are location, location, and location, then **Treasure Mountain Inn** (800-344-2460) at the top of Main Street is a winner. These are studio and one- and two-bedroom condos with full kitchens. Each of the three buildings has a coin-operated laundry, and there is a hot tub in the courtyard. Rates are $79–$270.

The bargain spots are dormitory digs and rooms in the **Chateau Après Lodge** (649-9372) with room rates of $42–$82, and $20 for a dorm bed. Another choice is **Budget Lodging,** 649-

2526 or (800) 522-7669, with hotel rooms to four-bedroom units for $30 to $900. It also has a hot tub and laundry facilities.

Near the Resort Center you'll find another cluster of hotels and condos. The best is the **Silver King Hotel**, 649-5500 or (800) 331-8652. This condominium hotel is about 100 yards from the lifts and at the hub of the transportation system. Amenities include an indoor/outdoor swimming pool and underground parking. Some units have private hot tubs. Rates: $80–$600.

The **Resort Center Lodge and Inn** is the second choice for luxury. It literally surrounds the base area lifts. Call (800) 824-5331 or 649-0800. Lots of amenities, including spas, health club, pool, steamroom and concierge. Rates for hotel rooms to four-bedroom units: $49–$1,289.

Shadow Ridge is the other top property near the lifts; (800) 451-3031 or 649-4300. It has a sauna, hot tub, laundry and parking. Hotel rooms to three-bedroom condos: $49–$580.

The Snow Flower is 100 feet from the beginner area. Call (800) 852-3101 or 649-6400. There are single-person jetted hot tubs in each unit, outdoor pools and underground parking. Studios to five-bedroom units go for $55–$645.

For more economical condos, try the renovated **Edelweiss Haus** across the street from the lifts and the Silver King Hotel. Call (800) 438-3855 for reservations only or 649-9342 to contact anyone in the hotel. There are heated outdoor pool and hot tub. Rates for hotel rooms to two-bedroom condos are $50–$300.

The final main cluster of hotels serving Park City is just outside downtown. Here try the **Inn at Prospector Square** (800) 453-3812 or 649-7100. This group of condos includes use of its athletic club in the rates, $49–$400. **The Yarrow Hotel** (800) 327-2332 or 649-7000, is considered a good family accommodation. Children under 12 stay free and the hotel sits in the middle of shopping, movies and restaurants. It is on the shuttlebus route, about a five-minute ride from Park City's Main Street. Rates: $89–$389. The 200-room **Olympia Park Hotel**, (800) 234-9003 or 649-2900, with swimming pool and exercise room, has hotel rooms and suites: $49–$399.

The Homestead is a rambling country resort 25 minutes from Park City in the town of Midway. This 109-year-old restored country inn is charming, with cross-country skiing and snowmobiling. This is one of the Great Inns of the Rockies, rated Four Diamond by AAA. Ski packages include breakfast and dinner, seven nights lodging, skierized rental car, five days of downhill skiing at any Utah area listed in this book, two hours of snowmobiling or cross-country skiing with pass and rentals for about $870 per adult, and $475 per child based on double occupancy. Non-package rates are $75–$295 for B&B; suites and condos also are available. Call (800) 327-7220 or 654-1102.

For luxury condos and houses at affordable prices as well as a chance to get some last-minute or off-peak bargains in the entire Park City area, call **Accommodations Unlimited**, (800) 321-4754. The staff is helpful and will offer suggestions for all aspects of your Utah vacation from skiing to après-ski.

Accommodations—Deer Valley

All lodging in Deer Valley is costly. Even in the value season, the least expensive starts at about $190 per night. Accommodations have the same high quality one finds at the resort itself, and much of it is slopeside, so if it's in your budget, book it. If not, stay in Park City. The skiing is a short bus ride away.

Top dog is the **Stein Eriksen Lodge**; (800) 453-1302 or 649-3700. Think of any luxury or service and you will probably find it—heated sidewalks between buildings, fireplaces in the rooms, maids twice a day, fresh terrycloth robes, floor-to-ceiling windows. The lodge put about $1.5 million into renovations last year. Room rates start at $400 a night and one-bedroom suites top out at about $875, except during Christmas.

After Stein's the places to stay on the mountain are the **Stag Lodge** (800) 453-3833 or 649-7444 and the **Goldener Hirsch** (800) 252-3373 or 649-7770, offering the elegance and service of a top Austrian hotel at midmountain in Deer Valley. Rates start at $300 during the regular season.

The **Pinnacle Condominiums** with three- and four-story living rooms are spectacular inside and out. Closer to the lifts—actually ski-in/ski-out properties—are the **Pine Inn** and **La Maçonnerie**. All units have private spas. Rates start at $550.

The most economical Deer Valley condos are the **Snow Park** units, where a one-bedroom without hot tub is $240 in the regular season.

For reservations for these properties and others, call **Deer Valley Lodging**, (800) 453-3833 or 649-4040 or **Deer Valley Central Reservations** at (800) 424-3337 or 649-1000.

Dining—Deer Valley

The best dining is in the Silver Lake part of Deer Valley. To get there in the evenings from Park City if you don't have a car, take the free Park City Transit buses, which run until 10:45 p.m. To make advance dinner reservations from anywhere in the United States, call (800) 424-3337 (424-DEER).

The **Mariposa** at Silver Lake Lodge is the gourmets' top choice. The restaurant is highly rated in many restaurant surveys. Reservations are a must (645-6715).

The **Glitretind Restaurant** in Stein Eriksen Lodge offers meals with a Norwegian flair. This is not the place to come if pinching pennies, but well worth the cost. Entrées range from $19 to $32. Don't expect to leave for less than $100 for two. Reservations required: 649-3700.

Glitretind's all-you-can-eat skier's buffet for $21.95, however, rates as an affordable and unforgettable eating experience. There is a chef cooking made-to-order pasta dishes, a carving table, various salads and cold meats, and delectable desserts. Unless you are more disciplined than we were, forget trying to ski for at least an hour after leaving this banquet.

The Seafood Buffet at Snow Park Lodge, spread out Mondays through Saturdays, gets rave reviews from everyone who has had the chance to sample the fare. Adults pay $38 and children $20, and it's all you can eat. Reservations: 645-6632.

McHenry's in the Silver Lake Lodge serves moderately priced lunches and dinners in a casual atmosphere.

For breakfast, head to the buffet at the **Snow Park Restaurant** and for lunch choose the **Silver Lake Restaurant**. The food is laid out like a magazine illustration, a spectacular presentation. These cafeteria-style restaurants glisten with shiny brass and sparkling glass, and the cooks decked out in kitchen whites complete with toques add another touch of class.

Dining—Park City

There are nearly 70 restaurants in Park City. After sampling scores of them and conferring with knowledgeable locals about the rest, here's our verdict.

For its inventive southwestern cuisine and funky yet quaint atmosphere, the **Barking Frog** is our favorite, with entrées in the $13–$20 range. This excellent restaurant enjoys stellar word-of-mouth advertising, so call for reservations (649-6222).

The other two restaurants that vie for best-in-town honors are **Alex's** on Main Street (649-6644) for a French menu, and **Adolph's** just outside town on the golf course (649-7177) for German and American cuisine. Entrées on both menus average $20 and higher. A bit outside the mainstream is the **Snowed Inn**, which has gourmet food in an elegant old Victorian setting. There are two seatings each night: a four-course meal at 6:30 p.m. and a seven-course dinner at 8:30 p.m. You'll need your own transportation. Reservations required; call 649-6368.

Mileti's on Main Street, 649-8211, serves the town's best Italian food. **Ichiban Sushi** on Main Street, 649-2865, is perhaps unique in the United States, with a Japanese-trained female sushi chef. Even Japanese visitors eat here. **Cisero's** on Main Street (649-5044) serves great Italian food.

The **Grill at the Depot** (649-9108), in the historic train station at the foot of Main Street, uses open grills for thick slabs of meat and wild game.

More recommendations are: **Nacho Mama's** (645-8226; the last four digits spell "TACO") for highly recommended southwestern/ Mexican food; and **Baja Cantina** (649-2252) at the Resort Center and the **Irish Camel** (649-6645) on Main

Street for good drinks and acceptable Tex-Mex food. For very reasonable Tex-Mex in a rowdy atmosphere try **El Cheapo's** at the top of Main Street in the Treasure Mountain Inn (649-0883). **The Eating Establishment** (649-8284) is a locals' cheap-eats favorite, as is the **Park City Pizza Company** (649-1591) on the center of Main Street. **Texas Red's Pit Barbecue** (649-7337) is one of the deals of the century, with 16-ounce T-bone steaks on the menu at $14.95. **The Yarrow** (649-7000) offers a family bonanza with all-you-can-eat prime rib buffets every Friday and Saturday. **The Grub Steak** (649-8060) also gets high marks from families. Finally, the **Riverhorse Café** (649-3536) on Main Street is a can't-miss choice for anyone who enjoys a no-fuss, low-key-elegant atmosphere.

We do on-mountain lunch alerts only when there is a special experience. In the case of Park City, **Mid-Mountain Restaurant** qualifies because of its setting. Reached on Webster Run near the bottom of Pioneer lift, this beautiful building nestled in the trees was formerly a lodge for miners. It was moved from the Angel Station on the gondola and fully restored. Even though it's a cafeteria, we like the history of the place and the touch of recorded classical music played on the expansive deck.

Après-ski/nightlife

Despite rumors of the Utah party blahs, Park City has some of the best nightlife of any ski town.

Immediate après-ski centers are **Steeps** and the **Baja Cantina**, both located in the Resort Center, and downtown at **Cisero's** where the happy hour can get very lively. **The Coyote Grill** in the Resort Center attracts a quieter crowd.

If you're thirsting for something a little different, try the **Wasatch Brew Pub** at the top of Main Street, where you can watch the brewing process even as you reap its yeasty rewards. The owner grew up in Milwaukee, and he makes beer just the way his grandfather taught him.

A hot nightspot is **The Black Pearl,** which features live entertainment nightly. It attracts the occasional celebrity—our spies spotted Madonna and San Antonio Spurs star Dennis Rodman back when they were a twosome.

The Club caters to a fairly young crowd and is a good place for singles. The dance floor upstairs, where the motif is velvet bordello, is a place to see and be seen. **The Alamo** next door is your basic saloon, with pool, loud music and louder conversation. **Cisero's** on Main Street is one of the best spots to meet other singles and dance a bit with a mixed crowd ranging from 20s to 40s. **Steeps** in the Resort Center is another main dancing hub of Park City. Here bands often play and there is plenty of room to dance and a great good-time crowd. The age group is similar to Cisero's. **The Down Under** normally has acoustic guitar. **Adolph's**, with piano music, has been recommended for quieter evenings.

When the 60-year-old **Egyptian Vaudeville Theater** has shows, it makes a nice evening's entertainment.

Child care

The Park City Chamber of Commerce can refer visitors to several child-care facilities or babysitting services. Call (800) 453-1360 or locally, 649-6100.

Other activities

Shopping: For a town the size of Park City, the shopping is rather so-so; nice, but nothing exceptional. Among the exceptions: **Hay Charlie's** on Main Street is an unusual store with Western apparel, and **Park City Antiques, Inc.** is worth a look if you like Old West collectibles. Main Street has interesting **art galleries** with differing collections. Deer Valley has several very upscale boutiques. Just off Interstate 80 at the Park City exit is a **factory outlet** center with 48 stores.

Park City's history is celebrated with a new activity, **Park City Silver Mine Adventure,** which is scheduled to open in fall, 1995. Visitors will be able to tour a miner's house, take an underground tour of an actual silver mine, dig for gemstones and precious metals, and hear about the people who struck it rich. All-inclusive tickets are expected to sell for $12.95 for adults and $9.95 for seniors and children younger than 12. Exhibit-only tickets are $6.95 and $5.50 respectively. Call 649-8011.

Another unusual activity: **Do-it-yourself ski jumping.** Yes, you can fly off the end of a ramp just like the Olympians do (okay, you'll be on a much smaller ramp, but it will feel like the 90-meter jump, let us assure you). The **Utah Winter Sports Park**, built for the 2002 Winter Olympics, gives ski jumping lessons for $20 for adults; $12 for ages 12-17 and $8 for kids 11 and younger (helmets included). A group of ski journalists (we were there) did it last winter—without any après-trips to the hospital. All kidding aside, if skiing has lost some of its thrill, you'll find it here. The park is worth a tour even if you don't jump. It will be the competition site for Olympic freestyle skiing, ski jumping, bobsled and luge. Call 649-5447.

Park City's ski calendar has some unusual events. For the past few years, the **World Cup** ski racing tour has opened here over the Thanksgiving weekend. Deer Valley hosts an annual **Tournament of Champions,** featuring former Olympic or World Cup champions in head-to-head competition each December. The **Sundance Film Festival** is in late January, showcasing new films from around the world.

Many companies offer **sleigh rides, snowmobile tours** and **hot-air balloon trips**. If you need the information in advance, call the Park City Chamber of Commerce for references, (800)

453-1360; when you're in town, check the Yellow Pages or ask your hotel concierge.

Park City Racquet Club (645-8807) has indoor tennis courts, volleyball and aerobic workouts. The **Prospector Athletic Club** has health club facilities; 649-6670.

Park City Visitor's Information Center and Museum is open Monday through Saturday, 10 a.m. to 7 p.m., Sundays noon to 6 p.m. It is packed with history of the Old West and has a self-guided city tour, with background on historical buildings.

Getting there and getting around

Getting there: Park City is 30 miles east of Salt Lake City, by Interstate 80 and Utah 224. The drive from the airport to Park City takes 45 minutes. Ground transportation makes frequent trips from the airport for $32–$36 round-trip. Providers include **Lewis Brothers Stages,** (800) 826-5844 or 649-2256 in Park City, 359-8347 in Salt Lake City; **Park City Transportation,** (800) 637-3803 or 649-8567; **Summit Transportation,** (800) 388-5289 or 649-3292; and **All Resort Express** (800) 457-9457 or 549-3999. If you arrive without reservations, go to the transportation counter at the Salt Lake International Airport and a representative will put you on the next available van. Call 48 hours in advance for Park City-to-airport reservations.

Getting around: To rent or not to rent a car? Our recommendation: if you're staying close to the town center or near a stop on the free bus line, do without. The town bus system has four routes with buses that come by about every 20 minutes from 7:40 a.m. to 12:30 a.m. If you plan to take a side trip to one of the Cottonwood Canyons ski resorts, the airport transportation companies have vans that will take you for about $20 round-trip.

Information/reservations

Park City has no single central reservations number, but these agencies can book just about every aspect of your trip. Ask about special ski packages: **Park City Ski Holidays;** (800) 222-7275; 649-0493. **Deer Valley Central Reservations** (800) 424-3337 (424-DEER); 649-1000.

Information: **Park City Area Chamber of Commerce/Convention and Visitors Bureau,** 1910 Prospector Avenue, P.O. Box 1630, Park City UT 84060; (800) 453-1360 or 649-6100.

All area codes are 801 unless otherwise noted.

Alta, Utah

It's hard to find a skier who is ambivalent about Alta. They either adore this place, tell all their friends and come back year after year, or they decide no thanks, this just ain't my cup of tea.

Alta, you see, is as lovably eccentric as your maiden aunt, the one who still has doilies to protect the upholstery on her overstuffed armchairs and who still listens to old Bing Crosby records on her aging turntable—despite your offer to buy her a CD player with remote control (*and* the Crosby CDs). "The music sounds just fine, dear," she says as she feeds you home-baked cookies and real hot chocolate. "I don't want you to spend all your money on me."

Alta, you see, has resisted installing high-speed chair lifts, building high-rise hotels and throwing away money on slick magazine ads. "The snow skis just fine, dear," Alta seems to say as she spoils you with 500-plus inches of fluffy Utah powder spread over 2,200 acres of terrain. "I don't want you to spend all your money on me."

And you won't. The lift ticket is $25, the rock-bottom lowest for a major ski resort (going by acreage and vertical drop) in North America. If you want more sophisticated facilities, no problem. Head next door to Snowbird—and be ready to pull a few more bills from your wallet.

Alta's low-key attitude is rooted in its history. In half a century of mining, Alta went from obscurity to boom, followed by outrageous scandal when the mines suddenly collapsed in the early 1900s. At a time when glamorous international figures were being courted by the new Sun Valley, Alta was born from the simple desire of Salt Lake residents to have a place where they could ski without having to climb uphill. Beginning in 1939 using its old ore tram, Alta has pulled nearly four generations of skiers up to its ridges. It still bears the original name, Alta Ski Lifts, without the word "resort" anywhere in sight.

Alta Facts
Base elevation: 8,550'; Summit elevation: 10,650'; Vertical drop: 2,100 feet
Number of lifts: 12—2 triple chairs, 6 double chairs, 4 surface lifts
Snowmaking: 25 acres Total acreage: 2,200
Uphill capacity: 9,100 per hour Bed base: 1,136

Alta provides a fine contrast to its neighbor Snowbird, just a mile down the road in Little Cottonwood Canyon. Where Snowbird with its high-occupancy tram and multistory hotel is high-tech, Alta with its serviceable lifts and multitude of mountain inns is homey.

And you probably will forgive Alta for not keeping up with the trends. Of the skiers we know who have been here, the vast majority return or intend to. Must be that no-fuss, home-baked warmth.

Where to ski

Powder is what Alta is all about. Not just because it gets a lot, but because, with its terrain of tree skiing and sheltered gullies, it tends to keep it longer. While most skiers are swishing down groomed runs a couple of days after a storm, the Alta cognoscenti are secretly diving into snow pockets in side canyons and upper elevations.

Alta, like Snowbird, is a what-you-see, you-can-ski resort, with many ways down that aren't named on the trail map. Be individual. Be creative. That's the spirit of Alta.

The ski area has a front and backside, and two base stations. Wildcat Base is the first one you reach. It has basic facilities—ticket office, restrooms, ski patrol. The Albion Base houses the Children's Center, Ski School and retail and rental operations. Albion is where you go to find the beginner slopes, but it has expert terrain at higher elevations. Albion and Wildcat are connected by a long, nearly level, two-way transfer rope tow, the only "lift" of its type we've ever seen. Just grab the rope and let it pull you to the other side.

Uphill from the Wildcat Ticket Office, Wildcat and Collins lifts serve advanced runs on the right side—narrow trails, bump runs, and many glades—with intermediate and more advanced runs on the left. Those to the left are wider, the main intermediate route down being Meadow.

From the left of these two lifts, skiers can access an entirely different ridge, West Rustler, by taking the Germania lift. That means more steep and deep at Eagle's Nest and High Rustler for experts, and intermediate slopes with less intimidating names like Ballroom and Mambo. The line at Germania lift may appear daunting on powder days but rarely averages more than ten minutes, although if there's powder on weekends, it can crank up to twenty.

From the top of Germania Pass the runs down the front side return you to Wildcat base area; runs down the back return you to Albion, or give access to the Sugarloaf and Supreme lifts. Skiers wishing to cross back into the Germania area must do an extensive traverse around the rim of a huge bowl. It has a superb view, and you may be tempted to stop to admire it. Keep going;

the view won't whoosh by. Though the ski area raised the Sugarloaf side 100 feet in 1993, it's still a slow traverse. The only other Albion-to-Wildcat route is at the base on the transfer tow.

From the Albion base station, Sunnyside and Albion lifts are slow riders across gentle terrain, a wide, rolling beginner's playground. At the top of those lifts, intermediates and experts can take Supreme lift to Point Supreme, the 10,650-foot summit, and from there have plenty of steep tree skiing to the left in an area near the boundary called Spiney Ridge. Some sections are known as Piney Glades and White Squaw. It's all known as steep, and tremendously popular with Salt Lake skiers. Up here you can ski all day without ever going the same way twice.

Also midmountain on the Albion side is Sugarloaf lift, which serves expert bowls as far as the eye can see (and good intermediate terrain). Swooping down into a gully to the left of the lift as you descend usually gives you powder pockets. A day or two after a storm, try Devils' Castle, the steeps under the rocks accessible from Sugarloaf.

To follow the sun, start the morning on Sugarloaf, then move to Germania on the front side at midday, and finish on Supreme.

Alta's gate skiing is at the Sunnyside lift and is open Friday and Saturday. The $5 ($7 for unlimited runs) race fee is payable at the race arena.

Mountain rating

Alta is a great place for any level of skier. Experts have powder and steeps. By itself, Alta is an expert's delight, and together with neighbor Snowbird, few other groupings can match it. The major difference is vertical drop—the Snowbird tram opens almost 3,000 feet of continuous expert vertical, versus the maximum expert drop of about 1,000 at Alta.

Intermediates have wonderful slopes here, plus a few very gentle pitches off to one side in the Albion area that don't get groomed—a super place to take your first powder turns. Alta doesn't skimp on grooming—we found the intermediate and beginner runs quite negotiable.

Given the choice between Snowbird and Alta, beginners definitely should start here. Not only are the slopes less intimidating, but so are the skiers (we're talking fashion and attitude here, not ability). The mile-long beginner run serviced by the Albion lift can make a beginner feel like a real skier—and that's what the sport is all about.

Snowboarding

Not permitted. Head over to Snowbird.

Lessons (94/95 prices)

Bearing the name of Alf Engen, the Norwegian ski jumper who came to Utah in 1930, the ski school is recognized within the industry for its contributions to the development of professional ski instruction. More than 100 instructors are quite a sizable squad for a resort this size. **Private lessons** are $55 for an hour, $165 for a morning and $140 for an afternoon, or $275 for all day. Two-hour **group lessons** are $23.

Afternoon workshops focusing on specific skills are called **Bumps Bumps Bumps, Conditions du Jour,** and **Diamond Challenge,** and are $30 for two and a half hours; meet at the blue and white signs below the base of Germania lift.

Lower-level ski lessons meet at the base of the Albion lift, while upper skill levels meet at the base of the Germania lift.

Children's lessons for ages 4–12 are $23 for a two-hour lesson. All-day packages with lunch, four hours of skiing and early dropoff and late pickup are $58 for ability levels 1–2, $75 for levels 3–4, and $80 for levels 5–9.

Child care

Alta's child care center is a state-licensed facility owned and operated by Redwood Pre-School, Inc. (742-3042). It has programs for children aged 3 months to 12 years that include lunch and play and/or on-snow activities. Children's ski lessons are available from the Alta ski school.

All-day infant care by reservation only is $50, $220 for five days. All-day child care with lunch is $35, $150 for five days.

Lift tickets (94/95 prices)

	Adult	Child (Up to 12) Senior (60+)
One day	$25	$25
Three days	$75 ($25/day)	$75 ($25/day)
Five days	$125 ($25/day)	$125 ($25/day)

Yes, we could have skipped the chart in this particular chapter, but we wanted to underscore Alta's sensible approach to pricing: management skips all the discount gimmicks, figures out what it will take to run the place, and charges everyone the same low price. They figure that everyone—adults, children and seniors—occupy one spot on the lifts, so all should be charged the same amount. And just in case you were wondering if a family can still save money here when there is no child discount, a family of four (two adults and two kids between 6 and 12) pays $500 to ski five days at Alta, $540 at Snowbird and $580 at Park City (based on 94/95 prices, and including multi-day discounts).

Half-day tickets are available for $19, and Alta accepts Visa and MasterCard (not the case a few years ago).

Accommodations (94/95 prices)

Something very important to know: as a general rule, Alta's lodges do not accept credit cards, though they do accept personal or travelers checks. Hotels will automatically add a 15 percent service charge, as well as local taxes. Ask whether your room has a private bath—some of them do not.

Rustler Lodge (742-2200, 800-451-5223) is midway between the Albion and Rustler/Wildcat base areas. It has an outdoor pool, saunas and hot tubs. Prices include breakfast and dinner, per person double occupancy, starting at $99 per night for a room without private bath, $125 and $145 for rooms with bath.

Alta Peruvian (800-453-8488 reservations only; 742-3000) has similar amenities, features movies each night, and is a short walk from the Wildcat base (or you can take the lodge's free shuttle). The rates include breakfast, lunch, dinner and lift ticket. (Food's great, by the way.) Dorm rooms are $80; double rooms with private bath range from $112 to $145 (per person, double occupancy). One- or two-bedroom suites also are available, as are multiday discounts. No credit cards accepted; personal or travelers checks are fine, as is cash.

The Alta Lodge (800-707-2582, reservations only; 742-3500) is a 57-room mountain inn with saunas, hot tubs, and several common areas, including a library. Skiers grab a rope tow at the end of the day to get back up a small hill to the lodge. Breakfast and dinner are included in the price, and the food is excellent. Daily room rates (based on double occupancy) are $205 for a room with a sink; $225 for a room with private bath. Single-occupancy and dorm rates are available; call for those. No credit cards; use personal or travelers checks, or greenbacks.

Goldminer's Daughter (742-2300 or 800-453-4573 for reservations only), named after a huge mining claim, is closest to the Wildcat lift. You can step out your door into the lift line, and drop by your room between runs for a hat or neck gaiter. All rooms have private bath. Per-person double occupancy rates with breakfast and dinner are $115 to $129. Dorm rooms are $79.

Snow Pine Lodge (742-2000) is Alta's oldest and smallest. It was extensively renovated a few years ago, and has an outdoor hot tub, Scandinavian sauna and a warm and homey atmosphere. Rates (per person, double occupancy) are $108-$118 for a room with private bath, $80-$97 for a shared-bath room, and $72 for a bed in the men's or women's dorm.

Two large condominiums, **Hellgate** (742-2020) and **Blackjack** (742-3200) are located between Alta and Snowbird, with Blackjack better situated for skiing between the two resorts and therefore slightly higher, although Hellgate has van service to the ski areas. Studios range from $125 to $155; one-bedrooms sleeping four, $125 to $245; two-bedrooms sleeping six, $240 to $300; three-bedrooms, $300 to $370. There is no service charge.

Dining

At Alta you eat in your condo or your lodge, and if you're headed for a condo, stop in Salt Lake for groceries.

On the slopes, **Chic's Place** is a fine and unpretentious restaurant with a good view.

Après-ski/nightlife

Bring your own. There's nothing going on but what visitors cook up—either in their condo or the lodge's common rooms. If a little bit of nightlife is all you need, head to Snowbird. But if your ski vacation is not complete without a vigorous night of dancing, stay in Salt Lake City and take the ski bus up here (see the Salt Lake City chapter for details).

Other activities

Shopping: A few shops in the Little Cottonwood Canyon area have local handicrafts, artwork and books, but this isn't why skiers come here. You can always take a bus down to Salt Lake City for a day of heavy-duty shopping.

Heliskiing is available in Little Cottonwood Canyon from Wasatch Powder Birds, 742-2800.

Getting there and getting around

Getting there: Salt Lake City is a major airline hub, so flights are numerous from every corner of the continent. Amtrak's California Zephyr and Desert Wind also stop here.

Alta is 25 miles southeast of Salt Lake City in Little Cottonwood Canyon on State Highway 210. Driving time from the city or the airport is one hour, with the most direct route from the airport east on I-80, south on I-215, Exit 6 to Wasatch Blvd., then follow the signs to Alta and Snowbird.

Getting around: Ground transportation from the airport or the city is frequent and plentiful. If you fly in, don't bother renting a car. Most of Alta's lodges have shuttles to get you to the slopes or to visit neighboring restaurants. If you are staying in Salt Lake City, take the Utah Transit Authority bus or a Lewis Brothers SkiExpress van to Alta. (See Salt Lake City chapter).

Bus service links Alta and Snowbird for $1.

Information/reservations

The **Alta Reservations Service** is the central reservations agent for Alta; call 942-0404, or call the individual lodges' 800 numbers if you've decided where to stay. The agency can also arrange rental cars and rooms in Salt Lake City. **Alta Ski Lifts** is at 742-3333. Recorded **snow report** is 572-3939.

All area codes are 801 unless otherwise noted.

Snowbird, Utah

Deep powder with fast ascents and descents are the hallmarks of Snowbird. If you're a powder devotee, Snowbird is Mecca: every powder skier should make at least one pilgrimage. An eight-minute tram ride takes you to the summit to experience what has earned Snowbird its reputation as the top powder-skiing resort. (You can ski Snowbird's entire 3,100-foot vertical drop in one continuous, thigh-burning run, too.) Nearby ski areas get nearly as much snow (500-plus inches) and it is equally dry, but frequent visitors here would probably bet their North Face powder suits that Snowbird's snow is a droplet or two drier and a flake or three deeper. We've heard Canadian heli-skiing guides measure their powder by Snowbird standards, as in, "Ayuh, it's good, but it's not quite Snowbird powder." It's hard to imagine a more flattering comparison.

Snowbird's look and atmosphere are quite distinctive among American ski resorts. There is no town here, just a shopping center, a skyscraper hotel and a couple of condo complexes. Facilities are sleek and high-tech.

Where to ski

To get the lay of the land at Snowbird, understand first the function of the tram. Mounting one lower peak, hanging across a cirque and rising to the 11,000-foot summit, it brings 125 skiers at a time to Hidden Peak, unseen from the base lodge. On powder days, when the first tram arrives, there's a dash for the slopes. Skiers hurl their equipment and then themselves over the railings to make the first tracks. After this thrill, things calm down a bit and decisions can be made whether to get equipment on quickly and be the first of the 125-person group down The Cirque or wait a bit, let others dash, and then go where they don't.

The choices are to drop under the tram into Peruvian Gulch, with intermediate, advanced and expert routes down, or to head left into the Little Cloud area.

Snowbird Facts
Base elevation: 7,900'; **Summit elevation:** 11,000'; **Vertical drop:** 3,100 feet
Number of lifts: 8–1 aerial tram, 7 double chairs **Snowmaking:** Minimal
Total acreage: 2,000 **Uphill capacity:** 9,000 per hour **Bed base:** 1,800+

Most tram riders opt for Peruvian. Intermediates peel off the upper ridge at Chip's Run, often marked with large orange balls to indicate the easiest way down. Chip's offers a few expert options en route. Experts tackle The Cirque, a plunge that drops into almost 3,000 vertical feet of expert slopes. You can choose a run about as steep as you want, some with chutes that hold only powder enough to slow your virtual freefall. Anyone who has dropped down Upper Silver Fox, Great Scott or Upper Cirque deserves to be treated with reverence—they're using up the extra lives they were blessed with.

From the tram ridge, Primrose Path is an unrelenting black diamond, normally the choice of those who think twice about tiptoeing around The Cirque. Here at Snowbird what you can see, you can ski. So pick your own way.

Should you decide to drop over to the Little Cloud side of Hidden Peak, the skiing is somewhat tamer—tamer by Snowbird standards. It's a wide scoop carved out of the side of the mountain, with cliffs above and swoops below. Road To Provo, the highest black run, skirts the top of the bowl and then drops down a third of the resort's distance to Little Cloud lift, which goes back to the top, or halfway down to the Mid Gad Restaurant. Regulator Johnson charts a steeper, more direct route from the summit to either destination.

Five lifts stretch out of Gad Valley. Wilbere is short and primarily serves beginners and intermediates. Mid Gad and Gad I lifts rise higher to serve wide intermediate slopes. One run is called Big Emma which, though very wide and rated green, will give beginners a good test, as its pitch might rate it blue at any other area. You get more vertical for your ride on Gad I and can access some mid-mountain expert runs.

A good starter for upper intermediates is Bassackwards, or they can stretch themselves on a black run called Carbonate, where they'll get the feel of a steeper, but not terrifying, pitch. The expert terrain is up higher at Gad II lift, which opens narrower trails through the trees and over megabumps (it also is off-limits to snowboarders). Gadzooks, Tiger Tail, Black Forest and Organ Grinder are equal challenges. Three groomed intermediate runs start at the top of Gad II, Bassackwards, Election and Bananas.

Never-evers and unconfident beginners should stay on Chickadee until they've learned a modicum of control. This slope is devoted to first-timers and small children and located in back of the Cliff Lodge.

A coin-operated race course is between Wilbere and Mid Gad lifts, accessible from either. Several runs are designated as Family Ski Zones and are marked on the trail map with dotted lines.

Note: We recommend that first-time visitors explore the mountain with the Host and Hostess Program, free introductory tours of the mountain that take skiers to the part best suited to their abilities. Tours meet on the plaza level of the Snowbird Center and leave daily at 9 a.m., 10 a.m. and 1 p.m. The hosts sort out the groups by skill level and then move to appropriate terrain, so faster skiers aren't held back and slower skiers aren't terrified. It's also a great way to meet people.

If you want to avoid crowds, start at 9 a.m. and ski Gad II and Little Cloud until 11. Then for the next hour and a half, work the Gad Valley chairs. Between 12:30 and 1:30 the lines lighten up and you can go back to the top. Remember, however, that even a 20-minute wait for the tram is equivalent to two lifts; you get more skiing for your wait. If you want to ski in the sun, the Gad Valley lifts are more protected and get morning sun. In the afternoon, head up to Little Cloud.

Mountain rating

Experts, you have arrived. A healthy half of Snowbird terrain is for you. These are not public-relations black diamonds, either—they are tough. You will leave exhilarated or frustrated, depending on whether you attacked them or they attacked you.

Intermediates, expect to be pushed. Owner Dick Bass, who has climbed the highest mountain on every continent, affirms, "What we gain too easily, we esteem too lightly." Let that be your rallying cry. You will improve, a phenomenon you may not recognize until you go back to ski those home slopes you thought were a challenge. Intermediates will be comfortable on both blues and greens here. If Snowbird exhausts you or you're here for a week and know all the routes in your comfort zone by heart, go next door to Alta, which has more mellow intermediate trails.

Beginners, you can learn here, but it will be a challenge. Chickadee is gentle enough, but it's a big jump after that. This mountain is wonderful, but isn't built for beginners. We want you to ski a second time, so go to Alta or Solitude for your baptism.

Snowboarding

Snowboarding is permitted on most of the mountain. The one place it can't be done is Gad II. A snowboard park has been added off the Little Cloud chair lift. Snowbird has a few flat stretches, which snowboarders hate because they must unbuckle to push themselves across; ask a mountain host how to avoid them. Instruction and rentals are available.

Lessons (94/95 prices)

Adult **group lessons** (called Super Class) are $55 for all day; $45 for afternoon classes for never-evers to low intermediates.

Private lessons in skiing, telemarking or snowboarding are $65 per hour ($5 between 9 and 10 a.m.); two to five people can split a $90 charge. A three-hour lesson is $180; $240 for two to five skiers.

Snowbird has several **special workshops**. The **Mountain Experience** allows skiers of advanced or expert level to join a Snowbird guide and launch an assault on the entire mountain for $65 for one day, $290 for five days. **Silver Wings** presents skiers over 50 with the opportunity to ski with people of the same ability and age group for $55 a day, $144 for three days, $240 for five days. Other clinics teach style, bump skiing, racing and snowboarding. A four-day women's seminar also is offered several times a season for $295, which covers everything except lifts and lodging.

For **children**, the **Chickadee Program** has 90-minute lessons for age 3–4 beginners for $45. Two children per instructor means this is a very popular program, so sign up in advance. **Super Class** is for children and teens aged 5 to 15. A full-day Super Class can be arranged through Camp Snowbird for $65, which includes lunch. Half days are also available.

Snowbird Ski School has three one-stop registration locations for ski school and purchasing lift tickets. (Tickets are not included in the lesson price, but the Chickadee chair for never-evers and children does not require tickets.) The offices are on Level 1 of the Cliff Lodge, the Plaza Deck of the Snowbird Center and the Alpine Room, Level 2 of the Snowbird Center. For more information or reservations, call 742-2222, ext. 5170.

Child care

Snowbird offers its lodge guests licensed day care at the **Camp Snowbird Children's Center** at the Cliff Lodge. Charges for the 94/95 season were $50 a day, with lunch, for ages 6 weeks to 2 years; $48 for ages 2 and 3, and $36 for ages 4–12. Multi-day discounts are available. Babysitting is $9 an hour, a little more for an additional child.

Reservations are required. Call the Children's Center at 742-2222, ext. 5026, or you can make reservations when you book your vacation at (800) 453-3000.

Lift tickets (94/95 prices)

	Adult	Child (6–12) Senior (62–69)
One day	$40	$26
Three days	$99 ($35/day)	$66 ($21/day)
Five days	$165 ($35/day)	$110 ($21/day)

These are the prices with tram access. For chairs only, the one-day prices are $33 and $21 respectively.

Children under 12 staying at Snowbird ski free when an accompanying adult purchases a lift ticket. Seniors 70+ ski free.

Accommodations (94/95 prices)

All lodging at Snowbird is within walking distance of the base lifts. Call (800) 453-3000 or (801) 742-2222. Winter season is mid-December through March; value season is late November through mid-December and April. Additional accommodations, accessible by shuttlebus, are plentiful in Salt Lake City.

The Cliff Lodge spreads like eagle's wings at the base of Snowbird. Inside, there's an 11-story atrium, a renowned spa, and a glassed-in rooftop with a heated pool that overlooks the slopes. The views are spectacular, the service extraordinary, the rooms comfortable—and so accessible to the slopes.

The 27,000-square-foot **Cliff Spa**, on the top floor of the hotel, has a wide variety of treatments for body, face, hair and nails, as well as a full exercise facility. Packages are offered, or services can be booked individually. Call 742-2222, ext. 5900 for spa, ext. 5960 for the salon.

Rooms with picture windows opening from the shower into the sleeping area add a touch of whimsy as well as a view. Room rates are $189 a night in winter season, and $110 in value season. One- and two-bedroom suites cost $509 and $799 a night in peak season or $270 and $425 in value season. Children under 12 stay and ski free with adults.

The lodge has gender-segregated dorm rooms with four single beds and lockable closets for each occupant. A lounge has a TV, video games, ping-pong and pool tables. Dormitory space costs $27–$57 a night, depending on the season.

The Lodge at Snowbird, **The Inn**, and **The Iron Blosam** are three condominium complexes with similar layouts. They are not as elegant as the Cliff Lodge, but are well maintained, roomy and comfortable. Amenities include outdoor swimming pools, indoor hot tubs and saunas. Rates are $194 a night for an efficiency, $363 for a one-bedroom; and $532 for one-bedroom with loft. Value season rates are $99, $187 and $275.

Dining

On the mountain, **Peak Express** at the top of the tram serves premium coffees, espresso and light snacks. The **Mid-Gad Restaurant** has a basic lunch menu of burgers, pizza, etc.

The Aerie on top of the Cliff Lodge is the most elegant for exquisite dining and dancing. The **Atrium** at lobby level serves cocktails and hefty buffet breakfasts and lunches. **The Mexican Keyhole**, also in the Lodge, offers Mexican and Southwestern fare. At the Iron Blosam Lodge, **Wildflower Ristorante & Lounge** serves outstanding Northern Italian cuisine. **The Lodge Club** in the Lodge at Snowbird has a good light dinner.

Other restaurants are in the base facility, Snowbird Center. **The Steak Pit** serves steak and seafood. There's usually a wait, but it's worth it. **The Forklift** is a breakfast and lunch spot with easy access to the slopes yet with a carpeted restaurant atmosphere. For cafeteria service, **The Rendezvous** has the usual, plus a well-stocked salad island. It also serves breakfast.

Pier 49 San Francisco Sourdough Pizza has pizza with lots of toppings, and **Birdfeeder** has gourmet coffees and light snacks.

Après-ski/nightlife

Snowbird's nightlife is on the very quiet side. For the liveliest après-ski, try **Tram Club**, located on the bottom floor of the Snowbird Center, with space-age decor and a picture-window view of the tram's huge operating gears. The **Wildflower Lounge** is mellow. In the evening, **The Aerie** has a bar with quiet piano music. At night, **Tram Club** is your best bet for dancing.

Surprisingly, Snowbird has its own microbrew beer. It's labled, creatively, Snowbird Beer. I'd vote for Cirque Chaser, Snowbird Suds, Peruvian Pale, Tram Tamer or Aerie Ale

Remember: you are in Utah, so the nightspots are "private clubs" that charge a $5 two-week membership fee. One card is valid for all the clubs at the Cliff Lodge and covers six people. Also, a warning: the only way to walk between the Cliff Lodge and Snowbird Center is across the Chickadee beginner slope. During the day you dodge skiers and snowboarders; at night it can be slippery. Pack your deep-tread après-ski boots or ride the Alta-Snowbird shuttle ($1 charge), which stops at both locations. This is something we wish Snowbird would remedy: it's a royal pain.

Other activities

Snowbird is not a good place for non-skiers unless they will spend considerable time at the Cliff Spa (see Accommodations). The only other diversion is **shopping**, and a champion browser will finish off the dozen or so shops in half a day.

Little Cottonwood Canyon has no cross-country skiing or snowmobiling, but spectacular **helicopter skiing** is available from Wasatch Powderbird Guides; 742-2222, ext. 4190.

Getting there and getting around

Getting there: Salt Lake City is a major airline hub, so flights are numerous. Amtrak's California Zephyr and Desert Wind lines also stop here (at 4 a.m., but the fare is cheap).

Snowbird is 25 miles southeast of Salt Lake City in Little Cottonwood Canyon. Driving time from the city or the airport is one hour, with the most direct route from the airport east on I-80, south on I-215, Exit 6 to Wasatch Blvd., then follow the signs.

Getting around: Ground transportation from the airport or the city is marvelous. If you fly in, don't bother renting a car—Snowbird is entirely walkable. If you plan to ski a lot of other Utah areas, stay in Salt Lake City (see Salt Lake City chapter).

Bus service links Alta and Snowbird for $1.

Information/reservations

Central reservations number is (800) 453-3000. The resort address is Snowbird Ski and Summer Resort, PO Box 929000, Snowbird UT 84092-9000; 742-2222. Area code is 801.

Big Cottonwood Canyon, Utah

Solitude Ski Resort and Brighton Ski Resort

Of any 10 skiers waiting at a bus stop in downtown Salt Lake City for the Utah Transit Authority ski express, it's a sure bet that seven will board the Snowbird/Alta bus to Little Cottonwood Canyon. The other three will board the Brighton/Solitude bus to Big Cottonwood Canyon.

If you're one of the three, be prepared for a silent judgment of your skiing ability by the Snowbird/Alta seven.

One will start the waiting-for-the-bus small talk. "Where are you headed?" he'll ask with a jaunty smile, perhaps with the thought that his group may invite you along on their search for the Steep and Deep.

"Solitude," you answer with an equally jaunty smile.

Your questioner's smile fades as his eyes take in your clothing, how far above your head your skis extend, and whether there is a tell-tale rental-shop sticker at the binding. He's too polite to ask, "If you can't handle Snowbird or Alta, then what are you doing on *those* skis?"

Big Cottonwood Canyon's reputation as the place where the locals learn to ski has more to do with prices than terrain. Solitude's ticket is $29 and Brighton's is $28.

Neither area is as vast as the ski areas in the neighboring canyon. But to dismiss these two areas as a playground where beginners whet their appetites for the real thing is to woefully underestimate the terrain. Solitude's Honeycomb Canyon has slopes that will bring out the adrenaline in the best of skiers. Brighton's expert offerings are fewer, but available.

Solitude Ski Resort

Solitude steadily has made improvements, such as a complete and award-winning re-design of the trail and lift system and an on-mountain restaurant, that should bring it into the Utah big leagues very soon. Next on the list is a new base village, including slopeside condominiums and hotel rooms.

Solitude's lift layout has a logical progression from beginner to expert areas. Beginners start on the Link chair, a slow-moving lift that serves a nearly flat, very wide, isolated run, Easy Street.

Solitude Facts

Base elevation: 7,988'; **Summit elevation:** 10,035'; **Vertical drop:** 2,047 feet
Number of lifts: 7—1 quad superchair, 2 triple chairs, 4 double chairs
Snowmaking: 80 acres **Skiable acreage:** 1,200
Uphill capacity: 10,750 per hour **Bed base:** 12,000 in Salt Lake City, plus 18 condo units scheduled for completion December 1995

When skiers conquer Link, the next step is the Moonbeam II chair, where Little Dollie, Pokey Pine and Same Street will take them back down gently. Next is either the Apex or Sunrise chair, where one green trail is surrounded by lots of blue.

The next level is the Powderhorn or Eagle Express chairs, where there are no green runs, just blue with a few black. If you can handle that, then you're ready for the Summit chair. From the top of the Summit chair, you can go one of three ways.

The first takes you back down to the Summit chair on upper intermediate runs like Dynamite and Liberty. Eventually you'll meet the runs off the Sunrise chair, which head back to the base.

Way Number Two heads toward Brighton on the intermediate SolBright trail. You can go all the way over to Brighton, or head down Corner Chute, a cleared but steep black-diamond run clearly visible from the Summit chair; you might also go into Headwall Forest, where you pick your own line through the trees, or jump into a couple of long steep narrow chutes.

The third option will take you into Honeycomb Canyon, a wonderful playground for advanced intermediates to experts. Woodlawn is a marked run that follows the canyon floor. On the map it's a blue line, a black line overlapping it. Check the grooming report before you head in: when groomed, the Woodlawn is a great advanced-intermediate run—otherwise, it's expert all the way, with some gigantic mogul fields and a short but extremely steep section that looks like it might be a small waterfall in the summer.

The canyon sides are an expert's delight. From the top, traverse until you find a line you like, then go for it. Honeycomb Canyon also can be reached from the Eagle Ridge run in the main part of the ski area, but this entry is strictly double-diamond through trees.

Mountain rating

Solitude is one of the few ski areas in the United States that has excellent terrain for all skier levels.

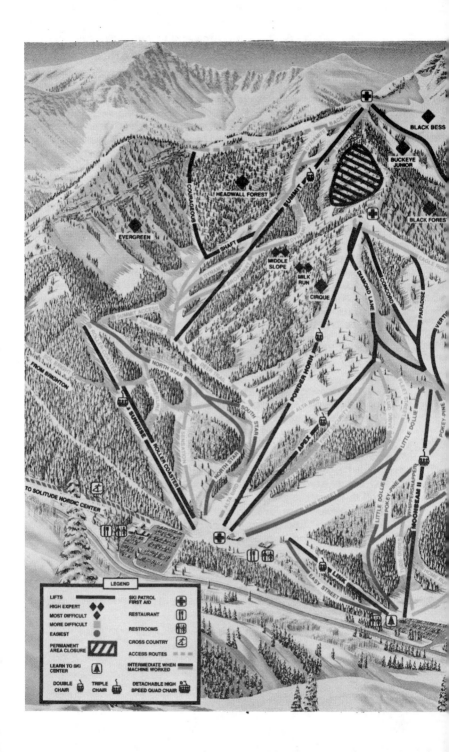

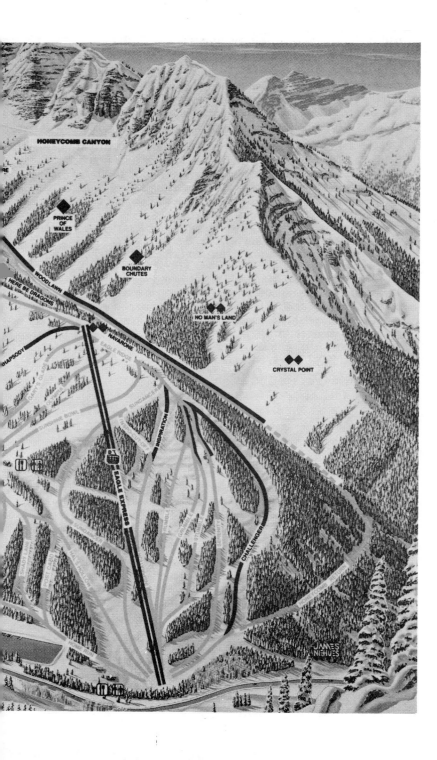

Snowboarding

Snowboarders are welcome Mondays through Thursdays, anywhere on the mountain; other days, it's skiers only. Solitude has no special snowboard facilities, such as a park or halfpipe.

Cross-country (94/95 prices)

Located at 8,700 feet between Solitude and Brighton, the Solitude Nordic Center's Silver Lake Day Lodge is a spectacular setting for cross-country skiing or snowshoeing. It has 20 km. of prepared trails for both classic and skating styles, plus ski and snowshoe rentals, lessons, light snacks and guided backcountry tours.

Trail passes are $8 for those aged 11 to 64, and free for those older or younger. A half-day pass is $6.

A very popular program is the Solitude Yurt. You ski to a yurt, a round tent-like building native to Central Asia. There you have a gourmet meal and ski back (it's a beginner trail both ways). Reservations are a must for this, and don't be too disappointed if you can't get in. Salt Lake City residents really enjoy it and hog many of the available spaces. The cost is $50 per person, but no children younger than 8 are allowed. Call 534-1400 for reservations. For this or other information about the Nordic Center, call (800) 748-4754, ext. 5774.

Lift tickets (95/96 prices)

	Adult	Junior (11–13) Senior (60–69)
One day	$32	$23
2 of 3 days	$56 ($28/day)	$46 ($23/day)
3 of 5 days	$84 ($28/day)	$69 ($23/day)

Two children 10 and younger ski free with a paying adult, while seniors 70 and older ski free. A beginner-lift ticket is $16, and a Big Cottonwood Canyon interconnect ticket, valid at Solitude and neighboring Brighton is also available.

Lessons (94/95 prices)

A **beginner package** including rentals, lift ticket and a lesson is $40. **Group lessons** are $40 for two and a half hours, but offered only in the afternoons. All-day lessons starting at 10:15 a.m. are $50. **Private instruction** is $60 per hour for 1-3 persons; $80 for 4-6 persons.

The Moonbeam Learning Center and Ski Academy is for **children** 4 to 12 years old. A full-day lesson with lunch is $55; a half-day without lunch is $35.

The school also offers **special workshops** for women, snowboarding, Nordic and racing at various times. Call for details, (800) 748-4754, ext. 5730.

Brighton Ski Resort

Most of the cabins you'll see in Big Cottonwood Canyon have been in Utah families for generations. Families came here to rough it on winter holidays and Brighton is where they came to

---

Brighton Ski Resort Facts
Base elevation: *8,755';* **Summit elevation:** *10,500';* **Vertical drop:** *1,745 feet*
Number of lifts: *7–2 quad superchairs; 2 triple chairs, 3 double chairs*
Snowmaking: *25 percent* **Total acreage:** *850*
Uphill capacity: *11,000 per hour* **Ski area bed base:** *12,000 in Salt Lake City*

---

ski. Brighton has retained that hardy pioneer atmosphere, even though recent improvements, such as two high-speed quad chairs and a new base lodge, have brought it into the modern ski world. Despite those high-priced improvements, Brighton's $28 per day lift ticket is the second-lowest in Utah—just three dollars more than Alta (which has no speedy lifts).

Good beginner runs descend from the Majestic chair, and from the Snake Creek chair, which goes to the top of the mountain. Beginners should keep an eye out so they don't get onto an intermediate trail: greens and blues do a lot of intertwining here.

Intermediates have the run of practically the whole area. The Snake Creek chair is a little less crowded than the Crest Express high-speed quad and the Majestic chairs. On this side of the area you'll find heavily wooded, fairly narrow runs. On the other side of the parking lot is the Millicent Chair and its wide-open terrain underneath. It's a little steeper over here, but with fewer trees.

Experts should try a short but heart-stopping run called Hard Coin off the Snake Creek chair. The trees are so thick you can hardly pick a line, but it's a marked trail. The Millicent side of the ski area is steeper and has some nice terrain.

Intermediates and advanced skiers also have an area served by the Great Western chair, Brighton's second high-speed quad. The longest run, Elk Park Ridge, is an intermediate cruiser that descends 1,745 vertical feet.

Mountain rating

Good for beginners and intermediates, and getting better for advanced and expert skiing, although not quite up to the level of the other Cottonwood Canyons resorts.

Snowboarding

O.K. everywhere. Rentals and lessons are available. Brighton has two halfpipes and a snowboard park. Because not all Utah resorts allow snowboards, this is a very popular spot with boarders.

Lift tickets (94/95 prices)

Skiers aged 11 to 69 ski for $28. Ages 10 and younger ski free, two children per paying adult with no restrictions or blackout dates. Skiers 70 and older ski free. Brighton does not sell multiday tickets, but half-day tickets are available. A beginner lift pass, good on two lifts, is $20.

Brighton also has about 175 acres of beginner and intermediate night skiing every day except Sunday.

Lessons (94/95 prices)

A **beginner package** including rentals, beginner lift ticket and a lesson is $30. **Group lessons** are $18, and lessons are offered at night, too. **Private instruction** is $45 per hour, with each additional person $20. (Parent and child together is $50.)

Kinderski is for **children** 4 to 7 years old. Lessons are one hour and 45 minutes, and cost $21 without equipment, $29 with. A full day with lunch is $55.

Child care

Neither area has child care.

Accommodations

Most skiers stay in Salt Lake City (see that chapter). The **Brighton Lodge** is a small, cozy lodge at the base of the lifts with heated outdoor pool, Jacuzzi and bar. Rates are $75 per night for a room, $99 for a suite and $45 for an economy hostel. Call (800) 873-5512 or (801) 532-4731.

Das Alpen Haus (649-0565) is a charming B&B near the foot of Brighton. Four suites are each named after a Swiss ski resort, and the atmosphere is decidedly Swiss Alpine. Prices range from $110 to $180 for two.

Getting there and getting around

Getting there: Solitude and Brighton are about 23 miles southeast of Salt Lake City in Big Cottonwood Canyon on State Highway 190. The most direct route from the airport is east on I-80, south on I-215, Exit 6 to Wasatch Blvd., then follow the signs to Solitude and Brighton.

Salt Lake City is a major transportation hub, so flights are numerous and Amtrak also serves the city.

Getting around: The Utah Transit Authority has excellent inexpensive bus service from downtown Salt Lake City hotels. If you stay at one of the Brighton lodges, you'll need a car for evening. Dining options in the canyon are slim, so your best bet will be to drive into Salt Lake City.

Information

Solitude, Big Cottonwood Canyon, Box 21350, Salt Lake City, UT 84121 (801-534-1400; sales office 800-748-4754.)

Brighton Ski Resort, Brighton, UT 84121 (800-873-5512 outside Utah, 801-532-4731 in the state).

The local area code is 801.

Schweitzer Mountain Resort Idaho

Owner Bobbie Huguenin predicts Schweitzer will someday be known as the Nordstrom of ski areas' because of its great product and customer service. It's a worthy goal for this 30-year-old "overnight sensation" of destination ski areas. That goal already is getting recognition: readers of *Snow Country* magazine rated Schweitzer third in customer service among Northern Rocky Mountain resorts behind heavyweights Deer Valley and Sun Valley. The magazine also calls Schweitzer "the resort with the greatest potential.".

But even with all the positive press Schweitzer has had in recent years, it's still very uncrowded. One skier per acre (2,350) is a good-sized crowd here. Its acreage is second largest in Idaho (Bogus Basin is slightly larger), and its vertical drop of 2,406 feet is second only to Sun Valley's 3,400.

Schweitzer also has big plans for the future. Right now, the resort has only one slopeside hotel and some condos in the village, but a European-style village with shops, restaurants and lodging is planned for the near future. Many visitors stay in Sandpoint, 11 miles away on the shore of beautiful Lake Pend Oreille. This is the sort of place that people visit and then try to figure a way to move there. The town reportedly has more real-estate agents per capita than the national average, and a steady stream of building permits being filed.

Where to ski

Compared to Rocky Mountain resorts, Schweitzer's elevation (6,400 feet) is not high, but it gets plenty of snow from its position in the Selkirks. Sometimes the snow is dry and fluffy when the storms come from the north, but more often it is wet and dense. It's drier than the Cascade Concrete that falls on Washington

---

Schweitzer Facts
Base elevation: 3,994' **Summit elevation:** 6,400'
Vertical drop: 2,406 feet **Number and types of lifts:** 6—1 quad superchair, 5 double chairs **Acreage:** 2,350 skiable acres **Snowmaking:** On beginner runs only
Uphill capacity: 7,092 skiers per hour
Bed Base: 2,762 pillows at base, 5,200 in Sandpoint

and Oregon areas, but still wet enough to have earned the local term, Panhandle Premix. The views are outstanding. From the top of Schweitzer, skiers can look east into Montana's Cabinet Range and north to the Canadian Selkirks. The view of big Lake Pend Oreille is memorable.

Fog and/or clouds can be a problem at any Northwest ski area, especially one close to a body of water like Lake Pend Oreille. If the day's ski report says, "Fog levels moving up and down," believe it.

Schweitzer's runs and chutes are steepest at the top of its two broad ski bowls, North and South. The bowls are separated by the Great Divide run, a long wide ridge that gives you a continuous option to head down into either bowl.

Chutes await advanced skiers in the South Bowl, reached by either Chair 1 or The Great Escape Quad. There are so many they're lettered A Chute, B Chute, rather than named. Upper Stiles and the adjacent Headwall Chutes are gonzo favorites.

There is some double-black skiing from the rim of South Bowl, but most experts will head up the Great Escape and turn right to North Bowl. Patient trekkers will be rewarded by the Siberia Chutes.

Intermediates can wind their way down from the South Bowl summit, but are advised to unload midway on the Snow Ghost chair heading toward the summit of North Bowl. The runs under the Timber Cruiser chair are a favorite for this ability level. This is where skiers will find the resort's newest blue-square run, Cathedral Aisle. Fans of Zip Down should be pleased. It runs outside the old Zip Down boundary and is a fair bit longer.

Advancing beginners won't be able to get to the top, but can get a view by unloading midway up Chair One and heading down Gypsy.

The Enchanted Forest and Happy Trails are perfect for children. Both run the length of the Musical Chairs Chair, which goes right by the windows of the 40,000-square-foot Headquarters Day Lodge. The Enchanted Forest, with kid-high, widely-spaced mounds that children can go over or around, is barred to adults and jealous snowboarders.

Night skiing, until 8 p.m. Thursday through Saturday, takes place below Chair 1's midway and below the lodge on Happy Trails. Night skiing is free with a day lift ticket.

Mountain rating

Schweitzer offers a lot for most skiing levels, especially intermediate to expert. It also has a wonderful learning area, served by a separate chair and completely isolated from other traffic. Better yet it is below the base area, so that never-evers can start out skiing, rather than sidestepping up the hill or riding a lift.

Cross-country

The mountain maintains 8 km. of free Nordic trails that leave directly from the village base area; beginners shouldn't attempt them, however. Schweitzer rents cross-country gear and snowshoes.

Snowboarding

Snowboarders have been welcomed by Schweitzer since the sport began. A youth club, the Schweitzer Stormriders Club, works with adults to develop a racing team.

Boarders can reach the Schweitzer halfpipe by unloading at Chair 1's Midway station, and riding down Midway to Jam Session, below the NASTAR course. Lessons and rentals are available.

Lessons (94/95 prices)

Schweitzer offers lessons for all levels of snowboarders, Alpine skiers, telemarkers and cross-country skiers. **Group lessons** cost $18, morning or afternoon. **Private lessons** cost $50 per hour ($40 per hour at 9 a.m.).

Children's lessons are $45 for ages 7-11 and $40 for ages 5-6. This is a full day program that includes lunch, lessons and lift ticket. Ages 3 1/2 to 6 can opt for half day of child care and an afternoon lesson for $45.

Special programs include workshops for women and technique clinics that cater to the day's snow conditions.

Child care (94/95 prices)

Kinder Kamp child care offers nursery and day camp starting at age 3 months. For children still in diapers, the costs are $35 a full day, $23 for half day. Out of diapers it's $27 and $19 respectively. Lunch is $5 extra.

Lift tickets

	Adult	Student (7–12)
One day (95/96)	$34	$20
Three days (94/95)	$90 ($30/day)	$69 ($23/day)
Five days (94/95)	$135 ($27/day)	$100 ($20/day)

Students at the upper end of the 7–12 age range should bring student ID. Seniors 65 and older ski for $25 ($63 for three days and $90 for five), and children 6 and younger ski free. In many of the lodging packages, children 12 and under stay and ski free.

Night skiing, which starts at 3 p.m., is $15 for adults and $10 for students and seniors, but is free with a day ticket.

Schweitzer has a snow check program, where a customer can return a lift ticket within one hour of purchase and get a coupon good for another day. Any reason is accepted: one couple complained they couldn't see the Lake Pend Orielle. The skiing was fine, but the lake was fogged in. They got their snow checks.

Accommodations

At the ski area: **The Green Gables Lodge** (800-831-8810) has 82 rooms, 36 with kitchenettes and eight with Jacuzzis. A new pool with three hot tubs and a heated deck and cabana was set for completion in summer 1995. Children 12 and under stay free with their parents, and ski free with a minimum four-night package. Lodging-for-two packages start at $139 per night.

About 50 condos are also for rent at the ski area.

In Sandpoint: Lodging here is inexpensive (many rooms less than $100 a night) and fairly basic, ranging in size from the four-room lakeside **Whitaker House** B&B (263-0816) to the 60 rooms of the **Lakeside Inn** (800-543-8126) and **Super 8 Motel** (800-843-1991). The **Quality Inn** (800-635-2534) has the region's only indoor pool. **Connie's Best Western** (263-9581; 800-282-0660) has a hot tub and heated outdoor pool, and a location right in town. The **Edgewater Resort Inn** (800-635-2534) also is on the lake. Several Sandpoint hotels offer ski packages.

Dining

Jean's Northwest Bar & Grill, in the Green Gables Lodge, is best for fresh seafood (cold water prawns sautéed with northwest peaches, $14.95) and game (medallions of venison loin sautéed with blackberries, cassis and fresh rosemary, $17.95). The pastas are good, too.

Schweitzer Village's **St. Bernard** has Southwest, Italian, Mexican and Cajun entrees, all for under $10.

On Highway 200 at the north end of the lake, diners are well rewarded for the drive to **Trestle Creek Inn** (555 Highway 200 E., Hope, 264-5942). The accent is on fresh ingredients, including the home-baked breads. You'll find pastas ($12–$15) jumbo Florida shrimps ($16.95), New York Strip steak ($19.25), and the house specialty The Hollandse Biefstuk ($16.95).

For serious northern Italian food, go to **Ivano's** (124 S. Second, 263-0211) in Sandpoint. House specialties are veal, chicken, fish and pasta. **The Donkey Jaw Restaurant & Lounge** (212 Cedar St., 265-2243) is for the nachos/burgers/taco crowd. Most prices are less than $5.

Après-ski/nightlife

Jean's Bar is a very happy place for après-ski with an excellent wine list. Also on the mountain, the **Club St. Bernard** has a quiet atmosphere, good for conversation, and pool and bar games. Cocktails are served 4 p.m. to closing. In Sandpoint, **Roxy's** (215 Pine St., 263-6696) has live bands Wednesday through Saturday.

Other activities

The Sandpoint Winter Carnival (800-800-2106), usually held the third week in January, has snow sculpture extravaganzas, ice skating parties, a "Taste of Sandpoint" on the Cedar Street Bridge, a Parade of Lights and a host of special events on Schweitzer Mountain.

The Green Gables Lodge activities desk can arrange Norwegian Fiord horse sleigh rides through an old-growth hemlock forest ($10 each) and guided snowmobile tours from one hour ($35) to all day ($150).

Recommended **shopping** includes Annie's Gifts in the Green Gables Lodge, The Company Store at 218 Cedar St., the Dann Hall Studios at 202 1/2 S. First St. for its astounding photographs of Idaho taken earlier this century, and The Bridge, a group of shops on a bridge, slightly reminiscent of the Ponte Vecchio in Florence.

Heli-skiing packages are available through the Monarch West Lodge (800-543-8193) in Sandpoint. Ontrak Airservice has access to 300,000 acres of the Idaho Panhandle between Schweitzer and the Canadian border. Overnight packages start at $290 each, including continental breakfast.

Getting there and getting around

Getting there: Schweitzer is a seven-hour drive from Calgary or Seattle. It's 75 miles northeast of Spokane by Highway 95. From Sandpoint drive north on 95 for two miles and left on Schweitzer Cutoff Road. After half a mile, go right at Boyer Avenue, then left about three quarters of a mile later onto the Schweitzer access road. The resort is eight miles from that point.

Five major airlines serve Spokane International Airport, where four-wheel-drive cars can be rented for $45–$85 per day.

Sandpoint is on the Amtrak Empire Builder route. The train comes through at 1 a.m., but it can be an inexpensive option for Seattle and Portland skiers.

Schweitzer will arrange ground transportation from the airport and Amtrak depot.

Getting around: Some Sandpoint hotels offer ski shuttlebus service, but most people will want their own wheels—the town is a little too spread out for walking.

Information/reservations

Call **Schweitzer Mountain Resort** at (800) 831-8810 for information and reservations for all on-mountain lodging and ski programs.

Call the **Greater Sandpoint Chamber of Commerce** at (800) 800-2106.

The local area code is 208.

Silver Mountain Resort
Idaho

Silver Mountain, near Kellogg in Idaho's Silver Valley, is rapidly becoming another mining-town-turned-ski-resort success story, just like Park City, Aspen and Ketchum. Skiers tend to visit here for a few days and never leave. The attitude is cheerful, upbeat, and very infectious.

Silver's original name was Jackass Ski Bowl, and you can still buy patches bearing that name for $5 at the local museum. The name honored the discoverer of the metal that brought riches to the valley more than a century ago. Local legend says a donkey got away from its owner, scampered up a hill, and was standing on a rock with a silvery glint when the owner caught up with it. Bunker Hill Mine, which also took lead, zinc and copper from the hillsides, ran the ski area for employee recreation and changed the name to Silverhorn. But in the early 1980s the price of silver plunged and Bunker Hill closed.

What the company left behind was a white-knuckle road up to the ski area (later condemned by the city) and a Superfund cleanup site of astounding proportions. The town decided to build a four-season resort, serviced by an aerial gondola to take skiers from the valley floor to the ski area. In late 1987, Kellogg got a federal grant to fund the gondola's construction; however, it had to be matched with private money. Part of it came from Kellogg residents, who taxed themselves $2 million to build the 3.1-mile lift, the longest single-stage gondola in the world. Silver Mountain began ski operations in 1990.

The gondola descends low over the houses and yards of the town of Wardner before climbing to Silver's "base area," called Mountain Haus, at 5,700 feet. (A hefty portion of Silver's terrain is below the Mountain Haus, which gives the area its 2,200-foot

---

Silver Mountain Facts

Base elevation: 4,100' **Summit elevation:** 6,300' **Vertical drop:** 2,200 feet
Number and types of lifts: 7–1 eight-passenger gondola, 1 quad, 2 triple chairs, 2 double chairs, 1 surface tow **Acreage:** 1,500 skiable acres
Snowmaking: 10 percent **Uphill capacity:** 8,200 skiers per hour
Bed base: None on mountain, 1,500 in Kellogg; Wallace and Coeur d'Alene.

vertical drop.) The gondola is the only way in and out of the ski area.

The support base in Kellogg is building, but slowly because of the economic downturn and unsureness over the Superfund cleanup. Land and housing are still cheap compared to other ski resorts. That's an opportunity for a skier with a bit of cash.

The record skier day for Silver was 3,200, not overwhelming for its lift capacity of 8,200 per hour. Its total visitor count grows each season as the word gets out. For now, Silver is an uncrowded and inexpensive ski vacation with lift ticket prices $10–$15 lower than most Colorado and California high-end resorts. Lodging is reasonable too.

Where to ski

Silver has two connected peaks, Kellogg and Wardner. The gondola deposits skiers and snowboarders at Mountain Haus on the Kellogg side. From here they can fan out in several directions.

Day fog can cause night ice when the thermometer dips. Until it softens up, stay on the groomed runs (most on the Kellogg side). Centennial and Tamarack are safe bets on the Wardner side.

Silver has a lot of serious terrain, including monster glade skiing. For advanced skiers, the run rating always depends on snow conditions. On fresh powder days, take Silver Belt to Rendezvous on the Kellogg side. For great thrills on the Wardner side, cut down anywhere from the early section of the Wardner Peak Traverse. The best skiing on powder days is off the scree slopes between the tops of Chairs 4 and 2.

Experts love Silver Mountain. They can take the Wardner Peak Traverse to an inspirational knob with a stupendous view of the Silver Valley below. Some nice black-diamond runs go back down to the Shaft and Chair 4.

Terrible Edith, reached by green-circle Noahs which descends from Mountain Haus, is one of those runs that makes you feel like you're skiing down a globe. It's like Dave's Run at Mammoth Mountain—the farther down you go, the steeper it gets, until finally you see the cat track below. At that point, you're only halfway down.

As good as Silver is for experts, it also offers a lot for beginners. Chairs 1, 2, 3, and 5 at the Mountain Haus base area all serve beginner terrain. Below the lodge, Ross Run is a wide beginner favorite, allowing crossover to Noahs and back again, ending on Dawdler with a choice to return to Chair 5 or Chair 3.

Silver Belt, from the triple Chair 2, is a wide and terrific intermediate warmup run. At the Junction you can turn down Saddle Back for a bumpier ride, or take a hard left on the Cross Over Run to the Midway load station on Chair 4 for a ride to Wardner Peak. From the top, there are several trails back to

Midway. Only advanced skiers pass Midway and keep going down through the Shaft to the Chair 4 base.

Most skiers ski the Kellogg side, so to avoid even a mirage of crowds, ski the Wardner side. Lift lines are rarely a problem, but the gondola queue can back up for downloading at closing time (remember, you can't ski to the gondola base). To avoid morning clog, ride up a half hour early for breakfast at Mountain Haus.

Silver has some nice surprises. One is the free ski wax, right by the free ski check at Mountain Haus. Another is the guarantee: if snow conditions don't please you, return your lift ticket to the gondola base within an hour and a half and get a pass for another day.

Mountain rating

All levels will have fun here. Experts will like Wardner Peak's runs and the North Face Glades on Kellogg Peak. Intermediates have most of Kellogg and quite a bit on Wardner, while beginners have a mostly isolated section under the gondola and around Mountain Haus.

Cross-country

Silver has no cross-country skiing, but telemark lessons are offered at the ski school.

Snowboarding

Because snowboarders were ripping through yards in the little town of Wardner under the gondola, it's now illegal to ski or snowboard in town, but there's plenty of space on the mountain and boarders are welcomed on all runs.

Lessons (94/95 prices)

Group instruction for ages 12 and older is $15 for two hours and $23 for four, for Alpine ski, telemark or snowboard lessons. A lift/lesson package for skiers and snowboarders is available for $39 at the Gondola Base ticket window.

Private lessons cost $30 per hour, with each additional student $12. An early-bird lesson at 9 a.m. is $20.

If you have never skied before, Silver Mountain offers a heck of a deal for ages 5 to adult. For $20 you get a two-hour lesson, rental equipment, lift ticket (which you get after the lesson) and a coupon for a follow-up lesson. For snowboarders, the cost is $23 and available for ages 12 and older.

The SKIwee lesson program is offered for children ages 5–11. Full day costs $25 for ages 5–6, and $40 for ages 7–11 for lifts, lesson and lunch. Half day also is available.

Child care

Minor's Camp Daycare, for ages 2 through 6, costs $30 for a full day and $20 for additional siblings. It includes lunch and a snack, games in the Camp Terrain Garden and ski equipment.

Half day, which also includes lunch, is $20 ($12 for other siblings). Children in Minor's Camp Daycare who want to ski can get a one-hour private lesson, equipment included, for $12. The instructor will pick up and drop off the child in Minor's Camp.

Lift tickets (95/96 prices)

	Adult	Child (7–12)
One day	$31	$18
Three days	$84 ($28/day)	$42 ($14/day)
Five days	$140 ($28/day)	$70 ($14/day)

Juniors (ages 13–21) and seniors (65 and older) ski for $24; $21 per day for multidays tickets. Children 6 and younger ski free.

Accommodations

The closest lodging is in Kellogg, where the gondola starts. So although Silver Mountain doesn't have slopeside lodging per se, some accommodations are within walking distance to the gondola. Skiers also can stay in Coeur d'Alene, about 35 miles away.

Patrick's Inn and Steakhouse (786-2311 or 800-766-9386) has a two-day, two-night early-in-the-week package that includes lodging and lift tickets for $80 each based on double occupancy. Frequently Patrick and his wife Nancy will take skiers on mountain tours to find the best runs.

The gondola base **Super-8 Motel** (783-1234 or 800-785-5443), with indoor pool and spa, is brand-new and has a midweek package of lift and lodging for $50 each, including continental breakfast.

Kellogg also has one- and two-bedroom condos at **Silver Ridge Mountain Lodge** (800-979-1991) and homes (call 800-435-2588 or 208-784-1166), plus several other motels, such as **The McKinley Inn** (786-7771 or 800-686-6432), and the **Silverhorn Motor Inn** (783-1151 or 800-437-6437), both of which have ski packages.

Ten miles east on I-90 is the mining town of Wallace. The **Best Western Wallace Inn** (800-643-2386) has Silver Mountain packages available from $49.95 per person per day, including round-trip shuttle to the ski area, based on quad occupancy. The Wallace Inn has 63 rooms, an on-site restaurant, heated indoor pool with Jacuzzi, sauna, steam rooms and a fitness center. The Best Western management also runs the **Jameson Hotel**, a historic and delightful lodge that may be open this winter, "depending on traffic," said manager Rick Shaffer. Call the same 800 number if historic digs appeal to you.

The **Coeur d'Alene Resort** (800-688-5253), a hugely popular summer golf resort on the shore of Lake Coeur d'Alene, has a ski package where children 17 and under stay and ski free. Two-day packages start at $149 per person double occupancy on weekdays and $179 on weekends, and include lodging, lift tickets, continental breakfast and round-trip shuttle to Silver Mountain, about 35 miles away. On Fridays through Sundays, the resort also shuttles skiers to Schweitzer Mountain, which is about an hour's drive. Advantages to staying here include more to do at night (including an indoor mall attached to the hotel), a lower elevation and the resort itself, which is quite luxurious and a huge bargain in winter.

Dining

In town, **Patrick's Inn and Steakhouse** (786-2311) is both a B&B and a restaurant. Patrick says, "I've eaten my way through most ski hill restaurants in the West, and we decided to offer on our menu what we as skiers like to eat." And that is Steak Patrick, a tenderloin filet wrapped in bacon, smothered with crab meat and topped with Bearnaise sauce, $16.95.

Good family fare is found at the gondola base, second floor, in **Timbers Cantina**. Timbers has a full range of Mexican and Southwest food, plus steaks, chicken sandwiches and burgers. Timbers features live entertainment on some weekends until 1 a.m.

The Enaville Resort (682-3453), Exit 43A off I-90, is always a happy discovery for skiers new to the Kellogg area. Known locally as the Snake Pit, it's more of a destination dinery than a resort. Over its 115-year history, the Snake Pit accommodated a lot of people for a lot of purposes, but sleeping through the night was never one of them. Enjoy an appetizer of Rocky Mountain oysters before moving on to buffalo burgers and barbecue.

Après-ski/nightlife

Not a strong point. At the end of the day, hang around the food court or go up to **Moguls Lounge** for some après-ski. Moguls is open until 5 p.m.

At night or for après-ski, **Patrick's Inn** is a fun place to hang out, mostly because of its proprietor. Patrick's has renovated its basement and put in a bar called The Out of Bounds. The **Timbers Cantina** at the gondola base is open with live music on the weekends. It closes at 8 p.m. weekdays and at 10 p.m. Friday and Saturday.

Other activities

Snowmobiling is very big in Wallace (where it's legal on city streets), ten miles east of Kellogg on I-90, and also at Lookout Pass, ten miles past Wallace on the Montana border. Lookout has a snowmobile camp and access to 600 miles of snowmobile trails. There are several special events and rides January through April every year. Phone (800) 643-2386 for more information (Best Western Wallace Inn is a headquarters of sorts for snowmobiling with free, secure snowmobile storage.)

Perhaps symbolic of the new Kellogg spirit are the life-size sculptures-from-scrap on view downtown—they were made by Dave Dose, a high school teacher and county commissioner with a sense of humor. **Shopping** in Kellogg is sparse. We recommend **Bitterroot Stoneware and Pottery** if you are looking for handmade gifts by Idaho artists.

At Cataldo, five miles west of Kellogg and 24 miles east of Coeur d'Alene on I-90 (Exit 39), sits the **Mission of the Sacred Heart**, Idaho's oldest building, finished in 1853. It was all hand built without nails, and the walls are a one-foot-thick mixture of mud, twigs and straw, covered with boards inside and out. Tours are available, and the mission is open year-round, 9 a.m.–5 p.m. in winter, admission $2 per vehicle.

Getting there and getting around

Getting there: Silver Mountain is at Kellogg, Exit 49 of I-90. It is 70 miles east of Spokane Airport, which is served by Horizon, Delta, Northwest, Continental, United and Southwest. The interstate is well maintained, and Silver Mountain's parking lot is a block off the freeway, so a four-wheel-drive car isn't necessary. However, you can rent one at the airport for $45–$85 per day. The Coeur d'Alene Resort will shuttle guests from Spokane Airport with prior arrangement. **Silver Service** (800-686-6432) run through the McKinley Inn, picks up passengers headed to Kellogg; reservations are required.

Getting around: It's possible to survive without a car, especially if you stay at the Coeur d'Alene Resort, but you will probably want one.

Information/reservations

Silver Mountain Ski and Summer Resort is located at 610 Bunker Ave., Kellogg, ID 83837-2200. Phone: 783-1111.

Lodging Information: Kellogg Chamber of Commerce, 784-0821; Coeur d'Alene Visitor's Bureau 664-0587.

Local area code is 208.

Sun Valley
Ketchum, Idaho

Sun Valley may provide America's perfect ski vacation. It has a European accent mixed with the Wild West. It is isolated, yet comfortable; rough in texture, but also refined; Austrian in tone, cowboy in spirit.

Ageless would be the one word to describe Sun Valley Village, America's first ski resort, built in 1936 by Union Pacific tycoon Averell Harriman. It exudes restrained elegance with the traditional Sun Valley Lodge, walking village, steeple, horse-drawn sleighs and steaming pools.

In contrast, the town of Ketchum is all-American West, a flash of red brick, a slab of prime rib, a rustic cluster of small restaurants, shops, homes, condos and lodges. It's the town of Ketchum that actually curls around the broad-shouldered ever-green rise of Bald Mountain, known as Baldy to locals. Each snow ribbon dropping from the summit into the valley leads to the streets of Ketchum.

This is Hemingway country. When he wasn't hobnobbing with Ingrid Bergman, Gary Cooper and Howard Hawks, he wrote most of *For Whom The Bell Tolls* in the Sun Valley Lodge, where the photos on display show Darryl Zanuck and other Hollywood celebrities who first made the place famous. Sun Valley has developed or trained many famous winter-sport athletes: the late Gretchen Fraser, who was the first American Olympic ski champion in 1948; Christin Cooper, a 1984 silver Olympic medalist; and Picabo Street, who won a silver at the 1994 Olympics and is the only American to win the overall World Cup downhill title; and ice skaters Peggy Fleming, Dorothy Hamill and Scott Hamilton, Olympic champions all.

The Sun Valley Company keeps the skiing as up-to-date as any in America. They claim the world's largest computerized

---

Sun Valley Facts
BALDY: Base: 5,740'; Summit elevation: 9,140'; Vertical drop: 3,400 feet
DOLLAR: Base: 6,010'; Summit elevation: 6,638'; Vertical drop: 628 feet
Number of lifts: 17–7 quad superchairs, 5 triple chairs, 5 doubles
Snowmaking: 30 percent   Total acreage: 2,054 skiable acres
Uphill capacity: 26,380 per hour   Bed Base: 6,000

snowmaking system, which covers more than half of Bald Mountain's groomed terrain, ensuring Thanksgiving and Christmas skiing. The area that put up the world's first chair lift now has seven quad superchairs, including one that rises a whopping 3,144 vertical feet in 10 minutes. In the past few years Sun Valley has built new lodges at the base of Warm Springs and one atop Seattle Ridge overlooking the bowls.

Places like Elkhorn, on the opposite side of Dollar Mountain, are strewn with condo projects, but the community as a whole has maintained its dreamy, hilly, tucked-away atmosphere. Sun Valley, 60 years old, has managed to age gracefully without losing any of the magic it had in its youth.

Where to ski

The main drawback to Sun Valley is the split in the ski areas. Baldy is a mountain for intermediates and advanced skiers. Never-evers, beginners and lower intermediates can't really enjoy this mountain and will end up skiing at Dollar/Elkhorn on the other side of town, so there is no easy way or convenient place for lower-level skiers to meet with their upper-level friends for lunch or après-ski. Sun Valley says this problem will be solved with its beautiful new River Run Lodge and Skier Services building at the base of the green-circle River Run trail. Ski school will be located there, and a beginner area reportedly is being developed. Until we see it work, though, we still believe Dollar is a better place to learn because of its gentler overall terrain and less high-speed skier traffic.

Baldy's terrain is best known for its long runs with a consistent pitch that keeps skiers concentrating on turns from top to bottom, rather than dozing off on a flat or bailing out on a cliff or wall. Mile-long ridge runs lead to a clutch of advanced and intermediate bowls. There are short and long black-diamond challenges, and plenty of cruising territory.

Trails are not apt to be quite so wide as at other Rocky Mountain resorts, but they're a lot wider than the ones in New England, and these trails are for the most part long, very long. Many skiers note, after skiing at Baldy for a day, that intermediate here would be rated expert at most other areas they've skied.

Limelight is a long, excellent bump run for skiers with strong knees and elastic spinal columns. Of the other black descents, the Exhibition plunge is one of the best known. Fire Trail, on the ski area boundary, is a darting, tree-covered descent for those who can make quick, flowing turns. The Seattle Ridge trail curves around the bowls with hypnotic views. The bowl area below, rarely mentioned by most ski writers, is a joy. It has something for every level of skier (except beginners and lower intermediates) and portions catch the sun throughout the day.

Warm Springs has some marvelous intermediate and advanced cruisers such as Warm Springs, Greyhawk, and Flying Squirrel.

If you want to follow the sun, start your day in the River Run area, then shift to the runs dropping off Seattle Ridge and finish up cruising the Warm Springs face.

Beginners have a whole mountain across the valley, Dollar/Elkhorn. The terrain here is perfect for teaching skiing and good for intermediates perfecting technique or starting out in powder. Skiing on the Dollar side of this mountain is shorter and more limited than on the Elkhorn face, which offers a small bowl with greater pitch and more challenging runs.

Cross-country (94/95 prices)

The Sun Valley/Ketchum area has about 210 km. of trails overall. The closest facilities are at the **Sun Valley Nordic Center** (622-2250 or 622-2251). Here near the Sun Valley Lodge, 40 km. of cross-country ski trails are groomed and marked for difficulty. They range from easy to isolated forest escapes. There is a half-track width for children as well as a terrain garden. The daily trail fee is $11, with discounts for half day, children and seniors. Group and private lessons are available.

The Blaine County Recreation District grooms the **North Valley Trails**, which consist of more than 100 km. of groomed trails in the Sawtooth National Recreation Area supported by set trail fees or donations. The largest is **Galena Lodge** (726-4010; grooming report: 726-6662) with 50 km. of trails, a full restaurant and a ski shop. It also has a 4 km. snowshoe trail. A popular event is dinner, followed by moonlit skiing. Adult trail passes are $5; children 16 and younger ski for $1. Rentals and lessons are available, and every Wednesday you can ski with a ranger and learn about natural history or wildlife. These tours are free with trail pass. Galena is 24 miles north of Ketchum on Highway 75.

Wood River Trails features 30 km. of trails winding around Dollar Mountain and from Ketchum to Hailey and Bellevue. **Lake Creek** has 15.5 km. of trails, and three other areas have less than 10 km. each. The **Boulder Mountain Trail** stretches 30 km. from the Sawtooth National Recreation Area headquarters eight miles north of Ketchum to Easley Hot Springs and Galena, and is groomed all winter, snow conditions permitting.

Avalanche and snow conditions are available 24 hours a day from the Ketchum Ranger District at 622-8027, while North Valley Trails maintains a grooming hotline, 726-6662.

For backcountry tours through the largest wilderness area outside Alaska, contact either **Sun Valley Trekking** (788-9585) or **Sawtooth Mountain Guides** (774-3324). Both feature hut-to-hut skiing and the opportunity to stay in yurts as well.

Snowboarding

Sun Valley describes itself as snowboard friendly. Private lessons for all abilities are available on Dollar and Baldy Mountains, with reservations required and made through the Sun Valley Ski School. Snowboard clinics cost $35 for two hours.

Lessons (94/95 prices)

Adult **group lesson** prices are $42 for one day (3 hours), $112 for three days and $166 for five days (15 hours). **Children's lessons** run four hours each day and include a supervised ski break. They cost $58 for one day, $152 for three days, and $230 for five days. SKIwee programs are available for children.

The Sun Valley Ski School (622-2248 or 622-2231) has several **specialized clinics.** Racing clinics run three hours per day. Cost is $48 for one day, $90 for two days, $130 for three days, and $195 for five days. A women's clinic for upper intermediates is held five times during the season—call for exact dates. **Private lessons** cost $68 per person for one hour to $185 for three hours in the morning ($160 for three hours in the afternoon). An all-day private lesson costs $310.

Child care

Sun Valley's Playschool, located on the Sun Valley Mall, offers supervised activities, hot lunches and ice skating. Reservations are required. Call 622-2288.

Lil'Annie's Day School (726-1411) is geared for ages 2 1/2 to 5 years. Call for reservations and programs.

Lift tickets (94/95 prices)

	Adult	Child (Up to 11)
One day	$47	$26
3 of 4 days	$135 ($45/day)	$70 ($23.33/day)
5 of 6 days	$220 ($44/day)	$110 ($22/day)

These are prices for tickets valid both at Baldy and Dollar. If you ski only at Dollar Mountain, prices are: one-day adult $24, three-day adult $60, one-day child $17, three-day child $45.

Skiers 65 and older enjoy a discount. Children 12 and younger ski and stay free when they are with a parent in a Sun Valley Resort hotel or condo or any participating property in Ketchum, Elkhorn or Warm Springs. Unfortunately, blackout periods for this offer are the Christmas/New Year holiday, most of February and half of March.

Accommodations (94/95 prices)

The **Sun Valley Lodge** is the heart of the resort, a place to relax on terrace overlooks and in grand sitting rooms beneath coppery chandeliers. Gleaming outside is a skating rink once ruled by ice queen Sonja Henie. *Sun Valley Serenade*, the '40s movie romance starring Henie and John Payne and featuring music by Glenn Miller, is still shown in the village Opera House. The village is a 3,000-acre Alpine enclave of archways, wall paintings, snow sculptures, and spruce foliage.

Standard rooms at the **Sun Valley Lodge** begin at $125 per night and go up to $299 for parlor suites. Four-night ski packages, including three-day lift tickets, start at $313 per person, double occupancy. Longer packages also are available. Because the Lodge was built well before the time of group tourism, each room is unique and pricing depends on room size and such added factors as view and balcony. **The Sun Valley Inn** runs $99 for a standard room to $160 for a deluxe room. Packages are available. Condos run $110 to $280; condo suites $100 to $360. Call (800) 786-8259 (800-SUN-VALY).

Elkhorn Resort and Golf Club, near Dollar Mountain, provides its own resort hotel world away from Ketchum and Sun Valley. Name performers play during the winter season and the health club is well outfitted. Rates range from $98 to $225. Call 622-4511 or (800) 355-4676 (800-ELKHORN).

Knob Hill Inn is one of the Ketchum area's most luxurious inns. The building is so Austrian you feel as if you've stepped out of your car into the Tyrol. The inn is No Smoking throughout. Room rates, with full breakfast, start at $160 for plenty of space and a king bed and range up to $300 for the Penthouse Suite. Call 726-8010 or (800) 526-8010.

The Idaho Country Inn is set on a knoll halfway between Ketchum and Sun Valley. Each of the ten rooms is individually decorated to reflect the Idaho heritage, as the Shoshone Room, Wagon Days Room, and Whitewater Room. Breakfasts here are fabulous and the hot tub sits on a hill behind the inn with a wonderful view. Rooms start at $125 and top out at $185 in high season. Call Terry or Julie Heneghan at 726-1019.

River Street Inn is resembles a charming New England B&B. It is within walking distance of the center of town. Rooms feature Japanese soaking tubs. Rates including breakfast range from $115 to $155. Call 726-3611.

Pinnacle Inn, across the street from Warm Springs base, is one of Ketchum's most convenient properties to the skiing. This is a collection of studio, one- and two-bedroom apartments with a complimentary breakfast in the restaurant in ski season. Rates are from $150 to $395 per night, with the more expensive apartments accommodating at least two couples. Call 726-5700 or (800) 255-3391.

The Tyrolean Lodge, a Best Western only 400 yards away from the River Run lift, has an Alpine atmosphere with wood-paneled ceilings and downy comforters dressing the beds. A champagne continental breakfast is served. Regular rooms are about $90. Call 726-5336 or (800) 333-7912.

Clarion Inn (formerly the Boulder Mountain Hotel) is a basic hotel with a large outdoor Jacuzzi and full breakfasts. Room doors open to outdoor walkways and the decor is simple. Prices are $90–$125. Call 726-5900 or (800) 262-4833.

Christophe Condominiums and Hotel features roomy condominiums with underground parking. A fire truck races guests back and forth to the lifts as well as the town bus. Rates for simple rooms for two are $75–$90; one-bedroom deluxe condos are $155–$200, with two bedrooms $205–$270. Call 726-5601 or (800) 521-2515.

Tamarack Lodge is smack in the middle of town with a hot tub and indoor pool. Good for families, with microwaves, refrigerators and coffee makers. It doesn't get any more convenient than this for nightlife and dining. Rooms with fireplaces cost more. Rates are $89–$119. Call 726-3344 or (800) 521-5379.

Condominiums:

River Run Lodge is a cluster of family-perfect condos within walking distance of River Run lifts. There is a big outdoor hot tub and units have VCRs. Rates for one-bedroom units with bunks and sleep sofa are $125; for two-bedroom units you'll pay $165–$300. Call 726-9086 or (800) 736-7503.

Sun Valley Resort has condominiums surrounding the Sun Valley Village. Studios start at $110 per night; four bedrooms are $280–$385, and one-, two- and three-bedroom units cost $160–$240. Call 622-4111 or (800) 786-8259 (800-SUN VALY).

Dining

On the mountain:

With the building of the Warm Springs and Seattle Ridge lodges in 1992 and 1993, and the River Run lodge this season, came excellent restaurants. Skiers can settle down to a lunch of prime rib, salmon, stone-fired pizza and many other delights, while enjoying panoramic views.

In Sun Valley Village:

The **Sun Valley Lodge** dining room has old-time elegance and is the only spot in the community with live music and dancing with meals. Specialties include Steak Diane, Chateaubriand Béarnaise Bouquetière, and fresh Idaho trout or poached salmon, all at about $22–$25.

The **Ram** attached to the Sun Valley Inn serves basic fare ranging from pasta to chops and steaks. The **Ore House** also serves steaks, chicken and fish, filling and well-prepared but nothing to write home about. **Gretchen's** in the Lodge has a fine dinner menu, and serves breakfast and lunch. The **Konditorei** has an Austrian flavor and excellent lunches, such as hearty soups served in a bread bowl next to a mountain of fruit.

In Ketchum

Sun Valley has some of the best restaurants in any ski resort in America; anyone with fine dining on his or her mind will not be disappointed. The region's real gourmet action takes place here. The price ranges we give here are a rough guide.

Entrées in the $15–$25 range:

Michel's Christiania (726-3032) run by Michel Rodigoz, serves fine French cuisine. **Evergreen** (726-3888) has an elegant setting of wood, crystal and glass for what many claim is Ketchum's best food and unarguably the town's best wine list. **Soupçon** (726-5034) has a boldly creative cuisine prepared in a tiny rustic house.

Felix (726-1166) in the Knob Hill Inn has an excellent continental menu and fine service in a very Austrian setting. **Mango** (726-8911) serves French/California cooking.

Entrées from $10–$15:

Salvatore's (726-3111) serves Italian food the way it's supposed to be prepared. Atmosphere is a bit L.A. but the food is perfecto. **The Sawtooth Club** (726-5233) has a great bar with cozy couches in front of a roaring fireplace and a series of small dining rooms tucked above and behind the bar. The food is excellent and very reasonable.

The Pioneer Saloon, (726-3139) a local hangout going back into Ketchum history, is known for its prime rib. **Ketchum Grill** (726-4660) has a daring, innovative menu with flavor mixtures that will keep your tastebuds tingling, and **China Pepper** (726-0959) is the place to head for spicy Thai and Chinese food.

Most entrées less than $10:

Globus Noodle (726-1301) has Chinese/Thai fare. All reports are good from locals and tourists alike.

Louie's (726-7775), in an old church, is a favorite family Italian place with a wide-ranging menu and super pizza. The Eggplant Parmesan is also excellent. Though Louie's has a longer history, locals rave about **Smoky Mountain Pizza** (622-5625) for great, very affordable Italian fare and massive salads. **Piccolo Pasta** (726-9251) has slightly more expensive Italian cooking in a cozy dining room, with fine light homemade pastas.

The **Warm Springs Ranch Restaurant** (726-2609) serves a wide-ranging menu and features mountain trout you can see swimming in pools near the cozy cabin.

The spot for excellent and inexpensive Mexican food is **Mama Inez** (726-4213) at the start of Warm Springs Road, or head to **Desperado's** (726-3068) just behind the visitor's center on Fourth Street. For slightly more expensive Mexican that is more Tex than Mex try **Tequila Joe's** (622-4511) in the Elkhorn Resort and Golf Club.

Breakfast is an important institution with most skiers. At the Sun Valley Lodge **Gretchen's** (622-2144) has plentiful fare with moderate prices and **Konditorei** (622-2235) in the Sun Valley Village has good breakfasts. The **Lodge Dining Room** (726-2150) serves an excellent Sunday brunch.

The best, however, are downtown in Ketchum. Locals seem split on the question, but they center on **The Kitchen**, the **Buffalo Café** and the **Kneadery**. All three are open for lunch as well. **The Kitchen** (726-3856) has a dozen varieties of omelets, with pancakes, waffles and a selection of specials served in an airy southwestern pale-colored room. Don't expect any bargains here—prices just about match Sun Valley Lodge. **The Kneadery** (726-9462) is a touch less expensive with a much cozier woodsy atmosphere. The champion bargain breakfast is found at the **Buffalo Café** (726-9795) with its Baldy Breakfast Special featuring pancakes, eggs, bacon and sausage for $3.95.

One more eatery we should mention: Directly across the street from the new Warm Springs Lodge at the base of Baldy is a Ketchum institution, **Irving's Red Hot** stand, where you can get great hotdogs. "The Works" (a dog smothered in fixings and chips) for only $2 is a lunch bargain that can't be beat.

Special Dining Experiences

One evening dining adventure that should not be missed is the horse-drawn sleigh ride to, and dinner at, **Trail Creek Cabin**. The cozy rough-hewn cabin dates from 1937 and seems even cozier after the brisk half-hour sleigh ride from the Sun Valley Inn. The cabin can be reached by sleigh, car or cross-country skis. For the sleigh ride, reservations should be made 72 hours in advance, but you can always check for open space; call 622-4111. The sleigh ride costs $13. Dinners range from $16 to $22, more or less.

A Winter's Feast is an evening of gourmet dining in an authentic Mongolian yurt (726-5775). You can ski to the yurt along a trail lit by torches or ride in on a sleigh drawn by horses (the sleigh ride is extra). Choose from four menus—salmon, beef, tuna, or lamb—each costing $60, plus wine and gratuity.

Après-ski/nightlife

Ketchum and Sun Valley have highly unusual après-ski, with major comedy and cabaret shows beginning at 5 p.m. and playing to 7 or 8. Sun Valley's historic landmark, the **Ram Bar**, has the **Mike Murphy** comedy show for a $7 cover. A free jazz concert is every Friday at the **Galleria**. Check the schedule for *Sun Valley Serenade* and Warren Miller movies at the **Opera House** in Sun Valley starting at 5 p.m. And the **Duchin Room** in the Lodge has music starting at 5 p.m.

If you are staying in Warm Springs, or wander over to the **Baldy Base Club** or **Apples** for good après-ski crowds.

The Vuarnettes, a local comedy act, perform regularly at the **Elkhorn Resort and Golf Club** during ski season.

Sun Valley's hottest nightclub belongs to none other than Bruce Willis, an occasional resident of this resort town. His **Dyn-o-mite Lounge** opened in late 1994 on Main Street at the site of the old Silver Creek outfitters store, and became an instant magnet because of Willis' ability to draw world-class bands to the establishment. The Dyn-o-mite sports a retro feel, with an intimate atmosphere and 1960s decor (but not 1960s prices).

At the somewhat roomier western bar **Whiskey Jacques** patrons can listen to live music and dance inside an authentic log building. A staple of Ketchum's nightlife since 1979, Whiskey's is a hangout for locals and visitors.

The Pioneer Saloon is famous for its steaks, prime rib, and imaginative 18th-century decorations (mounted elk and moose). The saloon gets very crowded very early on weekends.

Another popular spot is **The Casino**, so named because there used to be rows of slot machines where the tables now stand (gambling is now illegal in this part of the country). It's something of a departure from the more intense nightclubs in the area, with the dance floor replaced by pool tables.

For more sedate and elegant night action try the **Duchin Room** at the Lodge, which features the Joe Foss Trio until 1 a.m.

The Sun Valley Wine Company, with reportedly the largest wine selection in Idaho and a light dinner menu, is located above the liquor store on Leadville Street in Ketchum.

Remember—if you are staying in Sun Valley or Warm Springs and plan on partying in Ketchum, the KART bus system stops running at midnight, but A-1 Taxi and Baldy's Express Taxis are available until closing.

Other activities

Shopping opportunities are extensive in this long-time resort community. A couple of shops worth highlighting: **The Toy Store**, for unique and educational toys from around the globe; **Wild Willows**, a fun gift store; and **Angel Wings**, a gift store that specializes in angel paraphernalia.

Art galleries are another center of Ketchum's cultural life. Fourteen galleries are members of the Sun Valley Art Gallery Association (726-2602). They provide a beautiful brochure with a gallery map and offer guided evening gallery walks about a dozen times during the year.

Ballooning and **snowmobiling** are available through Mike Mulligan (726-9137). **The Sun Valley Athletic Club** (726-3664) is open to visitors with daily, weekly and monthly rates. It is a full club with child care, massage, aerobics, weights and swimming. You may even have the chance to work out with Arnold Schwarzenegger, who often hangs out here in his sweats.

Sun Valley Heli-Ski (622-3108) offers backcountry ski adventures for all levels of skiers. **Soaring** or winter glider rides are available through Sun Valley Soaring (726-3054).

The Community Library (726-3493) is a wonderful resource in Ketchum. The special collections on the history of skiing in Sun Valley make it a perfect stop for anyone interested in the history of the area.

Sun Valley Center For Arts and Humanities has performances and showings during the ski season. Call 726-9491 for a schedule or the Chamber of Commerce, 726-3423.

Getting there and getting around

Getting there: Sun Valley is not easy to reach. Almost all air connections require another hour or more of bus transfer. The closest airport is Friedman Memorial, 12 miles south of the resort in Hailey, served by Horizon Air and Delta's SkyWest Airlines. When it is open everything works well, but weather often closes it and it cannot handle big jets. Most guests arrive by jet at Twin Falls, about 90 minutes away, and some arrive in Boise, about three hours away. Last season, United operated weekly nonstop flights from Chicago and Los Angeles to Twin Falls, and threw in the ground transportation in the ticket price.

Several properties provide complimentary transportation, or use **A-1 Taxi**, 726-9351, or **Baldy's Express Taxi**, 720-2650. **Sun Valley Stages** (800) 821-9064, or locally 383-3085 in Boise or 622-4200 in Sun Valley, runs one bus a day between Boise and Sun Valley, which takes about three hours. Cost is $35 each way or $60 round trip; call for departure times.

Mike Mulligan Luxury Limo (726-5466) provides service serving Hailey, Twin Falls and Boise Airports. **Town and Country Tours** (788-2012) provides private transfers to Twin Falls, Hailey and Boise.

Charter bus service is available to Sun Valley from Boise, Idaho Falls, Twin Falls, and Salt Lake City. Call **Teton Stages** at 529-8036 or (800) 285-8036, or check with Sun Valley Stages.

Getting around: Get around the town and the ski areas with the free KART shuttlebus linking Sun Valley, Ketchum and Baldy about every 20 minutes.

Information/reservations

For **information and reservations** call (800) 786-8259 (800-SUN VALY). For the **snow report** call (800) 635-4150. The address is Sun Valley Resort, Sun Valley, ID 83353.

You can also book Sun Valley and Ketchum lodging through **Chamber of Commerce central reservations.** Call (800) 634-3347, fax (208) 726-4533, or write to Sun Valley-Ketchum Chamber of Commerce, PO Box 2420, Sun Valley, ID 83353

Local area code is 208.

Other Idaho ski areas

Bogus Basin Boise ID (800) 367-4397;
6 lifts, 45 trails, 1,800 vertical feet

Bogus Basin, where counterfeit gold was manufactured in the Western gold rush days, has no counterfeit ski slopes. Sixteen miles north of Boise and 168 miles west of Sun Valley, it is an area known to skiers who go beyond the big-name resorts in search of excellent sleepers. Bogus has first-rate glade skiing and its night skiing is up there with any in the country. Several black runs as well as intermediates and beginners are lighted, twelve in all. They take a skier through enchanted forests to the backside and flanks of a low but wide mountain crown (7,590 feet at Shafer Butte, the summit), offering scintillating city, valley and mountain views. Bogus Basin is open from 10 a.m. to 10 p.m. seven days a week, so that a skier hot for vertical feet can find true exhaustion. An impressive 2,600 skiable acres (Sun Valley has 2,054) offers a great variety of terrain. The ski school, with 130 instructors, is one of the largest in the Northwest. The mountain has two restaurants and the 70-unit Pioneer Inn halfway up the slopes; lift lines are rare.

Brundage Ski Mountain McCall, ID;
(208) 634-4151 or (800) 888-7544
6 lifts, 36 trails, 1,800 foot vertical

Payette Lake, which Brundage overlooks, is an unknown Lake Tahoe. It is beautiful and sparsely populated, with many outdoor activities including good intermediate downhill skiing. Numerous local skiers have been in the Winter Olympics, and every February the town has a Winter Carnival. From the top of the mountain you can see the Salmon River Mountains, Payette Lakes, Oregon's Eagle Cap Wilderness and the Seven Devils towering over Hells Canyon, America's deepest river gorge. The skiing on 1,300 acres is pleasant and uncrowded, with occasional challenging drops, but mostly cruisers.

Brundage has a reputation for some of the lightest powder in the Pacific Northwest, and the mountain offers snowcat skiing, either for day trips or an overnight trip with lodging in a Mongolian-style yurt. Other accommodations are in McCall, about a 15-minute drive.

The Big Mountain
Whitefish, Montana

True ski-resort discoveries are getting harder to find. If you live in a state or province along the U.S.-Canadian border west of the Great Lakes, you probably already know about this friendly, low-key spot with skiing that stretches on forever. You probably don't want us to tell anyone in the rest of either country about it. We understand, and of course, we'll keep your secret.

If you are a skier who wants lots of terrain to explore and an on- and a no-fluff off-slope atmosphere, you should head for this aptly named ski resort tucked into the far northwest corner of Montana.

This is an area popular with Seattle, Calgary and northern Midwest skiers. Many hop on Amtrak's Empire Builder, which on its every-other-day run between Seattle and Chicago dumps a load of eager skiers in the town of Whitefish within sight of The Big Mountain's trails.

Though sometimes the resort and the community business leaders long to see their name in the various annual listings of top ski resorts (acreage-wise, this ranks in the top ten, maybe even top five, depending on how one counts), most other times, they'd rather just keep it the Northwest's little secret. Many folks here are expatriates from other ski areas that were once as laid-back and unpretentious as The Big Mountain is now.

The best way in and out of the area is still by train (though Northwest flies nonstop from Minneapolis once a week), and the most popular nightlife event is the weekly Frabert award party at the Bierstube (more on that later). Everything is clean and comfortable, but you won't find concierges and valet parking. This is a down-home, comfortable place where a fur coat would look out of place except on a grizzly-bearded mountain man.

The ski area is eight miles from the town of Whitefish, up a winding access road that can be a bit scary in bad weather. At

---

Big Mountain Facts
Base elevation: 4,700'; **Summit elevation:** 7,000'; **Vertical drop:** 2,300 feet.
Number and types of lifts: 9,—1 quad superchair, 1 quad, 4 triples, 1 double and 2 surface lifts **Acreage:** 3,000 skiable acres
Snowmaking: 1 percent, three trails, top to bottom
Uphill capacity: 12,000 skiers per hour **Bed base:** 1,500 on mountain

the ski area base is a cluster of six hotels and condo properties and a few restaurants and bars. In Whitefish are more hotels, the best restaurants, shopping and the biggest variety of nightlife.

The weather here is a mix of the Rockies and Pacific Northwest maritime, called "inland maritime," and it creates spectacular snow ghosts at the summit, trees encased in many layers of frost. The climate also means plenty of snow. Somehow it produces fantastic light powder, but without the sunshine you'll find in the southern Rockies. If you forget your sunscreen you'll probably survive, but don't forget your goggles. Pack your sunglasses too—sunny days do occur, and when they do, the skiing is spectacular.

Where to ski

Ski anywhere you dare. This is not a resort limited to cut trails and in-bounds bowls. Within the marked boundaries are 3,000 acres of sprawling terrain; another 1,000 acres is in the permit area. The Big Mountain ski school offers free tours of the mountain daily.

The main access to The Big Mountain is the high-speed superchair, The Glacier Chaser, which moves skiers up 2,200 feet of vertical to the summit. If you ski straight ahead when you get off the superchair you'll drop down the north slope, a mostly intermediate series of runs alternating with tree-studded steeps. The return to the summit is by Chair 7.

If you make a U-turn when you get off the Glacier Chaser you'll reach wide well-groomed intermediate trails. Toni Matt, The Big Ravine or MoeMentum (formerly North Bowl; named for Olympic downhill champ Tommy Moe, who trained on the run in his younger years) are all perfect for power cruising with wide GS turns. Toni Matt, Inspiration and the Big Ravine provide top-to-bottom cruising.

All of these groomed runs are surrounded by fields of powder and thousands of trees beckoning to advanced and expert skiers. Good Medicine defines The Big Mountain experience. This is more an area of the mountain than a defined run through the trees. Through the entire Good Medicine area skiers can choose how tight they want their trees, and they have plenty of opportunities to bail out onto the groomed trails. Locals also can direct you to Movie Land, which starts with dense trees and then opens for great steep tree skiing before ending on Easy Street.

For big-air fans, The Big Mountain has a cornice next to the Summit House. Runs from this cornice, and almost all skiing to the left of the superchair, end up on Easy Street.

Low intermediates will spend most of their time on Chair 3, but they should make a few runs off Chair 2 or the T-bar before they try The Glacier Chaser. Chair 2's runs are equivalent in pitch to the blue runs off the front of the summit, but much shorter. This lower-mountain area is also lighted for night skiing. When you're ready to try the summit runs, try the North Slope runs first. The toughest part will be the upper part of MoeMentum, which can build formidable moguls by afternoon.

Never-evers and beginners have an excellent learning area, separate from other skiers, on the gentle trails under Chair 6. This area has the advantage of heading *down* from the base area, so first-timers can start without riding a lift.

Mountain rating

This is a wide-open, ski-anywhere-you-can mountain with consistent pitch and the added intrigue of nature's own slalom course through acres of frosty pines. Tree skiing makes this a delight for advanced skiers. Intermediates have long runs they'll dream about for days. Chair 6 serves a good beginner area. In short, this mountain satisfies the needs of every ability.

Cross-country

The Big Mountain has excellent cross-country for all levels. Next to the ski area, **The Big Mountain Nordic Center** has 10 km. of trails just below Chair 6. Lessons and rentals are available (862-1900). Trail fees are $5 for adults, $2 for juniors (13-18), $1 for children (7-12) and free for anyone younger when accompanied by an adult. Downhill ski pass holders can use the cross-country trails free.

Grouse Mountain Lodge (862-3000) in Whitefish has 15 km. of groomed cross-country trails and the town's only night skiing with 2.4 km. lighted.

The **Izaak Walton Inn** (888-5700), 62 miles east on Highway 2, has 30 km. of groomed trails as well as guides who take skiers into the Glacier National Park wilderness. Guides for groups of two or three cost $75 per person and $60 each for groups of four or more.

Glacier National Park provides a natural cross-country paradise. Here the unplowed park roads and trails provide kilometer after kilometer of ungroomed passages into the heart of the mountains. Check with the communications center (888-5441) or the park rangers for weather and snow conditions.

Snowboarding

The entire mountain is open for snowboarding. The rental shop has equipment and the ski school offers a two-hour group lesson for $23. The Whitetail run on the north side of the mountain has a snowboard park. Steve Persons of Whitefish, a World Cup snowboarding multi-medalist, teaches periodic snowboard camps.

WATERCOLOR BY BARBARA MELLBLOM

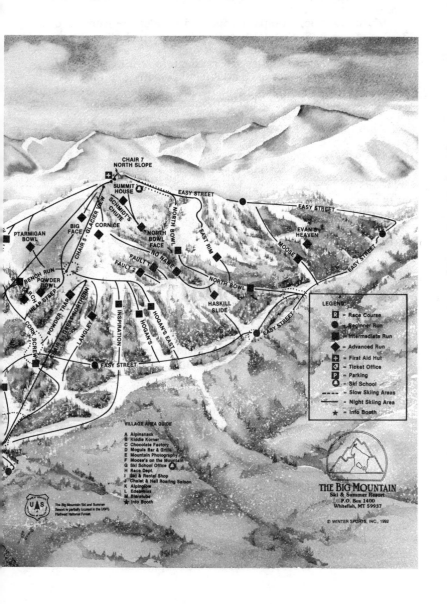

The Big Mountain
Ski & Summer Resort
P.O. Box 1400
Whitefish, MT 59937

© WINTER SPORTS, INC., 1992

Lessons (94/95 prices)

Group lessons for adults cost $23 for a half day and for a full day $34. Lesson packages for three half-day lessons are $63; three full days, $94. Seniors receive a 50 percent discount on group lessons.

Workshops for bumps, steeps and powder are from 1:30 to 3:30 p.m. for $23. Special beginner lessons including lifts and lessons cost $23 for a two-hour session.

Private lessons require reservations (862-2909). Rates are $52 for an hour ($16 for each additional person), $73 for one and a half hours ($21 each additional), $115 for a half day ($32 each additional), and $250 for a full six-hour day ($50 each additional). Beginner private lessons are $94 for two hours.

Special workshops include snowboard camps and women's weeks.

Children's lessons start at 3–4 years of age. For those 4–6, one- or two-hour Platter Lift Lessons cost $12.50 per hour. The program for younger children is in conjunction with the Kiddie Korner Day Care Center, and teaches basic skiing lessons and snow fun.

The full-day ski school program for older children includes five-hour lessons for $36 and half-day lessons for $19. Lift tickets are extra. Lunch is optional and costs an additional $6.50.

Child care

The main day care facility on the mountain is the **Kiddie Korner Child Care Center** (862-1999). It takes infants and toddlers, either half day or full day. Reservations are recommended for all children and required for infants younger than 12 months and non-walkers. Lunches are provided for a nominal fee; parents can also provide lunch or take their children out to lunch. Babysitting also is available; call for details and rates.

Lift tickets (95/96 prices)

	Adult	Child (7–12)
One day	$38	$20
Three days	$105 ($35/day)	$57 ($19/day)
Five days	$165 ($33/day)	$95 ($19/day)

Ages 13–18, college students and 62 and older pay $28 per day. Children 6 and younger ski free. Night skiing costs $12 for everyone, but with a day or multi-day ticket, it's free.

Skiers may ride the platter lift and Chair 6, which service the most gentle terrain, without charge. Also, day and multi-day ticket holders may ride the Glacier Chaser to the Summit House for dinner without charge on Wednesday and Saturday nights. (the Glacier Chaser turns into a gondola for night riding). Other passengers headed for the summit at night pay $6.

Accommodations

The properties located at The Big Mountain village may all be reserved by calling 862-1960 or (800) 858-5439. Lower rates are available before Christmas, in January and in April; higher rates apply in the last two weeks of December.

The **Kandahar Lodge** (862-6095) at the ski area looks like a mountain lodge should—wooden beams, spacious public areas and a soaring stone fireplace. The rooms are large, the food good and the location right on the slopes. A shuttle takes guests to the base area and at the end of the day skiers can glide right to the door. Rates vary from $124 to $184 per night.

In the center of the ski area village is the **Alpinglow Inn** (862-6966). This lodging has beautiful views from the restaurant and perhaps the most convenient location for skiers. Several of the rooms are packed with beds and the decor is basic paneling, but you can't beat the location. Rates are $83–$158.

The **Hibernation House** (862-3511) is the economy bed-and-breakfast. Rooms house as many as five guests and there is also an indoor hot tub. Rates are $64–$94.

Anapurna Properties and **Big Mountain Alpine Homes** are the two main condo and home management companies. Anapurna guests have access to the only indoor pool on the mountain. Rates go from $120 per night for a studio to $410 for the larger units and larger private homes.

The **Edelweiss** in the base area (862-5252), has hotel rooms for $115 with two-bedroom, two-bath condos going for $290.

In Whitefish, the **Grouse Mountain Lodge** (862-3000 or 800-321-8822) is the most comfortable and convenient hotel. Its rooms are spacious and a shuttlebus takes guests to the mountain every morning. Cross-country skiing is right out the back door and downtown is only a short walk or ride away. Regular season double room rates are $60–$119.

The **Log House on the Hill** (862-1071) is a four-bedroom, two-bath home that sleeps 12 and has a hot tub. Rates start at $150 per night.

The **Pine Lodge-Quality Inn** (862-7600) boasts an indoor-outdoor pool with connecting swim channel, hot tub and free continental breakfast. Rates are $63–$179.

Good Medicine Lodge (862-5488) is built of cedar timbers and has a rustic and informal atmosphere. Rooms are decorated in a Western-Native American motif with fireplaces and solid wood furnishings. Rates are $75–$85, including breakfast.

The **Garden Wall Inn** (862-3440) is an antique-filled B&B only a block from the city shuttle. This is great for couples. Rates are $95–$105 per night per double with breakfast.

The **Castle Bed and Breakfast** (862-1257), in the National Register of Historic Places, is one of Montana's most unusual buildings. The living room is massive with a great fireplace. The house has three guest rooms, one with private bath, two with shared bath. Double rooms with breakfast are $52 to $95 a night.

Dining

The **Summit House** serves dinners with a Glacier Park peak view on Wednesday and Saturday nights from 5:30 to 9 p.m. The Glacier Chaser chairs are replaced by gondola cars to whisk diners up the mountain. Call 862-2900 for reservations.

At the base of the ski area the best food can be found at **The Hellroaring Saloon** (named for the mountain range west of town, not the customer behavior) or **Mogul's Bar and Grill**. Though both are casual, Mogul's is a little more upscale; Hellroaring has a great neighborhood atmosphere. Others in the base area include the **Café Kandahar**, **Alpinglow Restaurant** with a great view, and the **Bierstube** for Back Door Burgers.

The bulk of restaurants are found in Whitefish. The finest dining in the area is at **Logan's Bar and Grill** in the Grouse Mountain Lodge (862-3000) or across the street in the **Whitefish Lake Restaurant** (862-5285) at the golf course. **The Two Moon Café** (862-7580) serves fresh pasta, chicken and fish entrées and great salads. It doesn't have a liquor license, but you can bring your own bottle of wine. **The Glacier Grande** (862-9400) combines nightlife with Southwest dinners.

Dos Amigos (862-9994) is a basic Tex-Mex spot with a fine selection of imported beers. At **Rocco's** (756-5834) you'll find good Italian seafood dishes as well as traditional Italian pastas and chicken, steak and veal. **The Coyote Roadhouse** (837-4250) is the spot to head for Cajun cooking and super-fresh fish. **Stumptown Station** (862-4979) grills up great steaks. **Jimmy Lee's** (862-5303) is the recommended Chinese restaurant if you have a craving for a stir-fry, straw mushrooms or Szechwan duck.

For breakfast, the place to see and be seen is **The Buffalo Café** (862-2833) in Whitefish. If you can get a seat and listen a bit you'll hear about everything happening in town. Try the Buffalo Pie, layers of hashbrowns, ham, cheese and poached eggs, or order the Cinnamon Swirl French Toast; get a side order of chorizo if you decide to stick with basic eggs. It's open for lunch as well. If you can't get a seat there, try the new **"Out of the Blue" Bakery** with great huevos rancheros and baked goods.

Montanans like good coffee and beer. Whitefish has four drive-through espresso establishments and many restaurants have microbrews on tap.

Après-ski/nightlife

If you enjoy a wacky, let-it-loose style of après-ski and nighttime fun, The Big Mountain has one of the best places in the country, **The Bierstube** at the ski area base. Hundreds of ski-club T-shirts (some quite risqué) hang from the rafters; owner Gary Elliott has boxes of 'em and rotates them every so often.

Among the various pranks and ceremonies is the Frabert Award, presented each week to the employee or visitor who does the biggest goof-up. Other pranks are legendary, but why ruin the fun for those of you who are Bierstube virgins? When ski clubs are in town and The Bierstube has a live band, the dancing goes full-blast until closing.

The Hellroaring Saloon, also at the ski area base, is the original Chalet, built in the 1950s. It still looks like an old ski bar from the inside. Best deal: if you buy a Hellroaring baseball cap ($20) you get free beer every day you wear it to the bar. Also on the mountain, **Moguls Bar and Grille** has entertainment nightly.

It's worth a visit to the **Palace Bar** on Central Avenue in Whitefish just to see its carved mahogany bar that dates back to the turn of the century. Until the health department said it couldn't, the Palace Bar also hosted the once-famous white mouse races.

The Great Northern Bar and Grill on Central Avenue offers live music from Thursday to Saturday and acoustic open-mike on Tuesday. Locals come for the burgers and wide selection of microbrewery beers and stay for the music.

Other Whitefish nightlife choices are on Central Avenue. Having all the bars lined up makes it easy to check out the scene and decide where you want to set up camp. Choose from **Glacier Grande, The Remington, Bulldog Saloon, Casey's** or **Stumptown,** all notable in their own way, and a good time for those cruising for rock or country music and drinks.

For more mellow evenings try the tipple and the band at **Logans Bar** in the Grouse Mountain Lodge. For a real cowboy evening, complete with live foot-stomping music and longneck beer bottles you can slip in your back pockets, head to the **Blue Moon Nite Club** in Columbia Falls at the intersection of Highways 2 and 40.

Other activities

Shopping: Quite limited at the base area. Whitefish's Central Avenue has many art galleries and stores that stock Western clothing, jewelry and crafts. **Montana Coffee Traders,** on Highway 93 south of town, has many Montana food gift items, such as huckleberry syrup.

Near the ski area, Old West Adventures has **sleigh rides** through the forests to an Old West roadhouse where hot drinks are served. On Thursday night the ride includes dinner and singing as well as a historical narrative about opening the West. Call 862-2900 for reservations.

Downtown in Whitefish sleigh rides leave the Grouse Mountain Lodge for a 20-minute ride to a camp near Lost Coon Lake. Call 862-3000 for reservations.

Snowmobiling is well organized in this part of the country. Groomed trails are maintained and a guide is available from the Flathead Convention and Visitors Association at (800) 543-3105. Several trails climb to the summit of The Big Mountain.

Snowcat powder skiing is also offered in areas of the mountain not yet served by lifts. Snowcat tours are four hours; call 862-2909 for rates.

Dog sledding adventures provide a fun 12-mile tour of the wilderness. Call 881-2275 for more information.

Getting there and getting around

Getting there: The nearest airport, **Glacier Park International** in Kalispell, is 19 miles south of the resort. However, service in and out is limited to twice a day on Delta from Salt Lake City and to several Horizon Air commuter flights from nearby airports. Northwest has a Saturday flight nonstop from Minneapolis and may add more for 95/96. Glacier Park International is the nearest airport for private pilots.

Train transportation via Amtrak's Empire Builder stops four times a week from Seattle and Portland to the west and from Chicago and Minneapolis to the east.

Driving to The Big Mountain is along some of North America's most scenic highways. Access from Banff or Missoula is by Highway 93. Highway 2 runs east and west through Kalispell. Whitefish RV Park is on Highway 93 south.

Getting around: If you stay and play at the mountain, you won't need a car. To get between mountain and town, you can take **Whitefish Area Rapid Transit** (WART), which has five daily runs. In winter, the schedule works well for those staying in Whitefish and riding the bus to ski, but it's impossible for mountain lodgers who want to party late at night in town (the last run back to the mountain is about 5:30 p.m.). Taxi service also is available.

Information/reservations

The Big Mountain maintains a central reservations system for all lodging on the mountain. Call 862-1960 or (800) 858-4157.

For information about activities in Kalispell and Whitefish contact the **Flathead Convention and Visitors Association at** (800) 543-3105 or 756-9091. The **Whitefish Chamber of Commerce** provides information at 862-3501.

The area code is 406 unless otherwise noted.

Big Sky, Montana

Tucked into Montana's southwest corner is a dormant volcano, perhaps ready to erupt into the big-time ski resort scene. Big Sky, with its impressive Matterhorn-shaped peak scraping the heavens at 11,166 feet, is a serious skier's mountain, bare bones and low on frills. Don't expect valet service from the parking-lot attendant, luxury day lodges or amenities of fancy resorts. You can expect spectacular scenery, friendly locals, a laid-back atmosphere, and starting this season, more vertical feet of slopes than any other American resort.

A seven-year building boom has seen Big Sky transformed from an intermediate mountain into one that also will challenge high-ability skiers. Big Sky has more than doubled its lift capacity in the last four years, which has opened a lot of variable expert terrain. The intermediate runs are still there, which makes Big Sky appropriate for both families and for those looking for real challenges.

You may hear a lot about Big Sky this season. By adding an aerial tram with two 15-passenger cars to the 11,150-foot level on Lone Peak, Big Sky will claim the longest vertical drop in the nation—4,180 feet, 41 feet higher than Jackson Hole. Most of the terrain under the tram will be tough, with pitches averaging 28 degrees. If you get to the top and find that the chutes, couloirs and steeps are over your head, no problem—admire the views of the nearby Spanish Peaks Wilderness area from the enclosed observation deck and ride back down. Also new this season is a double chair lift called Shedhorn, which opens 1,200 new acres of rolling intermediate terrain.

Big Sky is a true destination resort, far from large urban areas, yet an hour from the nearest jet airport. Visitors fly in from all over the country. Everything is available in the considerable space of a village that changes in appearance and attitude from rowdy and crowded in one section to stately and reserved in another. But it also has a European feel. Ski school director Hans Schernthaner is from Austria, and each year brings in

Big Sky Facts
Base elevation: 6,970'; **Summit elevation:** 11,150'; **Vertical drop:** 4,180 feet.
Number and types of lifts: 15—1 aerial tram, 2 4-passenger gondolas, 2 quad superchairs, 3 triples, 3 doubles and 4 surface lifts
Acreage: 3,500 skiable acres **Snowmaking:** 20 percent of trails
Uphill capacity: 16,510 skiers per hour **Bed base:** 3,540

English-speaking Europeans to teach. And each skier feeds a pass into machines that open gates for the lift, just as the computer systems in the Alps.

Big Sky now attracts nearly a quarter of a million skier visits. However, they are all swallowed by the 3,500-acre terrain. A big daily turnout is 3,000, meaning short lines for the gondolas. Nearly every visitor spends at least a day in Yellowstone, only an hour away.

Where to ski

Big Sky spans two mountains, Lone Peak and Andesite Mountain. Beginners and lower intermediates can enjoy gentle runs from Andesite's Southern Comfort triple chair. Sacajawea, El Dorado and Ponderosa appeal to families and young ones alike. Gentle rollers such as Mr. K, White Wing and Lone Wolf are reached via Gondola #1 or the Explorer Lift on Lone Peak

Advanced intermediates have a variety of terrain on both mountains. Skis run fast and long on Andesite's Bighorn, ElkPark and Ambush. Bump enthusiasts make tracks on Africa and MadWolf. Fine-tune your techniques on the manicured slopes of Tippy's Tumble, Lobo, Calamity Jane and Upper Morning Star.

Perhaps the most impressive ski terrain at Big Sky is the expansive bowl area, nestled in the heart of Lone Peak. Above treeline bowl beckon advanced skiers for untouched powder. A six-minute triple chair services this bowl area. Steep pitches and wide-open terrain can be found on the bowl's South Wall. The more adventurous can register with the ski patrol and test their skills in A-Z Chutes, the Pinnacles and the Big and Little Couloir, all out of bounds. Out-of-bounds skiing is permitted, but only with the right rescue equipment. If you want to ski this terrain, bring a transceiver and a shovel.

Experts should head to the vast terrain on Lone Mountain's north side, where a lot of locals ski. The Challenger chair climbs 1,750 steep vertical feet to open hair-raising black-diamond and double-black in-bounds terrain. This is some of the toughest in-bounds skiing in the country. Steep long pitches can be found on Big Rock Tongue, north-facing bowls greet skiers in Nashville Basin and narrow tree chutes are on Little Tree and Buttress Gully. Continue farther north and intermediates are treated to tamer terrain off the Iron Horse Quad lift. This is the first in a series of future lifts which will open up a new area called Moonlight Basin.

Mountain rating

Big Sky lives up to its name and is good for skiers of all abilities. The south side of Andesite Mountain is great for beginners because of the wide gentle slopes and because it gets a lot of sun. Intermediates have nearly half of Big Sky's terrain, but a caveat here: not all the blue trails are groomed, and some have cat-track runouts or are simply too short. Advanced and expert skiers have a lot of terrain—open bowls, chutes and couloirs—to play on. Bump enthusiasts might be a little disappointed here. Except for Mad Wolf (black diamond) and Africa (advanced blue), Big Sky doesn't get enough skiers to carve big moguls.

Cross-country

Nationally acclaimed **Lone Mountain Guest Ranch** offers 75 km. of international caliber Nordic skiing for all levels, with groomed diagonal and skating lanes. The trail system winds through open meadows and forested canyons, treating skiers to stunning views around every bend.

Lone Mountain Ranch teams with Alpenguide Tours of West Yellowstone to offer a variety of backcountry skiing, including snowcat tours into the interior of Yellowstone National Park, which allow beginners and experts a chance to view abundant wildlife, spouting geysers and other winter wonders of America's most beloved national park.

Deluxe cozy cabins with fireplace and full bath are available for weekly rental, including all meals, trail pass and evening programs for $1,250 to $2,500, depending on the number of people and cabin size. The Ranch has a Nordic shop with apparel, equipment and mementos. Trail pass is $10 for adults; children 12 and younger ski free; half day tickets available, as are group and private lessons (including a beginner package). Call 995-4644.

Snowboarding

No restrictions, and the resort has group and private lessons, rentals, repairs and two natural halfpipes.

Lessons (95/96 prices)

Big Sky has nearly 60 instructors, some of whom are English-speakers from the Alps. **Group lessons** cost $25 for half-day; $80 for four half-day sessions.

Private lessons cost $60 for an hour, $150 for half-day and $260 for a full-day lesson, with additional skiers paying extra.

Children's lessons are $38 for the day, without lunch, which is available at an extra charge. Ski Day Camp is for those aged 6-14, emphasizing fun and specific skills. Mini Camp is a program for ages 4-6, with sledding games and hot-chocolate parties in addition to ski time.

NASTAR races are $5 for two runs; $2 each additional run.

For information on lessons, call 995-5743.

Child care

The Big Sky Playcare Center (995-5847) takes infants and toddlers. Infant child care (younger than 18 months) requires a five-day advance reservation. For the toddlers, the center has an outdoor playground as well as indoor art, reading and play activities. Rates are $41 for a full day, $33 for half day, $55 for a full day of skiing and day care, or $8 per hour for hourly care. Reservations are suggested for all child care services and parents will need to bring some things, so call ahead.

Lift tickets (94/95 prices)

	Adult	Child (Up to 10)
One day	$38	Free**
Three days	$111 ($37/day)	
Five days	$175 ($35/day)	

Half-day tickets are sold, but are just $4 less. Other multiday rates also available. Skiers 70 and older ski for half price. Rates to ride the aerial tram had not been established at press time; call (800) 548-4486 for information.

**Up to two children ski free per paying adult, good every day of the season.

Accommodations

Big Sky is divided into three areas spanning nine miles—the Mountain Village, the Meadow Village and the Canyon. The farther you are from the lifts, the less you generally pay. These areas are serviced by a free shuttle system during the winter.

In the Mountain Village:

At the center of the Mountain Village are the 204-room **Huntley Lodge** and 92-suite **Shoshone Condominium Hotel**. The Shoshone is a luxury ski-in/ski-out hotel with condo-type units, lap pool, health club, steam bath and more. Rates are $220–$470. Call (800) 548-4486 or (406) 995-5000. The lodge has an outdoor pool, two Jacuzzis, sauna, game room and more. Rates are $101–$319. Packages available.

Condos are available through **Triple Creek Realty and Management Co.** (800-543-4362). If you want luxury, try the Beaverhead and Arrowhead condos, three and four bedrooms at $450–$525. Moderate two- and three-bedroom units are at Skycrest (underground parking and rates $320–$365) and Stillwater (studios and two-bedroom units at $130-$220).

Golden Eagle Condominium Rental (800-548-4488) rents units at Skycrest (served by the shuttle system), Bighorn (slopeside two-bedroom units at $250) and Hill (an eight-minute walk from the lifts; $105–$130 for a studio, with or without loft).

In the Meadow Village (six miles away):

New last season is **River Rock Lodge** (800-995-9966) described as a "boutique-style European hotel" with stone and log construction and beautiful interior decor. Its 29 rooms have rates of $95–$120, including continental breakfast.

The Golden Eagle Lodge (800-548-4488) offers budget-minded travelers clean, basic accommodations. The rooms have been renovated and expanded, and a full restaurant and bar are right there. There is a very friendly staff and rates are $40–$65.

Triple Creek Realty and Management Co. (800-543-4362) manages several condo complexes here, including Hidden Village, units set in the forest with in-house Jacuzzis and garage at $275–$350; Park, with head-on views of Lone Peak at $185–$280; or several others. **Golden Eagle Condominium Rental** (800-548-4488) has many condos on the cross-country trail system, and private homes, for $150–$400.

Also contact **Big Sky Condominium Management** (995-4560) or **River Rock Accommodations Management** (800-995-9966) for slopeside or Meadow Village accommodations.

In the Canyon (three miles from the Meadow Village, nine miles from the lifts, in the beautiful Gallatin River Canyon):

Buck's T-4 Lodge (800-822-4484), Big Sky's Best Western hotel, has two pool-size outdoor Jacuzzis, a large stone fireplace and a nationally acclaimed restaurant that specializes in wild game (see Dining). On the free shuttle route, the hotel has rates of $69–$99; kitchenettes for $125–$150.

Big Sky's only B&B, **The Rainbow Ranch** (995-4132), is 13 miles from the lifts. It has 12 rooms with private baths and full breakfasts included in the $45–$75 rate (for two people). Other places to stay 13–20 miles from the lifts are the **320 Ranch** (800-243-0320), with Montana-style log cabins, with or without cooking units, that sleep two to ten people. Rates: $68–$200. Budget accommodations ($65 or less) include the **Corral Motel** (995-4249) and the **Cinnamon Lodge** (995-4253), the latter of which has RV hookups for $15–$20.

Dining
In the Mountain Village:
Huntley Lodge (995-5783) is known for its fine dining—breakfast and dinner—and one of Montana's largest wine selections. In the Mountain Mall, **Whiskey Jack** has tableside slope views and an expansive outdoor deck for lunch or cocktails, and **M.R. Hummers** is known for its baby back ribs. **Buckskin Charlie's**, a casual spot for breakfast or dinner; with its full bar, popular with the younger budget-conscious crowd. Other lunch or snack spots: **Levinsky's** for pizza, **Scissorbills Bar and Grill** at the base of Silverknife ski run, or **Serendipity** for espresso and a muffin.

In the Meadow Village:
Intimate candlelight, linen service and sunset views of Lone Peak await at **First Place** (995-4244), behind the post office. It features American and Continental cuisine and famous desserts.

Edelweiss (995-4665) has excellent Austrian and German food. **Rocco's** (995-4200) has Mexican and Italian food with a full bar.

Lone Mountain Ranch Dining Room (995-2782) has a quiet, smoke-free environment in rustic elegance. Sleigh-ride dinners are offered here for about $50 per adult and $45 for kids. Call ahead as space is limited (995-2783). In the Westfork meadow, Guinness on tap and terrific pesto pizza are at **Uncle Milkies Pizza and Subs** (995-2900). Across the road, **Allgoods Bar and Grill** (995-2750) serve up hickory-smoked baby back ribs, chicken and pork, along with homemade stews and burgers. Breakfast and dinner daily and a pool table, darts and poker.

In the Gallatin Canyon:

Buck's T-4 Restaurant (995-4111) is the area's oldest and most popular dining establishment. Its specialties are wild game, Montana beef, veal and seafood. There's an extensive wine list and an original rustic bar built in 1946. If you're staying at the mountain or the meadow, ride the free shuttle. **320 Restaurant** (995-4283) serves breakfast and dinner daily in a nicely appointed Montana log cabin. Entrées are in the $13-$23 range, and sleigh ride dinners are nightly at $4 per person.

Budget eats can be found at the **Half Moon Saloon** (995-4533) for lunch and dinner, **Corral Bar and Cafe** (995-4249) for steaks, burgers and good local color, and the **Cinnamon Lodge and Restaurant** (995-4253) which features great Mexican food on Wednesday and Friday evening.

Après-ski/nightlife

Big Sky is known more for its slopes than its nightlife, but you can find a good time. First check Big Sky's local newspaper, *The Lone Peak Lookout*, which has entertainment listings.

The hub of night activity is the Mountain Village. Happy hour kicks off in **Chet's Bar**, in the Huntley Lodge, with the "Crazy Austrian" show (just go see it). Chet's also has poker games (legal in Montana). The **Whiskey Jack** frequently features nationally known recording artists, along with local bands. Covers range from free admission to $10. **Buckskin Charlie's** has live blues bands and drink specials on Monday nights. You can find a nice atmosphere and live jazz on weekends at **The Caboose**, downstairs in the Mountain Mall.

In the canyon, check out the **Buck T-4** game room, with pool tables, foosball and video games. On Tuesdays, it's $2 Night, with $2 pitchers of draft beer and two pizza slices for $2. Locals like the **Corral** and **The Half Moon Saloon**, with darts, pool, shuffleboard and local bands on weekends.

Other activities

Shopping: The Mountain Mall has various shops and boutiques. Plum Logo has Montana-made gifts and Big Sky T-shirts and souvenirs. The Lone Spur in the Shoshone Condominium complex is a good spot for high-quality western clothing, jewelry and gifts. In the Meadow Village, shop at Tick Ridge Traders, Presents, Northern Lights Trading Company, Willow Boutique and By Word of Mouth (which has a great wine selection and prices). Moose Rack Books has new, out-of-print and rare books in two locations, one at the mountain and another in the canyon. Also in the canyon is Sky Spirits, Big Sky's state liquor store, with a gift shop.

Snowmobiling in Yellowstone National Park is a major attraction. You can travel to Old Faithful in two or three hours and see buffalo, bald eagles, wild geese and moose. Most snowmobile shops offer a 10 percent discount with a Big Sky lift ticket and provide bus service from the resort and West Yellowstone. For information, Rendezvous Snowmobile Rentals, (800) 426-7669 or 646-9564; Snowmobile Yellowstone, (800) 221-1151; Yellowstone Adventures, (800) 231-5991 or 646-7735; West Yellowstone, (800) 541-7354 or 646-9695.

You can snowmobile nearer Big Sky with Canyon Rentals (995-4540) in Gallatin National Forest, half a mile south of the Big Sky entrance. Single riders are $79, doubles $105.

Rent snowshoes from the Lone Mountain Guest Ranch (995-4644) or Grizzly Outfitters (995-2939) for $8–$10 per day.

Dogsled rides are offered by Spirit of the North Dog Adventures (995-4644) with half-day tours at $89.

Winter fishing on the Gallatin River is available through Gallatin Riverguides (995-2290 or East Slope Anglers (995-4369), who have licenses, equipment rentals and supplies.

Getting there and getting around

Getting there: Northwest, Horizon Air, SkyWest, Frontier and Delta fly into **Bozeman Gallatin Field Airport,** an hour from the resort. (Northwest and Delta fly jets.) **4X4 Stage** shuttles passengers between the airport, the resort and West Yellowstone. Call 388-6404.

The resort is 45 miles south of Bozeman (and 50 miles north of West Yellowstone) on Highway 191 along the Gallatin River. Turn at the Big Sky entrance and drive to the Mountain Village.

Getting around: A car is optional unless you plan to do a lot of sightseeing or travel between the villages. You can get also manage with the free shuttlebus, which runs from 7 a.m.–11 p.m., beginning mid-December through the winter.

Information/reservations

Big Sky Ski & Summer Resort, (800) 548-4486 nationwide; 995-5000 in Montana. For group reservations and conferences, call (800) 548-4487.

The area code is 406 unless otherwise noted.

Taos, New Mexico

Taos Ski Valley is like no other ski resort in North America. The ski area is a little piece of the Alps, founded by a Swiss and surrounded by hotels and restaurants built by Frenchmen and Austrians. It's near the town of Taos, which is a rich mix of Spanish and Indian cultures, melded over the centuries to produce the Southwestern style. This style, in art, cuisine and architecture, isn't trendy here; it's the way things have always been. It is this exotic blend of the European and Southwestern that makes Taos Ski Valley unique in the ski world.

Taos Ski Valley holds another distinction: while many resorts walk a delicate marketing tightrope, touting whatever expert terrain they possess while trying not to scare anyone off, Taos seems to enjoy its tough reputation. Its marketers don't play up that image (word gets around among skiers), but they make no effort to refute it either. Instead they wisely advise visitors to meet the challenge by enrolling in Ski-Better-Week, a package of lessons, accommodations, meals and lift tickets.

Just about everybody at Taos enrolls in ski school. If you aren't part of a class, you feel like the kid that didn't get chosen for a sandlot baseball team. Après-ski talk centers on Ski-Better-Week anecdotes, and independents will sit at the bar with little to add.

Taos is one of a few remaining large ski resorts still run by a family—the Blake clan, now headed by Mickey, son of the late founder, Ernie. In the four decades since Taos opened, traditions have developed. One is the quest for hidden *porrons*, hand-blown Mexican glass flasks filled with martinis and buried in the snow under trees for classes to discover. Another is free hot chocolate in winter (lemonade in spring) in lift lines if they get too long (this happens most often at the base, where two non-high-speed quads must transport everybody in the morning). And the family-like ski classes everyone feel right at home.

Taos Facts
Base elevation: 9,207'; **Summit elevation:** 11,819'; **Vertical drop:** 2,612 feet
Number of lifts: 11—4 quad chairs, 1 triple chair, 5 double chairs, 1 surface lift
Percent snowmaking: 34 percent
Total acreage: 1,096 acres terrain, 687 acres of trails
Uphill capacity: 15,000 per hour **Bed Base:** 3,705 in Ski Valley and town

Where to ski

Two factors make Taos' intimidating topography approachable: a staff eager to help the newcomer and the outstanding instruction program. Every morning a crew of blue-jacketed hosts is stationed at ticket area, base, and the tops of all lifts to answer questions about lift lines and appropriate trails. Remember: an intermediate run like Lower Stauffenberg or Porcupine might be considered advanced elsewhere. Here, it is no disgrace to warm up on a green run—it's a good idea.

Taos' skiing is on two sides of a ridge marked by blue-square Bambi at the top and black-diamond Al's Run at the bottom. To the left of the ridge, as you look at the mountain, are wider, gentler runs such as Shalako Bowl, Honeysuckle, and Upper and Lower Totemoff. To the right of the ridge are narrower steeper runs like the dense, tree-filled Castor and Pollux, and intermediate trails such as Lower Stauffenberg and Powderhorn Bowl.

Smooth intermediate bowls can be found off the Kachina quad chair, the widest being Shalako. The least crowded bowl is Hunziker, named after a Swiss lift engineer, kept isolated by a short climb to its entrance. The Hunziker Bowl entices you with a mild concave slope, but just when you feel confident and relaxed, it drops off with the steepness of a waterfall and narrows down to force you into precision skiing in short turns.

For tree skiers, Taos has a special challenge, the twin runs Castor and Pollux. They hardly look like runs, just steep wooded parts of the mountain, unskiable, where some joker put a sign that looks just like a trail marker. The trees are two to 15 feet apart, and advanced classes regularly train here.

Powder skiing lasts on Highline Ridge and Kachina Peak. These are not for the faint of heart, for two reasons: they are double black diamonds and Kachina Peak is reachable only after an hour-and-fifteen-minute hike from the top chair at 11,800 feet to the ridge at 12,500 feet. You can, however, ski off Highline Ridge and West Basin Ridge after only a 15-minute hike. Skiers are advised to go with an instructor or a patrolman; at the very least, they must check in with the patrol at the top of Chair 6. The ski patrol will give you a rough screening to see if you can handle the double-diamond terrain. In any case you must ski the ridge with a partner.

Taos is rarely crowded: ticket sales are cut off at 4,800 although the mountain can accommodate many more. If you're looking for no people at all, the farthest run west, Lower Stauffenberg running into Don't Tell, will probably be empty. You definitely will find crowds twice a day: once in the morning as you board the two base lifts, and again in the afternoon. The only ways off the mountain are straight down the infamous Al's Run or a couple of other tough black-diamond routes, or on one of two green-circle cat trails, Whitefeather on the right and Rubezahl on the left. There's usually plenty of room on Al's Run, but not on Whitefeather and Rubezahl. Despite the slow-down efforts of ski hosts stationed every 20 feet or so, both runs resemble the Hollywood Freeway at rush hour, except that the faster skiers aren't stalled in traffic. They zip around the slower ones, gingerly wedging their way home. On busy days it's a mess.

Mountain rating

The name Taos Ski Valley is almost too genteel. It implies a softness to the slopes. Less appealing—but more accurate— would be Taos Ski Gorge. A whopping 51 percent of the runs are rated expert, but that doesn't mention that 19 of those 36 runs are double black diamonds.

While experts will adore Taos for its challenge, intermediates may be frustrated and beginners may be downright terrified. Most of the green-circle trails are narrow, high-traffic access runs to more challenging terrain. Many of the blue-square runs start off wide, but then get quite narrow in spots. Those narrow portions can build some menacing bumps.

We strongly recommend that lower-level skiers take lessons—not only to improve their skills but also to find the best part of the mountain for them. Only athletic beginners should attempt to learn here. Despite the highly regarded ski school, the jump from the tiny learning area to the mountain is enormous. Better learning terrain is at nearby Angel Fire (see the New Mexico chapter).

Skiers who are solid intermediate and above: rise up to meet Taos' challenge. If you normally ski blue runs at other resorts, you can ski Taos. It may be tough at first, but persist—you'll catch on. Taos can be an extremely rewarding ski experience *because* of its challenge. If you ski well here, you deserve to strut into the bar at the end of the day; there are few highs in skiing that top the successful conquest of this mountain. And if you don't, the mountain provides a convenient excuse.

Last suggestion: take a trail map and consult it often.

Cross-country

The nearest Nordic area is Enchanted Forest Cross-Country Ski Area, 40 miles northeast of Taos by Highways 522 and 38. Just below Bobcat Pass, 3 miles east of Red River, it has 34 km. of backcountry trails, some groomed, and an elevation of 10,300 feet. Trail rates are $9 for adults, with discounts for teens, seniors and children. At the headquarters at Miller's Crossing in downtown Red River, you can rent equipment (including pulks, which are sleds that allow adults to pull small children as they ski) and pick up trail maps. Call 754-2374.

Snowboarding

Not permitted. Monoskis and telemark skis are allowed.

Lessons (95/96 prices)

Ski-Better-Weeks are the core of the Taos ski experience, developed by former French Junior Alpine champion and ski school technical director Jean Mayer. Participants are matched for six mornings of intensive lessons, and they ski with the same instructor all week. Sixty-five percent of the participants are intermediate or higher.

Ski Week costs $360, lifts and lessons, for adults and teens. Children 6 to 12 can enroll for $384. Specialized Ski Weeks are offered for masters (age 50 and older) and women during certain weeks of the season. Prices vary. Many lodging properties offer the Ski Better Week as a package with meals and accommodations; indeed, you can't stay at Jean Mayer's Hotel St. Bernard unless you're signed up for the ski week.

Single **group lessons** (two hours, morning or afternoon) cost $29, three or more days are $25 per day.

Private lessons are $70 a person for the first hour, $45 each additional person or hour. An all-day private lesson is $325, with a maximum of three skiers; a half-day private lesson is $210.

The Yellowbird Special for **never-ever skiers** includes novice lift ticket, morning and afternoon lessons for $46; $52 includes equipment rental.

Super Ski Week is an intense ski week for adults who wish to focus seriously on improving their skiing. Skiers are analyzed, videotaped and put through what amounts to a mini ski-racing camp every morning and afternoon for a total of five hours. This is not a program for the timid or late-night party types—most participants have no energy left for anything but a quick bite to eat and then to bed. But most will find their skills much improved by the end of the week. It's offered at selected times and has varying costs, depending on the season.

Children's programs operate out of the Kinderkäfig children's center, where parents can also get ski rentals. (One disadvantage: the center is inconveniently located away from the main base area.) The Junior Elite program, ages 3 to 12, includes a two-hour morning lesson, lunch and afternoon supervised skiing for $65 a day. Younger children (ages 3–5) get a program that combines lessons, snow play and indoor activities. Reservations are recommended; call 776-2291.

The Ski School also has **special programs** in mogul introduction, mountain cruising, steep and deep, and telemark with a guide. The three-day programs cost $75.

Child care

The Kinderkåfig Children's Center also has infant and toddler care for ages 6 weeks to 2 years. For infants, there is a staff member for every two babies. Toddlers get planned activities and snow play. Rates including lunch and snacks are $50 a day, $30 per half day and $294 for six days. The program operates daily from 8:30 a.m. to 4 p.m.

Lift tickets (95/96 prices)

	Adult	Child (Up to 12)
One day	$38	$23
Three days	$105 ($35/day)	$60 ($20/day)
Five days	$175 ($35/day)	$100 ($20/day)

Seniors 65–69 ski for $18; 70 and older ski free. Taos also reduces its lift ticket price in January value season and the early and late season.

Accommodations

What gives Taos its European atmosphere is the emphasis on the complete week-long experience of lessons. The **Ski-Better-Week** packages include up to seven nights lodging (Saturday to Saturday), 20 meals, six lift tickets and six morning lessons. Prices range from $1,350 per person, double occupancy, at **Hotel St. Bernard** with three meals a day, to about $770 without meals at **Powderhorn Condominums.** Between these price extremes the Village has 11 other establishments, all but one offers the Ski Better Week package.

The **Hotel St. Bernard Condos** managed by Jean Mayer, Taos ski school technical director, offer the flavor of a European retreat. Dinner is in the famed Hotel St. Bernard, where the cuisine and ambiance are both legendary—and French.

Kandahar Condominiums on the slopes has hotel rooms as well as two-bedroom condos, which can also be booked with the Ski Week program (no meals). Per night: $159–$335, four to six per unit.

The Inn at Snakedance has 60 ski-in/ski-out rooms from $125 to $215 per night. Amenities include a spa with hot tub, sauna, exercise and massage facility; a slopeside library with stone fireplace, a glass-walled bar and a restaurants serving continental cuisine with a Southwest flair. Ski-Better-Week packages start at $1,276 per person.

The least expensive is the skiers' hostel, **The Abominable Snowmansion** (776-8298) in Arroyo Seco, nine miles from the Village, where the rates are under $25 for a dorm bed. Another bargain choice is the **Fraser House Hostel** in nearby Valdez, 776-5753.

Between the ski area and town is a bed-and-breakfast inn, the **Salsa del Salto.** Formerly the residence of Hotel St. Bernard owner Jean Mayer, it's now run by Jean's brother Dadou, a French-trained chef who cooks Salsa del Salto's gourmet breakfasts. Prices range from $85-$160 per room. B&Bs can be booked through the Taos B&B Association, (800) 876-7857.

The town of Taos offers a wide range of accommodations. Some have packages, but not the Ski-Better-Week package. (Remember, you can book the Ski-Better-Week separately.) Prices are generally less expensive than staying at Taos Ski Valley. ($55 to $395, depending on the luxury factor). At the northern edge of town, **Quail Ridge Inn** is a fully appointed condominium complex at a tennis ranch, including indoor and outdoor courts. Looking much like a pueblo, it exudes the Southwestern atmosphere. More information from 776-2211 or (800) 624-4448. Rooms at **El Pueblo Lodge** (800-433-9612) and the **Indian Hills Inn** (800-444-2346) are closer to the bottom of the price range. Other simple-yet-comfortable lodging is at the **Adobe Wall Motel** (758-3972) and the **Koshari Inn** (758-7199), both on Kit Carson Road, and a little farther from the ski area (and even less expensive), the **Taos Motel** (758-2524).

The Historic Taos Inn is the cultural center of Taos. The lobby, built around the old town well, is a gathering place for artists. Rooms feature adobe fireplaces, antiques, Taos-style furniture built by local artisans. Rates are $75–$160. Call (800) 826-7466 (800-TAOS-INN).

The **Sagebrush Inn** is an historic inn with a priceless collection of Southwestern art in the lobby and the best nightlife in town; $70–$140. Call (800) 428-3626 or 758-2254.

Reader recommendation: Frank Weymouth and Brenda Maille of Pelham, NH liked the condos at **Hacienda De Valdez**, located between the ski area and town, citing spaciousness, decor and friendly staff. They paid $190 per night, with two couples sharing the condo. Call (800) 837-2218 or 776-2218.

Taos Valley Resort Association, (800) 776-1111, or locally, 776-2233, can make all reservations and organizes all-inclusive three- to seven-day packages including air, transfers to Taos, lodging, lifts and lessons.

Dining

Because so many properties at Taos Ski Valley offer Ski-Better-Week packages, which include meals, most restaurants are operated by the lodges. It's still that way at the Hotel St. Bernard and Thunderbird Lodge. The best independent eateries in the village are **Rhoda's Restaurant, Dolomite** and **Tim's Stray Dog Cantina.** Rhoda's, named for Ernie Blake's wife, has many New Mexican specialties. Dolomite features Northern Italian pasta and pizza, but it's not a pizza joint—owner Karen Lubliner is a classically trained chef. At Tim's Stray Dog (an inevitable name: owner Tim Harter used to work at the Hotel St. Bernard, a.k.a. The Dog), try the Tequila Shrimp.

On the road into the valley, the **Casa Cordova** (776-2500) specializes in American and continental cuisine (entrées are $14-$20). The **Chili Connection** (776-8787) is known for its chicken chimichanga and Pollo Borracho Entrées run $7-$11. **Whitey's Brett House**, at the junction of Highways 64 and 150, serves continental cuisine in the $10-$18 range. Call 776-8545. **Renegade Cafe** at the Quail Ridge Inn (776-8319) specializes in Mediterranean-style food.

Taos has great variety. For the best burger in town, locals recommend the not-so-Southwest-sounding **Fred's Place** on S. Santa Fe Road (758-0514). The menu at the intimate **Apple Tree Restaurant** (758-1900) lists Southwestern dishes and continental cuisine. On the historic plaza, **The Garden Restaurant** (758-9483) offers New Mexican as well as American, Italian and French entrées; call 758-9483. **Doc Martin's** (758-1977) in the Taos Inn has creative Southwestern cuisine. **Michael's Kitchen** (758-4178) gets raves from locals for its breakfasts. The **Rancho de Taos House** (758-5089) has almost everything—Cajun, New Mexican, Italian, steaks. Another restaurant that gets high marks for dinner is **Roberto's**, which serves exceptional New Mexican dishes. Call ahead: 758-2434.

Après-ski/nightlife

Yawn. That is the sound of Taos' bone-tired skiers heading off to dreamland after dinner. The nightlife will never make any Top 10 lists.

After the lifts close, skiers will be found on the deck of the **Hotel St. Bernard**, the **Martini Tree Bar** at the Resort Center, or the **Twining Tavern** at the Thunderbird Lodge, sometimes with live music. The St. Bernard has live music every night—an eclectic mix of reggae, country, jazz, and acoustic guitar. The Thunderbird Lodge has live music in spurts. The Martini Tree has live music après-ski. **The Inn at Snakedance** has entertainment nightly.

Things are a little more lively in town. **The Sagebrush Inn** has Country & Western dances every night. The Kachina Lodge's **Cabaret Room** has a large dance floor for two-stepping, and **Ogelvie's Bar and Grill** in Taos Plaza is also hopping. For microbrew fans, **Eske's Brew Pub** off the Taos Plaza serves its own fresh beer brewed on the premises and pub fare.

Skiers and local artists mix at the **Adobe Bar** of the Taos Inn, which has been called the living room for artsy locals.

The *Taos News* has a weekly entertainment guide.

Other activities

Shopping: Georgia O'Keeffe and R.C. Gorman have made Taos legendary with art lovers. About 80 galleries are here, and the Quast Gallery has a Meet the Artist series at the ski area in winter. Taos is also where you will find extensive specialty shops, particularly around the plaza. A list is available from Taos Chamber of Commerce, 758-3873 or (800) 732-TAOS.

Fly fishing tours are offered in winter on the Red River by Los Rios Anglers, 758-2798.

Another unusual non-ski activity is a visit to **Taos Pueblo**, the 700-year-old home of the Tiwa Indians. In addition to the two massive adobe structures, the mission church of St. Francis of Assisi remains from the Spanish colonial era. The Tiwa Indians welcome visitors to their pueblo, their workshops, their ceremonies and sacred dances, except for a four- to six-week period each winter when the pueblo is closed for religious reasons. For exact dates, call the Taos Chamber of Commerce (800-732-8267). The pueblo is open from 9 a.m. to 4:30 p.m.

Getting there and getting around

Getting there: Taos Ski Valley is 135 miles—about three hours—north of Albuquerque, the nearest major airport. Rental car agencies are at the airport. If you choose to leave the driving to someone else, contact Faust's Transportation, 758-3410 in Taos or 843-9042 in Albuquerque; or Pride of Taos, 758-8340.

AMTRAK's Southwest Chief rolls from Chicago and Los Angeles. Train stations in Raton and Albuquerque are equidistant from Taos. Amtrak has ski packages, which we recommend because they provide connecting transportation, which is difficult to book on your own. Call American Rail Magic Tours at (800) 533-0363.

Getting around: If you are enrolled in a hotel-and-meals Ski Better Week package in Taos Ski Valley village and have no desire to go into the town of Taos 18 miles away, you won't need a car. If you want to visit the town, or aren't staying at the ski area, you'll need one. Overnight **RV parking**, without hookups, is permitted in the Taos Ski Valley parking lot.

Information/reservations

Address and phone: **Taos Ski Valley**, Box 90, Taos Ski Valley NM 87525; 776-2291. Snow report number: 776-2916.

Lodging reservations: **Taos Valley Resort Association**, (800) 776-1111.

Local area code is 505.

Ski Santa Fe, New Mexico

Take the brilliant sunlight of the high desert and a seemingly unlimited supply of fresh powder days. Add pre-Columbian Indian Pueblos, Spanish architecture, art galleries, a unique regional cuisine, and a skier-friendly mountain that will satisfy just about any taste, and you get Santa Fe.

Santa Fe offers enchanting contradiction. It is old and new, high mountain and flat desert, with cool winters that surprise out-of-staters who think of New Mexico as hot and dry. Skiing in this state is unlike anywhere else on the continent. To get a more foreign-feeling ski vacation, you'd need a passport.

Some ski vacationers think Taos is the only New Mexico ski area worth a long plane ride. Not so. If your main interest is racking up vertical feet, by all means head for Taos. Santa Fe (just an hour north of Albuquerque) is a better destination for those who prefer a balanced ski-and-sightseeing vacation. Santa Fe is one of the most culturally fascinating cities in the United States, it is loaded with great restaurants and things to do, and the ski area is a lot bigger than most people imagine.

Founded by Spanish conquistadors in 1610, 10 years before the pilgrims landed in Plymouth, Santa Fe is North America's oldest capital city. It is rich in history and culture, but of a different kind from mining-town ski areas.

When the Spanish arrived, the area was already populated with 100,000 Native Americans, who spoke nine languages and lived in some 70 multi-storied adobe pueblos, some still inhabited today. For the next 150 years, Santa Fe grew as a frontier military base and trading center, where Spanish soldiers and missionaries, Anglo mountain men and Native Americans mixed. In 1846, during the Mexican War, New Mexico was ceded to the United States and Santa Fe, at the end of the Santa Fe Trail, became a frontier town, hosting the likes of Billy the Kid and Kit Carson.

Ski Santa Fe Facts

Base elevation: 10,350'; **Summit elevation:** 12,000'; **Vertical drop:** 1,650 feet. **Number and types of lifts:** 7—1 quad superchair, 1 triple chair, 2 double chairs and 3 surface lifts **Acreage:** 590 in permit area **Snowmaking:** 30 percent **Uphill capacity:** 7,800 skiers per hour **Bed base:** 4,000 in Santa Fe

In the early part of this century, Santa Fe took on a new flavor. It became a magnet for men and women of the arts and literature. D.H. Lawrence, Ezra Pound, Willa Cather, Jack London and H.L. Mencken either lived or vacationed here. Artists Edward Hopper and Marsden Hartley spent time here, and Santa Fe was home to Robert Henri, George Bellows, Randall Davey, and Aaron Copland. Today this city of 60,000 is home to one of the world's premier art colonies, and it boasts an renowned opera company.

Where to ski

Ski Santa Fe sits 16 miles above the city. Though the mountain is known as a day-area destination for Santa Fe and Albuquerque skiers, out-of-town visitors will find a surprising amount of terrain.

All the mountain amenities, such as restaurants, ski rentals, child care, ski school and ticket sales, are at the base of the mountain just a few steps from the parking lot.

Beginners will be happiest on the lower part of the mountain, on the wide boulevard of Easy Street. Lower intermediates will find more challenges and a slightly steeper pitch on Open Slope and Upper and Lower Midland; if they're feeling adventurous, they should try Lower Burro for an exhilarating, winding trip through the trees on a mild pitch that even lower intermediates can handle. Intermediates will love it, too, though the access via Sunset requires some poling.

On a fresh powder day (once a week on average), local intermediates and advanced skiers head straight for the Tesuque Peak triple chair, to 12,000 feet and the top of the mountain. To the right of the lift (as the trail map reads) is Gayway, a glorious groomed pitch with several spicy turns, that gives new meaning to the term spectacular scenery. On a clear day, it almost gives the feeling of flying, thanks to the 150-mile vista as the trail drops away. Parachute, which parallels Gayway, is a groomed black diamond with a somewhat steeper pitch.

For the most part, the mountain's expert terrain is to the left of the Tesuque Peak chair. With fresh snow, locals go first to Columbine, Big Rocks and Wizard. These runs all check in as very steep, for advanced skiers only. Roadrunner is the expert bump run directly under the Tesuque chair. Tequila Sunrise and Easter Bowl have the best glade skiing.

On the far side of the mountain, reached by the Santa Fe Super Chief quad, Muerte and Defasio offer isolated trail skiing for advanced skiers. Middle and Lower Broadway give the same thing to intermediate skiers.

While there are hopes to overcome environmental objections and put in a lift in the Big Tesuque Bowl, for the moment the intrepid ski into this area via Cornice (once skiers leave Cornice, they are outside the ski area's permitted boundary). Big Tesuque skiers find natural powder, bowl skiing and trees. The bowls empty onto the area's entrance road, three miles below the base area. You must then hitchhike back up to the base area. First-timers should go with a local who knows this area: it's genuine backcountry, it's big and people occasionally get lost.

Mountain rating

We had pre-judged Ski Santa Fe to be a small, gentle day area. It's not. It definitely has enough terrain to keep a skier of any level happy for three to four days. Its gladed runs are great, though short; and Big Tesuque Bowl when skiable, is an adventure. Santa Fe could use an isolated beginner area; its green-circle trails are right in the line of traffic coming back to the base. To be fair, the ski area realizes this shortcoming and would very much like to add a 75-acre beginner's area; however, environmental activists are fighting Ski Santa Fe's master plan, which now is moving slowly through the U.S. Forest Service approval process.

Combined with Santa Fe's outstanding sightseeing opportunities, this is an excellent destination for skiers who don't want to be on the mountain every day (or all day). One warning: Ski Santa Fe has one of the highest lift-served elevations in the nation—12,000 feet on top, 10,350 at the base. Those susceptible to altitude problems should take note.

Cross-country

Santa Fe has no groomed or tracked trails. However, there are maintained backcountry trails in the surrounding Santa Fe National Forest. Aspen Vista Road, two miles below the ski area, is a popular and moderately difficult seven-mile trail. Black Canyon Campground, eight miles up the ski road, is a popular area for beginners. Maps and specific information are available from the National Forest Service at 988-6940. For trail and snow conditions in the Santa Fe National Forest call 984-0606.

Snowboarding

Boarding is allowed. Depending on conditions, Santa Fe opens a snowboard park. The area also hosts workshops, daily lessons and competitions. A learn-to-snowboard package with an all-day lesson, lifts and rentals is $69.

Lessons (95/96 prices)

Group lessons: Adult skiing or snowboarding (all day) $42; adult (half day) $26. A never-ever skier package with all-day lesson, beginner lift and rentals is $53. **Private lessons:** $60 per hour, each additional person is $26; two-hour are $100, additional skiers, $53; half-day lessons (three hours) are $142, additional person, $68.

Special clinics include a women's program, racing classes, segregated classes for those 50 and older, mogul clinics, telemark lessons and powder workshops. Prices vary, and not all are offered every week. Check with the ski school at 982-4429.

Children's ski school: Ages 3–9, all-day including lunch, $56 (add $10 for rental equipment). Half-day programs are $40. Children aged 3 and 4 have half-day lessons, with play activities in the afternoon, while the older children have morning and afternoon ski lessons. Three- and four-year-olds also can enroll in a snowplay program that includes some ski play, but not formal lessons. That program costs $48 for the day, including snacks, lunch and activities.

Child care

The ski area's Chipmunk Corner, located beneath the ticket booths, takes children aged 2 months to 3 years. All-day supervision and activities costs $44; $32 for half-day. The nursery is small, so during peak vacation times make your reservation when you book your hotel. Reservations required at all times; call 988-9636.

Lift tickets (95/96 prices)

	Adult	Child (Up to 12) Senior (62–71)
One day	$37	$23
Three days	$104 ($34.66/day)	$65 ($21.66/day)
Five days	$166 ($33.20/day)	$103 ($20.60/day)

A ticket valid only on the beginner lift is $20. Skiers 72 and older and kids shorter than 46 inches in ski boots ski free.

Accommodations

Ski Santa Fe has no base lodging, but even if it did, you'd want to be in Santa Fe for dining, shopping and the museums. More than 70 hotels, motels, inns, condominiums and B&Bs serve Santa Fe visitors. Winter is low season, so bargains abound. Expect to pay about $40–$69 a night for a hotel on the Cerrillos Road strip.

A downtown hotel on or near the Plaza usually will range from $75 to $200 (or higher for deluxe rooms). Lift-and-lodging packages can cut these prices considerably. Downtown is where the best restaurants, shopping and nightlife are concentrated.

La Fonda Hotel is the historic place to stay. An inn of one sort or another has been on this site for 300 years (Billy the Kid worked in the kitchen here washing dishes). The current La Fonda incarnation was built in the 1920s. Rooms are $105–$165 a night, with three-day ski packages (four nights' lodging) in the $400–$500 range per person. If you don't stay, at least stroll through and take a look—they don't make them like this anymore.

The way they make them now is across the Plaza from La Fonda. **The Inn of the Anasazi** is the politically correct place to stay. Before building, the owner consulted with Native American holy men. The hotel's restaurants use vegetables grown by local organic farmers. Leftovers are given to a homeless shelter and everything is recycled. However, this is a very expensive place to stay and eat ($199 and up), perhaps not the best choice for skiers who won't be in their rooms much.

Stay in a village of adobe cottages, most featuring their own Indian kiva fireplaces, at **La Posada**, a short walk from the Plaza. On the grounds of the Staab House, a Victorian mansion, the rooms feature traditional elements of adobe construction and lush grounds. Ski packages start at $332.

Excellent B&Bs are **Adobe Abode, Alexander's Inn**, the spacious **Dancing Ground of the Sun**, the quilt-filled **Grant Corner Inn**, the intimate **Inn of the Animal Tracks** and the classy **Water Street Inn**.

Other accommodations to consider are the new **Hotel Plaza Real**, the historic **Hotel St. Francis** and the adobe **Inn on the Alameda**. For families try the **El Rey Inn, Garrett's Desert Inn**, the **Fort Marcy Compound Condominiums**, and the **Otra Vez** condos.

Many of the chain hotels, such as **Comfort Inn, Days Inn, Holiday Inn** and **Hampton Inn,** have adopted the local adobe architectural style and are a little less expensive and conveniently located on Cerillos Road, handy for getting to the ski area but out of walking range for downtown.

For information on any of the lodging and ski packages available in Santa Fe call (800) 776-7669 (800-776-SNOW) or the Santa Fe Visitors Bureau at (800) 777-2489 (800-777-CITY).

Dining

On the mountain, skiers have two choices. **La Casa Cafeteria** in the base lodge called La Casa Mall, and **Totemoff's Bar and Grill** at the base of the Tesuque Peak Chair. La Casa, with a French chef, offers a variety including a pasta bar and a daily special such as fresh salmon with lemon tarragon. Its breakfast burrito is awesome, but only for brave palates. Totemoff's features burgers (beef and chicken), salads, pasta, cocktails and a sun deck.

Back in the city, Santa Fe cooks. Including fast food, Santa Fe has nearly 200 places to strap on the feed bag. From traditional New Mexican cuisine to steaks and seafood, Santa Fe has more food variety than you could consume in a year and far more good restaurants than we have room to recommend.

The Pink Adobe, 406 Old Santa Fe Trail (983-7712) is a local favorite dining spot and is therefore sometimes difficult to get in. They specialize in New Mexican and Creole foods, and reservations are necessary. Prices are moderate to expensive.

Tomasita's Cafe, 500 S. Guadaloupe (983-5721) is fast food with a twist. It's good, portions are large. service is friendly, and it's a favorite of Santa Fe families, so prepare to wait. It is inexpensive, and has some of the best New Mexican fare in town.

Don't hesitate to join the tourists at **The Ore House**, upstairs at 50 Lincoln Ave. (983-8687) on the Plaza. Known for its seafood, its bar features big sink-in chairs, free après-ski snacks and uniquely flavored margaritas.

Locals recommended tiny **Pasqual's**, 121 Don Gaspar (983-9340) for breakfast, but it's good anytime for delicious and beautifully presented New Mexican cuisine. Call for dinner reservations or expect to wait a long time. If you want to meet people, ask to be seated at the communal table. We met two locals, two Japanese and two Brits at our meal.

Locals also recommended the **Coyote Cafe**, 132 W. Water St. (983-1615). The main dining room has a fixed-price menu and modern Southwestern cuisine, while those in the bar can order a la carte. If you go in without reservations, they look at you as if you are *loco*. Prices are expensive. Another recommendation from locals in the upper price range, is **Santacafe**, 231 Washington St. (984-1788).

Some moderately priced restaurants are **Maria's New Mexican Kitchen**, 555 W. Cordova Rd. (983-7929), **Blue Corn Cafe** 133 Water St. (984-1800), or **Tommy's Bar and Grill**, 208 Galisteo St. (989-4407), where the gourmet salads are a meal.

If you are in town at lunch time, go stand in line with the locals at **Josie's Casa de Comida**, 225 E. Marcy (983-5311). The regional dishes are excellent and its homemade desserts are legendary. Josie's is very inexpensive, but closed on weekends.

Après-ski/nightlife

Santa Fe has the usual live bands, bars and places to dance. But it has some unusual off-slope activities as well.

To work out the kinks of a fresh powder day, stop at **Ten Thousand Waves** (988-1047, 982-9304) for a relaxing hot tub under the stars. About three miles from the Plaza, Ten Thousand Waves is a Japanese-style hot tub resort, with kimonos, sandals, massage and sexually segregated dressing rooms. There are seven private tubs and one communal tub.

For elegant après-ski (you can go in ski clothes), head for **Inn of the Anasazi** or **La Posada**, both close to the Plaza. At the latter, ask the bartender about the resident ghost, a lady that was featured on the TV show "Unsolved Mysteries."

In Santa Fe, a wonderful place to mix dinner with entertainment is at **La Casa Sena** (988-9232) in the historic Sena Plaza, a stately adobe built as a family home in the 1860s. The restaurant features New Mexican specialties—and singing waiters and waitresses. For about $20, you can eat, drink and hear an exceptional dinner theater show, belted out between courses. Children are welcome, reservations a must.

A new dinner theater (open in summer of 1995) is the **Old Santa Fe Music Hall**. Like La Casa Sena, the actors also are your waiters. They perform a vaudeville-style musical revue with a Western/Santa Fe theme. Call (800) 409-3311 or locally, 983-3311 for reservations and show times.

Other activities

Shopping: It's much cheaper to ski all day here than venture into Santa Fe's many shops and galleries. That warning said, more than 100 **galleries** feature Native American crafts and art, as well as fine art on a par with galleries in New York, Florence or Paris. On weekends, you can find bargains and excellent workmanship when Native American artisans sell their wares on blankets in front of the 480-year-old Palace of the Governors, a long-standing Santa Fe shopping tradition.

The **museums** in Santa Fe are first rate. Buy a three-day pass for $5, which will admit you to all of them. Must-sees are the Museum of International Folk Art (strong in area Spanish art), the Palace of the Governors (for local history) and the Museum of Indian Arts and Culture. Art lovers should visit the Museum of Fine Arts (with several Georgia O'Keeffe paintings) and the Center for Contemporary Arts.

Exercising: For $8 a day, the 19,000-square-foot Santa Fe Spa, 786 N. St. Francis Dr. (984-8727), has state-of-the-art exercise equipment, a heated indoor lap pool, massage staff, free child care and more.

Eight **Indian pueblos** are near Santa Fe. The San Idefonso Pueblo, famous for its distinctive pottery style, is the most scenic. Its annual festival to honor its patron saint is in late January and features traditional clothing and dances.

Call the **Santa Fe Visitors Bureau** (984-6760; 800-777-2489) for more information on these and other activities.

Getting there and getting around

Getting there: Santa Fe is 60 miles north of Albuquerque (the nearest major airport) on I-25. The ski area is 16 miles from town on Highway 475.

Getting around: Getting around Santa Fe and to and from the ski area is difficult without a car, though a shuttle service is available from the airport to major hotels. The airport in Albuquerque has the leading rental agencies.

Information/reservations

Ski Santa Fe: 982-4429 or (800) 982-7669.

Santa Fe Convention and Visitors Bureau: 984-6760 or (800) 777-2489.

The local area code is 505.

Other New Mexico ski areas

These ski areas allow snowboarding and offer lessons and ski packages. Children's ski instruction starts at age 3 or 4. Those with day care for younger children are noted.

Angel Fire, Angel Fire, NM; (800) 633-7463
6 lifts, 67 trails, 2,180 vertical feet, 375 skiable acres

This four-season resort 22 miles east of Taos is well suited for beginners and intermediates. Its relatively gentle terrain attracts many multi-generational families, who cruise down the green-circle Headin' Home run from the summit to the base as if they had been skiing all their lives. Angel Fire has challenging runs too, but it will make lower-level skiers feel like champs. Child care starts with infants. If you are planning to spend the night check into the 157-room Legends Hotel (800-633-7463) right at the base of the ski area.

Red River, Red River, NM; (505) 754-2223
7 lifts, 55 trails, 1,600 vertical feet, 270 skiable acres

Another family-oriented area, 37 miles northeast of Taos. Terrain leans toward beginner and intermediate. The ski area is smack in the town's center, which means 90 percent of the town's 6,400 beds—rustic cabins to luxurious condos—are within a mile of the slopes. A Nordic ski area is nearby. Day care is available. To reserve ski packages, call (800) 331-7669.

Sandia Peak Ski Area, Albuquerque, NM; (505) 242-9133
6 lifts, 25 trails, 1,700 vertical feet, 200 skiable acres

Sandia Peak is Albuquerque's playground. Just east of New Mexico's largest city, it has runs for all levels. Take the Sandia Peak Aerial Tramway, a tourist attraction the year round. For lodging information call (800) 473-1000.

Ski Apache, Ruidoso, NM; (505) 336-4356
10 lifts, 53 trails, 1,900 vertical feet, 750 skiable acres

Located in south-central New Mexico, 200 miles from Albuquerque, this resort is owned and operated by the Mescalero Apache Indian tribe. The ski area has no lodging, but there is plenty in Ruidoso, 16 miles away. Ski Apache's terrain is 45 percent advanced, but the beginner and intermediate trails have a good reputation for being well groomed. Some steep runs are winch-groomed. The view from the 11,500-foot peak is reportedly spectacular. Ski Apache also has the state's largest and oldest program for disabled skiers. For lodging information call (800) 545-9011; for ski packages, call (505) 336-4356.

StoryBook Cabins (505-257-2115) or the Best Western Swiss Chalet Inn (505-258-3333 or 800-477-9477) are recommended. Tribal-owned Inn of the Mountain Gods (800-545-9011) has ski packages and shuttles to the resort 20 miles away.

Ski Rio, Costilla, NM; (800) 227-5746
6 lifts, 2,150 vertical feet, 700 skiable acres

The most northerly of New Mexico's ski areas, Ski Rio was recently re-opened after being closed for most of four seasons. It got an area-wide facelift, including an improved base lodge and extended snowmaking. With its 700 acres and a remote location (close to the Colorado border off State Route 196), skiers will have the mountain to themselves.

Ski Rio has a very unusual attraction, a snow skate park with obstacles and terrain specific to snow skates, which look like ski boots with slick bottoms. The terrain is mostly wide and good for cruising, and a great place to learn, as Ski Rio uses the Perfect Turn® instructional program, which emphasizes total positive reinforcement. Ski Rio also has child care starting at 12 months.

Arizona Resorts

Sunrise Park Resort, McNary AZ; (602) 735-7669
11 lifts and tows, 60 trails, 1,800 vertical feet, 800 skiable acres

Today the White Mountain Apache Tribe owns and operates Apache Sunrise, by far the state's largest ski area. It is 215 miles east of Phoenix, about a five-hour drive. Three ski mountains feature wide-open runs and lifts than can take 15,000 skiers per hour. The base area at 9,200 feet rises to an 11,000-foot summit. Much of the terrain is intermediate, with a few challenging advanced drops. Weather this far south is often good, and snowfall averages 250 inches a year.

Fairfield Snowbowl, Flagstaff AZ; (602) 779-4577
4 lifts, 32 trails, 2,300 vertical feet, 196 skiable acres

The San Francisco Peaks rise abruptly above Flagstaff, 140 miles north of Phoenix. They provide the most challenging skiing in Arizona and some of the best views anywhere. Terrain is rated 30 percent beginner, 40 percent intermediate, 30 percent advanced. The altitude is surprising for a state known for its deserts and canyons—the base area is 9,200 feet and climbs to 11,500 feet. From the top of Mount Agassiz the view includes the Grand Canyon slash, red rocks of Sedona, and mountains outside Kingman. The Earth's curvature is visible from this lofty perch. Snowbowl has 196 skiable acres, with 65 of those acres at Hart Prairie, a beginner's slope just down the road from lifts. Hart Prairie has a modern lodge with room for 500 people; the Agassiz Lodge, at the base of the higher lifts, is nearly four decades old and tight on space.

Mt. Bachelor, Oregon

Mt. Bachelor is not your typical mountain. Many peaks are difficult to distinguish from neighboring summits, which may be just a few feet higher or lower. But Mt. Bachelor, a stately volcanic cone that is part of the Cascades mountain range, rises from Oregon's high desert, visible for miles in every direction.

On the eastern side of the Cascades, where snow falls lighter and drier than at other northwestern resorts, Mt. Bachelor has become a popular destination for western skiers. Despite no on-mountain lodging and little hot nightlife, Mt. Bachelor attracts skiers with a dependable 16-foot snowpack, clear, dry air, average daytime winter temperatures of 26 degrees and fine skiing from early November to July.

Visitors should keep in mind that all that snow results from a lot of storms, and winds often close the Summit Express chair, a high-speed quad to the 9,065-foot, treeless summit. An average stormy day brings winds of 60 to 70 miles per hour (the record is more than 200 mph), and those summit winds can kick up "ground blizzards" where the snow swirls into a whiteout six feet high. (Visibility is usually better lower on the mountain, where the ski trails are protected by trees.) But when the weather is clear and you're standing on top, you can see California's Mt. Shasta 180 miles to the south. That view, most commonly seen in spring, is worth a lot.

Though the volcano is extinct, the thinking of Mt. Bachelor's management is anything but. This is a resort that has been quick to embrace new concepts in the ski industry, such as electronic ticketing, a revolutionary ski school and high-speed quad chairs.

Although it is on the cutting edge of ski industry trends, Mt. Bachelor manages to keep its atmosphere very untrendy. No one notices or cares whether your ski clothes match, or even how hot a skier you are.

Mt. Bachelor Facts
Base elevation: 5,800'; **Summit elevation:** 9,065'; **Vertical drop:** 3,265 feet
Number of lifts: 12—6 quad superchairs, 3 triple chairs, 1 double chair, 2 surface lifts
Snowmaking: none **Acreage:** 3,200 lift-accessed skiable acres
Uphill capacity: 21,000 per hour **Bed base:** 7,500

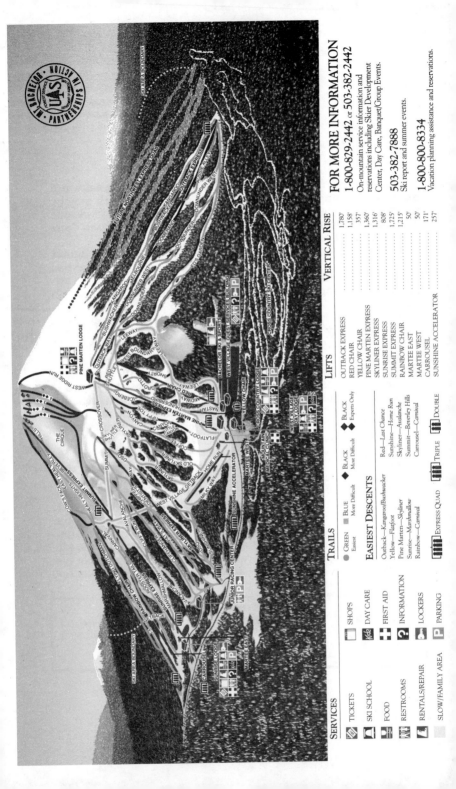

SERVICES

⛷ TICKETS	🏠 SHOPS		
⛷ SKI SCHOOL	👶 DAY CARE		
🍴 FOOD	✚ FIRST AID		
🚻 RESTROOMS	❓ INFORMATION		
🔧 RENTALS/REPAIR	🔒 LOCKERS		
SLOW/FAMILY AREA	P PARKING		

TRAILS

● GREEN
Easiest

■ BLUE
More Difficult

◆ BLACK
Most Difficult

◆◆ BLACK
Experts Only

EASIEST DESCENTS

Outback—Kangaroo/Bushwacker
Yellow—Flatfoot
Pine Marten—Skyliner
Sunrise—Marshmallow
Rainbow—Carnival

Red—Last Chance
Sunshine—Home Run
Skyliner—Avalanche
Summit—Beverley Hills
Carrousel—Carnival

EXPRESS QUAD   TRIPLE   DOUBLE

LIFTS   VERTICAL RISE

LIFTS	VERTICAL RISE
OUTBACK EXPRESS	1,780'
RED CHAIR	1,158'
YELLOW CHAIR	357'
PINE MARTEN EXPRESS	1,360'
SKYLINER EXPRESS	1,316'
SUNRISE EXPRESS	808'
SUMMIT EXPRESS	1,725'
RAINBOW CHAIR	1,215'
MARTEE EAST	50'
MARTEE WEST	50'
CARROUSEL	171'
SUNSHINE ACCELERATOR	257'

FOR MORE INFORMATION

1-800-829-2442 or 503-382-2442
On-mountain service information and
reservations including Skier Development
Center, Day Care, Banquet/Group Events.

503-382-7888
Ski report and summer events.

1-800-800-8334
Vacation planning assistance and reservations.

Where to ski

Mt. Bachelor is best suited to intermediates. The Outback Express, the longest chair lift on the mountain with a 1,780-foot vertical rise, serves excellent intermediate runs. From this chair, Boomerang is the only run rated black, and it parallels the lift. One blue-square run, Down Under, often is left ungroomed for mogul enthusiasts.

Other popular chairs for intermediates are the Pine Marten Express and the Skyliner Express. Old Skyliner, off the Pine Marten chair, has some marvelous dips and rolls—far more fun than the usual freeway design of many intermediate trails.

Most of the lower mountain is sheltered by trees, but some runs, such as Flying Dutchman and Tippytoe, give the exuberance of upper-mountain skiing. You usually can find moguls on Grotto, Canyon and Coffee Run, all off the Pine Marten chair.

When the Summit Express is open, experts should head for it. The steepest descent is through The Pinnacles, a jagged rock formation reached by a 150-foot hike from the top of the lift, then across the broad, ungroomed expanse of Cirque Bowl. Next might well be Cow's Face, far to the left of Summit Chair, steep but smooth. Because it's unknown to many skiers, it doesn't get carved into moguls, but wind packs it hard.

The longest continuous vertical (3,100 feet) can be had by taking the Summit chair off the backside, occasionally traversing right and ending up at the bottom of the Outback chair.

Intermediates can experience the heady sensation of being on the summit and still get down safely using the broad Healy Heights and Beverly Hills, which are always groomed. In fact, intermediates can't get into trouble at Mt. Bachelor: anything beyond their skill requires a knowledgeable decision to get into it—for example, the hike up to The Pinnacles.

Between the Outback and Red chairs is an unusual geologic feature, a lone cinder cone. It's not served by a lift, so powder lasts there until it's wind-packed. By getting up a head of steam from Leeway, skiers can swoop up nearly two-thirds of the way and climb the rest.

Never-evers get a treat at Mt. Bachelor: a high-speed quad chair, Sunshine Accelerator. High-speed quads move very slowly for loading and unloading, which makes them ideal for those learning the tricks of riding chair lifts. But these are expensive pieces of equipment, and it is rare for a ski area to spend that kind of money for learners. Green-circle trails descend from every lift except the Summit and Outback chairs. More difficult trails are on either side, funneling the faster skiers away from those still learning to control their turns.

Mountain rating

Most of the terrain is ideal for intermediates. Experts probably will feel restless after a weekend—they'll have to discover the pleasures of the backside and Cinder Cone.

Cross-country (94/95 prices)

The **Mt. Bachelor Rossignol Cross-Country Center,** across the parking lot from the West Village base lodge, has 56 km. of machine-set trails. There are 12 loops, from the easy 1-km. First Time Around to the challenging 12-km. Oli's Alley. The 6-km. intermediate trail, called Zigzag, leads to a heated shelter with good views. The center has equipment rental, clothing and accessories, repairs, trail and lesson information and lunch.

All-day passes are $9.50 for adults, $4.50 for children 7 to 12. Half-day rates start at noon—$8 for adults, $3.50 for children. Ages 65 and older pay $5.75 all day, or $4.25 half day. Children younger than 7 ski free.

Mt. Bachelor also operates 20 km. of groomed tracks at **Sunriver Resort,** about 14 miles from the downhill area. All-day tickets purchased here can be used at the Mt. Bachelor Nordic facilities in the afternoon, and vice-versa. Tickets at Sunriver are $8 for adults, $3.50 for kids.

Snowboarding

No restrictions. The resort offers lessons based on its Perfect Turn® learning program. A never-ever lesson is $50, including a two-hour clinic and full-day lift ticket and rental board.

Lessons (94/95 prices)

Mt. Bachelor is one of only a handful of ski resorts to offer a revolutionary ski-teaching philosophy called Perfect Turn®. Learning is based on total positive reinforcement, and based on our firsthand experience, it works. See the "Clinics For Advanced Skiers" section in our "Skiing is for Everyone" chapter.

Perfect Turn sessions for levels 4–9 (low intermediate to expert) cost $24, $20 with a dated performance card from your previous Perfect Turn lesson. Levels 1-3 are $32 for a lesson only; $40 for lesson, ski rental and lift pass.

Private lessons are $40 per hour; $10 for additional skiers. A private lesson with video analysis is $50.

Children's programs are for ages 4–12, based on the same positive approach as the adult Perfect Turn. Learning groups are formed according to age, ability and maturity in the skiing environment. Rates are $60 for lesson, rentals, lifts and lunch; $47 for half-day without lunch. Brand-new skiers can get the half-day package for $40. You must have your child registered by 9:45 a.m. at either the West Village or Sunrise Skier Development Centers.

Special programs include women's clinics, NASTAR, and coin-operated race courses.

Child care

A state-licensed day care center for children 6 weeks to 7 years operates at both West Village and Sunrise Lodges. Rates are $31 per day for all ages; a box lunch is $5 more. Reservations are recommended. Call 382-2442 or (800) 829-2442.

Lift tickets (95/96 prices)

	Adult	Child (7–12)
One day	$35	$19
Three days	$96 ($32/day)	$43 ($14.33/day)
Five days	$152 ($30.40/day)	$67 ($13.40/day)

Ages 65 and older ski for $20 a day; 6 and younger ski for free. Other multiday tickets are available.

If you usually ski fewer than ten runs per day, Mt. Bachelor's SkiData lift system could prove more economical. It tallies your points with each lift ride, until the points you paid for are gone. Use unused points the next day—or even next season—the tickets are fully transferable and are good for three years. The 200-point ticket is $35, while a 400-point ticket sells for $69. Currently, 16 percent of Bachelor's skiers use the point system. Those who ski all day long should stick to the all-day ticket.

Accommodations

Mt. Bachelor's nearest accommodations are several miles away in or near Bend.

The most extensive lodging complex is **Sunriver**, a resort community 18 miles from Mt. Bachelor and 15 miles south of Bend. The complex has a private airport, many activities, restaurants and stores. A shuttle runs throughout the expansive resort complex, and another shuttle runs between Sunriver and Mt. Bachelor (and costs $7, though this fee is included in some packages). This may be enough for some people, but it's tough to get to Bend. Rates run from $85 to $260 for rooms, private homes and condos. Call (800) 547-3922; in Oregon, (800) 452-6874.

Inn of the Seventh Mountain is Mt. Bachelor's closest lodging, with restaurants, a grocery store that stocks nearly 99 brands of beer, a skating rink, hot tub, snowmobile and sleigh rides, as well as a shuttle to the mountain. Economy rooms are $58, three-bedroom condos are $268, with many offerings and ski packages in between. Call (800) 452-6810 in the U.S.; (800) 874-9402 from Canada.

Bend's most deluxe accommodations are **River House**, nestled along the river close to restaurants and entertainment. Pool, indoor and outdoor spas and a Nautilus exercise room make this a mini-resort in the heart of town. Nightly rates range from $52 for two people to $92 for a river-view suite with three queen beds, two rooms and kitchen. (800) 547-3928; or 381-3111.

Bend has many more places to stay, plus five RV parks, and several more within 25 miles. Phone the **Bend Visitors' Information Center** for more information, 382-3221, or use the **Central Oregon Recreation Association** toll-free number: (800) 800-8334 to book lodging, packages and transportation.

Dining

A team of three searched diligently for great food at this resort without success. Overall, the cooking is basic and prices are based more on atmosphere rather than the chef's creativity.

Although you'll pay more at elegant **The Riverhouse Restaurant** (389-8810), good seafood is moderately priced at **McGrath's Publick Fish House** (388-4555), which has several unusual entrées, especially those from Northwestern waters.

Pine Tavern Restaurant (382-5581), with the twin pine trees shooting out of the dining room roof, serves great steak, ribs, lamb and prime rib. **Rosette** (383-2780) rustles up a Mediterranean-Northwest cuisine and more lamb dishes than most restaurants. It's quiet and sophisticated.

For ethnic food, try **Chan's** (389-1725) for Szechwan, Hunan and Cantonese; **Murrieta's** (389-1800) in Sunriver for Mexican food; or **Giuseppe's** (389-8899), *Pacific Northwest* magazine's "best ethnic" restaurant, for Italian. **Stuft Pizza** (382-4022) gets raves for its pizza, calzone and sandwiches.

Deschutes Brewery & Public House (382-9242), in the center of downtown Bend, has four to six of its handcrafted brews on tap. The beer is great; the meals are so-so.

For breakfast, try **The West Side Bakery & Cafe** on Galveston for its eggs-and-pancake menu and its fun decor (amusing knickknacks on the walls and ceiling, and a model train that runs through its three dining rooms at just below ceiling level), or **Café Paradiso** on Bond Street, which opens at 8 a.m. with the best smelling coffee in town and pastries.

Après-ski/nightlife

Mt. Bachelor is not known for an exciting après-ski atmosphere, nor is Bend noted for dynamic nightlife, though both can be found. The **Castle Keep Lounge** in the lower level of the West Village lodge offers lively après-ski with occasional live music. Also check **The Riverhouse** and **E.L. Bender's** in town.

Later, you'll find dancing at **Willie D's, The Shilo Restaurant and Lounge, Pasha's** and **The Riverhouse**, all in Bend; **Owl's Nest Lounge** at the Sunriver Resort and **Josiah's** at Inn of the Seventh Mountain. Most of the live music is weekends only, but Willie D's rocks all week long. For quieter evenings, try **Café Paradiso** in Bend, a European-style coffee house with acoustic music. **Pine Tavern Restaurant** has a mature adult atmosphere overlooking Mirror Pond. **Stuft Pizza** in Bend has comedy on Saturdays, and big-screen sports other nights.

Other activities

Shopping: Bend Factory Outlets, a 27-store outlet mall on Highway 97 south of Powers Road, has name brands such as Carter's Childrenswear, London Fog, Eddie Bauer and Bass Shoes. The real draw, though, are two **Columbia Outfitters** skiwear factory outlets, one downtown on Bond Street and the other at 55 N.W. Wall Street. Columbia makes a very practical ski clothing component system with zip-in fleece jacket liners that can be worn separately. Here, they are bargain priced.

Sunriver and Inn of the Seventh Mountain have **ice skating, horseback riding, sleigh rides** and **snowmobiling**.

The Oregon Trail of Dreams Training Camp offers **dogsled rides** by dogs that are training for Alaska's famed Iditarod race. Rates are $60 for adults; $30 for children less than 80 pounds. Call 382-2442 or (800) 829-2442.

The U.S. Forest Service, with a desk on the lower floor of Mt. Bachelor's West Village lodge, has several interpretive programs, including a **snowshoe tour** with a USFS naturalist.

Getting there and getting around

Getting there: Mt. Bachelor is 21 miles southwest of Bend, Oregon, on the scenic Cascade Lakes Highway. Take Highways 26 and 97 from Portland, 162 miles away. State Highway 126 comes from Eugene (132 miles).

United Express and **Horizon Air** have flights into Redmond/Bend Airport (16 miles from Bend) from many West Coast cities. **Amtrak** (800-872-7245, 800-USA-RAIL) provides daily service on the Coast Starlight, which runs from Los Angeles to Seattle. The closest stop is Chemult, 60 miles south of Bend. Arrange ahead for taxi pickup.

Getting around: A car is helpful. If you don't have one, be sure to stay in lodgings with some kind of shuttle service. Mt. Bachelor operates a free park-and-ride operation during the height of the season from its office on 14th Street in Bend, but you'll need a way to reach it.

Information/reservations

Central Oregon Recreation Association (800-800-8334) will assist with lodging, ground transportation and ski packages. In Oregon call 382-8334, or write Central Oregon Recreation Association, P.O. Box 230-97709, Bend, OR 97709.

Mt. Bachelor, P.O. Box 1031, Bend, OR 97701-1031; The ski report phone is 382-7888; Mt. Bachelor's toll-free number is (800) 829-2442.

All area codes are 503 unless otherwise noted.

Mt. Hood Region, Oregon

Portland skiers jokingly call these "our little day areas," but the three ski areas within 15 miles of each other on the shanks of Oregon's most beautiful mountain, Mt. Hood, offer a fine range of skiing experiences for destination skiers too.

Most skiers come from Portland for the day or from Seattle for a night or two. Most of the lodging is in the resort town of Hood River, famed for windsurfing and about 35 miles from Mt. Hood Meadows. Other lodging is closer, but limited. But the skiing is quite varied and abundant. Best of all, it's within an hour's drive of a major airport, Portland International.

Too bad the region doesn't market interchangeable lift tickets, because it has promise as a no-frills ski destination. The ski terrain and conditions can keep up the enthusiasm of advanced skiers for days at a time, with naturally rugged terrain that hasn't been dynamited to a freeway finish. We found plenty of what we like to ski, as well as some great terrain for the lower ability levels at Timberline and Mt. Hood Meadows.

Timberline

Timberline is known for its historic lodge and summer skiing. The lodge is a beauty, and we offer more detail in the accommodations section of this chapter. Timberline was the continent's first ski area to offer lift-served summer skiing, and now more than 50,000 skiers come each summer. The Palmer Snowfield has a steady pitch at the advanced intermediate level. It's challenging enough for you to find World Cup ski racers from several countries practicing technique. In winter, though, the Palmer chair is closed (too much snow, though ski-area officials keep exploring ways to keep it open) and Timberline becomes a great beginner and intermediate area.

Timberline Facts

Base elevation: 5,000'; Summit elevation: 8,500' summer, 7,000' winter; Vertical drop: 2,000 feet winter, about 1,500 feet summer (varies)
Number and types of lifts: 6 - 1 quad superchair, 1 triple chair and 3 double chairs. A fourth double chair and the superchair are used in summer.
Acreage: 1,000 (31 trails) Percent of snowmaking: None
Uphill capacity: 6,500 skiers per hour in winter; 8,000 in summer
Bed base: 71 rooms on mountain

Where to ski

Most Timberline skiing is below the main lodge, but few experiences in the skiing world match a ride up the Magic Mile Super Express to the bottom of the Palmer Snowfield. The original Magic Mile lift was the second ski lift in the country, after Sun Valley's. Silcox Hut, which served as the original top terminus and warming hut, was recently restored. Below the Timberline Lodge are many blue and green runs, with a few short black diamonds. The webbed trail system between the trees makes each run feel like a wilderness excursion.

Snowboarding

Timberline has gone all-out for snowboarders. In winter the ski area has a Bone Zone, a snow park to challenge the best riders. The base of Paint Brush Glade has a halfpipe. Lessons and rentals are available. Timberline is known for its summer camps on the snowfield. The U.S. Snowboard Training Center is there during the summer. Call (800) 325-4430 for information.

Lessons (94/95 prices)

Timberline has the SKIwee program for kids (ages 4–12), and charges $60 per day. Adult group lessons (ages 9 and older) cost $17 for 90 minutes. Private lessons are $35 for an hour.

Lift tickets (94/95 prices)

Adults $28, children (7–12) $18, valid 9 a.m. to 5 p.m. Other adult ticket prices range from $10 to $22, depending on time of day and day of the week. Timberline has night skiing until 10 p.m.

Mt. Hood Meadows

Mt. Hood Meadows is the big guy in the area, actually the largest "day" hill in the country. Its ski school is highly regarded in mountain circles, and the terrain has the most variety of the three Mt. Hood areas.

Mt. Hood Meadows Facts
Base elevation: 4,523'; **Summit elevation:** 7,300'; **Vertical drop:** 2,777 feet
Number and types of lifts: 11 - 3 quad superchairs, 1 quad chair, 5 double chairs, 2 surface lifts **Acreage:** 2,150 skiable acres (142 acres of night skiing)
Percent of snowmaking: None **Uphill capacity:** 16,181 skiers per hour
Bed base: None on mountain; closest 13 miles away in town of Government Camp, or 35 miles away in Hood River

---

Where to ski

Mt. Hood Meadows has by far the most varied terrain of the three ski areas and is huge, as big as all but the biggest Western destination resorts. Adventurous skiers enjoy the chain of chutes and bowls into Heather Canyon, reached from either the Cascade Express superchair or the Shooting Star quad chair. The favorite intermediate area is under the Hood River Meadows chair, affectionately called "Herm" for its initials, HRM. Beginners have the runs under the Daisy, Buttercup and Red chairs; the last is next to the snowboard halfpipe. Night skiing is in the vicinity of the main lodge.

Snowboarding

Mt. Hood Meadows has a groomed halfpipe plus a few natural ones, plenty of freeriding terrain and jumps. Rentals and lessons are available.

Lessons (94/95 prices)

Mt. Hood Meadows charges $25 for a 90-minute **group lesson. Private lessons** are $40 an hour, $25 for each additional person. A full-day program for **children** 4-6, called Kidski, costs $65 (ages 7-12, $75), including lift ticket, lesson, rentals and lunch. Half-day children's lifts-lessons-rental package is $45 for ages 4-6; $51 for first through eighth grades. **First-Timer packages** (all-inclusive) cost $30 for Alpine, $30 for Nordic, and $40 for snowboarding.

Lift tickets (94/95 prices)

Tickets are $32 per shift for adults. (Shifts are 9 a.m.-4 p.m., 11 a.m.-7 p.m., and 1-10 p.m.) Ages 65 and older ski for $20 per shift, while ages 7-12 ski for $20 any time during the day/night. Children 6 and younger ski for $6. Night tickets (4-10 p.m.) cost $16 for any age. Half-day price is $27.

Mt. Hood Ski Bowl

Mt. Hood Ski Bowl claims to be America's largest night-skiing area. It certainly offers quite a bit under the lights, including some truly steep black-diamond runs. It also emphasizes ski racing, with programs for a variety of age groups.

Mt. Hood Ski Bowl Facts

Base elevation: 3,566'; **Summit elevation:** 5,066'; **Vertical drop:** 1,500 feet
Number and types of lifts: 9 - 4 double chairs, 5 surface lifts
Acreage: 620 skiable acres **Percent of snowmaking:** 25 percent
Uphill capacity: 4,600 skiers per hour
Bed base: Several inns and lodges in Government Camp

Where to ski

Mt. Hood Ski Bowl is gaining a reputation for challenging ski runs with the addition of its outback area and 1,500 feet of vertical reached from Upper Bowl. The mountain is now rated at 40 percent expert, but the 60 runs have enough variety for all skills. Though beginners have some nice terrain, Ski Bowl's lift unloading ramps are sometimes black-diamond affairs, with steep pitches and some sharp turns.

Snowboarding

At Ski Bowl, the Multopor side and the Outback are favorites. Ski Bowl sells a $10 snowboard lift ticket good on a surface lift that services a halfpipe and obstacle course. Lessons are by appointment.

Lessons (94/95 prices)

Ski Bowl, with 100 ski instructors, has classes in racing, freestyle, cross-country and snowboarding. Group lessons cost $15, private lessons $30 for an hour. Ski Bowl also teaches lessons at night by appointment.

Lift tickets (94/95 prices)

Adults $23 ($13 nights), children (11 and younger) $16 ($11 nights). Like Mt. Hood Meadows, Ski Bowl sells shift tickets: Opening to 4:30 p.m., 11 a.m. to 7 p.m., 1 p.m. to close. An adult day+night ticket is $28.

Cross-country

Timberline has telemark lessons, weekends only, but no groomed cross-country trails. **Mt. Hood Meadows** has 15 km. of groomed Nordic track at the base of the Hood River Meadows lift, with rental equipment and instruction. Trail passes are $7, and the cross-country center is open Wednesdays through Sundays.

The **Mt. Hood National Forest** has nearly 200 km. of cross-country trails. The Trillium Lake Trail is normally groomed and tracked weekly. Maps are available at any ranger station.

Accommodations

The only slopeside lodging in the region is **Timberline Lodge**, 6,000 feet in the middle of the ski area and a National Historic Landmark. Built by the Works Progress Administration in 1937, it is filled with stunning artistic details, such as carved stairway banisters, colored linoleum wall murals and wrought-iron fireplace decor made from old railroad tracks. Rates range from $90 to $160 for rooms with private baths. Eleven chalet rooms with a shared bathroom and shower across the hall go for $60. Though Christmas season is sold out 15 months in advance, try to book a few days the week before the traditional Christmas vacation when the decorations are in place. (800) 547-1406; 231-5400 from Portland.

Also at Timberline is a unique group lodging opportunity: **Silcox Hut.** The 46-year-old newly restored hut was the terminus for the original Magic Mile chair lift. Now bunkrooms accommodate up to 24 guests (minimum 12, $65 per person, including dinner and breakfast). Call 295-1827 for reservations.

Other lodging is in the town of Government Camp, across Highway 26 from Ski Bowl. Our favorite is **Falcon's Crest Inn,** a delightful bed-and-breakfast run by Melody and Bob (BJ) Johnson. Its five rooms ($90 to $139) have private baths and varying decor (safari, 1920s, etc.). In December, every room of the inn has a uniquely decorated Christmas tree. Call 272-3403 or (800) 624-7384.

Those who prefer a little more privacy than a B&B affords can go across the street to the **Mt. Hood Inn**. This modern hotel has rooms with continental breakfast starting at $90 per night. Rooms with Jacuzzi tubs are $135. Midweek one-night ski packages start at $99 per couple. 272-3205 or (800) 443-7777.

Other lodging at Government Camp includes **Huckleberry Inn**, with rooms well under $100 and a dorm for $15 per person, 272-3325; or **Thunderhead Lodge Condominiums**, 272-3368.

The Resort at the Mountain is 20 minutes down-mountain from Timberline (and 45 minutes from the Portland airport). Here you can golf (27 holes) and ski in the same day. Ski packages start at $128 per couple. 622-3101 or (800) 669-7666.

Eleven miles from Mt. Hood Meadows toward Hood River on Highway 35 is the **Inn at Cooper Spur**. It has 1,200-square-foot log cabins that sleep seven and a group of hot tubs embedded in what may once have been a tennis court. Phone 352-6037. Mt. Hood Meadows has several **ski/lodging packages** with Hood River B&Bs, inns and hotels, starting in the $50–$60 range per person, double occupancy. Phone (800) 929-2754.

Central Oregon Reservations (800) 443-7777 can help with accommodations in the region.

Dining

Timberline Lodge has an elegant restaurant, the **Cascade Dining Room**, that serves meals at set times. The salmon and lamb are excellent. The **Blue Ox Deli** downstairs is sort of a theme bar of Paul Bunyan proportions, decorated with murals and original glass work by Virginia Vance. **Wy'East Lodge**, across the street, has several nice places for lunch.

Mt. Hood Meadows has two lodges, each with several eateries. North Lodge has the **Finish Line** for a great lunch, après-ski nibbles and drinks, and a view of the whole area. South Lodge has **Micro Pub & Sausage Haus**, with a good variety of microbrewed beer. You also can buy pizza cooked to order, espresso or latté, and pasta in the various restaurants.

Ski Bowl has more typical ski-cafeteria food in its two lodges, and warm food at the mid-mountain warming hut. Beer and wine are available at the **T-Bar** in the East Lodge, and there's a full bar, the **Beerstube**, in the West Lodge.

In Government Camp, **Falcon's Crest Inn** serves a fixed-price gourmet dinner ($26.95 to $28.95). Call 272-3403 or (800) 624-7384. **Huckleberry Inn** has a coffee shop open 24 hours a day, and is the place for a hearty breakfast. **Mt. Hood Brew Pub**, next to the Mt. Hood Inn, has microbrewed beer, espresso bar, local wines and a pub menu.

In the town of Hood River are several good restaurants, among them **Big City Chicks** (1302 13th St.) for "healthy foods of the world" such as rum-soaked Bajan chicken and Veggie Enchiladas Mole in polenta tortillas.

Après-ski/nightlife
Generally, the choices are night skiing and sleeping. Exceptions are the **Ram's Head Bar** or **Blue Ox Bar** at Timberline and the **Mt. Hood Brew Pub**, all of which are relaxed as opposed to lively.

Other activities
Not much, at least up on the mountain. Hood River has some nice boutique shopping.

Getting there and getting around
Getting there: U.S. Highway 26 east from Portland passes Mt. Hood Ski Bowl, 53 miles from Portland. For Timberline, turn left off the Highway and continue for six miles. To get to Mt. Hood Meadows, go through Government Camp to Highway 35, then turn left. It's 68 miles from Portland. An alternate route to Meadows is to take Interstate 84 east from Portland, following the Columbia River to the town of Hood River, where you turn south on Highway 35 for another 35 miles.

Getting around: A car is vital; however, those trying to rent may find themselves in a Catch-22 situation. Tire chains are a necessity, because the snow is wet and slippery. You can get a $50 fine if you're caught without them (or four-wheel-drive) when "Traction Devices Required" signs are posted. The Portland airport has five rental-car agencies. All but National will permit chain installation as long as you pay for any damage to the car. You must buy the chains, but the agencies will not reimburse you for the cost. (And just what are you going to do with a set of used tire chains?) Better to rent a four-wheel-drive car. All but Avis have them.

All the Mt. Hood ski areas are in Sno-Parks, which require parking permits. They cost $1.50 per day, $2.50 for three days, $9 for the year, and are available at the ski areas and at many stores on the way to the mountains.

Information/reservations
Mt. Hood Meadows, P.O. Box 470, Hwy. 35, Mt. Hood, OR 97041-0470. Office: 337-2222; snow phone: 227-7669.

Timberline, Government Camp, OR 97028. Office: 272-3311; snow phone: 222-2211. Timberline Lodge reservations: (800) 547-1406.

Mt. Hood Ski Bowl, P.O. Box 280, Government Camp, OR 97028. Office: 272-3206; snow phone: 222-2695.

Area codes are 503 unless otherwise noted.

Crystal Mountain, Washington

When the weather is right, the snow is deep, and avalanche danger is not too great, hardcore skiers from all over the West Coast beam themselves to Crystal for unparalleled skiing. The terrain is steep and thrilling, and there's enough of it to keep the adrenaline rushing all day. There's enough snow too, often 12 feet deep at the top.

It's Washington state's only destination Alpine ski resort, just 90 minutes from Seattle. The on-mountain condos, lodges and restaurants delight local skiers who would otherwise have to leave the state for a ski vacation.

Crystal Mountain is a favorite vacation spot for some Canadian ski-hill employees. They don't want their names used, but whole groups of British Columbia liftees and front office personnel can't wait for their annual midwinter ski vacations to Crystal. Their reasoning: Snow conditions at Crystal, near Mount Rainier, are consistently drier and more stable than in British Columbia, and they prefer Crystal's ambiance.

As befitting its Seattle ties, Crystal operates an espresso sled—a portable coffee cart to which skiers can schuss for a caffeine jolt. Another service is Crystal's plainclothes skiers who keep an eye on decoy skis they plant in public racks in an effort to catch thieves. Lock your skis, nonetheless.

Where to ski

The beginner lift at Crystal, called Discovery, inspires confidence. Blue runs make up another 37 percent of Crystal's 2,300 acres, and black-diamond runs are a whopping 43 percent. That high expert percentage is partly because of the 1,000 skiable acres in the back-country areas, both north and south. It's the kind of terrain that is out of bounds at most ski areas—woods, chutes and steep bowls. The backcountry isn't always open, nor is it patrolled regularly, but it's a major attraction for experts when the ski patrol opens the gates.

Crystal Mountain Facts
Base elevation: 4,400' **Summit elevation:** 7,002' **Vertical drop:** 3,102 feet
Number of lifts: 11–1 quad superchair, 1 quad, 3 triple chairs, 5 double chairs, 1 surface lift **Snowmaking:** 1.3 percent (30 acres near the base)
Acreage: 2,300 **Uphill capacity:** 15,600 skiers per hour **Bed base:** 720

The mountain boasts 3,100 vertical feet and 307 inches of annual snowfall. Thanks to Crystal's quad superchair, skiers can get to the top—7,000 feet—in 13 minutes. By skiing connecting trails, you can take a three-mile nonstop run to the bottom. Club Vertical, a frequent-skier program, is popular: for a $25 membership fee, skier days and accumulated vertical are electronically tabulated. Top numbers win prizes.

Cross-country

There are no cross-country trails, rentals or lessons, but $5 will buy a one-time lift ticket to access a backcountry lake trail.

Snowboarding

Crystal is snowboard heaven for sure, dude. Pacific Northwest snowboarders have gravitated to freeriding, and Crystal has woods, ridges and carving slopes that keep them coming back for more. Boarder Zone, next to the Quicksilver Chair, has banks, rails, obstacles and a double halfpipe.

Lessons (95/96 prices)

First-time skiers or snowboarders can take a two-hour lesson for $39 that includes a lift ticket and rental gear. The four-hour version is $10 more.

The **Kids' Club** lesson program is divided into ages 4–6 and 7–11, half day or full day. Rates include all-day lift ticket but not rentals. Half day, ages 4–6, costs $30; all day, $52. Half day, ages 7–11, costs $39; all day, $52. For children aged 3–4, the Lil' Otter special, $52 for all day, combines snow play and skiing, ski equipment, all-day supervision and lunch.

Adult group lessons for skiers and snowboarders are called Skill Improvement sessions. They cost $25 for a two-hour session; $35 for four hours. **Private lessons** (one hour, one or two people) are $39 at 9 a.m. or 3:30 p.m.; $45 at other times.

Inquire at the booth at the top of the Skid Row run for Quick Tips, which are half-hour on-mountain ski consultations. A one-run video-taped evaluation costs $5.

Child care

Crystal has programs for children aged 6 months to 7 years. Programs for ages 2–7 are daily; programs for infants are on non-holiday weekdays only. Full-day care costs $46 for infants up to 2 years; $39 for toddlers in diapers, $35 for potty-trained toddlers. The child care phone number is 663-2265.

Lift tickets (95/96 prices)

	Adult	Child (7–11)
Weekend day	$33	$22
Monday/Tuesday	$20	$20
Wednesday-Friday	$24	$24

Holidays are priced at the weekend rates. Ages 62-69 ski for $28 weekends. Night skiing (weekends and holidays only, 4-10 p.m.) is $16. Skiers age 70 and older and 5 and younger pay $5 any time. Return your lift ticket within 75 minutes for any reason and you will get a voucher for any other day.

Accommodations

All lodging at Crystal is within walking distance of the slopes. The three hotels and 96 condominiums vary widely in styles and prices, from $40 for two with a shower down the hall in the Alpine Inn Hotel, to $165 for a Crystal Chalet condo.

Lodging can match most budgets. Packages are available for two to five days. For reservations: **Alpine Inn Hotel**, 663-2262; **all other lodging**, 663-2558. Call either number for $49 midweek specials, including lift tickets (restrictions apply).

The parking lot has 21 RV hookups, $10 per night each.

Dining

Restaurants cater to both the white-linen and take-out crowds, with rustic dining, a cafeteria and après-ski hors d'oeuvres lounges in between. A favorite of the play-hard crowd is the **Snorting Elk Cellar** in the Alpine Inn.

Summit House, a rustic dining lodge at 6,872 feet, serves a passable version of the now-famous Northwest cuisine, but the main attraction is the view of Mount Rainier. It's more than 14,000 feet up, but looks like you could reach out and touch it.

Après-ski/nightlife

The Saloon brings in live bands to appease powder hounds who still have energy at day's end. Tuesday is comedy night.

Other activities

It's not widely known, but a Crystal lift ticket entitles the bearer to enjoy the swimming pool, hot tub, sauna and showers for $2. In the Crystal Inn, these facilities are open seven days a week, noon to 10 p.m. Massages are available but extra.

Getting there and getting around

Crystal is 76 miles southeast of Seattle, bordering the east side of Mount Rainier National Park. Drive south on I-5 from Seattle, take Exit 142 east to Auburn, Highway 164 to Enumclaw, and Highway 410 east to the Crystal Road.

Bus service from Puget Sound to Crystal Mountain is available on the Crystal Mountain Express. Call (206) 455-5505 for information and reservations.

Information/reservations

Snow condition hot line: 634-3771; Crystal Mountain office and ski school, 663-2265; rental shop: 663-2264. Lodging reservations: 663-2558. The local area code is 360.

Mt. Baker, Washington

Tucked onto the side of a mountain in the northwest corner of Washington state is a resort with possibly the deepest snow of any ski hill in the country. At Mt. Baker, anything less than 100 inches at the lodge is considered slight. The ski area is not actually the 10,778-foot volcano of the same name. It's on an arm of 9,127-foot Mt. Shuksan, one of the most photographed mountains in the world, also one of the most listened to, since its careening chunks of steep glacial avalanche can be seen and heard for miles around (they're well out of the ski area, so no worries, mate). But imagine the thrill of witnessing one from a chair lift.

In an era when smaller ski hills and non-destination resort ski areas are disappearing—there are 35 percent fewer resorts than ten years ago—Mt. Baker's success is an exception. Location, location and location, between Seattle and Vancouver, B.C., have a lot to do with it, but the main ingredient is the average annual 750-inch snowfall.

World champion snowboarders practice regularly at Mt. Baker and live in the nearby town of Glacier. Aside from the abundant snow, a main attraction for snowboarders is the halfpipe, the only natural one in the region. Starting from the top of the Shuksan Chairs, it follows a creek bed for a few hundred yards and is normally buried under 20 feet of snow. The halfpipe is the site of the annual Mt. Baker Legendary Halfpipe Banked Slalom Snowboard Competition. The January event has earned a national reputation, attracting riders from all over the U.S., Canada and Europe.

Mt. Baker's two quad lifts in three years and its expanded intermediate terrain are meeting skier hopes. Now, even on record skier days (more than 4,000 skiers is always a record) lift lines never top five minutes.

Mt. Baker Facts
Base elevation: 3,750' Summit elevation: 5,250'
Vertical drop: 1,500 feet Number and types of lifts: 9 - 2 fixed-grip quads, 6 double chairs, 1 rope tow Acreage: 1000 skiable acres No snowmaking Uphill capacity: 6,000 skiers per hour
Bed Base: none at ski area, 300 in Glacier, 17 miles down-mountain

Its terrain helps too. It offers all-day possibilities to beginners, intermediates, and advanced skiers and snowboarders alike, with plenty of gentle groomed slopes, steeps, chutes, and woods that bring out the pioneer spirit. The new slopeside White Salmon Day Lodge, with spectacular views of Mt. Shuksan, opened late last season. It's three miles closer to Glacier, with full food service and espresso, beer and wine. The Cascadian architecture on the building is full of pleasant surprises, from the paw prints in the restrooms to salmon sculptures in the railings to hand-carved animal newel posts. Rental equipment and instruction are available only at the upper Heather Meadows Base Area.

One drawback to the low elevation of the ski area is that the freezing level can yo-yo, and marginally cold days can turn snow to rain without notice. Some ski patrollers keep a few sets of dry clothes in the aid shacks.

Where to ski

Newcomers sometimes have a tough time figuring how to get back to the Heather Meadows Base Area, because everywhere they ski takes them farther away. With 1,000 acres to play with, that doesn't sound likely, but the ski area is laid out over two mountains, the Pan Dome side and the Shuksan side. Four chairs serve each side, but Shuksan is by far the more popular. It has the heaviest-duty terrain for snowboarders under the double Shuksan chairs and the gentlest groomed slopes for beginners and intermediates.

Chairs 7 and 8 now expand the Shuksan possibilities, but beginners may want to avoid Chair 8 for the time being—its terrain is mostly intermediate. The ride, however, rivals Blackcomb's Jersey Cream Express Chair for the majestic view of its mountain ridges to the left, past the ski area boundary at Rumble Gully.

The Pan Dome side, served by Chairs 1, 2, 3 and 6, is for the mogul bashers and chute shooters, but beginners can easily get back to the lodge on the Austin and Blueberry runs. The signage is good, but don't follow tracks or other skiers if you don't know where they're going. You may end up on steep Pan Face or unmapped places called Rattrap and Gunbarrel. The ski patrol performs award-winning rescues on icy crags that are best avoided.

Mountain rating

"Of my 100 deepest powder days in the last 20 years, 80 of them have been at the Mt. Baker Ski Area," said a local powderhound and heli-skier. The challenge is to pick your days carefully and finish your skiing by 10:30 in the morning, when the runs are skied out.

Mt. Baker's 1,000 acres of skiable terrain are rated at seven percent expert, 21 percent advanced, 42 percent intermediate and 30 percent novice.

Cross-country

Mt. Baker grooms a short Nordic trail loop to the north and west of the main upper parking lot. Elevation is about 4,000 feet and the trail is gentle. There is a $3 charge. The road ends at the ski area, so touring opportunities are all down-mountain on logging roads.

Snowboarding

In the old days of snowboarding, about ten years ago, Mt. Baker snowboarders were carving turns where even the ski patrol would rather not go. In effect, they opened new terrain within the boundaries and so helped skiers improve their skills. There were only a handful of boarders then; now they're a quarter of the mountain's business.

"No chute too steep, no powder too deep," is the motto of the Mt. Baker Hardcore, a group of local snowboarding enthusiasts headed by extreme shredmaster Carter Turk. He co-produced "Baked," a 45-minute video of serious and not-so-serious snowboarding that challenges Warren Miller for astounding feats and offbeat humor. It's one of many videos that attract snowboarders to the Mt. Baker region.

The annual Mt. Baker Legendary Banked Slalom takes place in late January every year. Billed as not for the squeamish, the race is a luge-like run with 10- to 20-foot banked walls. The 29 gates are positioned on the walls. It's not hard to figure how a Mt. Baker snowboarder won the extreme championship in Alaska.

Lessons (94/95 prices)

The Komo Kulshan Ski Club is starting its 43rd year of ski instruction at the Mt. Baker Ski Area. Komo Kids, as the learners are called, beef up their skills in what may be the best **children's ski program** in the Northwest. It's an eight-week series of weekend lessons that runs in January and February every year. Lessons are given by PSIA-certified instructors of the Mt. Baker Instruction Programs. Cost is $125 for the season, plus lift tickets.

Adult ski and snowboard **group lessons** start daily at 10:30 a.m. and 12:45 p.m. and cost $18 for each person ($15 for age 15 and younger). **Private lessons,** available any time, for any age or ability, cost $45 for one hour before 9 a.m. and $50 after that.

Mt. Baker's clinics show how to handle variable daily conditions, and special clinics focus on women, Nordic skiing and the handicapped (a SKIable Adaptive Program is for skiers who require adaptive equipment).

Child care

Day care is available in the lodge at the upper base area for children older than 2 who are toilet trained. Cost is $4 per hour. Ski lessons are offered for children older than 4. All-day supervision includes ski lessons, lift tickets and lunch.

Lift tickets (95/96 prices)

	Adult	Youth (7–15) Senior (60–69)
Weekend/holiday day	$28	$20.50
Midweek day	$18.50	$13.50

People 70 and older, or 6 and younger, ski free.

Mt. Baker is open daily through February, then it closes Mondays and Tuesdays through March. (It stays open daily through both U.S. and Canadian spring breaks, which are usually at different times.) In April it's open Fridays and weekends only.

Accommodations

Self-contained campers are welcome to spend the night in the parking lot (no hook–ups, no charge), but the nearest accommodations are 17 miles down the Mt. Baker highway in Glacier.

Mt. Baker Lodging (599-2453), in Glacier, rents vacation houses, from cedar cabins to large-group chalets, all with kitchens and fireplaces, from $89 to $225.

The **Mt. Baker Chalet**, at Mile Post 33 on the Mt. Baker Highway at the west end of Glacier, has 20 cabins and condos ranging in price from $50 to $225 per night. Call (800) 258–2405.

The **Snowline Inn**, sort of a two-story condo/hotel, rents studio units for two people for $65. Condo loft units for two rent for $85. Call (800) 228–0119.

Bellingham, 56 miles from the ski area on I-5, has a wider range of accommodations, including Best Westerns and B&Bs. **The Hampton Inn**, near the Bellingham Airport, has fitness and business centers, free shuttles and tasteful rooms starting at $64 for two or more people. Those older than 50 pay $59 for any room for up to four people. Rates include a 21-item free continental breakfast. Call (800) 426-7866 (800-HAMPTON). The **Bellingham-Whatcom Convention & Visitors Bureau** can be reached for more information at (800) 487–2032.

Dining

The mountain day lodge has a brown-bag room, a cafeteria-style restaurant and a taproom. Fast foods are available at the **Razor Hone Cafe**, at the foot of the Shuksan Chairs.

For dinner you can't beat **Milano's Cafe & Deli** in Glacier. Milano's specialty is fresh-made pasta at very reasonable prices. The salmon ravioli and tomato sauces regularly draw raves, and the Caesar salad may be the best in the region. There's an excellent selection of Italian wines and regional micro beers. The atmosphere is excitedly post-ski, but most of the staff are snowboarders. Milano's is at 9990 Mt. Baker Highway, Glacier, WA 98244. Call 599-2863.

For a calmer environment, at one of the highest rated restaurants in the Pacific Northwest, try **Innisfree** just down the highway. Go for the full dinner, or sample the quicker "After Ski at Innisfree." Before 5:30 p.m. you can order appetizers from the dinner menu at 10 percent off: Thai Chicken, Sweet Potato Agnoloti and Chèvre-filled Artichoke Hearts are but a few. Innisfree grows most of its own organic vegetables. Its address is 9393 Mt. Baker Hwy., Glacier, WA 98244. Call 599-2372.

Après-ski/nightlife

All evening excitement takes place in the town of Glacier, 17 miles down the mountain. The **Chandelier Restaurant** has an active party lounge. Because of all the Canadians, you'll learn to say "give me a beers" and "eh" a lot.

Other activities

Anything you can do in a national forest you can do here, but you have to bring your own gear—snowmobiles, for example. Groomed trails leave Glacier in all directions, but no place rents the equipment. Ice skaters even hike up to Alpine lakes, and backcountry tourers go everywhere. The ski area rental shop has Redfeather snowshoes for those pesky "deep stuff" days.

The **Air Bears Freestyle Ski Club** (6742 Enterprise Rd., Ferndale, WA 98248; 384-6801) offers coaching in freestyle skills. One coach was in the 1992 Winter Olympics and the other spent three years as a circus aerialist.

Getting there and getting around

The Mt. Baker Ski Area is at the end of the Mt. Baker highway, 56 miles east of Bellingham, I-5 Exit 255. No public transportation serves the ski area. The drive from Bellingham takes one and a half hours, from Seattle three hours and from Vancouver, B.C., two hours.

Bellingham International Airport is served by Horizon and United Express. Rental cars are available at the airport.

Information/reservations

Mt. Baker offices are in Bellingham, at 1017 Iowa St., Bellingham, WA 98226; call 734-6771. The recorded snow condition number is 671-0211. Mt. Baker's on-mountain office at the upper base has a cellular phone for public use.

The **Bellingham-Whatcom Convention & Visitors Bureau** can be reached for information on lodging, travel and entertainment at (800) 487–2032.

The local area code is 360.

Seattle Day Areas
Alpental/Snoqualmie/Ski Acres/Hyak
Stevens Pass

Only 50 miles of interstate highway lies between The Pass (Alpental/Snoqualmie/Ski Acres/Hyak) and Seattle. No wonder *Ski* rated these areas Number One for accessibility. Seattle is one hour away on I-90, which slices through Snoqualmie Pass revealing the Snoqualmie, Ski Acres and Hyak ski areas all in a row on the right. Alpental is a mile off the highway to the left. All are owned by Ski Lifts Inc. of Seattle, and collectively, the four-area group is called The Pass. It's the largest skiing complex in the state and claims to offer more night skiing—900 acres—than anywhere in the country. All but Hyak are open at night, but not all on the same nights. That's true for days too, but the schedule is impossible to memorize. Remember—any two or three of The Pass are open at any given time (except on non-holiday Mondays, when Ski Acres is the only one open), and one lift ticket plus the free shuttle will get you anywhere that's open.

One drawback, though. You've heard about the rain in Seattle? Snoqualmie Pass base elevation of 3,200 feet isn't all that high, and the freezing level yo-yos up and down. There's plenty of snow—about 170 inches each winter—but sometimes it's wetter than you'd like.

Stevens Pass is 78 miles from Seattle on Highway 2. Though young skiers get tired of hearing about the good old days, how the first lift was a rope tow powered by a V-8, so skiers wouldn't have to hike uphill any more, that's just how **Stevens**

The Pass Facts
Base elevation: 3,200'; Summit elevation: 5,400';
Vertical: 2,200' Alpental, 1,040' Ski Acres, 900' Snoqualmie, 1,080' Hyak.
Number and types of lifts: 33 total for all 4 areas - 1 quad chair, 4 triple chairs, 18 double chairs, 10 surface lifts. **Acreage:** 1,916 downhill acres, 2,000 Nordic-skiing acres.
Snowmaking: None **Uphill capacity:** 30,140 skiers per hour.
Bed base: 80 units at Snoqualmie Pass

Stevens Pass Facts
Base elevation: 4,061'; Summit elevation: 5,800'; Vertical drop: 1,979 feet **Number and types of lifts:** 11–1 fixed-grip quad, 4 triples, 6 doubles
Acreage: 1,125 acres. **Snowmaking:** None **Uphill capacity:** 14,350 per hour

Pass began, back in 1937. Now it has 11 lifts. Stevens is a bit of heaven that's very popular with Seattle area skiers.

Heading up toward Stevens Pass in the winter gives rise to thoughts of skiing the constellation of runs served by the Southern Cross and Jupiter chairs. Polaris Bowl, Andromeda Face and Pegasus Gulch beckon with their own siren songs of snow heaven.

Where to ski

Alpental (closed non-holiday Mondays) is for teenagers at heart. It's steep and undisciplined, and encourages you beyond its northern boundaries to the Great Scott Traverse. It's unpatrolled, and it's not always advisable to ski there, but big bowls, ridges, bluffs and couloirs all dump you eventually into Trash Can, the safest route out. But wait—it's just as treacherous within the boundaries. Alpental's Internationale run is considered by most Washington skiers to be the steepest, longest (2,200 feet), most exciting, and best run in the state. Luckily, it's wide; even so, the ski patrol closes it on icy days. To the right is an even steeper run, Adrenaline. To the left is Widow Maker, a jump. Then there's Lower Internationale, which opens into a wide bowl with tree skiing on the right side, moguls in the middle and a short chute on the left.

Snoqualmie (closed non-holiday Mondays) features gentle runs with names like Over Easy and Easy Rider, but there are plenty of blue runs over most of the north-looking face. Beaver Lake Chair, near the top, serves the expert terrain. The weekend crowds following backward-skiing uniformed leaders would make you think everybody in Seattle is taking a lesson.

Ski Acres (closed non-holiday Tuesdays) is mostly very gentle terrain where Seattle's beginners learn to ski. There are several serious black diamond runs from the very top of the ridge, reached by the Triple 60 Chair, but a cat track to the base lets nervous types off the hook.

Hyak (only open weekends and holidays, between Christmas and mid-March) is on the "dry" side of the pass. It has a regular following that likes the 1,000-foot continuous vertical drop on the front side and the backside-to-frontside treed runs— no crowds. The snowboard halfpipe is also on the backside.

At **Stevens Pass** the favorite areas for venturesome skiers are Mill Valley, with its black-diamond Borealis run, and the chutes reached by the 7th Heaven Chair. The Southern Cross Chair is 1,000 feet shy of a mile long, but if you swerve back and forth between the trees, you can easily double the distance back down to the bottom. Southern Cross and Jupiter lines are the shortest during lunch. The Way Back trail, above Mill Valley's Corona bowl, is part of the gentle intermediate route to the valley floor. It's called the Way Back because beginners and intermediates can turn right onto Skid Road and descend gracefully to the base area. The Double Diamond run leading to the base area is in fact a double diamond. Adjacent woods make for some good off-piste skiing when the snow is fresh.

Mountain ratings

The Pass has enough terrain variety to keep most skiers happy for a day or two. The three on the south side of the highway have connecting trails, and there's something to be said for skiing more than one hill in a day. Clearly, Alpental is for the intermediate to expert skier. Only 10 percent of the terrain is rated beginner.

At Stevens Pass, the 26 major runs are about one-third advanced, but the only chair for beginners to avoid is 7th Heaven. All others have easy, or at least intermediate, ways down.

Cross-country

The Ski Acres and Hyak Cross Country Center (closed non-holiday Tuesdays) is located at the base of Ski Acres Silver Fir Chair, the closest one to Hyak. Skiers can access the trail system from either Ski Acres XC Center (a zoo) or the Hyak base area, which is less crowded with better parking. Rentals, food and lessons are available at both access points. A $9 lift/trail ticket buys two round trips on the Silver Fir Chair to access the 2,000-acre, 55-km. trail system in the Ollalie Meadows and Rockdale Lake areas. Day or night fees on the lower 5-km. trail system are $4. Children 5 and younger ski free day or night.

Stevens Pass has a Nordic center with rentals and lessons, open 9 a.m. to 4 p.m. Friday through Sunday plus holidays, and more than 27 km. of groomed trails for both striding and skating. Regional biathlons are held here. The newly enlarged center is five miles east of the Stevens Pass parking lot. Trail passes cost $6 for adults, $5 for seniors and children aged 7-12. It's free for children 6 and younger and seniors 70 and older.

Snowboarding

Snowboards are welcome everywhere; in fact, Northwesterners feel they own the sport because so many champions train in the region. At Snoqualmie, a race course built for a freestyle competition stayed and became known as "Jellystone" in honor of the respected Snowboard Park Rangers.

Stevens Pass is a regional favorite, especially on powder days. Plenty of trees challenge technical turning skills and lots of open terrain and bowls supply the fun.

Lessons

The **Skiforall Foundation** is the state's premier ski school for people with disabilities. It was once named the Most Outstanding Therapeutic Recreation Program by the Washington Parks and Recreation Department. The foundation's position is that no human handicap can prevent you from enjoying some variety of snow sport. For more information, call 462-0978.

In addition, there are 34 ski schools on The Pass, including race camps, gate running and instructor training, as well as snowboarding and cross-country lessons. All four areas have beginner specials that include gear, passes and lessons. Call: Alpental, 434-6364; Snoqualmie, 434-7669, ext. 3242; Ski Acres, 434-6400; Hyak Ski School (downhill and cross-country), 391-2782; Ski Acres/Hyak Cross-Country Center, 434-6646.

Stevens Pass has lessons in all ski and snowboard disciplines in its 24 adult and 13 children's ski schools. Two entry-level specials for skiers and snowboarders, daily at 9:30 a.m. for skiers and 11:30 a.m. for snowboarders, include all equipment, a one-hour group lesson and a Daisy Lift (vertical rise is 308 feet) ticket. Non-holiday weekdays cost $24 for skiers and $30 for snowboarders. Weekend and holiday costs are $32 for skiers or $36 for snowboarders. Specials are available at the ski rental desk in the West Lodge.

Child care

Snoqualmie and **Ski Acres** both offer child care. The cost for toddlers aged 1 to 2 years is $30 for the day or $4 an hour. For pre-schoolers it's $25 a day or $3.50 an hour. During the week (non-holiday), a day or night lift ticket and child care together cost $30. Add $5 for toddlers. You must register at the child care office in Ski Acres' Main Lodge (at the Holiday Chair) or at Snoqualmie's child care center in the USFS Visitors Information Center near Alpenhaus Lodge. Call 434-7669, ext. 3349 or 3301 for information or to make reservations.

Stevens Pass child care, weekends and holidays only, accepts toilet-trained children between the ages of 30 months and 7 years. Call 973-2441 for information.

Lift tickets (94/95 prices)

The Pass

	Adult/Child (7+)	Senior (62-69)
Weekend day	$27	$20
Monday/Tuesday	$14	$14
Wednesday/Thursday	$16	$14
Friday	$18	$14

Children 6 and younger pay $5. Skiers 70 and older always ski free with ID. Add $2 if you also want to extend your ticket to nights. Night tickets alone range from $14-$18, depending on day of week. The Pass offers a $5 single-ride ticket so you can check conditions. Take the stub back within an hour and you get a $5 credit toward a lift ticket, either same day or another.

Stevens Pass

	Adult	Child (7–12)
Weekend day + night	$31	$24
Monday/Tuesday	$15	$12
Wednesday-Friday	$20	$20

Stevens Pass is open daily 9 a.m. to 10 p.m. Subtract $3 for weekend afternoon + night skiing; subtract another $3 for weekend night skiing. Night skiing (5–10 p.m.) costs $10 Sunday through Thursday. Those 62–69 pay $26 for the weekend day + night ticket; the $3 discount then applies for other times. Skiing is free for children 6 and younger and seniors 70 and older.

Accommodations

The Summit Hotel has the only lodging in Snoqualmie Pass. The inn has a hot tub, sauna, heated pool and restaurant. The 80 rooms range in price from $59 for one person to $102 for four. Call (360) 434-6300. RV parking in the pass is allowed, but there are no hookups.

Stevens Pass has no lodging, but self-contained RVs are welcome in the designated parking lot. Leavenworth, 37 miles east on Route 2, is a full-blown tourist town with lodging galore, mostly in the Alps tradition. Austrian atmosphere is offered by the **Hotel Pension Anna,** a No Smoking lodging at 926 Commercial St. It has 11 rooms with elegant Austrian furnishings. Rates are $65 and up. Call (509) 548-5807 for information or reservations. For information on other Leavenworth lodgings, call Bavarian Bedfinders at (800) 323-2920.

Skykomish, in the other direction, 16 miles west on Route 2, has the **Skyriver Inn** on the Skykomish River. It's a AAA-Two-Diamond lodging with rates starting at $47.50 for a queen bedroom with a parking lot view (rooms with river views cost $5 more). All units have a little refrigerator and coffee maker, and some have kitchenettes ($5 extra). A complete apartment that sleeps six adults comfortably costs $77.50. Call 677-2261 for reservations.

Dining

Webb's Bar & Grill in **Snoqualmie's** Alpenhaus Lodge is the place for healthy food. The same lodge also has a cafeteria. **Alpental** has a food service and lounge in Alpental Lodge and Denny Mountain Lodge. **Ski Acres** has a deli in the cross-country center, Bonanza Snack Bar at the Bonanza Chair, and a tavern and lounge in the Main Lodge. **Hyak** has a cafeteria and lounge in the Day Lodge.

There are three lodges at **Stevens Pass**. The Short Run Deli in West Lodge has good made-to-order sandwiches, soups and baked potatoes. The T-Bar Restaurant is a rustic full-service place. It specializes in ribs and chicken and has a soup-and-salad bar. The Mountain Express Restaurant, in the East Lodge, offers day-skier food—burgers, fries and chili.

Après-ski/nightlife

The Pass is an overgrown day area. It's only an hour's drive to Seattle. However, there is Saturday music at Alpental and Snoqualmie.

At Stevens Pass, with the night lights on, skiing itself is the nightlife. But there is a sports TV bar, Cloud Nine in the East Lodge. The Soft Landing Lounge, in the West Lodge, features live band entertainment and comedy shows.

Other activities

Shopping: On the way to The Pass is **Great Northwest Factory Stores**, a 40-store, name-brand outlet center that includes Great Outdoor Clothing Co., Bass Shoe, B.U.M. Equipment and others. Take Exit 30 from Interstate 90.

Snowflake Tubing and Snow Play, just across the street from Ski Acres, has a groomed tubing hill. Two double rope tows slide you back up the hill for a $6.50 ticket (5 and younger free). It's open Friday through Sunday, and holidays; night tubing until 10 p.m. Fridays and Saturdays. Bring your own tube (free air) or rent one on site for $5.50.

Stevens Pass has only skiing to offer.

Getting there and getting around

The Pass: Take I-90 east from Seattle. For Alpental and Snoqualmie, take Exit 52. For Ski Acres, take Exit 53. For Hyak, take Exit 54. Some problems every so often with slick roads. A free shuttle runs between the various ski areas at The Pass.

Stevens Pass: On U.S. Route 2, 78 miles northeast of Seattle, or 64 miles east of I-5 at Everett. It's not served by public transportation. Ninety school and ski club buses in the parking lot might suggest otherwise, but you've got to drive yourself there. The crowds are astounding on sunny holiday weekends. The road itself has improved dramatically in recent years, to the point where some truckers prefer it to I-90 for winter travel over the Cascades. A highway reader board in Monroe, where Everett and Seattle traffic join, alerts drivers about road and parking conditions ahead.

Information/reservations

The Pass expanded snowline: 236-1600, for conditions, rates and special events. The Pass office: 232-8182. Alpental Lodge: 434-6112; Snoqualmie Lodge: 434-6161; Ski Acres Lodge: 434-6671; Hyak Lodge: 434-7600.

Stevens Pass: Snow conditions recording, from Seattle 634-1645. Offices and information, 973-2441. Address is P.O. Box 98, Skykomish, WA 98288.

Local area code is 360, unless otherwise noted.

Jackson Hole, Wyoming

These are some of the contradictions you'll find on a winter vacation to Jackson Hole:

• This is one of the biggest ski areas in the United States: second-highest vertical at 4,139 feet, more than 2,500 acres of terrain and 10 lifts. But when you look across the valley at the Tetons, you can't pick out the ski area. There are no telltale white ribbons cut through heavily forested terrain. The Tetons are largely treeless, but the trees that are there are nicely spread out, forming natural paths. From a distance, Jackson Hole's runs, chutes and bowls disappear, and all you see are some of the most rugged and beautiful mountain peaks in the world.

• Fat wallets and fancy ski clothes don't seem to impress anyone here. A duct-tape patch is a badge of honor, not a reason to buy new ski clothes. This also is one of the few resorts in the world where ski-in lodging starts at $14 per night. And yet the town of Jackson has impressive shopping and art galleries where you can drop a thousand dollars in no time flat.

• Employees at the shops, restaurants and hotels in town are friendly without being overbearing, with the relaxed, unflappable attitude you find in the off-season at other ski resorts. The attitude comes naturally, because winter *is* the off-season in Jackson. Every summer, this charming little town is overrun by tourists headed for two national parks, Grand Teton and Yellowstone. Jackson residents seem to feel that if they can survive four months of bumper-to-bumper RVs, a few hundred thousand skiers and snowboarders are a piece of cake. Two wonderful things result from this backward calendar: hotel rooms are relatively cheap, and everyone is happy to see you. (The town is 12 miles from the ski resort town, which is called Teton Village. And of course, winter is high season there.)

• You've probably heard about the Hole's menacing terrain,

Jackson Hole Facts

Base elevation: 6,311'; **Summit elevation:** 10,450'; **Vertical drop:** 4,139 feet
Number and types of lifts: 10—1 aerial tram, 2 quad chairs, 1 triple chair,
4 double chairs, and 2 surface lifts
Acreage: 2,500 skiable acres **Percent of snowmaking:** 2 percent (about 80 acres)
Uphill capacity: 8,624 skiers per hour **Bed base:** 10,000

how it eats up skiers at the summit and spits them out at the
base. Yes, it has gnarly slopes—they don't sell "I Survived the
Tram" ski pins here for nothing. Yet it also has some excellent
learning terrain—long gentle wide runs, where you might even
catch a glimpse of a moose calf as he runs to join his mother.

Where to ski

Jackson Hole's 4,139-foot vertical drop is the second-largest
in the United States. (It lost the spot at the top of the list this
year when Big Sky, Montana installed an aerial tram to its
summit. However, you cover Jackson Hole's vertical with one
tram ride, while it takes three lifts to do it at Big Sky) Fully half of
Jackson Hole's 2,500 acres is marked with a black diamond. It's
no wonder the area has a reputation for steep, exciting skiing.

But the other half of that 2,500 acres is *not* black diamond.
Even better, most of the tough stuff is completely separate from
the easier runs—intermediates seldom have to worry about
getting in over their heads.

Skiing is spread across three areas. Rendezvous Mountain is
where you'll find Jackson Hole's tram and a lot of chutes, cliffs,
bumps and steep faces. Apres Vous Mountain has 2,170 vertical
feet of beginner and intermediate terrain, and Casper Bowl has
wide intermediate runs, sprinkled with a few advanced.

One surprising feature of Jackson Hole is its excellent
beginner terrain. The base of Apres Vous mountain has several
long wide gentle green runs, perfect for learning and served by
the Teewinot and Eagle's Rest chairs.

Though Jackson Hole is a marvelous place for beginners, it's
tough for lower intermediates. It's a big step from those gently
undulating green-circle slopes to Jackson Hole's blues. Although
the upper parts of Apres Vous and all of Casper Bowl are wide
and groomed, they have a much steeper pitch than blues at
other resorts, enough to intimidate some lower-level skiers.

Good intermediates will have a ball. Follow the solid blue
lines for groomed terrain and the broken blue lines for
ungroomed powder or bumps. You'll run out of gas before you run
out of terrain.

Still too tame for you? Then board the big red tram for the
4,139-foot, 12-minute rise to the top of Rendezvous Mountain.
This is where the big boys and girls go to play. Because area
management charges an extra $2 for each tram ride on top of
your lift ticket, you really have to want to be here. (You can get
unlimited tram access for an extra $3, but one time down may be
enough.) And be forewarned: The "easiest" way down from the
summit is Rendezvous Bowl, a huge, treeless face littered with
gigantic moguls. Head the opposite direction and you'll face
Corbet's Couloir. Much-photographed Corbet's is a narrow,
rocky passage that requires a 10- to 20-foot airborne entry.

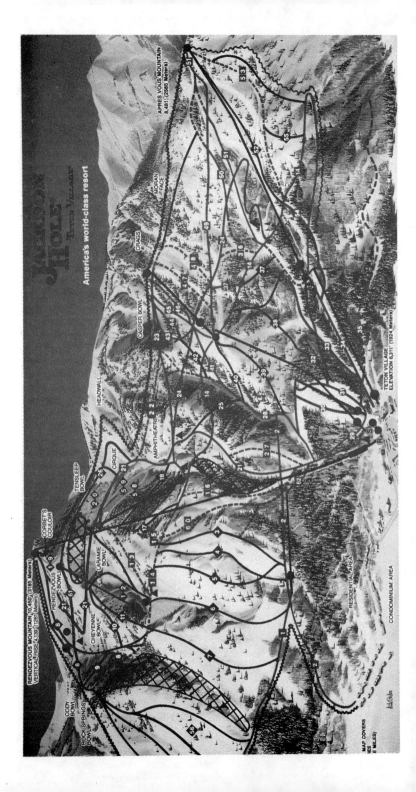

TRAIL DIFFICULTY SYMBOLS

● EASIEST

■ MODERATELY
   DIFFICULT

■ MORE DIFFICULT—
   VARIED TERRAIN PLUS
   SNOW CONDITIONS
   FOR THE BETTER THAN
   AVERAGE SKIER

◆ MOST DIFFICULT—
   EXPERT

◆ MOST DIFFICULT—
   EXPERT USE EXTRA
   CAUTION

TRAIL NAMES

1. Union Pass Traverse
2. Way Home
3. North Colter Ridge
4. Buffalo Bowl
5. South Colter Ridge
6. Rawlins Bowl
7. Lower Sublette Ridge
8. Rendezvous Trail
9. Bivouac
10. Bird In The Hand
11. Pepi's Run
12. Alta Chutes
13. Grand
14. South Pass Traverse
15. Gannett
16. Lower Tram Line
17. Riverton Bowl
18. Thunder
19. East Ridge Traverse
20. Expert Chutes

21. Gros Ventre
22. Nez Perce Traverse
23. Amphitheatre Traverse
24. Solitude Traverse
25. Avalanche
26. Downhill
27. Slalom
28. Sundance Gully
29. Eagle's Rest Cutoff
30. Eagle's Rest
31. Pooh Bear
32. Antelope Flats
33. Lower Werner
34. Lower Teewinot
35. Cross Country Ski Trail
36. Solitude Cutoff
37. Ashley Ridge
38. Beaver Tooth
39. Jackson Face
40. Nez Perce
41. Blacktail

42. Surprise
43. Camp Ground
44. Timbered Island
45. Easy Does It
46. Lift Line
47. Sleeping Indian
48. Wide Open
49. Togwotee Pass Traverse
50. Moran
51. Upper Teewinot
52. Upper Teewinot
53. St. Johns
54. Teewinot Gully
55. Secret Slope
56. North Hoback
57. South Hoback
58. Tower Three Chute
59. Paint Brush
60. Lander Bowl
61. Changing Rock
62. U.P. Connection

LIFTS

	AERIAL TRAM	2.4 Miles Long
	12 Minutes	4,139' Vertical Rise
1.	EAGLE'S REST DOUBLE CHAIR	2,260' Long
	5 Minutes	330' Vertical Rise
2.	TEEWINOT DOUBLE CHAIR	3,060' Long
	7 Minutes	425' Vertical Rise
3.	APRES VOUS DOUBLE CHAIR	5,000' Long
	10 Minutes	1,745' Vertical Rise
4.	THUNDER DOUBLE CHAIR	3,770' Long
	8 Minutes	1,466' Vertical Rise
5.	CASPER BOWL TRIPLE CHAIR	3,450' Long
	8 Minutes	1,046' Vertical Rise
6.	CRYSTAL SPRINGS DOUBLE CHAIR	4,113' Long
	9 Minutes	1,196' Vertical Rise
7.	UPPER SUBLETTE RIDGE QUAD CHAIR	4,108' Long
	9 Minutes	1,630' Vertical Rise
*8.	RENDEZVOUS BOWL SURFACE LIFT	2,714' Long
	5 Minutes	824' Vertical Rise
9.	UNION PASS SURFACE LIFT	1,360' Long
	2 Minutes	150' Vertical Rise

* This lift does not operate during periods of adverse wind,
weather or snow conditions.

Another face of the mountain are the Hobacks, a spacious area that offers some of the best lift-served powder skiing in America. Experts looking for a warmup should try Rendezvous' longest run, Gros Ventre, which starts out in Rendezvous Bowl, winds across the tops of Cheyenne and Laramie bowls, then mellows just enough the rest of the way down to earn a blue rating on the trail map. It may look bright blue on the map, but it's a lot darker under your skis.

Mountain rating

Color Rendezvous Mountain and the Hobacks jet black, with occasional slashes of navy-blue advanced intermediate. Casper Bowl is for intermediates up to experts, depending on the grooming. Casper's groomed runs (a solid blue line on the trail map) are a cruising delight. The ungroomed blues (a dotted line) are just plain hard work, worthy of advanced skiers. Apres Vous is fantastic for advanced intermediates but so-so for advancing beginners. Never-evers will do fine the first couple of days, but beginner terrain is quite limited.

Snowboarding

Snowboarding is permitted everywhere. A couple of natural halfpipes are Sundance Gully and Dick's Ditch. The ski school gives snowboard lessons and local shops rent boards.

Nearby skiing

The **Snow King Ski Area** is in downtown Jackson, about 12 miles from Jackson Hole. Sixty percent of its 400 acres is rated advanced, thanks to a north-facing slope that plunges 1,571 feet. Its only green-rated terrain is a catwalk that traverses the mountain from the summit to the base. Because it is so steep, always shaded and often icy, locals call it "Eastern skiing out West." This small town area is a great practice hill with a steep consistent pitch. Lift tickets are $25 for adults; kids 14 and younger and seniors 60 and older, $16. The hill is open for night skiing Tuesday through Saturday, and tickets are $12 after 5:30 p.m.

Cross-country

Jackson Hole has some of the most beautiful natural surroundings in the United States. Nordic skiers can strike out for marked trails in Grand Teton or Yellowstone National Parks, or try one of the six touring centers in Jackson and Grand Targhee.

The **Jackson Hole Nordic Center** (307-739-2629) serves as the hub of the Nordic systems in Teton Village with 20 km. of groomed track. Because it is next to the downhill ski area, it has telemark lessons as an option. Full-day beginner group lessons, half-day lessons for other levels and private instruction are available, as are guided excursions into the backcountry of Grand Teton National Park. Rentals also are available.

Other touring centers are **Spring Creek** (733-8833), **Teton Pines** (733-1005) and **Togwotee Mountain Lodge** (543-2847 or 800-543-2847).

Lessons (95/96 prices)

The ski school is not only the place to get instruction (and that isn't a bad idea, given Jackson Hole's extreme terrain), but it is also the place to engage a knowledgeable mountain guide. Jackson Hole's nooks and crannies can best be enjoyed with someone who knows how to reach them.

Adult **group lessons** are $50 for a full day (morning and afternoon sessions) and $40 for morning or afternoon. Three-day morning group-lesson packages are $100, and other multi-day discounts are available. **Private lessons** are given most commonly in a two-hour morning lesson for $120 for one skier, $150 for two to three and $190 for four to six people. Afternoon private lessons are slightly cheaper.

Jackson Hole has many **special workshops** such as instruction for disabled people, the Mountain Experience for advanced to expert skiers that show them the best terrain and snow conditions and various camps for women, racing and teens offered at specified times of the season. Guides can be hired for $190 for a full day ($35 more for each additional skier), $110 for morning half day and $100 for afternoon half day ($30 each additional skier). Reservations are recommended.

The SKIwee program for **children** ages 6 to 13 has all-day group lessons running $35. A three-day SKIwee package is $150, with lunch an additional cost (or kids can pack a lunch and stay with the supervised group). The resort also has ski lessons and day care for ages 3-5 as part of its day care program. This program is $64 for all day and $48 for a half day.

You can make reservations for any ski school program including mountain guides by calling 739-2610.

Child care (95/96 prices)

Day care for ages 2 months to 5 years is $55 for a full day; $42 a half day. Parents must provide formula or food for infants; toddlers get lunch and a snack in the price. Reservations are suggested, call 739-2691.

For babysitting at your hotel or condo, call **Babysitting Service of Jackson Hole**, 733-0685; (800) 253-9650. This service, which is a member of the Jackson Hole Chamber of Commerce, has mature sitters, some of whom are certified in first aid and child CPR.

Lift tickets (95/96 prices)

	Adult	Child (Up to 14) Senior (65+)
One day	$45	$24
Three days	$132 ($44/day)	$71 ($23.66/day)
Five days	$210 ($42/day)	$105 ($21/day)

These prices include unlimited tram access. Tickets for chair lifts-only are $3 less per day for everyone. As noted above, each tram ride is $2 additional, and for many people one run down from the tram will be plenty of excitement. If in doubt, buy a chair lift ticket. You can always later upgrade it to unlimited access for $3 more.

You can buy a Jackson Hole Ski Three five-day voucher book for $210 ($42 per day). At Jackson Hole, it's valid for a lift ticket and unlimited aerial tram. At Snow King, it buys a lift ticket and dinner at Rafferty's Restaurant in Snow King Resort. At Grand Targhee, it's valid for a lift ticket and the round-trip bus transportation from Jackson.

Accommodations

Choose from three locations: Teton Village at the base of the slopes, with fewer restaurants and nightlife options; the town of Jackson, with lots of eating, shopping and partying, 12 miles from skiing; or hotels, condos and two fine resorts between the two. Bus transportation between town and ski area is readily available.

Teton Village: The following lodging properties are all within steps of the slopes and each other, so the choice is on facilities or price rather than location. Most of these properties have ski packages; we list nightly room rates here.

Alpenhof (733-3242; 800-732-3244) is the most luxurious of the hotels. Built in peaked-roof Alpine style with lots of exposed and carved wood, it has an excellent restaurant and a large lounge that is a center of relaxed après-ski activity. Some of the 40 guest rooms have fireplaces. The hotel has a heated outdoor pool, Jacuzzi, sauna and game room. Room rates range from $89 to $402, depending on size of room and season; standard rooms in regular season are $141.

The Best Western Inn at Jackson Hole (733-2311 or 800-842-7666) has the most spacious rooms available (short of condos). Many have kitchenettes, fireplaces and/or lofts. It has two restaurants, a heated outdoor pool and hot tub. One possible drawback: every time you leave your room, you step outside. That means bundling up to go to the hot tub or restaurant. Room rates are $75-$225; standard rooms in regular season are $125-$150.

Sojourner Inn (733-3657 or 800-445-4655) started out as a European lodge but additions have turned it into a rambling hotel with pool, sauna and Jacuzzi. The rooms in the original building tend to be small, with not much space for ski luggage and paraphernalia; but the ones in the newer wing are larger and more modern. Room rates are $85-$260; standard rooms in regular season are $125-$145.

The Hostel (733-3415) has some of the most inexpensive slopeside lodging in the United States—$43 per night per room with one or two skiers; $56 per room for three or four (that's $14 per night!) Rooms are quite spartan, but have private baths and maid service; amenities include a large lounge and game area and laundry facilities.

The Village Center Inn (733-3155) has 16 one- and two-bedroom units, some with lofts, in a building next to the aerial tram. These are basic and unfancy. Rates range from $88 to $106. **Crystal Springs Inn** (733-4423) has 15 basic rooms that go for about $80 a night.

Condominiums and private homes are available through Teton Village Property Management (800-443-6840; 733-4610) and Jackson Hole Property Management (800-443-8613; 733-7945). Rates range from $100 to $650 per night.

Town of Jackson: Many of these accommodations also offer ski packages. All listed here are within a block of the public bus service to Teton Village unless noted.

One of the best, with a great location just off the main square, is the **Wort Hotel**, an 1880s-style, four-diamond AAA-rated hotel that is just off the main square. Nightly rates are $130-$170; a suite is available for $295. Close by is the Silver Dollar Bar, with its curving bar inlaid with 2,032 uncirculated 1921 silver dollars.

Snow King Resort is the largest hotel with 204 rooms ranging from $90 to $170. It has restaurants, a pool, indoor ice rink, game and fitness rooms and more. It is several long blocks from downtown, but right next to the Snow King Ski Area, which has night skiing. Rooms range from $100 to $170; suites and condos also are available for higher prices.

Two excellent B&Bs are **Rusty Parrot Lodge** (733-2000) and **Davy Jackson Inn** (739-2294 or 800-584-0532). Both have inviting rooms with down comforters, some with fireplaces. Rusty Parrot has more of a country, lodgepole pine decor, while Davy Jackson leans toward Victorian, but you can't go wrong at either. Rates, which include full breakfasts, are $145–$175. Rusty Parrot is about two blocks from downtown and half a block to the bus stop; Davy Jackson is three long blocks to downtown and a long block to the bus stop.

Between downtown and the ski area:

Two newer hotels are **Wyoming Inn of Jackson** (800-844-0035; 734-0035) and **The Best Western Lodge at Jackson Hole** (800-458-3866; 739-9703) located practically next door to each other on Broadway (Highway 89) heading toward Teton Village from downtown. **Wyoming Inn** is beautifully decorated with antique reproduction furniture, but has no pool or hot tub (though some rooms have Jacuzzis). It serves a continental breakfast, but there is no restaurant. Rates are $129–$169.

The Lodge at Jackson Hole (there also is a Jackson Hole Lodge, which is quite different) is a delight for children, because its exterior is decorated with carved and painted bears and raccoons, that hang from poles and peek from benches and mailboxes. Rates are $129–$149. Though it has a swimming pool and hot tub, it also has no restaurant.

One of the best spots to see the ragged Grand Teton Mountain and its equally beautiful neighboring peaks is at the **Spring Creek Resort**, atop the East Gros Ventre Butte, which blocks the view of Grand Teton from most of Jackson. The resort has luxurious hotel rooms, condos and houses for rent, a marvelous gourmet restaurant and unsurpassed views of the Jackson Valley, Grand Teton and the ski area. Rates are $150–$190 per night. Shuttles to town and the ski area are provided. Call 733-8833 or (800) 443-6139.

On Teton Village Road a few miles from the ski area and town is **Teton Pines Resort**. Though it perhaps is better known for its summer activities, including a stunning 18-hole golf course, it is open in winter and has ski packages. The amenities list goes on and on: free pick-up from the airport, free indoor tennis, use of a neighboring athletic club, in-room continental breakfast, an excellent gourmet restaurant, 14 km. of cross-country trails, pool and hot tub. Rooms are spacious and beautiful and are about half the summer rates at $160 per night. Call 733-1005 or (800) 238-2223.

Jackson has many other lodging choices. Call **Jackson Hole Central Reservations** (800) 443-6931 for information on winter packages. This agency can book your entire trip, from airline tickets to activities.

Dining

Jackson has more than 80 restaurants. All the best ones used to be in town, but now there are some outstanding ones in the outlying areas.

Teton Village: At the elegant end of the spectrum are the **Alpenhof Hotel Restaurant** (733-3462), a quiet, genteel place that serves German and Austrian specialties, or **Jenny Leigh's** (733-7102) at the Inn at Jackson Hole, which specializes in wild game entrées.

At the other extreme is **The Mangy Moose** (733-4913), beloved for its salad bar, down-home steak-and-seafood menu, and lively atmosphere, or **Beaver Dick's** (733-7102), with a bar menu and enough stuffed animal heads to buy the local taxidermist a slopeside mansion. Somewhere between is **Dietrich's Bar & Bistro** (733-3242), also in the Alpenhof Hotel, or **The Sojourner Inn's Steak & Pasta House,** (733-3657) where steaming plates of pasta warm a crisp winter night. Fondues are served each Friday.

Jackson: For casual inexpensive dining, it's **Bubba's** heaping plates of "bubbacued" ribs, chicken, beef and pork. No sense in giving you the phone number (it's at 515 W. Broadway), because Bubba's doesn't take reservations. Be prepared to wait, and while you do, send a member of your party across the street to the liquor store—Bubba's is BYOB.

Other casual places are the **Calico Pizza Parlor** (733-2460) and **Mountain High Pizza Pie** (733-3646). **Nani's Genuine Pasta House** (733-3888) and **Anthony's** (733-3717) got raves from locals for their authentic Italian regional cooking. **Lame Duck** (733-4311) has the best reputation for Chinese cooking.

A good choice on the elegant end is **The Range** (733-5481), which last year was located in Teton Village but moved to 225 Noah Cache St. in Jackson. It serves a five-course fixed-price (about $36), American regional cuisine dinner from an open-style kitchen, and also serves lunch and à la carte entrées. Other upper-scale choices are **Off Broadway Grille** (733-9777) for pastas, fresh seafood and meats; and **The Blue Lion** (733-3912), known for its roast rack of lamb.

For breakfast, try **The Bunnery** (733-5474), which has excellent omelets, whole-grain waffles and bakery items; **Jedediah's Original House of Sourdough** for superb sourjack pancakes and other breakfast meals or **Bubba's** for hearty fare. Locals recommend **Shades Cafe** (733-2015) for gourmet coffees, espresso and lattes. The coffee is fine, but we found the breakfast lacking (mushy waffles).

Between town and the ski area:

For excellent dining, **the Granary** (733-8833) at Spring Creek Resort is hard to beat. Entrées include such as medallions of elk. Another top choice is **The Grille at the Pines** (733-1005) at the Teton Pines Resort, with a beautiful dining room and extensive wine list. **Stiegler's** (733-1071) has specialties from owner Peter Stiegler's home in Austria.

Gouloff's (733-1886), across the street from the Teton Pines, has interesting game dishes such as pheasant-stuffed chicken and moose medallions (as well as pasta, beef and lamb) The Mexican restaurant with the best reputation is **Vista Grande** (733-6964).

For more ideas, pick up a copy of the Jackson Hole Dining Guide or browse through the rack of business-card-sized menus at your hotel (an excellent idea other resorts should use).

Après ski/nightlife

In Teton Village the rowdiest spot by far for après-ski and nightlife is **The Mangy Moose.** Close behind is **Beaver Dick's** at the Inn at Jackson Hole with its sports bar atmosphere. **Dietrich's** at the Alpenhof is much more sedate.

In town, **The Million Dollar Cowboy Bar** attracts tourists who love saddle bar stools, the silver dollars in the bar surface, and live Country & Western bands. Try it, corny as it sounds. **The Silver Dollar Bar** is similar, with more silver dollars in the bar. **The Shady Lady Saloon** at the Snow King Resort has live entertainment several nights a week. **Jackson Hole Pub & Brewery** has good microbrews, and hopes for live entertainment for the 1995-96 ski season, pending a permit from the city.

Other activities

Shopping here is what it should be at all resort towns—a selection of high-quality, moderately priced goods with friendly, helpful sales personnel. Shopaholics should stay in town (the Wort Hotel is right at the center of the action). The covered wooden sidewalks encourage window shopping, even when it snows. There are far too many good shops to single out any of them, but you'll find art galleries, plenty of Western clothing and items made from elk antlers.

Several unusual activities center around Jackson's abundant wildlife. You can take a sleigh ride through the **National Elk Refuge.** Between 7,000 and 9,000 elk winter in the valley, eating the hay provided by their human friends and going calmly about their business as the sleigh passes. The cost is about $8 for adults and $4 for ages 6-12. Reservations required; call 733-9212.

An outstanding educational tour is offered through the **Great Plains Wildlife Institute.** On the institute's wildlife spotting tours, you ride with a biologist to help spot the location and numbers of various wildlife. A four-hour tour costs $65 for adults and $35 for adult-accompanied children aged 3–12, with snacks provided. Full day and multiday tours also are offered. On our tour we saw bison, elk, eagles, moose, deer, bighorn sheep, trumpeter swans and pronghorn. Everyone gets to use binoculars and a powerful spotting scope for up-close viewing. Call 733-2623.

The unique **National Wildlife Art Museum** (733-5771) features the nation's premier collection of fine wildlife paintings, sculptures and other art, some dating back 170 years. Though the museum has been around since 1987, it moved into dramatic new quarters in 1994 across from the elk refuge.

Horse-drawn **dinner sleigh rides** are offered by Spring Creek Resort (733-8833) and Solitude Cabin (733-6657).

Other activities include **dogsled rides,** snowmobile excursions to **Granite Hot Springs, helicopter touring and skiing,** and of course, nearby **Grand Teton and Yellowstone National Parks.**

Getting there and getting around

Getting there: American, Delta, Skywest, GP Express (the Continental Connection), United and United Express serve the Jackson Hole airport. The town is 10 miles south of the airport, and Teton Village is 12 miles farther via Highways 89, 22 and 390.

Getting around: Whether to rent a car is a toss-up. Skiers can get along fine without one, though if you plan to do a lot of restaurant or nightlife hopping, or skiing at Grand Targhee or Snow King, you may want one. Unless you are used to driving steep Rocky Mountain passes, we recommend that you take the bus to Grand Targhee in snowy weather.

Warning for motorists: Highway signs say nothing about the ski areas. From town, follow signs for Teton Village to get to Jackson Hole ski area, and for Wilson when driving to Grand Targhee.

Southern Teton Area Rapid Transit (START) buses run frequently between Jackson and Teton Village at a cost of $2 each way, to 10 p.m. in ski season. Jackson Hole Transportation runs airport shuttles.

Information/reservations

Jackson Hole Central Reservations, 800-443-6931, for airline tickets, lodging, lifts, activities and transfers.

Jackson Hole Ski Corporation: P.O. Box 290, Teton Village, WY 83025; 733-2292. Snow conditions: 733-2291.

Local area code is 307.

Grand Targhee, Wyoming

If you like to ski or snowboard in powder snow but can't afford a heli-trip, Grand Targhee is the next best thing. About 500 inches of snow falls here each winter, and when it does, Targhee's groomers don't exactly work overtime. You gotta love a ski resort that designates beginner, intermediate and advanced powder areas on its trail map.

Did we scare away those of you who still flounder in fluff? Don't flip the page yet. This is one of the two best lift-served resorts in America to learn powder skiing. (Ironically, Alta, Utah is the other; Grand Targhee's address is Alta, Wyoming.) The trouble with powder at other resorts is you usually find it only on the steepest slopes, and it's tough to get a feel for loose snow when you're also struggling with the pitch. Grand Targhee leaves powder on some of its gentle, rolling terrain too, so anyone who wants to conquer powder will never have a better chance.

If you are an intermediate, rent a pair of "fat skis" and cut loose. These boards make all the difference in the world. One of our contributors, who can't make it 50 feet in deep powder on regular skis without falling, skied for four straight hours at Targhee on fat skis, giggling with delight at every turn. If you really don't want to deal with powder, Targhee grooms a few paths from the top of each lift.

The best part of this powder paradise is you won't have to share this fresh pillowy snow with the masses, because this resort is grandly isolated. Grand Targhee is in Wyoming, but the only way to get here is through Idaho. Its huge bowls of snow are on the western slope of the Tetons, which hug the border between the two states.

Targhee was the name of a local peacekeeping Indian chief who lived in the area more than 100 years ago (you'll see his portrait painted on one of the buildings). Grand, of course, comes from the 13,770-foot Grand Teton Peak. From here, you see the peak's less photographed but equally impressive west face.

Grand Targhee Facts

Base: 8,000'; **Summit elevation:** 10,200'; **Vertical drop:** 2,200 feet
Number of lifts: 4–3 double chairs, 1 surface lift
Snowmaking: none   **Total acreage:** 1,500 skiable acres   **Bed Base:** 432

When Averell Harriman was scouting for his dream resort in the 1930s, he narrowed it down to Targhee and the site that became Sun Valley. Local ranchers and farmers opened Targhee as a ski resort about 25 years ago. About eight years ago Boston architect, Mory Bergmeyer and his wife Carol, a management consultant, bought Grand Targhee after taking a ski trip there. The duo has modernized the facilities without sacrificing the splendid serenity.

Targhee is close to ranch country, and many of its employees herd cattle or grow potatoes in the snowless months. A good number have never lived anywhere else. Though not talkative, they are quite friendly.

No ski area is perfect for everyone, however. If you go stir-crazy without a variety of restaurants and other things to do, we suggest you stay in Jackson and spend one day of your vacation here. But if you'd like to completely unwind, ski during the day, read a good book at night and head home new and invigorated, this is the place.

Where to ski

Three chair lifts open high, broad descents mostly above treeline. However, 1,500 acres are more than you might expect from three chairs. Most of the skiing is for intermediates, with few narrow trails. Lifts can handle 3,600 skiers an hour, but on a big day at Targhee the crowd is 1,600.

Our stat box for this chapter shows the statistics for Fred's Mountain, which is lift-served. It has excellent cruiser runs and good bump slopes. Targhee doesn't have enough skiers per acre to make bumps, so the groomers make their own on the Big Thunder run. Widely spaced and perfectly symmetrical, they are excellent for beginning mogul skiers and those whose knees can't take the pounding of skier-made bumps. There is also tree skiing here and there. The resort grooms about 300 acres of runs; the rest—1,200 acres—is left to accumulate powder.

Peaked Mountain has an additional 1,500 acres, entirely reserved for snowcat skiing. Ten skiers per snowcat, with two guides, head out to enjoy this snowy playground. The longest run is 3.2 miles and covers slightly more than 2,800 vertical feet.

Snowboarding

The area has a gradual, groomed halfpipe. Snowboarding is allowed on all of Fred's Mountain.

Cross-country

The Targhee Nordic Center has 15 km. of track groomed for touring and skating. The trails wind through varied terrain, offering beautiful vistas of the Greater Yellowstone area as well as meadows and aspen glades. Trail passes are $7 a day, $4 for a senior or child; children 5 and younger ski free.

The Nordic Education Center teaches telemarking as well as touring and skating techniques. Group lessons are $20 and private lessons $45 an hour.

Half-day guided tours are offered into the backcountry for $65 for one person, $45 each for two. A snowshoe tour focuses on wildlife, with the guide pointing out tracks and explaining how animals survive the winter. This tour is $60 for one person, $35 each for two.

Lessons (95/96 prices)

Many instructors have stayed on at the Ski Training Center since its first season in 1969. The training center is noted for its teaching of lessons with a coaching approach.

Adult group lessons are $20.

Children's lessons for ages 8–12 and 13–16 are $35 for a half-day; $60 for a full day, and include lessons, lift ticket and lunch. Children's programs for ages 3–7 are $60 for a full day; $35 for half day, including lessons, lifts, lunch and day care activities.

Private lessons run $40 an hour, $15 for each additional person.

Targhee runs a half-day **powder skiing** instructional trip for intermediate or better skiers for $130 each if three people go, $150 for two and $248 for one. Grand Targhee also has several **special clinics** such as Extreme Skiing and WomenSki The Tetons.

Child care (95/96 prices)

Babies' Club takes ages 2 months to 2 years for $36 per day, $24 per half day. Kid's Club is for ages 3 to 7. Day care only is $32 per day, $20 per half day. The program includes two snacks and lunch in the full day, a snack for half day. Reservations are required; call (800) TARGHEE (827-4433). The child care center is open on Saturday nights so parents can spend time together.

Lift tickets (95/96 prices)

	Adult	Child (6–14) Senior (60–69)
One day	$32	$18
Three days	$87 ($29/day)	$54 ($18/day)
Five days	$135 ($27/day)*	$90 ($18/day)

For day skiers, children 5 and younger and seniors 70 and older ski free.

*Those who ski more than one day at Grand Targhee probably are staying there, too. In those cases, Targhee's lodging-lift packages are the most economical and practical. On all Targhee lodging packages, children 14 and younger stay and ski free, one child per paying adult.

A full day of snowcat skiing, including lunch, snacks and beverages served in a Snowcat Skiing souvenir mug, is $185; $160 for Targhee package lodging guests. Half day is $130.

If you are staying in Jackson and coming here for a day, buy your ticket in advance at Grand Targhee ticket outlets in Jackson or Teton Village. You'll save $3. Call 733-3101 in Jackson to find the nearest ticket outlet. Or, you can buy a Jackson Hole Ski Three book of five vouchers for $210, valid at Jackson Hole, Grand Targhee and Snow King (Jackson's in-town ski hill). When you use the voucher here, it includes the round-trip bus ride from Jackson, or a lesson (see the Jackson Hole chapter for more information on the vouchers).

Accommodations

The village sleeps 432 people at two hotel-type lodges and a 32-unit, multi-story condo building. All are within easy walking distance to lifts and base facilities. Nightly rates per room at the lodges run $59 to $172, at the condos $134 to $408.

Packages that include ski tickets and two group lessons are offered for seven nights and six days, five nights and four days, and three nights and three days.

For the hotel and motel rooms, regular season packages per person for two people range from $172 to $317 for three days, $253 to $488 for five nights and four days, and $357 to $681 for seven nights and six days.

For the Sioux Lodge condo lofts, regular season packages per person for two people range from $282 to $368 for three days and three nights, $399 to $570 for five nights and four days, and $557 to $794 for seven nights and six days.

Call (800) 827-4433 (800-TARGHEE) for information.

Dining

There's not much variety in this small village, but a lot of quality.

Skadi's is Targhee's finest restaurant, with entrées such as rack of lamb, whiskey chicken, shrimp scampi and poached salmon, all in the $12-$24 price range. Skadi's also serves breakfast and lunch. **Cactus Kitchen** is the spot for good family dinners, such as cheese enchiladas, pork chops and applesauce or prime rib.

Wild Bill's Grille in the Rendezvous Lodge has pizza, a soup and salad bar, sandwiches and Mexican food for breakfast and lunch, while the **Trap Bar** serves basic grilled sandwiches, burgers and chicken, plus après-ski snacks. **Cicero's** is a delightful spot for a healthy breakfast or lunch, with items such as pastries and soups, blueberry cornmeal waffles, trout and scambled eggs, veggie stir-fry and a stuffed baked potato. Sue Cicero will improvise meals for those on restricted diets, and she has Kix, Cheerios and Frosted Flakes on the breakfast menu for those picky kids who won't eat anything else. Cicero's serves dinner Thursdays through Sundays.

Après ski/nightlife/other activities

This is not Targhee's strong point. The **Trap Bar** has live music, there is an outdoor **heated swimming pool** and **hot tubs**, and **complimentary movies**. You can take a **sleigh ride** or go **snowmobiling. Souvenirs** can be found in Targhee's small general store or its ski clothing shop, High Country Colors. Mustang Sally's is a tiny boutique with some very fine clothing and jewelry made by Wyoming artisans.

If you need more than this, stay in Jackson, about an hour's drive.

Getting there and getting around

Getting there: Targhee is served by airports in Jackson, Wyoming and Idaho Falls, Idaho. Jets fly into both airports and resort shuttles pick up guests by reservation. You can rent cars at either airport or at Grand Targhee.

Targhee is just inside the Wyoming border on the west side of the Tetons, accessible only from Idaho. From Jackson, follow signs to Wilson on Highway 22, then go north on Highway 33 at Victor, Idaho. Turn east at the small town of Driggs (the sign is on the roof of a building), and drive 12 miles to the ski area. About eight miles from Driggs, you will start to suspect you're lost, but keep going—you can't make a wrong turn.

Coming from Idaho Falls, take Highway 20 to Rexburg, and turn east on Highway 33 to Driggs. Grand Targhee is 42 miles northwest of Jackson, 87 miles northeast of Idaho Falls and 297 miles north of Salt Lake City.

Getting around: If you are spending your entire vacation at Grand Targhee, don't rent a car. There's nowhere to drive. If you stay in Jackson, we recommend you ride the Targhee Express bus that picks up in Jackson and at Teton Village. It's $15 round trip; buy tickets at one of several locations (call 733-3101). The highway between Jackson and Grand Targhee is steep going over Teton Pass (up to 10 percent grade). We caution against staying at Targhee and driving to Jackson for the nightlife—if you want Jackson's nightlife, stay there.

Information/reservations

Grand Targhee Ski & Summer Resort, Alta, WY 83422; (800) 827-4433 (800-TARGHEE) or 307-353-2300.

The local area code is 307.

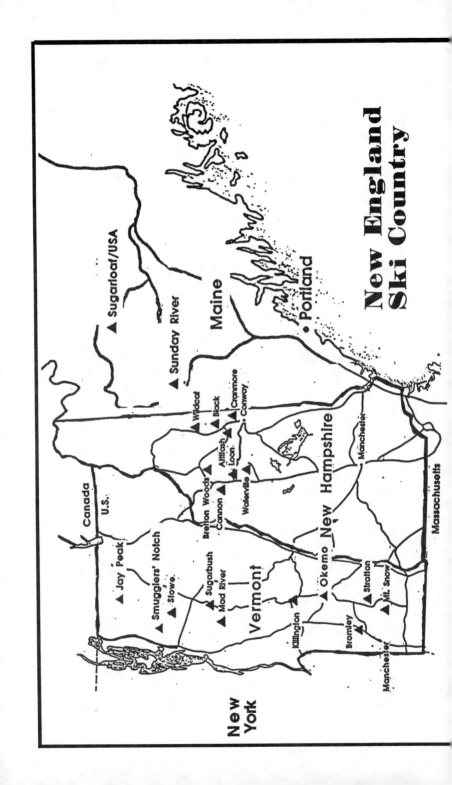

Sugarloaf/USA, Maine

Nestled in the Carrabassett River Valley in western Maine, Sugarloaf/USA is a condo-studded ski resort near the small town of Kingfield. This is a major mountain, more than 2,800 feet of continuous skiable vertical. Sugarloaf's slogan is "Size, Snow and Service"—according to our researchers, The Loaf lives up to it.

First-time visitors get a jaw-dropping first impression of Sugarloaf at one particular curve of Route 27, called "Omigosh!" corner. This unobstructed look shows a very big, very well utilized mountain. Runs snake down from the crown in every direction. Because each of these many runs has its own unique twists and turns, Sugarloaf offers a variety of skiing that goes beyond its already impressive size. As one guide put it, "Sugarloaf not only has good uphill capacity, it has exceptional downhill capacity too." The resort claims to have the lowest skier-per-acre ratio in the East.

Because it faces north toward the nearby Canadian border, Sugarloaf does not have an overabundance of sunshine. This, combined with its high latitude and elevation, means big natural snowfalls that come early and stay late. When sunshine comes in March and April, Sugarloaf is a favorite spring skiing spot.

Where to ski

This is a good all-around mountain for any level of skier, but what sets it apart is that it has enough steep and challenging runs to keep experts happily banging the boards all day. In addition to more than 500 acres of classic wooded New England ski trails, Sugarloaf also has 80 to 100 acres of treeless snowfields at the summit, where experts can experience Western-style, open-bowl skiing.

Experts will need little assistance to figure out where to ski. Double-diamond on the trail map is the honest truth.

Sugarloaf/USA Facts
Base elevation: 1,400'; **Summit elevation:** 4,237'; **Vertical drop:** 2,837 feet.
Number and types of lifts: 14—1 four-passenger gondola, 1 quad superchair, 2 quad chairs, 1 triple chair, 8 double chairs, 1 surface lift
Skiable acreage: 525 acres; **Snowmaking:** 95 percent
Uphill capacity: 20,035 skiers per hour **Bed base:** 6,000

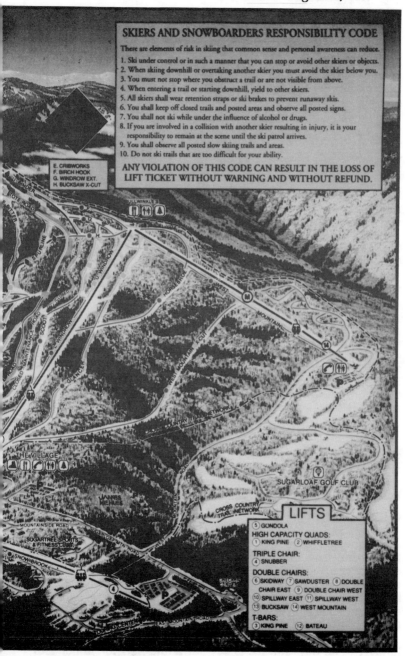

SKIERS AND SNOWBOARDERS RESPONSIBILITY CODE

There are elements of risk in skiing that common sense and personal awareness can reduce.

1. Ski under control or in such a manner that you can stop or avoid other skiers or objects.
2. When skiing downhill or overtaking another skier you must avoid the skier below you.
3. You must not stop where you obstruct a trail or are not visible from above.
4. When entering a trail or starting downhill, yield to other skiers.
5. All skiers shall wear retention straps or ski brakes to prevent runaway skis.
6. You shall keep off closed trails and posted areas and observe all posted signs.
7. You shall not ski while under the influence of alcohol or drugs.
8. If you are involved in a collision with another skier resulting in injury, it is your responsibility to remain at the scene until the ski patrol arrives.
9. You shall observe all posted slow skiing trails and areas.
10. Do not ski trails that are too difficult for your ability.

ANY VIOLATION OF THIS CODE CAN RESULT IN THE LOSS OF LIFT TICKET WITHOUT WARNING AND WITHOUT REFUND.

E. CRIBWORKS
F. BIRCH HOOK
G. WINDROW EXT.
H. BUCKSAW X-CUT

SUGARLOAF GOLF CLUB

CROSS COUNTRY TRAIL NETWORK

LIFTS

⑤ GONDOLA

HIGH CAPACITY QUADS:
① KING PINE ② WHIFFLETREE

TRIPLE CHAIR:
④ SNUBBER

DOUBLE CHAIRS:
⑥ SKIDWAY ⑦ SAWDUSTER ⑧ DOUBLE CHAIR EAST ⑨ DOUBLE CHAIR WEST
⑩ SPILLWAY EAST ⑪ SPILLWAY WEST
⑬ BUCKSAW ⑭ WEST MOUNTAIN

T-BARS:
③ KING PINE ⑫ BATEAU

Steep black runs beckon from the summit on both sides of the gondola, though the ones on the left are more difficult. The blacks down to the King Pine quad are all sweet and steep, if a little short. Bump monkeys should head for Choker on this side of the mountain, or to Skidder on the west side; groomers are under orders not to touch these trails, nor Ripsaw, Bubblecuffer and Winter's Way.

Advanced intermediates will find that they can handle most of the single-diamond blacks on this mountain. The Narrow Gauge run from the Spillway East chair is particularly worthy, and because it is officially rated for World Cup racing, in early season you may find yourself skiing next to the U.S. Ski Team.

The entire section served by the Whiffletree high-speed quad is an intermediate's playground. On the other side of the mountain the Tote Road stretches from the top of the gondola and winds down three miles to the village area.

At the base of the mountain, beginners will find the very broad and very gentle Boardwalk run, or West Mountain, under the chair by that name. Those looking for a little more challenge graduate to the paths from the top of Bucksaw chair, which is more than a mile long. Try skiing the trails served by the Bucksaw chair for end-of-the-day cruising.

S-K-I, the company that owns Killington and Mount Snow/Haystack in Vermont, Waterville Valley in New Hampshire and Bear Mountain in California, bought a majority interest in Sugarloaf two years ago and last season installed a high-speed quad to service 60 new acres of blue and black terrain. Sugarloaf's base area is planned to double in size in a westerly direction, toward the Bucksaw lift. The expansion will allow for new skier services, restaurants, shopping and lodging.

Snowboarding

Allowed on the entire mountain. Sugarloaf has two halfpipes, one of which is 400 feet in length and has walls 15 feet high. It also has a seven-acre snowboard park with 20- to 30-foot snow mounds, rails, staircases and barrels for bonking and sliding. Rentals and lessons are available.

Cross-country

Sugarloaf has 85 km. of trails groomed with double tracks and lanes for skating. The **Sugarloaf Ski Touring Center** is the largest and most complete in Maine. The center is off Route 27, south of the Sugarloaf access road. Three trails offer access from the resort's lodging facilities and the village area. The center also has a lighted Olympic-sized outdoor skating rink and a 6,000-square-foot lodge with a giant fireplace, a south-facing deck, and food and drink at the Klister Kitchen, a locals' favorite.

Group lessons are $14 an hour. Private lessons are $25 an hour. The all-day trail fee is $10 for adults, $8 for junior and senior citizens. Equipment rentals are $14 a day for adults and $10 for juniors and seniors. Call (207) 237-2000.

Multiday ticket holders may exchange a day of downhill for a day of cross-country including trail fee, lesson and equipment. Exchange tickets at the guest services desk in the base lodge.

Lessons (95/96 prices)

Group lessons are free in all lodging packages arranged through (800) 843-5623 (800-THE LOAF). Otherwise they cost $25 per two-hour course for adults and teens. Learn-to-ski packages include rental equipment, lessons and a beginner-lift ticket. The never-ever level gives access to three lifts for $35.

Private lessons are $45 an hour, or $50 per day per person for five or more people.

Children's lessons include the Mountain Adventure program for kids 7–12, costing $41 a day, including lunch, lifts and rentals. Ages 4–6 are in Mountain Magic, which costs $52 for a full day including lunch. Half days cost $41 for Mountain Adventure and $37 for Mountain Magic. Register at the ski school desk or in the Mountain Magic room in the base lodge.

Special programs concentrate on skills such as bumps, telemarking, powder or hard carving. Peak Performance workshops are scheduled for the second weekend in December and the last week in February, and feature Skiing For Women, Ski Challenge and Snowboard Challenge.

Child care

Moose Alley is a special kids-and-instructors-only section of the mountain where kids can do some controlled tree skiing.

There are children's activities every night except Sunday in the Mountain Magic Room in the base lodge. Ages 5–12 have one type of activity, while teens do something else. Examples include games and G- or PG-rated movies for the young set, and skating, dances, Wallyball games (a volleyball-type game played on a racquetball court) and PG-13 movies for the teens.

The child care facility takes children from 6 weeks to 5 years. Full-day rates are $42 and half days are $37. Each additional day is $48; additional half days are $33.

Lift tickets (95/96 prices)

	Adult	Child (6–12) Senior (65+)
One day (94/95)	$43	$24
Three days	$117 ($39/day)	$63 ($21/day)
Five days	$175 ($35/day)	$95 ($19/day)

Midweek day prices are about ten percent less. Teen prices (ages 13–18) are $93 for three days and $145 for five. Children 5 and younger ski free.

Accommodations

Sugarloaf is a planned condominium community in the mold of Keystone or Copper Mountain. That said, it is one of the more tasteful layouts we've seen, with the central village blending in well with the overall environment. **The Sugarloaf Mountain Hotel** is the centerpiece of the Alpine village. Most weekend rates are $110–220 and weekday rates of $100–210. The slightly more modest **Sugarloaf Inn** has a quaint New England inn feel. The Sugarloaf Inn offers packages that include ski lessons and use of the Sugarloaf Sports & Fitness Club, with pool, spas, massage therapy, tanning beds, exercise equipment and indoor racquetball and squash courts. Daily rates, per-person, double-occupancy, range from $89 to $150, depending on the season.

More than 900 condo units are spread throughout the resort, all designed so skiers can ski back to their lodging. (Not all have lift access, but a shuttle runs from the lodging to the lifts.) Families like the **Gondola Village** units because they are close to the state-licensed child-care facility. The **Bigelow, Snowflower** and **Commons** units are more luxurious, and the **Sugartree** units offer easy access to the health club.

The resort has an RV parking area serviced by lifts.

Dining

Sugarloaf is a compact resort, but has no fewer than 18 eateries. The **Truffle Hound** (235-2355; reservations suggested) has elegant continental dining. **Gepetto's,** Maine Restaurant Association's 1993 Restaurant of the Year, gets raves for its teriyaki steak. Our favorite for fine dining and atmosphere was the **Seasons** at the Sugarloaf Inn (237-2000). For pizza or burgers in a homey, noisy atmosphere, try **The Bag and Kettle** (locals call it The Bag.). You can rate the local talent on Blues Monday while eating a Bag-burger and get the lore of Sugarloaf from the locals. The deck at **The Black Bear Café** is a major lunch spot and the place to mingle. For an English pub experience, try **Theo's Restaurant,** where the Sugarloaf Brewing Company peddles its wares.

No trip to a Northeast ski area is complete without a visit to an authentic New England inn, and the **The Inn on Winter's Hill** in Kingfield is worth the 15-mile drive. Sitting on the hill named after Sugarloaf's founder, Amos Winter, the inn has an excellent restaurant, **Julia's** (265-5426). Proprietors Richard and Carolyn Winnick will gladly conduct tours of this fully renovated inn. **One Stanley Avenue** features a unique menu full of Maine-grown fare and has many loyal customers who think it's the best in the state, and the **Herbert Hotel** is also worth a visit.

In Eustis, 11 minutes north of Sugarloaf, two restaurants are worth checking out: **The Trail's End** for steaks and the **Porter House** for home cooking with big portions. **Tufulio's** and **Hugs** in the Carrabassett Valley span the gamut of Italian dishes served in a casual atmosphere.

Après-ski/nightlife

Sunny days bring the après-ski crowd to the decks of **The Black Bear Café** or **The Bag.** **Gringo's** has good Tex-Mex bar munchies and frequent live music in its **Widowmaker Lounge.**

The hot spot for live music and dancing at night is the aforementioned **Widowmaker Lounge.** For a more subdued atmosphere, try the **Sugarloaf Inn** or **The Double Diamond** in the Sugarloaf Mountain Hotel.

On Route 27 in the valley, you'll find the locals at **Carrabassett Yacht Club** or at **Judson's Motel,** the latter a favorite with UMaine and Colby College students.

Teenagers can head to **Rascals,** an alcohol-free teen spot with a DJ and dance floor. Younger teens have **Pinocchio's,** with video games, pinball and board games to keep them entertained.

Other activities

Shopping: The village has several shops, including **Pat Buck's Emporium,** a gift store that features handcrafted items by Maine artisans (including beautiful knitted sweaters); and **Gold/Smith Gallery,** with gold and silver jewelry, photo frames, and similar items. In Kingfield you'll find **Scent-sations** in the Herbert Hotel, where you choose your favorite scent and the store will put it into lotions, shampoos and body oils.

Dogsledding, horse-drawn sleigh rides, snowmobiling, snowshoeing, ice fishing and skating are among the activities that Sugarloaf Guest Services can arrange (237-2000).

Getting there and getting around

Getting there: By car, take I-95 north to Augusta, Route 27 through Farmington and Kingfield. Or take the Maine Turnpike to the Auburn exit, Route 4 to Farmington and Route 27 through Kingfield. The drive is about two and a half hours from Portland.

The closest commercial airport is the Portland International Jetport. Sugarloaf has a shuttle, **Riverbend Express,** that runs to and from it twice daily. Call (207) 628-2877 (628-BUSS) for information and reservations.

Getting around: A car is optional—about everything in the resort is within walking distance. A shuttle runs on weekends and is on call during the week.

Information/reservations

Sugarloaf USA: RR 1 Box 5000, Carrabassett Valley, ME 04947. Phone: (207) 237-2000. **Lodging reservations:** (800) 843-5623 (800-THE-LOAF) For lodging reservations in the area, usually at lower prices, call the Sugarloaf Chamber of Commerce at (800) THE-AREA (843-2732).

Area code is (207).

Sunday River, Maine

Sunday River, just outside of Bethel and tucked against the New Hampshire border, is a pleasant blend of old New England tradition with modern ski condominiums. Bethel is a typically picturesque New England town, complete with white-steepled church and ivy-covered prep school. The main street is lined with historic buildings, and the village common is anchored by the 75-year-old Bethel Inn.

The Sunday River Ski Resort rises six miles to the north, a 90-minute drive from the Portland airport and about three and a half hours from Boston. As you drive up the access road to the base area, you see condominium complexes, but they don't assault you; they blend with the trees and hills.

The resort doesn't have a main center. Three separate base lodges—South Ridge, Barker Mountain, and White Cap—provide basic cafeteria and sports shop facilities. South Ridge Lodge is the hub, housing the ski school, the corporate offices and a grocery store. The condo complexes are small centers to themselves, with most boasting an indoor or heated outdoor pool, hot tubs and saunas. A sense of quiet results: the bustle of people created by a town or central hub is dispersed into the condominiums.

It may be quiet, but Sunday River isn't dull. Something always seems to be happening here—ski terrain expansions, new lifts, a new hotel, a new way of teaching skiing, and a new ski train from Portland. Last season, the resort opened its seventh mountain peak as the first phase of a huge expansion called Jordan Bowl. This year's addition will be a new expert area called Oz. Off the mountain, its Bethel Station project now has a train station (more on that later), a four-screen movie theater and a new restaurant.

Sunday River is the flagship resort for LBO Holding, which also owns Attitash/Bear Peak and Sugarbush, and is acquiring Cranmore, all in New England. All the mountains have season

Sunday River Facts
Base elevation: 790'; **Summit elevation:** 3,140'; **Vertical drop:** 2,350 feet
Number of lifts: 16—3 quad superchairs, 5 quads, 5 triples, 2 doubles, 1 handle tow
Percent of snowmaking: 90 percent of trails **Total acreage:** 640 skiable acres
Uphill capacity: 30,000 per hour **Bed base:** 5,300 on mountain; 2,000 nearby

pass options for inter-resort skiing, and all offer a frequent skier program called the Edge Card, which rewards participants with free ski days. And all will benefit from Sunday River's snowmaking expertise. Last season, which was uncommonly dry and warm in New England, Sunday River lost just 12 of its 80 trails during the worst of the January thaw, and was back in full operation three days after it ended.

Where to ski

The original base area was Barker Mountain. But since 1985 Sunday River has opened five new mountain peaks. The resort's seventh peak, Jordan Bowl, opened in the 94/95 season, is a huge cirque to the west of the Aurora Peak area. The Jordan Bowl area ultimately will have up to six lifts and at least 250 acres of trails.

Beginners start on Sundance and then have the entire South Ridge area to practice linking their turns. Twelve beginner runs in the South Ridge area are serviced by a detachable quad, a triple and a double chair. Lower intermediates can also head to the White Cap quad and enjoy the relatively mellow Moonstruck, Starburst and Starlight runs.

Once a skier is past the basic snowplow and into stem christies, the rest of Sunday River beckons. The North Peak triple chair opens long practice runs like Dream Maker and Escapade. Lollapalooza, the green-circle trail in Jordan Bowl, "is like Dream Maker on steroids," as one frequent Sunday River skier said. It is long and wide with great views, but not a trail that beginners should start out on because the upper part can get bumped up on busy days, and probably should have a blue rating. Below this, though, it's quite mellow.

The Aurora area, served by a fixed quad chair and a triple chair, provides experts with plenty of challenge. This area now is accessible to lower-level skiers because of an extension of Sirius from the top of Spruce Peak across Vortex to Lights Out. Also, a green route goes from North Peak to the Aurora Peak base area.

But Aurora is still the spot to find tough skiing. it also has a double-diamond glade that runs from Lights Out to the base of Vortex. And Northern Lights offers an easier way down the mountain, though it's no stroll through the park. Celestial, reached from Lights Out, may be the nicest of the four gladed trails Sunday River opened last season. It starts out steep and wide, but mellows and narrows as you go down.

From the top of Barker Mountain a steep trio—Right Stuff, Top Gun and Agony—provide advanced skiers long sustained pitches. Agony and Top Gun are premier bump runs. Right Stuff is a cruiser early in the day after it's been groomed, but normally develops moguls by afternoon. Tree skiing fans will find a new gladed area—Last Tango—between Right Stuff and Risky

Business. This black-diamond natural slalom area is the gentlest and most spacious of the resort's five mapped glades. Though it's not particularly steep, it's tight. A work road about two-thirds of the way down allows skiers to bail out onto Right Stuff. Those who continue through the trees will find the terrain getting steeper and tighter. If you're less than an expert, you won't have much fun on Last Tango's lower third.

From the top of Locke Mountain, T-2 plunges down the tracks of an old T-bar providing a direct fall-line drop and a spectacular view of Bethel, the valley and Mt. Washington.

Halfway down Cascades, skiers can take a right turn onto Tempest (this trail is a steep intermediate in the morning, but bumped by afternoon), which together with Wildfire and the short Jibe, is served by the Little White Cap quad (Lift 9). Another advanced intermediate trail is Monday Mourning, which starts out steep and wide but mellows near the end, where the NASTAR course is located.

In the morning the sun shines on upper intermediate and advanced skiers heading up the White Heat quad. The White Heat run is a wide swath straight down the mountain from the peak of White Cap. Double-diamond Shockwave offers 975 vertical feet of big bumps and steep pitches. On the opposite side of White Heat, Obsession is a regulation GS trail. Two gladed areas called Hardball (skier right) and Chutzpah (skier left) start out deceptively mellow and open-spaced, but watch out. Technically, they are the most demanding on the mountain.

Mountain rating

Sunday River is perfect for beginners, with one of the most extensive lift-served beginner areas in New England. The ski school here has the best approach to learning in the industry and guarantees you learn to ski in a day, or your money back—last year out of 7,000 beginners only a handful failed.

Intermediates get a mountain full of terrain. Experts will find super steeps and monster bumps on Aurora Peak, Barker Mountain and White Cap.

Sunday River's snowmaking system is one of the best and biggest anywhere. Better yet, the resort is not subject to water restrictions as is the case in much of the East.

Cross-country

Though Sunday River does not have a dedicated cross-country center, this area of Maine is known for some of the best Nordic skiing in New England. The **Bethel Inn Cross-Country Ski Center** behind the hotel links up with 40 km. of marked and groomed trials. They have rentals, lessons and evening sleigh rides. The Bethel Inn also has facilities for instructing in telemark. Call 824-2175.

Trail fees are $11. Midweek, the trail fee is also good for entrance to the recreation center, with outdoor heated pool, sauna and fitness center, until 2 p.m.

The **Sunday River Ski Touring Center** (824-2410) is run by the Sunday River Inn on the Sunday River access road. It has 40 km. of groomed and tracked trails.

Carter's Cross-Country Ski Center (539-4848) off Route 26 in Oxford provides another alternative for skinny skis.

Forty-five minutes from Bethel is the **Jackson Ski Touring Center**. See the Mt. Washington Valley chapter for details of its ski touring programs.

Snowboarding (95/96 prices)

Sunday River has welcomed snowboarders for a long time, and decided to quit isolating boarders in a park. Instead, it has put park-style elements throughout the trail system, and skiers can use them, too. Rentals and lessons are available; a learning program, including board, boots and limited lifts, costs $40. Clinics are $32.

Lessons (95/96 prices)

The Sunday River Ski School teaches **group lessons** using a program it created. Called Perfect Turn®, it combines state-of-the-art ski technique with state-of-the-art educational theory. Sunday River has no lessons or teachers, but rather clinics and ski pros (like golf or tennis pros). This is not just a semantics change: Perfect Turn is so revolutionary that other ski areas are buying the rights to use it in their ski schools. Those areas include Mt. Bachelor, Oregon; Blue Mountain, Ontario; and Jiminy Peak, Massachusetts. We have taken these lessons and recommend them highly (see Everybody Skis chapter).

Perfect Turn has 10 levels of clinics. Levels 1–3, for never-evers to beginners, are 90 minutes to two hours. The package includes the clinic, a lift ticket for the South Ridge and North Peak and rental equipment, costing $40 for Level 1. Sunday River guarantees Level 1 skiers that they will be able to ride a lift, turn and stop by the end of the clinic, or they can repeat it free or get their money back. Levels 2–3 cost $23 per level.

Clinics for other levels normally last 75 minutes with a maximum of six skiers. Skiers head for the North Peak lodge, where they watch a short video that demonstrates various levels of skiing ability. Once they see a skier on the video who skis as they do, they know what level clinic to take. The video eliminates the "ski-off," which usually takes up about 40 minutes of a two-hour lesson, and starting on the mountain eliminates the lift ride to where the teaching begins. Clinics run about every half hour throughout the day and cost $23. Sunday River also is a demonstration center for the new Elan SCX "hourglass" ski, which is designed to make carving a turn very easy. Those in Perfect Turn clinics can use the skis free of charge.

Private clinic prices are $50 an hour for one.

Sunday River also has **special workshops** for specific groups such as women and 50+ skiers, all lasting about two hours and costing $30.

A Woman's Turn program, offered on weekends and a couple of times during holiday weeks, gives intermediate and advanced skiers a chance to perfect their turns. Also, Janet Spangler conducts a week-long women's program about four times per season.

Sunday River's **children's lessons** start with the Tiny Turns program, an hour of private instruction for ages 3 and 4 with a half- or full-day session in day care. The private clinic is $28 if the child is registered in day care; otherwise, the clinic cost is the regular private rate.

SKIwee is for youngsters 4 to 6 years of age. Mogul Meisters is for those 7 to 12 years of age. All day in either program, including lunch, lifts and equipment, costs $59. The morning or afternoon programs, without lunch, cost $48.

Child care

Day care covers ages 6 weeks to 2 1/2 years. The hourly rate is $7.50. Bring diapers, formula and food for infants. All-day programs cost $41 including lunch, and half-day programs are $22 for older toddlers. There are discounts for additional children in the same family. Call for reservations, especially on weekends (824-3000).

Lift tickets (95/96 prices)

	Adult	Child (6–12)
One day (94/95)	$43	$25
Three days	$124 ($41.33/day)	$77 ($25.66/day)
Five days	$206 ($41.20/day)	$127 ($25.40/day)

Midweek adult prices are $39 (94/95 price). Children 5 and younger ski free with parent. Seniors 65 and older ski for half the adult price of the day.

Accommodations (94/95 prices)

The Summit Hotel and condominiums are the most convenient to the slopes. But Bethel also has a group of excellent bed-and-breakfasts and old country inns. If you are planning a Sunday River vacation call the central reservations number, which will handle everything from air travel to day care.

The resort has built a ski dorm within walking distance of the slopes, designed primarily for groups.

The **Summit Hotel and Conference Center** is a trailside oasis with a 25-meter heated outdoor pool, athletic club, fine dining, and conference and banquet facilities in five meeting rooms and two ballrooms. Rates, which include lift tickets, start at $89 midweek and $129 weekend, per person for a double-occupancy unit. The **Snow Cap Inn** provides less luxury a short walk from the slopes (rates per person, double occupancy, $79 midweek, $99 weekend, including lift tickets) and the **Ski Dorm** next door offers affordable digs ($23 midweek, $34 weekends and holidays, no lift tickets) for single skiers.

Locke Mountain Townhouses are the most upscale, but hard to get, with the ideally located **Merrill Brook** condominiums not far behind. Condominium units are all convenient to the slopes and all have trolley service. Rates include lift tickets and are per person, based on maximum occupancy for the unit. They start at $69 midweek, $89 on weekends.

In Bethel the **Bethel Inn** (824-2175) has old stylish atmosphere and first-rate rooms. The rates include breakfast and dinner. Double rates run $60 to $125 per person. The inn also has a cross-country center and health club; see Cross-country section for more details.

The **Douglass Place** is Bethel's original bed-and-breakfast (824-2229). The proprietor has many tales to tell. **The Four Seasons** is in an old elegant building with excellent French cuisine (824-2755 or 800-227-7458). **The Sudbury Inn** has one of the best restaurants in town and a favorite watering hole (824-2174). **The Holidae House** in Bethel has drawn praise for its beautiful decor (824-3400). These B&Bs cost about $90–$140 per night.

Less than a mile from the base of the mountain, the **Sunday River Inn** (824-2410) offers a relaxed setting reminiscent of the great ski lodges of the '60s. It also operates the closest cross-country center. All rates include breakfast and dinner and range from about $40 for a dorm room where you bring your own sleeping bag to about $75 per person for a private-bath suite. Shared-bath rooms also are available.

Additional lodging can be arranged through Sunday River's reservation line (800) 543-2754 or the Bethel Area Chamber of Commerce, (207) 824-3585.

Dining

Legends in the Summit Hotel has a great menu and wine list. The **Fall Line** in the Fall Line Condominiums is convenient and serves good food. **Rosetto's Italian Restaurant** in the White Cap Lodge is open for dinner daily and for lunch on weekends and holidays.

Saturday's in the South Ridge base is packed for lunch and dinner with good reason. **The Peak Lodge and Skiing Center**, at the summit of North Peak, is a popular lunch spot with a giant deck. **BUMPS! Pub**, in the White Cap Lodge, serves a pub menu which should be avoided unless you're starving.

In Bethel try the **Sudbury Inn** and the **Bethel Inn**. The Sudbury recently renovated its dining room, making it evern more attractive. Downstairs, **Sud's Pub** is popular for après-ski and pub food. For French cuisine head to **L'Auberge**. **Mother's** on Upper Main Street is a favorite of students from the Gould Academy as well as skiers. The **Moose's Tale** in the brew pub serves an eclectic menu of basic fare. Locals tell us the **Sunday River Brewing Company** now serves food worthy of its excellent on-premise-brewed ales. **Skidders** makes fantastic deli take-out. The best pizza is reportedly in West Bethel at **The Only Place**, and the best breakfasts are at the **Red Top Truck Stop**, which opens at 5 a.m. for local loggers.

The newest restaurant in Bethel, the **Iron Horse** at Bethel Station, is housed in authentic railroad cars. Part of the experience includes the 7:45 p.m. freight train that rumbles by on the next track.

Après-ski/nightlife

If you strike it rich you may find midweek action at Sunday River and in Bethel, but the real fun heats up on weekends.

Immediate après-ski, when found, is at the base of the slopes. Try the **Barker Mountain Base Area**, which has mellow acoustic guitar on weekends, or **BUMPS!** at the White Cap Lodge for libations. **Saturday's** is the liveliest of the mountain spots. In town head to the **Sunday River Brewery** or **Sudbury's**.

At night, **BUMPS!** has bands on weekends and comedy nights planned for Tuesdays. The crowd tends toward young. The **Sunday River Brewery** has live music and excellent homemade brew. Downtown, the **Backstage** usually has karaoke during the week, with Country & Western and rock 'n' roll bands on weekends. It also has the only pool tables in town. **Sudbury's** has bands ranging from blues to bluegrass. A more sedate crowd fills **Legends** at the Summit Hotel for its acoustic music.

Other activities

Shopping: Bethel has some unusual shops, such as **Bonnema Potters**, with highly distinctive pottery depicting the Maine landscape; and **Mt. Mann**, a native gemstone shop. On Church Street, **Samuel Timberlake** produces fine reproductions of Shaker furniture.

At the ski area, **swimming pools and saunas** are in virtually every condominium complex. Guests staying at the few condos that don't have them have use privileges at nearby complexes. The ski dorm has video games and pool tables.

Other activities include **horse-drawn sleigh rides** (make reservations at the Guest Services Desk) and **ice skating** at the White Cap Base Lodge. Skating hours vary; rental skates are available. On weekends and holidays, teens can enjoy their own night club called **MVP's** and kids age 6–12 can attend **Camp Sunday River**, an evening of supervised activities.

Getting there and getting around

Getting there: Sunday River is in western Maine an hour and a half from Portland and three and a half hours from Boston. From I-95, Exit 11 in Maine to Route 26 north, continue to Bethel, then take Route 2 six miles north to Sunday River.

RV parking, no hookups, is allowed in designated parking areas at the resort. An RV park is also at White Birch Camping, in Shelburne on Route 2.

The most convenient commercial airport is Portland International Jetport, 75 miles from Sunday River. Private pilots can land in Bethel. **Bethel Express Corporation** will pick up from either airport by reservation (824-4646).

Perhaps the most fun way to Sunday River is by train. The **Sunday River Silver Bullet Ski Express** runs between Portland and Bethel. A bus transports skiers from Bethel to the slopes. Call the ski resort for schedules and fares.

Getting around: During the main part of the season, on-mountain transportation between the base areas is quite good on shuttlebuses that look like old trolley cars. The shuttle loop expands to include the condos at night. In shoulder season, the mountain shuttles are by request only. Several off-mountain properties, such as the Sunday River Inn and the Bethel Inn, have shuttle service to and from the slopes. Midwinter, you can get along without a car, but they're nice to have, especially if you want to go to Bethel. Early or late season, you'll need one.

Information/reservations

Sunday River Resort Reservations: (800) 543-2754.

Ski Report and Information: (207) 824-6400; (617) 666-4200; (508) 580-0666. **Address:** Sunday River Ski Resort, PO Box 450, Bethel, ME 04217. Administration phone: (207) 824-3000.

Local area code is 207.

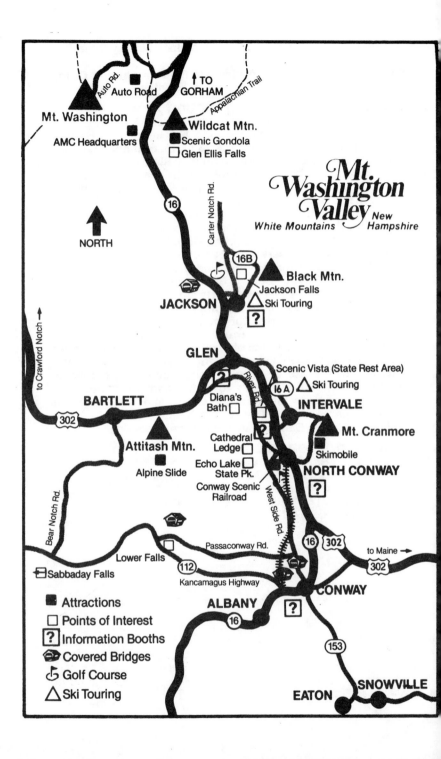

Mt. Washington Valley
New Hampshire

Wildcat, Cranmore, Attitash Bear Peak
Black Mountain, King Pine
Jackson Touring

These five relatively small ski areas, set into spectacular White Mountain terrain, combine with the Jackson Ski Touring Foundation (one of the world's best cross-country trail systems), the wild skiing on Mt. Washington, and the year-round resort attractions of Mt. Washington Valley, to make a multifaceted destination resort.

This was a destination resort long before anyone came here to ski. A quarter century before the Civil War, fashionable northeasterners started coming here for the summer, first by stage line and then by railroad and carriage, to meet Hawthorne and Emerson, watch Bierstadt paint his mountain landscapes, beat the heat, and find suitable husbands for their daughters. Many of the grand old hotels they visited have been brought up to date to add their charm to the mix of condos, motels, country inns, and B&Bs.

Legends of the early days of skiing—the late Thirties—surround you. Ride up the Wildcat gondola and look back at the fantastic bulk of Mt. Washington with its huge scooped-out ravines. This is hallowed ground, where Toni Matt on his wooden boards schussed over the Tuckerman headwall in one long arc to win the 1939 Inferno race, summit to base in six and a half minutes.

Most of all, what makes this area one of the pioneers of downhill skiing in America is the Eastern Slope Ski School, founded by Carroll Reed. This is where the Arlberg method of ski instruction was introduced to North America by Benno Rybizka, and by his Austrian teacher, the famous Hannes Schneider, who was released by the Nazis in return for banking concessions.

If anyone wants a break from downhill skiing, this is the place. The prime summer activities of hiking, climbing, and camping out are pursued in the snow-and-ice season by local and visiting fanatics. You can even practice your rock-climbing skills on an indoor wall.

Restaurants, many of them tucked into the tiny country inns or restored barns in the valley, are world class and have acknowledged gourmet reputations. In fact, this valley is home to one of the most famous cooking schools in the country.

Besides the skiing, picturesque inns and tempting restaurants, there are more tax-free factory outlet stores concentrated in Conway and North Conway than in any other area of the United States, making the region a top shopping destination.

Where to ski

Wildcat: For more than a decade, Wildcat has been voted the ski area with the most spectacular scenery in the Northeast, with beautiful views across Pinkham Notch to towering Mt. Washington and Tuckerman Ravine. Wildcat is known as an untamed resort, but in the past few years Wildcat has smoothed some of the bumpy runs. Now the groomers roll all but two of the trails. The trails themselves have also been widened and straightened extensively. However, this resort is still best for strong intermediate to expert skiers.

The skiing is tempered by three factors: the cold, the wind and the pitch of the slopes. The cold, wind and capricious weather changes of nearby Mt. Washington are among the most extreme in North America, so Wildcat skiers need to be dressed properly for changing conditions. The plus side to inclement weather, of course, is a lot of natural snow; Wildcat often is the last New Hampshire ski area to close. Though Wildcat's slopes are wider than they used to be, the area still has a reputation for steep and narrow—in short, classic New England skiing.

Intermediates should be able to handle the groomed trails covered by snowmaking. For the best intermediate way down the slopes, head to the Polecat side of the gondola; for a descent where it is prudent to pay attention to the details of skiing, loop to the opposite side. Intermediate and beginner trails exist, but skiers at Wildcat are probably there for the challenge. (Wildcat allows beginners free skiing on the Snowcat Novice Area served by its own triple chair.)

Wildcat Facts

Base elevation: 1,950'; Summit elevation: 4,050'; Vertical drop: 2,100 feet.
Number and types of lifts: 6—1 gondola, 4 triple chairs, 1 double chair
Acreage: 120 acres, 15 miles of trails Percent of snowmaking: 100 percent
Uphill capacity: 8,500 skiers per hour Bed base: 6,500+

Attitash Bear Peak: Just west of Glen on Route 302 in Bartlett, Attitash Bear Peak is a great intermediate mountain. It's not too big and not too steep, and has great snowmaking. Recent expansion has added some steep black diamond trails, as well as even more intermediate runs. This season Attitash

Bear Peak plans to add three to five new trails, a new base lodge and a quad superchair lift.

Attitash Bear Peak has a protected learning slope with triple chair, and there are several beginner trails around the Borvig lifts. Ptarmigan is supposed to be one of the steepest trails in New England, but it is manageable for good intermediates because of the elbow room on the run. The rest of the mountain is enough to keep 80 percent of skiers perfectly satisfied, with Northwest Passage serving up great cruising. Bear Peak offers trails averaging 150 feet in width as well as two black diamonds, Kachina and Myth Maker, that have gradients of 40 to 45 percent.

Attitash Bear Peak is one of the few ski areas in the country that supplements its traditional all-day lift ticket with a computerized point ticket allowing skiers to pay by the vertical foot. Called the Smart Ticket®, it's transferable and is good for two years from purchase date. It's an excellent choice for those who only want to ski a few hours.

Attitash Bear Peak Facts
Base elevation: 550'; **Summit elevation:** 2,300'; **Vertical drop:** 1,750 feet.
Number and types of lifts: 7–1 quad chair, 2 triple chairs, 4 double chairs
Acreage: 180 skiable acres **Percent of snowmaking:** 98 percent
Uphill capacity: 7,900 skiers per hour **Bed base:** 1,100 at base; 12,000 in region

Cranmore Facts
Base elevation: 497'; **Summit elevation:** 1,697'; **Vertical drop:** 1,200 feet.
Number and types of lifts: 5–1 triple chair, 4 double chairs
Acreage: 185 skiable acres **Percent of snowmaking:** 100 percent
Uphill capacity: 3,500 skiers per hour **Bed base:** 6,500+

Cranmore: Now in its 57th year of operation, Cranmore is one of the oldest resorts in America, one that features good balanced terrain. If you arrive in North Conway in the evening, you can't miss it: the lights for night skiing, which lasts until 9 p.m., are visible from a long way off and add one more festive ingredient to the town. Because it's right in North Conway, it has the potential to attain a European-style relationship with the town. Over the past five seasons, Cranmore has invested more than $11 million in various lift, terrain, base lodge and lodging facilities, plus a snowboarding halfpipe.

This ski area, along with neighbor Attitash Bear Peak, has become part of a chain of New England ski resorts that also includes Sunday River in Maine and Sugarbush in Vermont. It appears that Attitash and Cranmore will be marketed as one resort for the 95/96 season, and Cranmore will be added to The Edge, this group's frequent-skier program. Details were still in the works at press time, but for visitors to the Mt. Washington Valley this alliance should be a nice benefit.

Black Mountain: This ski area on Route 16B may be the best place in the valley for beginner lessons and family skiing. From the front side of the mountain, facing Whitneys' Inn, the area is reminiscent of a country club, but behind the ridge reached by the double chair are 26 sunny and sheltered south-facing trails ranging from beginner to advanced intermediate. Next to the Jackson Ski Touring area, Black Mountain has also become a center for cross-country skiers interested in trying out telemark skiing. Finally, Black Mountain's southern exposure provides a warmer place to ski when it's just too cold at other areas.

Snowboarding isn't allowed on Black Beauty or Lower Black Beauty trails, but the area has a 350-foot halfpipe.

Black Mountain's Family Passport allows two adults and two children 15 and younger to ski for $75 per day, some holiday periods excluded.

Black Mountain Facts
Base elevation: 1,300'; Summit elevation: 2,350'; Vertical drop: 1,050 feet.
Number and types of lifts: 4—1 triple chair, 1 double chair, 2 surface lifts.
Acreage: 85 trail acres Percent snowmaking: 98 percent
Uphill capacity: 3,700 skiers per hour Bed base: 1,500+

Mt. Washington: If you like to get to the top the old-fashioned way (you *climb* it) try the famous spring skiing in Tuckerman Ravine; all winter, there's the Sherburne Trail and several other areas. Start from Pinkham Notch Camp (see Other Activities). Note: please heed all information about weather and avalanche conditions. Mt. Washington has a reputation for some of the most vicious weather and quick changes anywhere.

King Pine: This small area has a modest vertical drop, but for those just starting out and parents who want to keep an eye on young children, an unintimidating area is preferable. King Pine does have one steep trail—reportedly one of the steepest in the state—but top-level skiers are better off somewhere else. King Pine is adjacent to the Purity Spring Resort, which has slopeside lodging and ski packages.

King Pine Facts
Base elevation: 500'; Summit elevation: 850'; Vertical drop: 350 feet.
Number and types of lifts: 4—1 triple chair, 1 double chair; 2 J-bars
Acreage: 60 skiable acres Percent of snowmaking: 95 percent
Uphill capacity: 4,000 skiers per hour Bed base: 6,500+

Snowboarding
New Hampshire law requires snowboarders to have a leash or strap tethering the board to their leg. All these ski areas welcome boarders, and some have specific facilities for them.

Cross-country

Jackson Ski Touring Foundation, Box 216, Jackson, NH 03846, on Route 16A (383-9355) is a mecca for Nordic skiers. It has more than 154 km. of groomed and backcountry trails, country inns are spaced throughout the region, and Mt. Washington towers above.

Mt. Washington Valley Ski Touring Association, Box 646, Intervale NH 03845 has over 60 km. of trails. For ski school, rentals, or snow conditions, call (800) 282-5220.

The Appalachian Mountain Club maintains a network of ski touring trails radiating from the AMC Camp at Pinkham Notch; about 7 km. are rated Easiest or More Difficult (requiring skills up to a strong snowplow and step turn), but about 40 km. are rated Most Difficult, with long challenging hills and narrow trails. AMC also has unusual dining; see that section for more details. Call: 466-2721.

The Nestlenook Inn (383-9443), also in Jackson, offers 35 km. of touring winding through its 65-acre farm.

Purity Spring Resort, home of the King Pine ski area, has 25 km. of groomed and tracked trails near Madison. Rentals and lessons available. Call (800) 373-3754 or (603) 367-8896.

Great Glen Trails is a cross-country facility, new last season, at the base of Mt. Washington. It has 10 km. of tracked and skate-groomed trails and another 6 km. that are skate-groomed. The base lodge has retail, rentals (with Fischer Revolution short skis), food and instruction. One loop and the learning area have snowmaking. Call 466-2333.

Lessons

All the areas have extensive ski schools. Most of the prices are from last season; as always, use them as a guideline.

Group lessons are $20 per session at Wildcat, $20 at Attitash Bear Peak Cranmore, $17 at Black and $14 at King Pine.

Private lessons are $45 per 90 minutes for one student at Wildcat; $40 an hour at Attitash Bear Peak, $35 at Cranmore, $32 at Black and $29 at King Pine.

Children's lessons (all include lessons, lift ticket, and rentals; most full day programs include lunch; lower price range is for half day) are $50–40 at Wildcat's SKIwee program, $55–$45 at Attitash Bear Peak Cranmore (rentals are $5 extra), $38–$45 at Black and $25–$45 at King Pine.

Learn-to-ski packages (rentals, lifts and lessons) are $36 at Wildcat, $37 at Attitash Bear Peak Cranmore, and $40 weekend, $35 midweek at Black.

Child care

Prices for child care are $15–$30 per day; call for more information. Children's instruction programs start at age 4 or 5 at these areas (call for specifics).

Attitash Bear Peak Cranmore has the Attitots nursery that accepts children from 6 months to 5 years. A snow-play program for ages 1–3 is designed to introduce children to skiing. Reservations recommended: 374-2368. Cranmore has a nursery for children of walking age or older, with lunch and snacks. Day care is $6 pre hour and $40 for a full day with lunch. The second from the same family child saves 50 percent.

Wildcat's Kitten Club nursery has child care for 18 months to 12 years (younger with advance notice). Cost is $35 per day and $20 per half day.

Black Mountain also has nursery facilities for infants 6 months or older. Facilities are limited, so reservations are suggested.

King Pine takes infants to age 6 for $3.50 an hour (minimum two hours) or $18 for the day (infants $2 extra).

Lift tickets

Attitash Bear Peak: Adults, $38, weekends and holidays ($31 midweek); children (12 and younger); $23 ($20 midweek). On Sunday, children 12 and younger pay their age to ski. Attitash Bear Peak also sells an electronic ticket that allows skiers to pay by the run; a good choice for those who don't get full value from an all-day ticket.

Cranmore: Price structuring for 95/96 will change quite a bit now that the ski area has been acquired by the Sunday River ski resort group. Expect prices to be similar to, or combined with Attitash Bear Peak.

Wildcat (95/96): Adults, $38, weekends and holidays; Children (6-12) and seniors (65 and older), $22 weekends. Midweek, everyone 6 and older skis for $19. Children 5 and younger ski free with a ticket-holding parent, and skiers 70 and older can ski free midweek. Two-day weekend tickets are $64 for adults ($32 per day) and $40 for kids and seniors ($20 per day). On Wednesdays two can ski for $32.

Black Mountain charges $30 for adults on weekends and $14 midweek. Ages 6-15 pay $20 on weekends; $14 midweek. Ages 65+ pay $25 on weekends, free midweek. Black sells a family ticket for $75 which includes two adults and two juniors.

King Pine (95/96): Lift rates are $25 for adults on weekends, $16 weekdays. Kids (12 and younger) ski for $10 a day midweek, $16 weekends. Night skiing (Tuesday, Friday, Saturday and holidays): $12 adults, $8 children.

The **Ski New Hampshire** five-day midweek ticket is valid at 18 New Hampshire resorts and costs $169 for adults. One child

12 and younger may ski free with each paying adult. Additional junior passes are $80. Blackout dates are Dec. 25-29, 1995 and Feb. 19-23, 1996.

Accommodations

Accommodations in the Mt. Washington Valley are among the best in skidom if you like rustic, romantic, tiny country inns and bed-and-breakfast establishments. You won't find high-rises, but great old historic inns accommodate those who prefer a large-hotel resort feel. Also, the valley has moderately priced motels suitable for families. Condominiums exist, but for the most part are concentrated at a few base areas. For lodging information or reservations, call the **Mt. Washington Valley Chamber of Commerce** at (800) 367-3364.

Stonehurst Manor, North Conway NH; 356-3113 or (800) 525-9100, was created from a turn-of-the-century mansion that belonged to the Bigelow family of carpet fame. It is still manorial—the setting, rooms and restaurant are absolute elegance. A room is $95; master bedroom with balcony or the suite is $145. Make sure you are staying in the manor; there is also a motel nearby with some lodging. Ask about the winter packages.

Sheraton Inn North Conway (800-648-4397; in New Hampshire 356-9300) at Settlers' Green in downtown North Conway, with 200 rooms and suites, is handy to all the best outlet stores as well as the rest of North Conway. It has saunas, whirlpools, swimming pool, fitness center and ice skating. Children younger than 17 stay free. Rates are $79–$175.

White Mountain Hotel and Resort (356-7100 or 800-533-6301) at the foot of Cathedral Ledges (the enormous sculptured granite cliffs you see from all North Conway), is reached by taking River Road off Route 16, then West Side Road to Hale's Location. The views back across the valley toward Cranmore are unmatched. Rates are $69–$139.

The Eastern Slope Inn Resort (356-6321 or 800-258-4708) in the heart of North Conway is a palatial New England Inn. This establishment has a bit of everything needed in a hotel. Rooms, suites and townhouses in winter cost $86–$242 a night per room.

The Eagle Mountain Resort, Jackson (383-9111; for reservations, 800-966-5779), is one of those lovingly restored classic 19th-century resort hotels; weekend, $95-$140; slightly lower midweek. Children 12 and younger free, sleeping in existing beds; additional adults, $15 per person daily.

The Wentworth Resort Hotel, Jackson Village (383-9700 or 800-637-0013), is a grand old hotel in the elegant tradition. Rooms are spacious, furnished with antiques and equipped with period baths. Room rates are $95–$130 a night. Ask about the three- and five-day midweek cross-country packages that include lodging, breakfast and dinner.

The Christmas Farm Inn, Jackson Village; (383-4313 or 800-443-5837) is a cluster of buildings around a larger house, each as quaint as the next. The main inn has nine rooms, and the other buildings house larger rooms and small apartments. This is as convenient as it gets for the Jackson Ski Touring trails. All rates include breakfast and dinner. A 15 percent service charge and taxes will be added to your bill. Double-occupancy room rates are $136–$190, depending on location.

The Wildcat Inn and Tavern, Jackson Village (383-4245 or 800-228-4245), was built a hundred years ago, was once the original Carroll Reed Ski Shop, is now old-shoe comfortable and delightful. Right across the street are the Jackson Touring Foundation and Jack Frost Ski Shop. Double occupancy costs $64–$84. Numerous multiday packages available.

Eastern Inns, North Conway (356-5447 or 800-628-3750), is a very handy family-oriented motel at the northern end of North Conway Village with an enormous parking lot, fireplace in the lobby, heated swimming pool, video game room, and sauna. Rooms cost $59–$110.

For smaller, cozier bed-and-breakfast establishments, **The Buttonwood Inn**, North Conway (356-2625 or 800-258-2625), is tucked in the woods with cross-country skiing from the back door. Room rates are in the $66-$160 range.

The Eastman Inn (356-6707 or 800-626-5855) just south of the North Conway village on the main road, is a B&B with 14 rooms in one of the oldest houses in town, newly restored with antique charm. Rates per room are $60-$80. Breakfast with waffle irons practically at your table is superb.

The Cabernet Inn (356-4704 or 800-866-4704) is a charming 1842 Victorian cottage that now is a nine-bedroom B&B. Each room has a private bath, and the inn has a full country breakfast. It's on Route 16 just north of Conway Village, and the rates are $69–$169. Some rooms have whirlpools or fireplaces.

The Scottish Lion is on the main drag in North Conway (356-6381). B&B rates are $59–$75 per couple per room. Cross-country is right out the back door. Rooms are filled with antiques and have canopy beds.

Ellis River House in Jackson (383-9339 or 800-233-8309), overlooks the Ellis River, has 18 rooms, some with whirlpool tubs and/or fireplaces, and also has some of Jackson's most popular touring outside the door. Rates: $89–$199.

Riverside Country Inn (356-90600) has been called the most romantic of the country inns. It has seven rooms and doesn't mind kids or dogs. It's on Route 16A in Intervale. Rates are $45–$95.

The Notchland Inn (374-6131 or 800-866-6131) on the "quiet side" of the valley, Route 302 outside Bartlett, is a romantic setting with 11 rooms, all with fireplaces. It has a hot tub, skating and cross-country skiing from the door. B&B rates are $110–150 per couple; half-board rates are $150–$190.

Red Jacket Mountain View (356-5411 or 800-752-2538), is a rambling, low, motel-like building with some loft rooms and bunk beds good for families. It has a panoramic view of the mountains, indoor pool and hot tub. Rates: $89–$154.

For slopeside condos, **Mt. Cranmore Condominiums** (356-6851 or 800-786-6754) are right at the base and room rental includes guest privileges at the Cranmore Recreation Center (see Other Activities). Representative winter rates are: two bedrooms and loft $175 weekday, $225 weekend, $1,025 per week (based on four people per unit); three bedrooms, and loft $255 weekday, $350 weekend, $1,625 weekly (based on eight). Add $15 for each additional adult.

Attitash Mountain Village (356-6851 or 800-786-6754) has generous amenities, such as an indoor pool, hot tubs, sauna, a skating pond, exercise room, restaurant and lounge. Sample rates from a wide selection: one-bedroom unit sleeping 6–8, $115–$135 midweek, $179–$199 weekend; three-bedroom unit sleeping 10–14, $239–$259 midweek, $309–$339 weekend.

To be really close to Mt. Washington, and for a head start if you're climbing, skiing, or using its cross-country trails, there's the **Joe Dodge Lodge** (466-2727) at Pinkham Notch, run by the Appalachian Mountain Club, with room for 104. The two-, four- and five-bunk rooms are simple, and rates include either one or two meals. Lodging and breakfast on a weekend, for example, are $38–$50. The public room has a fireplace, library, board games, and a well-used piano.

Dining

Mt. Washington Valley is home to some of the best restaurants in the nation. Competition between restaurants is so intense that locals call it the War of the Chefs.

The Bernerhof, 383-4414, has its own nationally famous cooking school and serves some of the best gourmet meals in the country, let alone the valley.

In Jackson, **The Christmas Farm Inn** (383-4313), **The Inn at Thorn Hill** (383-4242), **Wentworth Resort Hotel** (383-9700), and **Wildcat Inn and Tavern** (383-4245), as well as **Stonehurst** (356-3113) and **The 1785 Inn** in North Conway (356-9025) are all major "War of the Chefs" combatants.

For more down-to-earth meals, try the **Scottish Lion** (356-6381) or the **Red Parka Pub** (383-4344) for great barbecued spare ribs (no reservations; expect up to a two-hour wait on Saturday nights). **Bellini's** (356-7000) and **Merlino's** (356-6006) are best for Italian food, **Horsefeathers** (356-2687) and **Delaney's Hole in the Wall** (356-7776), both in North Conway, for basic American and the **Shannon Door Pub** (383-4211) for Irish entertainment and pizzas.

The best pizza is probably found at **Elvio's** (356-3307) on Main Street. **Peaches** (356-5860) on Main Street has a good breakfast. Other recommended breakfast spots: **Yesterday's** (383-4457) in Jackson, **Stanley's** (383-6529) in Glen and **Sugar House Eatery** (356-6295) in North Conway.

The **Appalachian Mountain Club** (466-2721) at the base of Mt. Washington in Pinkham Notch gets rave reviews for a slightly different dining experience. Meals are served family-style—a great way to meet some new friends. Wednesdays are International Dinner Series, featuring a different country's cuisine and a slide show and talk from area residents who have traveled abroad. Available spots fill up days in advance, perhaps partly because of the price: adults $10, kids 12 and younger $5.

Another combination of dinner and entertainment is at **Mystery Dinner Theater** (356-5411) at the Red Jacket Inn in North Conway every Saturday night. Diners can eat, drink and be Perry (Mason, that is) for a comedic mystery dinner show.

Après-ski/nightlife

One of the best ski bars in the country is the **Red Parka Pub**, which offers lively après-ski and then into the wee hours. Something is happening every night, and its informalstyle runs to beer served in Mason jars, and vintage skis and creative license plates from all over covering the walls. On nights when there is no live music, live comedy or a movie is featured.

Barnaby's Restaurant has live music in its new dance club, Club Picasso, daily until 1 a.m. and is normally packed with a just-over-21 crowd and loud rock music. The place to be in Jackson is the **Wildcat Tavern** where folk rock is served up on weekends. On Friday and Saturday nights, **Horsefeathers** at North Conway hops, and the **Up Country Saloon** has live dance music. Locals hang out in **Hooligans**, **Horsefeathers** and **Delaney's Hole in the Wall** in North Conway.

Other activities

Shopping: This is probably the best at any ski area in the nation because of more than 150 factory outlets and New Hampshire's sales-taxless status. The area also has many unusual boutiques with creative gift items. Stop by the chamber of commerce in North Conway and pick up a shopping guide; there are far too many stores to list here.

The **Mt. Cranmore Sports & Fitness Center**, 356-6301 at Cranmore base, is a huge all-season facility, with indoor and outdoor tennis courts, pool, aerobics classes, steamroom and sauna. It is also home to the largest (30 x 40 feet) indoor climbing wall in the Northeast. Classes are available through International Mountain Climbing School (356-6316).

Eastern Mountain Sports in The Eastern Slope Inn also has a range of winter climbing and hiking programs, including ice-climbing instruction, ascents of Mt. Washington, and traverses of the Presidential Range; 356-5433.

The Appalachian Mountain Club has an active winter schedule of courses and workshops on ski touring, snowshoeing, avalanches, and much more. The club's maps and guidebooks to these mountains are an unrivaled gold mine of indispensable information. Headquarters in the area is at Pinkham Notch, almost across the road from Wildcat. Call 466-2721.

Take a sleigh ride in the valley. Try Nestlenook's horse-drawn sleigh (383-0845). Ice skating rinks are in Jackson, North Conway and Conway, and at several resorts. King Pine ski area has dogsled rides.

Getting there and getting around

Getting there: The Mt. Washington Valley is 140 miles north of Boston. The closest airports are Portland, Maine, with major airline service from all over the country and Pease Airport in Portsmouth, New Hampshire, served by Business Express/Delta Connection. Each is about a 90-minute drive from North Conway. Manchester Airport, farther south in New Hampshire, is served by US Air, United, Continental Express and Business Express/Delta Connection, and is about a two-hour drive.

The best route from Boston is up I-95 to Route 16, then north on 16/302. An alternate route is to come north on I-93 and take Route 104 to Route 25 to Route 16, and on to North Conway. From Portland, follow 302.

North Conway is notorious for its weekend traffic jams going through town. Most visitors approach from the southern side, and most of the ski areas are on the northern side. It can take an hour to get through town. Try to drive during minimal traffic—at night or midday.

Getting around: Bring a car.

Information/reservations

The **Mt. Washington Valley Chamber of Commerce** can make reservations at local hotels and inns. Call (800) 367-3364.

Attitash Bear Peak Travel and Lodging Bureau: 374-2368 or (800) 223-7669 (SNOW).

Wildcat reservations: 466-3326 or (800) 255-6439.

Cranmore Ski and Stay: 356-5543 or (800) 543-9206.

Black Mountain information: 383-4490.

King Pine/Purity Spring Resort: 367-8896 or (800) 373-3754 (FREE-SKI).

Jackson Lodging Bureau: (800) 866-3334.

Local area code is 603.

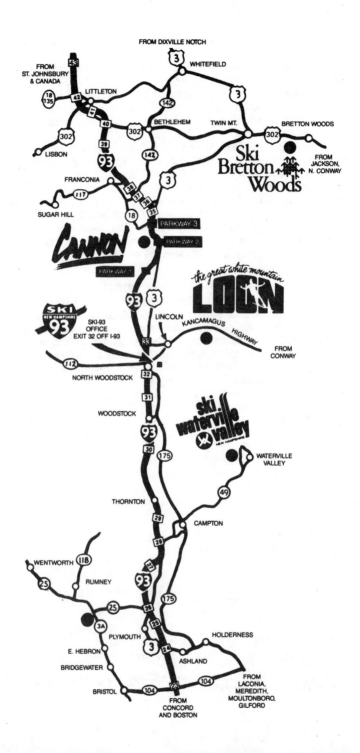

Ski 93
New Hampshire
Waterville Valley, Loon, Cannon, Bretton Woods

Waterville Valley, Loon Mountain, Cannon Mountain and Bretton Woods are all within 30 to 45 minutes of one another, accessible by I-93—hence their group marketing umbrella, Ski 93. Waterville is the most self-contained, while Loon has almost too much condo development; Cannon is the most historic and untamed; and Bretton Woods is tame but elegant.

You can ski them all with a five-day midweek lift ticket called the Family Pass, interchangeable at most New Hampshire resorts. It allows skiing at 18 areas, guaranteeing that a skier will never have to ski the same trail twice in one week or even two. The cost is $169 for adults, and free for one child skiing with a paying adult. (Additional child passes are $80.) You can buy the pass on any midweek day; it is then valid for five consecutive midweek days. Blackout periods are Dec. 25-29 and Feb. 19-23.

Waterville Valley

Waterville Valley is one of the best known mountains in New England, largely because of the publicity from staging more than 30 World Cup ski races in the past quarter century. (Waterville founder Tom Corcoran finished fourth in the 1960 Olympic giant slalom.) Though the area is well suited for racing, it isn't what we would want for an entire week of skiing. For an extended weekend, though, it can be a lot of fun. Waterville Valley is sufficiently self-contained that most visitors, once they enter, do not venture any farther than the slopes, just a short shuttlebus ride away. There are a lot of other things to do, too, such as cross-country skiing, shopping and a huge sports complex, with indoor and outdoor swimming pools, tennis, squash and racquetball courts, and indoor track. There is also an indoor skating rink.

Waterville now belongs to the same ski resort family as Killington, Mount Snow, Sugarloaf and Bear Mountain. In the past, one of Waterville Valley's main strengths has been family skiing. This continues. Facilities for children, such as the sports center with children's pool, the skating rink, video arcade, affordable children's menus, and sleigh rides all are important ingredients when young children are considered. When combined with its renowned ski school and the compact village, this resort shines for kids and families.

Waterville Valley Facts
Base elevation: 1,984'; **Summit elevation:** 4,004' **Vertical drop:** 2,020 feet.
Number and types of lifts: 13—1 quad superchair, 3 triple chairs
5 double chairs, 4 surface lifts
Acreage: 255 skiable acres **Percent snowmaking:** 96 percent
Uphill capacity: 15,660 skiers per hour **Bed base:** 2,500

Where to ski

Skiing is solid intermediate. These trails were cut more recently than the Front Four at Stowe or the trails down Cannon, so they are not New England's typical steep and narrow—there's elbow room and a chance to check out the slope before committing to the fall line again.

The Valley Run is a beginner/lower intermediate heaven with enough width to allow skiing for a couple of days down different sections. Beginners have a small area with a separate chair lift. One of the toughest runs, True Grit, develops major moguls and drops down the Sunnyside face. Two former tough mogul runs, Ciao and Gema, now are groomed daily. Such trails as White Caps, Sel's Choice, Old Tecumseh and Tippecanoe are intermediate and advanced playthings.

Snowboarding

Snowboarders have a large park, the Boneyard, on the Lower Periphery trail (to the right of the trail map). It features terrain and objects for sliding, bonking and the other things freestyle boarders enjoy. New Hampshire law requires snowboarders to have a board leash or strap.

Cross-country (95/96 prices)

Waterville has 105 km. of trails, 70 of which are groomed and tracked for skating as well as traditional skiing through the White Mountain National Forest.

Rentals and lessons are available, and new for 1995/96 will be guided cross-country and showshoe tours for all levels and ages. Trail fees: weekends, $11 for adults, $8 for children 12 and under; midweek, $8 and $6. A one-day beginner package, including pass, lessons and equipment, costs $33 for adults, $25 for children.

Lessons (95/96 prices)

Regular one-and-a-half-hour **group lessons** cost $24 per session. **Private instruction** is $50 an hour for one skier, $80 for two to five. Vacation option packages, including three full days of lessons (two sessions per midweek day), cost $69; five full days (two sessions per midweek day) cost $95.

For **children**, the SKIwee program costs $60 a day for ages 3 to 5, lunch extra; and $45 a day for Mountain Cadets (ages 6–8) and Mountain Scouts (9–12), including lift ticket, but lunch extra.

Child care (95/96 prices)

Two nurseries at the base area are available for children from 6 months to 4 years. All-day cost for ages 6 months to 2 years is $38, two days $74, three days $110 and five days $182. Space is guaranteed only with a reservation. Call 236-8311, ext. 3196 or 3197.

Lift tickets (95/96 prices)

	Adult	Child (6–12)
One day	$43 (weekend)	$28
Three days	$105 ($35/day)	$70 ($23.33/day)
Five days	$148 ($29.60/day)	$80 ($21.60/day)

Teen (13-19) prices are $38 for one day, $149 for five days. The one- and three-day prices are for weekends; midweek prices are $5–$8 per day lower across the age board. Kids 5 and younger ski free anytime. Waterville often runs a Kids Ski Free promotion when parents buy multi-day lodging packages; ask about this.

Loon Mountain

Loon has some of the most convenient accommodations in New Hampshire. This resort is a behemoth—at least in lodging. It's one of the few resorts where the bed base is almost double the lift capacity, which has created crowded conditions at times. Fortunately, Loon entered Phase II of its Loon 2000 expansion plan in summer 1995, with a $10 million project that included a quad superchair to replace two old double chairs in the West Basin Base Area, increase of snowmaking coverage to 97 percent, realignment of the Kissin' Cousin double chair which allowed creation of a dedicated learning area, and trail modifications to relieve congestion in high-traffic areas.

The area limits lift ticket sales to keep the mountain experience positive. Continued mountain improvements have meant the sold-out signs quit coming out every weekend; now it's about four days per season, with perhaps ten near-sellout days. The Unconditional Conditions Guarantee™ ensures you'll like the ski conditions or you'll ski free on your next visit.

Loon Mountain Facts

Base elevation: 950'; Summit elevation: 3,050'; Vertical drop: 2,100 feet.
Number and types of lifts: 8–1 gondola, 1 quad superchair, 2 triple chairs, 3 double chairs, 1 surface lift Acreage: 250 trail acres Percent snowmaking: 97 percent
Uphill capacity: 10,550 skiers per hour Bed base: 13,000

Where to ski

The intermediate runs are good and solid, with no expert surprises around the next clump of trees. Advanced North Peak runs are challenging and well removed from lower intermediate traffic. The steeps are there, but half the bumps are groomed out.

The upper trails are a bit twisted, narrow and seemingly undirected at the summit, but they open onto a series of wide intermediate pistes. A favorite is Flying Fox, a delightful cruise. Depending on snow conditions, skiers can link up with the West Basin via Upper Speakeasy, or they can drop down to the parking lot and take the 100-yard-long steam train ride to the adjacent base area. The West Basin area has another collection of intermediate trails.

The central portion of the mountain, serviced by the Seven Brothers triple chair, offers good intermediate-marked trails that advanced beginners can handle.

Realignment of the Kissin' Cousin double chair this season has given beginners and snowboarders a much improved learning area to the right of the West Basin.

Snowboarding

Snowboarding is allowed on the entire mountain. New features are a 2,500-foot snowboard park called Skid Row under the new quad superchair and a snowboard rental and hang-out area (it has a video arcade) called the Board Barn. New Hampshire law requires snowboarders to have a leg leash.

Cross-country

The Loon Mountain Cross Country Center has 35 km. of groomed and tracked trails 745-8111, ext. 5568. Children 5 and younger and seniors 70 and older ski free on Loon's cross-country trails.

Lessons (95/96 prices)

Loon's Ski School offers 90-minute **group lessons** for $24. Five sessions, $100. **Private lessons** are $55 an hour; $80 for one-and-a-half hours.

A **beginner special** for both skiers and snowboarders that includes equipment, all-day lessons and a limited lift ticket costs $52 per day. Enroll at either rental shop.

The **Specialty Ski Weeks** are reserved for skiers with truly advanced skills who want to fine-tune their tactics on all terrain and in all conditions. The three-day midweek program includes five hours of coaching each day, and is scheduled for various weeks throughout the season. Cost is $180.

Children 3 and 4 are enrolled in the P.K. Boo program. Full day lessons including lunch and lifts cost $55, half days $40. Children 5 and 6 are enrolled in the Kinder Bear Ski Camp. Full day lessons with lunch costs $65. There is also a Adventure Ski Camp class for ages 7 to 12, which includes lunch. This program groups children by ability level. Price is $73 a day.

Child care (95/96 prices)

The new Honeybear Nursery is located in the Mountain Club and welcomes kids 6 weeks to 8 years from 8:30 a.m. to 4 p.m.

Reservations are required (745-8111). Rates are as follows: half day, $30; one day, $45; each additional day is $40.

Lift tickets (95/96 prices)

Weekend prices	Adult	Child (6-12)
One day	$43	$27
Three days	$110 ($36.66/day)	$68 ($22.60/day)
Weekday prices		
One day	$36	$24
Three days	$96 ($32)	$63 ($21)
Five days	$144 ($28.80day)	$96 ($19.20/day)

Ticket sales are cut off after approximately 6,000 have been sold. To reserve tickets or ski rentals in advance by major credit card, call (603) 745-8111, ext. 5400.

Skiers aged 65-69 and 13-19 can ski for $30 midweek non-holiday, but for adult prices on weekends. Loon has a popular Saturday-Sunday ticket for $77 for adults, $48 for children; midweek discounts and other multiday rates are available. Children 5 and younger and 70 and older ski free.

The five-day price is for the New Hampshire Family Pass.

Cannon Mountain

Cannon Mountain is state-owned and has long been known by experts as one of the most challenging mountains in the East. It has a 2,146-foot vertical served by an 80-passenger tram. When skiing here you see no signs of civilization except for the ski lodge and lifts. Though once known as a mountain where grooming consisted of shoveling some snow under the lifts, Cannon now takes mountain preparation to heart. Of Cannon's 150 acres, 95 percent are covered by snowmaking. The trails are narrower in legend than they are in reality and the mountain can actually be skied by most intermediates. This is a place for advanced skiers to play and intermediates to push themselves.

A fixed-grip quad services the summit and exposes the skier to beautiful scenic vistas of the White Mountain National Forest. The Profile Trail presents the advanced intermediate with a well-groomed 2,400-foot thrill. The Upper Cannon, Tramway and Vista Way are all intermediate trails that are challenging but certainly negotiable, the steepest being Upper Cannon which offers New England-style steeps. Once down those trails, long and wide cruisers take you to the base.

Cannon Mountain Facts

Base elevation: 2,000'; Summit elevation: 4,146'; Vertical drop: 2,146 feet
Number and types of lifts: 6—1 aerial tram, 1 quad chair, 1 triple chair, 2 double chairs, 1 surface lift
Acreage: 150 trail acres Percent snowmaking: 95 percent
Uphill capacity: 6,000 skiers per hour Bed base: 13,000 nearby

The Front Five, as known to locals, are the intimidating trails seen from the highway. Three of them, Avalanche, Paulie's Folly and Zoomer, are marked black and rightfully so, especially Zoomer's bumps. The other two, Rocket and Gary's, have less pitch without the bumps.

Lessons (95/96 prices)

Learn To Ski (or Snowboard) For The Fun Of It includes up to three days of lift tickets, lessons and rental equipment for $35 per day. The first day includes two lessons, while the last two days include all-mountain lift tickets. Advanced skiers should check out the **Z-A-P Clinic**, which is a three-run private lesson: one run each down Zoomer, Avalanche and Paulie's Folly. It's offered Saturdays from 11 to 1, and you meet and pay the instructor at the top of the Zoomer chair lift. For other adult instruction programs, call the ski school.

For **children**, the SKIwee program costs $55 a day for ages 4 to 9, including lunch; and a similar program is available for children 10-12.

Child care (95/96 prices)

Child care programs are available for ages 12 months and older. All-day care is $35 with lunch.

Lift tickets (95/96 prices)

	Adult	Junior (6–12) Senior (65+)
One day	$37	$26
Two days	$65 ($21.66/day)	$45 ($15/day)
Three days	$90 ($18/day)	$62 ($12.40/day)

These are weekend prices; midweek discounts are available.

Bretton Woods

Bretton Woods has been more linked with the grand old Mount Washington Hotel and international monetary meetings than with skiing, which is relatively new at the resort. The skiing is mild and good for cruising. The resort also has a halfpipe for snowboarders. This mountain, like Waterville, is perfect for families and makes special efforts to ensure great family vacations.

Downhill variety is mixed with one of the best cross-country networks (outside of Jackson and Stowe) in New England, boasting 90 km. of prepared trails. The Nordic area is centered

---

Bretton Woods Facts
Base elevation: 1,600'; **Summit elevation:** 3,100'; **Vertical drop:** 1,500 feet
Number and types of lifts: 5–1 quad superchair, 1 triple chair,
2 double chairs, 1 surface lift **Acreage:** 175 trail acres **Snowmaking:** 98 percent
Uphill capacity: 7,300 skiers per hour **Bed base:** 3,000+

on the grounds of the Mount Washington Hotel, which provides a spectacular setting.

A beginner special costs $35 including trail pass, lessons and equipment; children 5 and younger ski free. Bretton Woods is noted for excellent children's ski programs. The Hobbit Ski and Snowboard School has ski lessons including lunch and rentals for $49; and similar snowboard lessons for $55.

Bretton Woods' nursery takes children 2 months to 5 years, $20 a half day and $30 a full day including lunch. An evening care program provides dinner, night skiing and indoor play for $34.

Lift tickets (95/96 prices)

	Adult	Junior (6-15)	Seniors (62+)
One day (weekend)	$38	$25	$25
One day (weekday)	$31	$15	$25
Two days (weekend)	$69	$45	$45
Five days (weekday)	$129	$70	$95

Ski 93 area accommodations

At the resorts

Waterville Valley: The **Golden Eagle Lodge** with 139 condominium suites features a distinctive design reminiscent of the turn-of-the-century grand hotels at the White Mountain resorts.

Additionally, Waterville has three hotel properties and four groups of condominiums all located in the valley. **The Snowy Owl** is perhaps the most charming and something of a modern country inn with breakfast. The **Black Bear Lodge** is slightly larger and more hotel-like, and the **Valley Inn and Tavern** operates as a country inn with rates that can include meals. All are in the same price range with two-day lodging and lift weekend packages starting at $129 (per person, double occupancy) and five-day midweek packages, starting at $319. On stays of three nights or more (non-holiday) at the Golden Eagle Lodges or Black Bear Lodge, kids stay and ski free.

Prices include entrance to the sports center and shuttle service. **Condominiums** are available and include access to the sports center.

Loon Mountain: The Mountain Club on Loon (800) 229-7829 or (603) 745-8111. This ski-in/ski-out property has everything under one roof—from parking to swimming pool, fitness club to restaurants. One problem: many of its rooms have a double Murphy bed with two small day beds along the windows. This arrangement is fine for couples, or for a family with young children, but it is awkward for two unrelated adults who don't want to sleep in the same bed. Package prices start at $79 per person, double occupancy.

Loon also has condominiums. Make reservations through the Mountain Club.

Bretton Woods: The premier property here is the restored 1896 **Bretton Arms Country Inn,** a National Historic Landmark next to the cross-country area and one of the most elegant and romantic inns in the state. Rates are about $115 per night. The **Bretton Woods Motor Inn** features less expensive accommodations between the downhill and cross-country areas. Bretton Woods also has a grouping of **townhouses.** All Bretton Woods properties can be reached through (800) 258-0330 or 278-1000. In winter the ski area provides shuttlebuses to and from the slopes.

In the region

Three motelish properties along Route 3 in Lincoln only minutes from Loon and Cannon join for advertising and offer similar accommodation with identical prices for the most part. Each has slightly different amenities. **Indian Head Motel Resort** off I-93, Exit 33 on Route 3 in Lincoln; (800-343-8000, 745-8000). This is one of the centers of après-ski action with live bands and a great ice-skating pond and attached cross-country trails. Room rates start at $89. **The Beacon,** (800-258-8934, 745-8118) on the same road as Indian Head, also has indoor tennis and the large indoor pools. Rates per person, double occupancy: $55, which includes lifts midweek and $60 per night with a two-night minimum and no lift ticket on weekends. **Woodward's Motor Inn** (800-635-8968, 745-8141) is the most family oriented. It has the area's only racquetball court and the best steaks in the region.

Just north of Franconia Notch and Cannon Mountain you'll find the **Red Coach Inn** (800-262-2493 (COACH-93), 823-7422) a modern hotel built behind a gabled cedar façade, a snowball's throw from the unspoiled New England town of Franconia (careful on the speed limit as you drive through). There is a large indoor pool and exercise room. Resorts most accessible from this hotel are Bretton Woods and Cannon, with Loon only a few minutes down I-93. Room rates are $70-$100.

The Woodstock Inn B&B (800-321-3985, 745-3951) A typical quaint New England lodge. The main building is more than 100 years old with no two rooms alike. You'll find them tucked under the rafters, some with private bath, or shared bath, all with casual charm. The restaurant in the front of the inn is one of Woodstock's most elegant; the one in the station at the rear is one of the town's liveliest. Rates per couple with breakfast: $55-$135. A room with a hot tub at the foot of your bed is a bit more.

Amber Lights Inn (726-4077) between Loon and Waterville has five relatively small rooms (four with shared bath) with big hospitality. Carola prides herself on providing one of the area's breakfast experiences with secret egg and cheese creations, homemade muffins and breads slathered with home-preserved jellies and jams. Children younger than 7 are discouraged. Room rates are $45-$60 with a continental breakfast and $55-$70 with the full breakfast (go for the latter).

Wilderness Inn B&B (745-3890) is run by the Yarnells, a couple with small children, who make other families with youngsters welcome in their house. Parents note: this place has laundry facilities! The B&B is only steps from the center of Woodstock, filled with shops and restaurants.

The Inn at Forest Hills (823-9550; fax 823-5555) is a newly restored English Tudor-style B&B built into a house which was once part of the grand Forest Hills Hotel. It provides a great New England tradition with fine breakfasts just about a mile from the village of Franconia on Route 142 heading toward Bethlehem. Room rates start at $60, double occupancy.

The Mulburn Inn (869-3389) is another B&B in a great Tudor-style setting with oak staircase and stained glass windows. Located in Bethlehem, once considered one of the fresh-air centers of New England, this home provides hospitality in the midst of a tiny New Hampshire town at the northern edge of Ski 93 only about 10 minutes from Bretton Woods. Rooms are in the $60-$90 range.

Dining

The most elegant dining experiences in the southern Ski 93 region can be found at the **William Tell** (726-3618) on Route 49 just outside Waterville Valley or at the **Woodstock Inn's Clement Room** (745-3951). The William Tell has a strong Swiss-German accent with excellent wines. The Clement Room is more eclectic with meals ranging from Jamaican Chicken to Veal Oscar. Both restaurants feature entrées in the $12-$19 range. The Woodstock Inn also serves great daily breakfasts as well as a fabulous weekend brunch; the William Tell is also known for its weekend brunch. For equally adventurous gourmet cuisine at the Bretton Woods end of Ski 93 try the **Bretton Arms Restaurant** (278-3000) in an elegant century-old atmosphere. Another spot recommended by locals for fine dining is **Sunset Hill House** (823-5522), which also has great views of the Franconia Range.

At Loon Mountain, try **Rachael's** (745-8111) or **The Granite Grille**, both at the Mountain Club. **The Common Man** (745-3463) offers good basic American dining with a roaring fireplace and rustic surroundings. For the place claimed by locals to have the best steaks, head to the **Open Hearth Steak House** at Woodward's Motor Inn. **Gordi's Fish and Steak House** (745-6635) is family-oriented and features Maine lobster and steaks. The **Tavern at the Mill** (745-3603) is set in a modernesque barn-like building, which is also one of the nightlife centers just outside Loon. **Truant's Tavern** (745-2239) serves clever dinner entrées in a mock schoolhouse atmosphere—drinking in class was never so much fun. The bar hops on weekends. **Woodstock Station** (745-3951), built in an old train station on Main Street, offers a creative menu of reasonable meals from meatloaf to Mexican. **G.H. Pizza** serves traditional and gourmet pizza, as well as hot and cold subs.

In Waterville Valley village family-style **Bull Moose Cafe** (236-4309) at Town Square serves American meals. On the other side of the Town Square is the **Common Man** with its American menu. Or head to **Chili Peppers** which has the area's best Mexican food. For pizza call **Alpine Pizza** at 236-4173. **Valley Inn** also offers good dining.

At Bretton Woods the **Top o' the Quad Restaurant** serves casual lunches and dinners Friday and Saturday with views of Mt. Washington's summit. Back down the mountain, try **Darby's Tavern** for hearty family dining, only a quarter-mile from the slopes. **Fabyans Station** is a good eatery in an old railroad station. In Franconia head to **Hillwinds**.

For breakfast head to **Jay's Sweetheart Diner, Pegs Place** or **The Country Mile** around North Woodstock. **The Millaway Cafe** in the Millfront Marketplace serves fresh and unusual pastries—and gourmet coffee. In Waterville test the Belgian waffles and pastries at the tiny **Coffee Emporium** in Town Square.

Après-ski/nightlife

After skiing at Loon head to the **Granite Bar in the Mountain Club** for good weekend entertainment and a decent quiet après-ski spot. The **Paul Bunyan Lounge** at the Octagon base has a young rowdy crowd.

Waterville now has a collection of bars in Town Square, each with slightly different après-ski. They are all within a few steps of each other. **Legends 1291**, the **Common Man**, plus the **Brookside Bar and Bistro** all serve up a good time, and later in the evening they stand in the same order, ranging from loud disco and rock to quieter moments. **Zoo Station** is an under-21 night club with dancing, video games and a juice bar. The **World Cup Bar and Grill** at the mountain has the normal collection of skiers for après-ski until 5:30 p.m.

Just down the road from Waterville on the way back to the interstate try the **William Tell** for a cozy quiet après-ski or the **Mad River Tavern** for a more raucous setting. Both have popular dinner menus.

The Woodstock area locals set up party camp at **Truant's Tavern** and **Woodstock Station** in Woodstock. **Gordi's Fish and Steak** in Lincoln serves up great munchies. **Indian Head**

Resort in Lincoln offers good après-ski. From Wednesday through Sunday, live bands rock the joint. The **Tavern Sports Bar** is a low-keyed darts, video game and pool hall. Downstairs the **Tavern at the Mill** has the area's best singles action with bands on weekends.

In Franconia (near Cannon), try **Village House**, a comfortable lounge with a lot of classic ski history and an evening entertainer who plays après-ski at the mountain's lounge; or **Hillwinds**, a large bar and lounge with live entertainment on weekends.

Other activities

Shopping: Waterville Valley's Town Square has several specialty shops worth a look. Lincoln, home of Loon Mountain, has some factory outlet stores, including New England's only North Face outlet, where we picked up some good buys on skiwear. The factory outlet bonanza of North Conway is 30 miles east of Bretton Woods. Absence of sales tax makes buying all the sweeter.

Waterville Valley has **sleigh rides** and an **indoor fitness center**, as well as a refrigerated ice arena for **skating**. Cannon is home to the **New England Ski Museum**, a collection of ski memorabilia well worth a brief visit. Though it's closed in winter, drive by **The Mount Washington Hotel & Resort** just east of the Bretton Woods ski area. Its setting against the towering Presidential Range makes a spectacular scene, especially at sunset when the snow-covered mountains turn pink.

The **Rocks Estate** in Bethlehem, on a hilltop about 10 miles from Cannon, has **sleigh rides** and offers some forestry-related activities, being owned by the Society For The Protection of New Hampshire Forests. Call (800) 639-5373.

Getting there and getting around

Getting there: Boston's Logan Airport is 130 miles away from the Ski 93 areas. Manchester Airport, 70 miles south, is serviced by Delta's Business Express, USAir, and United.

From I-93 heading north, Waterville Valley is 11 miles up Route 49 at Exit 28. Loon Mountain is on the Kancamagus Highway (Route 112) at Exit 32 in Lincoln. Cannon is visible from I-93 just north of Franconia Notch State Park, and Bretton Woods is on Route 302: take Exit 35 to Route 3, which meets Route 302 at Twin Mountain.

Getting around: A car is a necessity unless you stay close to the slopes at one resort and ski only there. On Saturday nights, Lincoln and North Woodstock run a "Jolly Trolley," designed to keep beverage imbibers out of their cars.

Information/reservations

Ski 93 Central Reservations handles 80 properties in the region and can arrange airline tickets, car rental, lift tickets and ski rentals, (800) 937-5493 (WE-SKI-93); in NH call 745-2409. **Lincoln-Woodstock Lodging Bureau** also is full-service and open seven days a week. It books lodging and packages throughout the Ski 93 region, as well as air tickets and rental cars. Call (800) 227-4191.

Waterville Valley Lodging Bureau handles information and reservations: (800) 468-2553 (GO-VALLEY). Resort offices: 236-8311; ski reports: 236-4144.

Loon Mountain Lodging Bureau at (800) 229-7829 for slopeside lodging. **Loon Mountain Resort** offices: 745-8111 locally; snow phone: 745-8100.

Bretton Woods Lodging Bureau at (800) 258-0330 or 278-1000; snow phone: 278-5051.

Cannon snowphone: (800) 552-1234 or 823-7771 locally.

Twin Mountain Lodging Bureau: (800) 245-8946 (TWIN).

The local area code is 603.

Hunter Mountain & Ski Windham
New York

These are the two closest large ski areas to New York City, only a two and a half hours' drive north. These resorts are in the midst of the rugged and rocky Catskills—home to such legends as Rip Van Winkle and the headless horseman of Sleepy Hollow. As far as skiing goes, the area woke with a vengeance almost thirty years ago. Trails were dynamited and dozed through rugged mountains, and snowmaking became an integral part of Eastern ski resorts.

The villages surrounding the mountains reflect the personalities of the local resort. Hunter and nearby Tannersville are basic rough Adirondack towns with supermarkets, bars, pubs, hotels and homes. Windham has a manicured look to it with pretty houses, no bars, delis rather than supermarkets and country inns instead of hotels. On the slopes, weekend crowds at Hunter reflect a rush-hour subway heritage. Windham skiers are far more sedate. At Hunter you may hear late-night beer-drinking songs and other sounds of merriment. In Windham the loudest midnight sound may be the snow guns, a passing car or water gurgling downstream.

Both Hunter Mountain and Ski Windham have the same amount of vertical and they are only ten miles apart. Hunter is by far the bigger operation—it is major league. It has become on of the snowmaking champions of the Northeast, shooting out mountains of snow and continually upgrading the system. Ski Windham offers good skiing but doesn't have the difficult terrain found at Hunter. Each area has a high-speed quad pumping skiers up the mountain and keeping lines manageable.

Hunter Mountain Facts

Base elevation: 1,600'; **Summit elevation:** 3,200'; **Vertical drop:** 1,600 feet
Number of lifts: 15–1 quad superchair, 2 triple chairs, 8 double chairs, 4 surface lifts
Percent snowmaking: 100 percent **Uphill capacity:** 18,000 per hour

Ski Windham Facts

Base elevation: 1,500'; **Summit elevation:** 3,100'; **Vertical drop:** 1,600 feet
Number of lifts: 7–1 quad superchair, 4 triple chairs, 1 double chair, 1 surface lift
Percent snowmaking: 97 percent **Total acreage:** 220 skiable acres
Uphill capacity: 11,800 per hour

Hunter's skiing is primarily solid intermediate with an advanced flair. Its toughest runs drop off the summit in the East. Hunter One is a mellow beginner paradise.

Ski Windham has a strong intermediate flavor but without Hunter's twists and turns and changing scenery. Its advanced trails are not as tough as Hunter's but will keep skiers happy for a few days and may be better for lower intermediates.

Both resorts are packed on weekends. If you can find any way to come at midweek the skiing is less crowded and everything's a bigger bargain.

Snowboarding

Snowboarding is allowed on the entire mountain at both Hunter and Ski Windham. Windham has just doubled the size of its snowboard park. There are lessons including packages for never-evers, and Small Class Sessions that meet three times a day. Rentals are also available at the mountain.

Lessons (94/95 prices)

Hunter: The Ski with a Pro Free program offers several runs with a pro every day (weather permitting) except Christmas and New Year's at 11:45 a.m. at the top of Snowlite Express.

Hunter has **beginner packages** that include everything one needs to learn to ski or snowboard for $45.

Private lessons cost $45 per hour for one, with each additional skier paying $20. A three-hour private lesson costs $120. Early a.m. and late p.m. private lessons only cost $35/person; additional skiers $15.

Children's ski school is open to children 5-12 and includes lifts, lessons, rentals, box lunch and supervision. Rates for the weekend day are $68; half day no lunch, $48. Full weekday is $48, half $35. Open 9:30 a.m. to 3:30 p.m.

Ski Windham (95/96 prices): This resort has a full ski school program as well. **Private lessons** run $38 an hour for one person, $65 for two, $80 for three. **Group lessons** are $19 per 1 3/4-hour session, or $85 for a book of five sessions, $170 for a book of ten lessons. The resort also has a full range of **programs for children 3–12.**

Child care

Hunter: The day care program can handle about 50 children. This service is for children 2–3 who have not yet begun to ski. It costs $30 for a full day (8:30 a.m. to 4 p.m.). A book of five days will cost $85. Lunch is not included. It can be purchased for $3 per day per child.

Ski Windham: The Children's Learning Center offers non-skiers and skiers a variety of activities, and for those who like to sprawl out on the floor when they draw or read, the floors are heated. Full-day/half-day programs: $44/$27 for non-skiers; $62/$40 for skiers without rentals; and $74/52 with rentals.

Lift tickets (95/96 prices)

Hunter: Full-day weekend/holiday lift tickets cost $41 adult, $28 junior (12 and younger); two days cost $76/$52, five days are $178/$120, and ten days $344/$230. These lift tickets are good anytime during this season.

Midweek non-holiday lift tickets cost is $34/22 for one day, $62/$42 for two days, $145/$95 for five days, and $280/$180 for ten days. There are special rates for Seniors (65 and older), teens (13–18) and students with valid college ID.

Ski Windham: A full-day ticket costs $38 adult/$33 junior (7–12) on weekends, and $31/$28 on weekdays. You can build your own ski week. The first day costs full price and you can buy additional days at a $2 discount.

On non-holiday weekdays, juniors ski free when accompanied by a paying adult (one child per adult). Children under 6 ski free anytime when accompanied by a ticketed adult.

Accommodations

Hunter: This ski area pioneered a bed-and-breakfast program that now has about 30 country inns participating. These B&Bs have prices starting at about $25. The program includes lift tickets and combined with the Kids Ski Free program is a money-saver.

Call (800) 775-4641 for lodging reservations. Try to stay at the actual resort villages—even Palenville, considered nearby by reservation agents, is at the bottom of a steep grade. Though they are "nearby," they are not very convenient.

We recommend these in the Hunter area: The **Scribner Hollow Lodge** with several upscale suites is perhaps the most luxurious. **Villa Vosilla** and the **Deer Mountain Inn** round out the top three. The **Liftside Condos** are very well appointed and convenient. There is a collection of excellent B&Bs such as the **Kennedy House** and **Washington Irving Lodge**; head to the **Hunter Village Inn** for more of a party atmosphere.

Ski Windham: Its reservation service (800-729-7549) has packages that include lifts, lodging and many discounts. The ski area owns the **Windham Arms Resort,** which offers country inn hospitality with regular shuttles to the ski area. Other accommodations within three miles of Ski Windham range from sprawling inns to B&Bs. **Antonio's Resort, Evergreen at The Thompson House, Christman's Windham House** and **Hotel Vienna** are good hotels in roughly descending order of luxury. B&Bs to try include **Albergo Allegria, Danske Hus** and **the Country Suite.** Rates start at $70 per night, double occupancy, weekends; $50 weeknights.

Dining

Scores of restaurants are in this region. Around Hunter the **Chateau Belleview** (589-5525) prepares fine continental cooking; **Swiss Chalet** has excellent cuisine; and **Deer Mountain Inn** is recommended by all the locals. For slightly less expensive fare try **P.J. Larkins** (589-5568), **Fireside** (263-4216), and **Pete's Place** (589-9840), all favorites with virtually everyone. Try the Crooked Cafe in Tannersville for breakfast.

Near Windham try **Brandywine** (734-3838) for well-prepared, affordable meals (Wednesday's pasta special is a real bargain) and **The Frog's House** (734-9817). These two spots got the nod from most locals. **Theo's** (734-4455) has tasty Greek food and **Thetford's** (734-3322) has great steaks and seafood. **Captain's Quarters** (734-3055) is the place to head for fish. **Temptations** at the Windham Arms Resort (734-3000) serves a '50s evening menu (tuna melt, grilled cheese, BLTs and clubs) in a pink, purple and chrome period decor. **Vesuvio** (734-3663) reputedly has the best Italian food in the area. **Chalet Fondue** (734-4650) has the best German menu in town, but locals from both areas recommended a trip to **Marie's Dream House** in Westkill (989-6565) for Austrian/German cooking that is worth the 20-minute drive. The best burger is charcoal grilled at **Jimmy O'Connor's** (734-4270). Try **Martin Sullivan's** (734-5714) daily specials for good-food bargains.

For breakfast try **Kountry Kitchen** in Hensonville or to the **Four Stars** (734-4600) or **Starlight Cafe** (734-9862).

Getting there and getting around

Getting there: The best access is up I-87 120 miles north of New York City. For Hunter Mountain, take Exit 20 at Saugerties and follow Route 32 to Route 32A to the area. To reach Ski Windham turn north on Route 296 off of Route 23A or if coming on the New York Thruway, take Exit 21 in Catskill and go west on Route 23 for 25 miles.

Both resorts provide buses from the New York City area. Hunter's bus leaves Mondays, Wednesdays, Fridays and Saturdays. Call (800) 552-6262 for information. Ski Windham's bus leaves Monday, Wednesday and Sunday. Call (516) 360-0369 or (718) 343-4444.

Getting around: At these resorts a car is virtually a must for getting around at night. .

Information/reservations

Lodging: For Hunter, call (518) 263-4641 or (800) 775-4641. For the Windham lodging service call (800) 729-7549 (729-SKIW).

Lake Placid/Whiteface
New York

As an area that would sit somewhere in the middle of the pack of northeast resorts based on its skiing alone, Lake Placid stands apart as a winter sports magnet. There's no doubt that the 1980 Winter Olympics were instrumental in establishing that reputation; nonetheless, plenty of past Olympic sites have retreat-ed into relative obscurity. At Lake Placid, the folks have picked up the the flame and run with it, so to speak. To fulfill the promise of Lake Placid so evident during the Olympics, they formed the Olympic Regional Development Authority (ORDA) to operate the multi-facility recreational area.

Because probably more world-class winter sports athletes still train and compete here than anywhere else in the free world (more than 8,000 a year) Lake Placid still has the feel of an Olympic village. Groups of young athletes are everywhere, and there always seems to be one championship or another underway. Even the athletes themselves revel in watching the daring if demented souls who soar off the Olympic jumps.

Lake Placid urges you at every turn to *participate*. In addition to the bobsled run and one of the most extensive and well-prepared cross-country ski circuits anywhere, you can experience the luge run at the Mt. Van Hoevenberg Olympic sports complex about eight miles away (this was the site of the 1983 World Cup Luge Finals). For the uninitiated, bouncing off the walls of a luge track is not unlike being in a pinball game played by unseen Nordic giants, with you as the ball. You have to experience it at least once. Of course, no one in their right mind would *want* to experience firsthand the thrill of being launched off a 120-meter ski ramp, but you can get a breathtaking perspective on that madness by taking the glass elevator 26 stories to the top. The $6 ticket, thankfully, is round-trip.

Lake Placid Facts
Base elevation: 1,200'; Summit elevation: 4,416'; Vertical drop: 3,216 feet
Number and types of lifts: 10–2 triple chairs, 7 double chairs , 1 rope tow
Acreage: about 158 acres Snowmaking: 93 percent
Uphill capacity: 10,115 skiers per hour Bed base: 5,000

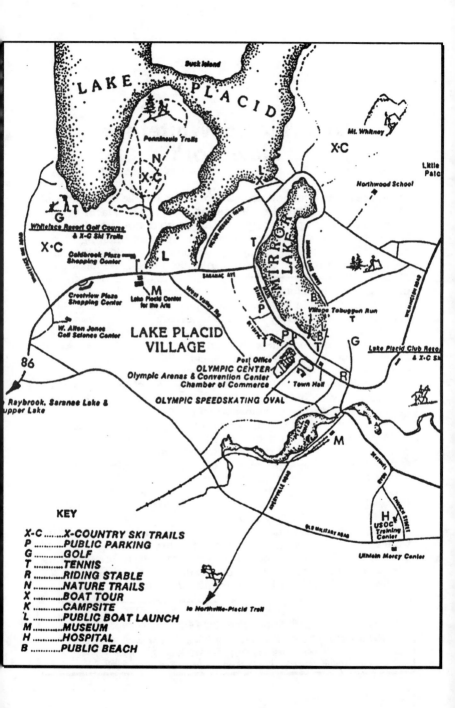

KEY

X-C ....**X-COUNTRY SKI TRAILS**
P ....**PUBLIC PARKING**
G ....**GOLF**
T ....**TENNIS**
R ....**RIDING STABLE**
N ....**NATURE TRAILS**
X ....**BOAT TOUR**
K ....**CAMPSITE**
L ....**PUBLIC BOAT LAUNCH**
M ....**MUSEUM**
H ....**HOSPITAL**
B ....**PUBLIC BEACH**

Back on Main Street, the town itself is dominated by the arena where America watched its Cinderella hockey team enter the history books in 1980. Wonderfully situated on Mirror Lake, the town is full of charm, if standing just one standard motel away from being truly quaint. For a relaxing afternoon away from the slopes, take a dogsled ride across the lake for the sheer novelty of it. At night many visitors will find both relaxation and exercise on the Olympic Oval (where Eric Heiden won five gold medals), lulled into an easy rhythm by the sharp scrape of their skates in the crisp night air. A personal favorite, however, is the nighttime toboggan run. As many as six of your entourage can ride together, clutching and yelping, as you shoot down the lighted ramp and spill suddenly out onto the darkness of frozen Mirror Lake with a giddy sense of fear and elation. It's another of those winter sports that had always *looked* or *sounded* like a lot of fun, but which you never quite got around to doing. Like so many other visitors, you'll find yourself running out of excuses at Lake Placid. "Come on," this area seems to beckon, "just do it."

Where to ski

With the greatest vertical drop of any mountain in the East (3,216 feet), Whiteface Mountain has some of the most worthy expert runs this side of the Mississippi. There's also a Medusa's head of excellent advanced and advanced-intermediate runs snaking down the forested slopes of Little Whiteface (a shoulder of the same mountain), and nearly all the bottom third of the mountain is wide-open and gentle—good for lower intermediates.

Like many Eastern mountains, Whiteface stands unshielded, lording it over a vast valley of forests and frozen lakes. That makes for some of the most spectacular views in the world, but winter winds do seem to whip across that valley and climb up the walls of Whiteface with predictable regularity. For many veteran Eastern skiers, the complaint about Whiteface has been that it's too often wind-blown, cold and icy. Having been there three times now, I would say that from my own experience Whiteface is, well, frequently wind-blown, cold and icy. You can't fault any area for unpredictable weather, and on an ideal day Whiteface comes close to being as good as it gets in the East. The local officials have also made a good-faith effort at countering icy slopes with increased snowmaking.

Beginners on Whiteface have a secluded area—off to the right looking up from the base, above Kids Kampus—reserved in their honor. The wide-open runs down to the bottom from the midstation are all suitable for lower intermediates, giving you a free run of half the mountain.

Intermediates should take the G-lift from the midstation up to the top of Little Whiteface. An observation platform just off to the left at the top of this double chair gives you an unparalleled view of the lakes and valley. Then try the snaking Excelsior run, which twists back down to the midstation. You can cut the rounded corners of this baby like a bobsled, choosing your own pace. After that warmup, tackle Paron's Run from the tip-top of Whiteface (Lift F—Summit Triple). Before this run was added four years ago, intermediates had no way to enjoy either the awe-inspiring view or best-in-the-East vertical available from the top of the mountain. Advanced skiers should also not miss the Empire and MacKenzie runs from the top of Little Whiteface. They're officially black, but under good conditions manageable.

Experts will want to spend their time on Cloudspin and Skyward, the men's and women's downhill Olympic runs respectively, at the top of Whiteface. These are sweethearts with plenty of pitch and moguls even for the hotdogs. Most of the runs down from Little Whiteface are also black, and they all have good grade.

Mountain rating

Whiteface is one of those rare mountains that has more to offer experts and beginners, with less in the middle range for true intermediates. Experts will find much of the upper half of the mountain challenging, though anything below the midstation is generally a wide-open cruise with very gentle grade. Beginners will thus find anything below midstation much to their liking. Intermediates will probably feel bored by most of the lower half of the mountain, and stretched by much of the upper. If you are ready to push yourself into the advanced stage, try Little Whiteface.

Cross-country

Here again, the folks at Lake Placid have built strongly on the foundation laid by the 1980 Winter Olympics, and the Mt. Van Hoevenberg complex offers cross-country skiing you are unlikely to find elsewhere—50 km. of marked trails that average 15 ft. wide, regularly groomed and patrolled; bridges built especially for cross-country skiers so you don't have to worry about traffic; snowmaking (5 km.), and emergency phones.

Within the complex are 10 marked loops offering one expert, six intermediate and three novice tours. Additional expert skiing is on the Porter Mountain racing loops. The start/finish stadium at the sports complex also features a ski shop, waxing room, small snack bar and warming room. Trail fees are $10 for adults and $8 for ages 6-12 and 62 and older. Children younger than 6 ski free.

Snowboarding

Snowboarding is permitted on all trails and lifts. Whiteface has lessons and rentals.

Lessons (94/95 prices)

The Whiteface Mountain Ski School has over 75 instructors and is affiliated with the Professional Ski Instructors of America (PSIA). They will tailor instruction to your particular needs, ranging from race packages, ski weeks and individual lessons, to special programs for juniors and children.

Group lessons cost $20 for 90 minutes. Multiple lessons can be purchased at discounts. Ski week packages begin with a wine-and-cheese party, and end with a race and party.

Private lessons are $40 an hour, with $25 for an extra person (limit of two). Discounts are offered on multi-hour lessons.

Race programs are offered through the Whiteface Alpine Training Center, and operated through the New York Ski Educational Foundation (NYSEF). They include electronic timing, bibs and printed results. You have to book at least two weeks in advance, however, by calling the NYSEF at 946-7001. The resort also has a coin-operated race program.

Children's programs include the Play & Ski packages offered at the Kids Kampus (just to the right of the main lodge area). The supervised program for children 4 to 6 includes indoor and outdoor activities, with instruction and nursery services. The drop-off area has adjacent parking. Half-day programs are $20. A full-day program costs $40 (including lunch). Children 6 and younger who can already ski can ride free on Whiteface's three lower lifts. Children's lessons for ages 7 to 12 are $25 half day and $45 a full day, lunch additional. For more about the children's program, 946-2223.

Child care

The Bunny Hutch gives children their own lodge and congregating area on the mountain, complete with a children's drop-off, adjacent parking for parents with children, a large nursery, children's rentals and an outdoor terrain garden.

The nursery is open daily for children aged 1 to 6, and the cost is $4 an hour or $25 per day per child, with lunch extra (supervisors can arrange for a variety of hot meals). Nursery service is offered daily 8 a.m. to 4.30 p.m.

Lift tickets (94/95 prices)

	Adult	Child (7–12)
One day	$37	$15
Three days	$102 ($34/day)	$45 ($15/day)
Five days	$150 ($30/day)	$75 ($15/day)

These are weekend and holiday prices; midweek prices are about $7 per day lower for adults. Children's prices remain the same. Seniors age 65–69 pay $20 any day. Ages 6 and younger and 70 and older ski free.

Early season specials run until just before Christmas, with adults paying $20 per day and juniors $15. In early March prices drop again, to $28 for adults and $15 for children.

Accommodations

Some of the larger hotels centered around the town of Lake Placid tend to be of the more modern franchise variety. Not so, however, the singular **Mirror Lake Inn** (523-2544), a traditional lodge right on the lake shore, and probably the finest overnight in the area. (It's rated Four Diamond by AAA.) The quaint New England-style exterior continues inside with antiques, chandeliers and mahogany walls. The inn also offers such modern amenities as indoor pool, whirlpool, sauna, health spa, and game room. The two restaurants include one of the best in town, with candlelight dining overlooking the lake. Room rates range from $86-$306, the latter for a suite.

The **Holiday Inn Sunspree Resort** (523-2556 or 800-874-1980) in the center of Lake Placid is the largest hotel in town (209 rooms). It features great views over the lake, rooms with refrigerators and microwaves, a large indoor pool with two-story ceiling, a game room for kids, a fitness center, and two restaurants, one of which becomes a nightclub on weekends. Rooms are in the $49 to $99 range; ask about ski packages.

The **Best Western Golden Arrow** (523-3353 or 800-582-5540) is on the lake with spectacular views and has an indoor pool, Jacuzzi, sauna, weight room, and racquetball courts. Room-with-view rates are as low as $60 midweek, and $118-$148 per room on weekends. Also boasting similar amenities is the **Lake Placid Hilton** (523-4411 or 800-755-5598), with two indoor pools and private balconies for each room with a view of the lake. The hotel's bed-and-breakfast package is quite popular, costing $86 for two, midweek. There is also a **Howard Johnson** (523-9555) in town.

The **Lake Placid Lodge** (523-2573, formerly Lake Placid Manor), is a classic Adirondack lodge with rustic rooms, fireplaces and exceptional French-American cuisine. The restaurant is open to the public.

Skiers on a budget should try the **Edge of the Lake Motor Inn** (523-9430), **Town House Motor Inn** (523-2532), **Alpine Air Motel** (523-2180), the **Econo Lodge** (523-2750), and the **Wildwood** on the Lake (523-2750), all of which have rooms for less than $100, some as low as $50.

The nearest RV park is KOA in Wilmington, NY.

Dining

Considered the best restaurant in the area, **Lake Placid Lodge** (523-2573, serves continental cuisine. Also upscale and excellent is the **Hungry Trout** (946-2217), specializing in, you guessed it, fish (entrées $12.95 and up). **The Charcoal Pit** (523-3050), open for about 35 years, charbroils lots of steaks and chops.

Solid German fare is available at slightly more moderate prices at the **Alpine Cellar** (523-2180). A full menu of schnitzels, sauerbraten and rippchen (smoked pork) are available starting around $10.95 per entrée. **Villa Vespa** (523-9959) features authentic Italian fare in the same price category. A personal favorite is the **Artist's Café** (523-9493) which features a prime location overlooking Mirror Lake, as well as steak and fish at reasonable prices: after a chilled dogsled ride on the lake, take a break with a bowl of their excellent onion soup. And no ski town is complete, of course, without an inexpensive Italian restaurant featuring pizza—**Mr. Mike's Pizza** (523-9770) takes care of that craving.

Après-ski/nightlife

Lake Placid is large enough to generate its own heat as a nightlife center, drawing not only the gypsy moths from the out-of-town vacationers, but also the local variety from the surrounding countryside. Because Whiteface lies separated from the town, however, most of the après-ski action is in the base lodge. **Steinhoff's** and **R.J. McDougall's**, just down the road from Whiteface are also good for an après-ski drink.

At night, the young and hot of foot head to **Mud Puddles**, on the side street next to the speed skating oval. High-tech disco gear is on full display around the dance floor. Most of the other nightlife action centers around the main hotels. **Cristy's** at the Holiday Inn features a large bar and even more generous dance floor, with music spun by a DJ (drink specials on Wednesday nights). **Roomers** at the Best Western also offers dancing to a DJ, or for a live band, try **Dancing Bears Lounge** at the Hilton.

Couples looking for a quieter nightspot should head for **The Cottage**, across the street from the Mirror Lake Inn. The fire's always going, and at sunset there's an excellent view of Mirror Lake and the surrounding mountains.

Other activities (94/95 prices)

Lake Placid is nothing *but* other activities. The **bobsled rides** at Mt. Van Hoevenberg Olympic Sports Complex are Tuesday through Sunday, 2-4 p.m., and cost $25 (including commemorative Olympic Bobsled Run pin).

Luge rides are offered on Saturdays and Sundays, 2-3 p.m., and cost $15 (for more information on both, 523-4436).

Tours of the **Olympic Jumping Complex**, with chair lift and elevator ride, cost $6 for adults, $4 for children and seniors.

The **Olympic Speed Skating Oval** is open for public skating 7-9 p.m. daily, and 1-3 p.m. on weekends (523-1655).

Operating hours for the **toboggan run** on Mirror Lake are Wednesday, 7–9 p.m., Friday, 7–10 p.m., Saturday noon–4 p.m. and 7–10 p.m., and Sunday noon–4 p.m. The charge is $3 for adults, $2 for children, and $3 for the toboggan rental.

The **Lake Placid Winter Olympic Museum,** with displays from the 1932 and 1980 Winter Olympics held at Lake Placid, is open Wednesday through Sunday. Admission is $3 for adults, $2 for seniors and $1 for children. Call 523-1655, ext. 226 for more information.

Getting there and getting around

Getting there: Commuter flights from several northeast cities serve Adirondack Airport, 16 miles away on Route 86 in Saranac Lake. Private planes can use Lake Placid Airport.

Trains stop at Westport on the New York City–Montreal line, and then passengers shuttle on a 40-minute ride to Lake Placid (523-4431 for the bus). There are special Amtrak Ski Packages, including rail fare, hotel accommodations, lift tickets and all transfers.

Getting around: It's about a ten-mile drive to both Whiteface (downhill) and Mt. Hoevenberg (cross-country) from the center of Lake Placid. Though regularly scheduled buses exist, it's best to have a car.

From the south, take Exit 24 (Albany) off the New York State Thruway (I-87). Take Northway (still I-87) to Exit 30, follow Route 9 north two miles to Route 73 and continue 28 miles to Lake Placid. From the west, take I-90 (NY State Thruway) to Exit 36 (Syracuse) for I-81. Follow I-81 north to Watertown, then east on Route 3 to Saranac Lake. Then take Route 86 east to Lake Placid.

Information/reservations

Contact the **Lake Placid Commerce and Visitors Bureau,** Lake Placid NY 12946; (800) 447-5224 (44-PLACID) or 523-2445.

The Olympic Regional Development Authority, Olympic Center, Lake Placid NY 12946; 523-1655, 800-462-6236, is the contact for information about the Olympic venues, including the ski area.

Local area code is 518.

Jay Peak, Vermont

Some skiers believe that the farther north they venture, the better the skiing will be. Jay Peak, a mere eight miles from the Canadian border in Vermont, fits that logic.

Ski Jay if you like adventure, spectacular scenery and an international flair. Ski somewhere else if you can't stand a long drive from big cities or you need to be pampered on the slopes.

Jay is a big mountain by Eastern standards, almost 4,000 feet high with a vertical drop of 2,150 feet and a cornucopia of skiing terrain. Jay gets lots of snow—an average of more than 300 inches.

Jay Peak has Vermont's only tram, a 60-passenger vehicle that whisks skiers from the base to the summit. If you are staying at the Hotel Jay, the tram is just outside your room.

Because of Jay's proximity to French-speaking Québec, 52 percent of its skiers hail from Canada and about half of those speak French. Get ready to hear a lot of French.

Where to ski

Jay has a low bed count; thus it is a day tripper's resort, with late-arriving crowds on weekends. Be smart and arrive early; try to catch the 8:30 a.m. tram to the summit. Enjoy the views of four states and Canada (don't forget your camera) and head over to Stateside area on the blue Vermonter trail. At Stateside you can ski some of Jay's most popular trails without any congestion or lift lines. Lines do form at the tram when all the late arrivals queue up, but Jay's trails are seldom congested thanks to being spread out.

The most challenging trails at Jay are mostly here at Stateside and serviced by the Jet Triple chair. The Jet Trail is a black diamond popular with locals. If you need more challenge and spice in your life, try the U.N., a gnarly, narrow, steep son-of-

---

Jay Peak Facts

Base elevation: 1,815'; **Summit elevation:** 3,968'; **Vertical drop:** 2,153 feet
Number and types of lifts: 6—1 tram, 1 quad chair, 1 triple chair,
1 double chair, 2 surface lifts
Acreage: About 325 trail acres **Snowmaking:** 80 percent
Uphill capacity: 7,200 per hour **Bed base:** 800 at resort; another 800 nearby

a-gun with hostile moguls. Catch it with good snow and you'll smile all day; catch it with tough Eastern conditions and you'll head for the base lodge for a couple of shooters. Next to the U.N. is Haynes, a black diamond similar to the Jet, but with more terrain changes at the top and wider and a tad easier at the bottom. Two other blacks off the Jet triple are somewhat similar. Both Derrick Hot Shot and Kitzbühel are New England narrow.

Skiers who want a more mellow descent should opt for the Montrealer connecting with Angel's Wiggle or the Northway. By now the latecomers will have formed a line at the Jet Triple and it's time to head to the Bonaventure chair for some great cruising on the Can Am. Or tackle the black-diamond River Quai under the tram into the milder Interstate to the tram base and perhaps a bite to eat.

If your timing is right, the surge of early lunch skiers will have already ascended the tram and your wait should be short. Your best bet following lunch is to take the Northway to Ullr's Dream, an intermediate trail that becomes a nice glade area halfway down. An alternative is the more difficult Beaver Pond Glade. Don't be surprised at the scarcity of skiers on this flank.

Jay is proud of its tree-skiing opportunities and even posts bilingual warning signs that explain the dangers and rules of skiing in the woods. Management reports that few accidents occur and that skiers love the ski-anywhere policy. Jay added about 30 acres of gladed trails last season.

Mountain rating

Jay is a good choice for intermediate to advanced skiers, particularly with the woods skiing available. The division is 20 percent beginner, 40 percent each intermediate and advanced.

Snowboarding

Jay encourages snowboarding and was one of the first to offer lessons by certified instructors. A halfpipe is featured, a Burton Demo Center and rentals.

Cross-country

Jay Peak has 20 km. of cross-country skiing on the mountain and another 200 km. locally. Telemarking is permitted at Jay and both instruction and rentals are available. A bonus for cross-country skiers at Jay is the vista at nearly every bend in the trail.

Lessons (95/96 prices)

Ski School Director Mickey Doheny and his assistant Dana Kennison have been at Jay for more than 20 years and have assembled a quality group of professionals with a high return rate. On weekends as many as 100 instructors are available for all skiing or snowboarding ability levels. A **private lesson** costs $36 per hour and a two-hour **group lesson** is $20.

Children's instruction starts at age 3. Morning lessons and afternoon activities are $20 for resort lodging guests and $30 for non-guests. Children 5–9 have the SKIwee program for $40 all day and $20 a half day, while youngsters 10–16 have the Mountain Adventure program, which gives them a choice of activities, such as skiing, snowboarding, snow skating and others. Three-day rate is $125; five-day $160, lift ticket extra (94/95 rates for all children's programs).

Child care (95/96 prices)
If you stay at Hotel Jay or the Jay Peak condos, child care for ages 2–7 is included with ski packages. Otherwise, it is $20 a full day, $10 a half day.

Lift tickets (95/96 prices)

	Adult	Child (6–12)
One day	$38	$26
Three days	$102 ($34/day)	$69 ($23/day)
Five days	$155 ($31/day)	$105 ($21/day)

These prices include the tram. Older than 65 and younger than 6 pay $5. Children's prices listed here are 94/95.

Accommodations
The 48-room **Hotel Jay** is convenience itself; it is the center of the base complex and houses guest services and the tram. Packages include lodging, lift tickets, breakfast and dinner, and children younger than 14 stay free. Free child care is offered 9 a.m. to 9 p.m. including supervised dinner for children. Two-day package is $239, per person, double occupancy; three days, $349; five days, $559.

The **Slopeside Condominiums** offer ski-in/out convenience and more space than the Hotel Jay, with equipped kitchens and fireplaces. Packages include lift tickets and lodging, but no meals. Two days, four persons per unit, $219 per person; three days, $289; five days, $419.

The **Black Lantern Inn** (326-4507, 800-255-8661) in Montgomery Village, nine miles from Jay on Route 118, was a stagecoach stop in the early 1800s. It's now a traditional country inn, some suites with whirlpool tub and fireplaces. Rates range from $65 to $85 per person, double occupancy with breakfast and dinner. B&B and no-meals rates also available.

The **Inglenook Lodge** (988-2880) on Route 242 less than a mile from Jay, is an 18-room lodge featuring Norwegian hospitality and the area's only indoor swimming pool. Rates range from $49 to $69 per person double occupancy.

The **Schnee Hutte Inne** (988-4020), also on Route 242 about a mile from the mountain, has a family atmosphere. The inn was remodeled in summer 1995 and the owners added a sauna among other improvements. Package rates for the 13 rooms are $35-$45 per person double occupancy, including a private room, private bath and breakfast. The proprietors also handle the adjacent **Trillium Woods Townhouses,** eight units with hot tub, sauna and fireplace.

The **Jay Village Inn** (988-2643) offers 15 private rooms with private bath in an authentic Vermont country inn. Package rates include a full country breakfast and are $75-$95 per night for a room for two and $90-$115 a night for a three-person room.

Dining/après-ski

Entrées at the **Hotel Jay** dining room include Steak Forestière sautéed with mushrooms and shallots and Pork Tenderloin Madeira. There are daily fresh fish specials.

The **Black Lantern** is known for its moderately priced but extraordinary fare, especially the Lamb Marguerite, which is marinated and broiled. A cozy bar attracts locals and guests.

The Belfry is a converted one-room schoolhouse five miles from the mountain with excellent seafood and inexpensive blackboard-style menus daily. Very casual—locals love it.

On the mountain, **après-ski** frivolities usually begin at the Golden Eagle Lounge in the base lodge, in the Hotel Jay or in the International Dining Room. The Inglenook Lodge usually has a guitar player around the big open hearth area.

Other activities

Shopping: Bogner, the upscale skiwear company, has one of its few factory outlets 20 miles away in Newport. Montgomery, nine miles away, has several shops with regional handicrafts.

Snowcat rides are available every Thursday. trips to a working farm take place on Wednesdays. Bonfire parties and Ski School parties take place at the end of the week. Contact the resort for specifics.

Getting there and getting around

Getting there: Jay Peak, located on Route 242, is approximately 65 miles northeast of Burlington, 90 miles southeast of Montreal and 210 miles north of Boston.

By air: Burlington International Airport has more than 60 daily flights on USAir, Continental, United, and Delta's Business Connection. Van service is available for hotel and condo guests for about $10. By train: Amtrak's Montrealer to St. Albans, Vt. Ground transportation for the 45-minute trip to Jay is available.

Getting around: If you're staying at the Jay Hotel or one of the slopeside condos and have no intention of exploring the area, you can get by without a car; otherwise, bring one.

Information/reservations

Jay Peak Resort: Box 242, Jay, VT 05859; Phone: (800) 451-4449; (802) 988-2611. Note: Canadian dollars are accepted at American face value for lift tickets only.

The local area code is 802.

Killington, Vermont

It's a good idea to carry a trail map at Killington. It is one of the biggest winter resorts in the United States. Superlatives are its specialty, and it claims the biggest, highest, fastest, steepest and largest in various categories as a key component of its marketing strategy. It leads the East, for example, in vertical drop (3,150 feet), lift capacity (36,627 skiers per hour) and longest ski season. (Killington strives to be the first ski area in the country to open—usually aiming for early October—and stays open until late May, sometimes June.) Its 162 trails cover six mountain peaks. Juggernaut, the longest ski trail in the U.S., meanders for 10 miles (granted, it's mostly suited to beginners and cross-country skiers). A mostly intermediate run, called the Four-Mile Trail, drops from Killington Peak to the Skyeship Base Station, down more than 3,000 feet of mellow vertical.

Killington trumpets its size proudly, but it also does so much so well. A vast snowmaking operation is why its season lasts seven months. All-inclusive packages offer some of the best deals in the country, with substantial savings over buying the components individually. Killington also has one of the best central reservations systems, which allows you to book everything from flights to car rental, lodging, child care and ski rental with one call: (800) 372-2007. And that trail map? One of the best, small enough to carry easily, but packed with info, including numbers to call if you lock your keys in your car.

The resort's shining new star is its eight-passenger gondola called Skyeship. Its individual cars are heated and have a closed-circuit radio system. Nice to look at, too—each car has been artfully painted with contemporary designs. Riders can get on and off the Skyeship at a mid-station near the base of the Needle's Eye double chair, but they don't have to. They can board at the base station and get off 12 minutes later at the top of Skye Peak, a rise of 2,520 feet. A note of clarification on our **stats:**

Killington Facts
Base elevation: 1,045'; Summit elevation: 4,195'; Vertical drop: 3,150 feet
Number and types of lifts: 20—2 gondolas, 2 quad superchairs, 5 quad chairs, 4 triple chairs, 5 double chairs, 2 surface lifts
Acreage: 860 trail acres Snowmaking: 64 percent
Uphill capacity: 36,627 skiers per hour Bed base: 4,800 (base), 19,000 (region)

The Skyeship is actually separate lifts, connected by a computerized transfer station. Because the two stages can operate independently, Killington counts them as two lifts (just in case you were wondering where the other gondola is).

Where to ski

The terrain is almost too sprawling to describe and make any sense of it. We'd suggest that you take the Meet the Mountains Tour, which leaves at 9:45 a.m. from the tour sign in front of the Resort Center at Snowshed. Guides will familiarize you with the area, and you'll pick up historical tidbits as you ski. The groups are assembled as much as possible by ability levels.

Killington has six separate base areas. Three of them are clustered within striking distance of the end of Killington Road. Snowshed and Rams Head are across the street from one another, and Killington base is just a bit up the road. Bear Mountain, home of the famed Outer Limits bump run, is on Bear Mountain Road off Route 4. The other two base areas are right off Route 4: the Skyeship Base Station, terminus for the long Juggernaut and Four-Mile trails and the spot to catch Skyeship; and Sunrise Mountain, which has mostly beginner trails.

Never-evers should start at the Snowshed learning area, where four lifts serve a very long, very wide and nicely isolated slope that has an excellent pitch for those just starting out.

The Rams Head double chair covers mainly beginner and intermediate terrain. Vagabond, off to the left of Rams Head chair, is an advanced run connecting with the Snowdon area. The Snowdon area is another cruiser's delight, and is served by two chairs from the base area and a Poma lift serving Bunny Buster, often used by the ski school. Highline and Conclusion are good advanced cruising runs with excellent pitch. Bunny Buster and Chute are similar but with a more mellow slope.

Between Snowdon Mountain and Killington Peak is some of the toughest terrain. The Canyon quad chair services this area for access to double-diamond Cascade, Downdraft, Double Dipper and Big Dipper Glade.

Skye Peak, where Killington added new terrain last season, has proved to be one of the most popular sections of the mountain. Experts and advanced intermediates can play on Ovation, Superstar and Skye Lark.

From the top of Skye Peak advanced skiers can drop down Skye Burst by following the Skye Peak quad. This connection is not recommended for lower intermediates because it leads to the Bear Mountain quad, which services good advanced and expert terrain. From the top of the Bear Mountain quad, skiers can descend Devil's Fiddle or loop in the opposite direction down Wildfire. For bumpers the real thrill is to drop directly under the chair lift and challenge Outer Limits.

Upon returning from Bear Mountain over to Skye Peak, intermediates may want to try the Needle's Eye, which drops beneath the second section of the Skyeship. A trip back up the Needle's Eye will put skiers back on Skye Lark or Bittersweet for a smooth cruise to the Killington Base Lodge or to Snowshed.

Beginner trails lead from all six interconnected peaks, which allows starting skiers the panoramic vistas and thrill of skiing from the summit, not possible at most areas where the upper-mountain trails are reserved for seasoned skiers.

Mountain rating

Overall, Killington rates as an excellent choice for beginner and intermediate. Advanced skiers will have a lot of fun in select areas such as Skye Peak, Bear Mountain and Killington Peak. Though experts will find no extreme skiing, they can find trails that will test them.

Cross country

Mountain Meadows Ski Touring (775-7077) has 40 km. of trails that meander across Kent Lake and through the surrounding forests. **Mountain Top Cross Country Ski Resort** (483-2311) in nearby Chittenden has 110 km. of trails; 40 km. of dual-set tracks and 2.5 km. of trails with snowmaking.

Both areas have rentals, lessons, ski shop and warming hut, and Mountain Top offers sledding and horse-drawn sleigh rides.

Trailhead Ski Touring Center in Stockbridge (746-8038) offers 60 km. of trails, with 35 km. groomed and 35 km. tracked. In Woodstock, the **Ski Touring Center** (457-2114) has 75 km. of trails, with 58 km. of groomed trails and 50 km. of tracked.

Snowboarding

Boarding is allowed on all sections of Killington. Lessons and rentals are available at Snowshed and Killington base lodges. Killington hosts a snowboard mogul contest on Outer Limits in the spring, and has a halfpipe and snowboard park.

Lessons (94/95 prices)

The Killington Ski School has several innovative systems: Mountain Training Stations have specially contoured snow and a ski drill set up at each one to improve certain skills, such as weight distribution and short-radius turns. As you progress from station to station, you actually teach yourself, based on the changing character of the snow. An instructor is available to coach students over the terrain. These stations are an integral part of the Killington learning method.

Learners have many alternatives, such as ski weeks, daily classes, individual lessons, advanced workshops, racing clinics and video workshops. For the ski week packages, ask a representative at central reservations to send a brochure.

Group lessons cost $23 per person. **Private lessons** cost $60 an hour; each additional person is $27. Two hours of private instruction cost $115 for one and $142 for two to five students. The full day costs $290 for one and $345 for two to five students.

For **children**, Superstars programs provide a full day of instruction, with lunch, for kids 6 to 12 years. The cost is $76 a day with lunch and $91 with lunch and rentals. The two-day program is $137, $153 with rentals. A five-day program costs $302, $342 with rentals.

Call the Killington Lodging Bureau at (802) 773-1330 to make reservations.

Child care (94/95 prices)

The Children's Center is located in the Snowshed Lodge. Killington takes children from 6 weeks to 12 years in the day-care program. The center is fully licensed.

Day care costs $45 per day and $30 per half day. Two-day rates: $56 for half days (no lunch), $85 for full days with lunch; $120 for five half-days, $180 for five full days.

First Tracks is an introduction to skiing program for children 3 to 5, which consists of two one-hour lessons in the terrain garden, rental equipment and snacks. The program costs $60 for a full day and $40 for a half day. Two-day weekend rates are $75 for half days (no lunch) and $112 for full days with lunch. The five-day program is $158 for half days, $236 for full days.

Reservations are required for the children's center. Call 422-6222. All-day programs run from 8 a.m. to 4 p.m. Add $5 for lunch to half-day programs. Parents must supply food and beverage for children 23 months and younger.

Lift tickets (94/95 prices)

	Adult	Child (6–12) Senior (65+)
One day	$46	$26
Two days	$81 ($40.50/day)	$40 ($20/day)
Five days	$180 ($36/day)	$90 ($18/day)

Lift ticket prices are normally packaged with lodging and lessons. Half-day and seven-day tickets also are available. Children 5 and younger ski free on Snowshed slope with a paying adult. These free tickets are available at the ski vacation center.

Accommodations (94/95 rates)

Killington has no quaint village. Killington Road is lined with hotels, restaurants, ski shops and discos from Route 4 to the main condominium complexes. None of the accommodations on the road are particularly luxurious—some are just the opposite. Consequently, Killington could never lay claim to being Vermont's best in the lodging department. If you're looking for a bargain, call the Killington Lodging Bureau and describe exactly what you want. The tradeoff is usually a longer distance to the lifts. You may make reservations for all these properties by calling (800) 372-2007. In general, two-night rates listed here are valid on weekends, while five-night rates are Sunday through Thursday. Call for specific rate information.

The top hotel on the mountain road at Killington is **The Inn of the Six Mountains** (800-228-4676 or 802-422-4302), with a 65-foot indoor lap pool, exercise room and frequent shuttles to the slopes. Rates for the five-day, five-night plan start about $280 per person, double occupancy, breakfast included.

Killington Village has good values and it may have the best location, with nearby athletic club facilities, some nightlife and an excellent shuttlebus system. Of the Village condominiums, the **Highridge** units are by far the most desirable. Other good choices are the **Sunrise** condos at the base of Bear Mountain and **The Woods at Killington**, which boasts private Jacuzzis and saunas, and a shuttle to the Snowshed Base.

Both the **Mountain Inn** and the **Cascades Lodge** are very convenient but they are also basic. The Cascades does have a nice indoor pool and the Mountain Inn has some of the best nightlife when the bar is hopping.

The Cortina Inn (773-3333), on Route 4 just past the Pico ski area, is perhaps the top upscale hotel in the area. It has a health club, pool, spa, two restaurants, children's activities on holiday weekends, and many large suites. Rates, per person double occupancy with breakfast: three nights, $177; five nights, $295.

The Vermont Inn (800-541-7795 or 775-0708), with 18 rooms and fireside dining, everything homemade, is a charming New England country inn. Breakfast and dinner are included in the rates. Costs for two people are $220 to $300 for two nights, and $450 to $650 for five nights. Fireplace rooms are available; ask for rates on those.

The Red Clover Inn (800-752-0571 or 802-775-2290) is five miles from Killington Road on 13 acres. This farmhouse estate has private baths, country decor and handmade quilts in each room. Room rates, including breakfast and dinner for two with entrées such as penne pasta and breast of Vermont pheasant, are $165-$250 on winter weekends, less midweek.

Another favorite is **The Summit Lodge** (422-3535). The food is excellent, the casual and friendly atmosphere infectious and the staff helpful. Double-occupancy rates, per person, with breakfast and dinner, are about $350 for five nights.

Of the other properties on Killington Road, **The Red Rob**, **Killington Village Inn** and **Chalet Killington** rate in that order. The food is reportedly best at the Red Rob, and both the Killington Village Inn and the Chalet offer a casual atmosphere. Rates include breakfast at the Red Rob and Chalet, and breakfast and dinner at the Killington Village Inn.

Near the base of the Killington Road is the **North Star Lodge** (422-4040), which has a pool and shuttle service, and is surrounded by good restaurants. Rates per person, double occupancy, no meals, are about $150 for three nights, $195 for five nights.

The Grey Bonnet (775-2537) on Route 100 north received numerous recommendations. There is a nice indoor pool, sauna and pub. Room with breakfast and dinner costs about $280 per person for five nights. You will need your car to get to the ski area.

To find real luxury make reservations at the **Woodstock Inn and Resort** in Woodstock, about 17 miles east of Killington. Rooms are cozy and beautifully decorated, with hand-stitched quilts on each bed. The dining room wine list has 184 selections, both foreign and domestic. Midweek, the inn has a very attractive package with downhill skiing at nearby Suicide Six or cross-country skiing at the Woodstock Ski Touring Center. Call (800) 448-7900.

Dining

The Killington area has more than 60 restaurants. The best in the area—ranked among the top in the nation by *Food and Wine* and *Condé Nast Traveler*—is **Hemingway's** (422-3886).

Our favorites are **The Summit** (422-3535, reservations suggested), an award-winning restaurant with a menu that changes nightly and a great wine list; **Jason's** (422-3303, reservations suggested) in the Red Rob for excellent Northern Italian food; the **Cortina** (773-3333) has excellent New England fare; and **The Vermont Inn** (800-541-7795 or 775-0708) has won awards for its fine formal dining. We haven't tried it personally, but the **Red Clover Inn**'s (775-2290) gourmet menu changes nightly and sounds delicious. **Churchill's House of Beef and Seafood** on Route 4 between Killington and Rutland is worth the drive for great food and an extensive wine list.

Claude's and **Choices** (422-4030) on the Killington Road were recommended by more than half-a-dozen locals. They are both in the same building and owned by the same chef. Claude's is the more elegant with entrées that include escargots, scallops and beef Wellington.

For restaurants a bit kinder to the budget: the **Wobbly Barn** is known for steaks and a great salad bar (no reservations); **Mrs. Brady's** and **The Grist Mill** are consistent; **Charity's** has specials every night for those hanging out after happy hour; and **The Back Behind Saloon** is inexpensive and getting more popular every year. All except the Back Behind Saloon are on the Killington Road—you'll find the saloon at the junction of Routes 4 and 100 at the foot of the Northeast Passage. .

Après-ski/nightlife

Immediate après-ski action can be found in **Charity's**. The **Nightspot** features a happy hour as well. It is a favorite locals' hangout on weekdays, with entertainment and dancing tourists extending into the evening on weekends. Après-ski at the mountain includes the Killington **Base Lodge** and the Snowshed **Pogonips**.

The **Pickle Barrel** has a lively happy hour with dancing later in the evening and is frequented by a young college crowd. **The Grist Mill** has karaoke music and more dancing tourists, this time singing as well. **Casey's Caboose** is a favorite locals' haunt with killer spicy buffalo wings. An older, quieter set meets at the **Summit** for happy hour.

For rowdy après-ski and then dancing to loud music, head to the **Wobbly Barn**. When the bar at the **Mountain Inn** has live entertainment, it's great fun.

Other activities

Shopping: In Killington, stop at the **Greenbrier Gift Shop** for handcrafted items and gourmet ware. Woodstock, about 17 miles east of Killington on Route 4, is one of Vermont's most beautiful villages and packed with art galleries and shops. Nearby Bridgewater has an outlet mall with about 60 stores.

The **Killington Village Health Spa** has a complete fitness center, pool, racquetball courts, steam rooms and Jacuzzis. Call 422-9370. An **outdoor skating rink** is below the Summit Lodge on the Killington Road. **Snowmobiling** is available in Rutland and Killington; call the Cortina Inn, 773-3333, or Killington Snowmobile Tours, 422-2121.

Getting there and getting around

Getting there: Killington is at the intersection of Routes 4 and 100 in central Vermont near the city of Rutland, about three hours from Boston and about 90 minutes south of Burlington. Green Mountain Limousine Service (773-1313) runs transfers from Burlington for $50 per person round-trip, and meets most flights. Thrifty Rental Cars has an office at the Inn of the Six Mountains.

Getting around: Bring or rent a car. Though you may not use it between your lodging and the slopes, Killington is very spread out, and you may want to visit one of the attractions nearby.

Information/reservations

For all information, reservations, and ski packages call (800) 372-2007. Killington and American Express co-produce an excellent pocket-sized guidebook; ask for a copy. Snow phone: 422-3261.

The local area code is 802.

Mount Snow/Haystack Vermont

Mount Snow/Haystack has the snowmaking efficiency of Killington, is closer to major cities than Stratton, and has just as careful grooming, but somehow this resort has remained about as down-home, folksy and unpretentious as all Vermont resorts should be. Thank heaven someone has kept a New England feel to the entire area. West Dover and Wilmington are true Vermont villages, without boutique-filled commercialism.

With the addition of Haystack Mountain a couple of seasons ago, Mount Snow now has 130 trails and 24 lifts—more than any area in the East. The two mountains are not interconnected by lifts, but a shuttlebus plies the route between the two bases.

Mount Snow works about as perfectly as any area in the country at making snow and moving skiers around on the mountain. It also has 86 trails, and quite uncharacteristic of New England, they are about 100 yards wide. As you look up at the mountain, the terrain is almost perfectly divided from right to left into expert, intermediate and beginner sections. Snowmaking blankets more than 80 percent of the mountain, providing snow from November through early May. Haystack has 1,400 vertical feet with 44 trails and six lifts.

Mount Snow's accommodations are in condos and lodges clustered at the base of the mountain, with more lodging within 10 miles of the resort. Though the mountain base has no village complex, West Dover (three miles) and Wilmington (nine miles) are traditionally quaint Vermont towns with shops, and white-steepled churches.

Where to ski

Just about any level of skier can ski Mount Snow anywhere. Solid intermediates can head to the North Face area, which is a

---

Mount Snow/Haystack Facts
Base elevation: 1,900'; Summit elevation: 3,600'; Vertical drop: 1,700 feet
Number of lifts: 24—1 quad superchair, 1 quad chair, 9 triple chairs,
10 double chairs, 3 surface lifts
Snowmaking: 83.5 percent   Trail acreage: 750 acres
Uphill capacity: 33,830 per hour   Bed Base: 12,000

grouping of isolated steeper runs, some of which are left to bump up. All the runs covering the face of the mountain and dropping to the village area are great cruisers. The names give you an idea of what to expect—Ego Alley, Sundance and Snowdance. This is the perfect place to dance on the snow.

The Sunbrook area, which catches the sun, is an ideal spot for lower intermediates. Beartrap, the one advanced trail in Sunbrook, with its south-facing exposure and snowmaking, is a haven for bump skiers. The resort pumps rock 'n' roll music from lift-tower speakers.

To the far south of the resort is Carinthia, which offers long mellow runs for advanced beginners, lower intermediates and those who want to have a playful cruise. There are enough zigs, zags and small drops to keep a skier awake.

Haystack's upper mountain has intermediate terrain. Advanced skiers and snowboarders should head for the Witches area. The lower mountain, segregated from the upper trails, is great for beginners.

Mountain rating

The emphasis is definitely on the intermediate. Advanced skiers and boarders can try some of relatively tough runs on the North Face of the resort, but if you are an expert, don't come out of your way to ski them—they're not that tough. Beginners and never-evers, get ready to improve—this mountain has just your kind of terrain.

Snowboarding

Snowboarding is allowed on both mountains. Mount Snow has a snowboard park, Un Blanco Gulch, located on the Canyon Trail, featuring side hits, a halfpipe, spines and plenty of jumps. Lessons are available through the ski school. Rentals are available at the Mount Snow Rental Shop and Cupola Ski Shop in West Dover.

Cross-country

Four major ski touring centers are near Mount Snow. The largest is **Hermitage Cross-Country Touring Center** (464-3511) on Coldbrook Road in Wilmington with 50 km. of trails that form a circle from the warming hut out to Mount Snow and back. **Sitzmark Ski Touring Center** (464-5498), **Timber Creek** (464-0999) and the **White House Touring Center** (464-2135) are others offering more than 60 km. of trails skewed toward the intermediate Nordic skier.

Lessons (94/95 prices)

Group lessons at Mount Snow take the form of 90-minute workshops for intermediates and advanced skiers called EXpress Customized Learning (EXCL). Each workshop has a maximum of six students and concentrates on two or three tips to help you improve. EXCL workshops are $23 ($25 on holidays). The price per lesson goes down the more lessons you take. Never-evers and beginners take traditional two-hour class lessons at the same price.

A two-hour **introduction to skiing** program is $45 including beginner lifts and equipment.

Private instruction costs $55 an hour for one student; additional students pay $30.

Children have the SKIwee program for ages 4–12, which offers a six-hour daily lesson including lunch for $77 for one day, $131 for two days, $187 for three days and $210 for five days.

Mount Snow has an unusual twist to children's skiing: Teddy Bear Weeks, four weeks of the season when children 12 and younger ski free for the week if they bring along a teddy bear. The activities include a forest safety talk by Smokey Bear, rides on a snow-grooming machine, a teddy bear ski race and an après-ski ice cream party. (Good luck getting your 11-year-old to take a teddy bear so you can save money on the lift ticket.)

Child care

The Mount Snow Child Care Center is one of New England's largest day-care centers. It provides care for children from 6 weeks to 8 years. There are separate rooms for infants and toddlers. Reservations are required; call 464-8501 or (800) 245-7669. Prices are $53 all day with lunch, or $232 for five days.

Lift tickets (94/95 prices)

	Adult	Child (Up to 12) Senior (65+)
One day	$45	$27
Three days	$110 ($36.66/day)	$59 ($19.66/day)
Five days	$175 ($35/day)	$90 ($18/day)*

*Children ski free when their parents purchase a five- to seven-day vacation package and when they are enrolled in SKIwee.

Adults ski for $40 midweek (except during holidays). Mount Snow has a discount card for college students called Extra Credit that allows for $27 lift tickets Sunday through Friday at Mount Snow, any day at Haystack. Call for details.

Those with full-price Mount Snow multiday tickets can ski at any of its sister resorts: Killington, Bromley, Waterville Valley or Sugarloaf. Multiday tickets also are valid at Haystack. Tickets to ski Haystack alone are $38 for adults on weekends, $29 midweek and $24 for juniors and seniors, $20 midweek.

Accommodations (94/95 prices)

At the base of the mountain are a group of condo projects and a luxury lodge that have shuttle service to the slopes. Most of the other accommodations line Route 100 between the slopes and the town of Wilmington, with some tucked on side roads back into the foothills.

All rates listed here are per person, non-holiday, based on double occupancy. The five-day Ski Week rate is Sunday through Thursday.

The Inn at Sawmill Farm, on Route 100 in West Dover, 464-8131. One of the nation's top country inns, it is in a class by itself. Entry is through a portion of the former barn. The rooms are spacious and feature dressing rooms off the baths. Small fireplace cottages have a sitting room and bedroom. The inn's sitting room provides a panoramic view, and the dining room serves some of the best meals in the valley.

The atmosphere is quite formal, with men required to wear jackets in the public areas and restaurant after 6 p.m. Children younger than 10 are not allowed. Weekend rates: doubles $270 including breakfast and dinner for two; cottages $290 including breakfast and dinner for two. The Inn at Sawmill Farm does not take credit cards.

Snow Lake Lodge, (800) 451-4211, or 464-7788. This sprawling 92-room mountain lodge is at the base of the main skiing area and has recently been renovated. The lodge has a fitness center, sauna, indoor hot tub, outdoor Jacuzzi, and après-ski entertainment each evening. The Sundance lift is 300 yards away or skiers can ride the free shuttle. The Snow Lake Lodge is excellent with children as well. Rates include breakfast and dinner. Two-day weekend, $165; five-day ski week, $273.

Andirons Lodge, Route 100, West Dover; 464-2114, or (800) 445-7669. This lodge is just two miles from the lifts. These are simple paneled rooms with double beds; some have additional twin beds. There is an indoor pool, a sauna and game room. The attached Dover Forge restaurant serves affordable meals. Rates: two-day weekend package, $92; five-day package, $148.

Matterhorn of Dover, on Route 100, West Dover, 464-8011 or (800) 497-1085. This has been lodging skiers for more than 20 years. The lobby has a two-story stone fireplace and the rooms are simple paneled rooms with cable TV, most with two double beds. Rates include breakfast and dinner. Two-day weekend, $118; five-day ski week, $199.

Nordic Hills Lodge, 179 Coldbrook Road, Wilmington; 464-5130 or (800) 326-5130. All rooms have cable TV. Rates include breakfast and dinner. Two-day weekend is $121; five-day ski week is $209.

Gray Ghost Inn, on Route 100, West Dover; 464-2474 or (800) 745-3615. This large country inn is operated by a British couple who have decorated some rooms with a country touch and others with mountain wood paneling. Many rooms have smaller or bunk beds for children. Rates include breakfast. Two-day weekend, $94; five-day ski week, $150.

Trail's End, Smith Road, Wilmington; 464-2727 or (800) 859-2585. This inn has 15 country-style rooms. Meals are served family style at three round tables, so that means visitors will probably return home with new friends. Rates include breakfast. Two-day weekend, $110; five-day ski week, $220.

Old Red Mill, Route 100 in the town of Wilmington about 15 minutes from the slopes; 464-3700 or (800) 843-8483. This inn, created from a former sawmill, is one of the bargains in the region. The rooms are small, most only about 7 by 12 feet with a double bed, toilet and shower, but all have TV. Larger rooms are available for families. The common areas, bar and dining rooms are rustic Vermont. Rates: two-day weekend, $80 room only; five-day ski week, $99.

Horizon Inn, 464-2131 or (800) 336-5513, Route 9 in Wilmington has an indoor heated pool, whirlpool, sauna and game room. The two-day weekend is $85 and five-day ski week, $108. No meals, but a bargain any way you look at it.

Best Western—The Lodge at Mount Snow, (800) 451-4289 or 464-5112, at the base of Mount Snow, has two-day weekend rates of $132; five-day ski package is $199, both with breakfast and dinner. Kids 12 and under stay and eat free midweek, excluding holidays.

Bed & Breakfasts

Mount Snow also has a group of charming and elegant bed and breakfast establishments. These B&Bs are smaller, most with fewer than 15 rooms.

The Doveberry Inn, on Route 100, West Dover; 464-5652 or (800) 722-3204. This eight-room inn was taken over about a year ago by Michael and Christine Fayette, both culinary-school-trained chefs. No children younger than 8 permitted. Per-person two-day weekend B&B is $110; five-day ski week is $225 with breakfast.

West Dover Inn, Route 100, West Dover; 464-5207 or (800) 732-0745. A historic country inn built in 1846 with 12 elegant rooms furnished with antiques, hand-sewn quilts, and color TVs. There are also two suites with fireplaces and whirlpool tubs. B&B rates: two-day weekend is $110; five-day ski week is $193.

The Red Shutter Inn, Route 9, Wilmington; 464-3768 or (800) 845-7548. This 1894 country home has been converted into an elegant country inn. There are only nine guestrooms. B&B rates: two-day weekend $95; five-day ski week is $190.

The Nutmeg Inn, Route 9W, Wilmington; 464-3351. Built in a 1770s home and decorated with country accents and quilts, this B&B has ten rooms and three fireplace suites. B&B rates: two-day weekend is $105; five-day ski week is $220.

The White House of Wilmington, Route 9, Wilmington; 464-2135. This is an upscale 23-room inn serving breakfast and dinner. Rates: two-day weekend is $198; five-day ski week, $445. Prices include breakfast and dinner; breakfast only packages also available.

Condominiums

Condo rates are per person, based on four people in a two-bedroom, two-bath unit, unless noted.

The Mount Snow Condominiums, 464-7788 or (800) 451-4211, are at the base of the lifts; only the Seasons complex is actually ski-in/ski-out and is the most highly recommended. These condos have an athletic center with indoor pools, saunas and hot tubs. A two-night weekend starts at $123; a five-day ski week runs $125. The Seasons complex prices are slightly higher.

Timber Creek Townhomes, 464-1222 or (800) 982-8922, are luxury condos located across Route 100 from the ski area. They have a fitness center and 18 km. of cross-country trails just outside. Shuttlebuses run between the complex and the ski area. The two-day weekend rate is $169; the five-day ski week costs $219.

Greenspring at Mount Snow, (800) 247-7833 or 464-7111, are upscale condos a mile from the slopes. This complex has the best athletic center in the area. Two-day weekend rate is $142; the five-day ski week costs $154.

Mount Snow has several packages that include lodging and skiing. For a **complete vacation planner** with descriptions of most area properties, write: Mount Snow, 105 Mountain Road, Mount Snow, Vermont 05356, or call (800) 245-7669 (245-SNOW).

Dining

The top dining experience (and the most expensive) is the **Inn at Sawmill Farm** (464-1130) which has 21,000 bottles in its wine cellar and gourmet continental dining with appetizers ranging from $6 to $14, entrées $22 to $30. As noted above, dining here is formal and jackets are required on all male guests (if you didn't bring one they do have a selection of blue blazers you can borrow). No credit cards accepted.

The Hermitage (464-3511) serves excellent meals at less stratospheric prices. This country inn has a very large dining room with some tables surrounded by overstuffed chairs. The walls are covered with the world's largest collection of hanging Delacroix prints. The wine cellar claims 40,000 bottles of 2,000 different labels. All game birds and venison are raised on the premises and jams, jellies and maple syrup are homemade. Entrées run from $14 to $25.

For other fine dining try **Betty Hillman's Le Petit Chef** (464-8437), **Two Tannery Road** (464-2707), and **Capstones** (464-5207), adjacent to the West Dover Inn. **Doveberry Restaurant** (464-5652) is small and intimate with husband-

and-wife chefs, culinary school graduates who have worked in Nantucket and San Francisco. The menu is Northern Italian.

The Deerhill Inn and Restaurant, (800) 626-5674 or 464-3100, on Valley View Road in West Dover features American cuisine. One dining room has a mountain view, the other a fireplace.

Fennessey's Parlor (464-9361) according to locals serves up consistently good food at reasonable prices. Decor is turn of the century.

For economical eats, try **Poncho's Wreck** (464-9320) with an eclectic dining room serving Mexican food, steaks, lobsters and fresh fish. Poncho's is a local institution. **B.A.'s Red Anchor** (464-5616), under the same ownership, serves its famous ribs and seafood specialties.

The Vermont House (464-9360) on Wilmington's main street, serves good food for cheap prices and is one of the locals' favorites. **Deacon's Den** (464-9361) is a good place for pizza, burgers and sandwiches right after skiing. **TC's Tavern** (464-9316) serves up good Italian food. **Giuseppe's** (464-2022) across from Poncho's in Wilmington cooks the best pizza in town. And for sandwiches and deli fare try **Julie's Cafe** (formerly Elsa's; 464-8624) on Route 100 in West Dover.

Après-ski/nightlife

Après-ski conversation opener: Did you know that Mount Snow was named for Reuben Snow, a farmer who used to own the land where the resort now sits?

Now that you know that, try it out at the **Cuzzins** at the Mount Snow main base lodge, where Bruce Jacques and the Invisible Band get the crowd jumping between 3 and 7 p.m. each Friday and Saturday. (Cuzzins is fairly rowdy on other days as well.) If you prefer something quieter, try **Snow Lake Lodge.**

At night, the hot spots are **Snow Barn** on Mount Snow, or **Deacon's Den,** both with live music and dancing. For a quiet drink, head for any of the finer restaurants listed in the dining section.

Every Saturday is Club Sundown for teens and young adults to age 20. A DJ spins the hot hits from 8 p.m. to midnight in the Carinthia base lodge. There is a nominal admission charge.

Other activities

Shopping: Though Wilmington has a few quaint shops, this is not a major activity at Mount Snow.

Adams Farm (464-3762), on Route 100 about five miles south of Mount Snow, is the place for horse-drawn sleigh rides. The farm has its own trail system with an old cabin where you stop for hot chocolate.

For snowmobiling, try High Country Snowmobile Tours (464-2108). Mount Snow has an ice skating rink for day and evening skating, and the Carinthia bunny slope is lit at night for sledding. You hike to the top and it's BYOS, though you may also use inner tubes and toboggans.

Getting there and getting around

Getting there: Mount Snow is the closest major Vermont ski resort to New York and Boston. It is on Route 100, nine miles north of Wilmington. Mileage from major cities: Boston, 127; New York, 213; Albany, 68.

The closest airports are Albany and Hartford's Bradley International, both about a 90-minute drive.

Getting around: Bring a car. If you stay close to the mountain, you won't need it during the day (shuttlebuses take you to and from the lifts), but you will want it at night.

Information/reservations

Contact the **Mount Snow Vacation Services** for one-stop reservations for everything from airline tickets to car rentals and lifts—(800) 245-7669 (245-SNOW).

For snow conditions, call 464-2151.

Local area code is 802.

Okemo Mountain, Vermont

Okemo Mountain deserves accolades for the greatest makeover of an under-utilized mountain and almost forgotten ski town. At one time Okemo had long, long surface lifts that often lifted skiers above the snow's surface. Today, however, Okemo proudly boasts 12 new lifts in as many years, including two comfortable high-speed quads. Okemo's natural terrain has been enhanced to provide entertainment and joy for all levels of skiers. Its commitment to improvements have given it 13 consecutive record seasons and garnered high rankings in several ski publications for snowmaking, grooming and customer service. Early and late each season, skiers remark how great the conditions are at Okemo, even when other eastern ski areas are struggling to put out a decent snow product. This is the key to Okemo's success.

Okemo will continue improving in 1995-96 with another increase in snowmaking capacity, and the start of a five-year construction on a new area called the Solitude Village Area. Located at the base of the Solitude Express quad, this will include a new chair lift serving four new trails; a development of condos, homes and townhouses, and a day lodge. Okemo last season added several new trails in the South Face area, mostly for upper-level skiers. It also introduced a teen lift ticket price that is between adult and child prices.

Where to ski

The trails are all very accessible and the lifts flow skiers conveniently around the mountain. Two quads rise from the base lodge to provide gentle skiing and access to the NASTAR Trail and to several clusters of condos and townhouses slopeside. There can be a slight logjam at these two lifts, but once up on the mountain, you can ski to a triple chair or two other quads that access the upper trails.

The Northstar Express high-speed quad draws the biggest crowd, but moves skiers up-mountain in a hurry. A less crowded

---

Okemo Facts

Base elevation: 1,150'; **Summit elevation:** 3,300'; **Vertical drop:** 2,150 feet **Number of lifts:** 12–2 quad superchairs, 5 quads, 3 triple chairs, 2 surface lifts **Snowmaking:** 95 percent **Total acreage:** 450 skiable acres **Uphill capacity:** 21,900 per hour option is to ski down another 100 yards to the seldom used Sachem quad, which serves as a good tune-up run down Ledges, a wide black-diamond mogul trail that can be skied by most upper intermediates. For a gentler descent, take the Upper and Lower Sachem or Easy Street.

Another ride on the Sachem chair allows a check on the Glades Summit quad chair. Occasionally it does not operate because of strong winds, but when it is running, prepare for a treat. Rimrock is a fine black-diamond run that is wide and varied in terrain. You can cruise it flat-out or enjoy the many subtle terrain changes characteristic of old Vermont trails. The only true double-black trails on the mountain are off this lift: Outrage and Double Black Diamond. Both are gladed, not particularly precipitous, but enjoyable and challenging with proper snow conditions. Two short trails off this lift, Triplesec and Challenger, add variety and usually have good snow cover.

Easily the most popular trail is World Cup, reasonably wide, constantly undulating and sheer pleasure. The Chief is one of Okemo's venerable runs. Still popular, it usually has more moguls than World Cup. The Chief, as most Okemo trails, is divided into upper and lower sections, with the lower part usually less challenging.

In the new South Face area, Wild Thing has lots of moguls. Advanced skiers also will enjoy steep Blind Faith and Punch Line. Dream Weaver is more than 6,000 feet long and offers nice intermediate cruising.

The Black Ridge triple chair often has short lines and great snow, because most skiers use the longer trails. Black Out and Sel's Choice are fine black-diamond trails and the Lower Wardance is a good race trail. The Green Ridge triple and the Solitude Peak high-speed chair have many runs for lower intermediates, especially Easy Rider, Heaven's Gate and Timberline.

Mountain rating

If there is a knock on Okemo it comes from the super-expert skiers who need more steeps and challenge than the resort has to offer. Experts enjoy Okemo at high speeds, intermediates and advanced skiers enjoy it at any speed, and beginners find that the great snow conditions help them advance more quickly.

Snowboarding

Okemo has a large snowboarding community not confined to the young and restless. Grey-haired ski patrollers and instructors foster a pro-boarding attitude. At the bottom of Sel's Choice are a snowboard halfpipe and park, off-limits to skiers. Boards, gear and rentals are available on the mountain, at the board center in Ludlow at Sport Odyssey and at Northern Ski Works. An Introduction To Snowboarding package is $50 for adults and $40 for juniors. It includes a beginner group lesson, rental equipment, and the use of Okemo's three lower-mountain lifts for the full day.

Cross-country

Fox Run Resort, just across from the Okemo entrance, has fine facilities with 32 km. of trails and a rental and repair shop.

Lessons (95/96 prices)

Okemo's ski school has become recognized as a leader in ski teaching and varied programs for all ability levels. Its director heads the children's committee of the Professional Ski Instructors of America and her involvement is reflected in the high marks accorded the SKIwee program at Okemo for kids 4–8 years old. The Young Mountain Explorers half- or full-day programs are available for children 8–12.

Okemo has several adult **specialized courses**. The Bump Series is offered on Sundays at 2 p.m. for competent skiers who would like to be more proficient in the bumps.

Women's Ski Spree is a five-day indulgence for women of all ability levels. Jennifer Speck supervises this program that includes three hours of daily instruction, a welcome party breakfast and lunch daily, guest speakers, video analysis, a farewell banquet and all female instructors. The cost is $475 for the five-day program, $325 for the three-day course, and $199 for a series of six Sunday lessons.

Group lessons start at $25 a day with discounts for multiday lessons and **private lessons** are $55 per hour with additional hours costing $35 and each additional skier charged $30 per hour.

Young Mountain Explorers ages 7–12 have supervised lesson programs for $63 a day or $25 for a half day with discounts for additional days.

Child care

Okemo provides child care for ages 6 weeks to 8 years. Kids 4 and older get an introduction to skiing through the SKIwee program and the use of mini-terrain gardens adjacent to the base lodge. You can peek in on your little one when you stop for lunch. Reservations for children's programs are recommended.

SKIwee pricing is $60 for a full day with lunch, $40 for a half day, $110 for two consecutive days, and $250 for five days.

Okemo has a unique Parent and Tot private lesson program for a parent and a child under 6. The cost is $65 per hour

Lift tickets (95/96 prices)

	Adult	Child (7–12)
One day (94/95)	$45	$28
Three days	$123 ($41/day)	$78 ($26/day)
Five days	$198 ($39.60/day)	$125 ($25/day)

Midweek adult prices (94/95) are $42; children, $25. Okemo also has teen prices for ages 13-18, which are $38 weekends, $35 midweek, $102 for three days and $165 for five days. Seniors 65 and over ski for child rates. Children 6 and younger ski free, and the beginner lift is free for all ages.

Accommodations

Okemo has many slopeside condos and townhouses. Per-person rates vary widely depending on proximity to the slopes and size, but a range would be $120-$185, off-mountain, to $210-$360 slopeside for a five-night ski week with breakfast and dinner included. The Okemo/Ludlow area, which includes Weston, Plymouth and Proctorsville, has 23 country inns, 16 bed-and-breakfast facilities, and 10 motels.

The **Castle Inn** on Route 131 in Proctorsville is an eye-catching edifice, having served as the Governor's mansion in days gone by. Weekend daily rate per room, double occupancy, breakfast and dinner, is about $180. The dining is truly gourmet and the 11 rooms quite elegant. Call 226-7222 for reservations.

The **Echo Lake Inn,** north on Route 100, is a charming New England inn with weekend rates of $110-$140 including breakfast and dinner or $90-$120 with breakfast. Presidents Coolidge and McKinley were guests here and the Coolidge family grounds are nearby. Call 824-6700 or (800) 356-6844.

The **Black River Inn** in Ludlow has a 1794 walnut four-poster bed in which Lincoln rested his 6-foot-4-inch frame. Weekend rates are $130-$160 with breakfast and dinner, and $85-$115 with breakfast. Call 228-5585 for reservations.

The **Cavendish Pointe Hotel** offers the full service of a 70-room country-style hotel, restaurant, lounge and game room. Daily weekend rate is $65-$85 per room, no meals. The hotel is on Route 103, two miles from Okemo. Call 226-7688.

The **Hawk Inn and Mountain Resort** has luxury country inn, home and townhouse facilities. This complex offers a resort feel and features indoor pool, sauna, Jacuzzis and fine dining. Bed and breakfast rates are $95-175 midweek and $125-$200 on weekends. Call 672-3811 or (800) 685-4295.

Dining

Priority's in the Village Center not only is a convenient spot for those staying on the mountain, but also has superb economical fare. The Pasta Diablo, with scallops and shrimp in a spicy red sauce, is great.

Nikki's at the foot of Okemo Mountain not only has a primo location, but a very good reputation. Nikki's is moderately expensive, but its Osso Bucco con Orechiette or steamed whole Maine lobster are favorites of the loyal repeat clientele. Nikki's desserts and extensive wine list add to its popularity.

Michael's Steak & Seafood restaurant on Route 103 just east of Ludlow is in a ramshackle sort of place that belies its true character. Many specials and the excellent cuts of steak bring back patrons for good dining at moderate prices.

North of Ludlow on Route 103 is **Harry's**, an understated place that has a high repeat business because of the moderate pricing ($9-$13) and an emphasis on international cuisine.

Après-ski/nightlife

For après-ski, try **Sitting Bull Lounge**, with a wide-screen TV and live music on weekends; **Priority's**, also with wide-screen TV and ski flicks; or **Dadds**.

Later in the evening, **Dadds** echoes reggae; **The Pot Belly** has country rock, '60s and '70s classics and karaoke on weekends; **Christopher's Sports and Spirits** for skill games and big-screen sports viewing; or **Northern Lights**, Ludlow's Western nightclub with live music on Fridays and Saturdays and a DJ/dance instructor on Sundays. Another hot spot is **Savannah's**, with live bands running the musical gamut from blues to rock. Savannah's has karaoke on select Friday nights, and unplugged musicians on Sundays. **Chuckles** is a favorite couples' spot because of its dance floor. **Old Farm House Inn** has rock and country groups, as well as a resident keyboard comic, Bob Emaa. **Cappuccino's** is a bistro with coffees and an occasional acoustic musician.

Other activities

Shopping: One of the best browsing stores in the Northeast, the **Vermont Country Store**, is in nearby Weston on Route 100. It's full of interesting and useful little items that are hard to find elsewhere, such as pant stretchers (wire frames that help natural-fiber pants dry without wrinkles) and Vermont Bag Balm, which helps heal sore cow udders and chapped hands. The store is open everyday except Sunday from 9 a.m. to 5 p.m.

Getting there and getting around

Getting there: Okemo is in south-central Vermont on Route 103 in Ludlow. The closest commercial airports are Hartford, Albany, Burlington or Boston. Burlington is the closest airport, about 90 minutes away, while Boston, the farthest, is about a three-hour drive.

Getting around: We recommend a car; though the immediate resort area is compact and easily walkable, you will want to try some restaurants, nightlife or activities nearby.

Information/reservations

Okemo Mountain Resort, Ludlow, VT 05149; 228-4041; snow report, 226-5222.

Lodging: (800) 786-5366 (800-78-OKEMO).

Local area code is 802.

Smugglers' Notch, Vermont

Big mountain skiing is the specialty of Smugglers' Notch. Its 2,610 vertical feet places second behind Killington for Vermont's longest vertical descent. Smugglers' has three mountains, one of which, Madonna Mountain, gives a 2,100-foot drop off one chair.

The area was named for the smugglers and bootleggers who brought in forbidden English goods in the War of 1812 and booze during Prohibition, storing the contraband in a cave between Madonna Mountain and Spruce Peak, the latter one of the peaks at Stowe. Though Route 108 passes Smugglers' and continues through the notch to Stowe, it is closed in winter.

Smugglers' started as a town-run area with two Poma lifts in 1954. It is now a premier four-season resort and has a strong reputation with families. Both *Family Circle* and *Better Homes and Gardens* chose Smugglers' in their separate listings as a top family vacation resort—the only ski resort to make both lists.

One feature that makes Smugglers' so great for families is its pedestrian-friendly village with stores, restaurants, an outdoor ice rink, sledding hill, indoor pool, saunas, steam baths, indoor and outdoor tennis, massage, crafts classes, sleigh rides, movies, parties for kids and adults and the largest licensed day-care facility in New England.

Where to ski

If you are a day visitor of intermediate skiing ability or better, resist the temptation to turn in at the main Village. Instead, continue up the hill to the top parking lot. Here you'll find fewer cars and a short walk to a point where you can ski right to the Sterling lift. This lift reaches 20 trails in the mellow category. Best of all, you can ski back to your car at day's end.

When you are sufficiently warmed up, seek out some real challenge from the top of Madonna Mountain. Three legitimate double-black-diamond trails beckon the true expert. Freefall is just that; the turns come quickly and you drop 10 to 15 feet with

---

Smugglers' Notch Facts
Base elevation: 1,030'; **Summit elevation:** 3,640'; **Vertical drop:** 2,610 feet
Number and types of lifts: 7–5 double chairs, 2 surface lifts
Acreage: 246 acres **Percent of snowmaking:** 61 percent
Uphill capacity: 6,250 per hour **Bed base:** 2,000

each turn. The F.I.S. trail sports a 41 percent gradient, and with the addition of top-to-bottom snowmaking has become a tad more civilized than in the past. Smugglers' grooms nightly, but some of the natural snow trails are left untouched. Management swears that many Mad River types ski Smugglers' for that very reason and the trails are posted as such. If you're hooked on glades, it's tough to find a better glade run than Doc Dempsey's. We just wish it were longer. Madonna has several other glade areas that aren't specified trails. The best bump runs are F.I.S., the middle portion of Upper Liftline, Smugglers' Alley, and Exhibition on Sterling Mountain.

Smugglers' and Stowe cooperate on a Ski-Over-The-Mountains lift ticket. For $30 on weekends and holidays and $26 weekdays, skiers on certain multiday packages at the two resorts can ski to the other resort by an intermediate trail, Snuffy's, and ski all day there. The connection is between Smugglers' Sterling Mountain and Stowe's Spruce Peak.

The third mountain at Smugglers' is Morse, with five trails ranging from beginner to expert. It is the best area for ski schoolers who want to avoid the hot-shots. If you are staying in the village, you'll need to ride to the top of Morse and ski down the green-circle Midway trail to get to the upper-mountain lifts. Return to the village is by the easy Meadowlark Trail or intermediate Northwest Passage.

Morse also is home to Mogul Mouse's Magic Lift, a half-speed double chair especially kind to beginners and young children. From the top of the lift winds the Magic Learning Trail, with nature stations, exploration paths and ski-through "caves."

Smugglers' has no high-speed quads or triple chairs, which sometimes contributes to moderate waits at the lift loading area. The tradeoff is that the trails are not congested.

Mountain rating

Smugglers' is good for all types of skiers. Fifty-four percent of the trails are rated intermediate, and many are well suited to recent ski-school grads. Advanced skiers have a quarter of the mountain, including ungroomed and gladed runs. Kids are all over the place here—a magnet for skiers who revel in a family atmosphere, but something to consider for single adults or couples who would rather have quieter surroundings.

Snowboarding

Snowboarders are welcome on all Smugglers' trails. Instructional programs focus on fun and safety. Snowboard camps are available for children 7 to 17.

Cross-country

More than 23 km. (about 14 miles) of scenic cross-country skiing on groomed and tracked trails is accessible from the main

Smugglers' area. The Nordic Ski Center offers rentals, lessons, skate skiing, backcountry and night tours, and snowshoe rentals and tours.

Lessons (95/96 prices)

Ski School Director Peter Ingvoldstad has been acclaimed as one of the most innovative teachers in the country. His techniques help children and adults learn the sport quickly.

Lessons are included with several lodging-and-lift packages at Smugglers'. **Children's programs** are divided into the following age groups: 3–6, 7–12 and 13–18. The teen program allows that age group to meet some new friends they can hang out with at the supervised evening teen activities.

Smugglers' has an innovative program called "Mom & Me/Dad & Me" that teaches parents how to teach their youngsters to ski. These lessons, essentially specialized private lessons, are for children aged 2 or older and a parent of at least intermediate skiing ability. Parents are taught games to make learning fun, and safety tips such as how to ride the lift with kids.

Group lessons (just short of two hours) are $24 and a one-hour **private lesson** is $45. **Special programs** include classes on style, terrain tactics, women's programs and programs for skiers 55 and older.

Child care

Alice's Wonderland Child Care is a major reason why *Family Circle* magazine chose Smugglers' as the top family resort for three years running. The facility accepts children 6 weeks to 6 years old and is staffed with professional care-givers who may also be hired for evening babysitting. Child care prices are $42 per day or $195 for five days.

Every night except Friday and Saturday, the center has Parents' Night Out, with dinner and activities for ages 3–12 so Mom and Dad can have some fun on their own.

Lift tickets (95/96 prices)

	Adult	Child (7–12)
Weekend day	$39	$26
Midweek day	$36	$26
Multiday	**	**

Children 6 and younger ski for free; those 65 and older ski for $29 a full day and $25 a half day. Morning or afternoon half day tickets are available.

**If you're staying for more than one day here, the wise move is to buy a lodging package that includes tickets and lessons. See the next section for more information.

Accommodations

At Smugglers' the primary and desirable place to stay is in the Resort Village. More than 2,000 beds are within walking distance of the lifts. Prices start at $399 per person (and $1,249 for a family of four) for a five-day Club Smugglers' package, including lifts and lessons. Packages include a welcome party, use of the pool and hot tub, family games nights, outdoor ice skating, family sledding parties, a weekly torchlight parade with fireworks finale, and a farewell party.

Condos at Smugglers' are spacious, clean and family-furnished—the furniture is sturdy and comfortable, without expensive bric-a-brac items at risk of being knocked over accidentally. Our condo was well stocked with family-style board games.

Smugglers' central check-in area is designed around the concept that once you check in, you have everything you need—lift tickets, instruction vouchers, rentals and day care. Computers at the front desk are tied to key areas such as the rental shop to make the resort very guest-friendly. During school vacations, however, the check-in area can get a bit backed up. If your vacation falls during this time, plan to have one parent stand in line while the other takes fidgety kids for a walk in the Resort Village. (If you check in at night, one parent can take the kids sledding, a resort spokeswoman said.) Remember, the payoff comes later—once you check in, you won't have to wait in line for tickets or lessons.

Dining

You never have to leave the Village to eat. The **Snowsnake Pizzeria** offers pizza, salads, calzones and stuffed breads with meat and veggie fillings—for eating there, taking out or delivery to your condo. The **Club Cafe**, with a view of the slopes, is open continuously for breakfast and lunch, including light fare and heart-healthy entrées. Families really enjoy the **Village Restaurant**, where kids on the FamilyFest® Package eat for half price when they are with their parents.

Restaurants dot the route between the resort and Jeffersonville, five miles away. Some examples:

Across from the entrance to the Village Center is the ever funky **Cafe Banditos** with low-cost Mexican food, hickory-smoked chicken and ribs and a children's menu. Down the road is the **Three Mountain Lodge**, eclectic dining in a classic log-lodge atmosphere. Steaks, seafood, veal, lamb, Vermont turkey and light meals are moderately priced.

Le Cheval D'Or, on Main Street in Jeffersonville, has been named one of 50 distinguished restaurants in the U.S. by *Condé Nast Traveler*, which praised it for its "woodsy, intimate dining room" and "lusty French food." Fresh salmon is cured and smoked on the premises. The cuisine combines French flair with New England ingredients, such as Vermont quail simmered in a rich red-wine sauce. Reservations are suggested (802-644-5556) and casual elegance is the suggested attire. Priciest place in town, but excellent value. On Parents' Night Out at Smugglers', Le Cheval d'Or picks up the tab for one child per family to stay at Alice's Wonderland Day Care.

Après-ski/nightlife

Smugglers' has great nightlife, but it's not of the typical "meet market" variety. Organized activities provide fun for all ages. Examples—a family sledding party on Wednesday nights on lighted Sir Henry's Hill; and Monday's Pictionary Family Tournament, featuring the popular draw-and-guess game.

For more traditional fun, try **The Club Cafe** for après-ski and nighttime entertainment such as karaoke on Wednesdays and dancing to DJ music on Saturdays. Saturday is also comedy night with the best comedians from the Northeast. **Banditos Cantina** turns into the liveliest weekend spot at Smugglers', with large-screen sports and music videos, pool table or live bands. Teens have the nightly Outer Limits Teen Center with music videos, snacks, and Wednesday and Saturday dance parties.

Other activities

Shopping: The Village Center has a few shops, stocked with necessities and typical T-shirt/hat/pin souvenirs. But if you want handmade Vermont crafts, you can make your own! Smugglers' has an unusual activity, **Artists in the Mountains**. Local artisans teach classes in traditional New England crafts, such as tin punching, basket weaving, stenciling and dried flower arranging. The classes include materials and cost $25-$35.

Getting there and getting around

Getting there: Smugglers' Notch is on Route 108 near Jeffersonville in northwest Vermont. Shuttles are available (24-hour notice required; book it when you book lodging) from the Burlington International Airport, 40 minutes away.

Getting around: Everything is within walking distance.

Information/reservations

Address and phone: Smugglers' Notch Resort, Smugglers' Notch, VT 05464; (802) 644-8851. Snow phone is (802) 644-1111.

For lodging reservations call (800) 451-8752 in the U.S. and Canada. In the United Kingdom, call toll-free 0800-89-7159. You can book everything, including airfare and transfers, with one phone call.

Stowe, Vermont

Stowe has an undeniable blue-blood lineage as one of the oldest and most distinguished Eastern ski resorts. Its ski patrol, founded in 1934, is the oldest in the United States, and its winter carnival is the longest running such event in the nation. In its early days, it was a definite "in" spot during the winter. For a period of time in the 1980s, Stowe let its slopeside facilities cross that invisible line separating quaint from antiquated. But management has kept up a steady stream of improvements for the past several years, with the idea of smoothing out some of the wrinkles of age without sacrificing the regal bearing and atmosphere—a job well done.

Those improvements have included more snowmaking, better lifts and updated skier base facilities. However, Stowe retained its long, narrow, twisting runs cut close into the surrounding forests—runs that are an important part of making Stowe a classic New England ski experience.

For those of you who are only familiar with the resort through photographs, Stowe appears to be a New England village nestled at the foot of a large ski mountain, with pubs and restaurants and boutique shopping clustered around a village square. That's the magic of telephoto lenses. The 200-year-old village of Stowe is typical New England in its look, with a charming white steepled church and a main street lined with historic buildings. But the town lies about seven miles away from the skiing at Mt. Mansfield and adjacent Spruce Peak. To truly enjoy all this area has to offer, you need a car. We realize that recommendation only contributes to increased street congestion, but the alternative is the Town Trolley, which runs the seven miles between the village of Stowe and Mt. Mansfield. It provides, in the understated words of a British journalist who begged a ride back into town with us, "an epic voyage." The trolley. Makes. A lot. Of stops. Between town. And. The. Mountain.

Stowe Facts

Base elevation: 1,390'; **Summit elevation:** 3,750'; **Vertical drop:** 2,360 feet.
Number and types of lifts: 11—1 quad superchair, 1 eight-passenger gondola, 1 triple chair, 6 double chairs, and 2 surface lifts
Acreage: 480 skiable acres **Snowmaking:** 73 percent
Uphill capacity: 11,465 skiers per hour **Bed base:** 5,000+

Where to ski

Part of the legend of Stowe revolves around its Front Face, and the fact that it features some of the steepest and most difficult runs in skidom. Having skied the Front Four is a badge of honor for northeast skiers, and deservedly so, given the nature of Goat, Starr, Liftline and National. Besides being steep, the head-walls are frequently draped with vintage New England ice and the trails are liberally moguled.

Experts who are gunning for all four should begin with National and Liftline. The resort's winch cats allow groomers to prepare these two from time to time, so this is a good place to get used to the considerable steepness of the Front Four. Starr is not groomed, and the view from the top of this run, as it disappears in a steep dive toward the base lodge area far below, is one you won't forget. If you haven't met your match by this time, then you're ready for Goat, a moguled gut-sucker no more than three to five bumps wide.

Another suggestion for the experts, who will find roughly 25 percent of the mountain catering to their desires, is a short but lovely little moguled path through tight trees called Centerline, just to the right of Hayride. Centerline was one of the runs that was widened and smoothed to remove the double fall line. Snowmaking also was added here, making it one of the early-season options for high-level skiers.

A very nice section of glade skiing through well-spaced trees is just off of the top section of Nosedive. Chin Clip from the top of the gondola is long, moguled, and moderately narrow, but it does not have quite the steep grade that the Front Four boast.

Intermediates will find that 59 percent of trails at Stowe are marked for their maximum enjoyment, including much of Spruce Peak. At Mt. Mansfield, ski to the right or left of the Front Four. Advanced intermediates will probably want to chance the tricky top part of Nosedive for the pleasure of skiing the long, sweeping cruiser that beckons further down. Going left from the top of the Forerunner Quad, take Upper Lord until it leads you to a handful of long excellent intermediate runs all the way to the bottom in Lower Lord, North Slope, Standard and Gulch.

From the quad, reaching the intermediate skiing under the gondola presents a small problem. The connection between these two parts of the mountain is not convenient unless you are an advanced intermediate willing to take a run down Nosedive, rated double-black at its top. (Yes it's narrow and the moguls get pretty big up there, but there's enough room to pick your way down. We got our advanced intermediate staff member down it before she realized its rating.) If you don't want to chance Nosedive, it's a hike from the quad area over to the gondola, or you can take the green-circle Crossover trail toward the bottom of the mountain, which allows skiers to traverse directly across the Front Four to the gondola base. If you want to work your way back from the gondola to the quad, take the Cliff Trail, which eventually hooks up with Lower Nosedive and dumps you at the base of the high-speed chair.

Across the parking lot is Spruce Peak with a small network of intermediate trails and Stowe's best beginner terrain. If you feel as though you need a little elbow room after too many tight New England trails, try Perry Merrill or Gondolier from the gondola, or cut turns about as wide as you want down Main Street on Spruce Peak.

The Big Spruce double is perhaps the coldest chair lift on the mountain, and certainly the oldest. The runs face south, so they lose snow earliest in the spring, and there is no snowmaking at the top of the mountain or on the long intermediate Sterling trail. Skiing upper Spruce Peak is like all skiing was in the old days—no snow from heaven, no skiing. When the snow is good and the wind isn't blowing, though, the mountain can be a cruiser's delight, and powder days are a real treat. From the top of Spruce Peak, skiers can cross over to Smuggler's Notch (see that chapter for more details on this interchangeable ticket).

Intermediates may also enjoy Stowe's night skiing. The upper portion of Perry Merrill and all of Gondolier are lit Wednesday through Sunday (seven nights during holidays) until 10 p.m. The ride up is in the warm gondola.

Beginners should start at the base area of Spruce Peak, then work up to the easy runs off the Toll House chair (Chair 5), then advance to Chair 4.

One route we would recommend to all levels is the four-mile-long, green-circle Toll Road, which starts at the top of the Forerunner quad and winds gently through forested slopes to the bottom. This is a marvelous trail for lower-level skiers, but more proficient ones will probably enjoy it, too—not for its challenge but for its beauty. You will ski through a canopy of trees. A little later, you'll ski by the small wood-and-stone Mountain Chapel, where on Sundays you can attend an informal church service accessible only to skiers. You just won't find this type of intimate experience out West.

Snowboarding

Stowe has a snowboard park, called the Flight Deck, on Lower Lord that includes jumps, rail slides and barrel bonks. A halfpipe, the only lit one in New England, is in the Midway base area. Professional instruction includes a never-ever program costing $49 for lift ticket and lesson, $69 with equipment rental. Snowboard clinics concentrate on halfpipe maneuvers, carving and pushing the outer limits.

Cross-country

Stowe has one of the best cross-country networks in the country. Four touring areas all interconnect to provide 132 groomed km. of trails, and an additional 107 km. in backcountry.

The Trapp Family Lodge (253-8511) organized America's first touring center and has 58 km. groomed and 48 km. tracked trails. The fee is $10 a day.

The Edson Hill Touring Center (253-7371) has 42 km. of trails with 20 km. trails groomed. Elevation varies from 1,400 feet to 2,100 feet. The fee is $6 a day.

Stowe Mountain Resort (253-3000) has 75 km. of trails, 35 km. of which are groomed. The daily fee is $10.

The Topnotch Resort (253-8585) has 40 km. of trails. Trail fee is $8.

Lessons (94/95 prices)

Need a little guidance getting down the Front Four? A **special workshop** concentrates on Goat, Starr, National and Liftline and costs $35 for three hours. Other clinics are a Breakthrough To Carving workshop for advanced intermediates for $35 and a Mountain Experience Week that works on mastering varying snow conditions and terrain while getting to know the mountain. The Mountain Experience Week is Monday through Friday afternoons, three hours daily, for $104.

Private instruction is available for $45 an hour, with $15 for each additional person. A full day of private instruction costs $210 and for two to five people, $310. **Group lessons** are $24 for one lesson, with each additional lesson $20.

The ski school has **children's programs** for those 3 to 12 years, headquartered at Spruce Peak. Full-day programs with lunch are $62, with each additional day $52.

Teens (13-16) at the intermediate or higher level have a program for $75 for the first day, $65 each additional day.

Telephone extension for the ski school is 3683 or 3682.

Child care

Kanga's Pocket takes children from 2 months through 6 years. A full day costs $48 ($42 for each additional day) and a half day is $32. Reservations are required; call 253-3000, ext. 2262. The children's center is at the Spruce Peak area.

Lift tickets (94/95 prices)

	Adult	Child (6–12) Senior (65+)
One day	$43	$24
Three days	$118 ($39.33/day)	$62 ($20.66/day)
Five days	$194 ($38.80/day)	$100 ($20/day)

These prices are valid in February and March. Early and late season prices are about $14 per day lower. January prices are about $6 per day lower and Christmas prices are a few dollars per day higher. Children 5 and younger ski free with paid parent or guardian.

Night skiing is $18 for adults and $16 for children. A twilight ticket, valid from 1 to 10 p.m., is $38 for adults, $22 for children.

Accommodations

Stowe features Added Value packages for downhill and cross-country skiing. Extras include night skiing, extra half days, lessons, etc. If you're staying at least three days, ask about these packages, either with individual lodges or better yet, the Stowe Area Association (800) 247-8693 (24-STOWE). Lodging ranges from small country inns and large resorts to hotels in the old New England tradition.

Ye Olde England Inne, on the Mountain Road; 253-7558 or (800) 477-3771. This is a favorite because it is bigger than a country inn and smaller than a full-fledged hotel. Recently restored, Ye Olde England is now considered one of the best lodgings in Stowe. It has been redone with an English country motif and lavish Laura Ashley touches. Because every room is decorated differently, call for specific differences. Room rates include breakfast. Just off the lobby is Mr. Pickwick's Polo Pub with a selection of more than 100 beers, eight available on tap. The pub also has a full selection of pub grub ranging from steak-and-kidney pie to haggis. Rates: $116–$150 per room, double occupancy.

Green Mountain Inn, Main Street; 253-7301 or (800) 445-6629. A charming old inn with a super location in the middle of town. The wide-planked floors are pine, as is the furniture, with many old four-poster canopied beds. Rooms that front on the street are a little too noisy for light sleepers; big delivery trucks rev their engines at the nearby stop sign starting at about 6 a.m. The hotel also has an annex that is not quite so quaint, but is off the main road. Room rates with breakfast are $100 to $205.

Butternut Inn, Mountain Road; 253-4277. A country inn in the classic sense. Of those we visited, the Butternut was our favorite in Stowe. It reflects the eccentricities of the owners, transplanted from Texas. The inn is No Smoking and no children are allowed. Every aspect of the inn is done nicely: its rooms are all different, guests are pampered, dinners are prepared only for the inn guests and include Angus beef and Tex-Mex, which alternate with more traditional New England fare. Anyone who wants everything done beautifully will appreciate the Butternut. Room rates: $95–$160 double occupancy with breakfast and après-ski snacks.

Ten Acres Lodge, Luce Hill Road; (800) 327-7357, or in Vermont, 253-7638. This country inn was converted from an 1840s farm house. As with all country inns, rooms vary in size, those in the main lodge are relatively simple, but the common areas on the first floor are beautiful. Ten Acres Lodge also has a group of eight modern units, called the Hill House, tucked into the woods behind the old farmhouse. These all have fireplaces in the rooms and share an outdoor hot tub. Rates, including breakfast: $75–$140 per room double occupancy.

The Gables Inn, on Mountain Road; 253-7730 or (800) 422-5371 (GABLES-1). Gables is what all friendly country inns should be. Not a quiet, stuffy place with antiques and Mozart playing, where you're afraid of breaking something. This is a real lived-in house, which helps everyone have a good time. The breakfasts are among the best in Stowe and guests wouldn't think of eating anywhere else—for dinner either. Room rates, based on double occupancy, $120–$200 per person with breakfast and dinner.

The Resorts

When the Trapp Family's life was dramatized in *The Sound of Music*, their everlasting fame was guaranteed. **The Trapp Family Lodge** (253-8511 or 800-826-7000), they established near Stowe upon arriving in the United States is a legend in its own right. Unfortunately, the original building burned down in the late 1970s, and was completely rebuilt from 1980 to 1983. It is still the most popular and upscale place to stay in the area, and is still in the family—it's now run by a son.

This is virtually a self-contained resort with an excellent cross-country center. The collection of restaurants is among the best in the area, and a modern pool and fitness center provide excellent amenities. Make reservations early because this lodge is normally full throughout the season (Christmas reservations should be made about a year in advance). Rates, with breakfast and dinner: $110–$139 per person, based on double occupancy.

Though not as famous as the Trapp Family Lodge, but much closer to the lifts and the town, **Topnotch at Stowe** (253-8585 or 800-451-8686; in Canada 800-228-8686), boasts the most extensive fitness center and spa in the area. Topnotch has rooms and condos, along with excellent meeting facilities. It also has the only four covered tennis courts in Stowe. Room rates: $154–$224 per person. Condos are higher.

The Inn at the Mountain, part of the Stowe Mountain Resort, is four-diamond rated by AAA, and we have no argument with that (800-253-4754). This beautiful inn and the surrounding condominiums (available through the same telephone number) comprise the only ski-in/ski-out facility in Stowe. The flavor is old-world New England warmth. The name of the Broken Ski Tavern in the Inn commemorates the founding of the first steel ski, which was introduced here. An early prototype is sitting in pieces above the fireplace. At breakfast, guests create their own omelets to order, and enjoy bread from the Inn's own bakery.

While the ambiance in the Inn may be old-world, the Fitness Center (free to all guests) across the parking lot is ultra-modern. There's universal weight training, free weights, workout rooms, aerobics classes, Stairmaster, Lifecycle and rowing machines, as well as a sauna and hot tub. Room and condo unit rates based on double occupancy and including breakfast and dinner range from $195 to $385.

The best family accommodations in Stowe are at the **Golden Eagle Resort Motor Inn**; 253-4811 or (800) 626-1010. This sprawling complex has more than a dozen buildings and facilities, from motel rooms with kitchenettes to apartments. Along with an excellent restaurant, The Alpine, the complex has an excellent fitness center with pool and hot tub facilities. It is all unpretentious and affordable. Because there are dozens of pricing options, the best bet is to contact the property and explain what you are looking for, but in general, room rates are $110–$170.

The **Stoweflake**, (253-7355 or 800-253-2232) down the road a bit from the Golden Eagle, is more upscale and has a pool and fitness center. Rates with breakfast and dinner based on double occupancy are $138–$186 a night, (without meals, $78–$138). A nice group of townhouse condominiums has studios to three-bedroom units for $150–$370.

The **Vermont Ski Dormitory** at the foot of Mount Mansfield offers bunk-style sleeping with shared bathroom facilities. Rates are about $35 a night with breakfast and dinner. Call (800) 866-8749 or 253-4010.

Dining

Stowe has long been famous for its cuisine. **Ten Acres** (253-7638) and **Isle de France** (253-7751) are considered by most to be the top gourmet spots in the area. Entrées at both restaurants range from $17 to $24. An up-and-coming restaurant is the **Blue Moon Café** (253-7006) with innovative fine dining. **Stubb's Restaurant** (253-7110) also gets good reviews.

The **Trapp Family Lodge** (253-8511) puts on an excellent Austrian-style meal for a fixed price of about $25. There normally is a choice of about a dozen entrées.

For a total dining experience, try the **Cliff House Restaurant** (253-3000) at the top of Stowe's gondola. A gourmet four-course meal awaits at $35 per person, plus tax and tip.

For alternatives that aren't budget-busters, try **Miguel's Stowe-Away** (253-7574) or the **Cactus Cafe** (253-7770) for Mexican food, **Restaurant Swisspot** (253-4622) for fondues and decadent Swiss chocolate pie, and **Gracie's** (253-8741) for great burgers and meat loaf. **The Shed**, which burned down two seasons ago, has rebuilt and added a microbrewery. It's still a great spot for steaks and prime rib. **Foxfire** (253-4887) has good

Italian food, as does **Trattoria La Festa** (253-8480). **The Whip** (253-7301) in the basement of the Green Mountain Inn is a good place for a light dinner or sandwiches. And **Mr. Pickwick's Polo Pub** (253-7064) is excellent. When your steak sandwich almost melts in your mouth, they're doing something right.

H.H. Bingham's (253-3000) in the Inn at the Mountain at the base of the Toll House lift, serves moderate continental cuisine with entrées in the $12 to $18 range; hearty lunches, too.

On-mountain, there are several choices for lunch and snacks. The **Midway Café and Bakery** in the Midway Lodge has fresh-baked pastries and muffins and gourmet coffee, the **Cliff House Café** at the gondola top is a nice atmosphere, and the **Broken Ski Tavern** at the Inn near the Toll House lift is quite relaxing and a little more upscale.

A breakfast favorite is **McCarthy's**, next to the movie theater, adjacent to the Baggy Knees complex. Also the breakfast at **The Gables** shouldn't be missed, especially on weekends.

Après-ski/nightlife

It's difficult to say exactly what ingredients go into making the perfect après-ski spot, but they are all there in just the right measure at the **Matterhorn Bar**. Located a few miles from the ski area on the mountain road, this raucous little roadhouse is packed and rollicking after the slopes close. There's a dance floor, a disc jockey, loud music, a rectangular bar that makes for easy circulation, pool tables, big-screen TV—all the ingredients. There's a more low-key après-ski meeting place at the mountain in the rustic **Broken Ski Tavern** at the Inn at the Mountain.

You can count the hot spots on one hand, and still have fingers left over. Stowe's college-crowd hangout is **B.K.B.'s**, which is the reborn Rusty Nail, which had burned down a couple of seasons ago. **Mr. Pickwick's Polo Pub** at the Olde England Inne gets a good pub crowd with its 120 different beers, and the bar at **Miguel's Stowe-Away** seems to be a singles meeting place.

Other activities

Shopping: Stowe has many fun shops and art galleries for browsing, most in town. **Shaw's General Store** is a century old and was the town's first ski shop. Other unusual shops are **Moriarty Hats & Sweaters** for custom knitted goods, and **Exclusively Vermont**, for various Vermont-made products.

Indoor tennis can be played at the Topnotch Racquet Club on the Mountain Road. Four Deco Turf courts are available as well as lessons for hourly fees. In the Village, Jackson arena has an Olympic-size **ice skating** rink. Call 253-6148.

Snowmobiles are available at Nichols Snowmobiles (253-7239) or from Farm Resort (888-3525). **Snowshoe** rentals and guided tours are available from Umiak Outdoor Outfitters, 253-2317.

Horse-drawn sleigh rides take place at Edson Hill Manor (253-7371), Stowehof Inn (253-9722), and Topnotch (253-8585).

Ben and Jerry's ice cream factory is just down the road in Waterbury and offers tours that include samples. Winter is not nearly so busy as summer, so it's a good time to take a tour.

Special events include the Stowe Winter Carnival, the oldest winter celebration in the country, normally the second half of January; the Stowe Challenge Cross-Country Races in February; and a Sugar Slalom race with sugar on snow at the finish line for skiers and watchers and the traditional Stowe Snow Beach Party, both in April.

Getting there and getting around

Getting there: Driving time to Stowe from Boston is about 3.5 hours; from Montreal, 2.5 hours. The resort is a few miles north of Waterbury Exit 10 on I-89.

Numerous flights arrive at the Burlington International Airport, which is 45 minutes from Stowe. All major rental car companies have offices there and most hotels have a transfer service. You can get discounts on flights and rental cars from the Stowe Area Association when you make your hotel reservations.

For skiers from Washington, Philadelphia or New York, the perfect prelude is a romantic trip aboard Amtrak's Montrealer, with comfortable private berths, helpful attendants to bring cocktails to your room, and the incomparable sensation of watching the moonlit landscape of New England whirl past your window to the lonely call of the train whistle. You arrive in Waterbury (15 miles from Stowe) early in the morning in plenty of time for a full day of skiing. Dinner and breakfast are included in the price, which will vary depending on place of origin. Reservations required.

Getting around: You can manage without a car, but we recommend one. The Town Trolley ($1 per single ride; $5 for a week-long pass) is fine for short jaunts, but a slow way to get to the mountain from town. Also, it doesn't operate at night.

Information/reservations

For the Stowe Area Association, call (800) 247-8693 (24-STOWE). Representatives can book rooms at 60 hotels, book flights and help with nearly every aspect of the vacation.

For slopeside accommodations at the Stowe Mountain Resort, call (800) 253-4764 (253-4SKI).

Stowe Mountain Resort recorded snow conditions: call 253-3600. Offices: 253-3000.

Local area code is 802.

Stratton Mountain, Vermont

Manchester is the quintessential Vermont town gone chic. A Vermont farmer arriving here would think he was in some Disney caricature of what Vermont *should* be. Tourists love it—outlets everywhere, gift shops, craft shops, antique shops, Orvis fly fishing on the Battenkill River, steepled churches, manorial hotels, charming country inns, gourmet dining. And it's all very upscale for the most part. Finding a place for a family with young children to stay can be a problem; you'll be relegated to motelish lodging or condos—forget the quaint inns. Weekend traffic is atrocious.

Stratton is an Alpinesque condo village at the base of the lifts that is, village-wise, to Vermont what Vail is to Colorado. Major changes are in store: Stratton has been acquired by Intrawest, parent company of Blackcomb and Panorama in British Columbia and Tremblant in Québec. Intrawest has won several awards for its ski-area design. Stratton will add New England's first six-passenger chair lift this season and increase snowmaking to 100 percent over the next two years. Future projects include a larger base lodge, a 1,000-seat summit restaurant and a "revitalization" of the village area.

Where to ski

This is a cruising mountain. The upper mountain has some steeps for advanced intermediates. Upper Lift Line to Lower Lift Line is made for big giant-slalom turns. Black Bear, Polar Bear, Grizzly Bear and Upper Tamarack—all served by the Grizzly double chair—are narrow runs in fine New England tradition with good vertical. Upper Kidderbrook to Freefall provides another good advanced cruise. Upper Standard starts steep but mellows at the bottom. The double-diamond trails are steep, with bumps that short skiers may have a hard time seeing over. Upper Spruce is the easiest of the double-diamond trails.

Stratton Facts
Base elevation: 1,872'; **Summit elevation:** 3,875'; **Vertical drop:** 2,003 feet
Number and types of lifts: 12—1 twelve-passenger gondola, 1 six-passenger high-speed chair, 4 quad chairs, 1 triple chair, 3 double chairs, 2 surface lifts
Acreage: 480 skiable acres **Snowmaking:** 80 percent
Uphill capacity: 21,000 skiers per hour **Bed base:** 8,000

The lower mountain and Sun Bowl are strictly for those who want to look good—very good. Stratton does its best to ensure that if a skier forgets to uplift in a turn he or she will still have a chance to get around.

Stratton has a wonderful feature for beginners: a Ski Learning Park with 10 gentle trails. It includes a terrain garden, where bumps and rolls are sculpted by the mountain staff, so beginners can practice their balance and independent leg action *before* they encounter bumps sculpted by hundreds of other skiers' skis.

Mountain rating

Stratton is one of America's best ego-inflating ski areas. Excellent grooming on the mostly mellow terrain makes it even easier. Experts can find some good challenges, but don't expect to be pushed.

Cross-country

The Manchester area offers an excellent series of trails through the surrounding hills.

Hildene (362-1788) is in Manchester Village with 15 km. of trails winding through the pine-covered estate of Robert Todd Lincoln.

Nordic Inn (824-6444), just east of Peru, has trails that wander into the Green Mountain National Forest.

The Stratton Ski Touring Center (297-4061) is located at the Sun Bowl and has 20 km. of tracked cross-country trails and 50 km. of backcountry skiing. Lessons and guided tours are available. Beginner terrain and great views are available at the Stratton Mountain Country Club, a separate area. Stratton plans eventually to link the two areas.

Viking Ski Touring Center (824-3933) in Londonderry provides 40 km. of groomed trails through woods and open fields.

Porc Trails (824-3933) are a series of ungroomed trails maintained by the West River Outing Club of Londonderry. If you intend to use them, make sure someone knows where you are and when you intend to return: the trails are not patrolled daily. Call for directions and parking locations.

Snowboarding

Stratton was one of the pioneers in this high-growth branch of the ski industry. Burton Snowboards, one of the earliest manufacturers, is headquartered in Manchester Center, and Stratton was one of the first major ski areas to allow the sport. Burton's founder, Jake Burton Carpenter, grew up skiing there. Stratton has a halfpipe, rentals and excellent instruction.

Lessons (95/96 prices)

Group lessons cost $25 and last an hour and 45 minutes. Ten sessions cost $210. The multi-lesson books are transferable, making them perfect for families. **Private lessons** cost $57 an hour, with additional skiers $28. Additional hours are discounted.

Children have the Big Cub and Little Cub programs, both with lunch and two lessons for $56. Big Cub is for children 7 to 12, Little Cub for ages 3 to 6.

NASTAR races cost $4 for adults and $3 for children younger than 19. A self-timed race course costs $1 a run or $8 for ten runs.

Child care

The Baby Cub program takes children from 6 weeks through 5 years; $45 includes lunch and a snack.

Lift tickets (95/96 prices)

Weekend rates	Adult	Child (7–12)
One day (94/95)	$43	$27
Three days	$132 ($44/day)	$80 ($26.66/day)
Five days	$210 ($42/day)	$122 ($24.40/day)

add 5% sales tax to these prices

These are weekend rates—midweek rates are 15–19 percent lower; other multiday rates are available. Children younger than 7 ski free. At Stratton skiers aged 65–69 ski for $33 on weekends; $27 midweek; those 70 and older ski for $20 any day.

Accommodations

For **Stratton Reservations** call (800) 843-6867. This toll-free number also handles several properties off the mountain and in Manchester as well.

The **Village Lodge** is smack in the middle of Stratton and is the premier property for location—walk out your door and you are a hundred yards from the gondola. The Village Lodge, with rooms decorated in subdued colors, has no amenities such as pool, dining room, or lounge; for those, take the shuttle to its larger sister hotel, the **Stratton Mountain Inn** in the center of the village with a spa, dining areas, lounges and a variety of rooms. A personal favorite is **The Birkenhaus**, which still has its old-world flavor with excellent service and European-style attention to making you comfortable. This is a small hostelry with the best food on the mountain. The **Liftline Lodge** provides Stratton's most economical lodging on the mountain and sprawls over several wings and buildings.

The **Mountain Villas** are a collection of condos suitable for families. Stratton Reservations has plenty of condos all within easy reach of the slopes. NOTE: The prices on these properties are significantly lower when you buy a Stratton Mountain package. Children younger than 6 stay and ski free anytime. Children 12 and younger stay free in the same room with their parents.

Manchester/Manchester Center

Manchester is filled with many tiny bed-and-breakfast establishments and New England hotels in the Currier and Ives tradition. Most discourage children, but if you brought children to these antique-filled houses, you would be a wreck before the trip was over.

Some of the best properties in the region are the **Wilberton Inn** (362-2500 or 800-648-4944) which is a classic, fashionable address; the **Equinox** (362-4700 or 800-362-4747, reservations only) grand, impressive and expensive (but surprisingly reasonable if you get a package deal); **The Inn at Manchester** (362-1793) a quaint, smaller country inn with 19 rooms; and **The Palmer House** (362-3600), an unpretentious hotel in Manchester Center with comfortable spacious country decor, four-poster beds, hot tub and sauna, built around a courtyard.

Though it's a few miles out of Manchester Center in the opposite direction from the two ski areas, **Barrows House** in Dorset (867-4455, 800-639-1620) is a good choice for anyone who seeks serene lodging. It is a beautifully restored 200-year-old country inn on expansive grounds, but is still close to Manchester Center's shopping and dining. Barrows House has a first-rate gourmet restaurant that is open to the public for breakfast and dinner, plus a tavern. Midweek lodging-and-meals packages are reasonably priced.

For families, try the **Aspen Motel** (362-2450), **Johnny Seesaws** in Peru (824-5533), and **The Red Sled** (362-2161). All are motelish and basic, but you won't have worry about breaking anything.

For **Manchester area central reservations**, call (802) 824-6915.

The closest RV park is in Dorset on Route 30.

Dining

In Manchester try these less formal, chef-owned eateries—**The Black Swan** (362-3807) which gets two thumbs up from everyone; **The Chantecleer** (362-1616) which is gourmet dining; **Dina's Restaurant** (362-4982) which presents American cuisine in an 18th-century farmhouse.

For family fare in Manchester strike out for the **Sirloin Saloon** (362-2600) with a rustic steakhouse atmosphere and a salad bar to write home about, and where children are readily welcomed. It is popular and mobbed on weekends. **Laney's Restaurant** (362-4456) has an open kitchen where you can see grilled items being prepared. **Gurry's Restaurant** (362-9878) is burgers and pizza but with specials that are kind to the wallet.

For Mexican and Cajun head into Manchester and try the **Park Bench Cafe** (362-2557). For popular Italian/American meals and pasta try **Garlic John's** (362-9843) which attracts massive crowds.

The best food on Stratton mountain is found in the **Birkenhaus**, which receives rave reviews from virtually everyone. The other on-mountain property that has attained a well-deserved niche in the hearts of the locals and repeat tourists is the **Liftline Lodge** with its special buffets—when liftline attendants say it's a deal, check it out.

A small restaurant not widely known is **Brush Hill** (896-6100) in West Wardsboro on Route 100, only eight miles away from Stratton Mountain Village. Ask a local how to find the back road to Mount Snow and take it. When you hit Route 100, turn right and it's a couple of hundred yards on your right. Chef Michael Sylva and his wife Lee have retreated to the woods from big-city restaurants to create their own Green Mountain cuisine. Dining here is by reservation only. Closed Mondays and Tuesdays.

Other top gourmet spots in the vicinity are **The Three O'Clock Inn** (824-6327) in an old restored farmhouse in South Londonderry; **Mistral's at Old Toll Gate** (362-1779) in the center of Manchester; **Barrows House** on Route 30 in Dorset and **The Dorset Inn** (867-5500) also on Route 30 and the oldest continuously operating inn in Vermont. Jackets are preferred in these. Most entrées will run $15 to $20. The two Dorset restaurants are about a 15-minute drive from Manchester Center in the opposite direction from the ski areas.

For more down-to-earth, out-of-Manchester fare try the **River Cafe** (297-1010) in Bondville with the best ribs in the area. Upstairs at **The Red Fox** (297-2488) in Bondville was recommended by just about every local and regular. **Jamaica House** (874-4400) in Jamaica has great Italian food and a homey bar. Across the street in Jamaica you find the **Brookside Steak House** (874-4271) right on the river with a giant salad bar.

For good simple sit-down food try **Jake's Marketplace Cafe** (824-3811) in Londonderry. **Johnny Seesaw's** (824-5533) in Peru has real Yankee cuisine.

Après-ski/nightlife

In Manchester the hottest pickup scene is at **Park Bench Café** with pitchers of margaritas, or try **Mulligans Bar** in Manchester Village. Once you get started just wander through town, bar to bar, until you find the spot with the evening's action.

At Stratton, when you get off the slopes, après-ski is on the packed deck of the **Bear's Den** with oom-pah-pah bands, in **Mulligans** serving 50 different types of beer, or **Cafe Applause** in the Stratton Mountain Inn. In the evenings the action continues in Mulligans (with live entertainment on weekends) and the Cafe Applause (great '50s and '60s jukebox if there's no live music) if you are staying on the mountain. Off the mountain, try the **Red Fox** down in Bondville for occasional music and dancing, or the **Jamaica House** for simple bar with TV action.

Other activities

Shopping: This is a major non-ski activity here. About 40 factory outlet stores are spread among five shopping centers and several stand-alone stores in Manchester and Manchester Center. Most are brand-name stores you'll find at other factory outlet centers, but a few are rare birds, such as The Down Outlet, Tse Cashmere and Orvis Catalog Outlet Store. These towns also have many boutiques and shops that stock handcrafted regional gift items, unusual clothing and other things you didn't know you needed until you saw them.

The **Stratton Sports Center** has facilities for indoor tennis, racquetball, indoor pool, hot tubs, saunas, fitness center, tanning salons, and massages.

Getting there and getting around

Getting there: Manchester Center is at the intersection of Routes 7A and 30 in southwestern Vermont. Stratton is on Route 30 about 15 miles east of Manchester. Look for the Stratton Mountain Road from Route 30. If you're heading straight for Stratton from I-91, take Exit 2 at Brattleboro, follow signs to Route 30, then drive 38 miles to Bondville and the Stratton Mountain Road.

The area is about 140 miles from Boston, 235 from New York City and 470 from Washington, D.C.

Getting around: Manchester and Stratton are about 90 minutes from the Albany airport and require a car for easy access.

Information/reservations

Stratton Mountain Resort information and mountain lodging reservations is (800) STRATTON (782-8866). If you want to make lodging arrangements in the Manchester area, call 824-6915.

Local area code is 802.

Sugarbush
Mad River Glen
Vermont

If Vermont is quintessential New England, then the Mad River Valley is a pretty fair candidate for quintessential Vermont. Its two main towns, Waitsfield and Warren, meet the visual requirements of anyone looking for the classic New England country town. Beautiful white and pastel clapboard houses fill the streets, historic buildings have lovingly been restored, and the narrow white-ribbon ski trails of Sugarbush stand out on the pine-green wooded slopes of 3,975-foot Lincoln Peak. Quaint country inns and charming excellent restaurants abound, yet condos and hearty-fare eating establishments meet the needs of skiers on a budget.

In the 1960s Sugarbush was dubbed Mascara Mountain for the proliferation of New York models who accompanied influential New Yorkers and Bostonians. Though a bit of that jet-set image lingers today, the resort has been positioning itself in the mainstream market by emphasizing its snowmaking, upper-end slopes and variety. More than any other resort area in Vermont, Sugarbush/Mad River Valley offers something for every level of skier at every level of accommodation luxury.

Where to ski

The skiing is on three separate mountains—Sugarbush South and Sugarbush North, which comprise the Sugarbush ski resort, and separately owned Mad River Glen on Route 17.

Each area provides a different experience. Heading the list of positives is the terrain, which goes from super gentle to super steep, and is well maintained. (Notice we did not say "groomed;" generally, both areas groom what needs to be groomed and leave alone what should be left alone.) Plodding lift systems used to

---

Sugarbush Facts
Base elevation: 1,485; **Summit elevation:** 4,135'; **Vertical drop:** 2,650 feet
Number and types of lifts: 18—4 quad superchairs, 3 quad chairs, 3 triples, 4 double chairs, 4 surface lifts
Acreage: 412 skiable acres **Snowmaking:** 68 percent
Uphill capacity: 24,363 skiers per hour **Bed base:** 6,600 (2,200 on mountain)

head the negatives list. However, Sugarbush is spending more than $13 million on improvements for this season, including seven new lifts. This takes Sugarbush from one high-speed quad to four in one year.

One of the speedy lifts—slightly more than two miles in length—will connect the two Sugarbush areas, North and South. At Sugarbush South, another high-speed replaces the Sugar Bravo triple and a third replaces the Gatehouse double. Also at South, a triple chair replaces the North Link Poma, which serves an intermediate-expert area. At North, the Green Mountain Express will be shortened and downgraded from a high-speed to create an expanded learning area. But Sugarbush North still will have a quad superchair—one of the speedsters will replace the North Ridge double chair. All in all, lift capacity will increase by 60 percent.

Sugarbush South is the larger of the two areas, with varying terrain. As you face the mountain, the runs to the left are generally the most difficult and those to the right are designed for beginners and lower intermediates. The runs served by Castlerock lifts are very black and no place for the timid.

For an intermediate a good start would be to take the Sugar Bravo chair, then traverse to the Heaven's Gate triple and the top of the mountain. From here take Upper Jester, rated blue (but barely more than a green), then choose from Downspout, Domino, Snowball, Murphy's Glades or Lower Jester. The most fun for intermediates on this part of the mountain is the terrain reached by the Sugar Bravo lift. Warning: there is a long runout at the bottom of Jester—be ready with your pushing technique.

The far right side of the area is served by the Gate House chair, then the North Link lift, which takes skiers even higher. Here intermediates will have relatively wide runs and good cruising. Beginners will want to stick to this section of the mountain, practicing on Pushover and Easy Rider and then graduating to Slowpoke and Sleeper.

Experts will find plenty of challenge. The entire Castlerock area offers narrow New England-style steeps, and if you are lucky the Castlerock run will occasionally be groomed, making for a heavenly smooth steep. Unfortunately the Castlerock lift is not on the improvement list and even when the resort is nearly empty at midweek the wait can be eight to 10 minutes.

From the top of Heaven's Gate experts can drop down a trio of short steeps directly below the lift or descend Organ Grinder with its tricky double fall line. To the left is the legendary Stein's Run with its steep moguled face and a trio of slightly less challenging expert runs.

Sugarbush North has wide-open cruising runs that a skier won't find at South or at Mad River Glen. This is primarily an intermediate playground, though the double blacks at the top—

F.I.S., Black Diamond, Exterminator and Bravo (the latter a single-diamond)—are among the toughest in New England. North also has more extensive snowmaking than South (76 percent is covered), though increased coverage at South is on this season's list of improvements.

On the map, the intermediate runs from the top of the Summit quad chair seem relatively short, but the map is misleading. The Rim Run connecting to Northway and then to either Which Way, Cruiser or North Star comprises one of the classic cruising runs in the United States. The other intermediate section is Inverness, served by a quad chair and offering a good training area. Beginners have an excellent area just to the left of the base with a T-bar and a short double chair.

Mad River Glen is a totally separate ski area and a throwback to earlier ski days. Mad River Glen prides itself on being tough (even the beginner trails here might be graded intermediate at Sugarbush), traditional (it's one of two areas in the nation with a chair lift for solo riders), natural (little snowmaking, combined with plenty of tight tree skiing), daring (can't imagine any other ski area with so much "out-of-bounds" skiing) and homey (skiers with serious tracks to carve have got to love a cafeteria with peanut-butter-and-jelly sandwiches to go).

Experts, real experts, have one goal: the top of the single chair. The lines do get long—very long. The ski patrol and lift operators scan the line and attempt to weed out beginners and lower intermediates who would have no business at the top. Meanwhile, the real experts happily wait—for them this is what skiing in the East is all about.

From the top of the single chair, experts can immediately drop down the Chute or the Fall Line, or if they are with a guide or local madman they can venture into the area called Paradise, entered by dropping down an eight-foot waterfall. Real experts: ask around for Octopus's Garden and the 19th and 20th holes. If you look like you know how to ski, a local may direct you there.

The single chair also has plenty of well groomed terrain for the solid intermediate. And guess what? It's not icy—Mad River Glen owner Betsy Pratt let her groomers know that this was her mountain, she wanted to ski it, and she didn't want to skate it. They found a way to scoop and buff the snow, when the weather cooperates it is surprisingly easy to ski. Antelope and Catamount are relatively moderate routes down the mountain.

Mad River Glen Facts
Base elevation: 1,637'; Summit elevation: 3,637'; Vertical drop: 2,000 feet.
Number and types of lifts: 4–3 double chairs, 1 single chair.
Acreage: about 95 skiable acres Snowmaking: 15 percent
Uphill capacity: 3,000 skiers per hour Bed base: 6,600

At the single chair midstation, tree skiing beckons through the Glades on one side of the lift line and Lynx on the other. More timid souls can traverse on Porcupine and drop down the wide-open Grand Canyon or thread through the narrow Bunny Run.

This brings you to the section served by the Sunnyside double chair. At the top of this sector, intermediates can turn to the left and drop down Quacky to Porcupine, Grand Canyon and Bunny, or they can go below the lift and to the right down a short series of expert trails, Panther, Partridge, Slalom Hill and Gazelle, most of which empty into Birdland.

Birdland is ostensibly the beginner area. Granted, there are Duck, Lark, Robin, Wren and Loon for beginners, but there are also lower intermediate tight runs like Snail and Periwinkle. Even though there are green circles at every fork in the trail, real intermediates can have plenty of fun here too. If you learn to ski here, nothing will daunt you elsewhere.

NOTE: Betsy Pratt has embarked on a plan to sell the ski area as a not-for-profit corporation through public shares— 2,000 of them at $1,500 each. Sales were doing well enough to keep the ski area open, but about thirty percent still needed to be sold. Before you make a special trip just to ski here (they don't make 'em like Mad River anymore, and a lot of people appreciate the rugged, nostalgic atmosphere), call ahead and be sure nothing drastic has happened.

Mountain rating

Experts: Head to Mad River Glen, the Castlerock section of Sugarbush South, and the short-but-steep Black Diamond and Upper FIS, plus Exterminator and Bravo at Sugarbush North.

Intermediates and cruise hounds: you'll have the most fun at Sugarbush North. If you're looking for day-long challenge, strike out for Mad River Glen and if you are just entering the intermediate ranks, test Jester and the Gate House area of Sugarbush South.

Beginners have their best area at Sugarbush North, and acceptable sections of Sugarbush South near Gate House. Never-evers should not start at Mad River Glen—take at least a week's lessons first.

Cross-country (94/95 prices)

The Sugarbush Winter Recreation Area, outside the Sugarbush Inn, has 25 km. of prepared trails across from the inn. Trail fees are $12 a day for adults, $8 for children, with reductions for guests staying in Sugarbush Resort properties. Equipment rentals, private lessons and group lessons are available. Other nearby cross-country areas are **The Inn at the Round Barn Farm** with 30 km. of groomed trails, rentals, instruction and snowshoe rentals ($8 trail fee, $4 for inn guests);

Blueberry Lake with 30 km. of trails ($9 fee); and **Ole's** (near the airport) with 35 km. and the most varied terrain in the area.

Snowboarding

Boarding is allowed everywhere at Sugarbush. Both Sugarbush mountains have halfpipes (the trail map pinpoints their location). South has one of the larger Eastern parks. World Cup riders helped design it, and boarders dubbed the park FRED, an acronym for Radical Extreme Descent, preceded by an expletive deleted. (Now you know.)

Snowboarding has been banned at Mad River Glen since the 93/94 season, when some impolite boarders ticked off the owner. That policy is unchanged.

Lessons (95/96 prices)

Because Sugarbush is owned by the Sunday River ski resort group, it also uses the excellent learning program that started at that Maine resort, Perfect Turn® (see the Everybody Skis chapter for an explanation). **Group clinics** are $24 for all levels except never-evers. **Guaranteed Learn to Ski,** which includes lesson, lifts and rentals, is $42 for level 1 skiers for never-evers; level 2 will be $52. **Private lessons** are $50 an hour; additional persons are $15. An all-day private lesson for one is $225, for two to four skiers, $310.

Children are divided into age groups for instruction. The Microbears program is for ages 2 1/2 to 4, with a little bit of skiing and day care for $53 full day, $39 half day. The Minibears program takes kids 4–6 years old for a combination of ski school and play activities for $58 full day, $39 half day. The Sugarbears program is for those 7–12 and costs $68 for a full day and $45 for half day, and the Catamounts program is for ages 13–16 and costs $75 for a full day. Children's programs include lunch and lift tickets, plus equipment for the 6-and-younger crowd. Multiday discounts are available except during holidays.

Mad River Glen has a ski school that, like the area, marches to its own drummer. Mad River offers weekday clinics, and private lessons with a maximum of four skiers per instructor. The ski school has offered bump and telemark clinics in the recent past; call the area to be sure they are still on for this season.

Mad River Glen also has beginner ski packages, ski programs for children aged 6–12 and NASTAR racing. When opened, two runs through the timed race course cost $5, with a dollar for each additional run.

Child care

The **Sugarbush Day School and Nursery** was the first child-care facility ever established at a ski resort. It takes children 6 weeks to 3 years. Two emergency medical technicians and a registered pediatric nurse are in residence. Toddlers get a pre-ski program that uses games on and off the snow to introduce skiing.

Full-day program with lunch is $48; half day is $35.

Mad River Glen has the Cricket Club Nursery for children 18 months to 6 years.

Lift tickets (95/96 prices)

Sugarbush

	Adult	Child (7–13) Senior (65–69)
One day (94/95)	$42	$23
Three days	$121 ($40.33/day)	$63 ($21/day)
Five days	$179 ($35.80/day)	$105 ($21/day)

Children 6 and younger and seniors 70 and older ski free. Sugarbush lowers ticket prices for adults in its Value Season, opening through mid-December and in April. Prices are higher during Christmas, New Year and Presidents' Day Weekend.

Mad River Glen

If Mad River opens as a coop ski ski area, these will be the lift ticket prices. If not enough members join the coop and the area is purchased by a larger resort, these prices will change dramatically. Call ahead.

	Adult	Junior (6–15) Senior (65–74)
One day	$26	$20
Three days	$74 ($24.66/day)	$56 ($18.66/day)
Five days	$*	$*

Adults pay $30 on holidays. Children 5 and younger will be issued a free ticket when skiing with a paying adult. Skiers 75 and older ski free.

* Skiers who buy a four-day lift ticket get their fifth, sixth and seventh days free.

Accommodations

This area has some of Vermont's finest country inn accommodations, all of which can be booked through Sugarbush Central Reservations, (800) 537-8427 (53-SUGAR), or call the inns directly.

Topping the list is recently restored **The Inn at the Round Barn Farm** a mile from Route 100 across the wooden bridge on East Warren Road (indeed, this rates with the best B&Bs we've seen anywhere in ski country). The farmhouse has been made into an elegant spacious, 11-room bed-and-breakfast. It is peaceful and quiet, strictly No Smoking, with children discouraged. Room rates for two people including breakfast, range from $95 for a small room with shower and private bath to $175 for the stunning Richardson Room with Vermont-made pencil post king bed, skylights, fireplace, oversized Jacuzzi and steam shower. There are 30 km. of cross-country tracks outside the door. Call 496-2276.

Tucker Hill Lodge (496-3983 or 800-543-7841), two miles from Sugarbush's lifts, has 22 rooms, each with a choice of breakfast alone or breakfast and a four-course dinner. Prices per day per person start at $124 for the room-and-meals deal.

If you like history, you'll adore **The Waitsfield Inn** (496-3979 or 800-758-3801) in the center of Waitsfield Village. It started life in the 1820s as a parsonage, was a sleeping-bag dorm for young skiers in the 60s and 70s, and is now a quaintly elegant 12-bedroom B&B. Each of the rooms is named for someone who lived in the house during the 19th century, and a booklet gives short biographies. A highlight is the inn's common area, a charming room built in what was once the stable. The inn is run by Steve and Ruth Lacey, he a droll Brit and she a bouncy Californian. Prices start at $130 for a room for two.

Other B&Bs that we found quite charming were **Lareau Farm Country Inn**, (496-4949) a roomy 14-bedroom inn connected to a popular weekend-only restaurant, the American Flatbread Kitchen; and **West Hill House** (496-7162), a four-bedroom (all with private bath) inn that has ski-stay packages starting at $62 per person per night, double occupancy.

The most luxurious full-service hotel property is the **Sugarbush Inn** located on the access road. Ski-and-stay packages start at $73 per person based on double occupancy. Though the inn and its 46 rooms are beautiful, the service was consistently underwhelming on our last stay here. The inn has a 25-km. cross-country trail system, indoor swimming pool, fitness center and saunas.

Another favorite is the **Weathertop Lodge** on Route 17 between Waitsfield and Mad River Glen (496-4909). Closer to Sugarbush resort you'll find Sugar Lodge at Sugarbush (800-982-3465) only a half mile from Sugarbush South, with a massive fieldstone fireplace. Rates at both are reasonable; call for current information.

Mad River Barn (496-3310) has spacious rooms and some of the best lodging food in the valley (both in quantity and quality). To stay here is a step into a wonderful 1940s ski lodge.

Families will want to check into the **Madbush Falls Country Lodge** on Route 100 (496-5557) or the **Hyde Away** (496-2322). Both are great spots for children and close to the slopes. The Hyde Away has become the favorite locals' dining hangout on Thursdays for Fish Night.

Of the condominiums in the Village at Sugarbush South, the most luxurious are the **Southface Condominiums** with hot tubs in each unit and a shuttlebus ride from the slopes. **The Snow Creek** condos are ski-in/ski-out, but you have the noise of snow guns at your back window during snowmaking operations. The

Paradise condos are newer but a good walk from the slopes; however, they have good shuttle service. **The Summit** units are roomy and **Castle Rock** condos are close to the slopes. **Unihab** looks like boxes stacked on one another, and **Middle Earth** condos are 10 minutes from the lifts and small.

Rates range from $126 for a one-bedroom in value season to $635 for a four-bedroom during holiday periods. Guests may use the indoor pool, indoor tennis, racquetball, squash courts, aerobics, Jacuzzi, steam room and Nautilus equipment at the Sugarbush Sports Center for an additional fee. These condos are close to the children's center.

Almost as close to the lifts as Sugarbush Village units is the newly completed **The Bridges Resort and Racquet Club.** This complex has racquetball courts and an indoor pool. Rates: two-bedroom, two-bath units start at $238. Call 583-2922 or (800) 453-2922.

Skiers heading primarily for Mad River Glen should check into the **Battleground** condos, starting at $184 for a two-bedroom unit. Call 496-2288 or (800) 248-2102.

Dining

With more than 40 eating establishments, the valley boasts a very high excellent-restaurant-per-skier ratio. The only other competition in New England is the Mt. Washington Valley in New Hampshire.

The top of the line is **Chez Henri** (583-2600) in Sugarbush Village at the base area of Sugarbush South. The restaurant manages to capture a true French bistro feeling—it is romantic and cozy, with low ceilings and a flickering fire. The owner, Henri Borel, personally greets guests and makes them feel at home. He also supervises the excellent wine selection. Chez Henri features lunch, fondue in the late afternoon, then dinner until 10 p.m. Entrées range from $13.50 to $22.

Sam Rupert's, down a driveway to the left as you approach the Sugarbush parking lot, has developed lots of fans and offers an eclectic menu rivaling any in the area along with a good reasonable wine list. Bill Brunell adds real magic to evenings twice a week.

The Common Man has attracted an excellent clientele and a reputation for good food. The atmosphere is great New England baroque barn with crystal chandeliers. Entrées generally range from $12 to $18; call 583-2800.

Tucker Hill Lodge on Route 17 between Waitsfield and Mad River Glen has one of the best reputations for dining in the valley. The menu changes every night of the week. Expect to pay between $16 and $24 for entrées. Reservations are suggested; call 496-3983. The downstairs lounge at Tucker Hill is called Giorgio's Cafe and serves Italian meals.

The **Terrace Room** at the Sugarbush Inn is intimate with continental dining. The menu changes daily depending on what foods are in season. The **Grill Down Under** is a more casual dining spot in the Sugarbush Inn and **Knickers** in the clubhouse at the Sugarbush Cross Country Center is enjoyable.

The **Bass Tavern** on the access road serves tasty heart-healthy creative meals ($10–$16) around a giant fireplace.

Mad River Barn Restaurant has a popular Saturday buffet, and dinners Sunday through Friday from 6:30 to 8 p.m. Meals are prepared by chefs from a nearby culinary school, Mary's in Bristol. Another Sugarbush tradition worth the effort is the **Flatbread Kitchen** open only on weekends at the Lareau Far Country Inn. Call 496-4949 to make sure they are serving.

For families out to stretch the budget and still get good wholesome food at reasonable prices, number one is the **Hyde Away** on Route 17. Thursday Fish Night is a big hit with locals. For simple quick food, try **The Den** on Waitsfield's main street, or **D.W. Pearl's**.

Good spots for breakfast are **D.W. Pearl's**, the **Hyde Away** and **Pepper's Restaurant** at Pepper's Lodge. The Mad River Barn lays out excellent homemade muffins and jams and serves only real maple syrup.

Après-ski/nightlife

Après-ski starts at the base lodges, which do booming business at the bar as the lifts close. Or head to **Chez Henri** where the bar fills up with people quietly drinking beer or wine. The **Hyde Away** is where you will find the locals; the **Blue Tooth** is most popular with tourists. The **Bass Tavern's** happy hour often will get rowdy. One or the other Sugarbush base lodges will usually have a live band for après-ski. On weekends try the **Sugarbush Inn** for a slightly more upscale crowd. If you are coming from Mad River Glen, the only place to stop is the **Mad River Barn**. The bar there looks like an old Vermont bar should look: moose head hanging over the fireplace, hunting scenes on every wall, big couches and stuffed chairs, wood paneling and a choice of bumper pool or shuffleboard.

In the evenings, **Gallagher's** has dancing with a mix of music from rock to country-rock and an interesting crowd. **Mad Mountain Tavern**, across from Gallagher's, is popular because of live music on weekends. **Chez Henri's** disco attracts a quieter slightly older group.

Other activities

Shopping: Waitsfield and Warren have art galleries, country stores and antique and collectible shops that are fun for browsing and buying. Most shops in tiny Warren Village within easy walking-distance of each other.

The **Sugarbush Sports Center** and the **Bridges Resort and Racquet Club** have various sports and exercise facilities.

Snowshoe treks are available from the summit of Sugarbush North to Sugarbush South. Call 583-0381.

Sleighrides and skijoring can be arranged at the Vermont Icelandic Horse Farm in Waitsfield. Call 496-7141. Other farms offering sleighrides are the Lareau Country Inn (496-4949) and Whispering Winds Farm in Moretown (496-2819).

Ice skating rinks are at Tucker Hill Lodge, Sugarbush Inn or the Skatium next to Grand Union in Waitsfield.

Mad River Flick (426-4200) has first-run movies, plus something at the concession stand most movie theaters don't offer: beer and wine.

Getting there and around

Getting there: Sugarbush is off Route 100, about 20 miles south of Waterbury. Burlington airport is about an hour away. Amtrak offers train-ski-lodging packages, with daily service from New York, Philadelphia and Washington, D.C. For information, call (800) 237-7547 for packages; (800) 872-7245 for train only.

Getting around: Sugarbush has four free shuttles: the Village shuttle, which connects several lodging properties with Sugarbush South; the Parking Lot Jitney, which circles each area's parking lot; the Intermountain Shuttle, which connects South and North; and the Fun Shuttle, which connects lodging at Sugarbush South with Waitsfield's downtown. The first two work fine. The Intermountain shuttle runs once per hour during the week; once per half hour on weekends. Get to the stop early. The nightly Fun Shuttle also runs once per hour from 6 p.m. to 12:30 a.m. For a one-time visit to town it's okay, but for more frequent visits, bring or rent a car.

You will need a car to get to Mad River Glen.

Information/reservations

Sugarbush Central Reservations will arrange all phases of your trip: (800) 537-8427 (53-SUGAR).

Snow phone: for Sugarbush call 583-7669; for Mad River Glen call 496-2001 or in Vermont 800-696-2001.

For **Mad River Glen** information call 496-3551.

The local area code is 802.

The Poconos, Pennsylvania

Honeymoon hideaways, major highways and big-city accessibility have make the hills of the Poconos in Northeastern Pennsylvania a convenient weekend area some of America's largest metropolitian areas.

The region has always had a hot honeymoon/weekend-getaway reputation with lodges offering heart-shaped beds and in-room spas. Beds of all shapes are not in short supply—you'll find 80,000 within an hour of the hills?.

Seven mountains—Alpine, Blue Mountain, Camelback, Jack Frost/Big Boulder, Shawnee and Tanglewood—are considered to be the main Pocono ski areas. Most are within 10 to 40 minutes of each other and only a few miles off the Pennsylvania Turnpike Northeast Extension, I-81, I-84 or I-80. The Poconos are about 90 minutes from New York City, less than 2 hours from Philadelphia and about 4 1/2 hours from the Baltimore/D.C. corridor.

By national standards, the Pocono ski areas would be deemed day areas owing to of their closeness to large cities and because the highest vertical drop is a meager 1,082 feet. But there also are trails, lifts and programs that can rival in their diversity many destination resorts.

Weekends tend to be crowded, very crowded. However, most areas have 100 percent snowmaking and state-of-the-art grooming, so surface conditions are reasonably good. Groomers will freshen up and snow guns fire if conditions fall apart too quickly. Most of the terrain is intermediate, with a few short-but-sweet black diamonds to keep the hot skiers happy, and plenty of beginner areas, often set apart.

Camelback Facts

*Base elevation: 1,250'; Summit elevation: 2,000'; Vertical drop: 800';
Number and types of lifts: 12-2 quad superchairs,7 doubles, 2 triples,1 surface lift. Acreage: 137 skiable acres. Snowmaking: 100 percent.
Uphill capacity: 18,600 per hour. Bed Base: 80,000 within 20 miles.*

Blue Mountain Facts

*Base elevation: 463'; Summit elevation: 1,543'; Vertical drop: 1,082';
Number and types of lifts: 7-1 quad superchair, 4 doubles, 2 surface lifts.
Acreage: 75 skiable acres. Snowmaking: 100 percent.
Uphill capacity: 8,600 per hour. Bed Base: 80,000 within 20 miles.*

The three most versatile areas are Blue Mountain, 20 minutes outside of Allentown, Pennsylvania; Jack Frost/Big Boulder, two hills practically across the road from each other where one ticket is good for both; and Camelback, with the most extensive trail system.

Where to ski

Blue Mountain: This ski area is closest to Philadelphia, and offers the highest vertical drop in the Poconos, 1,082 feet on Challenge. The pitch is steep and steady with moguls and a headwall near the bottom that will challenge the toughest. With ideal conditions, you might think you were skiing Vermont. This season a new intermediate trail, Paradise, will turn and snake from top to bottom and is fed by the Challenge quad superchair.

The area features night skiing seven nights a week and tickets are sold according to the hours you want to ski.

Jack Frost/Big Boulder: These two areas, marketed as the Big Two Resorts with an interchangeable lift ticket, are on opposite sides of Route 940 and a few miles from each other.

Big Boulder was one of the first Poconos ski areas and the to cover its trails with manmade snow. Today beginners and intermediates practice their skills day and night at Big Boulder on its 2,900-foot-long, 475-foot-high hill. If you arrive on a Friday night, you can ski to 10 p.m.

The Jack Frost lodge is at the top of the mountain. The 21 slopes and trails are straight, top to bottom, with variety in pitch. The mountain has two separate lift-served slopes for tubing.

Camelback: This area is the closest to metropolitan New York, and only about 20 minutes further from Philadelphia than Blue Mountain. It is an intermediate cruising heaven with 31 trails and a new high-speed quad. A second high-speed quad will open this season.

Although Margies and the Hump are rated expert, they tend to get slick early. The best skiing is on the intermediate trails, such as Interstate and Marc Antony. With the Stevenson high-speed quad, three new trails were added, including black-diamond 5,000-foot-long Cliffhanger which is F.I.S. rated (proper length, width and pitch to hold a professional race).

The trails are lighted for night skiing. Cameland, a special learning area, has been created for children ages 4–9.

Jack Frost Facts
Base elevation: 1,400'; **Summit elevation:** 2,000'; **Vertical drop:** 600 feet
Number and types of lifts: 7-1 quad superchair, 4 doubles, 2 triples
Acreage: 100 skiable acres   **Snowmaking:** 100 percent
Uphill capacity: 11,000 per hour   **Bed Base:** 80,000 within 20 miles

---

Big Boulder Facts
Base elevation: 1,700'; Summit elevation: 2,175'; Vertical drop: 475 feet
Number and types of lifts: 7-5 double, 2 triples. Acreage: 55 skiable acres.
Snowmaking: 100 percent. Uphill capacity: 8,900 per hour
Bed Base: 80,000 within 20 miles.

Mountain ratings

The Poconos are great for cruising intermediate terrain. Big Boulder has the best terrain for beginners. The longest trail is Bunny Shush, which covers 3,000 feet.

Best for advanced skiers are the three connecting slopes on East Mountain at Jack Frost, Challenge at Blue Mountain and Cliffhanger at Camelback.

Cross-country

Big Boulder offers a 3-km. trail at the top of the Edelweiss lift. The trail winds its way through Hickory Run State Park. Adjoining Jack Frost is a 15-km. trail winding through the open land surrounding the ski area.

Camelback and Blue have no cross-country skiing. However, many state parks and resorts near the ski areas have cross-country trails on them. You can call Pocono Mountain Tourist Bureau for a cross-country report at (717) 424-6050.

Snowboarding

At Camelback, The Glade has been turned into a snowboard park with a halfpipe.

At Big Boulder snowboarders are welcome to shred, hop, slide and jump at the Bonk Yard with its boxes, rail slides, barrels and truck tires.

Jack Frost snowboarders have two halfpipes, 400 and 500 feet in length.

Blue Mountain prohibits snowboarding. At all other theee areas boarders may ride anywhere on the mountains.

Lessons

Blue Mountain: Adult group lessons cost $16; children's group lessons are $13. Special clinics are available for women and for adults and children interested in racing. SKIwee is offered for children ages 4–12. The program includes instruction, lunch, progress report and SKIwee pin for $55 full day, $35 half day. Ski rentals are $11 extra.

Jack Frost/Big Boulder (94-95 prices) offers a Kids c'n Ski program. Kids 3–10 are given a three-hour lesson and a full-day lift ticket for $42 per child with rentals, $30 without rentals. Women's clinics, snowboarding and racing clinics offer an opportunity to master skills with those of similar abilities and interests. Group lessons are $60 for adults, $50 for children, and include a lift ticket.

Camelback has Cameland for children 4–9. They are supervised 9 a.m.–3:30 p.m. and get lift tickets, rentals and lunch for $65. Half day costs $50. Both packages provide three hours of instruction. Adult group lessons or racing clinics are $35 weekdays, $40 weekends, plus lift ticket.

Child care

Each area has amazing child-care deals during daytime skiing hours. At Camelback it's free for children 12 months or older on weekends 7:30 a.m.–5 p.m. and on weekdays 8:30 a.m.–5 p.m. At the Big Two for children 12 months and older, it's $6 half day, $10 full day, with each additional child half price when a parent buys a lift ticket. At Blue it's free during the week and $2 per hour on the weekend for children 6 weeks to 5 years old.

Lift tickets

Daily weekend prices	Adult	Child (6–12) Senior (60–69)
Blue Mountain	$38	$36
Jack Frost/Big Boulder	$37	$20 (6–10)
Camelback	$38	$32

Specific ticket information for each area:

Blue Mountain: Blue sells its tickets by full or partial days, with adult tickets ranging from $22 to $30 on weekdays, juniors $20 to $28. Special 20 percent discounts for women, college students, high-school students and ski club members are offered on certain days.

Jack Frost/Big Boulder (94/95 prices): Lift tickets are interchangeable at both areas. Night skiing is offered at Big Boulder only. Weekday prices: adult $30; children 6–10, $18. Various packages and combinations are available at a saving over single day tickets.

Camelback: Various combinations and multiday tickets are available. Midweek for adults is $32; children $26.

Accommodations

Although Jack Frost/Big Boulder claim that 50 percent of their skiers are multiday vacationers, most Pocono skiers come for the day. With 80,000 beds within an hour of any area, overnight accommodations in winter are guaranteed.

Jack Frost/Big Boulder have about 300 condos on-site. Midweek costs are about $99 per night, per person double occupancy (third person pays $49) and a two-night minimum. Lift tickets and dinner at the Blue Herron included (at Big Boulder); children under 12 sleep, eat and ski free. Call (800) 468-2442 or (717) 443-8425 for reservations.

With a Thursday or Friday night arrival and a minimum two-night stay, the third night is free and you get discounts on lift tickets.

Off mountain, **Split Rock Lodge and Convention Center** is a four-season resort with 400 rooms and amenities such as bowling, a movie theater, health club, pools, and nightly entertainment. Prices start about $84 per night per person, including breakfast, dinner and a lift ticket at Big Boulder. The weekend rate rises to $116 per person per night, and includes two meals, lift ticket, rentals and a lesson. Call (717) 722-9111 for current rates and reservations.

Mountain Laurel Resort, just off the Pennsylvania Northeast Extension and four miles from Jack Frost, has 253 rooms. Amenities include a pool, whirlpool, fitness center, restaurant, nightly entertainment, cross-country skiing and a weekend program for children of parents who want to skip away to ski. Call (717) 443-8411.

Blue Mountain has arranged ski-and-stay packages with 10 lodging properties. Their central reservations office can fill in the details.

The Inn at Jim Thorpe has a ski package including continental breakfast, welcome cocktail and ticket for $49 per person per weeknight and $58 on weekends. The Inn has a restaurant with Irish specials and a varied menu averaging $10.95 per entrée. Call (610) 325-2599.

Barnhouse Village, only nine miles from the slopes, offers 12 suites, shops, and a restaurant serving Pennsylvania Dutch food. Call (610) 837-1234.

About 20 minutes away in Allentown, the **Holiday Inn Conference Center** and the **Sheraton Allentown** offer a weekend special for $70 per night per person that includes a welcome reception, breakfast, buffet dinner and lift ticket. For reservations call (800) 383-1100.

Camelback has 450 rooms within 40 yards of the lifts including privately owned condos. Call 629-3661.

The Chateau at Camelback (closest to the slopes) has 151 rooms, weight room and swimming pool. Weekend package for two includes lift tickets and breakfast for $196, with dinner $247. Weekday package for two includes lift ticket and breakfast for $155; with dinner $200. Pay $50 extra and you can have a two-level suite that sleeps four, but meals and lift tickets are not included for the two extra sleepers. Call (800) 245-5900.

About 20 minutes away is **Pocono Manor,** with 255 double rooms. Built in 1902 and refurbished to modern standards, an indoor pool, sauna, Nautilus fitness center, hay rides, 40 miles of groomed cross-country trails and an ice skating rink. Cost is $71 per night per person mid-week, including breakfast and a lift ticket for Camelback. Weekends require a two-night stay at a cost of $84 per night per person inclusive. For reservations call (800) 233-8150.

In addition, strip motels, inns and B&Bs are available close to each area.

Dining

Blue Mountain: The closest thing to a gourmet experience is a drive to Allentown to take advantage of the nationally known restaurants on Route 145, such as Olive Garden, Chi Chi's, Chile's, Outback Steakhouse or Ground Round.

Camelback: Smugglers Cove (717-629-2277) on Route 611 in Tannersville has steaks, prime rib and seafood picked up fresh from New York's Fulton's Fish Market three times a week. Your best deal is the $8.95 early bird full dinner special, or try a pasta dish or the salad bar.

For Chinese and American, try **Pagoda** on Route 611 in Scotts Run with their Oriental gardens and 30-foot salt water aquarium. Call (717) 629-0250. **Fanucci's** on Route 611 in Swiftwater serves homemade pasta, seafood and veal.

Jack Frost/Big Boulder: The folks at the Big Two would like you to hang around and have dinner at the **Blue Herron Grille,** offering a traditional menu at $12–$18 per entrée. Close by on Lakeside Drive between Jack Frost and Big Boulder is **Close Quarters,** serving tasty Italian and American food in an upscale setting with prices of $15–$20 per entrée.   For reservations call (717) 722-8127.

Split Rock Lodge and **Mountain Laurel** have restaurants. For food, music and a holiday atmosphere, try **Shenanigans.** Entrées are $12 to $18. Call (717) 722-1100.

Aprés-ski/nightlife

Each area has its own aprés-ski crowd. Jack Frost brings in the locals along with the skiers at its **Elevation 2000 Bar,** which is open from 2–6 p.m. The **Blue Herron** downstairs at Big Boulder has music with a view of the slopes and stays open during night skiing hours. **Shenanigans,** just down the road on Lakeside Drive, has entertainment and music nightly on weekends.

Camelback's main lodge has music and entertainment on weekends from 2–6 p.m. For nightlife, head to Stroudsburg to **Hoopes** or **Vogue** on Main Street. Live bands, a D.J. and two dance floors keep things jumpin'.

Blue Mountain keeps its lodge open Thursday, Friday and Saturday nights to 11 with music and entertainment. Next stop is Allentown, if you still have energy.

Other activities

Many non-ski activities are offered at full-service resorts like Pocono Manor or Split Rock Lodge such as horseback riding, snowmobiling, cross-country skiing, health clubs or exercise rooms. But the Poconos are full of history with museums, historic mansions, craft shops and various points of interest.

Shoppers will like the Crossings, a discount outlet featuring 100 designer stores with deeply discounted merchandise. The Crossings is located at the juncture of the access road to Camelback and Route 611.

Getting there and getting around

Getting there: To reach Jack Frost/Big Boulder from New York, take Exit 43 from I-80. Jack Frost is five miles north by Route 115 then west on Route 940. Big Boulder is south of the interstate via Routes 115 and 903. To reach Camelback, take Exit 45 from I-80, then follow signs. Skiers coming from the south or heading to Blue Mountain should take the Northeast Extension of the Pennsylvania Turnpike to Exit 35 or 33 then follow the signs.

The ski areas are roughly 70 to 100 miles from Philadelphia, and 100 miles from New York City.

Check with ski shops for information about ski-club bus trips with lift tickets included. Ski clubs run regular trips to the Poconos and most will let non-members on the bus at least once.

Getting around: The best way to get to the Poconos is to drive. Without a car, transportation to the various resorts and restaurants is not possible. Adequate parking is available even on the most crowded weekends.

Information/reservations

Pocono Mountain Vacation Bureau has maps, brochures, lodging and general info. Call (800) POCONOS (800-762-6667).

For cross-country or tourist information call (717) 424-6050.

Blue Mountain, Palmerton, PA 18071; (610) 826-7700; snow report (800) 235-2226.

Jack Frost, Blakeslee, PA 18610; lodging (800) 468-2442; snow report (717) 443-8425.

Big Boulder, Lake Harmony, PA 18624; (717) 722-0100.

Camelback,Tannersville, PA 18272; (717) 629-1661; snow report (800) 233-8100.

Other Mid-Atlantic Resorts

Blue Knob, Claysburg PA, (814) 239-5111
7 lifts, 21 trails, 1,100 vertical feet

This mountain is in a part of Pennsylvania that gets more natural snow than the Poconos. The mountain has the lodge at the top. Beginner runs are at the top as well; toward the bottom the pitch becomes steeper. The resort is 150 miles from Philadelphia and 100 miles from Pittsburgh. Take the Bedford exit off the turnpike, then follow Rte. 220 north to Pavia and follow the signs.

Whitetail, Mercersburg PA, (717) 328-9400
6 lifts, 17 trails, 935 vertical feet

This is a fairly new resort, so the facilities are quite modern, including a quad superchair lift. Whitetail has a beautiful base facility and concentrates on giving Eastern skiers an upscale ski experience. In addition to having 100 percent snowmaking covering its 108 acres of trail, a children's center and 11,200 per hour skier capacity, it's just 90 minutes from the White House.

Elk Mountain Ski Area, Union Dale PA, (717) 679-2611
6 lifts, 25 trails, 1,000 vertical feet

This is, for Pennsylvania, a tough skier's mountain. The slopes are good for advanced skiers and solid intermediates who want some practice. Even the beginner trails are difficult. There is no real "resort area," but the region has about 50 hotels. Elk is in the northeast corner of Pennsylvania near Scranton.

Seven Springs, Champion PA, (814) 352-7777
18 lifts, 30 trails, 750 vertical feet
Hidden Valley, Hidden Valley, PA, (814) 443-2600
8 lifts, 16 trails, 610 vertical feet

These resorts are about three and a half hours from Baltimore and Washington and an hour from Pittsburgh. Seven Springs has the best base facilities and more difficult trails and Hidden Valley offers quieter surroundings. Trails at these two resorts will keep beginners and intermediates happy for a day or so. Seven Springs has the more difficult trails.

Snowshoe/Silver Creek, Snowshoe WV, (304) 572-1000
7 lifts, 33 trails, 1,500 vertical feet - Snowshoe
4 lifts, 14 trails; 663 vertical feet - Silver Creek

Snowshoe sits atop Cheat Mountain, topping off an inverted resort: the facilities are at the summit. The area often gets 200 inches of snow and has extensive snowmaking. This is the most elaborate and extensive resort in the South. The main problem is access: it's at the end of a 10-mile car path, but once there, every skier can enjoy the mountain.

Snowshoe bought nearby Silver Creek Resort, a terrific family area, during the 1992-93 season. Though the two areas are separate, a shuttle transports skiers the short distance. Silver Creek is less crowded, and the slopes are wider and better designed than at Snowshoe. The downside is the skiing is less challenging. One lift ticket is good at both areas.

Canaan Valley, Davis, WV, (304) 866-4121
21 trails, 3 lifts; 850 vertical feet

A long time favorite ski area for Washington skiers, Canaan (pronounced Kuh - NAAN) Valley ski area is located in a pristine wilderness area. Deer stroll in front of the park hotel. There is terrific cross country-skiing nearby. The downhill skiing is good with a variety of terrain for all levels.

Timberline Four Seasons Resort, Davis, WV (304) 866-4801
20 trails, 3 lifts; 1,084 vertical

This area was one of the first in the country to welcome snowboarders. It is a small family area, boasting a two-mile long beginner's run. It's usually uncrowded compared to next-door Canaan, and many of the skiers are resort property owners.

Wintergreen, Wintergreen VA (804) 325-2200
5 lifts, 10 trails; 1,003 vertical feet

Wintergreen is less than an hour south of Charlottesville along the famed Skyline Drive. While natural snow is limited, the manmade variety is religiously pumped out day and night. The lodge is rather upscale with boutiques and antiques. Most skiing is mellow, but The Highlands offers a thousand feet of bumps with limited crowds, thanks to good control by the ski patrol.

Wisp, McHenry, Maryland (301) 387-4911
5 chairs, 2 surface lifts; 23 trails on 80 acres; 610 vertical feet

Located above scenic Deep Creek Lake, Wisp is the closest thing below the Mason-Dixon Line to skiing Lake Tahoe. A solid family ski area with terrain for all levels; intermediates will especially enjoy cruising on the backside of the mountain.

Midwestern Resorts

The biggest Midwestern ski areas may not have the great verticals of mountains to the east and west, but they have enough terrain, fine facilities, and uphill capacity to tune anyone up for bigger adventures. The following are the best Midwestern ski destinations. Expect lift tickets to be between $25 and $30 everywhere except Michigan's Lower Peninsula, where weekend tickets will be in the mid-$30s. All the resorts offer midweek price incentives and stay-and-ski packages.

Michigan's Lower Peninsula:
Boyne Highlands and Boyne Mountain,
Harbor Springs and Boyne Falls MI (800) 462-6963 (GO-BOYNE)
55 trails; 520 vertical feet

The Mountain and **The Highlands** are about 30 minutes apart and exchange lift tickets. The Mountain's steep chutes and mogul fields are among the best in the region; Hemlock has long been the standard-bearer for Midwestern steep. The Mountain has the nation's only high-speed six-seat chair. The Highlands is a Michigan classic, with wide sweeping bowls and New England-style trails that slice through the woods. The Highlands added more beginner terrain and a new chair last season to complement its more demanding runs. Each resort has an uphill capacity of around 22,000 skiers per hour (tops in the Midwest). Boyne's snowmaking capabilities are legendary. Boyne Mountain routinely stays open on weekends through April.

Nubs Nob is just across the valley from the Highlands. Nubs offers the best trio of advanced slopes in the Lower Peninsula. Recent additions of intermediate and beginner terrain help round out the variety. It's the locals' choice, and one of the top day-trip areas in the Lower Peninsula. It has no lodgings.

Sugar Loaf, Cedar MI (616) 228-5461; (800) 748-0117
20 trails, 500 vertical feet

One of the most scenic resorts in the Lower Peninsula, the backdrop of Lake Michigan's blue-gray waters and the Manitou Islands offshore make it hard to keep your eyes on the slopes. A well-rounded area, The Loaf boasts some great steep with Awful-Awful and Manitou (Michigan's only FIS-sanctioned racing hill), and cruisers like Devil's Elbow and Sugar 'n' Spice. Gambling packages are offered at the Leelanau Sands Casino.

Crystal Mountain, Thompsonville MI (616) 378-2911
22 trails, 375 vertical feet

This skis much bigger than its 375-foot vertical. It's a great family area that offers solid intermediate slopes and lots of lower-level trails. As evidence of its appeal, Crystal ranks annually among the top 10 resorts nationally for NASTAR participants. It has a variety of lodging and a fitness center with pool.

Shanty Creek/Schuss Mountain, Ballaire MI
(616) 533-8621; (800) 348-4440; 30 trails, 450 vertical feet

This resort offers a nice weekend retreat. These two separate areas about five miles apart are now operated as one with interchangeable lift tickets. Shanty has the nicest lodging, but Schuss has the better skiing—a good skier will get bored quickly at Shanty.

Michigan's Upper Peninsula

This is a rugged land of dense forests, long winters, deep snows and a collection of ski areas called Big Snow Country. The region receives over 200 inches of snowfall annually. About a six- to seven-hour drive from Chicago, its center is Ironwood. These areas have enough variety to keep skiers happy for a weekend or a midweek trip.

Indianhead Mountain, Wakefield, MI
(906) 229-5181; (800) 346-3426 (3-INDIAN)
18 trails, 638 vertical feet

Indianhead runs are wide boulevards. It's an intermediate's dream—long, smooth runs—but they all look the same. The skier who likes a good challenge may get bored here but it is a great family area. The lodge and compact ski area sit atop the mountain. Runs fan out into the deep forests below, but all the lifts funnel back to the lodge on top.

Blackjack, Bessemer, MI (906) 229-5115; (800) 848-1125
16 trails, 465 vertical feet

Blackjack appeals to intermediate and advanced skiers, befitting its brawny lumberjack image. They will enjoy busting down some of the wide bump runs or exploring the many narrow chutes and trails that fork off the boulevards. The Black River meanders through the valley—very picturesque.

Big Powderhorn Mountain, Bessemer, MI
(906) 932-4838; (800) 222-3131; 23 trails, 600 vertical feet

This area offers a good variety of trails and the most uphill capacity in the immediate area (9,600 per hour). It has tree-lined trails, open bowls, rambling runs and narrow chutes to explore, plus the most slopeside lodging, restaurants and après-ski activity in the area.

Whitecap Mountain, Montreal, WI (715) 561-2227
32 trails, 400 vertical feet

Whitecap has had a facelift in recent years. Several new shops and a conference center have been added to the day lodge, but the expansion still preserves the Old-World charm. The most interesting mix of trails in the area drops down three peaks in every direction. It's the one place in the Midwest where a trail map comes in handy. Located in the Pekonee Mountains, it's in sight of Lake Superior on a clear day.

Porcupine Mountain, Ontonagon, MI (906) 885-5275
14 trails; 600 vertical feet

About 45 minutes north of Indianhead, Porcupine offers some of the most stunning Lake Superior views. It's almost perched on the shoreline, and the lake is in evidence on every run. Being state-owned, it offers the best lift rates in the area.

Minnesota

Blessed with superb ski terrain and consistently cold temperatures, northern Minnesota has some of the best snow conditions east of the Rockies, and the northwoods scenery is spectacular. What's here? Three excellent ski areas with big vertical drops (for the Midwest)—Giants Ridge, 550 feet; Spirit Mountain, 700 feet; and Lutsen, 800 feet. They are around Duluth and within an hour or so of each other.

Lutsen, Lutsen, MN (218) 663-7281
27 trails; 800 vertical feet

About an hour north of Duluth, Lutsen is the closest thing to true mountain skiing in the area. It has the only gondola in the Midwest. It will remind you of a New England ski area—three mountain peaks, long rock-ribbed trails flanked by birch and pine, and tight headwalls. Moose Mountain offers some great cruisers and breathtaking views of Lake Superior. The Mountain Inn and Village offers first-class slopeside lodging.

Spirit Mountain, Duluth, MN (800) 642-6377
20 trails; 700 vertical feet

Spirit Mountain has good vertical, long runs, snowy winters and great views of Duluth and the harbor perched on the Superior shoreline. The skiing is long on intermediate and beginner runs, without much variation in pitch and few twists and turns. A high-speed covered quad services the beginner trails—nice on cold days. An expert won't find challenge here.

Giant's Ridge, Biwabik, MN (218) 865-4143
19 trails; 500 vertical feet

About an hour's drive northwest of Duluth, this area is not as crowded as the other two. The trails soar off the crest and are varied in pitch, with a headwall here, a bowl there. The day lodge is first class, and so is the cross-country skiing.

Wisconsin

The skiing here has a certain ruggedness that you won't find in Michigan's Lower Peninsula. It's full of rocky outcroppings—spared the effect of the glaciers that spread over the upper Midwest some 10,000 years ago. It doesn't receive the natural lake-effect snow that Michigan gets, but the areas do an adequate job of snowmaking.

Devil's Head, Merrimac, WI (800) 338-4579 (DEVILSX)
21 trails; 500 vertical feet

In the beautiful Baraboo Bluffs overlooking the Wisconsin River Valley, this area has excellent beginner and intermediate skiing. One of the beginner runs is nearly two miles long. Its drawbacks are little advanced terrain and not much terrain variation. It is a full-service resort with a country-club atmosphere. Weekend crowds can be huge.

Located just down the road is **Cascade** with 460 vertical feet and a wide variety of skiing. It's straightforward skiing, with solid cruising and hefty faces for the bumps. It has more uphill capacity than Devil's Head (14,000 per hour), but weekend lines can still be long. These two resorts, located just three hours from Chicago, together are consistently rated the top day-trip destination in the Midwest.

Rib Mountain, Wausau, WI (715) 845-2846
13 trails; 624 vertical feet

Rib is the most European-feeling setting in the Midwest with the city nestled at the base of the mountain. It offers no-frills skiing with wide, western-like slopes. The narrow chutes off the Rib will entice advanced skiers. Lodging is available in the city.

Mt. La Crosse, La Crosse, WI (800) 426-3665
17 trails; 516 vertical feet

Skiers will find most of this area's runs are cut through rocky bluffs containing headwalls and chutes. It sits high atop a rugged bluff overlooking the Mississippi River. It has the only true double-black slope in the Midwest—Damnation.

Iowa and Illinois

A couple of good areas located in the tri-state corner are **Chestnut Mountain** (800-397-1320) near Galena, IL and **Sundown** (800-397-6676) near Dubuque, IA. They sit about 30 miles apart on bluffs overlooking the Mississippi River. Both have a 475-foot vertical and offer a good variety for all abilities. Their biggest drawback is lack of natural snow, but they do a good job with snowmaking.

Part of the charm of this area is that you can stay in and explore the historic river ports of Galena and Dubuque. Both have quaint B&Bs and country inns offering ski packages (800-747-9377). Riverboat gambling is a popular après-ski activity.

Alyeska, Alaska

Alyeska, 40 miles southeast of Anchorage, is an unusual ski resort: The base altitude is only 250 feet above sea level, the lowest of any major ski area in the world. Mt. Alyeska rises 3,939 feet, overlooking Turnagain Arm, a spectacularly beautiful extension that branches off Cook Inlet. The view from Alyeska is best savored from the Glacier Terminal at the top of the 60-passenger tram—mainly because if you see it for the first time while you're skiing, it will mesmerize you to the point where you're likely to run into someone or something. Another thing about Alyeska that's unusual: during the early part of the ski season, the ski "day" is about five hours long. Luckily, Alyeska has night skiing.

The lower half of the mountain is forested and the upper portion is above the tree line. Upper-mountain snow accumulations average 579 inches a season. On a mid-April visit there can be 20 feet of snow on the upper mountain.

Images of Alaska tend toward ice, sled dogs, igloos and pipeline construction in subzero weather. Anchorage reality is much different. Warm Pacific currents cause winter temperatures to average 10 to 30 degrees Fahrenheit. Anchorage also is a bustling city with many fun activities to keep its residents entertained during the long winter nights.

Alyeska itself has changed recently in a very big way, going from a rustic ski area to a luxurious resort. Change began in 1991 with a $70 million expansion program that came to fruition last season. The resort now has a 60-passenger tram transporting skiers more than a mile from the base to mid-mountain, a high-speed quad, a new beginner chair lift, a day lodge and an on-mountain restaurant with gourmet evening dining accompanied by that great view. In August, 1994, the final major component came on line: the 307-room luxury Alyeska Prince Hotel, which replaced a 27-room inn, which had been the only other lodging.

Alyeska Facts

Base elevation: 250'; **Summit elevation (lift-served):** 2,750'; **Vertical drop:** 2,500 feet
Number and types of lifts: 9–1 60-passenger tram, 1 quad superchair, 2 quad chairs, 3 double chairs, and 2 surface lifts
Acreage: 480 skiable acres **Snowmaking:** 12 percent
Uphill capacity: 9,450+ skiers per hour.

Where to ski

The quad superchair Spirit of Alyeska carries skiers 1,411 vertical feet to the top of the lift-serviced terrain, which is at the base of the Alyeska Glacier. Up here it's wide-open, above-treeline skiing. The entire 2,500 feet of vertical is skiable in one continuous run, with intermediate to super-expert pitch depending on your choice of route. Skiers and snowboarders also can hike to the 3,939-foot summit of Mt. Alyeska, where expert-level Glacier Bowl and the Headwall await.

Alyeska also has a unique combination of open bowl skiing and trails through the trees directly under Chairs 1 and 4. Beginners will stick to the area served by Chairs 3 and 7 and the surface lifts. Intermediates can take the new quad chair, drop into the bowl and ski whatever they can see. It doesn't take much judgment to figure out whether you are getting in over your head, and this bowl gives you plenty of room to traverse out of trouble. The bowl funnels into Waterfall and ends on Cabbage Patch before reaching the base area.

For intermediates taking the Spirit quad chair to the top of the resort, it's best to follow the Mitey Mite: swing left when you get off the chair. This takes you past the Glacier Express restaurant in the Glacier Tram Terminal, and back to the quad by three intermediate routes, or tip down South Face (very steep and ungroomed).

From the quad, experts can go right and drop down Gail's Gully or Prospector and take a gully left or right of Eagle Rock, then back to the quad. Experts willing to work can take the High Traverse from the quad, arcing through The Shadows between Mt. Alyeska and Max's Mountain, dropping down through new snow and open steeps; or continue over the ridge to find good steeps and a short section of gladed skiing on Max's Mountain (when opened by the ski patrol).

Mountain rating

Intermediates will have a field day, especially with the wide-open bowl skiing and spectacular views from the top of the Spirit quad. Experts have some good drops but the real challenge of Alyeska is the tremendous variety of terrain and snow conditions from top to bottom. Snow may be groomed, cut up or untouched. Often there is powder at the top moistening to mashed potatoes at the bottom.

Cross-country

The Nordic Skiing Association designed and prepared the 10-km. Winner Creek trail, which leaves from Alyeska's base and wanders through woods, across meadows and up and down gentle hills. The trail is not groomed. You can also skinny-ski around nearby Moose Meadow area—locals will point you there; it's not marked.

There are hundreds of kilometers of groomed cross-country trails in Anchorage at Kincaid, Russian Jack and Hillside Parks. The Chugach State Park hillside trails are easily accessible (with a 4-wheel-drive) wilderness areas. There's a Nordic resort at Hatcher Pass (an hour and a half north of downtown Anchorage) and more cross-country trails at Sheep Mountain Lodge, 50 miles north of Palmer.

Snowboarding

Alyeska permits snowboarding on all trails and has several natural halfpipes in its main bowl area. Lessons and rentals are available.

Lessons (95/96 prices)

You will meet some very interesting people teaching skiing. The half-dozen full-timers, all PSIA-certified, build houses, drive boats and catch salmon in the summer. Part-timers might be pharmacists, lawyers, pilots, mothers, purchasing agents, or firefighters.

Alyeska packages its ski and snowboard lessons, a real benefit for those traveling from the Lower 48. For example, adult intermediate and advanced skiers can get a **group lesson**, lift ticket and rentals for $55, a lesson and lift ticket for $45, or the lesson alone for $30. (The snowboard price is $60 in the first category, but the same in the latter two.) Beginners pay $35 for a ski ticket-lesson-rental package; snowboard novices pay $40; for the lesson alone for both groups, it's $25. You can add on an afternoon lesson for an extra $20.

Private lessons for skiing, telemarking, Nordic skiing or snowboarding are $40 an hour, $20 for extra students. The latter three are not regularly scheduled, so make reservations with the ski school in advance if you're interested. If you're enrolled in a private lesson, you can get a lift ticket for $15 and rental packages for $10 for skiing and $15 for snowboarding.

Children's lessons for ages 4-13 are part of the national SKIwee instruction program. Two-hour lessons are $20 for beginners; $25 for intermediate and up. Children can get packages similar to the adult programs that include rentals and lift tickets. The all-day program with lunch and lift ticket for ages 6-13 ranges from $50 to $60, depending whether the child needs rentals and his/her ability level. The children's programs are popular, so always try to make reservations (754-1111).

The **Challenge Alaska Adaptive Ski School**, a chapter of National Handicapped Sports, provides skiing for the disabled with support from Alyeska Resort. All disabilities, all ages, by reservation only. A skier with a disability, and ski buddy, may purchase discount lift tickets and rent adaptive ski equipment.

Open Tuesday-Sunday, usually December 15 to April 15. The Alyeska Price Hotel and Tramway are fully wheelchair-accessible, a resort spokesperson said, and Challenge Alaska has information on other wheelchair-accessible accommodations and amenities. Call: Challenge Alaska, Box 110065, Anchorage AK 99511-0065; (907) 563-2658; fax (907) 561-6142. Alyeska Ski School phone: 754-1111.

Child care

Here, Alyeska has a problem. Little Bears Playhouse day-care center is near the resort (783-2116), but it is normally full with local children. The staff may recommend other babysitters who live in the valley.

Lift tickets (94/95 prices)

	Adult	Child (8-12) Senior (60+)
One day	$29	$17
Two days	$54 ($27/day)	$32 ($16/day)
Three days	$79 ($26.33/day)	$47 ($15.66/day)

Though these prices seem a bit low for a resort, keep in mind that Alaskan winter days are shorter than they are farther south. Here, the lifts don't start running until mid-morning (about 10:30 a.m.). Children 7 and younger ski for $7. Students with ID pay $23 for day tickets. Night skiing on 19 trails (75 acres) runs Thursdays through Saturdays 4:30-9:30 from December through March: Adults—$14, children and seniors—$12.

Accommodations

The only lodging at the base of the resort is in the 307-room **Alyeska Prince Hotel** and privately owned condominiums, which may be rented through management agencies.

The Prince was built to be a self-contained resort. It's so new we haven't yet seen it, but all reports are quite positive. Rates are $160-$260 per night. Call (800) 880-3880 for reservations.

About 50 condominium units are managed by two firms, **Vista Alyeska Accommodations**, Box 1029, Girdwood AK 99587 (30 units), 783-2010, fax 783-2011. A condo sleeping six costs $175-$250 a night, a condo sleeping four costs $125 to $200 depending on amenities. Some have fireplaces, whirlpools, hot tubs and wet bars.

Alyeska has a few bed-and-breakfasts. See Anchorage Visitors Guide B&B section under "Alyeska" alphabetic listings.

The larger bed base is in **Anchorage**, a 35- to 55-minute drive depending on weather. Major hotels include the **Regal Alaskan, Hotel Captain Cook, Hilton, Holiday Inn, Sheraton** and **Westmark**. There are many other hotels and motels, and hundreds of bed-and-breakfast rooms (some with spectacular views) available through the B&B reservation services. See the free Visitors Guide, available throughout the area.

Dining

These are some of our favorite restaurants; see the Visitors Guide for more selections.

The Alyeska Prince Hotel's restaurants are: The **Pond Cafe**, the largest with seating for 164, serves breakfast, lunch and dinner with a California-Italian menu. The **Takanawa Sushi Bar** and the **Katsura Teppanyaki Room** are open for dinner five nights a week, but seat just 14 and 18 diners, respectively. The **Seven Glaciers Restaurant and Lounge** has casual fine dining in the evening at the second level of the Glacier Terminal at 2,300 feet. The view is incredible and the food is reportedly excellent. (Reservations: 754-2237).

Alyeska & vicinity: Perhaps the best restaurant in the area is the **Double Musky Inn**, a mile from the lifts on Crow Creek Road. It's mind-boggling to find great Cajun food in Alaska. Entrées from $18 to $30. No reservations, opens at 5 p.m.; closed on Mondays.

Turnagain House, a white-tablecloth restaurant looking out on Turnagain Arm halfway to Anchorage, has a reputation for fine seafood and other dishes with excellent service. Entrées $15 to $30. Call for reservations, 653-7500.

Chair 5, casual, less expensive, offers prime rib, halibut and a tasty, very spicy chicken jalapeño. Girdwood business district next to the Post Office.

The Bake Shop at the resort boardwalk has killer soups, energy-filled buttered sticky buns with fruit filling, and sandwiches. Walk in, meals $5-$9. Lots of locals, ski instructors and patrollers here.

Anchorage: For those with deep pockets and taste for the best, call the **Marx Brothers Cafe**, for inventive continental cuisine and impeccable service in a cozy frame-house setting which reminds us of a small New England inn. Reservations required. Most entrées $20-$30.

Likewise, the **Corsair**, with continental cuisine offered by owner Hans Kruger. The style is elegant—expect to spend the whole evening.

For Northern Italian, **Romano's** in midtown has a strong local following; no reservations. **Little Italy** in South Anchorage, closer to Alyeska, also is packed with locals, reservations taken and occasionally needed. Moderately priced, entrées $11-$21.

Also moderately priced with fresh seafood specials daily are **Simon & Seafort's Saloon & Grill** (livelier) and **Elevation 92** (quieter), around the corner from each other downtown. Also try **Jens' Restaurant & Gallery** and **Europa Cafe** in midtown.

Seemingly a hole in the wall, **Club Paris** is an intimate downtown steak house.

For great views, especially at cocktail time, try the top-floor **Crow's Nest** at the Hotel Captain Cook, or **Top of the World** in the Hilton. **Josephine's** in the Sheraton also has a view, but is open only for Sunday brunch. Reservations; bring $$$ if dining.

Many Japanese have settled in Anchorage, and good moderately priced restaurants such as **Akaihana, Tempura Kitchen, Daruma, Kumagoro, Shogun, Yamatoya** and **Ichiban** are the result. All offer tempura, sukiyaki and other cooked dishes as well as sushi and sashimi. **Thai Cuisine** has—surprise—Thai cuisine. There are good Chinese establishments and a few Korean.

Families should head to **Sourdough Mining Co.** (great ribs, corn fritters) **Gwennie's Old Alaska Restaurant** (breakfasts, sandwiches, historic photos), **Hogg Brothers** (wow omelets for working people), **Red Robin**, the **Royal Fork, Peggy's, Lucky Wishbone** (the best fried chicken), and **Arctic Roadrunner** (super burgers).

For margaritas and Mexican cooking: **La Mex, Garcia's, El Patio, Mexico in Alaska.** Nice places, not great cuisine.

Après-ski/nightlife

The **Aurora Bar and Lounge** in the Alyeska Prince Hotel has a moderately lively atmosphere in the bar, where skiers can watch sports on TV. The lounge is quieter, with a rock fireplace and comfortable sofas and chairs. For après-ski, head to the **Sitzmark Bar** at the base of Chair 3.

The **Double Musky** and **Chair 5** also have taverns. On the drive into Anchorage, the **Bird House** is a legendary sunk-in-the-ground log building. Try a drink, an incredibly hot pickle, and some conversation while trying to sit up straight. Bring a business card: you'll find out why. Look for the "Bar" sign and bird head on the building.

Anchorage has a highly developed nightlife and cultural scene, a legacy of the pipeline days, the long winter nights, and generous doses of oil patch money.

For theater, opera, drama and movies, buy the local newspaper (Daily News). There's a Friday morning entertainment tabloid that's very helpful. You'll be surprised at the visiting artists and productions at the Alaska Center for the Performing Arts downtown, or the University of Alaska in midtown.

Mr. Whitekeys' Fly By Night Club puts on a zany, hilarious show called (depending on the season) Christmas in Spenard, Springtime in Spenard, or Whale Fat Follies. Call 279-7726 for reservations. This may be the only bar in the world where you can order Spam with champagne, or Spam nachos. After the show, there's dancing to the Spamtones. Mr. Whitekeys, the owner, sponsored a climber eating a can of Spam on the summit of Mt. McKinley.

For loud rock and dancing try **Chilkoot Charlie's**, "where we cheat the other guy and pass the savings on to you." For quieter dancing and a slightly older clientele try **Legends** at the Sheraton, **Whale's Tail** at the Hotel Captain Cook, or the lounge at the Golden Lion Best Western. For country music head to **Last Frontier South**.

Other activities

For a **dogsled** trip, run by Bob Crockett's Chugach Express Dog Sled Tours, call 783-0887 for reservations; last-minute calls don't work. Trips and prices range from 30 minutes to 3 hours, $20 to $50+ per person.

The variety of other activities is staggering. Of course, Anchorage has many fine shops where you can buy native crafts, plus items from around the world, thanks to Anchorage's position as a stop on long-distance international flights. This city of 250,000 is the business, cultural, transportation and, to some extent, government center of the state. Use your Anchorage Visitors Guide, buy a newspaper, ask locals on the chair lift for their favorite things.

Getting there and getting around

Getting there: Alyeska is 45 miles south of downtown Anchorage. Get on Gambell Street south, which becomes the Seward Highway, Route 1, along Turnagain Arm. This spectacular drive is one of the best parts of the skiing experience at Alyeska, and if you see cars parked by the road near Falls Creek, stop—the drivers are watching Dall sheep. Toward spring you may see bald eagles as the fish return.

Getting around: If you stay at an Anchorage hotel, **Alaska Sightseeing** can take you to the resort with advance reservations. Ask at the hotel desk. Otherwise, you'll need a car. If you are driving on mountain roads, or on back roads in Girdwood, get a 4-wheel-drive vehicle. Locals do.

Information/reservations

Alyeska Resort, Box 249, Girdwood AK 99587; 754-1111, snow conditions tape 754-7669 (SKI-SNOW), fax 754-2200. Hotel reservations: (800) 880-3880.

Anchorage Convention & Visitors Bureau, 1600 A St. #200, Anchorage AK 99501. Phone the main office 276-4118, fax 278-5559, for a copy of the encyclopedic Anchorage Visitors Guide. Request first-class mail.

Questions and details: phone ACVB's Log Cabin Visitor Center (274-3531) or drop in at 4th and F downtown. There's also an Airport Visitor Center in the baggage claim area.

The local telephone area code is 907.

Canadian Resorts

Canada is a great destination for a ski vacation. Generally, the giant mountains and vast snowfields are in the West, while the narrow trails and quaint ski towns are in the East, just as they are in the U.S. But a Canadian ski vacation also has some very attractive differences. Some examples:

• Some of Canada's leading ski areas are in national parks. Banff and Jasper National Parks have four ski areas within their boundaries. The scenery is magnificent and wildlife sightings (elk, moose, bighorn sheep, etc.) are common.

• You can stay in an opulent, historic hotel, even if you're on a budget. The Canadian Pacific chain includes several grand hotels built to accommodate late 19th- and early 20th-century luxury rail travel. Some call them winter Snow Castles. In summer they are jammed with tourists willing to pay premium rates, but in winter, prices plummet—you can enjoy strolling through the expansive lobbies and pretend that you're skiing on trust-fund money or lottery winnings. These Canadian Pacific Snow Castles are described in the following chapters.

• Americans get the benefits of a foreign ski vacation without the jet lag. This isn't everyone's cup of tea, but we think it's fun to have multicolored money in our wallets instead of greenbacks, to calculate the exchange rate (especially when it's in our favor), to present our passports at the airport and, in the case of a Québec vacation, try to communicate in another language.

Prices are in Canadian dollars, which, at press time, was about $1.37 Canadian dollars for each U.S. dollar. Unless noted, prices do not include the G.S.T., Canada's Goods and Services Tax of 7 percent. Foreign tourists can get a G.S.T. refund for goods they take out of the country and on hotel rooms they pay for themselves (but not on rooms prepaid through a travel agent). You can't get refunds for meals or services such as transportation or lift tickets. Most hotels have refund forms.

Canada can be as cold as you've heard, or warmer than you imagined. We've skied in windbreakers in January, and huddled into fleece neck-warmers in a sudden April snowstorm. The best advice is to be prepared clothing-wise.

Travelers from the United States should bring a passport if they have one. Crossing the border is much easier and quicker with one than without, particularly when traveling by air.

Banff, Canada
Sunshine Village, Mystic Ridge & Norquay

Some places on Earth are so beautiful that they must be seen—words are inadequate to describe what unfolds before one's eyes. Banff National Park is one such place.

The Canadian Rockies are among the world's best known and most loved mountain ranges, and Banff National Park is the best known of the four national parks that stretch along the spiny border between Alberta and British Columbia. The Canadian government established Banff—the country's first—in 1885, and in 1984 the UN declared the four national parks—Banff, Jasper, Yoho and Kootenay—to be World Heritage Sites.

Today we think of national parks as places to be preserved; in both the U.S. and Canada strict regulations govern land use within their boundaries. But a hundred years ago, when Banff was newly established, the thinking was that a national park needed improvements such as tourist facilities for everyone to enjoy the spectacular scenery. Before that thinking changed, four ski areas were established within these parks, as well as some stunning hotels. This chapter profiles the two ski areas nearest the townsite of Banff, and in later chapters, we'll describe Lake Louise and Jasper.

Skiers and snowboarders owe it to themselves to take a trip here. Winter offers stunning vistas, but few crowds. Winter sports of all varieties are abundant. The summer tourist stampede has long subsided, residents are relaxed and friendly, and lodging prices are at rock-bottom, even in the most luxurious hotels.

For the first-time visitor, Banff is a good place to headquarter. The townsite—that's the word locals use, not town—is compact, yet filled with excellent restaurants, shopping and nightclubs. The two ski areas, one that overlooks the townsite and the other a few miles away, are quite good. We recommend that destination visitors also spend a day or two at Lake Louise, about 45 minutes away and the largest ski area.

Where to ski—Sunshine Village
Sunshine Village is the larger of the two Banff ski areas, 10 miles from the townsite. At the top of Lookout Mountain, nearly 9,000 feet above sea level, you will have crossed into British Columbia. Somewhere near your ski tips is the Great

Continental Divide itself. If you throw a snowball over your right shoulder, it will melt and find its way to the Pacific. Over your left, it will become one with the Atlantic. Scenery like this encourages such musings on fate and the cosmic wonders of North American geology.

It also encourages you to point your tips down and let that other cosmic force, gravity, take over. Skiing at Sunshine Village is wide-open, with an infinite number of ways down, some smooth, others moguled, all exhilarating.

Sunshine has the longest ski season in the region, sometimes even into June, and the most snow (360 inches as opposed to 120 and 140 at the other areas). Its reputation is based on its dramatic views—if the weather's clear.

Skiers arrive here by an unusual route: up a narrow canyon in a six-person gondola from the parking lot, around a sharp left turn and then fifteen more minutes, and *then* you're at what feels like a ski area base village. It's here at the Village that the play really starts, around a lodge, rental shop, general store, restaurant and the only slopeside lodging in the national parks. From here, a half dozen lifts and tows take off in all directions. Most people never ski all the way down until the end of the day; some not until the end of their vacation.

The Wheeler double chair and the Fireweed T-bar are down-mountain from the other lifts and permit skiers to enjoy the varied runs under the gondola. You can enjoy this area any time of the day, then ride the gondola to the top from its midstation, but most people play here in the afternoon on their way back down.

You'll find the most exhilarating skiing on the Great Divide Chair. Take Angel Express to get to it. Intermediates should first try the run down the face of Angel, called Ecstasy—just to get ready for the high country. From the top of Angel Express, it's wide-open above-tree-line skiing, with views of the Great Divide. Skiers at the blue level will find a bonanza.

The most challenging route from the Great Divide is far to the right toward the Tee-Pee Town chair as you head down.   Keep in mind there's a cliff edge. The appeal in getting as far out along the cliff edge as you dare is virgin snow, less trafficked. If you stay on the edge, you have to dip down a drop innocuously called The Shoulder. It's the only thing on the mountain labeled black

Sunshine Village Facts
Base elevation: 5,440'; Summit elevation: 8,954'; Vertical drop: 3,514 feet
Number of lifts: 13–1 gondola, 2 quad superchairs, 1 triple chair,
4 double chairs, 5 surface lifts
Snowmaking: none Skiable acreage: 2,200
Uphill capacity: 18,600 per hour Bed Base: 10,000 in Banff

which should be a double black. To avoid it, turn left and you'll negotiate only blacks, and find some great tree skiing.

Mogul runs can be found off the Tee-Pee Town Chair. If that's mild for you, take the WaWa T-bar on the opposite side of the Village up to a ridge with a left-hand dropoff called Paris Basin. It doesn't even look like a run, but they ski it. If you get there and decide against it, you can take an easy cat trail back down.

Sunshine has some flat spots to watch out for—most notably on Highway One, familiarly dubbed Tuck 'n' Pole by locals—if you don't tuck, you pole. Be sure to look far ahead coming off the Great Divide when you're headed back toward Strawberry Chair or you'll get caught on an up-slope.

The three-mile run at the end of the day from the Village down to the parking lot is a long luscious trip for beginners and a lovely end-of-day cruiser for intermediates. Advanced skiers can play on the occasional drops to the left, but they're short and eventually rejoin the ski-out.

To find powder just after a storm, head immediately to ByeBye Bowl (left, facing down off the Divide), but it gets blown off quickly. The day after a storm, try Paris Basin. To stay in the sun, ski Standish Face in the morning and Lookout Mountain (Great Divide) in the afternoon. A ski tour takes off from the upper gondola terminal at 9:50 a.m. and 12:50 p.m. daily.

Sunshine Village has exciting news for the 1995/96 season. It will open a high-speed quad lift on Goat's Eye Mountain in what may be the last ski development within the parks. Like Lookout, Goat's Eye is a craggy slab of a mountain, but with long fall-line runs and gradients that average 40 percent. Double black diamonds and plenty of glade skiing, as well as several intermediate runs, will add a tremendous amount of new terrain.

Mountain rating

With a whopping 60 percent of Sunshine's terrain marked intermediate, this a cruiser's mountain. The remaining 40 percent is divided evenly between beginner and expert. The percentage of expert terrain should increase with the addition of Goat's Eye, but this remains a well-balanced mountain.

Snowboarding

Snowboarders are welcomed, and rentals and lessons are available. One run loved by snowboarders and early intermediates is Dell Valley, a natural halfpipe near the Strawberry Triple Chair, where the g-forces will have you swooping up one side of a gorge, then turning to gain momentum on the down-slope to swoosh up the other side—just like the skateboarders.

Lessons (94/95 prices in Cdn$ plus GST)

Sunshine Village encourages the traditional **Ski Week,** an on-mountain week-long stay at the slopeside Sunshine Inn, by providing appealing packages including classes with the same instructor. Groups can be divided by ability level or by family, and the package includes evening activities as well. Five-night, six-day packages range $329–$499 per person double occupancy, depending on time of season and room.

Group lessons are $20. A never-ever package includes a longer lesson (two hours and a half), rentals and lift ticket for $43.

Private lessons are $45 per hour (plus $15 for an additional person); an early-bird private lesson starts at 9 a.m. for $30 per hour. Multi-hour discounts are available.

Children's programs: Three to six year olds just venturing onto the slopes can get a combo ski-and-play program for $27 for the full day (lunch is $5 extra) or $22 for half day. Equipment is included. Kids in that age group who already know how to ski can get a private one-hour lesson for $25, equipment and lift ticket extra. Young Devils is for 6–12 year olds just starting or well on their way. The price of $35 for full day includes lunch, $20 half day.

Child care

Care is provided for children 19 months to 6 years. Full day is $20, half day is $15, lunch is $5 extra. Reservations recommended; call (403) 762-6560.

Lift tickets (94/95 prices in Cdn$ with GST)

	Adult	Child (6–12)
One day	$38	$10
Three days	$105 ($35/day)	$30 ($10/day)
Five days	$155 ($31/day)	$50 ($10/day)

Students aged 13–25 and seniors 65 and older ski for $34. ($30 per day for three days; $27 per day for five.) Students need ID to qualify for the discount. Children 5 and younger ski free.

You can also buy a multiday Banff/Lake Louise Tri-Pass ticket, which we recommend for visitors. It is valid at Sunshine Village, Mystic Ridge & Norquay, and Lake Louise ski areas and includes bus rides from hotels to the ski areas. The cost is $46–$47 per day for adults, and $17 per day for children.

Where to ski—Mystic Ridge & Norquay

This small ski area with a big name packs a lot of punch for its size. A terrain expansion several years ago added some much-needed intermediate terrain, an area that contributed the Mystic Ridge part of the ampersanded moniker. The Norquay portion is what people can see from the townsite—long moguled ribbons that plunge right down its face and seem to hang right over the main street in Banff. If you're looking for a moderate challenge or a severe one, you can find it here, just four miles from Banff.

The view of Banff and the Bow Valley from the North American chair is spectacular, this is the lift that takes you to those bump ribbons. If the prospect of the run down puts your heart in your throat, you can ride back down the lift (many do).

Lone Pine is the name of that double-black mogul belt that plunges down a 35 percent gradient. Each year the area has a contest (Club 35,000) to see who can make the most consecutive runs in seven hours on this 412-meter, skeleton-jarring wall. Both men and women have done more than 20 trips, which says a lot for local physical fitness.

Another appeal for the adventure seeker is a chute on Norquay called Valley of the Ten, a narrow drainage perfect for avalanches and elevator skiers. To get to it, skiers at the top of North American chair drop off (correct terminology) to the left into a drop-out (accurate again) called Gun Run, the steepest thing on the mountain. For first-timers to the Norquay side, the easiest way down, still a tough black, is Memorial Bowl.

From the base the area look like a haven for mogul maniacs, but the terrain unseen from the base on the Mystic Express Quad is mainly intermediate with groomed runs. Three runs are partially groomed, leaving a choice of packed snow or powder.

Skiers wanting to stay in the sun all day have a challenge. Since at midday none of Mystic gets sun except the front two runs, Black Magic and Ka-Poof, both blacks, they'd better learn to ski bumps.

Mountain rating

Mystic Ridge & Norquay claims 11 percent beginner, 45 percent intermediate, 28 percent advanced and 16 percent expert. However, even the blues here are challenges, compared to most blues in the U.S. Intermediates should stick to the two quads, Mystic Express and Spirit. What's left for beginners is to poke around the base. Beginners are better off at Sunshine Village. The skier who will have a ball here is the intermediate to expert.

Snowboarding

Mystic Ridge & Norquay is a great supporter of the sport. Clinics are $25, $20 if you rent a board here.

Mystic Ridge & Norquay Facts
Base elevation: 5,350'; **Summit elevation:** 7,000'; **Vertical drop:** 1,650 feet
Number of lifts: 5–1 quad superchair, 1 quad chair, 2 double chairs, 1 surface lifts
Snowmaking: 90 percent of skiable terrain
Total acreage by trails: 162 acres skiable terrain
Uphill capacity: 6,300 per hour **Bed Base:** 10,000 in Banff

---

Lessons (94/95 prices in Cdn$ plus GST)

Learn-to-Ski packages for beginners are $30 for a 90-minute group lesson, lift ticket and equipment. Adult **group lessons** are $22 for a two-hour lesson. Children pay $17.

Private lessons are $35 per hour for adults, each additional person is $10 per hour and $15 for two. Before 10 a.m. or after 2:30 p.m., a private lesson is $29.

Mystic Ridge & Norquay participates in Club Ski, a three-day program of lessons with the same instructor and group, but skiing one day each at three resorts (see Lake Louise ticket section).

Child care

Children aged 19 months to 6 years are taken on a drop-in basis for $5 per hour per child, daily 9 a.m.–4 p.m. Options include lunch and combination snow play and ski instruction.

Lift tickets (95/96 prices in Cdn$ with GST)

	Adult	Child (6–12)
One day	$29.90	$13
Three days	$140 ($46.66/day)	$51 ($17/day)
Five days	$233 ($46.60/day)	$85 ($17/day)

Adult rates include night skiing, which is offered only on Wednesday until 9 p.m.. Students 13–25 with ID and seniors 55 and older ski for $25 (94/95 prices). Children 5 and younger ski free.

These multiday rates are for the Tri-Area Lift Pass, which is valid here, at Lake Louise and at Sunshine Village. The pass includes bus transportation and when used here, it also includes about $7 in other MR&N services.

Cross-country—Banff area

There are some lovely easy loops along the Bow River. Take Banff Avenue to the end of Spray Avenue, or turn left and cross the river. Trails wind through the whole area. **Parks Canada** puts out a very informative booklet on Nordic skiing in Banff National Park; you can obtain a copy for a small fee at the Banff Information Center, 224 Banff Ave., 9 a.m. to 5 p.m.

Banff Springs Golf Course Clubhouse offers ski and skate rentals, plus group and private lessons. Maps and information on trails are available at the Clubhouse.

Accommodations (prices in Cdn$ plus GST)

Rooms can be found for as little as $50, and even the premier locations are within most budgets.

The Sunshine Inn (800-661-1676) on the Sunshine Village mountain at the top of the gondola, is the only lodging in Banff National Park with ski-in/ski-out convenience. Rooms start at $80 per person in low season, then rise to $195 for larger rooms in regular season. All nightly rates include lift tickets, and the hotel runs a Ski Week program. .

All other lodging is in Banff, which has many nice places. That said, we strongly recommend the experience of staying at the **Banff Springs Hotel** (800-441-1414 in the U.S. and Canada; 762-2211) locally the cinnamon-colored castle perched on a small hill within walking distance of downtown. This is one of the Canadian Pacific Snow Castles.

You have seen this classic brick monolith in many photos, its steep pointed roofs rising from the brick-red nine-story walls, surrounding by evergreens and dramatic peaks. Its public areas are expansive, designed for turn-of-the-century mingling—we're talking a ballroom for 16,000.

Three-day ski-lodging packages, for example, start at about $180 Canadian per person. The hotel will open a full-service spa in fall, 1995.

Banff Park Lodge and Conference Center (800-661-9266; 762-4433) which hosts many cultural activities, is an expanse of cedar buildings in a wooded area two blocks from downtown. Rates are in the $50–$75 range.

The Mount Royal Hotel (800-267-3035; 762-3331) has a great location in downtown Banff, an excellent choice for those who enjoy nightlife. It gets a fair amount of street noise from Banff Avenue but has an exceptionally good restaurant. Rates are in the $50–$75 range.

The Inns of Banff (800-661-1272; 762-4581) a modern, multi-level lodge with balconies in most rooms, is a 15-minute walk from downtown. The rooms are fairly large and rates are $60–$100. .

High Country Inn (800-661-1244; 762-5084) on Banff Avenue is one of the least expensive, $50–$60 per night.

For information about other lodging, contact **Summit Vacations** (800-661-1676) a central reservations service that books lodging in Banff, Lake Louise and Jasper.

Dining

For those staying at Sunshine Village, the **Eagle's Nest Dining room** in the Sunshine Inn offers fine dining with lobster and filet mignon. **The Chimney Corner**, the inn's fireplace lounge, serves a sit-down lunch of croissants, soups, salads, pastas, ribs and steak sandwiches.

In the townsite of Banff, diners have a tremendous variety and number of restaurants to choose from. You will find almost every variety of ethnic food, as well as the familiar steak-and-seafood restaurants.

The Banff Springs Hotel alone has 12 restaurants, including **The Samurai** (762-6860), which serves Japanese cuisine including Shabu-Shabu, a healthy fondue broth. **The Pavilion** (762-6860) serves Italian dinners, while the **Alhambra Dining Room** (762-2211, ext. 6841) offers Spanish cuisine. If you like fondue, **Waldhaus** (762-6860) serves it and other traditional German, Austrian and Swiss fare at long tables that seat a dozen people.

Grapes (762-2211, ext. 6660) is the 26-seat wine bar, which also serves light meals to accompany its selection of fine wines from around the world. If beer is more to your liking, try **Henry VIII Pub** (762-2211, ext. 6577), which has British pub food.

Restaurants in the townsite of Banff, especially those on Banff Avenue, often are on the second floor above the shops. Sometimes the entrances are obvious, sometimes not.

Le Beaujolais (on Banff Avenue at Buffalo Street, 762-2712) received high praise for its French cuisine. Meals can be ordered à la carte, but the restaurant specializes in fixed-price, three- or five-course meals. You are likely to see diners in coats and ties, though neither is required. **Earls** (229 Banff Ave. at Wolf Street, 762-4414) got rave reviews from everyone for moderately priced Canadian beef steak, fresh salmon, pasta and thin-crust pizza.

For Italian, you can try **Giorgio's Trattoria** (219 Banff Ave. 762-5116) for Northern Italian gourmet pastas and pizzas, or **Guido's** (116 Banff Ave. above McDonald's, 762-4002) for more traditionally American Italian food, such as spaghetti, lasagna and chicken parmigiana. **Ticino** (205 Wolf St., 762-3848) specializes in dishes from the Italian part of Switzerland.

Coyotes Deli & Grill (206 Caribou St., 762-3963) serves breakfast, lunch and dinner at reasonable prices, with Southwestern, vegetarian and pasta dishes on the menu (also fresh-squeezed juices such as orange, apple and carrot). **The Bistro** (on the corner of Wolf and Bear streets, 762-8900) has tapas, pastas, crêpes, 22 wines by the glass and a very cozy atmosphere. **Grizzly House** (207 Banff Ave., 762-4055) also specializes in fondue and steaks, both beef and wild game.

One of the most fun places to eat breakfast, lunch or an informal supper is **Joe Btfsplk's Diner** (221 Banff Ave. 762-5529). Set in a 1950s-style diner decor complete with jukebox and Elvis posters, this restaurant serves huge portions (our pancakes measured nine inches in diameter).

For gourmet coffees and light snacks, try **Evelyn's Coffee Bar** on Banff Avenue, **Banff Coffee Company** on Bear Street, or **Jump Start Coffee and Sandwich Place** on Buffalo Street near the post office.

Reader recommendation: Eric Jon Knudtson of Calgary suggests Bumpers Inn for good steaks and ribs, The Paris Restaurant for classic food and Magpie & Stump for après ski.

Après-ski/nightlife

Après-ski is more quiet than rip-roaring in Banff, at least in our experience, but things really get going at night. Younger crowds probably will enjoy Banff nightspots, while mature skiers might be happier at the Banff Springs Hotel's many bars and lounges. The Happy Bus shuttles skiers to night spots around

Banff until midnight for $1.50. On nice evenings, you can easily walk between the Banff Springs Hotel and downtown.

At the hotel, **Whiskey Creek** attracts an aprés-ski crowd, as does the bar at **The Mt. Royal Hotel.** Crowds also start to gather at **The Rose and Crown**, an English-style pub with draught ale, a pool table, darts and an occasional live band.

At night, **Bumper's Loft Lounge** has a casual crowd, with live entertainment and ski movies. **Joshua's Pub** has Old Banff atmosphere, good food and Calgary's Big Rock ale on tap. **Wild Bill's** on Banff Avenue has Country & Western bands and a huge dance floor. **Barbary Coast** on Banff Avenue is billed as a sports bar, but the night we were there, it had a blues/soft rock band so excellent, we stayed to listen rather than do our bar-hopping research. **Eddy's Back Alley** on Banff Avenue with DJ dancing and occasional live bands got high marks from visitors in their early 20s. **Magpie & Stump** serves up great nachos and some of Banff's best aprés-ski. **Silver City** is where the younger set hangs out.

In the Banff Springs Hotel, the **Rob Roy Room** has dining and dancing and the **Rundle Lounge** has quiet music for hotel guests. At the **Waldhaus** at Banff Springs Golf Course, Happy Hans and Lauren, on accordion and trumpet, get everybody singing.

Other activities

Shopping: The Banff Springs Hotel has nearly 50 shops, many of which have unusual items such as regional handicrafts. Our favorite in the hotel was The Canadian Pacific Store, with items that reflect the bygone elegance of luxury train travel.

In the townsite, shopping is almost an athletic activity, with hundreds of shops lining Banff Avenue and its side streets. Most shops are clustered in little malls where you can enter the store from the inside on crummy days, or from the outside when the sun is out. Worth a drop-in: The Hudson's Bay Company, a department store famed for its blankets and Canada's oldest company, founded in 1670 and Roots Canada, for fine leather-and-cloth backpacks and handbags, and casual clothing.

For non-kitschy Canadian souvenirs: Orca Canada or Great Northern Trading Company (clothing, jewelry, knickknacks), Rocks and Gems (for inexpensive jewelry made from native Western Canadian gemstones), Bear Country Shirts (where we found the nicest quality T-shirts and sweatshirts) or A Taste of the Rockies (for gifts such as smoked salmon, jams and honeys).

Banff has much to do for non-skiers. Winter sports are numerous with skating (at Banff High School or the Banff Springs Hotel) snowshoeing (check with sports shops), dog sledding (762-3647) ice fishing (762-4936) and sleigh rides (762-4551). Yamnuska (678-4164) offers introduction courses to ice climbing and ski mountaineering. One of the most famous heli-skiing companies, Canadian Mountain Holidays, is headquartered here (762-7100). You also can go helicopter sightseeing with two companies, Alpine Helicopters (678-4802) or Canadian Helicopters (678-2207) to see the magnificent mountain peaks. Also on a nice day, take the Sulphur Mountain Gondola near The Banff Springs Hotel for a beautiful view. Adults $9, children $4. (762-2523).

Four museums of note: Banff Park Museum for the story of early tourism and wildlife management; Whyte Museum of the Canadian Rockies, for historic and contemporary art and historic homes; The Luxton Museum, for Plains Indians history and the Natural History Museum for local geology.

Getting there and getting around

Getting there: Calgary Airport is served by major airlines. Banff is 130 miles west of Calgary on the Trans-Canada Highway, an hour and a half drive. The Sunshine Village exit is five miles west of Banff; then five more miles to the gondola base parking area. Mystic Ridge & Norquay is on Norquay Road, one exit past the Banff townsite exit. Free ski shuttles pick up skiers at 11 Banff hotels and the bus depot.

Getting around: It is possible to ski Banff and Lake Louise without a rental car by using free shuttlebuses, **Happy Bus** ($1.50 a ride) in the area and **Pacific Western Transportation** (762-4558) or **Brewster Transportation** (762-6700) between the airport and Banff. For exploring, it's best to have a car.

Information/reservations

Sunshine Village, Box 1510, Banff, Alberta T0L 0C0; phone 762-6500, or (800) 661-1676 in the U.S. or Canada for Sunshine Inn reservations. **Mystic Ridge & Norquay**, Box 1258, Banff, Alberta, T0L 0C0; tel. 762-4421.

Summit Vacations is a central reservations service that books lodging in Banff, Lake Louise and Jasper, (800) 661-1676.

In Banff, use the **Super Line Talking Directory** to find out about all sorts of services, including road conditions, transportation, ski reports, activities, etc. Dial 762-9233 from a touch-tone phone and follow the instructions.

All prices are in Canadian dollars. (At press time, one U.S. dollar was worth $1.37 Canadian.)

Unless noted, the local area code is 403.

Lake Louise Ski Area
Banff Region, Canada

Even if Lake Louise Ski Area weren't one of Canada's largest, the scenery alone would be worth the visit. This was the last of the three ski areas to be developed in Banff National Park, starting in 1954. Today it is the largest, comprising two mountains and four faces. The expansiveness, together with the efficient lift system, allows skiers to get to the far reaches of the mountain quickly—if you can't get out of the base area on one of its three lifts in ten minutes, you get your ticket price refunded.

Where to ski

Lake Louise has three distinct areas: the Front Face, the Back Bowls and the Larch Area. First, the Front Face: Beginners enrolled in lessons will start on the Sunny T-Bar. Those with a little experience can progress to the Friendly Giant quad superchair and head down Wiwaxy, a 2.5-mile cruiser. Next step is Eagle Chair to try Deer Run and Eagle Meadows.

Intermediates should not miss Meadowlark, reached by the Eagle Chair, or Gully, reached from Top of the World. Advanced skiers can give the Men's Downhill or Ladies' Downhill trails a try to get an idea of what the big boys and girls ski when Lake Louise hosts World Cup races.

When skiers are ready to head for the Back Bowls, beginners should ride the Eagle Chair and take Pika down the back. Confident intermediates and advanced skiers can take Top of the World quad superchair, or ride the Olympic Chair from the base to the Summit Platter.

About the Platter: first off, realize that it used to be a T-bar until they decided the steepness demanded concentration, not conversation, so it's one up at a time now. The skiing here is nicely moguled, wide and above treeline—almost all black diamonds with a touch of blue. Intermediates can ride the Platter and head off the backside down Boomerang, an immensely fun

---

Lake Louise Facts
Base elevation: 5,400'; **Summit elevation:** 8,650'; **Vertical drop:** 3,250 feet.
Number and types of lifts: 11–2 quad superchairs, 1 quad chair, 2 triple chairs,
3 double chairs, 3 surface lifts **Acreage:** 4,000 skiable acres **Snowmaking:** 40 percent
Uphill capacity: 23,955 skiers per hour **Bed base:** 2,500 within 10 minutes

cruiser that seems to go on forever. If the weather is socked in, however, skip Boomerang. It will seem to go on forever in a bad way under those conditions.

From the Top of the World Chair, you have two choices: go back down the face, which is mostly intermediate terrain with touches of black, or dip down into the Back Bowls. Most of the advanced skiing is found here, with intermediate trails as well.

Experts: though you will like all of the Back Bowls, Paradise Bowl holds special attractions such as cornices, chutes and gladed areas. Just keep riding the Paradise Chair and you'll find them all. You'll find more glades under the Ptarmigan Chair, across the valley floor from the Larch Chair.

The Larch Area has the best intermediate skiing, as shown by the long lines at the only chair that serves it. However, the line moves fairly fast, and it's worth the wait. Wolverine, Larch and Bobcat are all long smooth cruisers. Advanced skiers also will like this. There's great tree skiing directly under the lift between Larch and Bobcat runs. From the top of the Larch Chair, you'll see that some powder freaks have hiked up to the 8,900-foot summit to leave tracks down Elevator Shaft Chute, between two rock outcroppings. The chute is within the ski area boundaries.

For a more modest thrill in a less traveled area, exit left off Larch Chair, then stay right and high on a gladed traverse until you find a deep powder bowl under Elevator Shaft. Called Rock Garden, it's not labeled on the map but it's in bounds, a hidden playground of loops, swoops, moguls and Cadillac-sized rocks.

If you want sun all day and want to ski the whole area, go to the Back Bowls in the morning, ski Larch midday and end up on the Front Face.

And if this is too much to remember, take a free guided tour by Friends of Louise. A crew of volunteers, the Friends guide skiers of all levels around this vast mountain. Tours leave at 9:30 a.m., 10:30 a.m. and 1 p.m. at Whiskyjack Lodge.

Mountain rating

A key factor in Louise's 60 years of skiing history is that skiers of all abilities have terrain suited to their skill level from all lifts except the Summit Platter. This makes it nice for groups of varying levels who want to ride together on the lifts.

Cross-country

Lake Louise has about 60 miles of groomed trails and access to hundreds of miles of backcountry trails. The ungroomed, well-marked trail to Skoki Lodge, a rustic log cabin (meaning no electricity, no plumbing, wood-burning stove), begins just above Temple Lodge at the ski area and heads up the valley and over Boulder Pass, seven miles one way. If you're not up for skiing so far into the wilderness, follow the gentle Shoreline Trail starting in front of Chateau Lake Louise, an easy mile and a half one way. Skiing on Lake Louise is not recommended.

A complex 13-mile network called Pipestone Loops starts four miles west of the Lake Louise Overpass on the Trans-Canada Highway. Although all are marked beginner, some are suitable for the intermediate.

There are probably half a dozen other trails in the area comprising a total of 50 miles of groomed touring. Rental shops, especially the one in Chateau Lake Louise that also rents clothing, can furnish trail maps.

Before setting out on any of the trails, check trail conditions at a park warden's office or by phoning 762-4256. Be aware that trail classification is done by healthy Canadians in good shape.

Snowboarding

Yes, everywhere on the mountain. There's a boarding park off Wiwaxy, reached by the Olympic Chair. Snowboard rentals and lessons are available.

Lessons (94/95 prices in Cdn$)

Group lessons (1.75 hours) cost $25, or $39 for two lessons taken the same day. **Private lessons** are $50 per hour, reduced to $39 if taken at 9 a.m. or 3 p.m.; extra skiers, $16 each.

Beginner's Special is a $32 one-day package including a 1.75-hour lesson, equipment rental and beginner area lift ticket. If you aren't skiing at the end of the lesson, you can take an afternoon lesson free. Arrive well before the lesson to pick up equipment.

The **Kinderski** program, ages 3-6, provides supervised day care, one ski lesson and indoor and outdoor play at the beginning and end of day. Cost is $27.

In the **Kids Ski** program, children aged 7-12 are guided around the mountain with instruction along the way for $19 for the morning or afternoon; $33 for full day. The program includes a lift ticket. Optional lunch is $5.

The **Club Ski Program** operates at Lake Louise, Sunshine Village and Mystic Ridge & Norquay. Groups of similar interest and expertise ski together with the same instructor for four hours a day at each of the three areas. A three-day program costs $139 (95/96 price). Club Ski Jr. for children 6–12 is $104, but you need to call ahead to confirm availability.

Child care (prices Cdn$)

Babies starting at 18 days to toddlers age 3 can be cared for at the nursery. Toddlers have their own play area. Children 3–6 get a combination of day care and one to two hours of ski lessons. The program includes a hot lunch. Infants under 19 months require reservations. Babies' care is $21 per day or $4 per hour, $3.75 per hour for toddlers. Day care for kids 3–6 is $3.50 per hour, with three-hour minimums.

Lift tickets (95/96 prices in Cdn$ including GST)

	Adult	Student/Seniors
One day	$42.50	$35
Three days	$120 ($40/day)	$89 ($29.67/day)
Five days	$195 ($39/day)	$146 ($29.20/day)

Students are 13–25 with ID and seniors are 65. Children 6–12 always pay $10 per day. Children younger than 6 ski free. Skiers interested in skiing at the Banff areas should buy the Tri-Area Pass, valid at all three ski areas. It includes bus transportation from hotels to the ski areas and other benefits; prices are listed in the Banff chapter.

Accommodations (Prices Cdn$)

The **Chateau Lake Louise** (800-441-1414; 522-3511 locally) is another of the Canadian Pacific "Snow Castles." Nested on the shore of Lake Louise, with the spectacular Victoria Glacier in the distance, this creamy yellow, multi-story hotel dates back to a log chalet built in 1890. Winter rates are a fraction of the summer prices: $110–$165 for most rooms, with two-night midweek ski packages starting at about $140 per person double occupancy. Some 500 guest rooms, restaurants, shops, Nordic ski center, masseuse, and free ski shuttles make this century-old Lady of the Lake up to date for skiers.

The **Post Hotel** (800-661-1586; 522-3989 locally) is a cozy, beautifully furnished 93-room log lodge with great views on all sides and fireplaces in 38 of the rooms, two of which are lovely riverside cabins with heated slate floors. It's personal and quiet, with the warmth and elegance provided by Swiss innkeepers. The buffet breakfast is a board of tasty delights. Except for Christmas, rates are in the $175–$225 range. There is a free ski shuttle.

Lake Louise Inn (800-661-9237; 522-3791) is a moderately priced family hotel with a noisy bar; $85–$145.

Deer Lodge (800-661-1595; 522-3747) near the Chateau, is its antithesis: No television, rustic, but great rooftop hot tub. It's old but well kept up; $65–$110.

Summit Vacations (800-661-1676) is a central reservations service that books lodging in Banff, Lake Louise and Jasper.

Dining

In the **Chateau** (call 522-3511 for all) the most elegant dining room is the **Edelweiss**, serving such entrées as salmon and duckling. The most popular restaurant is the **Walliser Stube Wine Bar** serving Swiss cuisine such as raclette and fondue. **The Poppy Room** is a family restaurant, cheery and light, the only one open for breakfast in winter. **Glacier Saloon** has a western theme, with steak sandwiches, finger food and salads. It's a little dark, so ask for a seat near the windows.

The Post Hotel (522-3989) is generally recognized as serving the finest Continental cuisine in Lake Louise. For a special occasion, this is a wonderful place.

Deer Lodge (522-3747) has homemade breads, patés, fish, veal and beef dishes as well as innovative specials and pastries.

Lake Louise Station (522-2600) is a restored railway station with views of the mountains and freight trains that rumble past. The menu is quite extensive, with pastas, lamb, Alberta steaks and fresh salmon, among other dishes.

Après-ski/nightlife

The **Sitzmark Lounge** is the après-ski spot at the mountain. It's on the third floor of the Whiskyjack Lodge at the base area and has an open fireplace.

Otherwise, après-ski and nightlife center in the hotels. At the Chateau, **The Glacier Saloon** has a lively atmosphere and dancing. For a quieter time, the **Walliser Stube** has a warm feel. In the Lake Louise Inn, **The Saddleback Lounge** is quiet and **Charlie II's** is noisy. The Post Hotel's **Outpost** is a cozy pub.

On Friday evenings, the **Brewster Cowboys Barbeque & Dance Barn** near the Chateau provides hearty cowboy food and lively Western entertainment. Tickets are $38 for adults and $27 for children, and include a sleigh ride to the barn.

Other activities

The Banff/Lake Louise area has many opportunities for other winter sports such as skating, snowshoeing, tobogganing and fishing; see the Banff chapter for phone numbers.

Getting there and getting around

Getting there: Lake Louise Village is 115 miles west of Calgary and 36 miles from Banff. Direct or one-stop flights connect Calgary with most major cities via seven airlines.

Getting around: Regular bus service is available from the airport direct to most hotels. The Lake Louise shuttlebus is free and operates from most hotels to the base of the ski lifts. Buy the Tri-Area ski pass and your bus transportation is included.

Information/reservations

Skiing Louise, Ltd. (Box 5, Lake Louise, Alberta T0L 1E0), (403) 522-3555.

Summit Vacations is a central reservations service that books lodging in Banff, Lake Louise and Jasper, (800) 661-1676.

The local area code is 403 unless otherwise noted.

Marmot Basin
Jasper, Alberta, Canada

The largest of the Canadian Rockies National Parks, Jasper is studded with lakes, threaded by cross-country trails, and decorated with spectacular drives such as the Icefields Parkway. Overloaded with tourists in the summer, it's delightfully uncrowded in the winter.

Marmot Basin has developed slowly. It has a hidden feel, far into the northland and separated from the hustle of Banff by a three-hour drive. It's far enough north, and far enough from a major airport (Edmonton three hours) that people aren't here by mistake or on a whim. They come for the scenery, the remoteness, the wonder of a herd of elk outside their chalet and the call of Canadian geese swooping over Lac Beauvert in the spring while the ski area still has winter snow.

The townsite of Jasper sprang up from a tent city in 1911, when the Grand Trunk Pacific Railway was laying steel up the Athabasca River Valley toward Yellowhead Pass, and its growth was rather helter-skelter. Hugging the Athabasca River and nestled against the train station, the town is relatively nondescript, consisting of clapboard cottages, a steepled Lutheran church, stone houses and lodgings with no single architectural scheme. It has a Great Plains small-town feel.

Where to ski

Two peaks, a handful of bowls and a wide ridge make up the ski area. The lower peak, Caribou Ridge, served by two chair lifts is only 7,525 feet high. Even so, it climbs above the tree line, a notably low topographical feature determined by lattitude.

Marmot, however, also has the excellent glade skiing off the triple chair and Kiefer T-bar which service Caribou Ridge. Directly below are black mogul runs, negotiable by a strong intermediate when groomed (this takes place about once a week)

Marmot Basin Facts
Base elevation: 5,640'; Summit elevation: 7,940'; Vertical drop: 2,300 feet
Number and types of lifts: 7–1 quad superchair, 1 triple chair,
3 double chairs, 2 surface lifts.
Acreage: 1,000 acres   Percent of snowmaking: 1 percent
Uphill capacity: 10,080 skiers per hour   Bed base: 5,500

but off to the right as you face downhill, advanced skiers can play in the trees in a black area misnamed Milk Run.

By staying high to the right, skiers can take another lift, Knob Chair, to gain 500 more vertical feet on Marmot Peak. The lift doesn't go all the way to the summit, but that doesn't stop hardy Canadians from hiking up, as their tracks on upper slopes testify. You can climb another 500 feet and still be in bounds. It's all Alpine bowls up here. Even intermediates can negotiate The Knob by a sinuous route down, but experts will want to drop into the fine powder in Dupres Bowl, a true scooped-out hollow, outrageously large, with Dupres Chute dividing it from Charlie's Bowl, a depression even steeper and farther away that stays untracked longer. This is what knowing skiers head for. It should be a double black; try telling that to Canadians. The most horrendous bump runs are just to the right of the Knob Chair— Knob Bowl and Knob Hill.

Stay high and even farther to the right from The Knob facing down. Here experts have an entirely different playground all to themselves—a ridge wide enough that some parts are treeless, like Thunder Bowl, others gladed, like Chalet Slope. Powder lasts the longest here because it takes you three lifts to arrive.

Intermediates and beginners will have the most fun on the lower mountain, where trees provide shelter from the sometimes fierce winds that block visibility on the naked summit.

Mountain Magic Tours are available and free daily, morning and afternoon. Tours leave from the Lower Chalet; check with Guest Services for times.

The area's one high-speed quad, Eagle Express, serves as the primary access chair to the upper-mountain lifts. That makes it a wait sometimes; don't come back to the base during peak loading times, like mornings before 9:30. There's rarely a wait on Caribou Chair on the lower mountain far to the right. It has terrain for all abilities and also will get you to the upper-mountain lifts. You can reach it directly by driving past the main lodge and heading for the farthest parking lot.

Mountain rating

Skiers of different levels can ride the same lifts, a factor which makes Marmot good family skiing. The terrain is evenly divided, with 35 percent beginner, 35 percent intermediate and 30 percent expert. Beginners have expansive mountain access, with 1,100 vertical feet on Eagle Express after they master terrain from the Red T-bar. They can even head up to Caribou Ridge for an above-treeline thrill where a high, wide trail, Basin Run, takes them safely back to the lower slopes.

Cross-country

This is prime ski touring country, and even if you've only done downhill, you'll want to try it. The scenery is guaranteed to draw you into the sport.

Jasper Park Lodge trails, about 19 km., are unparalleled for beauty and variety—lake shores, Alpine meadows and forests. They're gentle, groomed and easily accessible. The easiest is Cavell, a 5 km. lope with the elk. The perimeter loop samples a little of everything the Jasper Park Lodge trails offer.

Near Jasper Townsite, a good beginner trail is **Whistlers Campground Loop**, 4.5 km., level and lit for night skiing. **Pyramid Bench Trail**, rated intermediate and 4.7 km., overlooks the Athabasca River Valley. **Patricia Lake Circle**, 5.9 km. and rated intermediate (the recommendation is to follow the trail clockwise), provides several stunning views of Mt. Edith Cavell, the region's most prominent and dramatically sloped peak.

Trail maps are available in most lodgings. For **guided tours,** contact Beyond Bikes, 852-5922. You can get rentals and instruction here, too.

A full day's ski over Maccarib Pass from the Marmot Basin Road on the north shore of Amethyst Lake leads skiers to Tonquin Valley Lodge and hearty home-cooked meals and welcome beds. Contact Tonquin Valley Ski Tours, Box 550, Jasper, Alberta T0L 1E0; (403) 852-3909.

Snowboarding

Snowboarding has come to stay at Marmot. The New Ground Snowboard Cup is held in the spring and the area has a snowboard park. Lessons and rentals are available.

Lessons (95/96 prices in Cdn$ including GST)

Adult **group lessons** (age 13 and older) are $22 for two hours. Never-ever lessons that include lift pass and equipment cost $35 throughout the season.

Lessons for **children** 4-12 years are $15.

Ski Improvement Weeks include five two-hour sessions, Monday to Friday, video, a fun race and a Jasper Night Out. Adults are $90. Children 6-12 are $65.

Private lessons are $40 for an hour, $150 all day; additional skiers, $16 each per hour. **Specialty clinics** (moguls, racing, powder) are $22 per person with a minimum group of three.

Child care (95/96 prices in Cdn$ including GST)

Little Rascals, the indoor nursery, serves children 19 months through 5 years. It's $4 an hour, with supervision during the lunch hour, but lunch is an extra $4. All-day care is $22. Reservations: 852-3816.

Lift tickets (95/96 prices in Cdn$ including GST)

	Adult	Junior (6–12)
One day	$35	$14
Three days	$105 ($35/day)	$42 ($14/day)
Five days	$175 ($35/day)	$70 ($14/day)

Youth/student prices (ages 13–25) are $29 for a full day, but college-age students must be full time and present a valid student ID. Seniors aged 65 and older ski for $24 per day, and like the juniors, they get their fifth skiing day free. Children younger than 6 ski free.

Accommodations

Although **Jasper Park Lodge** (852-3301 or 800-441-1414) is also one of the Canadian Pacific Hotels, it's not in the grand-hotel style of the Chateau Lake Louise and Banff Springs Hotel. Rather, it's a grouping of traditional log cabins from the 1920s and new cedar chalets with spacious modern suites. (The older buildings have all been renovated and are thoroughly modern in the areas that count, such as bathrooms.) The lodging buildings are connected by pathways along Lac Beauvert to the main building, built like a Canadian hunting lodge, which houses all the restaurants, night spots and shops.

The lodge suggests all the best qualities you remember from youth summer camp, combined with the amenities you expect from a fine resort. Rates start under $100 before Christmas, and rise toward $220 for large suites in peak periods. Nordic and downhill ski packages are available. On the grounds, **Milligan Manor** is a restored eight-bedroom deluxe cabin overlooking the fairway and its resident elk herd.

All other lodging is in Jasper Townsite. **The Astoria** (800-661-7343; 852-3351) is a small hotel of character with elegantly renovated guest rooms, which rent for less than $100. **Chateau Jasper** (800-661-9323; 852-5644) has indoor pool and whirlpool, dining room, cocktail lounge and heated underground parking. Rooms and suites rent for $95–$205. **The Athabasca Hotel** (800-563-9859; 852-3386) one of Jasper's original lodgings, is close to the bus and VIA RAIL station. Rooms are $48–75; suites $170–$185. **Marmot Lodge** (800-661-6521; 852-4471) has rooms with kitchens and fireplaces; indoor pool, sauna and whirlpool on the premises. No charge for children under 12. Rooms cost $65–$135. **Pyramid Lake Resort** (852-4900) has skating and cross-country trails at your doorstep. Located five miles from the Townsite, it has a lovely view, private whirlpools, kitchenettes and fireplaces, as well as a restaurant on the premises. Bungalows range $50–$120.

Summit Vacations (800-661-1676) is a central reservations service for lodging in Banff, Lake Louise and Jasper.

Dining

At Jasper Lake Lodge, the **Beauvert Dining Room** overlooks the lake, is expansive, able to seat 800, but the **Edith Cavell** is the flagship restaurant, with white-glove tableside service, mahogany and silver, and a harpist playing. French veal and shrimp in a pastry are specialties. For breakfast, **The Meadows** features wholesome food in a country setting; food service continues all day.

In town, **Villa Caruso** (852-3920) serves steaks, prime rib, barbecued ribs, seafood and Italian dishes. It has live music and a beautiful view; make reservations. **Fiddle River Seafood Company** (852-3032) gets raves for creative fresh fish cooking. The **Amethyst Dining Room** (852-3394) serves light and healthy cuisine (beef, local fish) in an up-tempo casually elegant restaurant. Breakfast features omelets and a skier's buffet. A lovely buffet brunch on Sunday can be had at the Chateau Jasper's **Beauvallon Dining Room** (852-5644). Make reservations.

Athabasca Restaurant (852-3386) in Athabasca Hotel serves traditional Italian cooking in informal surroundings. **Mondi's Ristorante** (852-4070) makes its pasta and prepares sauces from scratch.

Mountain Foods Cafe, (852-4050) a sit-down or take-out restaurant, has affordable prices for its deli items. Pizza is at **Jasper Pizza Place** (852-3225), Greek cuisine at **L & W Restaurant** (852-4114), Japanese entrées and sushi bar at **Tokyo Tom's** (852-3780).

For great breakfasts, plus good food at other mealtimes, try **Papa George's Restaurant** in the Astoria Hotel (852-3351) or **Coco's Cafe** (852-4550), a European-style cafe with fresh baked goods, fruit pancakes, steamed eggs and gourmet coffees.

On the slopes, Marmot Basin has two food service areas. Upstairs in the Lower Chalet, **Country Kitchen** features pasta, sandwich bar and the local tradition, Marmot Basin Edible Soup Bowl—a delicious, hearty novelty. **Paradise Chalet**, mid-mountain, has a cafe and lounge. On busy days, lunch before 11:45 or after 1:15.

Après-ski/nightlife

Jasper is not known for rocking nightlife, but many of the in-town hotels have lounges. The **Atha-B Club** in Athabasca Hotel has the liveliest dancing in town; it also has **O'Shea's**, an Irish pub. **Whistle Stop** at Whistlers Inn is another good pub-type night spot with darts, pool table and big-screen sports; and **Dead Dog Saloon** in the Astoria Hotel has imported beer and is a popular locals' hangout. **Echoes Lounge** in Marmot Lodge has nightly entertainment.

At Jasper Park Lodge, the **Emerald Lounge** serves hearty après-ski snacks, and **Tent City** nightclub recalls the history of the lodge and has lively entertainment.

Other activities

Heliskiing in Valemount, British Columbia, 56 miles away along a scenic drive, is available mid-February to mid-April. Contact Robson HeliMagic at (604) 566-4700 for reservations, information, and car rental to the pickup site, an hour from town.

The usual winter sports are available here. Many operate at the Jackson Park Lodge, such as ice skating, snowshoeing, sleigh rides and something called kick sledding (a sleds used on frozen lakes, hard-packed snow and the skating lane of cross-country trails). Snowmobiling is not allowed within the national park, but a company offers guided tours about 70 miles from the townsite; call 852-6052.

Sightseeing companies run bus tours to some of the more scenic vistas, including the Icefields Parkway, which has ragged peaks, frozen waterfalls and glaciers as attractions. Call **Brewster Transportation**, 852-3332 or **Mountain Meadow Tours**, 852-5595 for details. On a cloudless winter day (unless it's right after a powder dump), ditch the skiing and take a drive along the Icefields Parkway (Highway 93)—you won't be sorry.

We always like to mention unique activities. Jasper has one that sounds ominous, but isn't, and it reveals incredible scenic wonders. **Canyon Crawls** are guided tours through Maligne Canyon where visitors walk (and crawl) 1.2 miles through a 6- to 20-foot-wide gorge on the frozen river. Attractions are ice caves, frozen waterfalls, towering canyon walls and splendid colors frozen into the ice. Insulated hiking boots and traction sandals are provided. It takes about three hours, but it's one of those once-in-a-lifetime activities that you'll brag about afterward. You must be in reasonable physical shape to crawl up some head-high waterfalls and squeeze through a few narrow spots. This usually is available only in January and February. Call **Maligne Canyon Tours** at 852-3370; or **Jasper Adventure Center** at 852-5595. The tour is $22 for adults, $11 for children with both companies.

A great time to visit is during the **Jasper in January festival**, which takes place mid- to late January. Lift tickets at Marmot Basin are discounted for adults and youth ($23 per day), and hotels mark down rooms as much as 30 percent off already low winter prices. The town throws in fireworks, snow sculpture contests, a parade and lots of other activities.

If you fly into Edmonton, spend some time there and tour the **West Edmonton Mall**, the second largest shopping mall in the world. Part shopping center, part amusement park, it covers 48 city blocks, has more than 800 stores, and includes (among other attractions) an indoor amusement park with a triple-loop roller coaster called Mindbender, a dolphin show, an 18-hole miniature golf course, an ice skating rink, and an indoor water park with enormous water slides, a giant wave pool and beach, and 85-degree temperatures. If you can swing the bucks, stay at the adjoining **Fantasyland Hotel**, where every floor is decorated in a theme such as Hollywood, Canadian Pacific Railway, Roman, Polynesian, etc.

Getting there and getting around

Getting there: Four major carriers fly into Edmonton, the closest city: Delta, American, America West and Northwest.

From Edmonton, Jasper is 270 miles west on Highway 16. By prearrangement, Jasper Park Lodge will send in a van for groups for a price of $15 to $20 each, depending on the size of the group. The ski area is 12 miles south of Jasper via Highway 93, 93A and Marmot Basic Road.

VIA RAIL operates service to Jasper from Edmonton and Vancouver, on its newly restored '50s-style art deco train, the Canadian. U.S. travel agents have more information. Greyhound operates daily service from Edmonton and Vancouver; call 421-4211. Brewster Transportation operates the Banff-Jasper Ski Bus and the Marmot Basin Bus Service from Jasper; call 852-3332.

Getting around: A car is best here. The ski area is a few miles from the town and lodging.

Information/reservations

For ski area information, write **Marmot Basin Ski-Lifts,** Box 1300, Jasper, Alberta T0E 1E0; call 852-3816.

Jasper Park Chamber of Commerce, (Box 98, Jasper, Alberta, T0E 1E0; call 852-3858) will provide information on activities. **Summit Vacations** is a central reservations service for lodging in Banff, Lake Louise and Jasper. Call (800) 661-1676.

Local area code is 403.

Red Mountain
British Columbia, Canada

Rossland, British Columbia, is gaining a reputation as the town where skiers stop for a day or two and never leave. Kiwis, Aussies, Europeans and a lot of Canadians stay in the small Kootenay town to ski the big peaks of Red Mountain Ski Resort.

Nancy Greene trained on Red, and went on to win Olympic gold in 1968. Kerrin Lee-Gartner, also from Rossland, did the same in 1992. In fact, Red Mountain claims to have contributed more skiers (27) to Olympic and World Cup competition than any other mountain in North America.

Until 1989, the mountain was owned and operated by a community ski club. Its casualness is appealing. Even today maps don't show boundaries, and skiers still explore the territory. Winter temperature at Red Mountain averages 20 degrees Fahrenheit, and typical season snowfall is 300 inches.

Where to ski

The twin peaks Red and Granite tower over Rossland from only two miles away, yet Granite's beginner trail is nearly five miles long. The reason is that trails and woods can be skied on all 360 degrees of the mountain.

Less of Red is available to skiers, but locals know a trail down the backside that leads to downtown Rossland. The trail has probably been there since the 1890s, when miners skied Red Mountain. The first Canadian downhill championships were held on Red in 1897. It was 50 more years before the first chair lift was built. Even today, Red and Granite don't have a lot of lifts, but these will take you anywhere you could want to go.

Thousands of acres of woods are dotted with private cabins, and 30 marked trails. There's no point in deciding on a favorite run through the woods, because you may never find it again—skiers who have worked here for years still find new routes.

Red Mountain Facts

Base elevation: 3,888' **Summit elevation:** Red: 5,205'; Granite: 6,699'
Vertical drop: 2,811 feet
Number and types of lifts: 6—3 triple chairs, 2 double chairs, 1 T-bar
Acreage: Hundreds (resort had no specific count) **Snowmaking:** None
Uphill capacity: 6,700 skiers per hour **Bed base:** 260 rooms within 8 miles

Skiers are advised to double up in the woods. A free Snow Host service is available to newcomers, and it's smart to take the tour. Even half the named runs are treed. But beginners needn't fear—there's plenty for them too, from every chair. On Red, Dale's Trail winds gently around like a logging road, and Little Red Run is served by the T-bar. On Granite, South Side Road winds from the Paradise side to the base, and Long Squaw and Easy Street combine for a gentle five-mile run.

Mountain rating

The runs are classified as 10 percent beginner, 45 percent intermediate and 45 percent advanced—lots of advanced terrain.

Cross-country (94/95 prices in Cdn$)

The **Blackjack Cross Country Ski Club** is across the road from Red Mountain Resort. It has 40 km. of tracks, most double-tracked with a skating lane. The trails wind through hemlock stands, past frozen beaver ponds, through open fields and some racing loops with steep ups and downs. Trail tickets, actually day memberships, cost $5, with a maximum family fee of $10.

For backcountry touring, skiers can buy a one-use-only lift ticket ($7) to gain access to 30 square miles from the top of **Granite Mountain**. It's smart to check first with the ski patrol on snow conditions.

Free cross-country skiing on tracks set after every snowfall is available 25 km. north of Rossland (on Highway 3B) in **Nancy Greene Provincial Park**. Trails are maintained by the Castlegar Nordic Ski Club. High Country Sports, at the base of Red Mountain, offers rentals and instruction.

Snowboarding

Red Mountain snowboard instruction methods have never failed to get beginners navigating gentle slopes within an hour. Riding the T-bar is tricky, but it's a good test of balance.

Red Mountain appeals to freeriders, because of the abundance of woods. A lot of the turns are tight, though; beginners ought to stay on the open slopes.

Lessons (95/96 prices in Cdn$)

Red Mountain Ski School is where many of Canada's ski instructors train and earn their ratings, CSIA Levels 1 through 4. The school also teaches coaches and snowboard instructors. Call the ski area for details and prices.

There's some serious teaching going on Red Mountain, and its high caliber is to the benefit of regular skiers. One-hour **private lessons,** by appointment only, cost $41 for one hour ($15 per additional person); discounts for additional hours. On Tuesdays and Thursdays a buddy can join your lesson free. Two-hour **group clinics** are $25 for ages 7 and older.

Children's lessons are for ages 3 1/2 to 6. A two-hour lesson with hot chocolate break is $30; an all-day program with lessons and daycare is $42 per day or $107 for three days.

The **Starter Pack** is a good program for never-evers. It includes a 90-minute lesson, rental equipment and T-bar lift ticket, and is $30.50 for ages 7-15 and $35.50 age 16 and older.

Specialty clinics are available through the sponsorship of Rossland businesses. A beginner snowboard package (lifts, lesson, rental) is $50 for ages 9 and older. Telemark lessons, on request, cost $96 for four hours, plus $49 for each additional person. Secret Stash explores the Red Mountain's hidden trails. Skiers go with a pro and pay $10 per hour each, minimum three skiers.

Child care

No infant or toddler care. Ski instruction starts at age 3 1/2 and is detailed in the Lessons section.

Lift tickets (95/96 prices in Cdn$)

	Adult	Child (7–12)
One day	$37	$20
Three days	$100 ($33.33/day)	$50 ($16.66/day)
Five days	$168 ($33.60/day)	$83 ($16.60/day)

Skiers 65 and older pay $25 full day, $65 for three days, $108 for five days. Students aged 13–18 ski for $32 full day, $85 for three days, $143 for five days. Children 6 and younger ski free. The five-day price that is for a book of five transferable tickets that do not have to be used on consecutive days. Half-day tickets also are available, and anyone can buy a beginner-lifts-only ticket for $10.

Accommodations

Red Mountain itself operates Central Reservations, and can book all travel, lodging and ski packages and arrangements. Its international toll–free number is (800) 663-0105.

The 67-room **Uplander Hotel** in downtown Rossland sets the standards for lodging and dining, and like every place else in town is five minutes from the slopes. Prices for a double room and lift tickets are $66 -$80 per person, plus 15 percent in taxes.

At the ski area is the **Red Shutter Inn**, with overnight prices starting at $51 including breakfast and taxes.

Three-bedroom cabins (ski in, walk up) cost $115 at the **Red Mountain Cabins & Motel**. The **Ram's Head Inn** is the place first-time visitors plan to try next time. It's a short walk from the lifts and is No Smoking, a new trend in Canada. Ski week packages start at $450. A double room is $190, with lift tickets.

In residential Rossland, the **Heritage Hill Inn** has rooms for $85 for two people, including breakfast but not lift tickets.

Dining

Sourdough Alley is the Red Mountain cafeteria, with the Rafter's Lounge upstairs specializing in pizzas and Mexican food. Soups, stews and sandwiches are at the **Paradise Lodge**, on the backside of Granite Mountain.

In town, the **Uplander** offers the widest array of food for serious diners. Its chef has been written up in big-city newspapers. She specializes in French, but her steaks and seafood keep 'em coming back.

In town try the **Flying Steamshovel Inn, Rockingham's Restaurant** (30 appetizers alone), and **Rossland Pizza** for Greek, Italian and pizza.

Après-ski/nightlife

In a town this size (4,000), the action is where you and your friends get together. The biggest party of the year is the **Winter Carnival** for three days near the end of January, and 1996 will be the 99th annual celebration, with skating parties, a snow sculpture contest, dances and other festivities. A peak experience is to stand on a downtown roof and watch the city parade go by, several times.

For Rossland pubs and lounges try the **Onlywell Pub, Rockingham's Restaurant** and **Powder Keg** at the Uplander.

Other activities

Shopping: Rossland has a small collection of unusual shops along Columbia Avenue, the main street.

Paragliding in tandem with a pro patroller is offered off the tops of Red ($35) and Granite ($60) on certain weekdays. **Ice skating,** with rentals, is at the Rossland Arena. **Heli-touring** the Red Mountain area costs $290 for up to six people.

Getting there and getting around

Getting there: Red Mountain is ten miles from the Canada-U.S. border, 125 miles north of Spokane. The airport in Castlegar, 20 miles north, is served by Air B.C. from Vancouver (90-minute flight) and Calgary. Shuttlebuses and rental cars are available.

Getting around: Though it's possible to fly in and stay at a place that will shuttle you to and from the slopes, we recommend a car for off-slope exploring.

Information/reservations

One call can do it all: (800) 663-0105. The local area code is 604, and all prices are in Canadian dollars.

Whistler/Blackcomb
British Columbia, Canada

Whistler/Blackcomb has emerged as one of the most popular resorts in North America; in most ski magazine surveys, it ranks Number One (or darn close). There are several reasons for this: twin mountains with the largest vertical drop on the continent (more than 5,000 feet for each), tremendous bowl skiing, runs that wind down the mountain seemingly forever—and to top it off, a marvelous three-village base area with lodging, restaurants and nightclubs, all within walking distance (cars are banned from Whistler Village center).

Generally, Whistler (the name most folks use for this two mountain resort) gets rave reviews, but the two drawbacks that come up most often in skier word-of-mouth are often made to sound worse than they are. One is Whistler's weather. Located relatively close to the Pacific Ocean at a low base altitude just over 2,000 feet, Whistler can get heavy rain or dense fog at times. Sometimes the weather at the bottom isn't always what's at the top. It may be raining in Whistler village, but snowing (or even sunny) on the summit. Crystal-clear, sunny days happen frequently, especially later in the season, and on those days skiing conditions are just awesome. Skiers will sometimes cite horrendous lift lines (primarily at base areas early in the morning) as the other problem, but in reality the few lines that develop look longer than the actual wait, thanks to several high-speed lifts at both areas.

Let's not forget, having considered the few drawbacks, that plenty of skiers adore Whistler/Blackcomb. This is one of the

---

Whistler Facts
Base elevation: 2,140'; **Summit elevation:** 7,160'; **Vertical drop:** 5,020 feet
Number of lifts: 13–1 10-passenger gondola, 4 quad superchairs, 3 triple chairs, 1 double chairs, 4 surface lifts **Snowmaking:** 7 percent
Acreage: 3,657 skiable trail acres **Uphill capacity:** 22,295 per hour **Bed Base:** 8,000+

Blackcomb Facts
Base elevation: 2,214'; **Summit elevation:** 7,494'; **Vertical drop:** 5,280 feet
Number of lifts: 13–1 8-passenger gondola, 6 quad superchairs, 3 triples, 3 surface lifts **Snowmaking:** 28 percent **Acreage:** 3,341 skiable trail acres
Uphill capacity: 27,112 per hour **Bed Base:** 8,000+

most international of ski resorts, attracting skiers from Australia, Asia, Europe, Latin America and the eastern regions of the U.S. and Canada.

The twin mountains of Whistler and Blackcomb, which rise above Whistler Village, are separately owned and managed. They are a bit like Siamese twins, joined at their bases, but distinct individuals, they fight like crazy over the skier population of the Pacific Northwest, but to the rest of the world they act as a single cooperative unit, knowing that tourists will ski both.

Whistler Mountain opened for skiing in 1966, 12 years before the village itself was built. Bowls, chutes, woods and trans-mountain runs were the standard. It was tough-guy stuff for the skiers of that day. Blackcomb Mountain opened in 1980, its ski run design reflecting the thinking that skiers preferred gentle fall-line skiing. Over the years, Blackcomb has added wilder terrain and Whistler has built gentle fall-line runs. Those who ski both frequently can tell the subtle differences, but to the occasional visitor the two mountains seem quite similar, especially now that skiers can get to Blackcomb by the Excalibur Gondola in the original Whistler Village.

Whistler Village is European-style, built to house, feed and amuse tourists. Whistler has some 75 restaurants and bars, and more than 100 shops. More than 2,700 rooms are in condos, B&Bs, lodges and hotels, and more are being built all the time.

There are now officially three villages in the valley: Whistler, Whistler North and Upper Village (the Blackcomb base). Each is about a five-minute walk from the others. New shopping opportunities open monthly, many of them too-familiar chain operations—Starbucks coffee, Holiday Inn, Eddie Bauer and the Hard Rock Cafe, to name a few. McDonald's gets some dirty looks, but its underground drive-through is a lifesaver when you're hurrying to get to the airport.

Where to ski

Ski both mountains; part of the appeal is to stand on one summit or ridge and look across the steep Fitzsimmons Valley at the runs of the other—to chart out where to go or gloat over where you've been. Both mountains offer complimentary tours, and they may be the best way for never-evers to learn their way around the slopes. Tours usually leave outside Pika's on Whistler and the Rendezvous on Blackcomb at 10:30 a.m. and 1 p.m.

Once you are up and out of the base areas, skiers and snowboarders spread out and there are few long lines except possibly at the Harmony Express on Whistler. On Blackcomb, head instead to the Crystal Ridge and Glacier Express chairs. From the Express, both glacier T-bars are easily accessible.

At Whistler, it's a good idea to start at the ten-person Whistler Village Gondola and take a speedy ride up 3,800 vertical feet to Roundhouse Station. Ascending over so much terrain, you'll think you're at the summit, but one glance out the gondola building reveals a series of five giant bowls above the treeline. These spread out from left to right: Symphony Bowl, Harmony Bowl, Glacier Bowl, Whistler Bowl and West Bowl (plus the unseen Bagel Bowl, far to the right edge of the ski boundary), all served by the Harmony Express.

Experts will pause just long enough to enjoy the view and then take Peak Chair to the 7,160-foot summit, turning left along the ridge to drop into Glacier Bowl. Or they'll do the wide mogul apron, Shale Slope, in upper Whistler Bowl, rest awhile at the ridge and then have another go below Whistler Glacier. There are no marked runs here—it's wide open. Be creative and let fly. Expert skiing off this summit is in West Bowl, but there are two intermediate ways down. One, Highway 86, is to the right of West Bowl, keeping to the ridge around Bagel Bowl instead of dropping in. The other is Burnt Stew, arguably the most scenic on the mountain. It goes high and wide off to the left of Harmony Bowl, sometimes flattening into a bit of a trudge. Reached by a long cat track looping behind the bowls, its views are dominated by the imposing Black Tusk peak.

If you want to know what skiing a distance of five miles feels like, take the Alpine T-bar from Roundhouse Station and turn right to find the bronze plaque identifying Franz's Run, one of the longest ski trails in North America. It turns and pitches and rolls and goes forever. Intermediates love it.

The World Cup course is a good challenge run for advanced intermediates. It starts at the top of the Orange Chair and goes a long, long way to the Whistler Creek Base Area.

Beginners won't be able to experience the upper bowls, but will find numerous easier routes down from the Roundhouse, which is, after all, more than 3,800 feet above the village.

Don't forget there's another whole mountain. Blackcomb's gondola, Excalibur, is just to the left of Whistler Mountain's 10-passenger lift. A high-speed quad at the top of the gondola connects skiers to Blackcomb's glacier skiing at the summit.

Another fast way up Blackcomb Mountain is on the speedy Wizard Express, a sleek quad with an aerodynamic Plexiglas windscreen that also keeps out the rain, which can be a menace at the 2,200-foot base area. At the top of the lift, 2,230 feet higher, you're still not halfway up the mountain. Hop on Solar Coaster, next to Wizard Express unloading area, for another 2,000 feet. Here at Rendezvous Restaurant are numerous routes down for all abilities.

To get into the wide-open above-treeline territory, take Expressway, a lazy beginner's traverse, to Seventh Heaven Express. That lift takes you to Mile High summit, where a free guided exploration of this upper terrain for intermediate and advanced skiers is available daily at 11 a.m. On the uphill ride, off to the right, you'll see the blacks of Xhiggy's Meadow. But once at the Mile High summit, the routes off the backside into Horstman and Blackcomb Glaciers give the feeling of being hundreds of miles into the wilderness. You can also reach these glaciers by taking the Glacier Express, which starts at the bottom of the Jersey Cream chair. While going down the spine off the backside of Horstman, keep to the left and peer over the cornice into the double-black-diamond chutes. Just seeing the abyss—or seeing someone hurl himself into it—gives quite a rush.

The best-known of these severe, narrow chutes is Couloir Extreme, formerly known as Saudan Couloir. The entry requires a leap of faith and skill. Nearby is Cougar Chute, also a double black. One of the most difficult chutes on the mountain is Pakalolo, which is very narrow and steep with rock walls on either side. "You don't want to miss a turn," a local says. Another, called Blowhole, drops from the trail leading to the Blackcomb Glacier from the Horstman Glacier.

A surprise for Blackcomb beginners is a sinuous run called Green Line. This takes off from the upper terminal of Seventh Heaven Express and follows the natural contours of the mountain from top to bottom on trails groomed daily. It's a thrilling way for beginners to do big-mountain skiing, but getting down, down, down may take all day. Another easy descent from the Hut is the Crystal Traverse run. It winds below the glaciers, becomes the Crystal Road and passes the Glacier Creek Lodge before joining Green Line two-thirds down the mountain.

Intermediates will especially love the runs off the Jersey Cream chair. They are wide and as smooth as the name implies.

Mountain rating

This resort has plenty of terrain for almost all skiers. When you ask locals which mountain they prefer, you get mixed responses. Even super experts have reasons for enjoying both, and intermediates will have a field day on either set of slopes. Beginners can have fun, especially because they can get down from the summit (and it's always fun to be able to get to the top), but the terrain for never-evers is only so-so. Other destination resorts of this size usually have a large isolated learning area easily accessible at the base. Neither of these mountains does.

Cross-country

Nordic skiing is available on the municipal **Lost Lake Trail**, 28 km. of double-tracked trails with a skating lane. Trails are well marked, and start a quarter-mile from the village. Trail passes are Cdn\$9, but skiing is free after 4 p.m. At night, a 4-km. stretch of trail is lit until 11 p.m. The Chateau Whistler Clubhouse, on the golf course, is a great rest stop, as is the log hut at Lost Lake. Call 932-6436 for conditions or information.

Most avid cross-country skiers take **BC Rail** to the Cariboo and the 100 Mile House. For information, contact BC Rail Passenger Services, Box 8770, Vancouver, B.C. V6B 4X6, or call 984-5426 or Great Escape Vacations at (800) 663-2515.

Snowboarding

Whistler Mountain picked four areas to sculpt for freeriders, gladerunners, waveheads and tricksters. It's a unique concession to snowboarders' needs, well ahead of the usual ski-area halfpipe. Adult camps (average age getting closer to 40) are available for $210, which includes Fresh Tracks Breakfast on the hill the second morning.

Blackcomb Mountain, home of five-time world snowboarding champion Craig Kelly's summer snowboard camps, has a big halfpipe near the top of the Catskinner Chair and a snowboard park on the lower half of Catskinner. The mountain attracts mostly freeriders. Never-ever lessons for $57, including Magic Chair lift ticket, board and boots, assure linked turns within 90 minutes.

Lessons (94/95 prices in Cdn$ plus GST)

Each mountain has its own ski and snowboard school, as well as a dual-mountain program called Ski Esprit, which combines guiding and instruction on both mountains. It costs $168 for three days and $199 for four (95/96 price).

At Whistler, the rate for a **group lesson** is $36, $70 for a private one-hour lesson and $122 for a two-hour private lesson. Never-evers pay $49 for a two-and-a-half-hour lesson, rentals and lift ticket (95/96 prices). At Blackcomb, the rate for a group lesson is $40. Private lessons are $70 for one hour, $122 for two hours. Never-evers pay $47 for the beginning lesson-lift-equipment package.

Both mountains offer **adult workshops** in parallel skiing, bumps, powder and racing. A two-and-a-half hour course is $40. At Whistler, Stephanie Sloan's Women Only ski and snowboard programs are offered six times a season. The three- or four-day programs (starting at $185 for skiers and $100 for snowboarders) stress motivation, fitness and nutrition. At Blackcomb, the Ladies Unlimited program for intermediate or advanced skiers is $165 for a two-day session, $195 for a three-day session, plus lift tickets.

Ski Scamps is the children's instructional program at Whistler. Wee Scamps (2-3 years) $48, provides lunch, snacks and skis. At Blackcomb, **Kids Kamp** operates Wee Wizards for 2 to 3 year olds for $50, including lunch and ski equipment rental. Super Kids for 4 to 12 year olds, Mini Masters for 7 to 10 year olds, and Super Stars for 10 to 13 year olds are all $36.50 a day, with half days and multidays available.

Child care

Whistler has no day-care facilities. Children's ski lessons start at age 2 with the Wee Scamps and Wee Wizards programs, which have morning ski lessons and afternoon activities and nap. If you are planning to take your young toddler here, be aware: not all 2-year-olds have the motor skills necessary to ski. Most ski areas start children's lessons at age 3 or 4.

Other options: On Saturdays and Sundays, the **Dandelion Day Care** center takes children aged three months to 5 years; call 932-1119. The Chateau Whistler and Delta Whistler Resort offer babysitting to their guests, and the Whistler Activity Center (932-2394) can refer you to other babysitting services.

Lift tickets (95/96 prices in Cdn$ plus GST)

	Adult	Child (7-12)
One day	$46	$20
Three days	$150 ($50/day)	$81 ($27/day)
Five days	$245 ($49/day)	$133 ($26.60/day)

The single-day rates are for each mountain, and are 94/95 prices. The dual-mountain lift ticket (listed here in the multiday rates) is the only one that makes sense for destination skiers.

Teens (13-18) ski for $135 on the dual-mountain three-day ticket, while ages 65 and older ski for $108. Children 6 and younger ski free.

Those who drive to Whistler can save about $5 per lift ticket by purchasing them at grocery stores in Squamish, a town about 25 miles south of the resort. Save-on-Foods (turn left at McDonald's) offers Whistler tickets, no grocery purchase required. Three miles north on Highway 99; Super-Valu sells Blackcomb tickets.

Accommodations (Prices in Cdn $)

Chateau Whistler (800-441-1414) is part of the Canadian Pacific Hotels (owners of Chateau Lake Louise and Banff Springs Hotel) with 350 rooms in 13 stories, an expansive sun deck stretching below the high turrets, two restaurants, night club and extensive health club. Rates: $175-$1,100.

Other than the Chateau, the largest deluxe lodging is **Delta Whistler Resort** (800-877-1133 from U.S., 800-268-1133 from Canada, or 932-1982) with 300 rooms, 30 percent of which are kitchen-equipped suites. Hotel rooms are $159-$275, studios are $189-$325, and a one-bedroom suite is $229-$395.

The **Glacier Lodge** (800-777-0185 or 932-2882) is decorated in pale plush. One-bedroom condominiums are $175-$370; two-bedroom, $235-$410. Lodge rooms are $95-$155. The **Crystal Lodge** (800-667-3363 or 932-1982) formerly known as the Nancy Greene Lodge, has 140 rooms from $79-$225. Cozy common areas around the fireplaces give a European atmosphere. Families who don't mind a slightly longer walk to the village center may find the large two-bedroom condominiums at **Tantalus Lodge** (932-4146) suitable for $99–$310.

The **Hearthstone** (800-663-7711 or 932-4161) rates range from $99 to $365 (the latter for a two-bedroom condo in high season). Rooms in the **Listel Whistler** (800-663-5472 or 932-1133) start at $119. Medium-priced units are available at **Mountainside Lodge** (932-4511) mini-kitchenette studios for $105–$275.

New last season is the **Holiday Inn SunSpree Resort** (800-229-3188) in Whistler Village Centre. Suite design is very imaginative, and maids are not allowed to use sprays in certain "allergy-free" rooms. Rates start in the $64–$129 range.

The **Edgewater** (932-0688) just north of Whistler, is on a peninsula of Green Lake, bordering a golf course and the River of Golden Dreams. Great for those who want luxury and no village hubbub.

The least expensive accommodations are outside the village at **Shoestring Lodge** (932-3338) offering dorm beds for $20 per night and twin or queen rooms for $80. **Whistler Resort and Club** (932-5756) has rooms for $80-$99 a night, depending on the season. Four dormitory lodges and a youth hostel have beds at about $20 a night—**Coast Mountain Lodge** (938-1280), **Fireside Lodge** (932-4545), **Southside Lodge** (932-2554), **UBC Lodge** (932-6604) and **Whistler Youth Hostel** (932-5492).

Whistler also has upscale B&Bs, owned and operated by families and sharing a central living area. These are located in residential areas and usually have no more than six rooms. Most have private baths. Rates vary $55–$180 and include breakfast. Ask for those with BC Accommodations approval.

Durlacher Hof (932-1924) is the genuine B&B article for skiers wanting an Austrian lodging experience. At the door, you swap your boots for boiled-wool slippers. Each of the seven rooms has its own bath and extra-long beds. Visiting celebrity chefs prepare dinner on the weekends. Room rates are $85–$180.

We have listed only a few of the many places to stay. To book any of these, and get other suggestions, call **Central reservations:** (800) 944-7853 (800-WHISTLER).

Dining

For years locals have said the **Rimrock Cafe and Oyster Bar** (932-5565) in Highland Lodge is the best restaurant in town. It is at Whistler Creek, a short ride away. Well-prepared seafood is complemented by an extensive wine list. **Les Deux Gros** (932-4611) is another favorite for the best in French fare. It's located about a mile south of Whistler in Twin Lakes Village.

Val d'Isère (932-4666) in the heart of Whistler Village features fine French cuisine. Umberto Menghi, a flamboyant Italian chef whose TV cooking show is popular in Canada, is well

known for his restaurants in Vancouver and two in Whistler—
Trattoria Di Umberto (932-5858) and **Il Caminetto Di Umberto** (932-4442). Continental cuisine is featured. Umberto's main man for 16 years, Mario Enero, broke off in January of 1993 and opened his own **La Rua** (932-5011). **Araxi** (932-4540), on the village square, serves Mediterranean dinners, imaginative pastas and pizza rusticas for $13.50 to $21.50.

At **Timberline** (932-5211) the quality meals are consistent and imaginative. The sunflower baked salmon with sweet pepper sauce is a favorite. **The Old Spaghetti Factory** (938-1921) in the Crystal Lodge has moderate prices as does **Evergreens** (932-7346) in the Delta Mountain Lodge. **The Keg** (932-5151) has good steaks and other basic American-type cooking.

On the Blackcomb side top dining spots are the **Wildflower** (938-2033) in the Chateau Whistler, **La Fiesta-Hot Rock Café** (938-2040) serving Mediterranean and Mexican cuisine (with excellent paella and heavy on the tapas), and **Monk's Grill** (932-9677) at the Wizard Lift base.

At the streetside entrance to the Le Chamois building is a Thai restaurant, **Thai One On** (932-4822). The menu is big, so ask if you're not sure. The Pak Tua Gai, peanut sauce on a bed of spinach with chicken, is a fine entrée for $10.95. Pad Thai Jay is a great-tasting vegetarian alternative for $6.95, especially washed down with Whistler's Mothers Ale. **Zeuski's** (932-6009) has moderately priced Greek food. The two restaurants have the same owner.

With more Japanese skiers than any other North American resort, Whistler also has excellent Japanese restaurants: **Sushi Village** (932-3330) and **Irori** (923-2221). For steaks cooked Japanese steakhouse-style, it's **Teppan Village** (932-2223) or **Nanbantei Yakitori** (938-3380) in Whistler North.

Moderate-priced dining is also available. **Jimmy D's Roadhouse** (932-4451) across from the conference center has affordable steaks, chicken and pasta. **Peter's Underground** (932-4811) is a family self-service restaurant serving large portions.

A short walk from the village area along Fitzsimmons Creek in the Fitzsimmons Lodge, **The Border Cantina** (932-3373) serves decent Mexican fare for *poco dinero*.

Good food is served on the mountains, too. The best on each are **The Raven's Nest**, at the top of the Quicksilver Express chair on Whistler Mountain, and **Christine's** in the back of the Rendezvous Lodge on Blackcomb (reservations are a good idea here; 938-7437). Eager skiers can board Whistler's gondola at 7:30 a.m. for an $8.95 buffet breakfast (lift ticket extra) and first rights to the ski runs. Whistler also offers **Moonlight Dine & Ski** four times per season, on full-moon nights only. Call 932-3434 for dates and cost. On the Blackcomb side, the Glacier Creek

Lodge has the **River Rock Grill** with potato bar, oriental noodle bar and a great array of pastas and pizzas. In the same lodge, the **Glacier Bite** has hearty soups and salads, with bistro-style counter service.

Après-ski/nightlife

Après-ski spills out onto the snow from **Longhorn Pub** at Whistler Village gondola base and **Merlin's** at Blackcomb. Both are of the beer-and-nachos variety with lively music. **Citta** in the center of Whistler Village is also a good après-ski spot.

For a quieter environment at the Whistler base area, **Crystal Lounge** from 3 to 6:30 p.m. hosts specialty coffees and guitar and piano music to help create a warm, gentle atmosphere. Creative aperitifs are mixed at **Planter's Lounge.** On the Blackcomb side, **The Mallard Bar** in the Chateau Whistler provides quiet piano music après-ski.

Later in the evening, the reggae and rock at **The Longhorn** starts at 9 p.m. and gets wailing by 10. Another disco is the **Savage Beagle**, and behind the Savage Beagle you'll find **Tommy Africa's** with a young crowd at the pool tables. The locals seem to congregate at **Garfinkle's** which has beer by the pitcher, TVs on almost every wall and a well-used dance floor.

Other activities

Shopping opportunities are plentiful, and new shops open all the time. At the Holiday Inn center, new shops are Cows, Helly Hansen and more. Below ground is the Whistler Adventure Club with an adventure booking office and store, an 18-lane bowling alley and a virtual reality theater.

Heli-skiing is offered by Tyax Heli-Skiing (932-7007), Whistler Heli-Skiing (932-4105), Western Canada Heli-Sports (938-1700) or Mountain Heli-Sports (932-3512). The same companies have scenic flights, as does Whistler Air (932-6615), which also features the option of landing on a glacier.

Hundred of miles of Whistler logging roads are accessible for snowmobiling from Highway 99. Whistler Snowmobile Guided Tours (932-4086) has three-hour guided tours several times a day, and two evening rides. Blackcomb Snowmobile (932-8484) is another company to try. Canadian Snowmobile Adventures (938-1616) offers luxury evening tours up Blackcomb Mountain.

Covered tennis courts are at the Delta Mountain Inn, ice skating and drop-in hockey take place at Meadow Park Arena (938-7275) a few miles north of the village and snowshoe treks are offered by Canadian Snowshoeing Services (932-7877). Sleigh rides are offered by the Whistler Outdoor Experience Company (932-3389).

The **Whistler Activity and Information Centre** (932-2394) provides information on these or other activities, as well as books reservations.

Getting there and getting around

Getting there: A recent open-skies agreement between the U.S. and Canada has resulted in direct flights to Vancouver from many cities and on many airlines. Canadian Airlines, Air Canada, American, Delta, Continental, Northwest, American Air, Horizon Air, Reno Air and United all have direct flights. The most scenic way to travel the 75 miles north to Whistler is to board **B C Rail**'s passenger trains, which have schedules designed to accommodate skiers. Trains leave North Vancouver at 7 a.m. daily, arriving at 9:34 a.m. They depart Whistler at 6:10 p.m. and return to North Vancouver at 8:35 p.m. Fare is $17 for adults, $8.50 for children younger than 12, one way. Taxis go from the airport to the train station and a bus picks up train passengers at several downtown locations.

Also, **Perimeter Transportation** leaves directly from the Vancouver Airport and goes to Whistler six times a day, with the last bus leaving at 11 p.m. Fare is $26.75 one way. Reservations are required. Call 261-2299.

Maverick Coach Lines operates from the downtown Vancouver bus depot at the corner of Dunsmuir and Georgia, and charges $13 one way. Call 255-1171. **Airport Express** shuttle will get you to the bus depot; call 255-1171. Skiers staying in Vancouver can hop the Blackcomb Ski Bus (622-8051) between 6 and 7 a.m. at various downtown hotels, ski all day and be back in Vancouver by 6 p.m., for $59 plus seven percent GST.

Allow plenty of time in the Vancouver Airport, both arriving and leaving, for customs declarations and currency exchange.

Getting around: Forget the car. You'll never use it while you're staying at Whistler Village.

Information/reservations

For specific information about each mountain, contact **Whistler Mountain Ski Corp.**, 932-3434 or 664-5614. Black-comb: **Blackcomb Mountain**, 687-1032 or 932-3141.

For general information and reservations, contact **Whistler Resort Association**, 4010 Whistler Way, Whistler, B.C. V0N 1B4; 932-3928 or toll-free in the U.S. (800) 944-7853. The toll-free number spells out "Whistler" (without the final letter).

All area codes are 604.

Québec Region
Canada

The closest thing to France in North America is the Canadian province of Québec. This section of Canada still speaks French as its primary language, maintains many French traditions and has managed to create a cuisine and way of life that still blend the rustic adventure of the New World and the sensibilities of Europe.

Québec offers more than a simple peek into a North American France. Here you can find some excellent skiing which, combined with the cities, the menus and the countryside, provides a vacation experience you'll remember long after the winter weather warms into summer.

Though much has been written about the French push for language purity in this region, the fact is that English is spoken virtually everywhere. French is still the *official* language and all signs are written in French, but at the resorts and in the cities, the natives are very friendly (at least to English-speakers from south of the border) and are more than willing to help make your vacation here enjoyable. It doesn't hurt to learn a few French phrases, and use them with a smile, however.

Québec City

Any visit to this province means a stop in Québec City with the historic, towering Château Frontenac on Place d'Armes surrounded by narrow cobblestone streets lined with boutiques and bistros. Between the *antiquittiés* and *galeries* you'll find delightful *patisseries* and *cafés* where you can enjoy a pleasant *gâteau avec café au lait*. Québec's version of Restaurant Row is rue St-Louis. For the latest in tourist kitsch souvenirs, walk down rue du Tresor. The nearby Ursuline Convent and Museum provides in sight into convent life of the 1600s and 1700s.

Below the Château Frontenac is the lower town. A short funicular will take you from the hotel to the oldest street in North America, **rue de Petit-Champlain**, running beside the towering town walls. The 1688 **church of Notre-Dame** still provides worship services as well as sightseeing. Stop in at the **Maison Chevalier**, a restored 18th-century house, and the **Place Royal**, once the heart of New France. The **Musée de Civilisation** showcases Québec history, art and culture.

Winter Carnival takes place annually around the end of February. It lasts ten days and always includes two weekends. If you are skiing at Mont-Sainte-Anne during that time you are in luck. The festival features parades, ice sculptures and music, with plenty of drinking and dancing—just imagine a Mardi Gras in the snow.

The main tourist office is at 60 rue d'Auteuil, just north of Grande Allée. A second tourist office is on Place d'Armes which deals with destinations in other parts of the province. Down in the Place Royal area, near the river, is another tourist office at 215 rue de Marché-Finlay in the Lower Town.

Montréal

This cosmopolitan center is the third largest French-speaking city in the world. Here the New World blends perfectly with the Old. Soaring skyscrapers stand side by side with Art Deco edifices but Vieux-Montréal, the center of government and commerce, still reminds visitors of the grand old days. Visit the Quai Jacques Cartier to see the evolving waterfront development—it now has art galleries, a flea market and a crafts center. See the **Place d'Armes**, site of Indian battles. Stop in at the neo-Gothic **Notre-Dame Basilica** opened in 1829. The **Montréal History Center** in the old fire hall on Place d'Youville provides a historic overview to the city.

Make sure to walk down **rue St-Denis** for its Latin Quarter appeal and wander down the pedestrian **rue Prince Arthur** for the latest in shopping.

Winter is the perfect time to visit *la ville souterraine*, or underground city, which has more than 1,000 shops, restaurants and bars, ten shopping plazas, six hotels and two train stations—all without stepping out into the cold weather.

For winter browsing there are plenty of ·museums (most closed on Mondays)—the Musée des Beaux Arts (the city's main art museum), the Contemporary Art Gallery, the Centre for Architecture, the McCord Museum, Saidye Bronfman Museum and the Château Dufresne Museum of Decorative Arts.

The main Montréal tourist office is at 1001 rue Square Dorchester. Other offices are at 174 rue Notre-Dame Est in Old Montréal and at the airport.

The ski resorts
Mont-Sainte-Anne

This is the town ski slope for Québec, only 25 miles east of the city. It has 2,050 vertical feet of skiing rising from the St. Lawrence River. The mountain has some of the most advanced lifts and ski pass systems in North America. The capacity of this lift system is an amazing 18,000 skiers per hour, so it's rare to find lift lines even on weekends, when Québec seems to come en masse to ski.

The views down to the river are spectacular. The skiing on more than 50 trails is perfect for virtually every level of skier. Hot experts will complain, but they do almost everywhere. The lift system includes bubble-topped high-speed quads and an eight-person gondola. Snowmaking blankets almost 90 percent of the terrain. *And* the computerized lift ticket system allows you to ski for a full week, full day, half day, a couple of hours, or any other combination you can dream up.

The Children's Center at the base of the mountain offers day care for children aged 6 months and older. A Kinderski school takes learners from 3 to 6 years of age.

Mont-Sainte-Anne, P.O. Box 400, Beaupré (Québec) G0A 1E0; (418) 827-4561, reservations: (800) 463-1568.

Tremblant

This Laurentian resort 80 miles north of Montréal was recently purchased by Intrawest, who own Blackcomb Mountain in British Columbia. Since then $258 million has been put into bringing this resort back to its former status as an elegant ski resort, and another $111 million will be invested in 1995-96. New facilities include a pedestrian village with ski-in/ski-out lodging, shops and restaurants; snowmaking; lifts; trails; and a mountain-top restaurant, *Le Grand Manitou.* In the last three years, Tremblant has received three National Ski Area Design awards from *Snow Country* magazine, which only gives out six awards per year for the entire continent.

Today the resort has 2,131 vertical feet of skiing with a very New England narrow-trail flavor. Though most of the mountain's slopes are just right for families and casual skiers, advanced and expert skiers will find new steeps, such as Zig Zag and Vertige on the South Side, and Dynamite on the North Side—all these were new in 93/94, and all are covered by snowmaking. Snowmaking now blankets about two-thirds of the 61 trails, about triple the coverage three years ago. Nine new lifts in the past three seasons—six of them high-speed quads—have increased lift capacity to 22,050 skiers per hour. If you haven't skied Tremblant in a while, it's time for a visit.

Tremblant, 3005, chemin Principal, Mont-Tremblant (Québec) J0T 1Z0; (819) 681-2000, reservations: (800) 461-8711.

Gray Rocks

Gray Rocks, a 75-mile drive north of Montréal on Highway 117, is a mouse compared to Tremblant and Mont-Sainte-Anne—it has 620 feet of vertical and four chair lifts. But this tiny resort has carved a big slice of the student skier market: the success of this Learn-to-Ski-Week concept is overwhelming, with more than 140,000 lessons given in this resort every season. Some ski writers claim this is a kinder, gentler resort, but lessons are not only for the timid first-time skiers. Here, skiers of every level are faced with a challenging week of perfecting technique.

Part of the success is the activity off the slopes. Where off-piste may mean deep powder at some resorts, at Gray Rocks it means good times. A week at Gray Rocks has been compared to a week-long party cruise with snow. Families are mixed with families. Singles are matched with other singles—*Glamour* at one time rated this one of the best single-man hunting grounds in North America. Groups eat together, sharing stories of the day's lesson and then the après-ski starts with creative alternatives to disco such as moonlight cross-country skiing, snow rafting races, beer fests, fashion shows, and pool parties.

Ski week prices range from Cdn$950 to Cdn$1,670 per person double occupancy. A special Thanksgiving weekend ski school is also available. You also can stay here without participating in Ski Week, opting for either downhill or cross-country skiing.

Gray Rocks, P.O. Box 1000, St. Jovite (Québec) J0T 2H0; (819) 425-2771, reservations (800) 567-6767.

Cross-country

Cross-country skiing is excellent throughout this province. Near Mont-Sainte-Anne is a network of 214 km. of marked and groomed trails including 100 km. reserved for skating. Terrain mix leans toward the difficult, but with plenty of kilometers for beginners and intermediates. You'll find heated cabins along the trails, a wilderness lodge with lessons as well as room and board, a chalet with cafeteria, ski school and other amenities plus a skating rink and toboggan run.

The region between Montréal and Tremblant claims 23 cross-country centers with more than 1,000 km. of trails. These trails connect inns, villages and other ski areas, making them well-suited for ski touring. Starting about 40 miles north of Montréal, try one of these major cross-country areas: Morin-Heights (150 km.), l'Estérel (95 km.), Far Hills (100 km.), Mont-Tremblant Park (160 km.), and Gray Rocks (90 km.).

Getting to Know You—365 questions and activities to enhance relationships

This little book gets right to the heart of successful relationships. Filled with hundreds of questions designed to smooth the path from chair-lift acquaintance to friend or long-term lover.
$6.95

Getting to Know Kids in Your Life

Interactive questions and activities to help grownups get to know children 3–7 years old better. **$6.95**

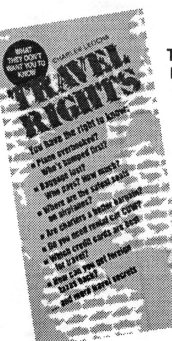

Travel Rights

Did you ever wonder exactly what are the rules regarding taking your ski equipment along on a plane? What happens if your skis and boots are lost or delayed? What should you do delayed by a snowstorm? What credit card helps get you home if you are injured skiing? This pocket-sized travel companion helps answer these and many more travel questions. This may be the best travel investment you make.
$7.95

In a bookstore near you or call 1-800-444-2524

"It's about time someone took women seriously on the slopes. Claudia Carbone has written a book every woman skier should read."
—*Snow Country*

"*WomenSki* invites women to take charge of their own ski equipment, their own physical and psychic comfort, their own ski lives."   —*Ski Magazine*

"Designed to demystify skiing... Equal parts resource manual and self-help handbook. A rousing pep talk for those who need it."
—*Skiing For Women*